Everyman's The
of English Words
and Phrases

Everyman's Thesaurus of English Words and Phrases

Revised from PETER ROGET
by D. C. BROWNING
MA (GLASGOW), BA, B. LITT (OXON)

SPHERE REFERENCE

A SPHERE BOOK

First published in Great Britain 1952 by J. M. Dent and
Sons Ltd in the Everyman edition
This edition compiled by D. C. Browning
Last Revised edition 1971
Published by Sphere Books Ltd 1981
Reprinted 1982, 1983, 1984 (twice), 1985 (twice), 1986, 1987,
1988, 1989

Printed and bound in Great Britain by
Richard Clay Ltd, Bungay, Suffolk
Set in Photon Times by Fleetlines Ltd, Southend-on-Sea,
Essex

0 86305 161 8

Sphere Books Ltd
A Division of
Macdonald & Co. (Publishers) Ltd
66/73 Shoe Lane, London EC4P 4AB
A member of Maxwell Pergamon Publishing Corporation plc

INTRODUCTION

It is just a hundred years since Roget's *Thesaurus of English Words and Phrases* was first published. In the course of that century of unprecedented development and change our language and vocabulary have undergone modifications and additions which have been dealt with from time to time in previous revisions of the work. But a new generation has grown up since the last recension, and the time seemed ripe for a more complete overhaul which would make it thoroughly up to date. Accordingly, the opportunity has been taken, in preparing this new single-volume edition, of giving the work as complete a revision as was possible, short of doing the whole compilation afresh. Every paragraph has been carefully reviewed, over 10,000 words and phrases have been added, and the articles have been 'tidied up' so that all additions follow the logical order which agrees with the original plan.

In the course of its century of use Roget's *Thesaurus* has come to be as widely accepted and as indispensable to writers as a dictionary and its system and arrangement have become so familiar that any radical alteration of them would lessen the value of the book to those who know their way about it from constant use. For that reason no attempt has been made to modify the main scheme which Roget originally laid down, and except for a few very minor alterations of numbering where the order had become confused the arrangement is the same as in previous editions. Within this scheme the articles have been greatly amplified and expanded, some of the pages containing up to a hundred fresh insertions.

The list of contents at the beginning sets out the plan of classification, and indicates the general divisions of the book. Readers who are interested in the detailed subdivisions of the classification will find them in the different paragraph headings, and the general principles of the work are explained in Roget's original Introduction, now printed at the end of the volume.

Technical Terms.

In giving some account of the additions which have been made, it is natural to start off with those technical terms which have been coined to fit modern scientific, political, and cultural developments. The wide range of the subjects covered is shown by these typical examples taken at random: *air-condition, airgraph, allergy, antibiotic, Appleton layer, bathysphere, Dadaism, deviationist, diarchy, displaced person, electrolysis, existentialism, fifth column, Gallup poll, geriatrics, Heaviside layer, hydroponics, intercom, ionosphere, iron curtain, libido, liquidate, parapsychology, psychotherapist, quisling, radar, robot, rotor, stratosphere, surrealism, telekinesis, television, troposphere, weather station.*

Aviation.

Along with the previous section may be grouped the very numerous terms which deal with recent developments in aviation and aerial warfare. These represent new types of aircraft: *autogiro, flying fortress, flying wing, jet aircraft, stratocruiser, stratoliner;* new types of weapon: *atom bomb, buzz-bomb, doodlebug, flying bomb, guided missile, V1, V2;* new names for personnel: *group-captain, wing-commander, squadron-leader, flight-lieutenant;* and for their evolutions: *air lift, bunt.* Finally there are words for the yet untried adventure of interplanetary voyaging: *astronautics, spacecraft, space ship, space travel.*

Everyday Neologisms.

In addition to words marking scientific advance there are also, of course, many neologisms reflecting change or fashion in everyday affairs, such as *baby-sitter, bingle, blurb, bottle-neck, bottle party, bulldozer, cannibalize, cartophily, embus, exclosure, frogman, green belt, infrastructure, jive, lumberjacket, nylons, phillumenist, play-pen, plug* (repeat), *prefab, pullover, quiz, screen* (test), *stockpile, totalizator, zipper.*

Slang Terms.

New slang terms form a considerable proportion of our additions, and among them will be noted a large number of service, particularly Air Force, coinages; the newest arm seems to have eclipsed the Navy in fertility of etymological invention. A few of the more recent terms are: *blah, browned off, bunce, chokka, dippy, erk, flap* (fuss), *flat out, flicks* (cinema), *gen, good show, hush-hush, It, Joe Soap, loopy, mike* (microphone), *never-never system, oodles, popsy, scarper, scatty, shemozzle, smashing, sprog, toffee-nose, twerp, whodunit,* and such phrases as *get cracking, get weaving, gone for a Burton, in a spin, it's in the bag, a piece of cake, shoot down in flames, step on it, tear off a strip, couldn't care less.*

Americanisms.

So many of our slang and other new words are borrowed from across the Atlantic that they demand a separate paragraph. A number of the commoner Americanisms had already been incorporated in the work, but fresh additions include *attaboy, bobbysoxer, boloney, bonehead, bughouse, burp, calaboose, chipper, come-back, cutie, didoes, doll up, faze, floosy, 'fraid-cat, G-man, gander* (look), *goo, grip-sack, haywire, hick, high-hat, hoodlum, hooey, hophead, jeep, jinx, josh, juke box, mazuma, mortician, motel, oomph, once-over, pan* (face), *pep, pinch-hitter, punk, rube, scram, screwball, simoleons, simp, smog, snoop, soup-and-fish, spondulics, stand-in, stooge, stuffed shirt, teenager, tuxedo, upstage, wisecrack, wop, yegg,* along with phrases like *cut no ice, hit the hay, out of kilter, stick one's neck out, take a run-out powder, give the frozen mitt.*

Scotticisms.

The opportunity has also been taken to insert a few of the terms in most common use north of the Tweed or wherever there are colonies of Scots. Only the most familiar words have been inserted, such as *ben, brae, callant, canny, clachan, clarts, dander, dunt, fash, flyte, glaur, gowk, havers, hoots, jalouse, kenspeckle, kittle, kyle, kyte, lum, ooss, pech, ploy, quaich, scunner, shilpit, shoogle, siller, skelp, skirl, smeddum, smirr, snowk, sonsy, speer, stot* (bounce), *stour, stramash, thole, thrapple, thowless, tirrivee, wean* (child), *wersh, wheesht.*

Nouns of Assemblage.

Among the more interesting old-fashioned additions may be mentioned the collection of nouns of assemblage in paragraph 72. In addition to the familiar *flock, herd, drove, pack,* there are listed the distinctive terms *sounder* (of swine), *skulk* (of foxes), *pride* (of lions), *charm* (of finches), *flush* (of mallards), *gaggle* (of geese), and *wedge* (of swans). To old patrons of the work this list should make up for the omission of the tedious and pointless catalogue of different methods of divination, from aeromancy to sciomancy, which was formerly given as a footnote under *Prediction* (511).

Changes and Excisions.

Very few changes have been made in the original grouping. The list of types of *tobacco-pipe* has been transferred from the *Air-pipe* paragraph to the *Tobacco* section, where it will naturally be more in keeping. The account of religious terms towards the end of the book has been rearranged so that *dissenters* and *nonconformists* are not grouped with *idolaters, fire-worshippers,* and other *heathens* under the comprehensive but hardly explicit heading of *Heterodoxy.* A number of foreign words and phrases have been omitted, particularly the more out-of-the-way Latin phrases, which are no longer so popular as in the days when Classics and culture were synonymous. Finally, many words like *caisson, chaperon, château,* which were formerly italicized as foreign are now printed in ordinary characters, having been accepted as English.

The Index

The opportunity has been taken of arranging the alphabetization of the references according to the up-to-date 'nothing-before-something' system set out in the pamphlet on Alphabetical Arrangement published by the British Standards Institution. By this system phrases are inserted in order after their initial word, and hyphened words are reckoned as two except when the initial component is merely a prefix. Every attempt has been made to render the index as complete as possible, and the process of hunting the required word in the body of the work has been further simplified by the insertion of numerous cross-references in those cases where one paragraph is closely related to others.

NOTE

Since the first publication of the single-volume edition in Everymans's Reference Library in 1952 several reprints and a substantial revision in 1962 have taken account of recent developments in English vocabulary.

Two hundred words or meanings have been inserted in their appropriate places throughout the various sections, and corresponding references have been added to the index. In 1955 separate sections were allotted to *Aircraft, Cinema* and *Radio*. The revision of 1962 reflected progress in space travel, radio, transport and jazz music, with such words as *astronaut, lunik, orbital; newscast, teleprompter, transistor; clearway, speedway, traffic warden; bebop, rock-and-roll, skiffle*. Also included were examples of terms coined for types of pompous circumlocution (e.g. *officialese, gobbledygook)*, and modern slang.

D. C. Browning having relinquished his editorship, the publishers' staff have continued the process of updating with numerous words in the same sections, and have added many more hitherto omitted from other sections. The present edition of the *Thesaurus* continues to record the neologisms of recent years in the *push-button* age, among them *bent, hippy, junkie, mini-, teach-in, whizz-kid* and everyday phrases such as *cliff-hanging, hive-off, industrial action, lean over backwards, steady as she goes*, and *at the end of the day*.

1971

CONTENTS

Everyman's Thesaurus
of English Words
and Phrases

CLASS I
WORDS EXPRESSING ABSTRACT RELATIONS

SECTION I—EXISTENCE

1°. *Being in the Abstract*

1 Existence *(Substantives)*, being, life, vital principle, entity, ens, essence, quiddity, subsistence; coexistence (120).

Reality, actuality, positiveness, absoluteness, fact, truth (494); actualization.

Presence; existence in space (186).

Science of existence, ontology; existentialism.

(Phrases) The sober reality; hard fact; matter of fact; the whole truth; no joke.

(Verbs) To be, to exist, have being, subsist, live, breathe, stand, abide, remain, stay, obtain, occur, prevail, be so, find itself, take place, eventuate, consist in, lie in; to vegetate, pass the time.

To come into existence, arise, come out, emerge, come forth, appear (448).

To bring into existence, produce, bring forth, discover (161), objectify.

(Adjectives) Existing, being, subsisting, subsistent, in being, in existence, extant, living, breathing, obtaining, prevailing, prevalent, current, afoot.

Real, actual, positive, absolute, essential, substantial, substantive, self-existing, self-existent; undestroyed, tangible, not ideal, not imagined, not supposititious, not potential, virtual, effective, unideal, true, authentic, genuine, mere, objective.

(Adverbs) Actually, really, absolutely, positively, etc., in fact, *de facto, ipso facto*.

(Phrase) In esse; cogito ergo sum.

2 Inexistence *(Substantives)*, non-existence, not-being, nonentity, *nihil*, nil, non-subsistence, nullity, vacuity, blank (4), negativeness, absence (187), removal (185).

Annihilation, abeyance, extinction (162); nirvana.

Philosophy of non-existence, nihilism.

(Phrases) No such thing; Mrs. Harris; 'men in buckram.'

(Verbs) Not to be, not to exist, etc.

To cease to be, pass away, perish, vanish, fade away, dissolve, melt away, disappear (449), to be annihilated, extinct, etc., to die (360), to die out.

(Phrases) To have no being; to have no existence; to be null and void; *non est*; to be no more; 'to leave not a rack behind'; to disappear into thin air; to be brought out of existence.

(Adjectives) Inexistent, non-existent, non-existing, etc., negative, blank, absent.

Unreal, potential, virtual, baseless, unsubstantial (4), imaginary, ideal, vain, fanciful, unpractical, shadowy, fabulous (515), supposititious (514).

Unborn, uncreated, unbegotten, unproduced, unmade.

Annihilated, destroyed, extinct, gone, lost, perished, melted, dissolved, faded, exhausted, vanished, missing, disappeared, departed, extinct, defunct (360).

(Adverbs) Negatively, virtually, etc.

(Phrase) In nubibus.

2°. Being in the Concrete

3 Substantiality *(Substantives)*, hypostasis, person, thing, being, something, existence, entity, reification, corporeity, body, physique, substance, object, article, creature, matter, material, stuff (316), substratum, protoplasm.

Totality of existences, world (318), continuum, plenum.

(Phrase) Something or other.

(Adjectives) Substantive, substantial, personal, bodily, tangible, true, real, concrete, corporal, corporeal, material, objective, hypostatic.

(Verbs) Substantialize, actualize, materialize, reify, embody.

(Adverbs) Substantially, etc., essentially.

------

4 Unsubstantiality *(Substantives)*, insubstantiality, nothingness, nihility, nothing, naught, damn-all, *nihil*, nil, nix, love, zero, cipher, a duck, duck's-egg, pair of spectacles; nonentity, nobody, no one (187).

A shadow, phantom, phantasm, phantasmagoria, dream, mockery, air, thin air, idle dream, pipe dream, castle in Spain (515), idle talk, ignis fatuus, *fata morgana,* mirage.

Void, vacuum, vacuity, vacancy, voidness, vacuousness, inanity, emptiness, hollowness, blank, chasm, gap, hiatus (198); empty space, ether.

(Phrases) Nothing at all; nothing whatever; nothing on earth; nothing under the sun; not a particle.

A man of straw; *vox et praetera nihil;* 'such stuff as dreams are made on.'

(Verbs) To vanish, fade, dissolve, evaporate.

(Adjectives) Unsubstantial, immaterial, void, vacant, vacuous, blank, null, inane, idle, hollow, airy, visionary (515).

3°. Formal Existence

Internal Conditions

5 Intrinsicality *(Substantives)*, in-being, immanence, inherence, inhesion, essence; essentiality, essentialness, subjectiveness, subjectivity, essential part, soul, quintessence, quiddity, gist, pith, core, backbone, marrow, sap, lifeblood; incarnation.

Nature, constitution, character, type, quality (157), temperament, temper, manner, spirit, ethos, habit, humour, grain, endowment, capacity, capability, moods, declensions, features, aspects, specialities, peculiarities (79), particularities, idiosyncrasy, idiocrasy, diagnostics.

(Verbs) To be innate, inborn, etc.

(Phrases) To be in the blood; to be born like that.

External Conditions

6 Extrinsicality *(Substantives)*, extraneousness, objectiveness, objectivity, accident, superficiality, incident.

(Adjectives) Derived from without, objective, extrinsic, extrinsical, extraneous, modal, adventitious, adscititious, incidental, accidental, nonessential, outward (220).

Implanted, engrafted.

(Adverb) Extrinsically, etc.

(Adjectives) Derived from within, subjective, intrinsic, intrinsical, inherent, essential, natural, internal, implanted, inborn, innate, inbred, engrained, inherited, immanent, indwelling, radical, constitutional, congenital, connate, hereditary, instinctive, indigenous.

(Phrases) In the grain; in the blood; bred in the bone.

Characteristic, peculiar, qualitative, special, diagnostic (79), invariable.

(Adverbs) Intrinsically, subjectively, substantially, at bottom, *au fond*, at the core.

4°. *Modal Existence*

Absolute

7 State *(Substantives)*, condition, category, class, kind, estate, lot, case, constitution, habitude, diathesis, mood, temper, morale.

Frame, fabric, structure, texture, contexture (329), conformation, organism.

Mode, modality, schesis, form, shape (240), figure, cut, cast, mould, stamp, set, fit, tone, tenor, trim, turn, guise, fashion, aspect, complexion, style, manner, character, kind, get-up, set-up, format, *genre*.

(Verbs) To be in a state, to be in condition, to be on a footing, etc.

To do, fare; to have, possess, enjoy, etc., a state, condition, etc.

To bring into a state, etc. (144).

(Adjectives) Conditional, modal, formal, structural, organic, textual.

(Phrases) As the matter stands; as things are; such being the case.

(Adverb) Conditionally, etc.

_____

Relative

8 Circumstance *(Substantives)*, situation, phase, position, posture, attitude, place, point, bearings, terms, fare, regime, footing, standing, status, predicament, contingency, occasion, juncture, conjuncture, emergency, exigence, exigency, crisis, pinch, impasse, pass, push, plight, fix.

(Phrases) How the land lies; how the wind blows; how the cat jumps.

(Adjectives) Circumstantial; given, conditional, provisional, modal, critical, contingent, incidental (6, 151), circumstanced, placed.

(Verb Phrases) To bow before the storm; to take things as they come; to cut one's coat according to the cloth.

(Adverbs) In or under the circumstances, conditions, etc.; thus; so; in such a case, contingency, etc.; accordingly, such being the case; since, sith, seeing that, as matters stand, as things go.

Conditionally, provided, if, an if, if so, if so be, if it be so, if it so prove, or turn out, or happen; in the event of, provisionally, unless, without.

(Phrases) According to circumstances; as it may happen, or turn out; as the case may be; *pro re nata*; wind and weather permitting; D.V.; rain or shine, sink or swim; at all events; other things being equal; *ceteris paribus*.

SECTION II—RELATION

1°. *Absolute Relation*

9 Relation *(Substantives)*, relationship, bearing, reference, standing, concern, cognation, correlation (12), analogy, affinity, homology, alliance, homogeneity, connection, association, approximation, similarity (17), filiation, affiliation, etc. (11, 166), interest, habitude; relativity.

Relevancy, pertinency, fitness, etc. (646, 23).

Aspect, point of view, comparison (464); ratio, proportion.

Link, tie (45), homologue.

10 Want or absence of relation.

Irrelation *(Substantives)*, disconnection, dissociation, disassociation, misrelation, independence, isolation (44), multifariousness, disproportion; commensurability, irrelevancy; heterogeneity, irreconcilableness (24), impertinence.

(Verbs) To have no relation with, or to, to have nothing to do with, to have no business there, not to concern, not to admit of comparison.

(Verbs) To be related, have a relation, etc., to relate to, refer to, have reference to, bear upon, regard, concern, touch, affect, have to do with, pertain to, belong to, appertain to, answer to, interest.

To bring into relation with, correlate, associate, connect, affiliate, link (43), bring near (197), homologize; to bring to bear upon.

(Phrase) To draw a parallel with.

(Adjectives) Relative, correlative, cognate, relating to, relative to, relevant, in relation with, referable to, pertinent (23), germane, belonging to, pat, to the point, apposite, to the purpose, apropos, *ad rem*, just the thing, quite the thing; pertaining to, appertaining to, appurtenant, affiliated, allied, related, implicated, connected, associated, *en rapport*, in touch with, bound up with, homological, homologous.

Approximate, approximative, approximating, proportional, proportionate, proportionable, allusive, comparable, like, similar (17).

(Adverbs) Relatively, thereof, as to, about, connecting, concerning, touching, anent, as relates to, with relation to, relating to, as respects, with respect to, in respect of, respecting, as regards, with regard to, regarding, in the matter of, with reference to, according to, while speaking of, apropos of, in connection with, inasmuch as, whereas, in consideration of, in point of, as far as, on the part of, on the score of, under the head of, *in re*; pertinently, etc. (23).

To isolate, separate, detach, disconnect, segregate (44).

(Adjectives) Irrelative, irrespective, unrelated, without reference, etc., to, arbitrary, episodic, remote, far-fetched, forced, out of place, out of tune (414), inharmonious, malapropos, irrelevant, foreign to, alien, impertinent, inapposite, extraneous to, strange to, stranger to, independent, paranthetical, incidental, outlandish, exotic, unallied, unconnected, disconnected, unconcerned, adrift, detached, isolated, insular.

Not comparable, incomensurable, inapplicable (24), irreconcilable, heterogeneous (83), uncomfortable.

(Phrases) Foreign to the purpose; nothing to the purpose; having nothing to do with; *nihil ad rem*; neither here nor there; beside the mark; *à propos des bottes*; dragged in by the scruff of the neck.

(Adverbs) Parenthetically, by the way, by the by, *obiter dicta, en passant,* incidentally, irrespectively, irrelevantly, etc.

---

11 Relations of kindred.

Consanguinity *(Substantives)*, relationship, kindred, blood, parentage (166), filiation, affiliation, lineage, agnation, connection, alliance, family connection, family tie, nepotism.

A kinsman, kinswoman, kinsfolk, kith and kin, relation, relative, friend, sibling, one's people, clan, connection, one's own flesh and blood, brother, sister, father, mother, uncle, aunt, nephew, niece, stepfather, etc., brother-in-law, etc., guid-brother, etc., cousin, cousin-german; first, second cousin; cousin once, twice, etc., removed; grand- or great-grandfather, etc., great-uncle, etc., a near relation, a blood-relation, a distant relation or relative, congener, collateral.

Family, issue, fraternity, sisterhood, brotherhood, parentage, cousinhood, etc.; race, stock, generation, sept, clan, tribe, strain.

(Verbs) To be related, to have or claim relationship with.

(Adjectives) Related, akin, consanguineous, congeneric, family, kindred, affiliated, allied, collateral, sib, agnate, agnatic, fraternal, of the same blood, nearly or close related, remotely or distantly related.

(Phrase) Blood is thicker than water.

12 Double relation.

Reciprocalness *(Substantives)*, reciprocity, mutuality, correlation, correlativeness, interdependence, interchange, interaction, reciprocation, etc. (148), alternation (149), barter (794).

(Verbs) To reciprocate, alternate, interchange, interact, exchange, counterchange, interdepend.

(Adjectives) Reciprocal, mutual, common, correlative, alternate, alternative; interchangeable, interdependent, international.

(Adverbs) Reciprocally, mutually, etc.

(Phrases) Mutatis mutandis; each other; vice versa; turn and turn about.

---

13 Identity *(Substantives)*, sameness, oneness, coincidence, coalescence, convertibility; selfness, self, ego, oneself, number one; identification, monotony; equality (27), tautology (104).

Synonym; facsimile (21), counterpart (17).

(Verbs) To be identical, to be the same, etc., to coincide, to coalesce.

To render the same.

To recognize the identity of, to identify, recognize.

(Adjectives) Identical, identic, same, self, selfsame, very same, no other, ilk, one and the same, ditto, unaltered, coincident, coinciding, coessential, coalescing, coalescent, indistinguishable, tantamount, equivalent, equipollent, convertible, much the same.

(Adverbs) All one, all the same, *ibidem*, ibid, identically, likewise.

(Phrases) Semper idem; toujours la même chose; alter ego; on all fours; much of a muchness.

14 Non-coincidence.

Contrariety *(Substantives)*, contrast, foil, set-off, antithesis, contradiction, opposition, oppositeness, antagonism (179, 708), distinction (15).

Inversion, reversion (218).

The opposite, the reverse, inverse, converse, antonym, the antipodes (237).

(Phrases) The reverse of the medal; the other side of the shield; the tables being turned.

(Verbs) To be contrary, etc., to contrast with, contradict, contravene, oppose, negate, antagonize, invert, reverse, turn the tables, to militate against.

(Adjectives) Contrary, opposite, counter, converse, reverse, antithetical, opposed, antipodean, antagonistic, opposing, conflicting, inconsistent, contradictory, contrarious, contrariant, negative.

(Phrases) Differing *toto caelo*; diametrically opposite; as black to white; light to darkness; fire to water; worlds apart; poles asunder.

(Adverbs) Contrarily, contrariously, contrariwise, *per contra*, oppositely, *vice versa*, on the contrary, *tout au contraire*, quite the contrary, no such thing.

---

15 Difference *(Substantives)*, variance, variation, variety, diversity, modification, allotropy, shade of difference, nuance; deviation, divergence, divarication (291), disagreement (24), dissimilarity (18), disparity (28).

Distinction, contradistinction, differentiation, discrimination (465); a nice or fine or subtle distinction.

(Phrases) A very different thing; a *tertium quid*; a horse of a different colour; another pair of shoes.

(Verbs) To be different, etc., to differ, vary, mismatch, contrast, differ *toto caelo*.

To render different, etc., to vary, change, modify, varify, diversify, etc. (140).

To distinguish, differentiate, severalize (465), split hairs, discriminate.

(Adjectives) Different, differing, disparate, heterogeneous, heteromorphic, allotropic, varying, distinguishable, discriminative, varied, modified, diversified, deviating, diverging, devious, disagreeing (24), various, divers, all manner of, multifarious, multiform, variform (81), variegated (440), diacritical.

Other, another, other-guess, not the same.

Unmatched, widely apart, changed (140).

(Phrase) As different as chalk is from cheese.

(Adverbs) Differently, variously, otherwise.

2°. *Continuous Relation*

16 Uniformity *(Substantives)*, homogeneity, homogeneousness, consistency, connaturality, conformity (82), homology, accordance, agreement (23), regularity (58), routine, monotony, constancy.

(Verbs) To be uniform, etc., to accord with, harmonize with, hang together, go together.

16A Absence or want of uniformity.

Non-uniformity *(Substantives)*, variety, multiformity (81), diversity, unevenness, irregularity, unconformity (83).

(Adjectives) Multiform, multifarious, various (81), diversified, inconsistent, of various kinds.

———

To become uniform, conform with, fall in with, follow suit.

To render uniform, to assimilate, level, smooth (255).

(Adjectives) Uniform, homogeneous, homologous, of a piece, of a kind, consistent, connatural, monotonous, even, unvarying, flat, level, constant.

(Adverbs) Uniformly, uniformly with, conformably (82), consistently with, in unison with, in harmony with, in conformity with, according to (23).

Regularly, at regular intervals, invariably, constantly, always, without exception.

(Phrases) In a rut (or groove); *ab uno disce omnes*; 'forty feeding like one.'

3°. *Partial Relation*

17 Similarity *(Substantives)*, resemblance, likeness, similitude, affinity, semblance, approximation, parallelism (216), analogy, brotherhood, family likeness; alliteration, head-rhyme, rhyme, pun, assonance, repetition (104), reproduction.

An analogue, copy (21), the like, facsimile, match, double, pendant, fellow, pair, mate, twin, *alter ego*, parallel, counterpart, brother, sister; simile, metaphor (521), resemblance, imitation (19).

(Phrases) One's second self; *Arcades ambo*; birds of a feather; *et hoc genus omne*; a chip of the old block; the very spit (and image) of.

(Verbs) To be similar, like, resembling, etc., to look like, resemble,

18 Dissimilarity *(Substantives)*, unlikeness, dissimilitude, diversity, divergence, difference (15), novelty (123), originality (515), disparity (28).

(Verbs) To be unlike, etc., to vary (15, 20).

To render unlike, to diversify (140).

(Phrase) To strike out something new.

(Adjectives) Dissimilar, unlike, disparate, of a different kind, class, etc. (75); diversified, novel, new (123), unmatched, unique, unprecedented (83).

(Phrases) Nothing of the kind; far from it; cast in a different mould; as different as chalk is from cheese.

(Adverb) Otherwise.

———

bear resemblance, favour, approximate, parallel, match, imitate, take after (19), represent, simulate, personate, savour of, have a flavour of, favour, feature.

To render similar, assimilate, approximate, reproduce, bring near, copy, plagiarize.

(Adjectives) Similar, like, alike, resembling, twin, analogous, analogical, parallel, allied to, of a piece, such as, connatural, congener, matching, conformable, on all fours with.

Near, something like, suchlike, mock, pseudo, simulating, representing, approximating, a show of, a kind of, a sort of.

Exact, accurate, true, faithful, close, speaking, lifelike, breathing.

(Phrases) True to nature; to the life; for all the world like; like as two peas; *comme deux gouttes d'eau*; cast in the same mould; like father, like son.

(Adverbs) As if, so to speak, as it were, quasi, as if it were, just as, after, in the fashion or manner of, *à la*.

---

19 Imitation *(Substantives)*, assimilation, copying, transcription, transcribing, following, repetition (104), duplication, reduplication, quotation, reproduction.

Mockery, mocking, mimicry, mimicking, echoing, reflection, simulation, counterfeiting, plagiarism, forgery, fake, fakement, acting, personation, impersonation, representation (554), copy (21), parody, paraphrase, travesty, burlesque, semblance, mimesis.

An imitator, mimic, impersonator, echo, cuckoo, parrot, ape, monkey, mocking-bird.

Plagiary, plagiarist, forger, counterfeiter.

(Phrase) O imitatores, servum pecus.

20 Non-imitation *(Substantives)*, originality, inventiveness, novelty.

(Adjectives) Unimitated, uncopied, unmatched, unparalleled, inimitable, unique, original, novel.

(Verb) To originate.

Variation *(Substantives)*, alteration, modification, difference (15), change (140), deviation (279), divergence (291); moods and tenses.

(Verbs) To vary, modify, change, alter, diversify (140).

(Phrase) To stear clear of.

(Adjectives) Varied, modified, diversified, etc.

(Adverbs) Variously, in all manner of ways.

(Verbs) To imitate, copy, plagiarize, forge, fake, reproduce, photograph, repeat (104), echo, re-echo, transcribe, match, parallel, emulate, do like, take off, hit off, reflect, mirror, model after (554).

To mock, mimic, ape, simulate, personate, impersonate (554), act, represent, adumbrate, counterfeit, parody, travesty, caricature, burlesque.

(Phrases) To take or catch a likeness; to take after; to follow or tread in the steps of, or in the footsteps of; to take a leaf out of another's book; to follow suit; to go with the stream; to be in the fashion.

(Adjectives) Imitated, copied, matched, repeated, paralleled, mock, mimic, parodied, etc., modelled after, moulded on, paraphrastic, imitative, mimetic, slavish, mechanical, synthetic, second-hand, imitable.

(Adverbs) Literally, verbatim, to the letter, *literatim, sic, totidem verbis,* so to speak, in so many words, word for word, *mot à mot* (562).

21 Result of imitation.

Copy *(Substantives)*, facsimile, counterpart, effigies, effigy, form, likeness, similitude, semblance, reflex,

22 Thing copied.

Prototype *(Substantives)*, original, model, pattern, standard, type, scale, scantling, archetype, protoplast, portrait, photograph (556), photostat, microfilm, enlargement, miniature, study, cast, autotype, electrotype, imitation, replica, representation, adumbration.

Duplicate, transcript, transcription, repetition (104), réchauffé, reflection, shadow, record, recording.

Rough copy, fair copy, revise, carbon copy, tracing, rubbing, squeeze, draft or draught, proof, pull, reprint.

Counterfeit, parody, caricature, burlesque, travesty, paraphrase, forgery.

antitype, module, exemplar, example, ensample, protoplast, paradigm, fugleman, lay figure.

Text, copy, design, plan, blueprint, keynote.

Mould, matrix, last, plasm, proplasm, mint, die, seal, stamp, negative.

(Verbs) To set a copy, to set an example.

_____

(Phrases) A second edition; a twice-told tale.

4°. General Relation

23 Agreement *(Substantives)*, accord, accordance, unison, uniformity, harmony, union, concord, concert, concordance (714), cognation, conformity, conformance (82), consonance, consentaneousness, consensus, consistency, congruity, congruence, congeniality, correspondence keeping, parallelism.

Fitness, pertinence, suitableness, adaptation, meetness, patness, relevancy, aptness, aptitude, coaptation, propriety, apposition, appositeness, reconcilableness, applicability, applicableness, admissibility, commensurability, compatibility, adaptability.

Adaptation, adjustment, graduation, accommodation, reconciliation, reconcilement, concurrence (178), consent (488), co-operation (709).

(Verbs) To be accordant, to agree, accord (714), correspond, tally, jibe, respond, harmonize, match, suit, fit, befit, hit, fall in with, chime in with, quadrate with, square with, cancel with, comport with, assimilate, unite with.

To render accordant, to adapt, accommodate, adjust, reconcile, fadge, dovetail, dress, square, regulate, comport, graduate, gradate, grade.

(Phrases) To become one; to fit like a glove; to suit one to a T.

(Adjectives) Agreeing, accordant, concordant, consonant, congruous, consentaneous, consentient, corresponding, correspondent, congenial,

24 Disagreement *(Substantives)*, discord, discordance, dissonance, disharmony, dissidence, discrepancy, unconformity, disconformity, nonconformity, incongruity, incongruence, *mésalliance*, discongruity, jarring, clashing, jostling (713), inconsistency, inconsonance, disparity, disproportion, disproportionateness, variance, divergence, jar, misfit.

Unfitness, repugnance, unsuitableness, unsuitability, unaptness, ineptitude, inaptness, impropriety, inapplicability, inadmissibility, irreconcilableness, irreconcilability, incommensurability, inconcinnity, incompatability, inadaptability, interference, intrusion, irrelation (10).

(Verbs) To disagree, belie, clash, jar, oppose (708), interfere, jostle (713), intrude.

(Phrase) To have no business there.

(Adjectives) Disagreeing, discordant, discrepant, jarring, clashing, repugnant, incompatible, irreconcilable, intransigent, inconsistent with, uncomformable, incongruous, disproportionate, disproportioned, unproportioned, inharmonious, inconsonant, mismatched, misjoined, misjudged, unconsonant, incommensurable, incommensurate, divergent (291).

Unapt, inapt, inept, inappropriate, improper, unsuited, unsuitable, inapposite, inapplicable, irrelevant, not pertinent, impertinent, malapropos, ill-timed, intrusive, clumsy, unfit,

harmonizing, harmonious with, tallying with, conformable with, in accordance with, in harmony with, in unison with, in keeping with, squaring with, quadrating with, falling in with, of one mind, of a piece, consistent with, compatible, reconcilable with, commensurate.

Apt, apposite, pertinent, germane, relating to, pat, bearing upon (9), applicable, relevant, fit, fitting, suitable, happy, felicitous, proper, meet, appropriate, suiting, befitting, becoming, seasonable, deft, accommodating, topical.

(Phrases) The cap fits; to the point; to the purpose; *rem acu tetigisti*; at home; in one's element.

unfitting, unbefitting, unbecoming, misplaced, forced, unseasonable, farfetched, inadmissible, uncongenial, illassorted, ill-sorted, repugnant to, unaccommodating, irreducible.

(Phrases) Out of season; out of character; out of keeping; out of joint; out of tune; out of place; out of one's element; at odds; a fish out of water.

(Adverbs) Discordantly, etc.; at variance with, in defiance of, in contempt of, in spite of, despite.

SECTION III —QUANTITY

1°. *Simple Quantity*

25 Absolute quantity.

Quantity *(Substantives)*, magnitude (192), amplitude, size, mass, amount, volume, area, quantum, measure, substance.

Science of quantity, mathematics.

Definite or finite quantity, handful, mouthful, spoonful, bucketful, pailful, etc.; stock, batch, lot.

(Adjective) Quantitative.

(Phrase) To the tune of.

26 Relative quantity.

Degree *(Substantives)*, grade, gradation, extent, measure, ratio, stint, standard, height, pitch, reach, sweep, radius, amplitude, magnitude, water, calibre, range, scope, shade, tenor, compass, sphere, rank, station, standing, rate, way, sort.

Point, mark, stage, step, position, slot, peg; term (71).

Intensity, might, fullness, strength (31), conversion (144), limit (233).

(Adjectives) Comparative, gradual, shading off.

(Adverbs) By degrees, gradually, *gradatim*, inasmuch, *pro tanto*, however, howsoever, step by step, rung by rung, bit by bit, little by little, by inches, inch by inch, by slow degrees, by little and little, in some degree, to some extent.

2°. *Comparative Quantity*

27 sameness of quantity or degree.

Equality *(Substantives)*, parity, coextension, evenness, equipoise, level, balance, equivalence, equipollence, equilibrium, poise, equiponderance, par, quits.

Equalization, equation, equilibration, co-ordination, adjustment, symmetry.

28 Difference of quantity or degree.

Inequality *(Substantives)*, disparity, imparity, imbalance, odds, handicap, bisque, difference (15), unevenness.

Preponderance, preponderation, inclination of the balance, advantage, prevalence, partiality.

Superiority (33), a casting vote; inferiority (34).

A drawn game or battle, a dead heat, a draw, a tie.

A match, peer, compeer, equal, mate, fellow, brother (17), equivalent, makeweight.

(Phrases) A distinction without a difference; a photo finish.

(Verbs) To be equal, etc., to equal, match, come up to, keep pace with; come to, amount to, balance, cope with.

To render equal, equalize, level, balance, equate, aequiparate, trim, dress, adjust, fit, accommodate, poise, square; to readjust, equipoise, equilibrate, set against.

(Phrases) To be or lie on a level with; to come to the same thing.

To strike a balance; to establish or restore equality; to stretch on the bed of Procrustes; to cry quits.

(Verbs) To be unequal, etc., to preponderate, outweigh, outbalance, overbalance, prevail, countervail, predominate, overmatch, outmatch (33).

To fall short of, to want (304), not to come up to.

(Phrases) To have or give the advantage; to turn the scale; to kick the beam; to topple over.

(Adjectives) Unequal, uneven, disparate, partial, unbalanced, overbalanced, top-heavy, lopsided, preponderating, outweighing, prevailing.

(Phrases) More than a match for, above par; below par; *haud passibus aequis.*

———

(Adjectives) Equal, even, quit, level, coequal, co-ordinate, equivalent, synonymous, tantamount, convertible, equipollent, equiponderant, equiponderous, square.

Rendered equal, equalized, equated, drawn, poised, levelled, balanced, symmetrical, trimmed, dressed.

(Phrases) On a par with; on a level with; much of a muchness; as broad as it is long; as good as; all the same; all one; six of one and half a dozen of the other; not a pin to choose between them; tarred with the same brush; diamond cut diamond.

(Adverbs) *Pari passu,* equally, symmetrically, *ad eundem,* practically, to all intents and purposes, neck and neck.

29 Mean *(Substantives)* medium, intermedium, compromise, average, norm, balance, middle (68), *via media, juste milieu.*

Neutrality, mediocrity, middle course, shuffling.

(Phrases) The golden mean; the average man; the man in the street.

(Verbs) To compromise, pair off, cancel out.

(Phrases) To sit on the fence; split the difference; strike a balance; take the average; reduce to a mean; to take a safe course.

(Adjectives) Mean, intermediate, middle, median, normal, average, mediocre, middling, ordinary (82), neutral.

(Adverb phrases) On an average; in the long run; half-way; taking the one with the other; taking all things together; in round numbers.

30 Compensation *(Substantives),* equation, commutation, compromise (774), indemnification, neutralization, nullification, counteraction (179), recoil (277), atonement (952).

A set-off, offset, makeweight, counterpoise, ballast, indemnity, hush-money, amends, equivalent.

(Phrases) Measure for measure; give and take; *quid pro quo;* tit for tat.

(Verbs) To compensate, make up for, indemnity, countervail, counterpoise, balance, compromise, outbalance, overbalance, counterbalance, counteract, set off, hedge, redeem, neutralize (27), cover.

(Phrases) To make good; split the difference; fill up; make amends.

(Adjectives) Compensating, compensatory, countervailing, etc., equivalent, equipollent (27).

(Phrase) In the opposite scale.

(Adverbs) However, yet, but, still, all the same, for all that, nevertheless, none the less, notwithstanding, be that as it may, on the other hand, although, though, albeit, *per contra*.

(Phrases) As broad as it's long; taking one thing with another; it is an ill wind that blows nobody any good.

Quantity by Comparison with a Standard

31 Greatness *(Substantives)*, largeness, magnitude, size (192), multitude (102), fullness, vastness, immensity, enormity, infinity (105), intensity (26), importance (642), strength.

A large quantity, deal, power, world, macrocosm, mass, heap (72), pile, sight, pot, volume, peck, bushel, load, stack, cart-load, wagon-load, truck-load, ship-load, cargo, lot, flood, spring tide, mobs, bags, oodles, abundance (639), wholesale, store (636).

The greater part (50).

(Verbs) To be great, etc., run high, soar, tower, transcend, rise, carry to a great height (305).

(Phrases) To know no bounds; to break the record.

(Adjectives) Great, gross, large, considerable, big, ample, above par, huge, full, saturated, plenary, deep, signal, extensive, sound, passing, goodly, famous, noteworthy, noble, heavy, precious, mighty (157), arch, sad, piteous, arrant, red-hot, downright, utter, uttermost, crass, lamentable, consummate, rank, thoroughpaced, thorough-going, sovereign, unparalleled, matchless, unapproached, extraordinary, intense, extreme, pronounced, unsurpassed, unsurpassable.

Vast, immense, enormous, towering, inordinate, severe, excessive, monstrous, shocking, extravagant, exorbitant, outrageous, whacking, thumping, glaring, flagrant, preposterous, egregious, overgrown, stupendous, monumental, prodigious, marked, pointed, remarkable, astonishing, surprising (870), incredible, marvellous, transcendent,

32 Smallness *(Substantives)*, littleness, minuteness (193), tenuity, scantness, scantiness, slenderness, meanness, mediocrity, insignificance (643), paucity, fewness (103).

A small quantity, modicum, atom, particle, molecule, corpuscle, microcosm, jot, iota, dot, speck, mote, gleam, scintilla, spark, ace, minutiae, thought, idea, suspicion, *soupçon*, whit, tittle, shade, shadow, touch, cast, taste, grain, scruple, spice, sprinkling, drop, droplet, driblet, globule, minim, dash, smack, nip. sip, scantling, dole, scrap, mite, slip, snippet, tag, bit, morsel, crumb, paring, shaving (51), trifle, thimbleful, toothful, spoonful, cupful, mouthful, handful, fistful.

Finiteness, a finite quantity.

(Phrases) The shadow of a shade; a drop in a bucket or in the ocean.

(Verbs) To be small, etc., to run low, diminish, shrink, decrease (36), contract (195).

(Phrases) To lie in a nutshell; to pass muster.

(Adjectives) Small, little, wee, scant, inconsiderable, diminutive, minute (193), tiny, minikin, puny, petty, sorry, miserable, shabby, wretched, paltry (643), weak (160), slender, feeble, faint, slight, scrappy, fiddling, trivial, scanty, light, trifling, moderate, low, mean, mediocre, passable, passing, light, sparing.

Below par, below the mark, under the mark, at a low ebb, imperfect, unfinished, partial (651), inappreciable, evanescent, infinitesimal, atomic, homoeopathic.

Mere, simple, sheer, bare.

incomparable, tremendous, terrific, formidable, amazing, phenomenal, superhuman, titanic, immoderate.

Indefinite, boundless, unbounded, unlimited, incalculable, illimitable, immeasurable, infinite, unapproachable, unutterable, indescribable, unspeakable, inexpressible, beyond expression, swingeing, unconscionable, fabulous, uncommon, unusual (83).

Undiminished, unrestricted, unabated, unreduced, unmitigated, unredeemed, untempered.

Absolute, positive, decided, staring, unequivocal, serious, grave, essential, perfect, finished, completed, abundant (639).

(Adverbs) In a great degree, much, muckle, well, considerably, largely, grossly, greatly, very, very much, a deal, not a little, no end, pretty, pretty well, enough, richly, to a large extent, to a great extent, ever so, mainly, ever so much, on a large scale, insomuch, all lengths, wholesale, in a great measure.

In a positive degree, truly (494), positively, verily, really, indeed, actually, in fact, fairly, assuredly, decidedly, surely, clearly, obviously, unequivocally, purely, absolutely, seriously, essentially, fundamentally, radically, downright, in grain, altogether, entirely, completely.

In a comparative degree, comparatively, *pro tanto*, as good as, to say the least, above all, most, of all things, pre-eminently.

(Adverbs) In a small degree, on a small scale, to a small extent, a wee bit, something, somewhat, next to nothing, little, inconsiderably, slightly, so-so, minutely, faintly, feebly, lightly, imperfectly, scantily, shabbily, miserably, wretchedly, sparingly, weakly, slenderly, modestly.

In a limited degree, in a certain degree, to a certain degree or extent, partially, in part, some, somewhat, rather, in some degree, in some measure, something, simply, only, purely, merely, in a manner, at least, at most, ever so little, thus far, *pro tanto*, next to nothing.

Almost, nearly, well-nigh, all but, short of, not quite, close upon, near the mark.

In an uncertain degree, about, thereabouts, scarcely, hardly, barely, somewhere about, say, more or less, *à peu près*, there or thereabouts.

In no degree, noways, nowise, nohow, in no wise, by no means, not in the least, not at all, not a bit, not a bit of it, not a whit, not a jot, in no respect, by no manner of means, on no account.

(Phrases) As little as may be; after a fashion; in a way.

Within an ace of; on the brink of; next door to; a close shave (or call).

In a complete degree, completely (52), altogether, quite, entirely, wholly, totally, *in toto, toto coelo*, utterly, thoroughly, out and out, outright, out and away, fairly, clean, to the full, in every respect, *sous tous les rapports*, in all respects, on all accounts, nicely, perfectly, fully, amply, richly, wholesale, abundantly, consummately, widely, as . . . as . . . can be, every inch, *à fond, de fond*, far and wide, over head and ears, to the backbone, through and through, *ne plus ultra*.

In a greater degree, even, yea, *a fortiori,* still more.

In a high degree, highly, deeply, strongly, mighty, mightily, powerfully (157), profoundly, superlatively, ultra, in the extreme, extremely, exceedingly, excessively, comsumedly, sorely, intensely, exquisitely, acutely, soundly, vastly, hugely, immensely, enormously, stupendously, passing, surpassing, supremely, beyond measure, immoderately, monstrously, inordinately, tremendously, over head and ears, extraordinarily, exorbitantly, indefinitely, immeasurably, unspeakably, inexpressibly, ineffably, unutterably, incalculably, infinitely, unsurpassably.

In a marked degree, particularly, remarkably, singularly, uncommonly, unusually, peculiarly, notably, *par excellence*, eminently, pre-eminently, superlatively, signally, famously, egregiously, prominently, glaringly, emphatically, strangely, wonderfully, amazingly, surprisingly, astonishingly, prodigiously, monstrously, incredibly, inconceivably, marvellously, awfully, stupendously.

In a violent degree, violently, severely, furiously, desperately, tremendously, outrageously, extravagantly, confoundedly, deucedly, devilishly, diabolically, with a vengeance, *à outrance*, like mad (173).

In a painful degree, sadly, grievously, woefully, wretchedly, piteously, sorely, lamentably, shockingly, frightfully, dreadfully, fearfully, terribly, horribly.

Quantity by Comparison with a Similar Object

33 Superiority (*Substantives*), majority, supremacy, primacy, advantage, preponderance, excess (641), prevalence, pre-eminence, championship.

Maximum, acme, climax, zenith, summit, utmost height, record, culminating point (210), the height of, lion's share, overweight.

(*Phrases*) A Triton among the minnows; cock of the walk; *ne plus ultra: summum bonum.*

(*Verbs*) To be superior, etc.; to exceed, surpass, excel, eclipse, transcend, top, overtop, o'ertop, cap, beat, cut out, outclass, override, outmatch, outbalance, overbalance, overweigh, overshadow, outdo; preponderate, predominate, prevail.

To render larger, magnify (194).

(*Phrases*) To have the advantage of; to have the upper hand; to bear the palm; to have one cold; to beat hollow; to take the shine out of; to throw into the shade; to be a cut above.

(*Adjectives*) Superior, greater, major, higher, surpassing, exceeding, excelling, passing, ultra, vaulting, transcending, transcendent, unequalled, unsurpassed, peerless, matchless, unparalleled, without parallel.

Supreme, greatest, utmost, paramount, pre-eminent, foremost, crowning, sovereign, culminating, superlative, topmost, top-hole, highest, first-rate, champion, A1, the last word, the limit.

(*Phrases*) *Facile princeps; nulli secundus; primus inter pares.*

(*Adverbs*) Beyond, more, over and above the mark, above par, over and above, at the top of the scale, at its height.

In a superior degree, eminently, pre-eminently, egregiously, prominently, superlatively, supremely, above all, of all things, principally, especially, particularly, peculiarly, *par excellence, a fortiori.*

34 Inferiority (*Substantives*), minority, subordination, shortcoming (304); deficiency, minimum.

(*Verbs*) To be less, inferior, etc., to fall or come short of, not to pass (304); to want, be wanting.

To become smaller, to render smaller (195); to subordinate.

(*Phrases*) To be thrown into the shade; to hide one's diminished head; to give a person best; to play second fiddle.

(*Adjectives*) Inferior, deficient, smaller, minor, less, lesser, lower, sub, subordinate, subaltern, secondary, second-rate, second-best.

Least, smallest, wee-est, minutest, etc., lowest.

(*Phrases*) Weighed in the balance and found wanting; not fit to hold a candle to.

(*Adverbs*) Less, under or below the mark, below par, at the bottom of the scale, at a low ebb, short of, at a disadvantage.

Changes in Quantity

35 Increase *(Substantives)*, augmentation, enlargement, extension, dilatation (194), increment, accretion, development, rise, growth, swell, swelling, expansion, aggrandizement, aggravation, rise, exacerbation, spread, climax, exaggeration, diffusion (73), flood-tide; accession (37).

(Verbs) To increase, augment, enlarge, amplify, extend, dilate, swell, wax, expand, grow, stretch, shoot up, mushroom, rise, run up, sprout, burgeon, advance, spread, gather head, aggrandize, add, superadd, raise, heighten, strengthen, greaten, exalt, enhance, magnify, redouble, aggravate, exaggerate, exasperate, exacerbate, escalate.

(Phrases) To add fuel to the flame; to pour oil on the flames.

(Adjectives) Increased, augmented, enlarged, etc., undiminished; cumulative; additional (37).

(Adverb) Crescendo.

36 Non-increase.
Decrease *(Substantives)* diminution, depreciation, lessening, reduction, abatement, bating, declension, falling off, dwindling, contraction (195), shrinking, attenuation, extenuation, anticlimax, abridgment, curtailment (201), coarctation, narrowing; deduction (38).

Subsidence, wane, ebb, decrement.

(Verbs) To decrease, diminish, lessen, dwindle, decay, crumble, shrink, contract, shrivel, fall off, fall away, waste, wear, wane, ebb, subside, decline, languish, wear off, run low, grow downward.

To abridge, reduce, curtail, cut down, pare down, subtract, shorten, cut short, dock (201), bate, abate, fritter away, attenuate, extenuate, lower, weaken, dwarf; to mitigate (174), to throw in the shade.

(Phrase) To hide its diminished head.

(Adjectives) Decreased, diminished, lessened, etc., shorn, short by, decreasing, on the wane.

(Adverbs) *Diminuendo, decrescendo.*

3°. *Conjunctive Quantity*

37 Addition *(Substantives)* adjection, introduction, superinduction, annexation, superposition, superaddition, subjunction, supervention, increment, accession, superfetation, corollary, reinforcement, supplement, accompaniment (88), interposition (228), insertion (300).

(Verbs) To add, annex, affix, superadd, supplement, reinforce, subjoin, superpose, throw in, clap on, tack to, append, tag, engraft, saddle on, saddle with, superinduce, introduce, work in, interleave, extra-illustrate, grangerize.

To become added, to accrue, advene, supervene.

(Phrase) To swell the ranks of.

(Adjectives) Added, annexed, etc., additional, supplementary, supplemental, suppletory, subjunctive,

38 Non-addition.
Subduction *(Substantives)*, subtraction, abstraction, deduction, deducement, retrenchment, removal, elimination, ablation (789), purgation, curtailment, etc. (36), garbling, mutilation, truncation, abscission, excision, amputation, detruncation, sublation, castration, apocope.

Subtrahend, minuend; decrement, discount.

(Verbs) To subduct, exclude, deduct, subtract, abscind, retrench, remove, withdraw, eliminate, bate, detract, deduce, take away, deprive of, curtail (36), garble, truncate, mutilate, eviscerate, exenterate, detruncate, castrate, spay, geld, purge, amputate, cut off, excise, cut out, dock, lop, prune, pare, dress, clip, thin, shear, decimate, abrade (330).

adscititious, additive, accessory, cumulative.

(Adverbs) Additionally, in addition, more, *plus*, extra, and, also, likewise, too, furthermore, forby, item, and also, and eke, else, besides, to boot, etcetera, and so forth, into the bargain, over and above, moreover.

With, together with, withal, along with, including, inclusive, as well as, not to mention, to say nothing of; jointly, conjointly (43).

39 Thing added.

Adjunct *(Substantives)*, additament, addition, affix, appendage, annex, suffix, postfix, inflexion, augment, increment, augmentation, accessory, item, garnish, sauce, supplement, extra, bonus (810), adjective, addendum, complement, corollary, continuation, increment, reinforcement, pendant, apanage.

Sequel (65), postscript, codicil, envoy, rider, corollary, heel-piece, tag, tab, skirt, flap, lappet, trappings, tail, tailpiece (67), queue, train, suite, cortège, accompaniment (88).

(Phrase) More last words.

41 Forming a whole without coherence.

Mixture *(Substantives)*, admixture, commixture, commixtion, intermixture, alloyage, marriage, miscegenation.

Impregnation, infusion, infiltration, diffusion, suffusion, interspersion, transfusion, seasoning, sprinkling, interlarding, interpolation, interposition (228), intrusion; adulteration, sophistication.

Thing mixed, a touch, spice, tinge, tincture, dash, smack, sprinkling, seasoning, infusion, suspicion, *soupçon*, shade, bit, portion, dose.

Compound resulting from mixture, blend, alloy, amalgam, magma, *mélange*, half and half, hybrid, *tertium quid*, miscellany, medley,

(Adjectives) Subtracted, deducted, etc., subtractive.

(Adverbs) In deduction, etc., less, *minus*, without, except, excepting, with the exception of, but for, barring, save, exclusive of, save and except (83).

40 Thing remaining.

Remainder *(Substantives)*, residue, remains, remnant, the rest, relics, leavings, heel-tap, odds and ends, cheese-parings, candle-ends, offscourings, orts.

Residuum, *caput mortuum*, dregs, refuse (645), scum, recrement (653), ashes, dross, cinders, slag, sediment, silt, alluvium, stubble; slough, exuviae, result, educt.

Surplus, overplus, surplusage, superfluity, excess (641), balance, complement, fag-end, stump, butt, rump, wreck, wreckage, ruins, skeleton.

(Verbs) To remain, be left, be left behind, exceed, survive.

(Adjectives) Remaining, left, left behind, residual, exuvial, residuary, sedimentary, outstanding, net, cast off, odd, over, unconsumed, surviving, outlying.

Superfluous, over and above, exceeding, redundant (641), supernumerary.

42 Freedom from mixture.

Simpleness *(Substantives)*, singleness, purity, clearness, homogeneity.

Purification (652), elimination, sifting, winnowing.

(Verbs) To render simple, simplify, sift, winnow, bolt, screen, sort, eliminate; to separate, disjoin (44).

To purify (652).

(Adjectives) Simple, uniform, of a piece, homogeneous, single, pure, clear, sheer, blank, neat, absolute, elemental, elementary; unmixed, unmingled, untinged, unblended, uncombined, uncompounded, undecomposed, unadulterated, unsophisticated, undiluted, straight.

Free from, exempt from.

(Phrase) Pure and simple.

pastiche, pasticcio, patchwork, odds and ends; farrago, jumble (59), mess, salad, sauce, hash, hodge-podge or hotchpotch or hotchpot, mash, mish-mash, job lot, omnium gatherum, gallimaufry, olla podrida, olio, salmagundi, pot-pourri, Noah's ark, cauldron, marquetry, mosaic (440), complex.

A cross, hybrid, mongrel, half-breed, Eurasian, mulatto, quadroon, octoroon, sambo.

(Phrases) A mingled yarn; a scratch team.

(Verbs) To mix, commix, immix, intermix, associate, join (43), mingle, commingle, intermingle, bemingle, interlard, intersperse, interpose, interpolate (228); shuffle together, hash up, huddle together, deal, pound together, stir up, knead, brew, jumble (59); impregnate with.

To be mixed, to get among, to be entangled with.

To instil, imbue, infuse, infiltrate, dash, tinge, tincture, season, sprinkle, besprinkle, suffuse, transfuse, attemper, medicate, blend, alloy, amalgamate, compound (48), adulterate, sophisticate, infect, cross, intercross, interbreed, interblend.

(Adjectives) Mixed, mingled, intermixed, etc., motley, miscellaneous, promiscuous; complex, composite, mixed up with, half-and-half, linsey-woolsey, mongrel, heterogeneous; miscible.

43 Junction *(Substantives)*, joining, joinder, union, connection, connecting, hook-up, conjunction, conjugation, annexion, annexation, annexment, attachment, compagination, astriction, ligation, alligation, colligation, fastening, linking, accouplement, coupling, matrimony (903), grafting; infibulation, inosculation, symphysis, anastomosis, association (72), concatenation, communication, approach (197).

Joint, join, juncture, pivot, hinge, suture, articulation, commissure, mitre, seam, stitch, meeting, reunion, mortise.

Closeness, firmness, tightness, compactness, attachment, communication.

(Verbs) To join, conjoin, unite, connect, associate, put together, embody, re-embody, hold together, lump together, pack, fix together, attach, affix, saddle on, fasten, bind, secure, make fast, grapple, moor, clench (or clinch), catch, tie, pinion, strap, sew, lace, string, stitch, tack, knit, tat, crochet, knot, button, buckle, hitch, lash, truss, bandage, braid, splice, swathe, gird, tether, picket, harness, inspan, bridge over.

Chain, enchain, shackle, pinion, fetter, manacle, handcuff, lock, latch,

44 Disjunction *(Substantives)*, disconnection, disunity, disunion, disassociation, disengagement, abstraction, abstractedness, isolation, insularity, oasis, separateness, severalness, severality.

Separation, parting, detachment, divorce, sejunction, seposition, segregation, insulation, diduction, discerption, elision, caesura, division, subdivision, break, fracture, rupture, dismemberment, disintegration, dislocation, luxation, severance, disseverance, severing, fission, scission, rescission, abscission, laceration, dilaceration, wrenching, abruption, disruption, avulsion, divulsion, tearing asunder, section, cutting, resection, cleavage, fissure, breach, rent, split, crack, slit, tear, rip, dispersion (73), incision, dissection, vivisection anatomy.

Anatomist, prosector.

(Phrase) Disjecta membra.

(Verbs) To be disjoined, separated, etc., to come off, fall off, get loose, fall to pieces.

To disjoin, disconnect, disunite, part, dispart, detach, separate, space, space out, cut off, rescind, segregate, insulate, dissociate, isolate, disengage, set apart, liberate, loose, set free (750), unloose, unfasten, untie, unbind,

belay, brace, hook, clap, together, leash, couple, link, yoke, bracket, hang together, pin, nail, bolt, hasp, clasp, clamp, screw, rivet, solder, weld, impact, wedge, rabbet, mortise, mitre, jam, dovetail, enchase, engraft, interlink, inosculate, entwine, enlace, interlace, intertwine, intertwist, interweave, interlock.

To be joined, etc., to hang or hold together, cohere (46).

(Adjectives) Joined, conjoined, coupled, etc., bound up together, conjunct, corporate, compact.

Firm, fast, close, tight, taut, secure, set, fixed, impacted, jammed, locked, etc., intervolved, intertwined, inseparable, indissoluble, inseverable, untearable.

(Phrases) Hand in hand; rolled into one.

(Adverbs) Conjointly, jointly, etc.

With, along with, together with, in conjunction with.

Fast, firmly, closely, etc.

————

disband, unfix, unlace, unclasp, undo, unbutton, unbuckle, unchain, unfetter, untack, unharness, ungird, unpack, unbolt, unlatch, unlock, unlink, uncouple, unpin, unclinch, unscrew, unhook, unrivet, untwist, unshackle, unyoke, unknit, unsolder, ravel out, unravel, disentagle, unpick, unglue, switch off, shut off.

Sunder, divide, subdivide, divorce, sever, dissever, abscind, cut, scissor, incide, incise, snip, nib, cleave, rive, slit, split, split in twain, splinter, chip, crack, snap, burst, rend, break or tear asunder, shiver, crunch, chop, cut up, rip up, hack, hew, slash, whittle, haggle, hackle, discind, tear, lacerate, mangle, mince, gash, hash, knap.

Dissect, cut up, carve, slice, castrate, detruncate, anatomize; take, pull, or pick to pieces; unseam, tear to tatters, tear piecemeal, divellicate, disintegrate; dismember, disembowel, eviscerate, disbranch, dislocate, joint, disjoint, behead, mince, break up, crunch, gride, comminute (330), vivisect.

(Phrase) To tear limb from limb.

(Adjectives) Disjoined, disconnected, etc., snippety, disjointed, multipartite, abstract, disjunctive, isolated, insular, separate, discrete, apart, asunder, loose, free, liberated, disengaged, unattached, unannexed, distinct, unassociated, unconnected, adrift, straggling, dispersed, disbanded, segregated.

Cut off, rescinded, etc., rift, reft.

Capable of being cut, scissile, fissile, discerptible.

(Adverbs) Separately, etc., one by one, severally, apiece, apart, adrift, asunder; in the abstract, abstractedly.

45 Connecting medium.

Vinculum *(Substantives)*, link, connective, connection, junction (43), conjunction, copula, intermedium, hyphen, bridge, stepping-stone, isthmus, span, girder.

Bond, filament, fibre (205), hair, cordage, cord, thread, string, packthread, twine, twist, whipcord, tape, ferret, raffia, line, snood, ribbon, riband, rope, cable, hawser, painter, halyard, guy, guy-rope, wire, chain.

Fastening, tie, tendril, tendon, ligament, ligature, strap, tackle, rigging, traces, harness, yoke, band, withe, withy, brace, bandage, roller, fillet, thong, braid, inkle, girth, cinch, cestus, girdle, garter, halter, noose, lasso, lariat, surcingle, knot, running-knot, slip-knot, reef-knot, sailor's knot, grannyknot, etc.

Pin, corking-pin, safety-pin, nail, brad, tack, skewer, staple, clamp, vice, bracket, cramp, screw, button, buckle, brooch, clasp, slide, clip, hasp, hinge, hank, bolt, catch, latch, latchet, tag, hook, tooth, hook and eye, lock, locket, holdfast, padlock, rivet, anchor, grappling-iron, stake, post, gyve, shackle (752).

Cement, adhesive, mucilage, glue, gum, paste, size, goo, solder, lute, putty, bird-lime, mortar, stucco, plaster, grout.

46 Coherence *(Substantives)*, cohehesion, adherence, adhesion, accretion, concretion, agglutination, conglutination, aggregation, consolidation, set, cementation, soldering, welding, grouting.

Sticking, clinging, adhesiveness, stickiness, gumminess, gummosity, glutinosity (352), cohesiveness, density (321), in separability, inseparableness, tenaciousness, tenacity.

Clot, concrete, cake, lump, conglomerate (321).

(Verbs) To cohere, adhere, stick, cling, cleave, hold, take hold of, hold fast, hug, grow or hang together, twine round.

To concrete, curdle, cake.

To glue, agglutinate, conglutinate, agglomerate, consolidate, solidify (321); cement, lute, paste, gum, grout, stick, solder, weld.

(Phrases) To stick like a leech; to stick like wax; to cling like ivy, like a bur, like a limpet.

(Adjectives) Cohesive, adhesive, cohering, tenacious, sticky, tacky, glutinous, gluey, gooey, gummy, viscous (352), agglutinatory.

United, unseparated, sessile, inseparable, inextricable, infrangible (321).

47 Want of adhesion.

Incoherence *(Substantives)*, nonadhesion, immiscibility, looseness, laxity, slackness, relaxation, freedom, disjunction.

(Phrases) A rope of sand; *disjecta membra*.

(Verbs) To loosen, make loose, slacken, relax, unglue, unsolder, etc., detach, untwist, unravel, unroll (44, 313), to comminute (330)

(Adjectives) Incoherent, immiscible, detached, non-adhesive, loose, slack, lax, relaxed, baggy.

Segregated, flapping, streaming, dishevelled, unincorporated, unconsolidated, uncombined.

(Phrase) Like grains of sand.

———

48 Combination *(Substantives)*, union, unification, synthesis, incorporation, amalgamation, coalescence, crasis, fusion, embodiment, conflation, absorption, blending, centralization; mixture (41).

Compound, composition, amalgam, impregnation, decompound, decomposite, resultant.

(Verbs) To combine, unite, unify, incorporate, amalgamate, synthesize, embody, unify, re-embody, blend, merge, fuse, absorb, melt into one, consolidate, coalesce, centralize; to impregnate, to put together, to lump together.

(Adjectives) Combined, compound, composite, coalescent, synthetic, synthetical, impregnated with, engrained.

49 Decomposition *(Substantives)*, analysis, resolution, dissolution, disintegration, catalysis, electrolysis, corruption (653), dispersion (73), disjunction (44).

(Verbs) To decompose, rot, disembody, analyse, electrolyse, decompound, resolve, take to pieces, separate into its elements, dissect, unravel (313), break up.

(Adjectives) Decomposed, etc., catalytic, analytic, analytical, corrupted, dissolved.

———

4°. *Concrete Quantity*

50 Whole *(Substantives)*, totality, integrity, integrality, allness, entireness, entirety, *ensemble*, collectiveness, individuality, unity (87), indivisibility, indiscerptibility, indissolubility; embodiment, integration.

All, the whole, total, aggregate, integer, gross amount, sum, sum total, *tout ensemble*, upshot, trunk, hull, skeleton, hulk, lump, heap (72).

The principal part, bulk, mass, tissue, staple, body, compages, the main, the greater part, major part.

(Phrases) The whole caboodle; the whole boiling.

(Verbs) To form or constitute a whole, to integrate, embody, aggregate, amass (72), to total, amount to, come to.

(Adjectives) Whole, total, integral, entire, one, unbroken, uncut, undivided, seamless, individual, unsevered, unclipped, uncropped, unshorn, undiminished, undemolished, undissolved, unbruised, undestroyed, indivisible, indissoluble, indissolvable, indiscerptible.

Wholesale, sweeping.

(Adverbs) Wholly, altogether, totally, entirely, all, all in all, as a whole, wholesale, in the aggregate, in the mass, *en masse*, in the lump, *en bloc*, on the whole, *in toto*, in the gross, *in extenso*, in the bulk, to the full, throughout, every inch.

(Phrases) The long and short of it; nearly or almost all; root and branch; lock, stock, and barrel; hook, line, and sinker; in the long run; in the main; neck and crop; from end to end; from beginning to end; from first to last; from head to foot; from top to toe; fore and aft; from alpha to omega.

51 Part *(Substantives)*, portion, item, division, subdivision, section, chapter, verse, extract, passage, gobbet, sector, segment, fraction, fragment, frustum, detachment, piece, bit, lump, chunk, dollop, scrap, whit, swatch, morsel, mouthful, scantling, cantle, cantlet, slip, crumb (32), fritter, rag, tag, shred, tatter, splinter, snatch, cut, cutting, snip, snippet, snick, collop, slice, chip, chipping, shiver, sliver, matchwood, spillikin, smithereens, driblet, clipping, paring, shaving, debris, odds and ends, oddments, sundries, detritus, lamina, shadow, flotsam and jetsam, pickings.

Parcel, share, instalment, contingent, compartment, department, dividend, dose, particular, article, clause, paragraph.

Member, limb, lobe, lobule, arm, branch, scion, bough, joint, link, ramification (256), twig, bush, spray, sprig, offshoot, leaf, leaflet, stump, stub, butt, rump, torso.

(Verbs) To part, divide, subdivide, break (44); to partition, parcel out, portion, apportion (786), to ramify, branch, branch out.

(Adjectives) Part, fractional, fragmentary, scrappy, lobular, sectional, aliquot, divided, multifid, partitioned, isomeric.

(Adverbs) Partly, in part, partially, piecemeal, in detail, part by part, by driblets, bit by bit, little by little, by inches, inch by inch, foot by foot, drop by drop, in snatches, by fits and starts.

---

52 Completeness *(Substantives)*, entirety, fullness, impletion, completion (729), perfection (650), solidity, stop-gap, makeweight, padding, filling up, integration, absoluteness, sufficiency; complement, supplement (39).

Fill, load, bumper, brimmer, bellyful, skinful.

53 Incompleteness *(Substantives)*, deficiency, defectiveness, shortcoming (304), unreadiness, defalcation, failure, imperfection (651), hollowness, patchiness.

Part wanting, omission, defect, break, deficit, ullage, caret, lacuna, hiatus (198).

(Verbs) To be complete, etc., suffice (639).

To render complete or whole, to complete, exhaust, perfect, finish, make up, fill up, charge, load, replenish, make good, piece out, eke out.

(Phrases) To give the finishing touch; to supply deficiencies; to go to all lengths; to go the whole hog; to thrash out.

(Adjectives) Complete, entire, whole (50), absolute, perfect, full, plenary, solid, undivided, with all its parts, supplementary, adscititious, thorough, exhaustive, radical, sweeping, searching; consummate, thorough-paced, regular, sheer, unmitigated, unqualified.

Crammed, saturated, brimful, chock-full.

(Adverbs) Completely, entirely, to the full, outright, wholly, totally, thoroughly (31), *in toto, toto caelo,* in all respects.

(Phrases) To the top of one's bent; up to the ears; *à fond*; from first to last; from beginning to end; *ab ovo usque ad mala.*

(Verbs) To be incomplete, etc., to fail, fall short (304).

To dock, lop, mutilate, garble, truncate, castrate (38).

(Adjectives) Incomplete, unfinished, imperfect, defective, deficient, wanting, failing, short by, hollow, meagre, insufficient, half-baked, perfunctory, sketchy, scrappy, patchy.

Mutilated, garbled, docked, lopped, truncated; proceeding, in progress.

(Phrase) Cetera desunt.

---

54 Composition *(Substantives),* make-up, constitution, constituency, crasis.

Inclusion, admission, comprehension, reception.

(Verbs) To be composed of, to consist of, be made of, formed of, made up of, be resolved into.

To contain, include, hold, comprehend, take in, admit, embrace, involve, implicate.

To compose, constitute, form, make, make up, fill up, build up, put together, embody.

To enter into the composition of, to be or form part of (51), to merge in, be merged in.

(Adjectives) Comprehending, containing, including, comprising, etc.

Component, constituent, formative, forming, constituting, composing, etc., belonging to, appertaining to, inclusive.

55 Exclusion *(Substantives),* nonadmission, omission, exception, rejection, proscription, repudiation, exile, banishment, excommunication.

Separation, segregation, elimination, seposition.

(Verbs) To be excluded from, etc., to be out of it.

To exclude, shut out, bar, leave out, omit, reject, repudiate, neglect, blackball; lay, put, or set apart or aside; segregate, pass over, throw overboard, slur over, neglect (460), excommunicate, banish, expatriate, extradite, deport, ostracize, relegate, rusticate, send down (297), rule out.

To eliminate, weed, winnow, screen, bar, separate (44), strike off.

(Phrase) 'Include me out.'

(Adjectives) Excluding, omitting, etc., exclusive.

Excluded, omitted, etc., unrecounted, inadmissible.

(Adverbs) Except, save, bar, barring, excepting.

---

56 Component *(Substantives)* component part, integral part, element, constituent, ingredient, member,

57 Extraneousness *(Substantives),* extrinsicality (5), exteriority (220).

limb (51), part and parcel, contents (190), appurtenance, feature, personnel.

A foreign body, alien, stranger, intruder, outsider, incomer, interloper, foreigner, dago, wop, *novus homo*, parvenu, immigrant, newcomer, new chum, pommy, greenhorn, tenderfoot.

(Adjectives) Extraneous, foreign, alien, tramontane, ultramontane, interloping.

(Adverbs) Abroad, in foreign parts, overseas.

SECTION IV—ORDER

1°. *Order in General*

58 Order *(Substantives)*, regularity, orderliness, tidiness, uniformity, even tenor, symmetry.

Gradation, progression, pedigree, line, descent, subordination, course, series (69), array, routine.

Method, disposition, arrangement, system, economy, discipline, pattern, plan.

Rank, station, hierarchy, place, status, stand, scale, step, stage, period, term (71), footing; rank and file, pecking order.

(Verbs) To be or become in order, to form, fall in, arrange itself, place itself, range itself, fall into its place, fall into rank.

(Adjectives) Orderly, regular, in order, arranged, etc. (60), in its proper place, correct, tidy, shipshape, trim, *en règle*, well regulated, methodical, business-like, uniform, symmetrical, systematic, unconfused, undisturbed, untangled, unruffled, unravelled, still, etc. (265).

(Phrases) In apple-pie order; Bristol fashion.

(Adverbs) Systematically, methodically, etc., in turn, in its turn.

Step by step, by regular steps, gradations, stages, periods, or intervals, periodically (138).

At stated periods (138), *gradatim, seriatim*.

(Phrase) Like clockwork.

59 Absence, or want of Order, etc.
Disorder *(Substantives)*, irregularity, asymmetry, anomaly, confusion, confusedness, disarray, untidiness, jumble, huddle, litter, lumber, farrago, mess, hash, clutter, pie, muddle, mix-up, upset, hotchpotch, hugger-mugger, anarchy, anarchism, imbroglio, chaos, tohubohu, omnium gatherum(72), derangement(61).

Complexness, complexity, complication, intricacy, intricateness, implication, perplexity, involution, ravelling, tangle, entanglement, snarl, knot, coil, skein, sleave, network, labyrinth, Gordian knot, jungle.

Turmoil, *mêlée*, tumult, ferment, stew, fermentation, pudder, pother, riot, uproar, bobbery, rough-house, rumpus, scramble, fracas, vortex, whirlpool, maelstrom, hurly-burly, bear - garden, Babel, Saturnalia, Donnybrook, pandemonium.

Tumultuousness, riotousness, inquietude (173), derangement (61), topsyturvydom (218).

(Phrases) Wheels within wheels; confusion worse confounded; most admired disorder; *concordia discors*; hell broke loose.

A pretty kettle of fish; a fine state of things; a how-d'ye-do; the fat in the fire; a bull in a china shop; the devil to pay.

The cart before the horse; hysteron proteron.

(Verbs) To be out of order, irregular, disorderly, etc., to ferment.

To derange, put out of order (61).

(Phrases) To be at cross-purposes; to make hay of.

(Adjectives) Disorderly, orderless, out of order, disordered, misplaced, out of place, deranged, disarranged (61), irregular, desultory, anomalous, untidy, sloppy, slovenly, tousled, straggling, unarranged, immethodical, unsymmetrical, unsystematic, unmethodical, undigested, unsorted, unclassified, unclassed, asymmetrical.

Disjointed, out of joint, out of gear, out of kilter, confused, tangled, involved, intricate, complicated, inextricable, irreducible.

Mixed, scattered, promiscuous, indiscriminate, casual.

Tumultuous, turbulent, riotous, troublous, tumultuary (173), rough-and-tumble.

(Adverbs) Irregularly, etc., by fits and snatches, pell-mell; higgledy-piggledy, hugger-mugger; at sixes and sevens; helter-skelter, harum-scarum, anyhow.

60 Reduction to Order.

Arrangement *(Substantives)*, disposal, disposition, collocation, allocation, distribution, sorting, assortment, allotment, apportionment, marshalling, alignment, taxis, taxonomy, gradation, organization, ordination; plan (626).

Analysis, sifting, screening, classification.

Result of arrangement, digest, synopsis, analysis, table, register (551).

Instrument for sorting, sieve, riddle, screen (260).

(Verbs) To order, reduce to order, bring into order, introduce order into.

To arrange, dispose, place, form; to put, set, place, etc., in order; to set out, collocate, pack, marshal, range, align (or aline), rank, group, parcel out, allot, distribute, assort, sort, sift, riddle.

To class, classify, categorize, file, string, thread, tabulate, pigeon-hole, catalogue, index, register, take stock.

To methodize, digest, regulate, size, grade, gradate, graduate, alphabetize, co-ordinate, systematize, organize, settle, fix, rearrange.

To unravel (246), disentangle, ravel, card, disembroil.

(Phrases) To put or set to rights; to assign places to.

(Adjectives) Arranged, methodical (58), embattled, in battle array.

(Phrase) A place for everything, and everything in its place.

61 Subversion of Order, bringing into disorder.

Derangement *(Substantives)*, disarrangement, misarrangement, displacement, misplacement, dislocation, discomposure, disturbance, bedevilment, disorganization, perturbation; shuffling, rumpling, embroilment, corrugation (258), inversion (218), jumble, muddle, disorder (59).

(Verbs) To derange, disarrange, misarrange, misplace, mislay, discompose, disorder, embroil, unsettle, disturb, confuse, perturb, jumble, tumble, huddle, shuffle, muddle, toss, hustle, fumble; to bring, put, or throw into disorder, trouble, confusion, etc., break the ranks, upset.

To unhinge, put out of joint, dislocate, turn over, invert; turn topsy-turvy; turn inside out (218), bedevil, throw out of gear.

To complicate, involve, perplex, tangle, entangle, embrangle (or imbrangle), ravel, ruffle, tousle, rumple, dishevel, muss, litter, scatter, make a mess of, monkey with, make hay of.

(Adjectives) Deranged, etc., disordered (59).

2°. *Consecutive Order*

62 Precedence *(Substantives)*, coming before, antecedence, antecedency, anteposition, priority (116), anteriority, the *pas*, the lead.

Superiority (33), precession (280).

(Verbs) To precede, come before, lead, introduce, usher in.

To place before; to prefix, affix, premise, prelude, preface, prologize.

(Phrases) To have the *pas*; to take the lead; to have the start; set the fashion; to open the ball.

(Adjectives) Preceding, precedent, antecedent, anterior, prior, previous, before, ahead of, leading.

Former, foregoing; coming or going before; precursory, precursive, prevenient, inaugural, prodromal, prodromic, preliminary, aforesaid, said, aforementioned, prefatory, introductory, prelusive, prelusory, proemial, preparatory, preambulatory.

(Adverbs) In advance, ahead, in front of, before, in the van (234).

---

64 Precursor *(Substantives)*, antecedent, precedent, predecessor, forerunner, pioneer, outrider, avant-courier, leader, bell-wether, herald, harbinger.

Prelude, preamble, preface, foreword, prologue, prodrome, protasis, prolusion, overture, premise, proem, prolepsis, prolegomena, prefix, introduction, heading, advertisement, frontispiece, groundwork (673).

(Adjectives) Precursory, prefatory (62).

66 Beginning *(Substantives)*, commencement, opening, outset, incipience, inception, inchoation, initiative, overture, exordium, introduction (64), inauguration début, onset, brunt, alpha.

Origin, source, rise, conception, birth, infancy, bud, embryo, germ, egg, rudiment, *incunabula*, start, cradle, starting-point, starting-post (293); dawn, morning (125).

63 Sequence *(Substantives)*, coming after, consecution, succession, posteriority (117), secondariness; following (281).

Continuation, order of succession, successiveness; alternation (138).

Subordination, inferiority (34).

(Phrase) Proxime accessit.

(Verbs) To succeed, come after, follow, come next, ensue, come on, tread close upon; to alternate.

To place after, to suffix, append.

(Phrases) To be in the wake or trail of; to tread on the heels of; to step into the shoes of; to assume the mantle of.

(Adjectives) Succeeding, coming after, following, subsequent, ensuing, sequent, sequacious, consequent, next; consecutive, amoebean, alternate (138).

Latter, posterior.

(Adverbs) After, subsequently, since, behind, in the wake of, in the train of, at the tail of, in the rear of (234).

---

65 Sequel *(Substantives)*, after-part, aftermath, suffix, successor, tail, runner-up, queue, train, wake, trail, rear, retinue, suite, appendix (39), postscript, epilogue, peroration, excursus, after-piece, tailpiece, tag, colophon, afterthought, second thoughts, *arrière pensée*, codicil, continuation, sequela, apodosis.

(Phrases) More last words; to be continued.

(Adjectives) Subsequent, ensuing (63).

67 End *(Substantives)*, close, termination, desinence, conclusion, finish, finis, finale, period, term, terminus, limit, last, omega, extreme, extremity, butt-end, fag-end, stub, tail, nib, tip, after-part, rear (235), colophon, coda, tailpiece, tag, *cul-de-lampe*, peroration, swan-song.

Completion (729), winding-up, *dénouement*, catastrophe, consummation, expiration, expiry, finishing

Van, vanguard, title-page, heading, front (234), fore-part, head (210).

Opening, entrance, entry, inlet, orifice, porch, portal, portico, gateway, door, gate, postern, wicket, threshold, vestibule, mouth, *fauces*, lips.

Alphabet, A B C, rudiments, elements.

(Phrase) The rising of the curtain; the thin end of the wedge.

(Verbs) To begin, commence, inchoate, rise, arise, originate, initiate, open, dawn, set in, take its rise, enter upon, embark on, set out (293), rcommence, undertake (676).

To usher in, lead off, lead the way, take the lead or the initiative; head, stand at the head, stand first, broach, set on foot, set a-going, set abroach, set up, handsel, institute, launch, strike up.

(Phrases) To make a beginning; to cross the Rubicon; to break ground; set the ball in motion; take the initiative; break the ice; fire away; open the ball; kick off; tee up; pipe up.

(Adjectives) Beginning, commencing, arising, initial, initiatory, initiative, inceptive, incipient, proemial, inaugural, inchoate, inchoative, embryonic, primigenial, aboriginal, rudimental, nascent, natal, opening, dawning, entering.

First, foremost, leading, heading, maiden.

Begun, commenced, etc.

(Adverbs) At, or in the beginning, at first blush, first, in the first place, *imprimis*, first and foremost, *in limine*, in the bud, in embryo.

From the beginning, *ab initio, ab ovo.*

stroke, knock-out, K.O., death-blow, *coup de grâce*, upshot, issue, fate, doom, Day of Judgment, doomsday.

(Phrases) The *ne plus ultra*; the fall of the curtain; *'le commencement de la fin.'*

(Verbs) To end, close, finish, expire, terminate, conclude; come or draw to an end, close or stop, be all over, pass away, give out, peter out, run its course; to say one's say, perorate, be through with.

To come last, bring up the rear.

To bring to an end, close, etc., to put a period, etc., to; to make an end of; to close, finish, seal, wind up, complete, achieve (729), crown, determine.

(Phrases) To cut the matter short; to shut up shop.

(Adjectives) Ending, closing, etc., final, terminal, eschatological, desistive, definitive, crowning.

Last, ultimate, penultimate, antepenultimate, hindermost, rear, caudal, conterminal, conterminous.

Ended, closed, terminated, etc., through.

Unbegun, fresh, uncommenced.

(Adverbs) Once for all, in fine, finally, at the end of the day, for good, for good and all.

---

68 Middle *(Substantives)*, midst, mean, medium, happy medium, *via media*, middle term, centre (223), *mezzo termine, juste milieu*, half-way house, hub, nave, navel, omphalos, bull's-eye, nucleus.

Equidistance, equator, diaphragm, midriff; bisection (91).

Intervenience, interjacence, intervention (228), mid-course (628).

(Adjectives) Middle, medial, median, mesial, mean, mid, middlemost, midmost, mediate, intermediate (29), intervenient, interjacent (228), central (222), equidistant, embosomed, merged.

Mediterranean, equatorial.

(Adverbs) In the middle, amid, amidst, midway, amidships, midships, halfway.

(Phrases) In the thick of; *in medias res.*

69 Uninterrupted sequence.

Continuity *(Substantives)*, consecution, consecutiveness, succession, suite, progression, series, train, chain, catenation, concatenation, scale, gradation, course, procession, column, retinue, cortège, cavalcade, rank and file, line of battle, array, pedigree, genealogy, lineage, race.

File, queue, echelon, line, row, rank, range, tier, string, thread, team, tandem, random, suit, flush, colonnade.

(Verbs) To follow in, form a series, etc.; to fall in.

To arrange in a series, to marshal (60); to string together, file, thread, graduate, tabulate.

(Adjectives) Continuous, sequent, consecutive, progressive, serial, successive, continued, uninterrupted, unbroken, entire, linear, in a line, in a row, etc., gradual, constant, unremitting, unintermitting, evergreen (110).

(Adverbs) Continuously, consecutively, etc., *seriatum*; in a line, row, series, etc., in succession, etc., running, gradually, step by step; uninterruptedly, at a stretch, at one go.

(Phrase) In Indian file.

70 Interrupted sequence.

Discontinuity *(Substantives)*, interruption, pause, period, interregnum, break, interval, interlude, episode, lacuna, cut, gap, fracture, fault, chasm, hiatus (198), caesura, parenthesis, rhapsody, anacoluthon.

Intermission, alternation (138); a broken thread, broken melody.

(Verbs) To be discontinuous, etc.; to alternate, intermit.

To discontinue, pause, interrupt, break, interpose (228); to break in upon, disconnect (44); to break or snap the thread.

(Adjectives) Discontinuous, inconsecutive, broken, interrupted, unsuccessive, desultory, disconnected, unconnected, fitful, spasmodic, sporadic, scattered.

Alternate, every other, intermitting, alternating (138).

(Phrase) Few and far between.

(Adverbs) At intervals, by snatches, *per saltum*, by fits and starts, *longo intervallo*.

---

71 Term *(Substantives)*, rank, station, stage, step, rung, round, degree (26), remove, grade, link, place, peg, mark, point, *pas*, period, pitch, stand, standing, status, footing, range.

(Verbs) To hold, occupy, find, fall into a place, station.

3°. *Collective Order*

72 Assemblage *(Substantives)*, collection, dozen, collocation, compilation, levy, gathering, ingathering, muster, round-up, colligation, contesseration, *attroupement*, association, concourse, conflux, convergence, meeting, assembly, congregation, at home (892), levee, club, reunion, gaudy, soirée, conversazione, accumulation, cumulation, array, mobilization.

Congress, convocation, convention, *comitium*, committee, quorum, conclave, synod, caucus, conventicle, eisteddfod, mass-meeting.

73 Non-assemblage.

Dispersion *(Substantives)*, scattering, dissemination, diffusion, dissipation, spreading, casting, distribution, apportionment, sprinkling, respersion, circumfusion, interspersion, divergence (291), demobilization.

Odds and ends, waifs and strays, flotsam and jetsam.

(Verbs) To disperse, scatter, sow, disseminate, diffuse, shed, spread, overspread, dispense, disband, disembody, distribute, dispel, cast forth; strew, bestrew, sprinkle, sparge, issue, deal out, utter, resperse, intersperse,

Miscellany, olla podrida, museum, *collectanea,* menagerie (636), Noah's ark, anthology, encyclopaedia, portfolio, file.

A multitude (102), crowd, throng, rabble, mob, press, crush, horde, posse, body, tribe, crew, gang, knot, band, party, swarm, school, shoal, bevy, galaxy, covey, flock, herd, drove, corps, troop, troupe, squad, squadron, phalanx, platoon, company, regiment, battalion, legion, host, army, division.

set abroach, circumfuse; to decentralize, demobilize; to hive-off.

(Phrases) To turn adrift; to scatter to the four winds; to sow broadcast; to spread like wildfire.

(Adjectives) Unassembled, uncollected, dispersed, scattered, diffused, sparse, spread, dispread, widespread, sporadic, cast, broadcast, epidemic, adrift.

(Adverbs) Sparism, here and there, *passim.*

A sounder (of swine), skulk (of foxes), pride (of lions), charm (of finches), flush (of mallards), gaggle (of geese), wedge (of swans).

Clan, brotherhood, fraternity, sisterhood, party (712).

Volley, shower, storm, cloud, flood, deluge.

Group, cluster, clump, set, batch, battery, pencil, lot, pack, budget, assortment, bunch, parcel, packet, package, bundle, fascicle, fascicule, *fasciculus,* faggot, wisp, truss, tuft, rosette, shock, rick, fardel, stack, sheaf, stook, haycock.

Accumulation, congeries, heap, hoard, lump, pile, rouleau, tissue, mass, pyramid, bale, drift, snowball, acervation, cumulation, glomeration, agglomeration, conglobation, conglomeration, conglomerate, coacervation, coagmentation, aggregation, concentration (290), congestion, omnium gatherum.

Collector, tax-gatherer, whip, whipper-in.

(Verbs) To assemble, collect, muster, meet, unite, cluster, swarm, flock, herd, crowd, throng, associate, congregate, conglomerate, concentrate, congest, rendezvous, resort, flock together, get together, reassemble.

To bring, get or gather together, collect, draw together, group, convene, convoke, convocate, collocate, colligate, round up, scrape together, rake up, dredge, bring into a focus, amass, accumulate, heap up, pile, pack, do up, stack, truss, cram, pack together, congest, acervate, coagment, agglomerate, garner up, lump together, make a parcel of; to centralize; to mobilize.

(Phrases) To heap Pelion upon Ossa; to collect in a drag-net.

(Adjectives) Assembled, collected, etc., undispersed, met together, closely packed, dense, crowded, serried, huddled together, teeming, swarming, populous.

(Phrases) Packed like sardines; crowded to suffocation.

74 Place of meeting.

Focus *(Substantives),* point of convergence, corradiation, rendezvous, home, headquarters, club, centre (222), gathering-place, meeting-place, trysting-place, rallying-ground, haunt, howff, resort, museum, repository, depot (636).

4°. *Distributive Order*

75 Class *(Substantives),* division, category, predicament, head, order, section, department, domain, province.

Kind, sort, variety, type, genus, species, family, phylum, race, tribe, caste, sept, clan, *gens,* phratry, breed, kith, sect, set, assortment, feather, stripe, suit, range, run.

Gender, sex, kin, kidney, manner, nature, description, denomination, designation, character, stamp, stuff, *genre.*
(Adjectives) Generic, racial, tribal, etc.
(Verbs) To classify, catalogue (60).

76 Inclusion *(Substantives)*, comprehension under a class, reference to a class, admission, comprehension, reception, subsumption.
Inclusion in a compound, composition (54).
(Verbs) To be included in, to come under, to fall under, to range under; to belong, or pertain to, appertain; to range with, to merge in, to be of.

77 Exclusion from a class *(Substantives)*, rejection, proscription.
Exclusion from a compound (55).
(Verbs) To be excluded from, etc.; to exclude, proscribe, debar, rule out, set apart (55).
(Phrase) To shut the door upon.
(Adjectives) Exclusive, excluding, etc.

To include, comprise, comprehend, contain, admit, embrace, receive; to enumerate among, reckon among, reckon with, number among, refer to, place under, class with or among, arrange under or with, take into account, subsume.
(Adjectives) Including, inclusive, all-embracing, congener, congeneric, congenerous, *et hoc genus omne*, etcetera.
Included, merged, etc.
(Phrase) Birds of a feather.

78 Generality *(Substantives)*, universality, catholicism, catholicity.
Every man, every one, everybody, all, all hands.
Miscellaneousness, miscellany, encyclopaedia, generalization, prevalence, drag-net.
(Phrases) The world and his wife; N or M.
(Verbs) To be general, common, or prevalent, to prevail.
To render general, to generalize.
(Adjectives) General, generic, collective, comprehensive, encyclopaedic, panoramic, bird's-eye, sweeping, radical, universal, world-wide, cosmopolitan, catholic, common, oecumenical, transcendental, prevalent, prevailing, all-pervading, epidemic, all-inclusive.
Unspecified, impersonal; every, all.
(Adverbs) Whatever, whatsoever, to a man; generally, universally, on the whole, for the most part.

79 Speciality *(Substantives)*, particularity, peculiarity, individuality, haecceity, thisness, personality, characteristic, mannerism, idiosyncrasy, trick, gimmick, specificness, specificity, eccentricity, singularity (83).
Version, reading (522).
Particulars, details, items, counts.
I, myself, self, I myself, *moi qui vous parle.*
(Phrases) *Argumentum ad hominem;* local colour.
(Verbs) To specify, particularize, individualize, realize, specialize, designate, determine.
(Phrases) To descend to particulars; to enter into detail.
(Adjectives) Special, particular, individual, specific, proper, appropriate, personal, private, respective, several, definite, determinate, especial, certain, esoteric, endemic, partial, party, peculiar, characteristic, distinctive, typical, unique, diagnostic, exclusive, *sui generis,* singular, exceptional (83).

This, that, yonder, yon, such and such.
(Adverbs) Specially, specifically, etc., in particular, respectively, personally, individually, *in propria persona.*
Each, apiece, one by one, severally, seriatim, namely, *videlicet,* viz., to wit.

5°. Order as regards Categories

80 Rule *(Substantives)*, regularity, uniformity, constancy, standard, model, nature, principle, the order of things, routine, prevalence, practice, usage, custom, use, habit (613), regulation, precept (697), convention, *convenances.*

Form, formula, law, canon, principle, keynote, catchword.

Type, archetype, pattern, precedent, paradigm, the normal, natural, ordinary or model state or condition; norm, control.

(Phrases) A standing order; the bed of Procrustes; laws of the Medes and Persians.

(Adjectives) Regular, uniform, constant (82).

81 Multiformity *(Substantives)*, variety, diversity, multifariousness, allotropy, allotropism.

(Adjectives) Multiform, variform, polymorphic, multifold, manifold, multifarious, multigenerous, omnifarious, omnigenous, heterogeneous, motley, epicene, indiscriminate, desultory, irregular, diversified, allotropic; different (15).

(Phrase) Of all sorts and kinds.

———

82 Conformity *(Substantives)*, conformance, observance, naturalization, harmony, convention (613).

Example, instance, specimen, sample, ensample, exemplar, exemplification, illustration, pattern (22), object lesson, case in point, quotation, the rule.

(Phrases) The order of the day; the common or ordinary run of things (23); a matter of course.

(Verbs) To conform to rule, be regular, orthodox, etc., to follow, observe, go by, bend to, obey rules; to be guided or regulated by, be wont, etc. (613), to comply or chime in with, to be in harmony with, follow suit; to standardize, naturalize.

To exemplify, illustrate, cite, quote, put a case, produce an instance, set an example.

(Phrases) To go with the crowd; to do in Rome as the Romans do; to follow the fashion; to swim with the stream; to keep one in countenance.

(Adjectives) Conformable to rule, regular, uniform, constant, steady, according to rule, *en règle, de rigueur,* normal, well regulated, formal, canonical, orthodox, conventional, strict, rigid, positive, uncompromising (23).

Ordinary, natural, usual, common, wonted, accustomed, habitual (613), household, average, everyday, current, rife, prevailing, prevalent, established,

83 Unconformity *(Substantives)*, nonconformity, unconventionality, informality, arbitrariness, abnormity, abnormality, anomaly, anomalousness, lawlessness, peculiarity, exclusiveness; infraction, breach, violation, of law or rule; individuality, idiosyncrasy, mannerism, eccentricity, aberration, irregularity, unevenness, variety, singularity, rarity, oddity, oddness, exemption, salvo.

Exception, nondescript, a character, original, nonesuch, monster, monstrosity, prodigy (872), *lusus naturae, rara avis,* freak, curiosity, crank, queer fish; half-caste, half-breed, cross-breed, mongrel, hybrid, mule, mulatto (41), *tertium quid,* hermaphrodite, sport.

Phoenix, chimera, hydra, sphinx, minotaur, griffin, centaur, hippocentaur, hippogriff, basilisk, cockatrice, tragelaph, kraken, dragon, wyvern, roc, sea-serpent, mermaid, merman, cyclops, unicorn.

(Phrases) Out of one's element; a fish out of water; neither one thing nor another; neither fish, flesh, nor fowl, nor good red herring; a law to oneself.

(Verbs) To be unconformable to rule, to be exceptional, etc.; to violate a law or custom, to stretch a point.

(Phrases) To have no business there; to beggar description.

(Adjectives) Unconformable, excep-

received, stereotyped, acknowledged, typical, accepted, recognized, representative, hackneyed, well-known, familiar, vernacular, commonplace, trite, banal, cut and dried, naturalized, orderly, shipshape, run of the mill.

Exemplary, illustrative, in point, of daily or everyday occurrence, in the order of things.

(Phrases) Regular as clockwork; according to Cocker (or Hoyle).

(Adverbs) Conformably, by rule, regularly, etc., agreeably to; in accordance, conformity, or keeping with.

Usually, generally, ordinarily, commonly, for the most part, as usual, *more solito, more suo, pro more*; of course, as a matter of course, *pro forma*.

Always, uniformly (16), invariably, without exception, never otherwise.

For example, for instance, *exempli gratia, inter alia*.

(Phrases) Ab uno disce omnes; ex pede Herculem; ex ungue leonem; birds of a feather.

tional, abnormal, anomalous, anomalistic, out of order, out of place, misplaced, irregular, unorthodox, uneven, arbitrary, informal, aberrant, stray, peculiar, funny, exclusive, unnatural, eccentric, unconventional, Bohemian, beatnik, hippy, yippy.

Unusual, unaccustomed, unwonted, uncommon, rare, singular, unique, curious, odd, extraordinary, strange, *outré*, out of the way, egregious, out of the ordinary, unheard of, queer, quaint, old-fashioned, unfashionable, nondescript, undescribed, unexampled, *sui generis*, unprecedented, unparalleled, unfamiliar, fantastic, newfangled, grotesque, bizarre, weird, eerie, outlandish, exotic, preternatural, unexampled, unrepresentative, uncanny, denaturalized.

Heterogeneous, heteroclite, amorphous, out of the pale of, mongrel, amphibious, epicene, half-blood, hybrid (41), androgynous, betwixt and between.

(Phrases) 'None but himself could be his parallel'; caviare to the general.

(Adverbs) Unconformably, etc.; except, unless, save, barring, beside, without, but for, save and except, let alone, to say nothing of; however, yet, but.

SECTION V—NUMBER

1°. *Number in the Abstract*

84 Number *(Substantives)*, symbol, numeral, figure, cipher, digit, integer, counter, a round number, notation, a formula; series.

Sum, difference, subtrahend, complement, product, factorial, multiplicand, multiplier, multiplicator, coefficient, multiple, least common multiple, dividend, divisor, factor, highest common factor, greatest common measure, quotient, sub-multiple, fraction, vulgar fraction, mixed number, numerator, denominator, decimal, circulating decimal, recurring decimal, repetend, common measure, aliquot part, reciprocal, prime number; permutation, combination, election.

Ratio, proportion, progression (arithmetical, geometrical, harmonical), percentage.

Power, root, exponent, index, function, logarithm, antilogarithm; differential, integral, fluxion, fluent; incommensurable, surd.

(Adjectives) Numeral, complementary, divisible, aliquot, reciprocal, prime, fractional, decimal, factorial, fractional, mixed, incommensurable.

Proportional, exponential, logarithmic, logometric, differential, fluxional, integral.

Positive, negative, rational, irrational, surd, radical, real, imaginary, impossible.

85 Numeration *(Substantives)*, numbering, counting, tale, telling, tally, calling over, recension, enumeration, summation, reckoning, computation, ciphering, calculation, calculus, algorism, dactylonomy, rhabdology.

Arithmetic, analysis, algebra, differential and integral calculus.

Statistics, dead reckoning, muster, poll, census, capitation, roll-call, muster-roll, account, score, recapitulation, demography.

Addition, subtraction, multiplication, division, proportion, rule of three, reduction, involution, evolution, practice, equations, extraction of roots, approximation, interpolation, differentiation, integration. ·

Abacus, logometer, ready-reckoner, slide-rule, sliding-rule, tallies, Napier's bones, calculating machine, tabulator, totalizator, totalizer, tote, cash-register.

(Verbs) To number, count, tell, tally, call over, take an account of, enumerate, muster, poll, run over, recite, recapitulate; sum, sum up, cast up, tell off, score, cipher, compute, calculate, reckon, estimate, figure up, tot up; add, subtract, multiply, divide; amount to.

Check, prove, demonstrate, balance, audit, overhaul, take stock.

(Adjectives) Numerical, arithmetical, logarithmic, numeral, analytic, algebraic, statistical, computable, calculable, commensurable, incommensurable, incommensurate.

86 List *(Substantives)*, catalogue, inventory, schedule, register, census, return, statistics, record (551), account, registry, syllabus, roll, terrier, cadastre, cartulary, tally, file, muster-roll, roster, rota, bead-roll, panel, calendar, index, table, book, ledger, day-book, synopsis, bibliography, contents, invoice, bill of lading, bill of fare, menu, red book, peerage, baronetage, Almanach de Gotha, Debrett, Domesday Book, prospectus, programme, directory, gazetteer, who's who.

Registration, etc. (551).

2°. *Determinate Number*

87 Unity *(Substantives)*, unification, oneness, individuality, singleness, solitariness, solitude, isolation (893), abstraction; monism.

One, unit, ace, monad.

Someone, somebody, no other, none else, an individual; monist.

(Verbs) To be alone, etc.; to isolate (44), insulate, set apart.

To render one, unify.

(Phrase) To dine with Duke Humphrey.

(Adjectives) One, sole, single, individual, apart, alone, lone, isolated, solitary, lonely, lonesome, desolate, dreary, insular, insulated, disparate, discrete, detached; monistic.

Unaccompanied, unattended, *solus*, single-handed, singular, odd, unique, unrepeated, azygous.

Inseverable, irresolvable, indiscerptible, compact.

88 Accompaniment *(Substantives)*, coexistence, concomitance, company, association, companionship, partnership, collaboration, copartnership, co-efficiency.

Concomitant, adjunct, context, accessory (39), coefficient, companion, attendant, fellow, associate, consort, spouse, colleague, collaborator, partner, copartner, side-kick, buddy, satellite, escort, hanger-on, parasite, shadow; travelling tutor, chaperon, duenna.

(Verbs) To accompany, chaperon, coexist, attend, associate or be associated with, keep company with, collaborate with, hang on, shadow, wait on, to join, tie together.

(Phrases) To go hand in hand with; to be in the same boat.

(Adjectives) Accompanying, coexisting, attending, attendant, concomi-

(Adverbs) Singly, etc., alone, by itself, *per se*, only, apart, in the singular number, in the abstract, one by one; one at a time.

One and a half, sesqui-.

———

tant, fellow, twin, joint, associated with, accessory.

(Adverbs) With, withal, together with, along with, in company with, collectively, hand in hand, together, in a body, cheek by jowl, side by side; therewith, herewith, moreover, besides, also, and (37), not to mention.

89 Duality *(Substantives)*, dualism, duplicity, twofoldness, doubleness, biformity; polarity.

Two, deuce, couple, brace, pair, dyad (or duad), twins, Siamese twins, Castor and Pollux, Damon and Pythias, fellows, gemini, yoke, span, file, conjugation, twosome; dualist.

(Verbs) To unite in pairs, to pair, pair off, couple, match, mate, bracket, yoke.

(Adjectives) Two, twain, dual, binary, dualistic, duplex (90), duplicate, dyadic, binomial, twin, tête-à-tête, Janus-headed, bilateral, bicentric, bifocal.

Coupled, bracketed, paired, etc., conjugate.

Both, both the one and the other.

90 Duplication *(Substantives)*, doubling, gemination, reduplication, ingemination, repetition, iteration (104), renewal.

(Verbs) To double, redouble, geminate, reduplicate, repeat, iterate, re-echo, renew (660).

(Adjectives) Double, doubled, redoubled, second.

Biform, bifarious, bifold, bilateral, bifacial, twofold, two-sided, two-faced, duplex, duplicate, ingeminate.

(Adverbs) Twice, once more, over again, *da capo, bis, encore*, anew, as much again, twofold (104, 136).

Secondly, in the second place, again.

———

91 Division into two parts.

Bisection *(Substantives)*, bipartition, dichotomy, halving, dimidiation, bifurcation, forking, branching, ramification, divarication, splitting, cleaving.

Fork, prong, fold, branch, Y.

Half, moiety, semi-, demi-, hemi-.

(Verbs) To bisect, halve, divide, split, cut in two, cleave, dimidiate, dichotomize.

To separate, fork, bifurcate, branch out, ramify.

(Phrases) To go halves; to go fifty-fifty; to split the difference.

(Adjectives) Bisected, halved, divided, etc., bipartite, bicuspid, bind, bifurcated, bifurcate, cloven, cleft, split, etc.

92 Triality *(Substantives)*, trinity.

Three, triad, triangle, triplet, trey, trio, tern, trinomial, leash, threesome, trefoil, triquetra, *terza rima,* trilogy.

Third power, cube.

(Adjectives) Three, triform, trine, trinal, trinary, ternary, ternal, ternate (93), trinomial, tertiary, tri-.

93 Triplication *(Substantives)*, triplicity, trebleness, trine.

(Verbs) To treble, triple, triplicate, cube.

(Adjectives) Treble, triple, tern, ternary, ternate, triplicate, trigeminal, threefold, third.

(Adverbs) Three times, thrice, threefold, in the third place, thirdly.

94 Division into three parts.

Trisection *(Substantives)*, tripartition, trichotomy; third part, third.

(Verbs) To trisect, divide into three parts.

(Adjectives) Trifid, trisected, tripartite, trichotomous, trisulcate, triform.

———

95 Quaternity *(Substantives)*, four, tetrad, quadruplet, quad, quartet, quaternion, foursome, square, tetragon, tetrahedron, tessara, quadrature; tetralogy.

(Verbs) To reduce to a square, to square.

(Adjectives) Four, quaternary, quaternal, quadratic, quartile, tetractic, tetra-, quadri.

96 Quadruplication.

(Verbs) To multiply by four, quadruplicate, biquadrate.

(Adjectives) Fourfold, quadruple, quadruplicate, fourth.

(Adverbs) Four times, in the fourth place, fourthly, to the fourth degree.

97 Division into four parts.

Quadrisection *(Substantives)*, quadripartition, quartering, a fourth, a quarter.

(Verbs) To quarter, to divide into four parts.

(Adjectives) Quartered, etc., quadrifid, quadripartite.

---

98 Five *(Substantives)*, cinque, cinqfoil, quint, quincunx, pentad, pentagon, pentahedron, quintuplet, quin, quintet.

(Adjectives) Five, quinary, quintuple, fivefold, fifth.

Six, half a dozen, hexad, hexagon, hexahedron, sextet.

(Adjectives) Senary, sextuple, sixfold, sixth.

Seven, heptad, heptagon, heptahedron, septet.

(Adjectives) Septenary, septuple, sevenfold, seventh.

Eight, octad, octagon, octahedron, octet, ogdoad.

(Adjectives) Octonary, octonal, octuple, eightfold, eighth.

Nine, ennead, nonagon, enneagon, enneahedron, novena.

(Adjectives) Enneatic, ninefold, ninth.

Ten, decad, decagon, decahedron, decade.

(Adjectives) Decimal, denary, decuple, tenfold, tenth.

Twelve, a dozen.

(Adjectives) Duodenary, duodecimal, twelfth.

Thirteen, a long dozen, a baker's dozen.

Twenty, a score, icosahedron.

(Adjectives) Vigesimal, twentieth.

Forty, twoscore.

(Adjectives) Quadragesimal.

Fifty, twoscore and ten.

(Adjectives) Quinquagesimal.

Sixty, threescore.

(Adjectives) Sexagesimal, sexagenary.

Seventy, threescore and ten.

Eighty, fourscore.

99 Quinquesection, etc.

(Adjectives) Quinquefid, quinquarticular, quinquepartite.

Sexpartite.

Septempartite.

Octopartite.

Decimation, tithe.

(Verb) To decimate.

Ninety, fourscore and ten.

Hundred, centenary, hecatomb, century. One hundred and forty-four, a gross.

(Verbs) To centuriate.

(Adjectives) Centesimal, centennial, centenary, centurial, centuple, centuplicate, hundredfold, hundredth.

Thousand, chiliad, millennium.

(Adjective) Millesimal.

Myriad, lac, crore.

Million, billion, trillion, etc.

3°. *Indeterminate Number*

100 More than one.

Plurality *(Substantives)*, a number, a certain number, a few, a wheen, a round number.

(Adjectives) Plural, more than one, upwards of, some, a few, one or two, two or three, umpteen, certain.

(Adverb) Etcetera.

101 Zero *(Substantives)*, nothing (4) nought (or naught), cipher; nobody, *nemo.*

(Adjectives) None, not one, not any, not a soul.

---

102 Multitude *(Substantives)*, numerousness, numerosity, numerality, multiplicity, majority, profusion, legion, host, a great or large number, numbers, array, power, lot, sight, army, sea, galaxy, populousness (72), a hundred, thousand, myriad, million, etc.

A shoal, swarm, draught, bevy, flock, herd, drove, flight, covey, hive, brood, litter, mob, nest, crowd (72).

Increase of number, multiplication, multiple; greater number, majority.

(Verbs) To be numerous, etc., to swarm, teem, crowd, come thick upon, outnumber, multiply, to people.

(Phrase) To swarm like locusts or bees.

(Adjectives) Many, several, a wheen, sundry, divers, various, a great many, very many, full many, ever so many, no end of, numerous, profuse, manifold, multiplied, multitudinous, multiple, multinomial, endless (105), teeming, populous, peopled.

Frequent, repeated, reiterated, outnumbering, thick, crowding, crowded; galore.

(Phrases) Thick as hail; thick as leaves in Vallombrosa; plentiful as blackberries; in profusion; numerous as the sands on the seashore; their name is Legion.

103 Fewness *(Substantives)*, paucity, a small number, handful, scantiness, rareness, rarity, thinness.

Diminution of number, reduction, weeding, elimination, thinning; smaller number, minority.

(Verbs) To be few, etc.

To render few, reduce, diminish in number, weed, weed out, prick off, eliminate, thin, thin out, decimate.

(Adjectives) Few, scanty, scant, rare, infrequent, sparse, scattered, hardly or scarcely any, reduced, thinned, etc.

(Phrases) Few and far between; you could count them on the fingers of one hand.

---

104 Repetition *(Substantives)*, iteration, reiteration, harping, recapitulation, run, recurrence (136), recrudescence, tautology, monotony; cuckoo-note, chimes, repetend, echo, burden of a song, refrain, jingle, renewal, rehearsal, réchauffé, rehash, reproduction (19).

Cuckoo, mocking-bird, mimic, imitator, parrot.

Periodicity (138), frequency (136).

(Phrase) A twice-told tale.

(Verbs) To repeat, iterate, reiterate, recapitulate, renew, reproduce, echo, re-echo, drum, hammer, harp on, plug, rehearse, redouble, recrudesce, reappear, recur, revert, recommence.

(Phrases) Do or say over again; ring the changes on; to harp on the same string; to din or drum in the ear; to go over the same ground; to begin again.

(Adjectives) Repeated, repetitional, repetitionary, repetitive, recurrent, recurring, reiterated, renewed, ever-recurring, thick-coming, monotonous, harping, sing-song, mocking, chiming; above-mentioned, said, aforesaid.

(Phrases) It's that man again; cut and come again; *cramoe repetita.*

(Adverbs) Repeatedly, often (136), again, anew, over again, afresh, ditto, *encore, de novo, da capo, bis* (90).

(Phrases) Toties quoties; again and again; in quick succession, over and over again; ever and anon; time after time; year after year; times out of number; *ad nauseam.*

105 Infinity *(Substantives)*, infiniteness, infinitude.

(Adjectives) Infinite, numberless, innumerable, countless, sumless, untold, unnumbered, unsummed, incalculable, unlimited, limitless, illimitable, immeasurable, unmeasured, measureless, unbounded, boundless, endless, interminable, unfathomable, exhaustless, termless, indefinite, without number, without limit, without end, unending.

(Adverbs) Infinitely, etc., without measure, limit, etc., *ad infinitum*, world without end.

SECTION VI—TIME

1°. *Absolute Time*

106 Duration *(Substantives)*, time, period, term, space, span, spell, season, era, epoch, decade, century, chiliad, age, cycle, aeon.

Intermediate time, while, interval, interim, pendency, intervention, intermission, interregnum, interlude, recess, break, intermittence, respite (265).

Long duration (110).

(Phrases) The enemy; the whirligig of time.

(Verbs) To continue, last, endure, remain, go on; to take, take up, fill or occupy time, to persist, to intervene.

To pass, pass away, spend, employ, while away or consume time, waste time.

(Adjectives) Continuing, lasting, enduring, remaining, persistent, perpetual, permanent (150).

(Adverbs) While, whilst, so long as, during, pending, till, until, up to, during the time or interval, the whole time or period, all the time or while, in the long run, all along, throughout, from beginning to end (52).

Pending, meantime, meanwhile, in the meantime, in the interim, *ad interim, pendente lite*, from day to day, for a time, for a season, for good, yet, up to this time.

107 Timelessness *(Substantives)*, neverness, absence of time, no time, *dies non.*

Short duration (111).

(Adverbs) Never, ne'er, at no time, on no occasion, at no period, nevermore, *sine die.*

(Phrases) On Tib's eve; at the Greek Calends; *jamais de ma vie*; 'jam every other day.'

108 Definite duration, or portion of time.

Period *(Substantives)*, second, minute, hour, day, week, fortnight, month, lunation, quarter, year, leapyear, lustrum, quinquennium, decade, lifetime, generation, century, age, millennium, *annus magnus*.

(Adjectives) Hourly, horary; daily, diurnal, quotidian; weekly, hebdomadal, menstrual, monthly, annual, secular, centennial, bicentennial, etc., bissextile, seasonal.

(Adverbs) From day to day, from hour to hour.

Once upon a time; Anno domini, A.D.; Before Christ, B.C.

108A Contingent Duration.
During pleasure, during good behaviour, *quamdiu se bene gesserit*.

110 Long duration.

Diuturnity *(Substantives)*, a long time, an age, a century, an eternity, aeon.

(Phrases) Temporis longinquitas; a month of Sundays.

Durableness, durability, persistence, lastingness, continuance, permanence (150), longevity, survival.

Distance of time, protraction, extension or prolongation of time, delay (133).

(Verbs) To last, endure, stand, remain, continue, abide, tarry, protract, prolong, outlast, outlive, survive; spin out, draw out, eke out, temporize, linger, loiter, lounge (275), wait.

(Phrase) To live to fight another day.

(Adjectives) Durable, of long duration, permanent, enduring, chronic, intransient, intransitive, intransmutable, lasting, abiding, persistent; livelong, longeval, long-lived, macrobiotic, diuturnal, evergreen, perennial, unintermitting, unremitting, perpetual (112).

Protracted, prolonged, spun out, long-winded, surviving, lingering.

(Adverbs) Long, a long time, permanently.

(Phrases) As the day is long; all the

109 Indefinite duration.

Course *(Substantives)*, progress, process, succession, lapse, flow, flux, stream, tract, current, tide, march, step, flight, etc., of time.

Indefinite time, aorist.

(Verbs) To elapse, lapse, flow, run, proceed, roll on, advance, pass, slide, press on, flit, fly, slip, glide, run its course.

(Adjectives) Elapsing, passing, etc.; aoristic.

(Adverbs) In course of time, in due time of season, in process of time, in the fullness of time.

(Phrase) Labuntur anni.

111 Short duration.

Transientness *(Substantives)*, transitoriness, impermanence, evanescence, transitiveness, fugitiveness, fugacity, fugaciousness, caducity, mortality, span, shortness, brevity.

Quickness, promptness (132), suddenness, abruptness.

A *coup de main*, bubble, Mayfly, nine days' wonder.

(Verbs) To be transient, etc., to flit, pass away, fly, gallop, vanish, fade, intromit.

(Adjectives) Transitory, transient, transitive, passing, impermanent, evanescent, fleeting, momentary, fugacious, fugitive, flitting, vanishing, shifting, flying, temporary, temporal, makeshift, provisional, provisory, rough and ready, cursory, galloping, short-lived, ephemeral, deciduous, meteoric.

Brief, sudden, quick, prompt, brisk, abrupt, extemporaneous, summary, hasty, precipitate.

(Adverbs) Temporarily, etc., *en passant, in transitu*, extempore.

In a short time, soon, at once, awhile, anon, by and by, briefly, presently, apace, eftsoons, straight, straightaway, quickly, speedily, promptly, presto, slapdash, directly,

day long; all the year round; the live-long day; hour after hour; morning, noon, and night; for good; for many a long day.

immediately, incontinently, forthwith; suddenly, *per saltum,* at one bound.

(Phrases) At short notice; the time being up; before the ink is dry; here to-day and gone to-morrow (149); *sic transit gloria mundi.*

112 Perpetuity *(Substantives),* eternity, sempiternity, immortality, athanasy, everlastingness, perpetuation.

(Verbs) To last or endure for ever, to have no end: to eternize, perpetuate.

(Adjectives) Perpetual, eternal, everlasting, sempiternal, coeternal; endless, unending, ceaseless, incessant, unceasing, uninterrupted, interminable, having no end, unfading, evergreen, never-fading, amaranthine, ageless, deathless, immortal, undying, never-dying, imperishable, indestructible.

(Adverbs) Always, ever, evermore, aye, for ever, for aye, for evermore, still, perpetually, eternally, etc., in all ages, from age to age.

(Phrases) For ever and a day; *esto perpetua*; for ever and ever; world without end; time without end; *in secula seculorum*; to the end of time; till Doomsday; till hell freezes; to a cinder.

113 Point of time.

Instantaneity *(Substantives),* instantaneousness, moment, instant, second, split second, minute, twinkling, trice, flash, breath, span, jiffy, flash of lightning, suddenness (111).

(Verbs) To twinkle, flash, to be instantaneous.

(Adjectives) Instantaneous, push-button, sudden, momentary, extempore.

(Phrases) Quick as thought; quick as a flash; quick as lightning.

(Adverbs) Instantly, momentarily, *subito*, presto, instanter, suddenly, plump, slap, slapdash, in a moment, in an instant, in a second, in no time, in a trice, in a twinkling, at one jump, in a breath, extempore, *per saltum,* in a crack, out of hand.

(Phrases) Before one can say 'Jack Robinson'; in a brace of shakes; between the cup and the lip; on the spur of the moment; in the twinkling of an eye; in a jiffy; in two ticks; on the instant; in less than no time; at one fell swoop; no sooner said than done.

114 Estimation, measurement, and record of time.

Chronometry *(Substantives),* chronology, horology, horometry, registry, date, epoch, style, era.

Greenwich, standard, mean, local, solar, sidereal time; summer time, double summer time.

Almanac, calendar, ephemeris, chronicle, annals, register, journal, diary, chronogram, time-book.

Instruments for the measurement of time, clock, watch, stop-watch, repeater, chronograph, chronometer, sextant, timepiece, dial, sun-dial, horologe, pendulum, hour-glass, water-clock, clepsydra; time signal.

Chronographer, chronologer, chronologist, time-keeper, annalist.

(Verbs) To chronicle, to fix or mark the time, date, register, etc., to bear date, to measure time, to beat time, to make time, to time.

(Adjectives) Chronological, chronometrical, chronogrammatical.

(Adverb) O'clock.

115 False estimate of time.

Anachronism *(Substantives),* error in time, prolepsis, metachronism, prochronism, parachronism, anticipation.

Disregard or neglect of time.

(Verbs) To anachronize, misdate, antedate, postdate, overdate, anticipate.

(Adjectives) Anachronistic, anachronous, misdated, undated, overdue, postdated, antedated.

(Phrases) To take no note of time; to prophesy after the event.

2°. Relative Time

1. TIME WITH REFERENCE TO SUCCESSION

116 Priority (*Substantives*), antecedence, anteriority, precedence, pre-existence.

Precursor, predecessor, prelude, forerunner (64), harbinger, antecedent; the past (122).

(*Verbs*) To precede, come before, forerun, pre-exist, prelude, usher in, dawn, announce (511), foretell, anticipate, forestall.

(*Phrases*) To be beforehand; to steal a march upon.

(*Adjectives*) Prior, previous, preceding, precedent, anterior, antecedent, pre-existent, pre-existing, former, foregoing, aforesaid, said, above-mentioned, prehistoric, antediluvian, pre-Adamite.

Precursory, prelusive, prelusory, proemial, introductory, prefatory (62), prodromal, prodromic.

(*Adverbs*) Before, prior to, previously, anteriorly, antecedently, aforetime, ere, ere now, erewhile, before now, heretofore, ultimo, yet, beforehand, above, *supra*.

(*Phrase*) Before the flood.

117 Posteriority (*Substantives*), succession, sequence, subsequence, supervention, sequel, successor (65), postlude.

(*Verbs*) To follow, come or go after, succeed, supervene, ensue.

(*Phrases*) To tread on the heels of; to follow in the footsteps of.

(*Adjectives*) Subsequent, posterior, following, after, later, succeeding, post-glacial, post-diluvial, post-diluvian, puisne, posthumous, post-prandial, post-classical.

(*Adverbs*) Subsequently, after, afterwards, since, later, later on, at a subsequent or later period, proximo, next, in the sequel, close upon, thereafter, thereupon, whereupon, upon which, eftsoons, below, *infra*.

———

118 The Present Time (*Substantives*), the existing time, the time being, the present moment, juncture, crisis, epoch, day, hour; the twentieth century.

Age, time of life.

(*Verb*) To strike while the iron is hot.

(*Adjectives*) Present, actual, current, existing, that is.

(*Adverbs*) At this time, moment, etc., now, at present, at this time of day, at the present time, day, etc., to-day, nowadays, instant, already, even now, but now, just now, upon which.

(*Phrases*) For the time being; for the nonce; *pro hac vice*; on the nail; on the spot; on the spur of the moment; now or never.

119 Time different from the present.

Different Time (*Substantives*), other time.

Indefinite time, aorist.

(*Adjective*) Aoristic.

(*Adverbs*) At that time, moment, etc., then, at which time, etc., on that occasion, upon, in those days.

When, whenever, whensoever, upon which, on which occasions, at another or a different time, etc., otherwhile, otherwhiles, at various times, ever and anon.

(*Phrases*) Once upon a time; one day; some other time; one of these days.

———

120 Synchronism (*Substantives*), synchronization, coinstantaneity, co-existence, coincidence, simultaneousness, coevality, contemporaneousness, contemporaneity, concurrence, concomitance.

Having equal times, isochronism.

A contemporary, coeval, coetanean.

(Verbs) To coexist, concur, accompany, synchronize.

(Phrase) To keep pace with.

(Adjectives) Synchronous, synchronal, synchronistic, simultaneous, coexisting, coincident, concomitant, concurrent, coeval, coetaneous, contemporary, contemporaneous, coeternal, isochronous.

(Adverbs) At the same time, simultaneously, etc., together, during the same time, etc., in the interim, in the same breath, in concert, *pari passu*; meantime, meanwhile (106), while, whilst.

121 Prospective time.

Futurity *(Substantives)*, the future, futurition, the approaching time, hereafter, the time to come, posteriority (117), after time, after age, the coming time, the morrow, after days, hours, years, ages; after life, millennium, doomsday, the day of judgment, the crack of doom.

The approach of time, the process of time, advent, time drawing on, the womb of time.

Prospection, anticipation, prospect, perspective, expectation (507), horizon, outlook, look-out.

Heritage, heirs, progeny, issue, posterity, descendants, heir apparent, heir presumptive.

Future existence, future state, postexistence, after-life, beyond.

(Verbs) To look forward, anticipate, forestall (132), have in prospect, keep in view, expect (507).

To impend, hang over, lie over, approach, await, threaten, overhang, draw near, prepare.

(Phrases) Lie in wait for; bide one's time; to wait impatiently; kick one's heels.

To be in the wind; to be cooking; to loom in the future.

(Adjectives) Future, to come, coming, going to happen, approaching, impending, instant, at hand, about to be or happen, next, hanging, awaiting, forthcoming, near, near at hand, imminent, threatening, brewing, preparing, in store, eventual, ulterior, in view, in prospect, prospective, in perspective, in the offing, in the wind, on the cards, that will be, overhanging.

Unborn, in embryo, in the womb of time.

122 Retrospective time.

Preterition *(Substantives)*, the past, past time, *status quo,* days of yore, time gone by, priority (116), former times, old times, the olden time, ancient times, antiquity, antiqueness, lang syne, time immemorial, prehistory.

Archaeology, palaeology, palaeontology, palaeography, archaism, retrospection, retrospect, looking back.

Archaeologist, antiquary, medievalist, palaeographer, palaeologist, Dr. Dryasdust.

Ancestry (166), pre-existence.

(Phrases) The good old days; the golden age; the rust of antiquity.

(Verbs) To pass, be past, lapse, go by, elapse, run out, expire, blow over; to look back, cast the eyes back, retrospect, trace back, dig up, exhume.

(Phrases) To have run its course; to have had its day.

(Adjectives) Past, gone, gone by, over, bygone, foregone, pristine, prehistoric, quondam, lapsed, elapsed, preterlapsed, expired, late, *ci-devant,* run out, blown over, that has been.

Former, foregoing, late, last, latter, recent, overnight, preterperfect, preterpluperfect, forgotten, irrecoverable, out of date.

Looking back, retrospective, retroactive, *ex post facto*; archaeological, etc.

Pre-existing, pre-existent.

(Adverbs) Formerly, of old, erst, whilom, erewhile, before now, time was, ago, over, in the olden time, anciently, in days of yore, long since, retrospectively, ere now, before now, till now, once, once upon a time, hitherto, heretofore, *ultimo.*

(Adverbs) Prospectively, hereafter, by and by, some fine day, one of these days, anon, in future, to-morrow, in course of time, in process of time, sooner or later, *proximo*, in after time.

On the eve of, ere long, at hand, near at hand, on the point of, beforehand, against the time.

After a time, from this time, henceforth, henceforwards, thence, thenceforth, thenceforward, whereupon, upon which.

(Phrases) All in good time; in the fullness of time.

The other day, yesterday, last night, week, month, year, etc.; just now, recently, lately, of late, latterly.

Long ago, a long while or time ago, some time ago.

(Phrases) Once upon a time; from time immemorial; in the memory of man; time out of mind.

Already, yet, at length, at last.

---

2. TIME WITH REFERENCE TO A PARTICULAR PERIOD

123 Newness *(Substantives)*, novelty, recentness, recency, modernity, freshness, greenness, immaturity, youth (127), rawness.

Innovation, renovation (660), renewal.

Nouveau riche, parvenu, upstart, mushroom; latest fashio, *dernier cri.*

(Verbs) Renew, renovate, restore (660), modernize.

(Adjectives) New, novel, recent, fresh, green, evergreen, raw, immature, untrodden, advanced, twentieth-century, modern, modernistic, avant-garde, neoteric, new-born, nascent, new-fashioned, up-to-date, new-fangled, vernal, renovated, brand-new, split-new, virgin.

(Phrases) Fresh as a rose; fresh as a daisy; fresh as paint; just out; spick and span.

(Adverbs) Newly, recently, lately, afresh, anew.

124 Oldness *(Substantives)*, age (128), antiquity, eld, ancientry, primitiveness, maturity, decline, decay, obsolescence; seniority, eldership, primogeniture.

Archaism, relic, antique, fossil, eolith; elder, doyen.

(Verbs) To be or become old, mature, mellow; to age, fade, decay.

(Adjectives) Old, ancient, antique, antiquated, out-of-date, of long standing, time-honoured, venerable, hoary, primitive, diluvian, antediluvian, fossil, palaeozoic, preglacial, palaeolithic, neolithic, primeval, primordial, prime, pre-Adamite, prehistoric, antemundane, archaic, classic, medieval.

Immemorial, inveterate, rooted, traditional.

Senior, elder, eldest, oldest, first-born (128).

Obsolete, obsolescent, out-of-date, stale, time-worn, faded, decayed, effete, declining, played-out, crumbling, decrepit (128), *passé.*

(Phrases) Nothing new under the sun; old as the hills; old as Methuselah; old as Adam; before the Flood; time out of mind; since the year one.

---

125 Morning *(Substantives)*, morn, morrow, forenoon, a.m., prime, dawn, daybreak, dayspring, peep of day, break of day, matins, aurora, first blush of the morning, prime of the morning, twilight, crepuscule, sun-rise, sun-up, cockcrow.

126 Evening *(Substantives)*, eve, e'en, decline of day, close of day, eventide, nightfall, curfew, vespers, evensong, dusk, twilight, gloaming, eleventh hour, sunset, sundown, afternoon, p.m., bedtime, midnight; autumn, Indian summer, St.

Noon, midday, noontide, meridian, fathers, forebears, fathers, ancestors, midsummer.

(Adjectives) Matutinal, auroral, vernal, midsummer.

———

127 Youth *(Substantives)*, infancy, babyhood, boyhood, juvenility, childhood, youthhood, juniority, juvenescence, adolescence (131), minority, nonage, teens, tender age, bloom, heyday, boyishness, girlishness.

Cradle, nursery, leading strings, pupilage, pupilship, puberty.

(Phrases) Prime of flower of life; the rising generation; salad days; schooldays.

(Adjectives) Young, youthful, juvenile, callow, sappy, beardless, under age, in one's teens, boyish, girlish, junior, younger.

(Phrase) In statu pupillari.

———

Martin's summer, St. Luke's summer, winter, the fall.

(Phrases) The witching time of night; the dead of night; blindman's holiday.

(Adjectives) Nocturnal, vespertine, autumnal, hiemal, brumal.

———

128 Age *(Substantives)*, old age, senility, senescence, oldness, longevity, years, anility, grey hairs, climacteric, decrepitude, hoary age, caducity, crow's feet, superannuation, dotage, anecdotage, seniority, green old age, eldership.

(Phrases) The vale of years; decline of life; the sere and yellow leaf; second childhood.

(Adjectives) Aged, old, elderly, senile, matronly, anile, in years, ripe, mellow, grey, grey-headed, hoary, hoar, venerable, timeworn, declining, antiquated, *passé*, rusty, effete, decrepit, superannuated.

Patriarchal, ancestral, primitive, older, elder, senior; eldest, oldest, first-born, bantling, firstling.

(Phrases) With one foot in the grave; marked with crow's feet; advanced in life, or in years; stricken in years; no chicken; long in the tooth; old as the hills.

———

129 Infant *(Substantives)*, babe, baby, nursling, suckling.

Child, bairn, wean, little one, brat, toddler, kid, chit, urchin, bantling, bratling, papoose, elf, piccaninny.

Youth, boy, lad, laddie, stripling, youngster, teenager, callant, younker, gossoon, nipper, whipster, whipper-snapper, schoolboy, young hopeful, hobbledehoy, cadet, minor.

Girl, lass, lassie, wench, miss, colleen, flapper, bobbysoxer, damsel, maid, maiden, *jeune fille.*

Scion, sapling, seedling, tendril, mushroom, nestling, chicken, larva, chrysalis, tadpole, whelp, cub, pullet, fry, foetus, calf, lamb, lambkin, colt, filly, pup, puppy, foal, kitten.

(Adjectives) Infantine, infantile, virginal, childish, baby, babyish, callow.

(Phrases) In leading-strings; at the breast; in arms; in one's teens; tied to mother's apron-strings.

———

130 Veteran *(Substantives)*, old man, seer, patriarch, greybeard, gaffer, grandsire, grandam, dowager, matron, crone, beldam, hag, sexagenarian, octogenarian, centenarian, oldster, old-timer, old stager, old buffer, fogy, geezer.

Methuselah, Nestor; elders, forefathers, forebears, fathers, ancestors, ancestry.

(Adjectives) Veteran, aged, old, grey-headed (128).

———

puerile, boyish, girlish (127), unfledged, new-fledged, kittenish,

131 Adolescence *(Substantives)*, puberty, pubescence, majority, adultness, maturity, ripeness, manhood, virility.

A man, adult (373), a woman, matron (374), *parti*; ephebe.

(Phrases) Prime of life; man's estate; flower of age; meridian of life; years of discretion; *toga virilis*.

(Adjectives) Adolescent, pubescent, of age, out of one's teens, grown up, mature, middle-aged, manly, virile, adult.

Womanly, matronly, nubile, marriageable, out.

3. TIME WITH REFERENCE TO AN EFFECT OR PURPOSE

132   Earliness   *(Substantives)*, timeliness, punctuality, readiness, promptness (682), promptitude, expedition, quickness, haste, acceleration, hastening, hurry, bustle, precipitation, anticipation, precociousness, precocity.

Suddenness, abruptness (111).

(Phrases) A stitch in time saves nine; the early bird catches the worm.

(Verbs) To be early, to be in time, keep time, be beforehand.

To anticipate, forestall, book, engage, bespeak, reserve.

To expedite, hasten, haste, quicken (274), press, dispatch, accelerate, precipitate, hurry, bustle (684).

(Phrases) To take time by the forelock; to steal a march upon; to be beforehand with; to be pressed for time.

(Adjectives) Early, prime, rathe, timely, timeous, punctual, matutinal, forward, ready, quick, expeditious, precipitate, summary, prompt, premature, precocious, prevenient, anticipatory, pre-emptive.

Sudden, abrupt, unexpected (508), subitaneous, extempore.

(Adverbs) Early, soon, anon, betimes, apace, eft, eftsoons, in time, ere long, presently, shortly, punctually, to the minute, on time, on the dot.

Beforehand, prematurely, before one's time, in anticipation.

Suddenly, abruptly, at once, extempore, instanter.

(Phrases) In good time; at sunrise; with the lark; early days.

On the point of; at short notice; on the spur of the moment; all at once; before you can say 'knife'; no sooner said than done.

133 Lateness *(Substantives)*, tardiness, slowness (275), delay, cunctation, procrastination, deferring, lingering, lagging, etc., postponement, dilatoriness, adjournment, shelving, prorogation, remand, moratorium.

Protraction, prolongation, leeway.

(Phrase) Fabian tactics.

(Verbs) To be late, etc., tarry, wait, stay, bide, take time, dally, dawdle, linger, loiter, lag, bide one's time, shuffle (275, 683).

To stand over, lie over, hang fire.

To put off, defer, delay, leave over, suspend, stave off, postpone, adjourn, carry over, shelve, procrastinate, temporize, stall, filibuster, prolong, protract, draw out, spin out, hold up, prorogue.

(Phrases) To tide it over; to bide one's time; to let the matter stand over; to sleep on it; to kick (or cool) one's heels.

(Adjectives) Late, tardy, slow, dilatory (275), posthumous, backward, unpunctual, procrastinatory, behind-hand, belated, overdue.

Delayed, etc., suspended, pending, in abeyance.

(Adverbs) Late, after time, too late, behind time; at length, at last.

Slowly, leisurely, deliberately.

(Phrases) Late in the day; a day after the fair; at the eleventh hour; after death, the doctor.

134 Occasion *(Substantives)*, opportunity, chance, opening, break, show, room, suitable or proper time or season, high time, opportuneness, tempestivity, seasonableness, crisis, turn, juncture, conjuncture.

Spare time, leisure, holiday (685), spare moments, hours, etc., time on one's hands.

(Phrases) Golden (or favourable) opportunity; the nick of time.

(Verbs) To use, make use of, employ, profit by, avail oneself of, lay hold of, embrace, catch, seize, snatch, clutch, pounce upon, grasp, etc., the opportunity.

To give, offer, present, afford, etc., the opportunity.

To time well; to spend or consume time.

(Phrases) To turn the occasion to account; to seize the occasion; to strike the iron while it is hot; to make hay while the sun shines; *carpe diem*; to take the tide at the flood; to furnish a handle for.

(Adjectives) Opportune, timely, well-timed, timeful, timeous, seasonable, happy, lucky, providential, fortunate, favourable, propitious, auspicious, critical.

(Adverbs) Opportunity, etc., on the spot, in proper or due time or season, high time, for the nonce.

By the way, by the by, *en passant, à propos,* parenthetically.

(Phrases) In the nick of time; on the spur of the moment (612); now or never; at the eleventh hour; time and tide wait for no man.

135 Intempestivity *(Substantives)*, untimeliness, unsuitable time, improper time, unseasonableness, inopportuneness, evil hour.

Hitch, impediment (706), check, *contretemps*.

(Verbs) To be ill-timed, etc., to mistime, intrude, come amiss.

To lose, omit, let slip, let go, neglect, pretermit, allow, or suffer the opportunity of occasion to pass, slip, go by, escape, lapse; to lose time, to fritter away time (683).

(Phrases) To let slip through the fingers; to lock the stable door when the steed is stolen.

(Adjectives) Ill-timed, untimely, untimeous, mistimed, unseasonable, out of season, unpunctual, inopportune, untoward, intrusive, too late (133), too early (132), malapropos, unlucky, inauspicious, unpropitious, unfortunate, unfavourable, unsuited, unsuitable.

(Adverb) Inopportunely, etc.

(Phrases) As ill luck would have it; in evil hour; after meat, mustard; a day before (or after) the fair.

3°. Recurrent Time

136 Frequency *(Substantives)*, oftness, recurrence, repetition (104), recrudescence, reiteration, iteration, run, reappearance, renewal, *ritornello, ritournelle*, burden.

Frequenter, *habitué*, fan, client.

(Verbs) To recur, revert, return, repeat, reiterate, reappear, renew, reword.

To frequent, resort to, visit, attend, haunt, infest.

(Adjectives) Frequent, common, not rare, repeated, reiterated, thick-coming, recurring, recurrent, incessant, everlasting, perpetual, rife; habitual (613).

137 Infrequency *(Substantives)*, rareness, rarity, uncommonness, scarcity, fewness (103), seldomness.

(Verb) To be rare, etc.

(Adjectives) Infrequent, rare, scarce, unfrequent, uncommon, unprecedented, unheard-of.

(Phrase) In short supply.

(Adverbs) Seldom, rarely, scarcely, hardly, scarcely ever, ever, hardly ever, not often, unfrequently.

Once, once for all, once in a way.

(Phrases) Once in a blue moon; angels' visits.

(Adverbs) Often, oft, oft-times, not infrequently, frequently, often-times, many times, several times, repeatedly.

Again, anew, afresh, *de novo*, ditto, over again, *da capo*, again and again, over and over, ever and anon, many times over, time after time, time and again, repeatedly (104).

Perpetually, continually, constantly, incessantly, everlastingly, without ceasing.

Sometimes, occasionally, at times, now and then, now and again, from time to time, at intervals, between whiles, once in a while, there are times when.

Most often, for the most part, generally, usually, commonly, most frequently, as often as not.

(Phrases) A number of times; many a time (and oft); times out of number.

138 Regularity of recurrence, punctuality.

Periodicity *(Substantives)*, intermittence, beat, ictus, pulse, pulsation, rhythm, lilt, swing, alternation, alternateness, bout, round, revolution, rotation, turn.

Anniversary, jubilee; silver, golden, wedding; centenary, bicentenary, tercentenary, etc.; feast, festival, birthday.

Regularity of return, rota, cycle, period, stated time, routine.

(Phrase) The swing of the pendulum.

(Verbs) To recur in regular order or succession, to come round, return, revolve, alternate, come in its turn, beat, pulsate, intermit; to regularize.

(Adjectives) Periodic, periodical, recurrent, cyclical, revolving, intermittent, remittent, alternate, every other, alternating, rhythmic, rhythmical, steady, punctual.

Hourly, daily, diurnal, tertian, quotidian, weekly, hebdomadal, fortnightly, bi-monthly, monthly, biannual, annual, yearly, biennial, triennial, centennial.

(Phrase) Regular as clockwork.

(Adverbs) Periodically, at regular intervals, at stated times, at fixed periods, punctually, from day to day.

By turns, in turn, in rotation, alternately, in shifts, off and on, ride and tie, hitch and hike.

139 Irregularity of recurrence uncertainty, unpunctuality, fitfulness.

(Adjectives) Irregular, uncertain, unpunctual, capricious, desultory, unrhythmic, unrhythmical, fitful, spasmodic, flickering, casual.

(Adverbs) Irregularly, etc., by snatches, by fits and starts, skippingly, now and then, occasionally.

SECTION VII—CHANGE

1°. *Simple Change*

140 Difference at different times.

Change *(Substantives)*, alteration, mutation, permutation, variation, modification, modulation, inflexion, mood, qualification, innovation, metastasis, metabolism, deviation, turn, diversion, inversion, reversion, reversal, eversion, subversion (162),

141 Absence of change.

Permanence *(Substantives)*, persistence, endurance, *status quo;* maintenance, preservation, conservation, conservatism, *laissez-faire,* rest, sleep, establishment, truce, suspension, settledness (265), perdurability, stability (150).

bouleversement, upset, organic, change, revolution (146), substitution (147), transposition (148), transit, transition.

Transformation, transmutation, transfiguration, metamorphosis, transmigration, transubstantiation, transmogrification, metempsychosis, avatar.

Vicissitude, flux, unrest (149); change of mind, tergiversation (607).

(Phrase) The wheel of fortune.

(Verbs) To change, alter, vary, modify, modulate, diversify, qualify, tamper with, edit, turn, shift, veer, tack, chop, shuffle, swerve, warp, deviate, turn aside, turn topsy-turvy, upset, invert, reverse, introvert, subvert, evert, turn inside out.

Form, fashion, mould, model, vamp, warp, work a change, superinduce, resume, disturb (61), innovate, reform, remodel, refound, new-model, modernize, revolutionize.

Transform, transume, transmute, transfigure, transmogrify, metamorphose, pass to, leap to, transfer.

(Phrases) To ring the changes; to turn over a new leaf; to introduce new blood; to shuffle the cards; to turn the corner; to wax and wane; to ebb and flow; *tempora mutantur; nous avons changé tout cela.*

(Adjectives) Changed, altered, new-fangled, warped, etc,; transitional, metamorphic, metabolic, metastatic.

(Adverb) Mutatis mutandis.

---

142 Change from action to rest.

Cessation *(Substantives)*, discontinuance, desistance, quiescence.

Intermission, remission, suspension, interruption, suspense, stand, halt, closure, stop, stoppage, pause, rest, lull, breathing-space, respite, truce, drop, interregnum, abeyance.

Comma, colon, semicolon, period, full stop.

(Verbs) To discontinue, cease, desist, break off, leave off, hold, stop, pause, rest, drop, lay aside, give up, have done with, stick, hang fire, pull up, give over, shut down, knock off, relinquish (624), surcease.

To come to a stand, or standstill, suspend, cut short, cast off,

(Phrase) The law of the Medes and Persians.

(Verbs) To remain, stay, stop, persist, tarry, hold, last, endure, continue, dwell, bide, abide, maintain, keep, hold on, stand, subsist, live, stand still, outlive, survive.

To let alone, let be.

(Phrases) To keep one's footing; to hold one's ground; to stick to one's guns; to stand fast.

(Adjectives) Persisting, etc., permanent, established, unchanged, unmodified, unrenewed, unaltered, fixed, settled, unvaried, intact, inviolate, persistent, stagnant, rooted, monotonous, unreversed, conservative, unprogressive, undestroyed, unrepelled, unsuppressed, unfailing, stationary (265), stereotyped, perdurable.

(Adverbs) In statu quo, for good, finally, at a stand, at a standstill, *uli possidetis.*

(Phrases) J'y suis, j'y reste; plus cela change, plus cela est la même chose; esto perpetua.

---

143 Continuance in action *(Substantives)*, continuation, perseverance, repetition (104), persistence, run.

(Verbs) To continue, persist, go on, keep on, abide, keep, pursue, hold on, run on, follow on, carry on, keep up, uphold, sustain, perpetuate, persevere, keep it up, stick it, peg away, maintain, maintain one's ground, harp upon, repeat (104), take root.

(Phrases) To keep the pot boiling; to keep the ball rolling.

(Adjectives) Continual, continuous, continuing, etc., uninterrupted, inconvertible, unintermitting, unreversed, unstopped, unrevoked, unvaried, unshifting, perpetual (112).

---

go out, be at an end; intromit, interrupt, arrest, intermit, remit; put an end or stop to.

To pass away, go off, pass off, blow over, die away, wear away, wear off (122).

(Phrases) To shut up shop; to stay one's hand; to rest on one's oars; to rest on one's laurels.

(Interjections) Hold! hold on! stop! enough! avast! *basta!* have done! a truce to! stop it! drop it! cheese it! chuck it! stow it! cut it out!

144 Gradual change to something different.

Conversion *(Substantives)*, reduction, transmutation, resolution, assimilation; chemistry, alchemy; growth, lapse, progress, becoming; naturalization.

Passage, transit, transition, transmigration, flux, shifting, sliding, running into, etc.; phase, conjugations; convertibility.

Laboratory, alembic, crucible (691).

Convert, pervert, vert, turncoat, renegade, apostate.

(Verbs) To be converted into; to become, get, wax, come to turn to, turn into, assume the form of, pass into, slide into, glide into, lapse, shift, run into, fall into, merge into, melt, grow, grow into, open into, resolve itself into, settle into, mature, mellow; assume the form, shape, state, nature, character, etc., of; illapse.

To convert into; to make, render, form, mould, reduce, resolve into; transume (140), fashion, model, remodel, reorganize, shape, modify, transmogrify; assimilate to; reduce to, bring to; refound, re-form, reshape.

(Adjectives) Converted into, become, etc., convertible, transitional.

(Adverbs) Gradually, *gradatim*, by degrees, step by step, by inches, inch by inch, by little and little, by slow degrees, consecutively, seriatim, *in transitu*.

145 Reversion *(Substantives)*, return, reconversion, relapse (661), recidivism, atavism, throwback, reaction, recoil (277), backlash, rebound, ricochet, revulsion, alternation (138), inversion, regression (283).

Reinstatement, re-establishment (660).

(Phrases) The turning-point; the turn of the tide; *status quo ante bellum*.

(Verbs) To revert, turn back, return to, relapse, recoil, rebound, react; to restore (660), to undo, unmake.

(Phrase) To turn the tables (719).

(Adjectives) Reverting, etc., restored, etc., regressive, retrogressive, atavistic, revulsive, reactionary.

(Interjection) As you were!

146 Sudden or violent change.

Revolution *(Substantives)*, counter-revolution, revolt, rebellion (742), transilience, jump, leap, plunge, jerk, start, spasm, convulsion, throe, storm, earthquake, catastrophe, cataclysm (173).

Legerdemain, conjuration, sleight of hand, hocus-pocus (545), harlequinade, witchcraft (992).

A revolutionary, revolutionist, counter-revolutionist, deviationist; the red flag.

(Verbs) To revolutionize, remodel, recast, refashion, reconstruct.

(Adjectives) Revolutionary, radical, extreme, intransigent, catastrophic, cataclysmic.

(Adverbs) Root and branch.

147 Change of one thing for another.

Substitution *(Substantives)*, commutation, supplanting, replacement, supersession, enallage, metonymy, synecdoche, antonomasia.

Thing substituted, substitute (634), succedaneum, makeshift, shift, apology, stand-in, pinch-hitter, locumtenens, representative, proxy; understudy, deputy (759), vice, double, dummy, changeling, scapegoat, stooge; stop-gap, jury-mast, palimpsest, metaphor (521).

(Phrase) Borrowing of or robbing Peter to pay Paul.

(Verbs) To substitute, put in place of, commute, supplant, cut out, change for, supersede, take over from.

To give place to; to replace.

(Phrases) To serve as a substitute, etc.; to do duty for; to stand in the shoes of; to take the place of.

(Adjectives) Substituted, etc., vicarious, subdititious, makeshift, provisional.

(Adverbs) Instead, in place of, in lieu of, in the room of, *faute de mieux.*

148 Double and mutual change.

Interchange *(Substantives)*, exchange, commutation, intermutation, reciprocation, transposition, permutation, shuffling, castling (at chess), hocus-pocus, interchangeableness, interchangeability.

Reciprocity (12), retaliation (718), barter (794).

(Phrases) A Roland for an Oliver; tit for tat; *quid pro quo.*

(Verbs) To interchange, exchange, bandy, transpose, shuffle, change hands, swap, dicker, permute, reciprocate, commute, counterchange.

(Phrases) To play at puss in the corner; to play musical chairs; to return the compliment; to give and take; you scratch my back, and I'll scratch yours.

(Adjectives) Interchanged, etc., reciprocal, mutual, commutative, interchangeable, intercurrent.

(Adverbs) In exchange, vice versa.

2°. *Complex Changes*

149 Mutability *(Substantives)*, changeableness, changeability, inconstancy, variableness, mobility, instability, unsteadiness, vacillation, unrest, restlessness, slipperiness, impermanence, fragility, fluctuation, vicissitude, alternation, vibration, oscillation (314), flux, ebbing and flowing, ebbs and flows, ups and downs, fidgets, fidgetiness, fugitiveness, disquiet, disquietude.

A Proteus, chameleon, quicksilver, weathercock, kaleidoscope, harlequin; the moon.

(Phrases) April showers; shifting sands; the wheel of fortune; the Cynthia of the minute.

(Verbs) To fluctuate, vary, waver, flounder, vibrate, flicker, flit, flitter, shift, shuffle, shake, totter, tremble, vacillate, ebb and flow, turn and turn about, change and change about.

150 Immutability *(Substantives)*, stability, unchangeableness, unchangeability, constancy, permanence, persistence (106), invariableness, durability, steadiness (604), immobility, fixedness, stableness, settledness, stabiliment, firmness, stiffness, anchylosis, solidity, aplomb, ballast, incommutability, insusceptibility, irrevocableness.

Rock, pillar, tower, foundation, fixture.

(Phrase) The law of the Medes and Persians.

(Verbs) To be permanent, etc. (265), to stand, stand fast, stand pat, remain.

To settle, establish, stablish, perpetuate, fix, set, stabilitate, retain, keep, hold, make sure, nail, clinch, rivet, fasten (43), settle down, set on its legs.

(Phrases) To build one's house on a rock; to weather the storm.

To fade, pass away like a cloud, shadow, or dream.

(Adjectives) Mutable, changeable, variable, ever-changing, inconstant, impermanent, unsteady, unstable, protean, proteiform, unfixed, fluctuating, vacillating, shifting, versatile, fickle, wavering, flickering, flitting, restless, erratic, unsettled, mobile, fluttering, oscillating, vibratory, vagrant, wayward, desultory, afloat, alternating, plastic, disquiet, alterable, casual, unballasted, volatile, capricious (608).

Frail, tottering, shaking, shaky, trembling, fugitive, ephemeral, transient (111), fading, fragile, deciduous, slippery, unsettled, irresolute (605), rocky, groggy.

Kaleidoscopic, prismatic, iridescent, opalescent, shot.

(Phrases) Unstable as water; changeable as the moon, or as a weathercock; *sic transit gloria mundi*; here to-day and gone to-morrow.

Present events

151 Eventuality *(Substantives)*, event, happening, occurrence, incident, affair, transaction, proceeding, fact, matter of fact, phenomenon, advent.

Business, concern, circumstance, particular, casualty, accident, adventure, passage, crisis, episode, pass, emergency, contingency, consequence (154).

The world, life, things, doings, course of things, the course, tide, steam, current, run, etc., of events.

(Phrases) Stirring events; the ups and downs of life; a chapter of accidents; the cast of the dice (156).

(Verbs) To happen, occur, take place, take effect, come, come of, become of, come about, come off, pass, come to pass, fall, fall out, run, be on foot, fall in, befall, betide, bechance, turn out, go off, prove, eventuate, draw on, turn up, crop up, supervene, survene, issue, arrive, ensue, arise, spring, start, come into existence, fall to one's lot.

(Adjectives) Immutable, incommutable, unchangeable, unaltered, unalterable, not to be changed, constant, permanent, invariable, undeviating, stable, durable (265), perennial (110), valid.

Fixed, steadfast, firm, fast, steady, confirmed, immovable, irremovable, rooted, riveted, stablished, established, incontrovertible, stereotyped, indeclinable, settled, stationary, stagnant.

Moored, anchored, at anchor, on a rock, firmly seated, deep-rooted, ineradicable.

Stranded, aground, stuck fast, high and dry.

Indefeasible, irretrievable, intransmutable, irresoluble, irrevocable, irreversible, inextinguishable, irreducible, indissoluble, indissolvable, indestructible, undying, imperishable, indelible, indeciduous, insusceptible of change.

(Phrases) J'y suis, j'y reste; stet; can the Ethiopian change his skin, or the leopard his spots?

Future events

152 Destiny *(Substantives)*, fatality, fate, doom, destination, lot, fortune, star, planet, preordination, predestination, fatalism, inevitableness, kismet, karma, necessity (601), after life, futurity (121).

(Phrases) The decrees of fate; the wheel of fortune.

(Verbs) To impend, hang over, overhang, be in store, loom, threaten, await, come on, approach, stare one in the face, foreordain, preordain, predestine, doom, must be.

(Phrase) To dree one's weird.

(Adjectives) About to happen, impending, coming, destined, imminent, inevitable, ineluctable, inexorable, fated, doomed, devoted.

(Phrases) On the cards; on the knees of the gods.

(Adverbs) Necessarily, inevitably.

(Phrases) What must be, must; *che sarà sarà*; 'It is written'; the die is cast.

To pass off, wear off, blow over.

To experience, meet with, go through, pass through, endure (821), suffer, fare.

(Adjectives) Happening, occurring, etc.; going on, current, incidental, eventful, stirring, bustling.

(Phrase) The plot thickening.

(Adverbs) Eventually, in the event of, on foot, on the *tapis*, as it may happen, happen what may, at all events, sink or swim, come what may.

(Phrases) In the course of things; in the long run; as the world wags.

SECTION VIII—CAUSATION

1°. *Constancy of Sequence in Events*

153 Constant antecedent.

Cause *(Substantives)*, origin, source, principle, element, occasioner, prime mover, *primum mobile*, spring, mainspring, agent, seed, leaven, groundwork, basis (215), fountain, well, fount, fountain-head, spring-head, author (164), parent (166), *fons et origo, raison d'être.*

Pivot, hinge, turning-point, key, lever.

Final cause, proximate cause, immediate cause, ground, reason, the reason why, the why and the wherefore, rationale, occasion, derivation, provenance.

Rudiment, germ, embryo, bud, root, *radix*, radical, etymon, nucleus, seed, ovum, stem, stock, trunk, taproot.

Nest, cradle, womb, *nidus*, birthplace, hot-bed, forcing-bed.

Causality, origination, causation, production (161), aetiology.

Theories of causation, creationism; evolution, Lamarckism, Darwinism, Spencerism, orthogenesis.

(Verbs) To be the cause of, to originate, germinate, give origin to, cause, occasion, give rise to, kindle, suscitate, bring on, bring to pass, give occasion to, produce, bring about, institute, found, lay the foundation of, lie at the root of, procure, draw down, induce, realize, evoke, provoke, elicit, entail, develop, evolve, operate (161).

To conduce, contribute, tend to (176); to determine, decide.

(Phrases) To have a hand in; to have a finger in the pie; to open the door to; to be at the bottom of; to sow the seeds of; to turn the scale.

154 Constant sequent.

Effect *(Substantives)*, consequence, product, result, resultant, resultance, upshot, issue, end (67), fruit, crop, aftermath, harvest, development, outgrowth, derivative, derivation.

Production, produce, work, handiwork, performance, creature, creation, offshoot, fabric, offspring, firstfruits, firstlings, output, *dénouement*, derivation, heredity, evolution (161).

(Verbs) To be the effect, work, fruit, result, etc., of; to be owing to, originate in or from, rise from, take its rise from, arise, spring, proceed, evolve, come of, emanate, come, grow, germinate, bud, sprout, stem, issue, flow, result, follow, accrue, etc., from; come to; to come out of, be derived from, be caused by, depend upon, hinge upon, result from, to be dependent upon, hang upon; to pan out.

(Phrase) To take the consequences.

(Adjectives) Owing to, due to, attributable to, ascribable to, resulting from, through, etc., all along of, hereditary, genetic, derivative.

(Adverbs) Of course, consequently, necessarily, eventually.

(Phrases) Cela va sans dire; thereby hangs a tale.

(Adjectives) Caused, occasioned, etc., causal, original, primary, primordial, having a common origin, connate, radical, embryonic, embryotic, in embryo.

Evolutionary, Darwinian; aetiological.

(Phrase) Behind the scenes.

155 Assignment of cause.

Attribution *(Substantives)*, theory, aetiology, ascription, reference to, rationale, accounting for, imputation to, derivation from, filiation, affiliation, genealogy, pedigree, paternity, maternity (166), explanation (522), cause (153).

(Verbs) To attribute, ascribe, impute, refer to, derive from, lay to, point to, charge on, ground on, invest with, assign as cause, trace to, father upon, account for, theorize, ground, etc.

(Phrases) To put the saddle on the right horse; to point out the reason of; to lay at the door of.

(Adjectives) Attributable, imputable, assignable, traceable, ascribable, referable, owing to, derivable from.

Putative, attributed, imputed, etc.

(Adverbs) Hence, thence, therefore, because, from that cause, for that reason, on that account, owing to, thanks to, forasmuch as, whence, *propter hoc*, wherefore, since, inasmuch as.

Why? wherefore? whence? how comes it? how is it? how happens it? how does it happen?

In some way, somehow, somehow or other, in some such way.

(Phrase) Hinc illae lacrimae.

---

156 Absence of assignable cause.

Chance *(Substantives)*, indetermination, accident, fortune, hazard, hap, haphazard, chance-medley, luck, lot, fate (152), casualty, contingency, adventure, venture, potluck, lucky dip, treasure trove, hit.

A lottery, toss-up, game of chance, *sortes Virgiliance, rouge et noir*, heads or tails, gambling (621), sweepstake.

Possibility, probability, odds, long odds, a near shave, bare chance.

(Phrases) The turn of the cards; a cast or throw of the dice; a pig in a poke; a blind date.

(Verbs) To chance, hap, turn up; to fall to one's lot, to be one's fate (152); to light upon; stumble upon.

To game, gamble, cast lots, raffle, play for.

(Phrases) To take one's chance; to toss up for; to chance one's arm; to take a flyer.

(Adjectives) Casual, fortuitous, random, accidental, adventitious, causeless, incidental, contingent, uncaused, undetermined, indeterminate, suppositional, possible (470); aleatory.

(Adverbs) By chance, by accident, perchance, peradventure, perhaps, maybe, mayhap, haply, possibly.

Casually, etc., at random, at a venture, as it may be, as it may chance, as it may turn up, as it may happen; as chance, luck, fortune, etc., would have it.

2°. *Connection between Cause and Effect*

157 Power *(Substantives)*, potentiality, potency, prepotence, prepotency, prepollence, puissance, strength (159), might, force, energy, metal, dint, right hand, ascendancy, sway, control, almightiness, ability, ableness, competency, efficiency, effectiveness, efficacy, efficaciousness, validity, cogency, en-

158 Impotence *(Substantives)*, inability, disability, disablement, impuissance, weakness (160), imbecility, paralysis, inaptitude, incapacity, incapability, invalidity, inefficacy, inefficiency, inefficaciousness, ineffectualness, disqualification, helplessness, incompetence.

(Phrases) A dead letter; waste

ablement; agency (170), casualty (153), influence (175), authority (737).

Capability, capacity, faculty, quality, attribute, endowment, virtue, gift, property.

Pressure, high pressure, mechanical energy, applied force, motive power.

(Verbs) To be powerful, etc., to gain power; to exercise power, sway, etc., to constrain.

To be the property, virtue, attribute, etc., of; to belong to, pertain to, appertain to, to lie or be in one's power.

To give or confer power, to empower, enable, invest, endue, endow, arm, render strong (159).

(Adjectives) Powerful, high-powered, potent, puissant, potential, capable, able, equal to, cogent, valid, effective, effectual, efficient, efficacious, adequate, competent.

Forcible, energetic, vigorous, nervous, dynamic, vivid, sturdy, rousing, all-powerful, omnipotent, resistless, irresistible, inextinguishable, sovereign, invincible, unconquerable, indomitable.

(Adverbs) Powerfully, etc., by virtue of, in full force.

159 Degree of power.
Strength (Substantives), energy (171), power (157), vigour, vitality, force, main force, physical force, brute force, spring, elasticity, tone, tension, tonicity.

Stoutness, sturdiness, lustiness, lustihood, stamina, physique, nerve, muscle, thews, and sinews, backbone, pith, pithiness.

Feats of strength, athletics, gymnastics.

Strengthening, invigoration, bracing, recruital, recruitment, refreshment, refocillation (689).

Science of forces, dynamics, statics.

Adamant, steel, iron, oak, heart of oak.

An athlete, gymnast, acrobat; an Atlas, a Hercules, Sampson, Cyclops, Goliath.

(Phrases) A giant refreshed; a tower of strength.

paper; brutum fulmen; blank cartridge.

(Verbs) To be impotent, powerless, etc.; to collapse, fail, flunk, break down, fizzle out, fold up.

To render powerless, etc., to deprive of power, disable, disenable, incapacitate, disqualify, unfit, invalidate, nullify, deaden, cripple, cramp, paralyse, muzzle, hamstring, bowl over, render weak (160).

(Phrases) To go by the board; to end in smoke.

To clip the wings of; spike the guns; to tie a person's hands; to put a spoke in one's wheel; to take the wind out of one's sails.

(Adjectives) Powerless, impotent, unable, incapable, incompetent, inadequate, unequal to, inefficient, inefficacious, inept, ineffectual, ineffective, inoperative, nugatory, incapacitated, harmless, imbecile, disqualified, disabled, armless, disarmed, unarmed, weaponless, defenceless; unnerved, paralysed, palsied, disjointed, nerveless, adynamic, unendowed.

(Phrases) Laid on the shelf; hors de combat; not having a leg to stand on.

160 Weakness (Substantives), feebleness, impotence (158), debility, atony, relaxation, helplessness, languor, slackness, enervation, nervousness, faintness, languidness, infirmity, emasculation, effeminacy, feminality, femineity, flaccidity, softness, defencelessness.

Childhood, etc. (127, 129); orphan, chicken.

Declension, loss, failure, etc., of strength, invalidation, delicacy, delicateness, decrepitude, asthenia, neurasthenia, anaemia, bloodlessness, palsy, paralysis, exhaustion, collapse, prostration, faintness, cachexy (or cachexia).

A reed, thread, rope of sand, house of cards; a weakling, sissy, jellyfish.

(Verbs) To be weak, etc., to droop, fade, faint, swoon, languish, decline, flag, fail, totter, drop, crock; to go by the board.

(Verbs) To be strong, etc., to be stronger, to overmatch.

To render strong, etc., to give strength, tone, etc., to strengthen, invigorate, brace, buttress, sustain, fortify, harden, case-harden, steel, gird up, screw up, wind up, set up, tone up.

To reinforce, refit, recruit, vivify, restore (660), refect, refocillate (689).

(Phrase) To set on one's legs.

(Adjectives) Strong, mighty, vigorous, stout, robust, sturdy, powerful, puissant, hard, adamantine, invincible, able-bodied, athletic, Herculean, muscular, brawny, sinewy, made of iron, strapping, well-set, well-knit, stalwart, doughty, husky, lusty, hardy, irresistible; strengthening, etc.; invigorative, tonic.

Manly, manlike, masculine, male, virile, manful, full-blooded.

Unweakened, unallayed, unwithered, unshaken, unworn, unexhausted, unrelaxed, undiluted, unwatered, neat.

(Phrases) Made of iron; as strong as a lion, as a horse; in great form; fit as a fiddle.

(Adverbs) Strongly, forcibly, etc., by main force, *vi et armis*, by might and main, tooth and nail, hammer and tongs, for all one is worth.

To render weak, etc., to weaken, enfeeble, debilitate, devitalize, deprive of strength, relax, enervate, unbrace, unman, emasculate, castrate, geld, hamstring, disable, unhinge, cripple, cramp, paralyse, maim, sprain, exhaust, prostrate, blunt the edge of, deaden, dilute, water, water down.

(Adjectives) Weak, feeble, debile, strengthless, nerveless, imbecile, unnerved, relaxed, unstrung, unbraced, enervated, nervous, sinewless, spineless, lustless, effeminate, feminine, womanly, unmanned, emasculated, castrated.

Crippled, maimed, lamed, shattered, broken, frail, fragile, flimsy, gimcrack, halting, shaken, crazy, shaky, paralysed, palsied, paralytic, decrepit, puny, shilpit, drooping, languid, faint, sickly, flagging, dull, slack, limp, spent, effete, weather-beaten, worn, seedy, exhausted, deadbeat, all in, whacked, done up, languishing, wasted, washy, vincible, untenable, laid low, run down, asthenic, neurasthenic, neurotic, rickety, invertebrate, feckless.

Unstrengthened, unsustained, unsupported, unaided, unassisted, defenceless, indefensible, unfortified, unfriended, fatherless, etc.

(Phrases) On one's last legs; the worse for wear; weak as a child, as a baby, as a kitten, as water; good or fit for nothing.

3°. *Power in Operation*

161 Production *(Substantives)*, creation, formation, construction, fabrication, manufacture, building, architecture, erection, edification, coinage, organization, putting together, establishment, setting up, performance (729), workmanship, output.

Development, breeding, evolution, flowering, genesis, generation, *epigenesis,* procreation, propagation, fecundation, impregnation, gestation, birth, bringing forth, parturition, growth, proliferation.

162 Non-production.

Destruction *(Substantives)*, waste, dissolution, breaking up, disruption, consumption, disorganization, falling to pieces, crumbling, etc.

Fall, downfall, ruin, perdition, crash, smash, havoc, desolation, *bouleversement, débacle,* upset, wreck, shipwreck, cataclysm, extinction, annihilation; doom, destruction of life (360), prang (716, 732).

Demolition, demolishment, overthrow, subversion, suppression, dismantling, cutting up, corrosion,

Theory of development, Mendelism, eugenics.

(Verbs) To produce, effect, perform, operate, do, make, form, construct, fabricate, frame, contrive, manufacture, weave, forge, coin, carve, sculp, chisel, build, raise, edify, rear, erect, run up, establish.

To constitute, compose, organize, institute, work out, realize, bring to bear, bring to pass, accomplish, bring off.

To create, generate, engender, beget, bring into being, breed, propagate, proliferate, conceive, bear, procreate, give birth to, bring forth, yield, flower, fructify, hatch, develop, bring up.

To induce, superinduce, suscitate (153).

(Phrases) To be brought to bed of; to usher into the world.

(Adjectives) Produced, etc., producing, productive of, etc., creative, formative, parturient, pregnant, *enceinte*, genetic; eugenic.

(Phrase) In the family way.

163 Reproduction *(Substantives)*, renovation, restoration (660), reconstruction, revival, regeneration, revivication, resuscitation, reanimation, resurrection, resurgence, reappearance, palingenesis, reincarnation, multiplication; phoenix.

(Verbs) To reproduce, revive, renew, renovate, rebuild, reconstruct, regenerate, revivify, resurrect, resuscitate, reanimate, reincarnate, quicken; come again into life, reappear

(Phrase) To spring up like a mushroom.

(Adjectives) Reproduced, etc., renascent, reappearing; hydra-headed.

———

erosion, crushing, upsetting, abolition, abolishment, sacrifice, immolation, holocaust, dilapidation, devastation, *razzia*, ravaging, extermination, eradication, extirpation, rooting out, averruncation, sweeping, etc., death-blow, *coup de grâce*, the crack of doom.

(Verbs) To be destroyed, etc., to perish, waste, fall to pieces, break up, crumble, break down, crack.

To destroy, do or make away with, demolish, overturn, upset, throw down, overthrow, overwhelm, subvert, put an end to, uproot, eradicate, extirpate, root out, grub up, break up, pull down, do for, dish, ditch, crumble, smash, crash, crush, quell, quash, squash, squelch, cut up, shatter, shiver, batter, tear or shake to pieces, tear to tatters, pick to pieces, put down, suppress, strike out, throw or knock down, cut down, knock on the head, stifle, dispel, fell, sink, swamp, scuttle, engulf, submerge, wreck, corrode, erode, consume, sacrifice, immolate, burke, blow down, sweep away, erase, expunge, liquidate, wipe out, mow down, blast.

To waste, lay waste, ravage, dilapidate, dismantle, disorganize, devour, swallow up, desolate, devastate, sap, mine, blow up, stifle, dispatch, exterminate, extinguish, quench, annihilate, kill (361), unroot, root out, rout out, averruncate, deracinate.

(Phrases) To go to the dogs, or to pot; to go to the devil, or to rack and ruin; to be all over with one.

To lay the axe to the root of; to make short work of; make a clean sweep of; to make mincemeat of; to scatter to the winds; cut up root and branch; knock on the head; to wipe the floor with; to knock into a cocked hat; to sap the foundations of; to nip in the bud; to strike at the root of; to pluck up by the root; to ravage with fire and sword.

(Adjectives) Destroyed, done for, dished, etc.; destructive, subversive, pernicious, ruinous, deadly, incendiary, demolitionary.

164 Producer *(Substantives)*, originator, author, artist, creator, prime mover, founder, workman, doer, performer, manufacturer, forger, agent (690), builder, architect, factor.

166 Paternity *(Substantives)*, fatherhood, maternity, motherhood, parentage, parent, father, sire, paterfamilias, pater, dad, daddy, papa, pa; mother, mamma, ma, mummy, mum, dam, materfamilias, mater, procreator, pregenitor, begetter, ancestor, ancestry, forefathers, forebears, grandsire; house parent, stem, trunk, stock, pedigree.

(Adjectives) Paternal, maternal, parental, fatherly, motherly, family, ancestral, patriarchal.

---

168 Productiveness *(Substantives)*, fecundity, fruitfulness, fertility, prolificness; creativeness, inventiveness.

Pregnancy, gestation, pullulation, fructification, multiplication, propagation, procreation.

A milch cow, rabbit, warren, hydra.

(Phrase) A land flowing with milk and honey.

(Verbs) To procreate (161), multiply, teem, pullulate, fructify, proliferate, generate, fertilize, impregnate, conceive.

(Adjectives) Productive, prolific, teeming, fertile, fruitful, luxuriant, fecund, pregnant, great, gravid, *enceinte*, with child, with young.

Procreant, procreative, generative, propagable, life-giving.

165 Destroyer *(Substantives)*, extinguisher, exterminator, assassin (361), executioner (975), ravager, annihilator, subverter, demolisher; iconoclast, vandal.

167 Posterity *(Substantives)*, progeny, breed, issue, offspring, brood, seed, litter, spawn, scion, offset, child, son, daughter, grandchild, grandson, granddaughter, etc., bantling, shoot, sprout, sprig, slip, branch, line, lineage, filiation, family, offshoot, ramification, descendant, heir, heiress, heir apparent, heir presumptive.

Straight descent, sonship, primogeniture, ultimogeniture.

(Adjectives) Filial, daughterly, dutiful, lineal, hereditary.

(Phrase) A chip of the old block; the rising generation.

169 Unproductiveness *(Substantives)*, infertility, barrenness, sterility, unfruitfulness, unprofitableness, infecundity, fruitlessness (645), non-agency.

(Verbs) To be unproductive, etc., to come to nothing.

To render unproductive, sterilize, castrate, spay, pasteurize.

(Adjectives) Unproductive, inoperative, barren, addled, infertile, unprolific, sterile, unfruitful, fallow, fruitless, infecund, issueless, unprofitable (645).

---

170 Agency *(Substantives)*, operation, force, working, strain, function, office, hand, intervention, intercession, interposition, exercise, work, swing, play, causation (153), impelling force, mediation (631), action (680).

Modus operandi, quickening power, maintaining power.

(Verbs) To be in action, to operate, function, work, act, perform, play, support, sustain, strain, maintain, take effect, quicken, strike, strike hard, strike home, bring to bear.

(Phrases) To come into play; to make an impression.

(Adjectives) Acting, operating, etc., operative, practical, efficient, efficacious, effectual, in force.

Acted upon, wrought upon.

171 Physical **Energy** (*Substantives*), force, power, activity, keenness, intensity, sharpness, pungency, vigour, strength, edge, point, raciness, metal, mettle, vim, dash, fire, punch, go, pep.

Seasoning, mordant, pepper, mustard, cayenne, caviare (392).

Mental energy (604), mental excitation (824), voluntary energy (682).

Exertion, activity, stir, bustle, hustle, agitation, effervescence, fermentation, ferment, ebullition, splutter, perturbation, briskness, voluntary activity (682), quicksilver.

(*Verbs*) To give energy, energize, stimulate, invigorate, kindle, galvanize, electrify, intensify, excite, exert (173).

(*Adjectives*) Strong, energetic, emphatic, forcible, forceful, active, keen, vivid, intense, severe, sharp, acute, pungent, poignant, racy, brisk, ebullient, mettlesome, enterprising, go-ahead, double-edged, double-barrelled, double-distilled, drastic, intensive, trenchant.

(*Phrases*) *Fortiter in re;* with telling effect; with full steam; at high pressure; flat out.

172 Physical **Inertness** (*Substantives*) inertia, *vis inertiae*, inertion, passiveness, passivity, inactivity, torpor, latency, torpidity, dullness, stagnation, deadness, heaviness, flatness, slackness, tameness, slowness, languor, lentor, quiescence (265), sleep (683), intermission (141).

Mental inertness, indecision (605), placidity (826).

(*Verbs*) To be inalert, inactive, passive, etc.; to hang fire, smoulder.

(*Phrase*) To sit on the fence.

(*Adjectives*) Inert, inactive, passive, torpid, flaccid, limp, lymphatic, sluggish, dull, heavy, flat, slack, tame, slow, supine, slothful, stagnant, blunt, lifeless, dead.

Latent, dormant, smouldering, unexerted, unstrained, uninfluential.

(*Adverbs*) Inactively, in suspense, in abeyance.

———

173 **Violence** (*Substantives*), inclemency, vehemence, might, impetuosity, boisterousness, abruptness, ebullition, turbulence, horseplay, bluster, uproar, shindy, row, riot, rumpus, fierceness, rage, wildness, fury, heat, exacerbation, exasperation, malignity, fit, paroxysm, orgasm, force, brute force, *coup de main,* strain, shock, spasm, convulsion, throe.

Outbreak, burst, outburst, dissilience, discharge, volley, explosion, blow-up, blast, detonation, rush, eruption, displosion, torrent.

Turmoil, tumult, storm, tempest, squall, hurricane, tornado, typhoon, cyclone, earthquake, volcano, thunder-storm.

A rowdy (949), berserk (or berserker), spitfire, fireeater, hellhound, fury, termagant, virago, vixen, hellcat, dragon, demon, tiger, beldam, Tisiphone, Megaera, Alecto, Maenad.

174 **Moderation** (*Substantives*), gentleness, temperateness, calmness, mildness, composure, sobriety, slowness, tameness, quiet (740), restfulness, reason.

Relaxation, remission, measure, golden mean, mitigation, tranquillization, assuagement, soothing, allaying, etc., contemperation, pacification (723), restraint, check (751), lullaby, sedative, lenitive, demulcent, palliative, opiate, anodyne, balm, opium.

Mental calmness (826).

(*Verbs*) To be moderate, etc., to keep within bounds or within compass, to settle down, to keep the peace, to sober down, remit, relent.

To moderate, soften, soothe, mitigate, appease, temper, attemper, contemper, mollify, lenify, tame, dull, take off the edge, blunt, obtund, tone down, subdue.

To tranquillize, assuage, appease, lull, cool, compose, still, calm, quiet,

(Verbs) To be violent, etc., to run high, ferment, effervesce, run wild, run riot, run amuck, rush, tear, rush headlong, bluster, rage, rampage, riot, storm, boil, fume, let off steam, foam, wreak, bear down.

To break out, fly out, bounce, go off, explode, displode, fly, fulminate, detonate, blow up, flash, flare, burst, burst out, shock, strain.

To render violent, sharpen, stir up, quicken, excite, incite, stimulate, kindle, lash, suscitate, urge, accelerate, foment, aggravate, exasperate, exacerbate, convulse, infuriate, madden, lash into fury, inflame, let off, discharge.

(Phrases) To break the peace; to see red; to out-herod Herod; add fuel to the flame.

(Adjectives) Violent, vehement, warm, acute, rough, rude, wild, boisterous, impetuous, ungentle, tough, brusque, abrupt, rampant, knock-about, rampageous, bluff, turbulent, blustering, riotous, rowdy, noisy, thundering, obstreperous, uproarious, outrageous, frantic, phrenetic, headstrong, rumbustious, disorderly (59).

hush, quell, sober, pacify, damp, lay, allay, rebate, slacken, smooth, soften, alleviate, rock to sleep, deaden (376), check, restrain, slake, curb, bridle, rein in, hold in, repress, smother, counteract (179).

(Phrases) To pour oil on the waves; to pour balm into; to throw cold water on.

(Adjectives) Moderate, gentle, mild, sober, temperate, measured, reasonable, tempered, calm, unruffled, tranquil, smooth, untroubled; unexciting, unirritating, soft, bland, oily, demulcent, lenitive, cool, quiet, anodyne, hypnotic, sedative, peaceful, peaceable, pacific, lenient, tame, halcyon, restful.

(Phrases) Gentle as a lamb; mild as milk.

(Adverbs) Moderately, gently, temperately, softly, etc.

(Phrases) Softly, softly, catchee monkey; *suaviter in modo; est modus in rebus.*

Savage, fierce, ferocious, fiery, fuming, excited, unquelled, unquenched, unextinguished, unrepressed, unbridled, unruly, boiling, boiling over, furious, outrageous, raging, running riot, storming, hysteric, hysterical, wild, running wild, ungovernable, unappeasable, immitigable, uncontrollable, insuppressible, irrepressible, raging, desperate, mad, rabid, infuriated, exasperated.

Tempestuous, stormy, squally, spasmodic, spastic, paroxysmal, convulsive, galvanic, bursting, explosive, detonating, volcanic, meteoric, seismic.

(Phrases) Fierce as a tiger; all the fat in the fire.

(Adverbs) Violently, etc., by force, by main force, like mad.

(Phrases) By might and main; tooth and nail; *vi et armis*; at the point of the sword, or bayonet.

4°. *Indirect Power*

175   Influence *(Substantives)*, weight, pressure, prevalence, sway, ascendancy (or ascendency), preponderance, predominance, predominancy, dominance, prepotency, importance (642), reign, ableness, capability (157).

Footing, hold, foothold, purchase,

175A Absence of Influence, impotence (158), weakness (160), inertness (172).

(Verb) To have no influence.

(Phrase) To cut no ice.

(Adjective) Uninfluential.

---

fulcrum, stance, *point d'appui, pou sto, locus standi,* leverage, vantage-ground; aegis, protection, patronage, auspices.

(Phrases) A tower of strength; a host in himself.

(Verbs) To have influence, etc., to have a hold upon, to have a pull, to gain a footing, work upon, take root, take hold, permeate, penetrate, infiltrate, prevail, dominate, predominate, outweigh, overweigh, carry weight, weigh, tell, to bear upon.

(Phrases) To be in the ascendant; to cut some ice; to pull wires; to pull the strings; to set the fashion; to have a voice.

(Adjectives) Influential, valid, weighty, prevailing, prevalent, dominant, regnant, predominating, predominant, prepotent, ascendant, rife.

(Adverb) With telling effect.

176 Tendency *(Substantives)*, aptness, proneness, proclivity, conduciveness, bent, bias, quality, inclination, trend, propensity, predisposition, leaning, drift, conducement, temperament, idiosyncrasy, vein, humour, mood.

(Verbs) To tend, contribute, conduce, lead, dispose, incline, trend, verge, bend to, affect, carry, promote, redound, to, subserve to (644), bid fair to, make for, gravitate towards.

(Adjectives) Tending, contributing, conducing, conducive, working towards, calculated to, disposing, inclining, bending, leading, carrying to, subservient, subsidiary (644, 707); apt, liable, prone, disposed, predisposed.

(Adverbs) For, whither, in a fair way to.

177 Liability *(Substantives)*, subjection to, dependence on, exposure to, contingency, possibility (156), susceptivity, susceptibility.

(Verbs) To be liable, etc., incur, to lay oneself open to, lie under, expose oneself to, stand a chance, to open a door to.

(Phrase) To stick one's neck out.

(Adjectives) Liable, apt, prone, subject, open to, incident to, exposed to, dependent on; answerable, accountable, responsible.

Contingent, incidental, possible, casual.

(Phrases) Within range of; at the mercy of.

5°. *Combinations of Causes*

178 Concurrence *(Substantives)*, co-operation, collaboration (709), union, agreement, consent (488), pulling together, alliance; complicity, connivance, collusion.

Voluntary concurrence (709).

(Verbs) To concur, co-operate, conspire, agree, conduce, contribute, unite, to pull together, hang together, join forces.

(Phrases) To have a hand in; to be in the same boat; to go hand in hand (709).

(Adjectives) Concurring, concurrent, conjoined, concomitant, associate, co-operating, conspiring, agreeing, correspondent, conformable,

179 Counteraction *(Substantives)*, opposition, antagonism, polarity, clashing, etc., collision, contrariety (14), resistance, interference, friction.

Neutralization, nullification, compensation (30).

Reaction, retroaction (277), repercussion, rebound, recoil, ricochet, counterblast.

Check, obstacle, hindrance (706); antidote, counter-irritant, preventive, corrective, remedy (662).

Voluntary counteraction (708).

(Verbs) To counteract, oppose, cross, contravene, antagonize, interfere or conflict with, collide with,

pulling together, etc., of one mind, in alliance with, with one consent, of one mind, with one accord.

———

clash, neutralize, undo, nullify, render null; to militate against, withstand, resist (719), hinder (706), repress, control, curb, check, rein in (174).

To react (277), countervail, counterpoise (30), overpoise.

(Adjectives) Counteracting, opposing, etc., counteractive, antagonistic, conflicting, reactionary, recalcitrant, opposite, retroactive, cohibitive, counter, contrary (14).

(Adverbs) Counter, notwithstanding, nevertheless, nathless, none the less, yet, still, although, though, albeit, howbeit, maugre, at all events.

But, even, however, in defiance of, in the teeth of, in the face of, in spite of, in despite of (708).

(Phrases) For all that; all the same; be that as it may; even so.

CLASS II

WORDS RELATING TO SPACE

SECTION I—SPACE IN GENERAL

1°. *Abstract Space*

180 Indefinite space.

Space *(Substantives)*, extension, extent, expanse, room, scope, range, purview, way, expansion, compass, sweep, play, amplitude, latitude, field, swing, spread, stretch; spare room, headway, elbow-room, freedom, house-room, stowage, roomage, margin.

Open space, void, space, vacuity (4), opening, waste, wilderness, moor, moorland, campagna, tundra.

Abyss (198); unlimited space, infinity (105).

(Adjectives) Spatial, two-dimensional, three-dimensional.

Spacious, roomy, commodious, extensive, expansive, capacious, ample.

Boundless, unlimited, unbounded, limitless, illimitable, infinite, uncircumscribed, shoreless, trackless, pathless.

(Adverbs) Extensively, etc., wherever, everywhere.

(Phrases) The length and the breadth of the land; far and near, far and wide; all over; all the world over; from China to Peru; from Land's End to John o' Groat's; in every quarter; in all quarters; in all lands; every hole and corner; here, there, and everywhere; from pole to pole; throughout the world; to the four winds; under the sun.

181 Definite space.

Region *(Substantives)*, sphere, ground, area, realm, quarter, district, orb, circuit, circle, compartment, domain, tract, department, territory, country, canton, county, shire, township, riding, hundred, parish, bailiwick, province, satrapy, *arrondissement*, commune, enclave, principality, duchy, kingdom, empire, dominion, colony, protectorate, mandate.

Arena, precincts, *enceinte*, walk, patch, plot, paddock, enclosure, field, compound.

Clime, climate, zone, meridian.

(Adjectives) Regional, territorial, provincial, parochial, local, etc.

Limited space, locality.

182 Place *(Substantives)*, spot, point, nook, corner, recess, hole, niche, compartment, premises, precinct, station, pitch, venue, abode (189).

Indefinite place.

(Adverbs) Somewhere, in some place, wherever it may be.

———

2°. *Relative Space*

183 Situation *(Substantives)*, position, locality, locale, status, latitude and longitude, footing, standing, post, stage, bearings, aspect, orientation, attitude, posture, lie, emplacement.

Place, site, station, pitch, seat, venue, whereabouts, direction, azimuth, etc. (278).

Topography, geography, chorography.

A map, chart, plan (554).

(Verbs) To be situated, to lie, to have its seat in.

(Adjectives) Local, topical; situate.

(Adverbs) In situ, here and there, *passim,* whereabouts.

184 Location *(Substantives),* localization, lodgment, deposition, reposition, stowage, establishment, settlement, fixation, grafting, insertion (300), lading, encampment, billet, installation.

A colony, settlement, cantonment.

A habitation, residence, dwelling (189).

(Phrases) Genius loci; the spirit of the place.

(Verbs) To place, situate, locate, localize, put, lay, set, seat, station, lodge, park, post, install, house, settle, stow, dump, establish, fix, root, plant, graft, stick in, tuck in, insert, wedge in, shelve, pitch, camp, posit, deposit, reposit, cradle, encamp, moor, pack, embed (or imbed), vest, stock, populate, people, colonize, domicile.

To billet on, quarter upon.

To pocket, pouch, put up, bag, load.

To inhabit, reside (186), domesticate, put up at, colonize.

(Phrase) To pitch one's tent.

185 Displacement *(Substantives),* dislodgment, eviction, ejectment (297), deportation, extradition, expatriation, banishment, exile.

Removal, remotion, transposition, relegation (270).

(Verbs) To displace, dislodge, unhouse, unkennel, break bulk, take off, eject, evict, chuck out, hoof out, expel, etc. (297), extradite, expatriate, banish, exile, relegate, oust, rusticate, ostracize, remove, transfer, transpose, transplant, transport (270), empty, clear, clear out, sweep off, sweep away, do away with, get rid of, root out, disestablish, unpeople, depopulate.

To vacate, leave (293), get out, heave out, bale out, lade out, pour out (297).

(Phrase) To make a clean sweep of.

(Adjectives) Displaced, etc., unhoused, houseless, homeless, stateless.

(Phrase) Like a fish out of water.

(Adjectives) Placed, located, etc., situate, situated, ensconced, nestled, embosomed, housed, moored, rooted, unremoved.

3°. *Existence in Space*

186 Presence *(Substantives),* occupancy, occupation, attendance, whereness.

Diffusion, permeation, pervasion, interpenetration, dissemination (73).

Ubiquity, ubiety, ubiquitousness, omnipresence.

(Verbs) To exist in space, to be present, attend, remain.

To occur in a place, lie, stand, occupy, colonize.

To inhabit, dwell, reside, live, abide, sojourn, lodge, nestle, perch, roost, put up at, hang out at, stay at,

187 Absence *(Substantives),* nonexistence (2), non-residence, non-attendance, alibi, absenteeism.

Emptiness, void, vacuum, voidness, vacuity, vacancy, vacuousness.

An absentee, truant, nobody, nobody on earth.

(Verbs) To be absent, not present, etc., vacate, to keep away, to keep out of the way.

(Phrases) Make oneself scarce; absent oneself; take oneself off; stay away; play truant; be conspicuous by one's absence.

stop at, squat, hive, burrow, camp, encamp, bivouac, anchor, settle, take up one's quarters, pitch one's tent, get a footing, frequent, haunt, tenant, take root, strike root, revisit.

To fill, pervade, permeate, penetrate, interpenetrate, infiltrate, be diffused through, be disseminated through, overspread, run through.

(Adjectives) Present, occupying, inhabiting, etc., moored, at anchor, resident, residentiary, domiciled.

Ubiquitous, omnipresent.

(Adverbs) Here, there, where? everywhere, in residence, aboard, on board, at home, afield, etc., on the spot.

(Phrases) Here, there, and everywhere; at every turn.

188 Inhabitant *(Substantives)*, resident, residentiary, dweller, indweller, occupier, occupant, lodger, boarder, paying guest, inmate, tenant, sojourner, settler, squatter, backwoodsman, national, colonist, denizen, citizen, cit, cockney, townsman, burgess, countryman, villager, cottar, compatriot, garrison, crew, population, people.

Native, indigene, aborigines, autochthones, son of the soil.

A colony, settlement, household.

Newcomer (57).

(Adjectives) Indigenous, native, aboriginal, autochthonous, domestic, domiciled, domesticated, domiciliary.

(Adjectives) Absent, not present, away, gone, from home, missing, non-resident.

Empty, void, vacant, vacuous, blank, untenanted, tenantless, uninhabited, deserted, devoid, unoccupied, unpeopled.

(Phrases) Nowhere to be found; A.W.O.L. (absent without leave); *non est inventus*; not a soul; nobody present; the bird being flown.

(Adverbs) Without, minus, nowhere, elsewhere, sans.

(Phrases) One's back being turned; behind one's back.

---

189 Place of habitation.

Abode *(Substantives)*, dwelling, lodging, domicile, residence, address, habitation, berth, seat, lap, sojourn, housing, quarters, accommodation, headquarters, throne, ark, tabernacle.

Nest, nidus, lair, haunt, eyrie (or aerie), den, hole, earth, warren, rookery, hive, habitat, haunt, resort, retreat, nidification, perch, roost.

Bivouac, camp, encampment, cantonment, castrametation, tent, marquee, teepee, igloo.

Cave, cavern, cell, grove, grot, grotto, alcove, bower, arbour, cove, chamber (191).

Home, fatherland, motherland, native land, country, homestead, homestall, fireside, snuggery, hearth, Lares and Penates, household gods, roof, household, housing; 'dulce domum', Blighty.

Building, structure, edifice, fabric, erection, pile, tenement, messuage, farm, farmhouse, steading, grange.

Cot, cabin, hut, shack, chalet, croft, shed, hangar, penthouse, lean-to, booth, stall, hovel, outhouse, barn, kennel, sty, coop, hutch, cage, cote, stable, garage, offices.

House, mansion, villa, flat, flatlet, prefab, maisonette, cottage, box, lodge, *pied-à-terre,* bungalow, hermitage, summer-house, gazebo, folly, rotunda, tower, temple (1000), château, castle, pavilion, court, hall, palace, kiosk, house-boat.

Inn, hostel, hotel, roadhouse, motel, tavern, caravansery, hospice, rest-house, dak-bungalow, barrack, lodging-house, guest-house, dosshouse, lodgings, apartments, diggings, digs.

Hamlet, village, clachan, thorp, dorp, kraal, borough, burgh, municipality, town, city, garden city, metropolis, suburb (227), conurbation, province, country.

Street, place, terrace, parade, road, avenue, row, lane, alley, court, wynd, close, yard, passage, rents, slum; square, polygon, quadrant, circus, crescent, mall, place, piazza, arcade, gardens.

Anchorage, roadstead, dock, basin, wharf, quay, port, harbour, haven.

(Adjectives) Urban, civic, metropolitan, municipal, provincial, rural, rustic, countrified; home-like, homy.

190 Things contained.

Contents *(Substantives)*, cargo, lading, filling, stuffing, freight, load, burden, ware (798).

191 Receptacle *(Substantives)*, recipient, receiver, reservatory, compartment (636).

Cell, cellule, loculus, follicle, hole, corner, niche, recess, nook, crypt, stall, pigeon-hole, lodging (189), bed, berth, bunk, doss, etc. (215), store-room, strong-room.

Capsule, vesicle, cyst, bladder, pod.

Stomach, belly, paunch, ventricle, crop, craw, maw, gizzard, bread-basket, kyte, ovary, womb (221).

Pocket, pouch, sporran, fob, sheath, scabbard, socket, bag, sac, sack, wallet, scrip, poke, kit, knapsack, rucksack, haversack, sabretache, satchel, cigar-case, cigarette-case, reticule, powder-box, flapjack, compact, vanity-case, vanity-bag, portfolio, budget.

Chest, box, hutch, coffer, case, casket, caddy, pyx (or pix), caisson, desk, davenport, escritoire, bureau, cabinet, reliquary; trunk, portmanteau, saratoga, grip-sack, grip, bandbox, valise, hold-all, attaché-case, dispatch-case, dispatch-box, writing-case, suit-case, dressing-case, kit-bag, brief-bag, brief-case, gladstone bag, boot, creel, crate, packing-case, snuff-box, mull.

Vessel, vase, bushel, barrel, canister, jar, can, pottle, basket, pannier, corbeille, punnet, hamper, tray, hod.

For liquids: cistern, reservoir, tank, vat, cauldron, barrel, cask, keg, runlet, firkin, kilderkin, demijohn, carboy, amphora, bottle, jar, decanter, carafe, tantalus, ewer, cruse, crock, kit, canteen, flagon, flask, flasket, thermos flask, vacuum flask, stoup, noggin, vial (or phial), cruet, caster, urn, samovar, billy.

Tub, bucket, pail, pot, tankard, beaker, jug, pitcher, mug, noggin, pipkin, gallipot, matrass, receiver, alembic, retort, test-tube, pipette, capsule, kettle, spittoon.

Bowl, basin, jorum, punch-bowl, cup, goblet, chalice, quaich, tumbler, glass, horn, can, pan, pannikin, plate, dish, trencher, tray, salver, patera, calabash, porringer, saucepan, skillet, casserole, tureen, saucer, platter, hod, scuttle, baikie, shovel, trowel, spoon, spatula, ladle.

Closet, cupboard, cellaret, chiffonier, wardrobe, bunker, bin, buffet, press, safe, sideboard, whatnot, drawer, chest of drawers, tallboy, lowboy, till.

Chamber, flat, storey, apartment, room, cabin, bower, office, court, hall, saloon, *salon*, parlour, state-room, presence-chamber, reception-room, drawing-room, sitting-room, living-room, gallery, cabinet, nursery, boudoir, library, study, snuggery, adytum, sanctum, den, phrontistery, lumber-room (636), dormitory, bedroom, dressing-room, refectory, dining-room, breakfast-room, billiard-room, smoking-room, pew, harem, seraglio, zenana.

Attic, loft, garret, cockloft, belfry, cellar, vault, hold, cockpit, ground-floor, *rez-de-chaussée*, basement, kitchen, kitchenette, pantry, scullery, bathroom, lavatory, water-closet, w.c., urinal, latrine, rear, toilet, convenience, comfort station, heads, thunder-box, offices.

Portico, porch, veranda, piazza, stoop, lobby, court, hall, vestibule, foyer, lounge, corridor, loggia, passage, anteroom, antechamber.

(Adjectives) Capsular, saccular, sacculate, recipient, ventricular, cystic, vascular, celled, cellular, cellulous, cellulose, camerated, chambered, locular, multilocular, roomed, two-roomed, etc., polygastric, pouched, marsupial.

SECTION II—DIMENSIONS

1°. *General Dimensions*

192 Size *(Substantives)*, magnitude, dimension, bulk, volume, largeness, bigness, greatness (31), expanse, amplitude, mass, massiveness.

Capacity, capaciousness, tonnage (or tunnage), calibre, scantling.

Average size, stock size.

Corpulence, adiposity, obesity, chubbiness, plumpness, *embonpoint*, stoutness, out-size; corporation, flesh and blood, brawn, brawniness.

Hugeness, vastness, enormousness, enormity, immensity, monstrousness, monstrosity; expansion (194) infinity (105).

A giant, Goliath, Brobdingnagian, Antaeus, Gargantua, monster, whale, leviathan, elephant, mammoth, colossus, tun, lump, chunk, bulk, block, boulder, mass, bushel, whacker, thumper, whopper, spanker, behemoth.

A mountain, mound, heap (72).

(Phrases) A Triton among the minnows; the lion's share.

(Verbs) To be large, etc., to become large (194).

(Adjectives) Large, big, great, considerable, bulky, voluminous, ample, massive, massy, capacious, comprehensive, mighty, king-sized.

Corpulent, obese, stout, fat, plump, rotund, buxom, sonsy, lusty, strapping, bouncing, portly, burly, brawny, fleshy, beefy, goodly, in good case, chopping, jolly, chubby, full-grown, chub-faced, lubberly, hulking, unwieldy, lumpish, husky, stalwart.

193 Littleness *(Substantives)*, smallness (32), minuteness, diminutiveness, exiguity, inextension, puniness, dwarfishness, epitome, duodecimo, rudiment, microcosm.

Leanness, emaciation, thinness, macilency, flaccidity, meagreness.

A dwarf, runt, pygmy, midget, Lilliputian, chit, bantam, urchin, elf, doll, puppet, skeleton, ghost, spindle-shanks, shadow, Tom Thumb, manikin, *homunculus*.

Animalcule, mite, insect, emmet, fly, gnat, midge, shrimp, minnow, worm, grub, tit, tomtit, mouse, small fry, smout, mushroom, pollard, millet-seed, mustard-seed, grain of sand, molehill.

Atom, point, speck, dot, mote, ace, jot, iota, tittle, whit, particle, corpuscle, electron, molecule, monad, granule, grain, crumb, globule, nutshell, minim, drop, droplet, mouthful, thimbleful, sprinkling, dash, suspicion, *soupçon*, minimum, powder (330), driblet, patch, scrap, chip, inch, mathematical point; minutiae.

(Phrases) The shadow of a shade; a drop in the ocean; chicken feed; tip of the ice-berg.

(Verbs) To be small, etc., to become small, contract (195).

(Adjectives) Little, small, minute, diminutive, inconsiderable, exiguous, puny, tiny, wee, weeny, teeny-weeny, petty, mini, minikin, hop-o'-my-thumb, miniature, bijou, *petite*, pygmy, undersized, half-pint, dwarf,

Squab, dumpy (202), tubby, roly-poly, pursy, blowsy.

Huge, immense, enormous, mighty, unbounded, vast, vasty, amplitudinous, stupendous, inordinate, herculean, thumping, whacking, whopping, monster; gigantic, giant-like, colossal, titanic, mountainous, elephantine, mammoth, cyclopean, Antaean, Gargantuan, Falstaffian, Brobdingnagian; infinite, unbounded.

(Phrases) Large as life; plump as a partridge; fat as a pig; fat as butter; fat as bacon.

---

194 Expansion *(Substantives)*, enlargement, extension, augmentation, increase of size, amplification, ampliation, aggrandisement, spread, increment, growth, development, pullulation, swell, dilatation, rarefaction, turgescence, turgidity, thickening, tumefaction, intumescence, swelling, tumour, diastole, distension, puffing, inflation.

Overgrowth, hypertrophy, overdistension, tympany.

Bulb, knot, knob (249).

Superiority of size.

(Verbs) To become larger, to expand, widen, enlarge, extend, grow, increase, swell (202), gather, fill out, deploy, dilate, stretch, largen, spread, mantle, bud, burgeon, shoot, spring up, sprout, germinate, vegetate, pullulate, open, burst forth, put on flesh, outgrow.

To render larger, to expand, aggrandize, etc., distend, develop, open out, broaden, thicken, largen, amplify, tumefy, magnify, rarefy, inflate, puff, blow up, stuff, cram, pad, fill out.

To be larger than, to surpass, exceed, be beyond, cap, overtop (206, 33).

(Adjectives) Expanded, enlarged, increased, etc., swelled out, swollen, distended, bulbous; exaggerated,

stunted, dwarfed, dwarfish, pollard, Lilliputian; pocket, thumb-nail, portative, portable, duodecimo.

Microscopic, infra-microscopic, evanescent, impalpable, imperceptible, invisible, inappreciable, infinitesimal, homoeopathic, atomic, corpuscular, molecular, rudimentary, rudimental.

Lean, thin, gaunt, meagre, emaciated, lank, macilent, ghostly, starved, starveling, fallen away, scrubby, reduced, shrunk, shrunken, attenuated, extenuated, shrivelled, tabid, flaccid, starved, skinny, wizen, wizened, scraggy, lanky, raw-boned, scrawny, spindle-shanked, lantern-jawed (203).

(Phrases) In a small compass; in a nutshell; on a small scale.

Worn to a shadow; skin and bone.

195 Contraction *(Substantives)*, reduction, diminution, decrease of size, defalcation, lessening, decrement, shrinking, shrivelling, systole, collapse, emaciation, attenuation, tabefaction, tabes, consumption, marasmus, atrophy; hour-glass, neck (203).

Condensation, compression, squeezing.

Inferiority of size.

Corrugation, contractility, astringency.

(Verbs) To become smaller, to lessen, diminish, decrease, dwindle, shrink, contract, shrivel, collapse, wither, wilt, lose flesh, wizen, fall away, decay, purse up, waste, wane, ebb, to grow less.

To render smaller, to contract, lessen, etc., draw in, to condense, reduce, · clip, compress, constrict, cramp, squeeze, attenuate, chip, dwarf, bedwarf, stunt, cut short (201), corrugate, crumple, crush, purse up, pinch (203), deflate.

To be smaller than, to fall short of, not to come up to.

(Phrases) To grow 'small by degrees, and beautifully less' (659); to be on the wane; to hide its diminished head.

(Adjectives) Contracting, etc., astringent, styptic, tabid, contracted, lessened, etc., shrivelled, wasted,

bloated, tumid, turgid, puffy, full-blown, full-grown, full-formed, over-grown, hypertrophied, pot-bellied, swag-bellied, dropsical, oedematous.

(Phrase) 'A-swellin' wisibly.'

196 Distance, *(Substantives),* remoteness, farness, longinquity, elongation, offing, removedness, parallax, reach, span.

Antipodes, outpost, outskirts, aphelion, apogee, horizon.

Separation (44), transference (270). Diffusion, dispersion (73).

(Phrases) Ultima Thule; ne plus ultra; the uttermost parts of the earth; the back of beyond.

(Verbs) To be distant, etc.; to extend to, stretch to, reach to, spread to, go to, get to, stretch away to; outgo, outstep (303); to go to great lengths.

To remain at a distance, keep away, stand off, keep off, keep clear, stand aloof, hold off.

(Adjectives) Distant, far, far off, remote, removed, distal, wide of, clear of, yon, yonder, at arm's length, apart, aloof, asunder, ulterior, transalpine, transatlantic, ultramundane, hyperborean, antipodean, hull down.

Inaccessible, un-get-at-able, out of the way, unapproachable, unreachable; incontiguous.

(Adverbs) Far, away, far away, afar, off, a long way off, afar off, wide away, aloof, wide of, clear of, out of the way, a great way off, out of reach, abroad.

Apart, asunder, few and far between.

Yonder, farther, beyond, *longo intervallo,* wide apart, poles apart.

(Phrases) Far and near; far and wide; over the hills and far away; a far cry to; from end to end; from pole to pole; from Indus to the Pole; from China to Peru; from Dan to Beersheba; to the ends of the earth; out of the sphere of; wide of the mark.

wizened, stunted, waning, ebbing, etc., neap, condensed.

Unexpanded, contractile, compressible.

(Phrase) Multum in parvo.

197 Nearness *(Substantives),* nighness, proximity, propinquity, vicinity, vicinage, neighbourhood, adjacency, closeness; perihelion, perigee.

A short distance, a step, an earshot, close quarters, a stone's throw, a hair's breadth, a span, bowshot, gunshot, pistol-shot.

Purlieus, neighbourhood, environs (227), vicinity, *alentours,* suburbs, whereabouts, *banlieue,* borderland.

A bystander, neighbour.

Approach, approximation, appropinquation, appulse (286), junction (43), concentration, convergence (290).

Meeting, *rencontre* (292).

(Verbs) To be near, etc., to adjoin, hang about, trench on, border upon, stand by, approximate, tread on the heels of, cling to, clasp, hug, crowd, get near, etc., to approach (287), to meet (290).

To bring near, to crowd, pack, huddle together.

(Adjectives) Near, nigh, close, close at hand, neighbouring, proximate, approximate, adjacent, adjoining, intimate, bordering upon, close upon, hard upon, trenching on, treading on the heels of, verging on, at hand, handy, near the mark, home, at the point of, near run, in touch with, nearish.

(Adverbs) Near, nigh, hard by, fast by, close to, next door to, within reach, within call, within hearing, within an ace of, close upon, at hand, on the verge of, near the mark, in the environs, round the corner, at one's door, at one's feet, at one's elbow, at close quarters; within range, pistol-shot, a stone's throw, etc.; cheek by jowl, beside, alongside, at the heels of, at the threshold.

About, hereabouts, thereabouts, in the way, in presence of, in round numbers, approximately, roughly, as good as, *à peu près* (32).

198 Interval *(Substantives)*, inter-space (70), break, gap, opening (260), chasm, hiatus, caesura, interstice, lacuna, cleft, fosse, mesh, crevice, chink, creek, cranny, crack, slit, fissure, scissure, chap, rift, flaw, gash, cut, leak, dike (350), ha-ha, fracture, breach, rent, oscitation, gaping, yawning, pandiculation, insertion (300), pass, gorge, defile, ravine, canyon (or cañon), crevasse, chimney, couloir, *bergschrund*, gulf, gully, gulch, nullah, strait, sound, kyle, frith, furrow *(see 259)*.

Thing interposed, go-between, interjacence (228).

(Verbs) To separate (44), gape, yawn.

---

199 Contiguity *(Substantives)*, contact, proximity, apposition, juxtaposition, touching, tangency, tangent, osculation, meeting (292), syzygy, coincidence, register, co-existence, adhesion (46).

Confine, frontier, demarcation, border (233).

(Verbs) To be contiguous, etc., to touch, meet, adhere, (46), osculate, coincide, register, coexist, join, adjoin, abut on, graze, border, march with.

(Adjectives) Contiguous, touching, bordering on, meeting, in contact, conterminous, osculating, osculatory, tangential, proximate.

(Phrases) Hand to hand; end to end; tête-à-tête; next door to; with no interval; in juxtaposition, apposition, etc.; in register.

2°. Linear Dimensions

200 Length *(Substantives)*, longitude, span, stretch.

A line, bar, rule, stripe, spoke, radius.

Lengthening, elongation, prolongation, production, producing, protraction, extension, tension, stretching.

(Verbs) To be long, etc., to extend to, reach, stretch to.

To render long, lengthen, extend, elongate, prolong, produce, stretch, draw out, protract, spin out, drawl.

(Phrase) To drag its slow length along.

(Adjectives) Long, longsome, lengthy, tedious, tiresome, wiredrawn, outstretched, lengthened, produced, etc., sesquipedalian, interminable, endless, unending, never-ending, there being no end of.

Linear, lineal, longitudinal, oblong.

(Phrases) As long as my arm; as long as to-day and to-morrow.

(Adverbs) Lengthwise, longitudinally, in a line, along, from end to end, endways, from stem to stern, fore and aft, from head to foot, from top to toe, cap-à-pie.

---

201 Shortness *(Substantives)*, brevity, briefness, a span, etc., *see* Smallness (193).

Shortening, abbreviation, abbreviature, abridgment, curtailment, reduction, contraction, compression (195), retrenchment, elision, ellipsis, compendium (596), conciseness (in style) (572).

(Verbs) To be short, brief, etc.

To render short, to shorten, curtail, abridge, abbreviate, epitomize, reduce, contract, compress, scrimp, skimp, boil down.

To retrench, cut short, cut down, pare down, whittle down, clip, dock, lop, poll, prune, pollard, crop, bob, shingle, bingle, snub, truncate, cut, hack, hew, foreshorten.

(Adjectives) Short, brief, curt, laconic, compendious, compact, stubby, squab, squabby, squat, chunky, stubby, stocky, dumpy, podgy, fubsy, skimpy, stumpy, pug, snub.

Oblate, elliptical.

Concise (572), summary.

---

202 Breadth *(Substantives)*, width, latitude, amplitude, diameter, bore, calibre, superficial, extent, expanse.

Thickness, crassitude (192), thickening, expansion, dilatation, etc. (194).

(Verbs) To be broad, thick, etc.

To broaden, to swell, dilate, expand, outspread, etc. (194); to thicken, incrassate.

(Adjectives) Broad, wide, ample, extended, fan-like, outstretched, etc.

Thick, corpulent, fat (192), squab, squabbly, squat, chunky, stubby, stocky, dumpy, podgy, fulsy, thickset.

(Phrases) Wide as a church door; thick as a rope.

———

203 Narrowness *(Substantives)*, slenderness, closeness, scantiness, exility, lankness, lankiness, fibrousness.

A line (205), a hair's breadth, a finger's breadth, strip, streak, vein.

Thinness, tenuity, leanness, meagreness.

A shaving, a slip (205), a mere skeleton, a shadow, an anatomy.

A middle constriction, stricture, neck, waist, isthmus, wasp, hourglass, bottle-neck, ridge, ravine, defile, gorge, pass (198).

Narrowing, coarctation, tapering, compression, squeezing, etc. (195).

(Phrases) A bag of bones; a living skeleton.

(Verbs) To be narrow, etc., to taper, contract, shrink.

To render narrow, etc., to narrow, contract, coarctate, attenuate, constrict, constringe, cramp, pinch, squeeze, compress, tweak, corrugate, warp.

To shave, pare, shear, etc.

(Adjectives) Narrow, strait, slender, thin, fine, tenuous, filiform, filamentary, filamentous, fibrous, funicular, capillary, stringy, wiredrawn, finespun, anguine, taper, dapper, slim, slight, gracile, scanty, scant, spare, delicate.

Meagre, lean, emaciated, lank, lanky, weedy, rangy, gangling, starveling, attenuated, pinched, skinny, scraggy, gaunt, cadaverous, skin and bone, raw-boned, scrawny, spindle-shanked (193), hatchet-faced, wasp-waisted, herring-gutted, spidery, spindly, reedy.

(Phrases) Thin as a lath; thin as a whipping-post; lean as a rake; thin as a thread-paper; thin as a wafer; thin as a shadow.

204 Layer *(Substantives)*, stratum, bed, zone, substratum, slab, escarpment, floor, flag, stage, course, storey, tier.

Plate, lamina, lamella, sheet, flake, scale, coat, pellicle, membrane, film, slice, shive, cut, shaving, rasher, board, plank, platter, trencher, spatula, leaf.

Stratification, scaliness, a nest of boxes, coats of an onion.

(Verbs) To slice, shave, etc.

(Adjectives) Lamellar, laminated, lamelliform, laminiferous, scaly, squamous, filmy, membranous, flaky, foliated, foliaceous, stratified, stratiform, tabular, nested.

205 Filament *(Substantives)*, line, fibre, fibril, tendril, hair, gossamer, wire, thread, cord, funicle, rope, yarn, string, twine (45), cilium, gimp.

Strip (51), shred, slip, spill, list, string, band, fillet, fascia, ribbon (or riband); roll, lath, slat, splinter, sliver, shiver, shaving, arborescence (256); strand.

A hair-stroke.

(Adjectives) Filamentary, fibrous, hairy, capillary, thread-like, wiry, funicular, stringy.

———

206 Height *(Substantives)*, altitude, elevation, eminence, pitch, loftiness, sublimity.

Stature, tallness, procerity, culmination (210).

A giant, grenadier, guardsman, colossus, giraffe.

Alp, mountain, mount, hill, butte, ben, brae, hillock, kopje, monticule, fell, moorland, hummock, knap, knoll, cape, headland, foreland, promontory, ridge, *arête*, peak, pike, uplands, highlands, rising ground, downs, dune, mound, mole, steep, bluff, cliff, crag, vantage-ground, tor, eagle's nest, aerie.

Orography, Orology.

Tower, pillar, column, obelisk, monument, steeple, spire, *flèche*, campanile, belfry, minaret, turret, cupola, pilaster, skyscraper.

Pole, pikestaff, maypole, flagstaff, topmast, topgallant mast, crow's nest.

Ceiling, roof, awning, canopy (*see* 210), attic, loft, garret, housetop.

Growth, upgrowth (194).

(Verbs) To be high, etc., to tower, soar, ride, beetle, hover, cap, overtop, culminate, overhang, hang over, impend, overlie, bestride, mount, surmount, to cover (222), perch.

To render high, to heighten, exalt (307).

To become high, grow, upgrow, soar, tower, rise (305).

(Adjectives) High, elevated, eminent, exalted, lofty, supernal, tall, towering, beetling, soaring, colossal, gigantic (192), Patagonian, culminating, raised, elevated, etc., perched up, hanging (gardens), crowning, coronary.

Upland, moorland, hilly, mountainous, cloud-touching, heaven-kissing, cloud-topt, cloud-capt, Alpine, subalpine, aerial; orographical.

Upper, uppermost (210), topgallant.

Overhanging, impending, incumbent, overlying, superincumbent, supernatant, superimposed, hovering.

(Phrases) Tall as a maypole; tall as a steeple; tall as a poplar.

(Adverbs) On high, high up, aloft, above, upstairs, overhead, in the clouds, on tiptoe, on stilts, on the shoulders of, over head and ears.

Over, upwards, from top to bottom, from top to toe, from head to foot, cap-à-pie.

(Interjection) Excelsior!

207 Lowness *(Substantives)*, lowlands, depression, a molehill, recumbency, prostration.

Dwarf, pygmy bantam, Lilliputian.

Lowlands; molehill.

A ground-floor, basement, cellar, *rez de chaussée* (191), hold.

(Verbs) To be low, etc., lie low, grovel, wallow, crouch, slouch, lie flat.

To lower, depress (306), take down a peg, prostrate, subvert.

(Adjectives) Low, low-lying, neap, nether, prostrate, flat, level with the ground, grovelling, crouched, crouching, subjacent, underground, underlying, squat.

(Adverbs) Under, beneath, underneath, below, down, adown, downstairs, below stairs, over head and ears, downwards, underfoot, at the foot of, underground, at a low ebb.

———

208 Depth *(Substantives)*, deepness, profundity, profoundness, depression, bathos, anti-climax, depth of water, draught.

A hollow, pit, shaft, well, crater, gulf, abyss, abysm, bottomless pit, hell.

209 Shallowness *(Substantives)*, shoaliness, shoals.

(Adjectives) Shallow, skin-deep, superficial, shoaly.

———

Soundings, submersion, plunge, dive (310).

Plummit, lead, sounding-rod, probe; bathymetry.

Bathysphere, diving-bell, caisson, submarine; diver, frogman.

(Verbs) To be deep, etc.

To render deep, etc., to deepen, sink, submerge, plunge, dip, dive (310).

To dig, scoop out, hollow, sink, delve (252).

(Adjectives) Deep, deep-seated, profound, sunk, buried, submerged, etc., subaqueous, submarine, subterranean, underground, subterrene, abysmal; bathymetrical, bathymetric.

Bottomless, soundless, fathomless, unfathomed, unsounded, unplumbed, unfathomable.

(Phrases) Deep as a well; ankle-deep; knee-deep; breast-deep; chin-deep.

(Adverbs) Beyond one's depth, out of one's depth, underground.

(Phrases) Over head and ears; to Davy Jones's locker; in the bowels of the earth.

---

210 Summit *(Substantives)*, top, vertex, apex, zenith, pinnacle, acme, climax, culminating point, apogee, pitch, meridian, sky, pole, watershed.

Tip, tiptop, crest, crow's nest, mast-head, truck, peak, turning-point, pole.

Crown, brow, nib, head, nob, noddle, pate.

Capital, cornice, sconce, architrave, pediment, entablature, frieze.

Roof, ceiling, thatch, tiling, slating, awning, canopy (222).

(Adjectives) Top, topmost, uppermost, tiptop, culminating, meridian, capital, head, polar, supreme, crowning, coronary.

(Phrase) At the top of the tree.

211 Base *(Substantives)*, basement, plinth, foundation, substratum, ground, earth, pavement, floor, paving, flag, ground floor, deck, substructure, infrastructure, footing, groundwork.

The bottom, rock-bottom, nadir, foot, sole, toe, root, keel.

Dado, wainscot, skirting-board.

(Adjectives) Bottom, undermost, nethermost, fundamental, basic.

---

212 Verticality *(Substantives)*, erectness, uprightness, perpendicularity, aplomb, right angle, normal, plummet, plumb-line, azimuth, circle.

Wall, precipice, cliff.

Erection, raising, rearing.

(Verbs) To be vertical, etc., to stand up, to stand on end, to stand erect, to stand upright, to stick up.

To render vertical, to set up, stick up, erect, rear, raise up, cock up, prick up, raise on its legs.

(Adjectives) Vertical, upright, erect, perpendicular, sheer, normal, straight, standing up, etc., up on end, bolt upright, rampant.

213 Horizontality *(Substantives)*, a level, plane, dead level, flatness (251).

Recumbency, lying, lying down, reclination, decumbence, decumbency, supination, resupination, prostration; spirit-level.

A plain, floor, level, flat, platform, bowling-green, billiard-table, plateau, terrace, estrade, esplanade, parterre, table-land (204, 215).

(Verbs) To be horizontal, recumbent, etc., to lie, recline, lie down, couch, sit down, squat, lie flat, lie prostrate, sprawl, loll.

To render horizontal, etc., to lay, lay down, lay out, level, flatten, prostrate, knock down, fell, floor.

(Adverbs) Up, vertically, etc., on end, up on end, endways, endwise.

(Phrase) Straight up and down.

(Adjectives) Horizontal, level, plane, flat, even, discoid.

Recumbent, decumbent, lying, prone, supine, couchant, couching, jacent, prostrate, squat, squatting, sitting, reclining.

(Adverbs) Horizontally, etc., on one's back, on all fours, on one's hunkers.

(Phrases) Like a millpond.

---

214 Pendency *(Substantives)*, dependency, suspension, hanging.

A pendant, pedicel, peduncle, tail, train, flap, skirt, plait, pigtail, queue, tassel, earring, pendulum.

A peg, knob, button, stud, hook, nail, ring, fastener, zipper, clip, staple, knot (45), tenterhook.

(Verbs) To be pendant, etc., to hang, swing, dangle, swag, daggle, flap, trail.

To suspend, append, hang, sling, hook up, hitch, fasten to.

(Adjectives) Pendent, pendulous, pensile, hanging, dependent, swinging, etc., suspended, etc., loose, flowing, caudal.

Having a peduncle, etc., pedunculate, tailed, caudate.

(Adverbs) Dingle-dangle.

(Phrase) In the air.

---

215 Support *(Substantives)*, ground, foundation, base, basis, *terra firma*, fulcrum, foothold, toehold, *point d'appui, pou sto, locus standi*, landing, landing-place, resting-place, ground-work, substratum, floor, bed, stall, berth, lap, mount.

A supporter, prop, stand, strut, stray, shore, boom, yard, outrigger, truss, sleeper, staff, stick, walking-stick, crutch, stirrups, stilts, alpenstock, baton, anvil.

Post, pillar, shaft, column, buttress, pedicle, pedestal, plinth (211), baluster, banister.

A frame, framework, scaffold, scaffolding, skeleton, cadre, beam, rafter, lintel, joist, jamb, mullion, corner-stone, stanchion, summer, girder, cantilever, sponson, tie-beam, (45), columella, backbone, keystone, axle, axle-tree, axis, fuselage, chassis.

A board, form, ledge, platform, floor, stage, shelf, hob, bracket, arbor, rack, mantel, mantelpiece, mantel-shelf, counter, slab, console, dresser, flange, corbel, table, trestle, shoulder, perch, truss, horse, easel, desk.

A seat, throne, dais, divan, musnud, chair, arm-chair, easy-chair, *chaise longue*, hammock-chair, deck-chair, bench, sofa, davenport, lounge, settee, chesterfield, couch, *fauteuil*, stool, tripod, footstool, *tabouret*, trivet, woolsack, ottoman, settle, squab, bench, saddle, pillion, dicky, hassock, pouffe, cushion, howdah.

Bed, bedstead, chair-bedstead, bedding, pillow, bolster, mattress, shakedown, tester, pallet, hammock, bunk, stretcher, crib, cradle, cot, palliasse, donkey's breakfast, sleeping-bag, flea-bag.

Atlas, Persides, Atlantes, Caryatides, Hercules, Yggdrasil.

(Verbs) To be supported, etc., to lie, sit, recline, lean, loll, lounge, abut, bear, rest, stand, step, repose, etc., on, be based on, bestride, straddle, bestraddle.

To support, bear, carry, hold, sustain, shoulder, uphold, hold on, upbear, prop, underprop, shore up, underpin, bolster up, pillow.

To give, furnish, afford, supply, lend, etc., support or foundations; to bottom, found, ground, base, embed.

(Adjectives) Supported, etc., astride, astraddle; fundamental, basic.

216 Parallelism *(Substantives)*, coextension.

(Verbs) To be parallel, etc.

(Adjectives) Parallel, coextensive.

(Adverbs) Alongside, abreast, beside.

(Phrases) Side by side; cheek by jowl.

———

Steepness, precipitousness, cliff, precipice, talus, scarp, escarp, escarpment; measure of inclination, clinometer.

Diagonal, zigzag, distortion, hypotenuse, angle (244).

(Phrase) The leaning tower of Pisa.

(Verbs) To be or render oblique, etc., to slope, slant, tilt, lean, incline, shelve, stoop, descend, bend, heel, careen, sag, swag, slouch, cant, sidle, skew, scarp, escarp, bevel, distort.

(Adjectives) Oblique, inclined, leaning, recumbent, sloping, shelving, skew, askew, skew-whiff, slant, aslant, slanting, slantendicular, plagioclastic, indirect, distorted, wry, awry, ajee, drawn, crooked, canted, tilted, biased, saggy, bevel, slouched, slouching, etc., out of the perpendicular, backhanded.

Uphill, rising, ascending, acclivitous.

Downhill, falling, descending, declining, declivitous, anticlinal.

Steep, abrupt, precipitous, break-neck.

Diagonal, transverse, athwart, transversal, antiparallel.

(Adverbs) Obliquely, etc., on one side, askew, edgewise, askant, askance, sideways, aslope, slopewise, all on one side, crinkum-crankum, asquint, at an angle.

(Phrase) Facilis descensus Averni.

217 Obliquity *(Substantives)*, inclination, slope, leaning, slant, crookedness, bias, bend, bevel, tilt, list, dip, swag, cant, lurch, skew, skewness, bevelling, squint.

Acclivity, uphill, rise, ascent, gradient, rising ground, bank, ramp.

Declivity, downhill, fall, devexity.

A gentle or rapid slope, easy ascent or descent, chute, helter-skelter, switchback, *montagnes russes*.

---

218 Inversion *(Substantives)*, contraposition, overturn, somersault (or somerset), *culbute*, subversion, retroversion, reversion, reversal, introversion, eversion, transposition, pronation and supination.

Anastrophe, metathesis, hysteron, proteron, spoonerism, palindrome.

(Verbs) To be inverted, etc., to turn turtle, loop the loop, bunt.

To render inverted, etc., to invert, reverse, upset, overset, overturn, turn over, upturn, subvert, retrovert, transpose, turn topsy-turvy, tilt over, *culbuter*, keel over, topple over, capsize.

(Adjectives) Inverted, inverse, upside down, topsy-turvy, top-heavy.

(Adverbs) Inversely, topsy-turvy, etc., inside out.

(Phrases) To turn the tables; to put the cart before the horse; to the

219 Crossing *(Substantives)*, intersection, decussation, transversion, convolution.

Reticulation, network, inosculation, anastomosis, interweaving, twining, intertwining, matting, plaiting, interdigitation, mortise (or mortice).

Net, knot, plexus, web, mesh, twill, skein, hank, felt, lace, tulle, wattle, wicker, basket-work, basketry, mat, matting, plait, trellis, lattice, grille, *cancelli*, grid, griddle, grating, gridiron, tracery, fretwork, filigree, reticle, diaper.

Cross, chain, wreath, braid, cat's-cradle, dovetail, Greek cross, Latin cross, Maltese cross, cross of St. Anthony, St. Andrew's cross, cross of Lorraine, swastika, fylfot.

(Verbs) To cross, lace, intersect, decussate, interlace, intertwine, inter-

right about; bottom upwards; head over heels; the wrong side up; base over apex.

———

twill, tangle, entangle, ravel, net, knot (43), dishevel, raddle.

twist, pleach, plash, entwine, enlace, enmesh, weave, interweave, inweave, twine, twist, wreathe, interdigitate, interlock, anastomose, inosculate, dovetail, splice (43).

To mat, plait, plat, braid, felt,

(Adjectives) Crossing, intersecting, etc., crossed, intersected, matted, etc., crucial, cruciform.

Retiform, reticulate, areolar, areolate, cancellated, grated, barred, streaked, traceried.

(Adverbs) Across, thwart, athwart, transversely, crosswise.

3°. Centrical Dimensions

1. GENERAL

220 Exteriority *(Substantives)*, externality, outness, outside, exterior, surface, superficies, superstratum, eccentricity, extremity, frontage.

Disk, face, facet, front (234), skin (222).

(Verbs) To be exterior, etc.

To place exteriorly, or outwardly, to turn out.

(Adjectives) Exterior, external, outer, outward, outlying, outdoor, outside, extramural, superficial, skin-deep, frontal, discoid, eccentric, extrinsic.

(Adverbs) Externally, etc., out, without, outwards, outdoors, abroad.

(Phrases) Out of doors; *extra muros; ab extra;* in the open air; *sub Jove; à la belle étoile;* al fresco.

221 Interiority *(Substantives)*, inside, interior, hinterland, back-blocks, interspace, substratum, subsoil.

Vitals, viscera, pith, marrow, heart, bosom, breast, entrails, bowels, belly, intestines, guts, innards, womb, lap, backbone, *penetralia*, inmost recesses, cave, cavern (191).

(Verbs) To be interior, internal, within, etc.

To place or keep within, to enclose, circumscribe (see 231, 232).

(Adjectives) Interior, internal, inner, inside, intramural, inward, inlying, inmost, innermost, deep-seated, intestine, intestinal, splanchnic, intercostal, inland, interstitial, subcutaneous, intrinsic.

Home, domestic, indoor.

(Adverbs) Internally, inwards, inwardly, within, inly, therein, *ab intra,* withinside, indoors, within doors, ben, at home, *chez soi,* up country.

222 Covering *(Substantives)*, cover, roof, ceiling, slates, tiles, thatch, cowling, canopy, baldachin, awning, tarpaulin, tilt, tent (189), lid, hatch, operculum (263), shed.

Integument, skin, tegument, pellicle, fleece, cuticle, scarf-skin, epidermis, hide, pelt, peel, crust, bark, rind, cortex, husk, scale, shell, carapace, capsule, coat, tunic, tunicle, sheath, case, casing, calyx, theca,

223 Centrality *(Substantives)*, centre (68), middle, focus, epicentre, hub, core, kernel, marrow, pith, nucleus, nucleolus, heart, pole, axis, bull's-eye, nave, navel, umbilicus, omphalos; concentration, centralization.

(Verbs) To be central, etc.

To render central, centralize, concentrate.

To bring to a focus.

(Adjectives) Central, centrical,

sheathing, scabbard, wrapping, wrapper, envelope, tarpaulin, cloth, table-cloth, blanket, rug, quilt, eider-down, coverlet, (or coverlid), counter-pane, carpet, drugget, oilcloth, wax-cloth, linoleum.

Superposition, coating, facing, veneer, paint, enamel, varnish, anoint-ing, inunction, incrustation, plaster, stucco, wash, parget, patina.

(*Verbs*) To cover, superpose, super-impose, overspread, over-canopy, wrap, lap, overlap, face, case, encase, veneer, pave, upholster.

To coat, paint, enamel, varnish, pave, plaster, beplaster, daub, be-daub, encrust, stucco, dab, smear, besmear, anoint, spray, do over, gild, japan, lacquer (or lacker), plate, electroplate, parget.

(*Phrase*) To lay it on thick.

(*Adjectives*) Covering, etc., cutaneous, dermal, cortical, cuticular, tegu-mentary, skinny, scaly, squamous, imbricated, epidermal, loricated, armour-plated, iron-clad.

middle, middlemost, midmost, me-dian, azygous, axial, focal, umbilical, concentric.

(*Adverbs*) Midway, centrally, etc.

224 Lining (*Substantives*), coating, facing, internal, incrustation, puddle, stalactite, stalagmite, wainscot, dado, wall.

Filling, stuffing, wadding, padding.

(*Phrases*) To line, encrust, stuff, pad, wad, face, puddle, bush.

(*Adjectives*) Lined, encrusted, etc.

---

225 Investment (*Substantives*), dress, clothing, raiment, drapery, costume, attire, toilet, trim, rig, rigout, fig, habiliment, vesture, apparel, underwear, full dress, evening dress, soup-and-fish, glad rags, dinner-jacket, tuxedo, fancy dress, accoutrement, outfit, wardrobe, trousseau, uniform, regimentals, battle-dress, kit, equip-ment, livery, gear, harness, turn-out, caparison, suit, dress suit, lounge suit, bathing suit, swim-suit, tweeds, flannels, rigging, trappings, slops, traps, duds, togs, clobber, frippery, bloomers, haberdashery, housing.

Dishabille, morning dress, dressing-gown, undress, mufti, civvies, rags, *négligé*, tea-gown.

Clothes, garment, garb, garniture, vestment, pontificals, robe, tunic, caftan, paletot, habit, gown, coat, dress-coat, claw-hammer, frock, stole, blouse, shirt-waist, toga, haik, smock-frock, kimono, bikini.

Cloak, opera-cloak, cape, mantle, mantlet, dolman, shawl, wrap, wrapper, veil, fichu, yashmak, tippet, kirtle, plaid, mantilla, tabard, burn-ous, overcoat, great-coat, British

226 Divestment (*Substantives*), nudity, bareness, nakedness, baldness, undress, dishabille, threadbareness.

Denuding, denudation, stripping, uncovering, decortication, peeling, flaying, excoriation, desquamation, moulting, exfoliation.

(*Verbs*) To divest, uncover, denude, bare, strip, unclothe, undress, unrobe, disrobe, disapparel, debag, disarray, take off, doff, cast off, peel, pare, decor-ticate, husk, uncoif, unbonnet, excoriate, skin, flay, expose, exfoliate, lay open, dismantle, unroof, uncase, unsheathe, moult, mew.

(*Adjectives*) Bare, naked, nude, stripped, denuded, undressed, un-clothed, unclad, undraped, uncovered, unshod, barefoot, bareheaded, un-bonneted, exposed, in dishabille, in buff, bald, threadbare, ragged, callow, roofless.

(*Phrases*) In a state of nature; stark-naked; *in puris naturalibus*; stripped to the buff; in one's birthday suit; bald as a coot; as bare as the back of one's hand; out at elbows.

---

warm, duffle coat, surtout, spencer, rain-coat, ulster, mackintosh, waterproof, oilskin, slicker, burberry, poncho, surplice, alb, cassock, pallium, etc., mask, domino, cardinal, pelerine.

Jacket, vest, under-vest, semmit, singlet, jerkin, lumberjacket, waistcoat, cardigan, sweater, jersey, pullover, slipover, jumper, windbreaker, windcheater, doublet, gaberdine, camisole, combinations, stays, corset, bodice, under-bodice, brassière, bra, corsage, cestus, petticoat, kilt, filibeg (or philibeg), stomacher, skirt, kirtle, crinoline, farthingale, underskirt, slip, apron, pinafore.

Trousers, trews, breeches, galligaskins, knickerbockers, plus-fours, knickers, drawers, scanties, pantaloons, pants, overalls, dungarees, boiler suit, rompers, unmentionables, inexpressibles, smalls, tights, bags, breeks, slacks, shorts, jeans, briefs.

Cap, hat, top-hat, silk hat, tile, bowler, panama, slouch-hat, trilby, Stetson, titfer, deerstalker, billycock, wide-awake, sou'wester, beaver, castor, bonnet, forage-cap, tam-o'-shanter, tammy, balmoral, glengarry, toque, sun-bonnet, hood, head-gear, head-dress, kerchief, scarf, muffler, comforter, boa, snood, coiffure, coif, skull-cap, calotte, biretta, cowl, chaplet, capote, calash, pelt, wig, peruke, periwig, toupee, transformation, chignon, turban, puggaree, fez, helmet, topi, shako, busby, képi, casque, beret.

Shirt, smock, shift, chemise, chemisette, nightshirt, nightgown, nightdress, pyjamas, bed-jacket, bed-gown, collar, cravat, neck-cloth, neck-tie, stock, handkerchief.

Shoe, pump, high-low, Oxford shoe, sabot, brogue, sand-shoe, plimsoll, rubbers, sneakers, boot, jack-boot, top-boot, Wellington, gumboot, slipper, mule, galosh, overshoe, legging, puttee, buskin, greaves, mocassin, gaiter, spatterdash, spat, stocking, sock, nylons, hose, sandal, clog, babouche.

Glove, gauntlet, mitten, sleeve, cuff, muff.

Outfitter, tailor, clothier, milliner, sempstress, costumier, hatter, hosier, shoemaker, cobbler.

(Verbs) To invest, cover, envelop, lap, involve, drape, enwrap, wrap up, lap up, sheathe, vest, clothe, array, enrobe, dress, dight, attire, apparel, accoutre, trick out, rig, fit out, fig out, caparison, adonize, dandify, titivate, don, put on, wear, have on, huddle on, slip on, roll up in, muffle, perk up, mantle, swathe, swaddle, equip, harness.

(Adjectives) Invested, clothed, arrayed, dight, etc., clad, shod, etc.; sartorial.

---

227 Circumjacence *(Substantives)*, circumambiency, encompassment, surroundings, environment, atmosphere, medium, setting, scene, outpost, skirt, outskirts, boulevards, suburbs, suburbia, rurbania, purlieus, precincts, faubourgs, environs, entourage, *banlieue*, green belt.

(Verbs) To lie around, surround, beset, set about, compass, encompass, environ, enclose, encircle, embrace, lap, gird, begird, engirdle, orb, enlace, skirt, twine round, hem in (231).

228 Interjacence *(Substantives)*, interlocation, intervention, insertion, interposition, interspersion, interpenetration, interdigitation, interpolation, interlineation, intercurrence, intrusion, obtrusion, insinuation, intercalation, insertion, intertwinement, interference, permeation, infiltration.

An intermedium, intermediary, a go-between, bodkin, intruder, interloper; interlude, episode; parenthesis, gag, flyleaf, *entresol* (68).

(Adjectives) Circumjacent, ambient, circumambient, surrounding, etc., circumfluent, circumferential, suburban, extramural, embosomed.

(Adverbs) Around, about, without, on every side, on all sides, right and left, all around, round about.

229 Outline *(Substantives)*, circumference, perimeter, periphery, ambit, circuit, lines, tournure, contour, profile, silhouette, sky-line.

Zone, belt, girth, band, baldric, zodiac, cordon, girdle, cingulum, clasp (247).

230 Edge *(Substantives)*, verge, brink, brow, brim, margin, marge, border, skirt, rim, side, mouth, jaws, lip, muzzle, door, porch, portal (260), kerb; shore, coast.

Frame, flounce, frill, ruffle, jabot, list, fringe, valance, edging, trimming, hem, selvedge, welt, furbelow.

(Verbs) to border, edge, skirt, coast, verge on.

(Adjectives) Border, marginal, coastal, skirting.

A partition, septum, panel, diaphragm, midriff, party-wall.

A half-way house, no-man's land.

(Verbs) To lie, come, or get between, intervene, intrude, butt in, slide in, permeate, put between, put in, interpose, interject, chip in, throw in, wedge in, thrust in, foist in, insert, intercalate, interpolate, parenthesize, interline, interleave, interlard, interdigitate, dovetail, sandwich, worm in, insinuate, obtrude (300), intersperse, infiltrate; to gag.

(Phrases) To put one's oar in; to stick one's nose into; to have a finger in the pie.

(Adjectives) Interjacent, intervening, etc., intermediary, intermediate, intercalary, interstitial, parenthetical, mediterranean.

(Adverbs) Between, betwixt, 'twixt, among, amongst, amid, amidst, midst, betwixt and between, sandwich-wise, parenthetically, between the lines, in the thick of.

———

231 Circumscription *(Substantives)*, limitation, enclosure, confinement, shutting up, circumvallation, entombment.

Imprisonment, incarceration (751).

(Verbs) To circumscribe, limit, delimit, localize, bound, confine, enclose, surround (227), compass about, impound, restrict, restrain (751), shut in, shut up, lock up, bottle up, dam, hem in, hedge in, wall in, rail in, fence, picket, pen, enfold, coop, corral, encage, cage, mew, entomb, bury, immure, encase, pack up, seal up, wrap up (225), etc.

(Adjectives) Circumscribed, etc., imprisoned, pent up (754), landlocked.

(Phrase) Not room to swing a cat.

232 Enclosure *(Substantives)*, envelope, case, box (191), pen, penfold, fold, sheep-fold, pound, paddock, enclave, *enceinte*, corral, ring fence, wall, hedge, hedgerow, espalier, exclosure, play-pen.

Barrier, bar, gate, gateway, door, barricade, cordon.

Dike (or dyke), ditch, fosse, moat.

Fence, pale, paling, balustrade, rail, railing, hurdle, palisade, battlement, rampart, embankment, breakwater, mole, groyne (717), circumvallation, contravallation.

233 Limit *(Substantives)*, boundary, bounds, confine, term, bourne, line of demarcation, termination, stint, frontier, border, precinct, marches, line of circumvallation, pillars of Hercules, Rubicon, turning-point, last word, *ne plus ultra*.

(Adjectives) Definite, conterminal, terminal, frontier.

(Phrases) To cross the Rubicon; thus far and no farther.

2. SPECIAL

234 Front (*Substantives*), face, anteriority, fore-part, front rank, foreground, van, vanguard, advanced guard, outpost, proscenium, façade, frontage, foreword, preface, frontispiece (64).

Forehead, visage, physiognomy, phiz, countenance, mug, dial, puss, pan, beak, rostrum, bow, stem, prow.

Pioneer, avant-courier (64).

(In a medal) obverse; (in a coin) head.

(*Verbs*) To be in front, etc., to front, face, envisage, confront, bend forward, etc.

(*Adjectives*) Fore, anterior, front, frontal, facial.

(*Adverbs*) Before, in front, ahead, right ahead, in the van, foremost, vis-à-vis, in the foreground, face to face, before one's eyes.

---

236 Laterality (*Substantives*), side, flank, quarter, hand, cheek, jowl, wing, profile, temple, loin, haunch, hip, broadside, lee-side, lee.

East, orient; West, occident.

(*Verbs*) To be on one side, etc., to flank, outflank, to sidle, skirt.

(*Adjectives*) Lateral, sidelong, collateral, sideling, bilateral, trilateral, quadrilateral, multilateral, many-sided, eastern, oriental, western, occidental, eastward, westward.

(*Adverbs*) Sideways, side by side (216), sidelong, abreast, abeam, alongside, aside, by the side of, to windward, to leeward.

(*Phrases*) Cheek by jowl; broadside on.

238 Dextrality (*Substantives*), right, right hand, dexter, offside, starboard, recto.

(*Adjectives*) Dextral, right-handed; ambidextrous, ambidexter.

235 Rear (*Substantives*), back, posteriority, the rear rank, rearguard, the background, heels, tail, scut, rump, croup, crupper, breech, backside, posterior, fanny, catastrophe, buttocks, haunches, hunkers, hurdies, hind quarters, *dorsum*, dorsal region, stern, poop, after-part, tailpiece, wake.

(In a medal) reverse; (in a coin) tail.

(*Verbs*) To be in the rear, behind, etc., to fall astern, to bend backwards, to back on.

(*Phrases*) Turn the back upon; bring up the rear.

(*Adjectives*) Back, rear, postern, hind, hinder, hindmost, sternmost, posterior, dorsal, after.

(*Adverbs*) Behind, in the rear, aft, abaft, astern, aback, rearward.

(*Phrases*) In the background; behind one's back; at the heels of; at the tail of; at the back of; back to back.

237 Antiposition (*Substantives*), opposite side, contraposition, reverse, inverse, antipodes, opposition, inversion (218).

Polarity, opposite poles, North and South.

(*Verbs*) To be opposite, etc., subtend.

(*Adjectives*) Opposite, reverse, inverse, antipodal, subcontrary.

Fronting, facing, diametrically opposite, vis-à-vis.

Northern, boreal, septentrional, arctic; southern, austral, antarctic.

(*Adverbs*) Over, over the way, over against, facing, against, fronting (234), face to face, vis-à-vis.

239 Sinistrality (*Substantives*), left, left hand, sinister, near side, port, larboard, verso.

(*Adjectives*) Sinistral, left-handed.

SECTION III—FORM

1°. *General Form*

240 Form *(Substantives)*, figure, shape, configuration, make, formation, frame, construction, conformation, cut, set, trim, build, make, stamp, cast, mould, fashion, structure.

Feature, lineament, phase (448), turn, attitude, posture, pose.

Morphology, isomorphism.

Formation, figuration, efformation, sculpture.

(Phrase) The cut of one's jib.

(Verbs) To form, shape, figure, fashion, carve, cut, chisel, chase, emboss, hew, rough-hew, cast, rough-cast, hammer out, block out, trim, work, lick into shape, knock together, mould, sculpture, sculp, grave, stamp.

241 Absence of form.

Amorphism *(Substantives)*, amorphousness, formlessness, shapelessness, disfigurement, defacement, mutilation (846).

Vandalism, vandal, Goth.

(Verbs) To destroy form, deform, deface, disfigure, disfeature (846), mutilate.

(Adjectives) Shapeless, amorphous, formless, unhewn, rough, rude, Gothic, unfashioned, unshapen, misshapen, inchoate.

(Adjectives) Formed, graven, etc., receiving form, plastic, fictile.
Giving form, formative, plastic, plasmatic, plasmic.

242 Regularity of form.

Symmetry *(Substantives)*, shapeliness, eurhythmy, uniformity, finish, beauty (845), proportion, balance.

(Adjectives) Symmetrical, regular, shapely, eurhythmic, well-set, uniform, finished, well-proportioned, balanced, chaste, classic.

(Phrase) Teres atque rotundus.

243 Irregularity of form.

Distortion *(Substantives)*, twist, kink, wryness, asymmetry, gibbosity, contortion, malformation, ugliness, etc. (846), teratology.

(Verbs) To distort, twist, wrest, writhe, wring, contort, kink, buckle.

(Adjectives) Irregular, unsymmetrical, asymmetrical, distorted, twisted, wry, awry, askew, crooked, on one side, misshapen, deformed, ill-proportioned, ill-made, round-shouldered, pigeon-chested, humpbacked, hunchbacked, gibbous, gibbose; knock-kneed, bandy-legged, bow-legged, club-footed, splay-footed.

(Phrases) All manner of ways; all over the place.

2°. *Special Form*

244 Angularity *(Substantives)*, angulation, angle, cusp, bend, elbow, knee, knuckle, groin, crinkle-crankle, kink, crotch, crutch, crane, fluke, scythe, sickle, zigzag, anfractuosity, refraction; fold (258), corner (182).

Fork, bifurcation, dichotomy.

Right angle (212), salient angle, re-entrant angle, acute angle, obtuse angle.

A polygon, square, rectangle, pentagon, hexagon, heptagon, octagon, nonagon, decagon, lozenge, diamond, rhomb, rhombus, rhomboid, parallelogram, gore, gusset, wedge.

Cube, parallelepiped, pyramid, prism, rhombohedron, tetrahedron, pentahedron, hexahedron, octahedron, dodecahedron, icosahedron.

T-square, set-square, protractor, goniometer, theodolite, sextant, quadrant, clinometer.

(Verbs) To bend, refract, diffract, fork, bifurcate, angulate, crinkle, crankle, splay.

(Adjectives) Angular, triangular, quadrangular, rectangular, bent, crooked, hooked, aduncous, aquiline, jagged, serrated, falciform, falcated, furcated, forked, bifurcate, zigzag; dovetailed, knock-kneed, crinkled, akimbo, geniculated, polygonal, trigonal, pentagonal, etc., fusiform, sagittate, arrow-headed, wedge-shaped, cuneate, cuneiform, splayed, angulate, cubical, pyramidal, rhombohedral, tetrahedral, etc.

245 Curvature *(Substantives)*, curvation, incurvity, incurvation, bend, flexure, flexion, hook, crook, camber, bending, deflexion, inflexion, arcuation, diffraction, turn, deviation, detour, sweep, sinuosity, curl, curling, winding, recurvature, recurvation, refraction, flexibility (324).

A curve, arc, circle, ellipse (247), parabola, hyperbola, catenary, festoon, arch, arcade, vault, bow, crescent, half-moon, lunette, horseshoe, loop, bight, crane-neck, conchoid, ogee.

(Verbs) To be curved, etc., to bend, curve, etc., decline, turn, trend, deviate, re-enter, sweep.

To render curved; to bend, curve, incurvate, camber, deflect, inflect, crook, hook, turn, round, arch, arcuate, bow, curl, recurve, loop, frizzle.

246 Straightness *(Substantives)*, rectilinearity, directness.

A straight line, a right line, a direct line; inflexibility (323).

(Verbs) To be straight, etc.

To render straight, to straighten, rectify, set or put straight, take the curl out of, unbend, unfold, uncurl, uncoil, unroll, unwind, unravel, untwist, unwreathe, unwrap.

(Adjectives) Straight, rectilinear (or rectilineal), direct, even, right, in a line; unbent; not inclining, not bending, not turning, not deviating to either side, undeviating, unturned, undistorted, unswerving.

(Phrases) Straight as an arrow; as the crow flies; in a bee line.

———

(Adjectives) Curved, vent, etc., curvilinear, curviform, recurved, recurvous, circular, oval (247), parabolic, hyperbolic, bowed, crooked, bandy, arched, vaulted, arcuated, camerated, hooked, falcated, falciform, crescent-shaped, semilunar, semicircular, conchoidal, lunular, lunulate, cordiform, heart-shaped, reniform, pear-shaped; bow-legged, bandy-legged, knock-kneed, devious.

247 Simple circularity.
Circularity *(Substantives)*, roundness, rotundity (249).

A circle, circlet, ring, areola, hoop, roundlet, *annulus*, annulet, bracelet, bangle, armlet, anklet, ringlet, eye, loop, wheel, cycle, orb, orbit, rundle, zone, belt, cordon, band, sash, girdle, cestus, cincture, baldric, bandolier, fillet, cummerbund, fascia, wreath, garland, crown, corona, coronal, coronet, chaplet, necklace, rivière; noose, lasso.

An ellipse, oval, ovule, ellipsoid,

248 Complex circularity.
Convolution *(Substantives)*, winding, wave, undulation, circuit, tortuosity, anfractuosity, sinuosity, involution, sinuation, circumvolution, meander, circumbendibus, twist, twirl, squiggle, curl, curlicue, curlie-wurlie, tirlie-whirlie, crimp, frizz, frizzle, permanent wave, perm, windings and turnings, *ambages*, inosculation, peristalsis.

A coil, reel, roll, spiral, helix, corkscrew, worm, volute, scroll, cartouche, rundle, scallop (or scollop), escallop.

cycloid, epicycloid, epicycle, semi-circle, quadrant, sextant, sector, segment.

(Verbs) To make round, round, circle, encircle, environ (227).

(Adjectives) Round, rounded, circular, annular, orbicular.

Oval, elliptical, elliptic, ovate, egg-shaped; cycloidal, etc., moniliform.

———

Serpent, eel, maze, labyrinth.

(Verbs) To be convoluted, etc.

To wind, twine, twist, coil, roll, turn and twist, weave, twirl, wave, undulate, meander, scallop, curl, crimp, frizz, frizzle, perm, inosculate, entwine (219), enlace, twist together, goffer.

(Adjectives) Convoluted, winding, twisting, contorted, waving, waved, wavy, curly, undulating, undulant, undulatory, undated, serpentine, anguilline, mazy, labyrinthine, Daedalian, tortuous, sinuous, flexuous, snaky, involved, sigmate, sigmoid, sigmoidal, vermiform, vermicular, peristaltic, meandrine; scalloped (or scolloped), wreathed, wreathy, crisped, crimped, frizzed, frizzy, frizzled, frizzly, ravelled, twisted, dishevelled (61).

Spiral, coiled, helical, turbinate.

(Adverb) In and out.

249 Rotundity *(Substantives)*, roundness, cylindricity; cylinder, barrel, drum, cylindroid, roll, roller, rouleau, column, rolling-pin, rundle.

Cone, conoid; pear-shape, bell-shape.

Sphericity, spheroidity, globosity; a sphere, globe, ball, spheroid, ellipsoid, drop, spherule, globule, vesicle, bulb, bullet, pellet, pill, clue, marble, pea, knob, pommel.

(Verbs) To form into a sphere, render spherical, to sphere, ensphere, to roll into a ball, round off, give rotundity, etc.

(Adjectives) Rotund, round, cylindric, cylindrical, cylindroid, columnar, lumbriciform; conic, conical, conoidal.

Spherical, spheral, spheroidal, globular, globated, globous, globose, ovoid, egg-shaped, gibbous, bulbiform, bulbous, bell-shaped, campaniliform, campaniform, campanulate, fungiform, bead-like, moniliform, pyriform, cigar-shaped.

(Phrases) Round as an apple, as a ball; *teres atque rotundus*.

3°. *Superficial Form*

250 Convexity *(Substantives)*, prominence, projection, swelling, gibbosity, bulge, protuberance, intumescence, tumour, cancer, tuberosity, tubercle, tooth, knob, excrescence, elbow, process, condyle, bulb, nob, nubble, node, nodule, nodosity, tongue, *dorsum*, hump, hunch, hunk, bunch, boss, embossment, bump, lump, clump, sugarloaf, point (253), bow, bagginess.

Pimple, wen, papula, pustule, carbuncle, corn, wart, polyp, boil, furuncle, fungus, fungosity, bleb, blister, blain, chilblain, bunion.

Papilla, nipple, teat, pap, breast,

251 Flatness *(Substantives)*, plane; horizontality (213), layer (204), smoothness (255); plate, platter, slab, table, tablet; level.

(Verbs) To render flat, flatten, smooth, level.

(Adjectives) Flat, plane, even, level, etc. (213), flush, scutiform, scutellate.

(Phrases) Flat as a pancake; flat as a flounder; flat as a board; flat as my hand; a dead flat; a dead level.

252 Concavity *(Substantives)*, depression, hollow, hollowness, indentation, intaglio, cavity, dent, dint, dimple, follicle, pit, sinus, alveolus, dug, udder, mamilla, proboscis, nose, neb, beak, snout, nozzle, belly, paunch, corporation, kyte, back, shoulder, elbow, lip, flange.

Peg, button, stud, ridge, rib, jetty, snag, eaves, mole, cupola, dome, balcony.

Cameo, high and low relief, bas-relief, *basso rilievo, alto rilievo*; repoussé work.

Mount, hill (206); cape, promontory, foreland, headland, ness, mull, salient, point of land, hummock, spur, hog's back, offset.

(Verbs) To be prominent, etc., to project, bulge, belly, jut out, bristle up, to hang over, overhang, beetle, bend over, protrude, stand out, stick out, poke out, stick up, start up, cock up, shoot up, swell.

To render prominent; to raise (307), to emboss, chase, stud, bestud, ridge.

lacuna, honeycomb, excavation, trough (259).

Cup, basin, crater, etc. (191); socket, thimble.

Valley, vale, dale, dell, dingle, coombe, strath, bottom, corrie, glade, glen, cave, cell, cavern, cove, grotto, grot, alcove, gully (198), cul-de-sac.

(Verbs) To be depressed, etc., to cave in, subside, retire.

To depress, hollow, scoop, gouge, dig, delve, excavate, dent, dint, stave in, mine, undermine, burrow, tunnel.

(Adjectives) Depressed, concave, hollow, stove in, retiring, retreating, cavernous, honeycombed, alveolar, cellular, funnel-shaped, infundibular, bell-shaped, campaniliform, porous (260).

———

(Adjectives) Convex, prominent, projecting, bulging, etc., bold, bossed, bossy, knobby, nubbly, lumpy, bumpy, nodose, embossed, chased, gibbous, salient, mamilliform, in relief, bowed, arched, bellied, baggy, cornute, odontoid, tuberous, tuberculous, ridged, ridgy.

---

253 Sharpness *(Substantives)*, keenness, pointedness, acuteness, acuity, acumination, spinosity, prickliness.

A point, spike, spine, spicule, needle, bodkin, (262), aiguille, pin, prickle, prick, prong, tine, caltrop, *chevaux de frise*, arrow, spear, bayonet, pike, sword, dagger (727), spur, rowel, barb, spit, cusp, horn, antler,

254 Bluntness *(Substantives)*, obtuseness, dullness.

(Verbs) To be blunt, etc., to render blunt, etc., to obtund, dull, take off the point or edge, turn.

(Adjectives) Blunt, obtuse, dull, bluff.

———

snag, tag, jag, thorn, brier, bramble, thistle, nib, tooth, tusk, denticle, spoke, cog, ratchet, comb, bristle, beard, awn, *arête*, crest, cone, peak, spire, pyramid, steeple, porcupine, hedgehog.

Cutlery, blade, edge-tool, knife, jack-knife, penknife, clasp-knife, bowie, jocteleg, chisel, razor, scalpel, bistoury, lancet, axe, hatchet, pole-axe, pick-axe, pick, mattock, spade, adze, coulter, ploughshare, scythe, sickle, reaping-hook, bill, billhook, cleaver, scissors, shears, sécateurs.

Sharpener, knife-sharpener, strop, hone, grinder, grindstone, whetstone, steel, emery, carborundum.

(Verbs) To be sharp, etc., to taper to a point, to bristle with.

To render sharp, etc., to sharpen, point, aculeate, set, whet, strop, hone, grind, barb, bristle up.

(Adjectives) Sharp, keen, pointed, conical, acute, acicular, aculeated, arrowy, needle-shaped, spiked, spiky, spicular, spiculate, mucronate, mucronated, ensiform, peaked, acuminated, salient, cusped, cuspidate, cuspidated, cornute, prickly, spiny, spinous, thorny, jagged, bristling,

muricate, pectinated, studded, thistly, briery, snaggy, digitated, barbed, spurred, two-edged, tapering, fusiform, dentiform, denticular, denticulated, toothed, odontoid, cutting, trenchant, sharp-edged.

Starlike, stellated, stelliform.

(Phrases) Sharp as a needle, as a razor.

255 Smoothness *(Substantives)*, evenness, level (213), polish, gloss, glossiness, sleekness, slipperiness, lubricity, lubrication (332), down, velvet, velveteen velour, silk, satin, plush, glass, ice, enamel, macadam.

Burnisher, calender, mangle, iron, file, plane, sandpaper, emery-paper, roller.

(Verbs) To smooth, smoothen, plane, polish, burnish, calender, mangle, enamel, glaze, iron, file, roll, lubricate, macadamize.

(Adjectives) Smooth, even, level, plane, sleek, slick, polished, glazed, glossy, sleeky, silken, silky, satiny, velvety, glabrous, slippery, oily, soft, unwrinkled.

(Phrases) Smooth as glass, as velvet, as satin, as soil; slippery as an eel.

---

256 Roughness *(Substantives)*, unevenness, asperity, rugosity, ruggedness, scabrousness, salebrosity, cragginess, craggedness, corrugation, nodosity, crispness, plumosity, villosity; grain, texture, nap, pile.

Arborescence, branching, ramification.

Brush, bur, beard, shag, whisker, dundreary, mutton-chop, sideboards, side-burns, down, goatee, imperial, moustache, feather, plume, crest, tuft, *panache*, byssus, hair, chevelure, toupee, wool, fur, mane, cilia, fringe, *fimbriae*, tress, moss, plush, velvet, velveteen, velour, stubble.

(Verbs) To be rough, etc.

To render rough, to roughen, crisp, crumple, corrugate, rumple.

(Adjectives) Rough, uneven, scabrous, gnarled, rugged, rugose, rugous, salebrous, unpolished, matt, frosted, rough-hewn, craggy, cragged, prickly, scrubby.

Arborescent, dendriform, arboriform, branching, ramose, ramulose, dendroid.

Feathery, plumose, plumous, plumigerous, tufted, fimbriated, hairy, ciliated, hirsute, flocculent, bushy, hispid, tomentous, downy, woolly, velvety, villous (or villose), bearded, pilous, shaggy, shagged, stubbly, fringed, befringed, setaceous, filamentous.

(Phrases) rough as a nutmeg-grater; like quills upon the fretful porcupine; against the grain.

257 Notch *(Substantives)*, dent, dint, nick, cut, indent, indentation, dimple.

Embrasure, battlement, machicolation, machicoulis, saw, tooth, sprocket, crenelle, scallop (or scollop).

(Verbs) To notch, nick, cut, dent, indent, dint, jag, scotch, slash, scallop (or scollop), crenelate.

(Adjectives) Notched, etc., jagged, crenate, crenated, crenelated, dented, dentated, denticulated, toothed, palmated, indented, serrated.

258 Fold *(Substantives)*, plication, plait, ply, crease, pleat, tuck, hem, flexion, flexure, joint, elbow, doubling, duplicature, gather, wrinkle, crow's-foot, rimple, crinkle, crankle, crumple, rumple, rivel, ruck, ruffle, ruche, dog's-ear, corrugation, flounce, frounce, lapel, pucker, crimp.

(Verbs) To fold, double, plicate, plait, crease, wrinkle, crinkle, crankle, curl, cockle up, cocker, rimple, frizz, frizzle, rumple, flounce, frounce, rivel,

twill, corrugate, ruffle, crimp, crumple, pucker, to turn down, turn under, tuck, ruck.

(Adjectives) Folded, dog's eared (or dog-eared), etc.

259 Furrow *(Substantives)*, groove, rut, slit, scratch, streak, stria, crack, score, rib.

Channel, gutter, trench, ditch, dike, moat, fosse, trough, kennel, chamfer, ravine (198), fluting.

(Verbs) To furrow, etc., flute, plough.

(Adjectives) Furrowed, etc., ribbed, striated, striate, sulcated, fluted, canaliculate, bisulcate, trisulcate, etc., corduroy, corded, corrugated.

260 Opening *(Substantives)*, hole, foramen, perforation, eye, eyelet, keyhole, loophole, porthole, scuttle, mouse-hole, pigeon-hole, eye of a needle, pinhole, peep-hole, puncture.

Aperture, hiatus, yawning, oscitancy, dehiscence, patefaction, slot, chink, crevice (198).

Window, light, fanlight, skylight, casement, lattice, embrasure.

Orifice, inlet, intake, outlet, mouth, throat, muzzle, gullet, weasand, nozzle, portal, porch, gate, lych-gate, wicket, postern, gateway, door, embouchure, doorway, exit, vomitory, hatch, hatchway, gangway, arcade.

Channel (350), passage, pass, tube, pipe, vessel, tubule, canal, thoroughfare, gut, fistula, ajutage, tap, faucet, chimney, flue, vent, funnel, gully, tunnel, main, adit, pit, shaft, gallery, alley, aisle, glade, vista, bore, mine, calibre, pore, follicle, porosity, porousness, lacuna.

Sieve, cullender, colander, strainer, tamis, riddle, screen, honeycomb.

Apertion, perforation, piercing, boring, mining, terebration, drilling, etc., impalement, pertusion, puncture, acupuncture, penetration (302).

Opener, tin-opener, key, master-key.

(Verbs) to open, ope, gape, yawn.

To perforate, lay open, pierce, empierce, tap, bore, mine, drill, scoop out, canalize, tunnel, transpierce, transfix, enfilade, rake, impale, spike, spear, gore, stab, pink, stick, prick, lance, puncture, riddle, honeycomb, punch, jab; uncover, unrip, stave in.

(Phrase) To cut a passage through.

(Adjectives) Open, pierced, perforated, etc., perforate, wide open, ajar, unclosed, unstopped, patulous, gaping, yawning, patent.

Tubular, tubulous, tubulate, tubuliform, cannular, fistulous, fistular, fistulate, pervious, permeable, foraminous, porous, follicular, cribriform, honeycombed, infundibular, windowed, fenestrated.

(Phrase) Open sesame!

261 Closure *(Substantives)*, occlusion, blockade, shutting up, filling up, plugging, sealing, obstruction, impassableness, blocking up, obstipation, constipation, blind alley, blind corner, cul-de-sac, impasse, caecum.

Imperforation, imperviousness, impermeability, imporosity.

(Verbs) To close, occlude, steek, plug, block up, fill up, blockade, obstruct, bar, stop, bung up, seal, clinch, plumb, cork up, shut up, choke, throttle, ram down, dam up, cram, stuff up.

(Adjectives) Closed, shut, unopened, occluded, etc., impervious, imperforate, caecal, impassable, invious, pathless, untrodden, unpierced, unventilated, impermeable, imporous, operculated, tight, watertight, air-tight, hermetic.

(Phrase) Hermetically sealed.

262 Perforator *(Substantives),* borer, auger, gimlet, stylet, drill, wimble, awl, bradawl, brog, scoop, corkscrew, dibble, trepan, probe, bodkin, needle, stiletto, lancet, punch, spike, bit, brace and bit, gouge, fleam.

(Verbs) To spike, gouge, scoop, punch, lance.

263 Stopper *(Substantives),* stopple, plug, cork, bung, spigot, spike, spile, vent-peg, stopcock, tap, stopgap, rammer, ramrod, piston, wad, dossil, wadding, tompion, stuffing, tourniquet.

Cover, lid, operculum, covering, covercle, door, etc. (222), valve.

A janitor, door-keeper, commissionaire, chucker-out, ostiary, concierge, porter, warder, beadle, Cerberus.

SECTION IV—MOTION

1°. *Motion in General*

264 Motion *(Substantives),* movement, transit, transition, move, going, etc., passage, course, stir.

Step, gait, stride, tread, port, footfall, carriage, transference (270), locomotion, travel (266), voyage (267).

Mobility, restlessness, unrest, movability, movableness, inquietude, flux; kinematics.

(Verbs) To be moving, etc., to move, go, stir, hie, gang, budge, pass, flit, shift, glide, roll, roll on, flow (347, 348), sweep along, wander (279), change or shift one's place or quarters, dodge, keep going.

To put in motion, impel, etc. (276); to propel, project (284); to mobilize, motorize.

(Adjectives) Moving, in motion, on the move, going, transitional; kinematic.

Shifting, movable (270), mobile, restless, nomadic, wandering, vagrant, discursive, erratic (279), mercurial, unquiet.

(Adverbs) In transitu, under way, on the move.

265 Quiescence *(Substantives),* rest, stillness, stagnation, stagnancy, fixedness, immobility, catalepsy, paralysis.

Quiet, quietness, quietude, tranquillity, calm, calmness, sedentariness, peace; steadiness, balance, equilibrium.

Pause, suspension, suspense, lull, stop, stoppage, interruption, stopping, stand, standstill, standing still, lying to, repose (687), respite.

Lock, deadlock, dead stop, embargo.

Resting-place, anchorage, moorings, bivouac, port (189, 666), bed, pillow, etc. (215).

(Verbs) To be quiescent, etc., to remain, stand, stand still, lie to, pull up, hold, halt, stop, anchor, stop short, stop dead, freeze, heave to, rest, pause, repose, keep quiet, take breath, stagnate, vegetate, settle; to mark time.

To stay, tarry, sojourn, dwell (186), pitch one's tent, cast anchor, settle, encamp, bivouac, moor, tether, picket, plant oneself, alight, land, etc. (292) ride at anchor.

(Phrases) Not to stir a peg (or step or inch); *'j'y suis, j'y reste';* to come to a standstill; to come to a deadlock; to rest on one's oars or laurels.

To stop, suspend, arrest, lay to, hold one's hand, interrupt, intermit, discontinue (142), put a stop to, quell, becalm.

(Phrases) To bring to a standstill; to lay an embargo on.

(Adjectives) Quiescent, still, motionless, moveless, at rest, stationary, untravelled, stay-at-home, at a stand, at a standstill, stock-still, standing still, sedentary, undisturbed, unruffled, fast, stuck fast, fixed, transfixed, rooted, moored, aground, at anchor, tethered, becalmed, stagnant, quiet, calm, breathless, peaceful, unmoved, unstirred, immovable, immobile, restful, cataleptic, paralysed, frozen, irremovable, stable, steady, steadfast.

(Phrases) Still as a statue; still as a post; quiet or still as a mouse.

(Interjections) Soho! stop! stay! avast! belay! halt! as you were! hold hard! hold your horses! hold on! whoa!

266 Locomotion by land.

Journey *(Substantives)*, travel, travelling, excursion, expedition, tour, trip, trek, circuit, peregrination, discursion, ramble, outing, pilgrimage, Odyssey, course, ambulation, march, route march, marching, walk, walking, promenade, stroll, saunter, dander, turn, trot, tramp, hike, stalk, noctambulation, perambulation, ride, equitation, drive, jogtrot, airing, constitutional, spin, jaunt, joy-ride, change of scene.

Roving, vagrancy, flit, flitting, migration, emigration, immigration, intermigration; *Wanderlust.*

Map, plan, itinerary, road-book, Guide, Baedeker, Bradshaw, A B C.

Procession, caravan, cavalcade, column, cortège.

Organs and instruments of locomotion, legs, feet, pins, stilt, skate, ski, snow-shoe, locomotive, vehicle (272, 273), velocipede, penny-farthing, bone-shaker, bicycle, cycle, bike, push cycle, tandem, tricycle, fairy-cycle, scooter.

(Phrase) Shanks's mare.

(Verbs) To travel, journey, trek, walk, ramble, roam, rove, course, wander, itinerate, perambulate, stroll, straggle, expatiate, range, gad about, gallivant, knock about, to go or take a walk, journey, tour, turn, trip, etc.; to prowl, stray, saunter, tour, make a tour, knock about, emigrate, flit, migrate.

To walk, march, counter-march, step, tread, pace, wend, wend one's way, promenade, perambulate, circumambulate, take a walk, go for a walk, take the air, trudge, trapes, stalk, stride, straddle, strut, foot it, hoof it, stump, clump, plod, peg along, bundle, toddle, patter, shuffle on,

267 Locomotion by water, or air, or through space.

Navigation *(Substantives)*, voyage, sail, cruise, Odyssey, circumnavigation, periplus, seafaring, yachting, boating; drifting, headway, sternway, leeway.

Natation, swimming, surf-riding.

Flight, flying, flip, volitation, aerostation, aeronautics, aerostatics, ballooning, aviation, gliding.

Space travel, astronautics.

Wing, pinion, fin, flipper; oar, scull, canvas, sail, rotor, paddle, punt-pole, paddle-wheel, screw, turbine, jet.

(Verbs) To sail, make sail, warp, put to sea, navigate, take ship, get under way, spread sail, spread canvas, carry sail, plough the waves, plough the deep, scud, boom, drift, course, cruise, coast, circumnavigate, aviate.

To row, pull, paddle, scull, punt, steam.

To swim, float, buffet the waves, skim, *effleurer*, dive, wade.

To fly, aviate, hedge-hop, be wafted, hover, soar, glide, wing; to flush.

(Phrases) To take wing; to take flight.

(Adjectives) Sailing, etc., seafaring, under way, under sail, on the wing, volant, nautical; airborne, aeronautic, aeronautical, aerostatic; astronautical.

(Phrases) In sail; under canvas.

tramp, hike, footslog, traverse, bend one's steps, thread one's way, make one's way, find one's way, tread a path, take a course, take wing, take flight, defile, file off.

Ride, jog on, trot, amble, canter, gallop, take horse, prance, frisk, tittup, caracole, have a run, ride and tie, hitch-hike, lorry-hop.

To drive, slide, glide, skim, skate, toboggan, ski.

To go to, repair to, resort to, hie to.

(Phrase) To pad the hoof; to hump bluey.

(Adjectives) Travelling, etc., ambulatory, itinerant, wayfaring, peripatetic, discursive, vagrant, migratory, nomadic, on the wing, etc., circumforanean, overland.

(Adverbs) By the way, *chemin faisant,* on the road, *en passant, en route,* on foot, afoot.

---

268 Traveller *(Substantives),* wayfarer, voyager, itinerant, passenger, commuter, tourist, tripper, excursionist, wanderer, rover, straggler, rambler, hiker, bird of passage, gad-about, globe-trotter, vagrant, tramp, hobo, bum, swagman, sundowner, vagabond, rolling-stone, nomad, pilgrim, hadji, palmer, runner, courier, pedestrian, peripatetic, emigrant, fugitive.

Rider, horseman, equestrian, cavalier, jockey, postilion, rough-rider, scout, motorist.

Mercury, Iris, Ariel.

269 Mariner *(Substantives),* navigator, seaman, sailor, seafarer, shipman, tar, old salt, bluejacket, marine, jolly, boatman, *voyageur,* ferryman, waterman, lighterman, bargee, gondolier, longshoreman, crew, oarsman.

An aerial navigator, aeronaut, balloonist, aviator, airman, flying man, pilot.

Astronaut, cosmonaut, spaceman.

---

270 Tranference *(Substantives),* transfer, displacement, metathesis, transposition (148), remotion, removal (185), relegation, deportation, extradition, conveyance, draft, carriage, carrying, convection, conduction, export, import.

Transmission, passage, transit, transition, ferry, transport, gestation, portage, porterage, cartage, carting, shovelling, shipment, transhipment, air lift, air drop, freight, wafture, transportation, transumption, transplantation, transfusion, translation, shifting, dodging, dispersion (73), traction (285).

(Verbs) To transfer, convey, transmit, transport, transplant, transfuse, carry, bear, carry over, hand over, pass forward, remove (185), transpose (148), shift, export, import, convey, conduct, convoy, send, relegate, extradite, turn over to, deliver, waft, ship, tranship, ferry over.

To bring, fetch, reach, draft.

To load, lade, charge, unload, shovel, ladle, decant, empty, break bulk.

(Adjectives) Transferred, etc., movable, portable, portative.

(Adverbs) From hand to hand, on the way, *en route, en passant, in transitu,* from pillar to post.

---

271 Carrier *(Substantives),* porter, bearer, coolie, *hammal,* conveyor, transport-worker, stevedore (690), conductor, locomotive (285).

Beast of burden, cattle, horse, blood-horse, arab, steed, nag, palfrey, galloway, charger, destrier, war-horse, courser, racer, racehorse, hunter, pony, filly, colt, foal, barb, jade, hack, *bidet,* pad, cob, tit, punch, roadster, goer, pack-horse, draught horse, cart-horse, post-horse, shelty, jennet, bayard, mare, stallion, gelding, gee-gee, gee, stud.

Ass, donkey, moke, cuddy, jackass, mule, hinny, sumpter-mule.

Camel, dromedary, llama, zebra, reindeer, yak, elephant, carrier-pigeon.

272 Vehicle *(Substantives)*, conveyance.

Carriage, caravan, van, furniture van, pantechnicon, wagon, stage-wagon, wain, dray, cart, float, trolley, sledge, sleigh, bob-sleigh, *luge*, toboggan, truck, tumbril, pontoon, barrow, wheelbarrow, hand-barrow, lorry.

Train, railway train, goods train, freight train, rolling stock, Pullman car, parlour car, restaurant-car, dining-car, diner, buffet-car, sleeping-car, sleeper, horse-box, cattle-truck, rail-car, tender.

Equipage, turn-out, carriage, coach, chariot, chaise, post-chaise, phaeton, curricle, tilbury, whisky, victoria, landau, brougham, clarence, gig, calash, dog-cart, governess-cart, trap, buggy, carriole, jingle, wagonette, jaunting-car, shandrydan, droshky, kibitka, berlin, stage, stage-coach, diligence, car, omnibus, bus, charabanc, brake, cabriolet, cab, hackney cab, four-wheeler, growler, fly, hansom.

Motor-car, motor, automobile, autocar, touring-car, tourer, sports car, torpedo, landaulette, limousine, saloon, sedan, two-seater, runabout, coupé, jalopy, tricar, motor-cycle, side-car, autocycle, moped, corgi, motor-bus, motor-coach, autobus, taxi-cab, taxi, motor-van, jeep; trolley-bus, tram-car, tram, street-car.

Tank, armoured car, half-track, amtrac, duck.

Bath-chair, wheel-chair, sedan chair, palanquin (or palankeen), litter, jinricksha (or rickshaw), brancard, stretcher, perambulator, pram, mail-cart, bassinette, baby-carriage.

Shovel, spoon, spatula, ladle, hod.

273 Ship *(Substantives)*, vessel, pottom, craft, shipping, marine, fleet, flotilla, squadron, three-master, barque (or bark), barquentine, brig, brigantine, schooner, sloop, cutter, skiff, yawl, ketch, smack, dogger, hoy, lugger, barge, wherry, lighter, hulk, buss, packet, clipper, rotor ship.

Navy, armada, warship, man-of-war, ironclad, capital ship, super-dreadnought, dreadnought, battle-ship, battle-cruiser, cruiser, frigate, corvette, gunboat, aircraft-carrier, monitor, torpedo boat destroyer, destroyer, torpedo boat, mine-sweeper, mine-layer, submarine, Q-boat, troop-ship, trooper, transport, hospital ship, flagship; ship of the line, first-rate, seventy-four, fireship.

Liner, merchantman, tramp, slaver, steamer, steamboat, steam-packet, paddle-steamer, stern-wheeler, screw-steamer, turbine, tender, tug, collier, whaler, coaster, tanker.

Argosy, bireme, trireme, quadrireme, quinquereme, galley, galleon, carrack, caravel, galliot, polacca, tartan, junk, praam, saic, dhow, proa, sampan, xebec.

Boat, motor-boat, long-boat, pinnacle, launch, cabin cruiser, yacht, shallop, jolly-boat, gig, funny, dinghy, bumboat, fly-boat, wherry, coble, cock-boat, punt, cog, kedge, out-rigger, catamaran, fishing-boat, coracle, hooker, life-boat, gondola, felucca, dahebeeyah, caique, canoe, dug-out, raft, float.

(Adverbs) Afloat, aboard.

273A Aircraft *(Substantives)*, flying machine, aeroplane, monoplane, biplane, seaplane, hydroplane, plane, flying boat, amphibian, air-liner, flying wing, stratocruiser, stratoliner, sky-master, jet aircraft, jet, turbo-jet, autogiro, helicopter, hoverplane, whirlybird, planicopter, glider; fighter, bomber, fighter-bomber, flying fortress, super-fortress.

Balloon, air-balloon, aerostat, Montgolfier, pilot balloon, blimp, kite, airship, dirigible, Zeppelin.

Space ship, rocket, sputnik, lunik, satellite.

(Adjective) Airborne; orbital.

2°. Degrees of Motion

274 Velocity (*Substantives*), speed, celerity, swiftness, rapidity, fleetness, expedition, speediness, quickness, nimbleness, briskness, agility, promptness, promptitude (682), dispatch, acceleration (684).

Gallop, full gallop, canter, trot, run, rush, scamper, scoot, scorch, hand-gallop, lope; flight, dart, bolt, dash, spurt, sprint.

Haste, hurry, scurry, bounce, bolt, precipitation, precipitancy (684), forced march, race, steeplechase, Marathon race.

Rate, pace, step, gait, course, progress.

Lightning, light, cannon-ball, bullet, wind, rocket, arrow, dart, quicksilver, telegraph, express train, clipper.

An eagle, antelope, doe, courser, racehorse, racer, gazelle, greyhound, hare, squirrel, bandersnatch.

Mercury, Ariel, Camilla.

Speed indicator, speedometer, tachometer, log, log-line.

(*Verbs*) To move quickly; to trip, speed, haste, hie, hasten, hurry, fly, press, press on, press forward, post, push on, whip, scamper, run, sprint, race, scud, scour, scurry, scuttle, spin, scoot, scorch, rip, clip, shoot, tear, whisk, sweep, skim, brush, glance, cut along, dash on, dash forward, trot, gallop, lope, rush, bound, bounce, flounce, frisk, tittup, bolt, flit, spring, boom, dart.

To hasten, accelerate, expedite, dispatch, urge, whip, forward, buck up, express, speed-up, hurry, precipitate, quicken pace, gather way, ride hard.

To keep up with, keep pace with, race, race with, outpace, outmarch, distance, outdistance, lap, leave behind, outrun, outstrip, gain ground.

(*Phrases*) To cover the ground; to clap on sail; take to one's heels; clap spurs to one's horse; to run like mad; ride hard; outstrip the wind; to make rapid strides; wing one's way; be off like a shot; run a race; stir one's stumps; do a scoot; get a move on; get cracking; step on it; give her the gun; let it rip.

275 Slowness (*Substantives*), tardiness, dilatoriness, slackness, lentor, languor (683), drawl.

Hobbling, creeping, lounging, etc., shambling, claudication, halting, walk, amble, jog-trot, dog-trot, mincing steps, foot-pace, crawl.

A slow-goer, dawdle, dawdler, lingerer, slow-coach, lame duck, drone, tortoise, snail, slug, sluggard, slacker.

Retardation, slackening, slowing down, delay (133).

(*Verbs*) To move slowly, to creep, crawl, lag, slug, drawl, dawdle, linger, loiter (683), plod, trudge, flag, saunter, lounge, lumber, trail, drag, grovel, glide, laze, amble, steal along, inch along, jog on, rub on, bundle on, toddle, waddle, shuffle, halt, hobble, limp, claudicate, shamble, mince, falter, totter, stagger.

To retard, slacken, relax, check, rein in, curb, strike sail, reef, slow up, slow down.

(*Phrases*) To 'drag its slow length along'; to hang fire; to march in slow time, in funeral procession; to lose ground.

To put on the drag; apply the brake; clip the wings; take in sail; take one's time; ca' canny; *festina lente*.

(*Adjectives*) Slow, slack, tardy, dilatory, easy, gentle, leisurely, deliberate, lazy, languid, drowsy, sleepy, heavy, drawling, leaden, sluggish, snail-like, creeping, crawling, etc., dawdling, lumbering, hobbling, tardigrade.

(*Adverbs*) Slowly, etc., gingerly, softly, leisurely, deliberately, gradually, etc. (144), *piano, adagio, largo*.

(*Phrases*) In slow motion; just ticking over; under easy sail; at a snail's pace; with mincing steps; with clipped wings; by degrees; little by little; inch by inch.

(Adjectives) Fast, speedy, swift, rapid, full-drive, quick, double-quick, fleet, nimble, agile, expeditious, prompt, brisk, frisky, hasty, hurried, flying, etc., precipitate, furious, light-footed, nimble-footed, winged, eagle-winged, mercurial, electric, telegraphic, light-legged; accelerative.

(Phrases) Swift as an arrow; as a doe, as a lamplighter; off like a shot; quick as lightning; quick as thought.

(Adverbs) Swiftly, with speed, speedily, trippingly, etc., full-tilt, full speed, apace, post-haste, *presto*, tantivy, by express, by telegraph, slap, slap-dash, headlong, hurry-scurry, hand over hand, at a round trot.

(Phrases) Under press of sail, or canvas; *velis et remis*; on eagle's wings; at the double, in double-quick time; with giant, or gigantic steps; *à pas de géant*; in seven-league boots; whip and spur; *ventre à terre*; as fast as one's legs or heels will carry one; *sauve qui peut*; the devil take the hindmost; *vires acquirit eundo;* with rapid strides; at top speed; in top gear; flat out; all out; like greased lightning; like the wind.

3°. Motion conjoined with Force

276 Impulse *(Substantives)*, momentum, impetus, push, impulsion, thrust, shove, fling, jog, jolt, brunt, throw, volley, explosion (173), propulsion (284).

Percussion, collision, concussion, impact, clash, encounter, cannon, carom, carambole, appulse, shock, crash, bump, charge, tackle (716), foul.

Blow, stroke, knock, tap, fillip, pat, rap, dab, dig, jab, smack, slap, hit, putt, cuff, bang, crack, whack, thwack, slog, belt, wipe, clout, swipe, clip, squash, dowse, punch, thump, pelt, kick, lunge, buffet, beating (972).

Hammer, mallet, mall, maul, beetle, flail, cudgel, bludgeon, life-preserver, cosh, baton, truncheon, knobkerrie, shillelagh, staff, lathi, cane, stick, club, racket, bat, driver, brassy, baffy, spoon, putter, cleek, iron, mashie, niblick, ram, battering-ram, monkey-engine, catapult, pile-driver, rammer, sledge-hammer, steam hammer.

Dynamics; seismometer.

(Verbs) To impel, push, give impetus, etc., drive, urge, hurtle, boom, thrust, elbow, shoulder, charge, tackle, jostle, justle, hustle, shove, jog, jolt, encounter, collide, clash, cannon, foul.

To strike, knock, tap, slap, dab, pat, slam, hit, bat, putt, rap, prod, jerk, dig, cuff, smite, butt, impinge, thump, bethump, beat, bang, whang, biff, punch, thwack, whack, spank, skelp, swat, lay into, shin, slog, clout, wipe, swipe, batter, dowse, baste, pummel, pelt, patter, drub, buffet, belabour, cane, whip (972), poke at, hoof, jab, pink, lunge, kick, recalcitrate.

To throw, etc. (284), to set going, mobilize.

(Adjectives) Impelling, etc., impulsive, impellent, impelled, etc., dynamic, dynamical.

(Interjections) Bang! boom! wham!

277 Recoil *(Substantives)*, retroaction, revulsion, reaction, rebound, bounce, stot, repercussion, ricochet, rebuff, reverberation, reflux, reflex, kick, springing back, ducks and drakes.

A boomerang, spring (325).

(Verbs) To recoil, react, spring back, fly back, bound back, rebound, stot, reverberate, repercuss.

(Adjectives) Recoiling, etc., on the recoil, etc., refluent, repercussive, reactionary, retroactive.

(Phrase) On the rebound.

———

4°. *Motion with reference to Direction*

278 Direction *(Substantives)*, bearing, course, route, bent, inclination, drift, tenor, tendency, incidence, set, leaning, bending, trend, dip, steerage, tack, steering, aim, alignment (or alinement), orientation, collimation.

A line, bee-line, path, road, aim, range, quarter, point of the compass, rhumb, great circle, azimuth, line of collimation.

(Verbs) To tend towards, go to, point to, or at; trend, verge, align (or aline), incline, conduct to, determine.

To make for, or towards, aim at, take aim, level at, steer for, keep or hold a course, be bound for, bend one's steps towards, direct or shape one's course.

To ascertain one's direction, orient (or orientate) oneself, to see which way the wind blows.

(Adjectives) Directed, etc., direct, straight, undeviating, unswerving, aligned (or alined) with, determinate, point-to-point.

(Adverbs) Towards, to, *versus*, thither, directly, point-blank, full tilt at, whither, in a line with, as the crow flies.

By way of, via, in all directions, *quaquaversum*, in all manner of ways, to the four winds.

———

280 Going before.
Precession *(Substantives)*, leading, heading.

Precedence in order (62), priority (116), precursor (64), front (234).

(Verbs) To precede, forerun, lead, head, herald, introduce, usher in (62), go ahead.

(Phrases) Go in the van; take the lead; lead the way; open the ball; have the start; to get before; steal a march.

(Adjectives) Preceding, leading, etc.

(Adverbs) In advance, before (62), in the van, ahead.

279 Deviation *(Substantives)*, swerving, aberration, obliquation, *ambages*, warp, bending, flexion, deflection, refraction, sidling, side-slip, skid, half-roll, barrel-roll, loop, straying, straggling, warping, etc., digression, circuit, detour, departure from, divergence (291), desultory motion; slice, pull, hook, leg-break, off-break, googly.

Motion sideways, side-step.

(Verbs) To alter one's course, divert, deviate, depart from, turn, bend, swerve, break, switch, skid, side-slip, zoom, bank, loop, bunt, jib, shift, warp, stray, straggle, sidle, diverge (291), digress, wander, meander, veer, wear, tack, yaw, turn aside, turn a corner, turn away from, face about, wheel, wheel about, steer clear of, ramble, rove, go astray, step aside, shunt, side-track, jay walk.

(Phrases) To fly off at a tangent; to face to the right-about; to go out of one's way; to lose one's way.

(Adjectives) Deviating, etc., aberrant, discursive, devious, desultory, erratic, vagrant, stray, undirected, circuitous, roundabout, crab-like, zigzag.

(Adverbs) Astray from, round about.

(Phrases) To the right-about; all manner of ways; like the knight's move in chess.

281 Going after.
Sequence *(Substantives)*, following, pursuit, chase, hunt (622).

A follower, pursuer, attendant, shadow, satellite, hanger-on, train.

Sequence in order (63), in time (117).

(Verbs) To follow, pursue, chase, hunt, hound, shadow, dog, tail, trail, lag.

(Phrases) Go in the rear, or in the wake of; tread in the steps of; tread on the heels of; go after; fly after; to follow as a shadow; to lag behind; to bring up the rear; to fall behind; to tail off.

(Adjectives) Following, etc.

(Adverbs) Behind, in the rear, etc.

282 Motion forwards.

Progression (*Substantives*), advance, advancement, progress (658), on-going, progressiveness, progressive motion, flood-tide, headway, advancing, etc., pursuit, steeplechase (622), journey, march (266).

(*Verbs*) To advance, proceed, progress, go, move, bend or pass forward, go on, move on, pass on, get on, get along, jog on, push on, go one's way, go ahead, forge ahead, make head, make way, make headway, work one's way, press forward, edge forward, get over the ground, gain ground, make progress, keep or hold on one's course, keep up with, get forward, distance.

(*Phrases*) To make up leeway; to go with the stream; to make rapid strides; to push or elbow or cleave one's way; to go full tilt at.

(*Adjectives*) Advancing, etc., progressive, go-ahead, avant-garde, profluent, undeviating.

(*Adverbs*) Forward, onward, forth, on, in advance, ahead, under way, straightforward.

(*Phrases*) *Vestigia nulla retrorsum; en avant.*

283 Motion backwards.

Regression (*Substantives*), regress, recess, retrogression, retrogradation, retreat, withdrawal, retirement, recession (287), refluence, reflux, retroaction, return, reflexion, reflex (277), ebb, countermovement, counter-march, veering, regurgitation, back-wash.

(*Verbs*) To recede, retrograde, return, rebound, back, fall back, fall or drop astern, lose ground, put about, go back, turn back, hark back, double back, countermarch, turn tail, draw back, get back, retrace one's steps, wheel about, back water, regurgitate, yield, give.

(*Phrases*) Dance the back step; beat a retreat.

(*Adjectives*) Receding, etc., retrograde, retrogressive, regressive, refluent, reflex, recidivous, resilient.

(*Adverbs*) Backwards, reflexively, to the right-about, about turn, *à reculons, à rebours.*

(*Phrase*) *Revenons à nos moutons.*

---

284 Motion given to an object in front.

Propulsion (*Substantives*), push, pushing (276), projection, jaculation, ejaculation, throw, fling, fillip, toss, shot, discharge, shy.

Ballistics, gunnery; *vis a tergo.*

Missile, projectile, shot, shell, ball, bolt, dart, arrow, bullet, stone, shaft, brickbat, discus, quoit, caber.

Bow, sling, pea-shooter, catapult etc. (727).

(*Verbs*) To propel, project, throw, fling, cast, pitch, chuck, bung, toss, lob, loft, jerk, jaculate, ejaculate, hurl, boost, bolt, drive, sling, flirt, flip, flick, shy, dart, send, roll, send

285 Motion given to an object behind.

Traction (*Substantives*), drawing, draught, pull, pulling, towage, haulage.

Traction engine, locomotive; hauler, haulier, tractor, tug; trailer.

(*Phrase*) A long pull, a strong pull, and a pull all together.

(*Verbs*) To draw, pull, haul, lug, drag, tug, tow, trail, train, wrench, jerk, twitch, yank.

(*Phrase*) To take in tow.

(*Adjectives*) Drawing, etc., tractile.

---

off, let off, discharge, fire off, shoot, launch, let fly, dash, punt, volley, heave, pitchfork.

To bowl, trundle, roll along (312).

To put in motion, start, give an impulse, impel (276), expel (297).

(*Phrases*) To carry off one's feet; to put to flight.

(*Adjectives*) Propelling, etc., propulsive, projectile, etc.

286 Motion towards.

Approach (*Substantives*), approximation, appropinquation, access, appulse, afflux, affluxion, pursuit (622), collision (276), arrival (292).

(*Verbs*) To approach, draw near, approximate, to near; to come, get, go, etc., near; to set in towards, make up to, snuggle up to, gain upon, gain ground upon.

(*Phrases*) To tread on the heels of; to hug the shore.

(*Adjectives*) Approaching, etc., approximative.

287 Motion from.

Recession (*Substantives*), retirement, withdrawal, retreat, retrocession (283), departure (293), recoil (277), decampment, flight, stampede, skedaddle.

A runaway, a fugitive.

(*Verbs*) To recede, go, move or fly from, retire, retreat, withdraw, come away, go or get away, draw back, shrink, move away.

To move off, stand off, draw off, buzz off, fall back, turn tail, march off, decamp, absquatulate, skedaddle, vamoose, sheer off, bolt, scram, hop it, beat it, slip away, run away, pack off, fly, remove, abscond, sneak off, slink away.

(*Phrases*) To take French leave; to cut and run; take to one's heels; to give leg-bail; take one's hook; *sauve qui peut*; the devil take the hindmost; beat a retreat; make oneself scarce; do a bolt; do a guy; make tracks; cut one's lucky.

(*Adjectives*) Receding, etc., fugitive, runaway (671).

288 Motion towards, actively.

Attraction (*Substantives*), drawing to, pulling towards, adduction, attractiveness, magnetism, gravity, gravitation.

A loadstone, magnet.

(*Verbs*) To attract, draw, pull, drag, etc., towards, adduce.

(*Adjectives*) Attracting, etc., adducent, attrahent, adductive, attractive, magnetic, gravitational.

(*Interjections*) Come! come here! approach! come near!

289 Motion from, actively.

Repulsion (*Substantives*), push (276), driving from, repulse, expulsion (297).

(*Verbs*) To repel, repulse; push, drive, etc., from, drive away, cold-shoulder, send packing.

(*Phrases*) To give the frozen mitt to; send away with a flea in one's ear; send to the right-about (678).

(*Adjectives*) Repelling, etc., repellent, repulsive, forbidding.

(*Interjections*) Get out! be off! scram! avaunt! (293, 297).

290 Motion nearer to.

Convergence (*Substantives*), appulse, meeting, confluence, concourse, conflux, congress, concurrence, concentration.

Resort, assemblage, synod (72), focus (74), asymptote.

(*Verbs*) To converge, come together, unite, meet, fall in with, close in upon, centre in, enter in, meet, come across, come up against.

To gather together, unite, concentrate, etc.

291 Motion farther off.

Divergence (*Substantives*), aberration, peregrination, wandering, divarication, radiation, ramification, separation (44), dispersion, diffusion, dissemination (73); deviation (279).

(*Verbs*) To diverge, divaricate, deviate, wander, stray (279), radiate, branch off, ramify, file off, draw aside.

To spread, disperse, scatter, distribute, decentralize, diffuse, disseminate, shed, sow broadcast, broadcast, sprinkle.

(Adjectives) Converging, etc., convergent, confluent, concurring, concurrent, centripetal, asymptotical.

---

292 Terminal motion at.

Arrival *(Substantives)*, advent, reception, welcome, return, disembarkation, debarkation, remigration.

Home, goal, resting-place, destination, journey's end, harbour, haven, port, dock, pier, landing-place, landing-stage, landing-ground, airfield, airstrip, airstop, airport, aerodrome, helidrome, terminus, station.

Meeting, rencontre, rencounter, encounter.

Caller, visitor, visitant, guest.

(Verbs) To arrive, get to, come, come to, reach, attain, come up with, come up to, catch up, make, fetch, overtake, overhaul.

To light, alight, land, dismount, disembark, debark, detrain, outspan, debus, put in, put into, visit, cast, anchor.

To come upon, light upon, pitch upon, hit upon, drop in, pop upon, bounce upon, plump upon, bump against, run against, run across, close with.

To come back, return, get back, get home, sit down.

To meet, encounter, rencounter, contact, come in contact (199).

(Phrase) To be in at the death.

(Adjectives) Arriving, etc., homeward bound.

(Adverbs) Here, hither.

(Interjections) Welcome! hallo! hail! all hail! good day ! good morrow! *ave!*

To part, part company, turn away from, wander from, separate (44).

(Phrase) To go or fly off at a tangent.

(Adjectives) Diverging, etc., divergent, radiant, wandering, aberring, aberrant, centrifugal.

(Adverb) Broadcast.

---

293 Initial motion from.

Departure *(Substantives)*, outset, removal, exit, exodus, decampment, embarkation, flight, hegira.

Valediction, adieu, farewell, goodbye, leave-taking, send-off; stirrup-cup, doch-an-doris, one for the road.

A starting point or post, place of departure or embarkation, airfield, terminus, etc. (292).

(Phrase) The foot being in the stirrup.

(Verbs) To depart, go, set out, set off, start, start off, issue, go forth, sally, debouch, sally forth, set forward, be off, move off, pack off, buzz off, scram, begone, get off, sheer off, clear out, vamoose, skedaddle, absquatulate.

To leave a place, quit, retire, withdraw, go one's way, take wing, flit, embus, inspan, entrain, embark, go on board, set sail, put to sea, weigh anchor, slip cable, decamp (671).

(Phrases) To take leave; bid or take adieu; bid farewell; to say goodbye; make one's exit; take a run-out powder.

(Adjectives) Departing, etc., valedictory, outward bound.

(Adverbs) Whence, hence, thence.

(Interjections) Be off! get out! clear out! scram! buzz off! hop it! beat it! begone! get you gone! go along! off with you! avaunt! away with you! go about your business!

Good-bye! bye-bye! 'bye! ta ta! farewell! fare you well! adieu! *au revoir! auf wiedersehen! a rivederci! bon voyage! vale! hasta la vista! sayonara!* so long! cheerio! chin-chin! tinkety-tonk! pip-pip! tootle-oo! bung-ho!

---

294 Motion into.

Ingress *(Substantives)*, ingoing, entrance, entry, introgression, admission, admittance, intromission,

295 Motion out of.

Egress *(Substantives)*, exit, issue, emersion, emergence.

Exudation, extravasation,

introduction, insinuation, insertion (300), intrusion, inroad, incursion, influx, irruption, invasion, penetration, interpenetration, infiltration, import, importation, illapse, immigration.

A mouth, door (260); an entrant.

(Verbs) To enter, go into, come into, set foot in, intrude, invade, flow into, pop into, insinuate itself, penetrate, interpenetrate, infiltrate, soak into; to put into, etc., bring in, insert, drive in, run in, wedge in, ram in (300), intromit, introduce, import, smuggle.

(Phrases) To find one's way into; creep into; worm oneself into; to darken one's door; have the entrée; to open the door to.

(Adjectives) Ingoing, incoming, penetrative, penetrant.

(Adverb) Inwards.

---

296 Motion into, actively.

Reception (Substantives), admission, admittance, importation, immission, introduction, ingestion, imbibition, absorption, resorption, ingurgitation, inhalation (300).

Eating, swallowing, deglutition, devouring, gulp, gulping, gorge, gorging, carousal.

Drinking, potation, sipping, supping, suction, sucking, draught, libation; smoking, snuffing.

Mastication, manducation, rumination, chewing; hippophagy, ichthyophagy, anthropophagy.

(Verbs) To admit, receive, intromit, import, ingest, absorb, resorb, imbibe, inhale, let in, take in, readmit, resorb, reabsorb, snuff up, sop up, suck, suck in, swallow, take down, ingurgitate, engulf.

To eat, fare, feed, devour, tuck in, gulp, bolt, snap, get down, pick, peck, gorge, engorge, fall to, stuff, cram, gobble, guttle, guzzle, wolf, raven, eat heartily, do justice to, overeat, gormandize (957), dispatch, discuss.

To feed upon, live on, feast upon,

transudation (348), leakage, seepage, percolation, distillation, oozing, effluence, efflux, effusion, drain, dropping, dripping, dribbling, drip, dribble, drainage, filtering, defluxion, trickling, eruption, outbreak, outburst, outpouring, gush (348), emanation, aura.

Export, expatriation, emigration, remigration, repatriation, exodus (293).

An outlet, vent, spout, tap, faucet, sluice, flue, chimney, pore, drain, sewer (350).

(Verbs) To emerge, emanate, issue, go, come, move, pass, pour, flow, etc., out of, find vent, pass off, evacuate.

To transude, exude, leak, seep, well out, percolate, transcolate, strain, distil, drain, ooze, filter, filtrate, dribble, trickle, drizzle, drip, gush, spout, run, flow out, effuse, extravasate, disembogue, debouch (348).

(Adjectives) Dripping, outgoing, etc., oozy, leaky, trickly, dribbly.

---

297 Motion out of, actively.

Ejection (Substantives), emission, effusion, rejection, expulsion, detrusion, extrusion, eviction.

Discharge, egestion, evacuation, vomition, eructation, belch; bloodletting, venesection, phlebotomy, tapping.

Deportation, exile, rustication, banishment, relegation, extradition.

(Phrases) The rogue's march; the bum's rush.

(Verbs) To emit, eject, expel, export, reject, discharge, give out, let out, cast out, clear out, sweep out, clean out, gut, fillet, wipe off, turn out, chuck out, elbow out, kick out, hoof out, sack, dismiss, bounce, drive out, root out, pour out, ooze, shed, void, evacuate, disgorge, extrude, empty, detrude, throw off, spit, spit out, expectorate, spirt, spill, slop, drain.

To vomit, spue, cat, puke, cast up, keck, retch, spatter, splutter, slobber, slaver, slabber, squirt, eructate, belch, burp, give vent to, tap, broach, open the sluices, heave out, bale out, shake off.

regale, carouse, batten upon, fatten
upon, dine, etc., browse, graze, crop,
chew, champ, munch, gnaw, nibble,
crunch, ruminate, masticate, mandu-
cate, mumble.

To drink, quaff, swig, booze, drench,
sip, sup, lap, drink up, drain up, toss off,
drain the cup, tipple (959).

(Phrases) To give entrance or admittance to; open the door to; usher in.

To refresh the inner man; restore
one's tissues; play a good knife and
fork; get outside of; wrap oneself
round.

To drink one's fill; wet one's whistle;
empty one's glass; crook or lift one's
elbow; crack a bottle.

(Adjectives) Admitting, etc., admitted, etc., admissible; absorbent,
absorptive.

Hippophagous, ichthyophagous, anthropophagous, herbivorous, gra-
minivorous, granivorous, omnivorous.

To throw, project (284); to push,
thrust (276).

To unpack, unlade, unload (270).

To banish, exile, extradite, deport;
ostracize, boycott, send to Coventry.

(Phrases) To send packing; to send
to the right about; to send about one's
business; to give the sack to; to show
the door to; to turn out neck and crop;
to make a clean sweep of; to send away
with a flea in one's ear.

(Adjectives) Emitting, etc., emitted,
etc.

(Interjections) Be off! get out!
scram! (293), scat! fade! chase yourself! *allez-vous-en!*

———

298 Food *(Substantives)*, pabulum,
aliment, nourishment, nutriment,
sustenance, sustentation, nurture, subsistence, provender, fodder, provision,
prey, forage, pasture, pasturage, keep,
fare, cheer, rations, diet, regimen.

Comestibles, eatables, victuals,
prog, grub, chow, chuck, toke, eats,
meat, bread, breadstuffs, cake, pastry,
viands, cates, delicacy, delicatessen,
dainty, creature comforts, belly-
timber, staff of life, dish, flesh-pots,
pottage, pudding, ragout, omelet,
sundae, kickshaws.

299 Excretion *(Substantives)*,
discharge, emanation, exhalation,
exudation, secretion, extrusion, effusion, extravasation, evacuation, faeces,
excrement (653), perspiration, sweat,
saliva, salivation, spittle, diaphoresis;
bleeding, haemorrhage, flux.

(Verbs) To emanate, exhale, excern,
excrete, exude, effuse, secrete, secern,
extravasate, evacuate, urinate, discharge, etc. (297).

———

Table, board, commons, good cheer, bill of fare, menu, commissariat,
table d'hôte, ordinary, cuisine.

Canteen, Naffy, restaurant, chop-house, café, cafeteria, eating-house,
tea-room, tea-shop, coffee-house, coffee-stall, bar, milk bar, snack bar,
public house, pot-house, ale-house, wineshop, brasserie, bodega, tavern
(189).

Meal, repast, feed, mess, spread, course, regale, regalement, entertainment, feast, banquet, junket, refreshment, refection; breakfast, *chota
hazri*, elevenses, *déjeuner*, lunch, bever, luncheon, tiffin, tea, afternoon tea,
five-o'clock tea, high tea, dinner, supper, whet, appetizer, aperitif, bait,
dessert, *entremet, hors d'oeuvre*, picnic, bottle-party, wayz-goose,
beanfeast, blow-out, tuck-in, snack, pot-luck table d'hôte, *déjeuner à la
fourchette*.

Mouthful, bolus, gobbet, sip, sup, sop, tot, snort, hoot, dram, peg,
cocktail (615), nip, *chasse*, liqueur.

Drink, hard drink, soft drink, tipple, beverage, liquor, broth, soup, etc.,
symposium.

(Phrases) A good tuck-in; a modest quencher.

(Adjectives) Eatable, edible, esculent, comestible, alimentary, cereal, culinary, nutritious, nutritive, nutrient, nutrimental, succulent, potable, drinkable.

298A Tobacco, the weed, bacca, baccy, honeydew, cavendish, bird's-eye, shag, virginia, latakia, perique, plug, twist.

Cigar, segar, cheroot, havana, manila, weed, whiff, cigarette, fag, gasper, stinker, coffin-nail.

Snuff, rappee.

A smoke, draw, puff, pinch, quid, chew, chaw.

Tobacco-pipe, pipe, briar, meerschaum, calabash, corncob, clay pipe, clay, churchwarden, dudeen (or dudheen), cutty, hookah, hubble-bubble, chibouque, narghile, calumet.

(Verbs) To smoke, chew, take snuff.

(Adjective) Nicotian.

300 Forcible ingress.

Insertion *(Substantives)*, putting in, implantation, introduction, interjection, insinuation, planting, intercalation, embolism, injection, inoculation, vaccination, importation, intervention (228), dovetailing, tenon, wedge.

Immersion, dip, plunge, bath (337), submergence, submersion, souse, duck, soak.

Interment, burying, etc. (363).

(Verbs) To insert, introduce, intromit, put into, import, throw in, interlard, inject, interject, intercalate, infuse, instil, inoculate, vaccinate, pasteurize, impregnate, imbue, imbrue, graft, engraft, bud, plant, implant, embed, obtrude, foist in, worm in, thrust in, stick in, ram in, stuff in, tuck in, plough in, let in, dovetail, mortise (or mortice), insinuate, wedge in, press in, impact, drive in, run in, empierce (260).

To immerse, dip, steep, immerge, merge, submerge, bathe, plunge, drop in, souse, douse, soak, duck, drown.

To inter, bury, etc. (363).

(Adjectives) Inserting, inserted, implanted, embedded, etc., ingrowing.

301 Forcible egress.

Extraction *(Substantives)*, taking out, removal, elimination, extrication, evulsion, avulsion, eradication, extirpation, wrench.

Expression, squeezing; ejection (297).

Extractor, corkscrew, pincers, pliers, forceps.

(Verbs) To extract, take out, draw, draw out, pull out, tear out, pluck out, extort, wring from, prise, wrench, rake out, rake up, grub up, root up, uproot, eradicate, extirpate, dredge, remove, get out (185), elicit, extricate, eliminate.

To express, squeeze out, wring out, pick out, disembowel, eviscerate, exenterate.

(Adjectives) Extracted, etc.

302 Motion through.

Passage *(Substantives)*, transmission, permeation, penetration, interpenetration (294), filtration, infiltration, percolation, transudation, osmosis (or osmose), capillary action, endosmosis (or endosmose), exosmosis (or exosmose), intercurrence; way, path (627); channel, pipe (350).

Terebration, impalement, etc. (260).

(Verbs) To pass, pass through, traverse, terebrate, stick, pierce, impale, spear, spike, spit (260), penetrate, percolate, permeate, thread, thrid, enfilade,

go through, cross, go across, go over, pass over, get over, clear, negotiate, cut across, pass and repass; work, thread or worm one's way, force a passage; to transmit.

(Adjectives) Passing, intercurrent, penetrative, transudatory, etc.

---

303 Motion beyond.

Transcursion *(Substantives)*, transilience, transgression, trespass, encroachment, infringement, extravagation, transcendence, enjambement, overrunning.

(Verbs) To transgress, overstep, surpass, overpass, overrun, overgo, beat, outstrip, outgo, outstep, outrun, outdo, overreach, overleap, outleap, pass, go by, strain, overshoot the mark, overjump, overskip, overlap, go beyond, outpace, outmarch, transcend, distance, outdistance, lap, encroach, exceed, trespass, infringe, trench upon.

(Phrases) To stretch a point; to steal a march on; to pass the Rubicon; to shoot ahead of; to throw into the shade.

(Adverbs) Beyond the mark, out of bounds.

304 Motion short of.

Shortcoming *(Substantives)*, failure, falling short (732), defalcation, default, backlog, leeway, incompleteness (53); imperfection (651); insufficiency (640).

(Verbs) To come or fall short of, not to reach, keep within bounds, keep within compass, to stop short, be wanting, lose ground, miss the mark.

(Adjectives) Unreached, deficient (53), short, minus.

(Adverbs) Within the mark, within compass, within bounds, etc., behindhand.

---

305 Motion upwards.

Ascent *(Substantives)*, rise, climb, ascension, upgrowth, leap (309).

A rocket, sky-rocket, lark, skylark; a climber, mountaineer, Alpinist, stegophilist.

(Verbs) To ascend, rise, mount, arise, uprise, go up, get up, climb, clamber, swarm, shin, scale, scramble, escalade, surmount, aspire.

To tower, soar, zoom, hover, spire, plane, swim, float, surge.

(Phrase) To make one's way up.

(Adjectives) Rising, etc., scandent, buoyant, floating, supernatant, superfluitant.

(Adverbs) Uphill, on the up grade.

(Interjection) Excelsior!

306 Motion downwards.

Descent *(Substantives)*, fall, descension, declension, declination, drop, cadence, subsidence, lapse, downfall, tumble, tilt, toppling, trip, lurch, *culbute,* spill, cropper, purler, crash.

Titubation, shamble, shambling, stumble.

An avalanche, landslip, landslide, debacle, slump.

(Phrase) The fate of Icarus.

(Verbs) To descend, come or go down, fall, sink, gravitate, drop, drop down, droop, decline, come down, dismount, alight, light, settle, subside, slide, slip, slither, glissade, toboggan, coast, volplane, dive (310).

To tumble, slip, trip, stumble, pitch, lurch, swag, topple, topple over, swoop, tilt, sprawl, plump down, measure one's length, bite the dust, heel over, careen (217), slump, crash.

To alight, dismount, get down.

(Adjectives) Descending, etc., descendent, decurrent, decursive, deciduous.

(Phrase) Nodding to its fall.

(Adverbs) Downhill, on the down grade.

307 Elevation *(Substantiveş)*, raising, lifting, erection, lift, uplift, upheaval, upcast.

Lift, elevator, hoist, escalator, crane, derrick, winch, windlass, jack, lever.

(Verbs) To elevate, raise, lift, uplift, upraise, set up, erect, stick up, rear, uprear, upbear, upcast, hoist, uphoist, heave, upheave, weigh, exalt, promote, give a lift, help up, prick up, perk up.

To drag up, fish up, dredge.

To stand up, rise up, ramp.

(Phrases) To set on a pedestal; to get up on one's hind legs.

(Adjectives) Elevated, etc., rampant.

(Adverbs) On stilts, on the shoulders of.

---

308 Depression *(Substantives)*, lowering, abasement, abasing, detrusion, reduction.

Overthrow, upset, prostration, subversion, overset, overturn, precipitation.

Bow, curtsy (or curtsey), genuflexion, obeisance, kowtow, salaam.

(Verbs) To depress, lower, let down, take down, sink, debase, abase, reduce, demote, detrude, let fall, cast down, to grass, send to grass.

To overthrow, overturn, upset, overset, subvert, prostrate, level, raze, fell; cast, take, throw, fling, dash, pull, cut, knock, hew, etc., down.

To stoop, bend, bow, curtsy (or curtsey), bob, duck, kneel, crouch, cower, lout, kowtow, salaam, bend the head or knee; to recline, sit, sit down, couch, squat.

(Phrases) To take down a peg; to pull about one's ears; to trample in the dust.

(Adjectives) Depressed, sunk, prostrate.

309 Leap *(Substantives)*, jump, hop, spring, bound, vault, saltation.

Dance, caper, curvet, caracole, *entrechat*, gambade, gambado, capriole, dido, demivolt.

Kangaroo, jerboa, chamois, goat, frog, grasshopper, flea, buck-jumper.

(Phrases) Hop, skip, and jump; on the light fantastic toe.

(Verbs) To leap, jump, bound, spring, take off, buck, buck-jump, hop, skip, vault, dance, bob, curvet, romp, caracole, caper, cut capers.

(Adjectives) Leaping, etc., saltatory, Terpsichorean, frisky.

---

310 Plunge *(Substantives)*, dip, dive, ducking, header.

Diver, frogman.

(Verbs) To plunge, dip, souse, duck, dive, plump, plop, submerge, submerse, bathe, douse, sink, engulf, founder.

---

311 Curvilinear motion.

Circuition *(Substantives)*, turn, wind, circuit, curvet, detour, excursion, circumbendibus, circumvention, circumnavigation, north-west passage, circulation.

Turning, winding, twist, twisting, wrench, evolution, twining, coil, circumambulation, meandering.

(Verbs) To turn, bend, wheel, put about, switch, circle, go round, or round about, circumnavigate, circumambulate, turn a corner, double a point, wind, meander, whisk, twirl, twist (248), twill; to turn on one's heel.

(Phrases) To lead a pretty dance; to go the round; to turn on one's heel.

(Adjectives) Turning, etc., circuitous, circumforaneous, circumfluent.

(Adverb) Round about.

312 Motion in a continued circle.

Rotation *(Substantives)*, revolution, gyration, roll, circumrotation, circumgyration, gurgitation, pirouette, circumvolution, convolution, turbination, whir, whirl, eddy, vortex, whirlpool, cyclone, anticyclone, tornado, typhoon, whirlwind, willy-willy, waterspout, surge, dizzy round, maelstrom, Charybdis.

A wheel, flywheel, screw, reel, whirligig, rolling stone, windmill, top, teetotum, merry-go-round, roundabout, gyroscope, gyrostat.

Axis, axle, spindle, pivot, pin, hinge, pole, swivel, gimbals, mandrel.

(Verbs) To rotate, roll, revolve, spin, turn, turn round, circumvolve, circulate, gyre, gyrate, gimble, wheel, reel, whirl, twirl, birl, thrum, trundle, troll, twiddle, bowl, roll up, furl, wallow, welter.

(Phrases) To box the compass; to spin like a top.

(Adjectives) Rotating, etc., rotatory, rotary, circumrotatory, turbinate, trochoid, vortiginous, vortical, gyratory.

(Phrase) Like a squirrel in a cage.

(Adverbs) Clockwise, with the sun, deiseal (or deisil); counter-clockwise, against the sun, withershins (or widdershins).

313 Motion in a reverse circle.

Evolution *(Substantives)*, unfolding, etc., development, introversion, reversion, eversion.

(Verbs) To evolve, unfold, unroll, unwind, uncoil, untwist, unfurl, untwine, unravel disentangle (44), develop, introvert, reverse.

(Adjectives) Evolving, evolved, etc.

(Adverb) Against.

———

314 Reciprocating motion, motion to and fro.

Oscillation *(Substantives)*, vibration, undulation, pulsation, pulse, systole, diastole, libration, nutation, swing, beat, shake, seesaw, alternation, wag, evolution, vibratiuncle, coming and going, ebb and flow, flux and reflux; vibratility.

Fluctuation, vacillation, dance, lurch, dodge, rolling, tossing, etc.

A pendulum, seesaw, rocker, rocking-chair, rocking-horse, etc.

(Verbs) To oscillate, vibrate, undulate, librate, wave, rock, swing, sway, pulsate, beat, wag, waggle, wiggle, wobble, shoogle, nod, bob, tick, play, wamble, wabble, waddle, dangle, swag, curtsy.

To fluctuate, vacillate, alternate, dance, curvet, reel, quake, quiver, quaver, roll, top, pitch, flounder, stagger, totter, brandish, shake, flicker, flourish, seesaw, teeter, move up and down, to and fro, backwards and forwards, to pass and repass, to beat up and down.

(Adjectives) Oscillating, etc., oscillatory, vibratory, vibratile, vibrant, vibrational, undulatory, pulsatory, pendulous, libratory, systaltic.

(Adverbs) To and fro, up and down, backwards and forwards, seesaw, zigzag, wibble-wabble.

315 Irregular motion.

Agitation *(Substantives)*, stir, tremor, shake, ripple, jog, jolt, jar, succussion, trepidation, quiver, quaver, dance, jactitation, jactitancy, restlessness, shuffling, twitter, flicker, flutter, bobbing.

Disturbance, perturbation, commotion, turmoil, welter, bobbery; turbulence, tumult, tumultuation, bustle, fuss, flap, tirrivee, jerk, throw, convulsion, spasm (173), twitch, tic, staggers, St. Vitus's dance, epilepsy, writhing, ferment, fermentation, efferverscence, ebullition, hurly-burly, hubbub, stramash, *tohu-bohu*; tempest, storm, whirlwind, cyclone (312), ground swell.

(Verbs) To be agitated, to shake, tremble, quiver, quaver, shiver, dither,

twitter, twire, writhe, toss about, tumble, stagger, bob, reel, sway, wag, waggle, wiggle, wobble, shoogle, dance, wriggle, squirm, stumble, flounder, shuffle, totter, dodder, shamble, flounce, flop, curvet, prance, cavort, throb, pulsate, beat, palpitate, go pit-a-pat, fidget, flutter, flitter, flicker, bicker, twitch, jounce, ferment, effervesce, boil.

To agitate, shake, convulse, toss, tumble, bandy, wield, brandish, flap, flourish, whisk, switch, jerk, hitch, jolt, jog, hoggle, jostle, hustle, disturb, shake up, churn.

(Phrases) To jump like a parched pea; to be in a spin; to shake like an aspen leaf; to drive from pillar to post.

(Adjectives) Shaking, etc., agitated, tremulous, shivery, tottery, jerky, shaky, shoogly, quivery, quavery, trembly, choppy, rocky, wriggly, desultory, subsultory, shambling, giddy-paced, saltatory.

(Phrases) All of a tremble or twitter; like a pea on a drum; like a cat on hot bricks; like a hen on a hot griddle.

(Adverbs) By fits and starts; subsultorily, *per saltum* (139).

CLASS III
WORDS RELATING TO MATTER

SECTION I — MATTER IN GENERAL

316 Materiality *(Substantives)* corporeity, corporality, materialness, substantiality, physical condition.

Matter, body, substance, brute matter, stuff, element, principle, parenchyma, material, substratum, frame, *corpus pabulum*, flesh and blood.

Thing, object, article, still life, stocks and stones.

Physics, somatology, somatics, natural philosophy, physiography, physical science, experimental philosophy, positivism, materialism.

(Verbs) To materialize, embody, incarnate, objectify, externalize.

(Adjectives) Material, bodily, corporeal, corporal, carnal, temporal, physical, somatic, somatological, materialistic, sensible, palpable, tangible, ponderable, concrete, impersonal, objective, bodied.

317 Immateriality *(Substantives)*, incorporeity, spirituality, spirit, etc. (450), inextension.

Personality, I, me, myself, ego.

Spiritualism, spiritism, idealism, immaterialism.

(Verbs) To disembody, spiritualize, immaterialize.

(Adjectives) Immaterial, incorporeal, ideal, unextended, intangible, impalpable, imponderable, bodiless, unbodied, disembodied, extra-sensory, astral, psychical, psychic, extramundane, unearthly, supernatural, supranatural, transcendent, transcendental, pneumatoscopic, spiritualistic, spiritual (450).

Personal, subjective.

———

318 World *(Substantives)*, nature, creation, universe; earth, globe, wide world, cosmos, sphere, macrocosm.

The heavens, sky, welkin, empyrean, starry heaven, firmament, ether; vault or canopy of heaven; celestial spaces, starry host, heavenly bodies, star, constellation, galaxy, Milky Way, *via lactea*, nebula, etc., sun, moon, planet, asteroid, planetoid, satellite, comet, meteor, meteorite, shooting star.

Zodiac, ecliptic, colure, orbit.

Astronomy, astrophysics, uranography, uranology, cosmology, cosmography, cosmogony; planetarium, orrery.

An astronomer, star-gazer, cosmographer; observatory.

(Adjectives) Cosmic, cosmical, mundane, terrestrial, terraqueous, terrene, telluric, sublunary, under the sun, subastral, worldwide, global.

Celestial, heavenly, spheral, starry, stellar, nebular, etc., sidereal, sideral, astral, solar, lunar.

319 Heaviness *(Substantives)*, weight, gravity, gravitation, ponderosity, ponderousness, avoirdupois, pressure, load, burden, ballast; a

320 Lightness *(Substantives)*, levity, imponderability, subtlety, buoyancy, airiness, portability, volatility.

lump, mass, weight, counterweight, counterpoise; ponderability.

Lead, millstone, mountain.

Balance, spring balance, scales, steelyard, weighbridge.

Statics.

(Phrase) Pelion on Ossa.

(Verbs) To be heavy, to gravitate, weigh, press, cumber, load.

(Adjectives) Weighty, heavy, ponderous, gravitating, weighing, etc., ponderable, lumpish, cumbersome, hefty, massive, unwieldy, cumbrous, incumbent, superincumbent; gravitational.

(Phrase) Heavy as lead.

A feather, dust, mote, down, thistledown, flue, ooss, fluff, cobweb, gossamer, straw, cork, bubble; float, buoy; featherweight.

(Verbs) To be light, float, swim, be buoyed up.

(Adjectives) Light, subtle, airy, vaporous, imponderous, astatic, weightless, imponderable, ethereal, sublimated, floating, swimming, buoyant, air-borne, portable, uncompressed, volatile.

(Phrases) Light as a feather; light as thistledown; 'trifles light as air.'

SECTION II—INORGANIC MATTER

1°. *Solid Matter*

321 Density *(Substantives)*, denseness, solidness, solidity, impenetrability, incompressibility, cohesion, coherence, cohesiveness (46), imporosity, impermeability, closeness, compactness, constipation, consistence, spissitude, thickness.

Specific gravity; hydrometer, araeometer.

Condensation, consolidation, solidification, concretion, coagulation, conglomeration, petrification, lapidification, vitrification, crystallization, precipitation, inspissation, thickening, grittiness, knottiness, induration (323).

Indivisibility, indiscerptibility, indissolubility.

322 Rarity *(Substantives)*, tenuity, absence of solidity, subtility, sponginess, compressibility; hollowness (252).

Rarefaction, expansion, dilatation, inflation, dilution, attenuation, subtilization.

Ether, vapour, air, gas (334).

(Verbs) To rarefy, expand, dilate, dilute, attenuate, subtilize, thin out.

(Adjectives) Rare, subtle, sparse, slight, thin, fine, tenuous, compressible.

Porous, cavernous, spongy, bibulous, spongious, spongeous.

Rarefied, expanded, dilated, subtilized, unsubstantial, hollow (252).

A solid body, mass, block, knot, lump, concretion, concrete, cake, clot, stone, curd, coagulum, clinker, nugget; deposit, precipitate.

(Verbs) To be dense, etc.

To become or render solid; solidify, solidate, concrete, set, consolidate, congeal, jelly, jell, coagulate, curdle, curd, fix, clot, cake, cohere, crystallize, petrify, vitrify, condense, incrassate, thicken, inspissate, compact, concentrate, compress, squeeze, ram down, constipate.

(Adjectives) Dense, solid, solidified, consolidated, etc., coherent, cohesive, compact, close, thick-set, serried, substantial, massive, lumpish, impenetrable, incompressible, impermeable, imporous, constipated, concrete, knotted, gnarled, crystalline, crystallizable, vitreous, coagulated, thick, incrassated, inspissated, curdled, clotted, grumous.

Undissolved, unmelted, unliquefied, unthawed,

Indivisible, indiscerptible, infrangible, indissolvable, indissoluble, insoluble, infusible.

323 Hardness *(Substantives)*, rigidity, rigescence, firmness, renitence, inflexibility, stiffness, starchiness, starchedness, temper, callosity, durity, induration, grittiness, petrifaction, etc. (321), ossification, sclerosis.

A stone, pebble, flint, marble, rock, granite, brick, iron, steel, corundum, diamond, adamant, bone, callus.

(Verbs) To render hard, harden, stiffen, indurate, petrify, vitrify, temper, ossify.

(Adjectives) Hard, horny, corneous, bony, osseous, rigid, rigescent, stiff, firm, starch, stark, unbending, unyielding, inflexible, tense, indurate, indurated, gritty, stony, proof, adamantean, adamantine.

(Phrases) Hard as iron, etc.; hard as a brick; hard as a nail; hard as a deal board; 'as hard as a piece of the nether millstone'; stiff as buckram; stiff as a poker.

---

325 Elasticity *(Substantives)*, springiness, spring, resilience, buoyancy, renitency, contractility (195), compressibility.

Indiarubber, rubber, caoutchouc, whalebone, elastic.

(Verbs) To be elastic, etc., to spring back, fly back, rebound, recoil (277).

(Adjectives) Elastic, tensile, springy, resilient, buoyant.

327 Toughness *(Substantives)*, tenacity, strength, cohesion (46), stubbornness (606).

Leather, gristle, cartilage.

(Verbs) To be tenacious, etc., to resist fracture.

(Adjectives) Tenacious, tough, wiry, sinewy, stringy, stubborn, cohesive, strong, resisting, resistant, leathery, coriaceous.

(Phrase) Tough as leather.

---

324 Softness *(Substantives)*, tenderness, flexibility, pliancy, pliableness, pliantness, litheness, pliability, suppleness, sequacity, ductility, malleability, tractility, extensibility, plasticity, inelasticity, laxity, flaccidity, flabbiness, limpness.

Clay, wax, butter, dough; a cushion, pillow, featherbed, down, padding, wadding, cotton-wool.

Mollification, softening, etc.

(Verbs) To render soft, soften, mollify, relax, temper, mash, pulp, knead, squash.

To bend, yield, give, relent, relax.

(Adjectives) Soft, tender, supple, pliable, limp, limber, flexible, flexile, lithe, lissom, *svelte*, willowy, pliant, plastic, waxen, ductile, tractile, tractable, malleable, extensile, sequacious.

Yielding, bending, flabby, flaccid, lymphatic, flocculent, downy, flimsy, spongy, oedematous, doughy, argillaceous, mellow; emollient, softening, etc.

(Phrases) Soft as butter; soft as down; soft as silk; yielding as wax; tender as a chicken.

326 Inelasticity *(Substantives)*, want or absence of elasticity, softness, etc. (324).

(Adjectives) Inelastic, ductile, limber, etc. (324).

---

328 Brittleness *(Substantives)*, fragility, crispness, friability, frangibility, fissility.

(Verbs) To be brittle, break, crack, snap, split, shiver, splinter, fracture, crumble, break short, burst, fly.

(Adjectives) Brittle, frangible, fragile, frail, jerry-built, gimcrack, shivery, fissile, splitting, splintery, lacerable, crisp, friable, short, crumbling.

(Phrases) Brittle as glass; a house of cards.

329 Texture *(Substantives)* structure, construction, organization, set-up, organism, anatomy, frame, mould, fabric, framework, carcass, architecture, *compages*; substance, stuff, parenchyma, constitution, intertexture, contexture, tissue, grain, web, warp, woof, nap (256).

Fineness or coarseness of grain.

Histology.

(Adjectives) Textural, structural, organic, anatomic, anatomical; fine, delicate, subtle, fine-grained; coarse, homespun, rough-grained, coarse-grained; flimsy, unsubstantial, gossamery, filmy, gauzy.

330 Pulverulence *(Substantives)*, state of powder, powderiness, efflorescence, sandiness, friability.

Dust, stour (or stoor), powder, sand, shingle, sawdust, grit, meal, bran, flour, limature, filings, debris, detritus, moraine, scobs, crumb, seed, grain, spore, atom, particle (32), flocculence.

Reduction to powder, pulverization, comminution, granulation, disintegration, weathering, subaction, contusion, trituration, levigation, abrasion, detrition, filing, etc. (331).

Mill, quern, grater, nutmeg grater, rasp, file, pestle and mortar.

(Verbs) To reduce to powder, to pulverize, comminute, granulate, triturate, levigate, scrape, file, abrade, rub down, grind, grate, rasp, mill, pound, bray, bruise, contuse, contund, beat, crush, crunch, scrunch, crumble, disintegrate, weather.

(Adjectives) Powdery, granular, mealy, floury, branny, farinaceous, furfuraceous, flocculent, dusty, sandy, sabulous, arenaceous, gritty, efflorescent, impalpable; pulverizable, pulverulent, friable, crumbly, shivery, pulverized, etc., attrite.

331 Friction *(Substantives)*, attrition, rubbing, massage, abrasion, rub, scouring, limature, filing, rasping, frication, elbow-grease.

Grindstone, whetstone, buff, hone, strop (253).

(Verbs) To rub, abrade, scratch, scrape, scrub, grate, fray, rasp, pare, scour, polish, massage, curry, shampoo, rub out.

332 Absence of friction.

Lubrication *(Substantives)*, prevention of friction, oiling, etc., anointment.

Lubricant, oil, lard, grease, etc. (356); synovia, saliva.

(Verbs) To lubricate, oil, grease, anoint, wax; smooth (255).

(Adjectives) Lubricated, etc.

2°. *Fluid Matter*

1. FLUIDS IN GENERAL

333 Fluidity *(Substantives)*, fluid (including both inelastic and elastic fluids).

Inelastic fluid.

Liquidity, liquidness, aquosity, a liquid, liquor, lymph, humour, juice, sap, blood, serum, serosity, gravy, chyle, rheum, ichor, sanies; solubility.

Hydrology, hydrostatics, hydrodynamics.

334 Elastic fluid.

Gaseity, vaporousness, flatulence, flatulency; gas, air, vapour, ether, steam, fume, reek, effluvium.

Smoke, cloud (353).

Pneumatics, aerostatics, aerodynamics; gas-meter, gasometer.

(Verbs) To be fluid or liquid, to flow, run (348).

(Adjectives) Liquid, fluid, fluent, running, flowing, serous, juicy, succulent, sappy, lush.

Liquefied, uncongealed, melted, etc. (335).

335 Liquefaction *(Substantives)*, liquescence, fusion, melting, thaw, deliquation, deliquescence, lixiviation.

Solution, dissolution, decoction, infusion, apozem, flux.

Solvent, menstruum, alkahest.

(Verbs) To render liquid, to liquefy, deliquesce, run, melt, thaw, fuse, solve, dissolve, resolve, to hold in solution.

(Adjectives) Liquefied, melted, unfrozen, molten, liquescent, liquefiable, deliquescent, diffluent, soluble, dissoluble.

(Verbs) To emit vapour, evaporate, to steam, fume, reek, smoke, puff, smoulder.

(Adjectives) Gaseous, aeriform, ethereal, aerial, airy, vaporous, vapoury, flatulent, volatile, evaporable.

336 Vaporization *(Substantives)*, gasification, volatilization, evaporation, distillation, sublimation, exhalation, volatility.

Vaporizer, retort, still.

(Verbs) To render gaseous, vaporize, volatilize, evaporate, exhale, distil, sublime, sublimate.

(Adjectives) Volatilized, etc., volatile, evaporable, vaporizable.

---

2. SPECIFIC FLUIDS

337 Water *(Substantives)*, heavy water, serum, lymph, rheum, whey.

Dilution, immersion, maceration, humectation, infiltration, sprinkling, washing, spraying, aspersion, affusion, irrigation, douche, balneation, bath, shower-bath, inundation, deluge (348), a diluent.

(Verbs) To be watery, etc., to reek.

To add water, to water, wet, moisten (339), dilute, dip, immerse, plunge, merge, immerge, steep, souse, duck, submerge, drown, soak, saturate, sop, macerate, pickle, blunge, wash, lave, springle, asperge, asperse, dabble, bedabble, affuse, splash, splatter, spray, swash, douse, drench, slop, slobber, irrigate, inundate, deluge, flood.

To take a bath, to tub, bathe, bath, paddle.

To syringe, inject, gargle.

(Adjectives) Watery (339), aqueous, aquatic, lymphatic, diluted, etc., reeking, dripping, sodden, drenched, soaking, sopping.

Wet, washy, sloppy, squashy, splashy, soppy, soggy, slobbery, diluent, balneal.

(Phrases) Wet as a drowned rat; soaked to the skin; wet as a rag; wet through.

338 Air *(Substantives)*, common air, atmospheric air.

The atmosphere, troposphere, tropopause, stratosphere, ionosphere, Heaviside layer, Appleton layer; the sky, the ether, the open air, ozone, weather, climate.

Meteorology, climatology, isobar, barometer, aneroid barometer, weather-glass, weather-chart, weather station, weather ship.

Exposure to the air or weather, airing, weathering (330).

(Verbs) To aerate, oxygenate, arterialize, ventilate, air-condition.

(Adjectives) Containing air, windy, flatulent, aerated, effervescent.

Atmospheric, airy, open-air, *plein-air,* alfresco, aerial, aeriform; meteorological, barometric, weather-wise.

(Adverbs) In the open air, *à la belle étoile, sub Jove.*

339 Moisture *(Substantives)*, moistness, humidity, dampness, damp, wetness, wet, humectation, madefaction, dew, muddiness, marsh (345).

Hygrometer, hygrometry, hygrology.

(Verbs) To be moist, etc.

To moisten, wet, humectate, sponge, damp, dampen, bedew, imbue, infiltrate, imbrue; soak, saturate (337).

(Adjectives) Moist, damp, watery, humid, wet, dank, muggy, dewy, roral, rorid, roscid, juicy, swampy (345), humectant, sopping, dripping, sodden.

(Phrase) Wringing wet.

340 Dryness *(Substantives)*, siccity, aridity, drought.

Exsiccation, desiccation, arefaction, drainage.

(Verbs) To be dry, etc.

To render dry, to dry, dry up, sop up, swab, wipe, blot, exsiccate, desiccate, dehydrate, drain, parch.

(Adjectives) Dry, anhydrous, dehydrated, arid, dried, etc., unwatered, undamped, waterproof, husky, juiceless, sapless; siccative, desiccative.

(Phrases) Dry as a bone; dry as dust; dry as a stick; dry as a mummy; dry as a biscuit; dry as a limekiln.

---

341 Ocean *(Substantives)*, sea, main, the deep, brine, salt water, blue water, high seas, offing, tide, wave, surge, ooze, etc. (348).

Hydrography, oceanography.

Neptune, Thetis, Triton, Oceanid, Nereid, sea-nymph, siren, mermaid, merman, dolphin; trident.

(Phrases) The vasty deep; the briny; the ditch; the drink.

(Adjectives) Oceanic, marine, maritime, thalassic, pelagic, pelagian, seagoing, hydrographic.

(Adverbs) At sea, on sea, afloat.

342 Land *(Substantives)*, earth, ground, terra firma, continent, mainland, peninsula, delta, alluvium, polder, tongue of land, neck of land, isthmus, oasis.

Coast, shore, seaboard, seaside, seabank, strand, beach, bank, lea.

Cape, promontory, etc. (250), headland, point of land, highland (206).

Soil, glebe, clay, humus, loam, marl, clod, clot, rock, crag, chalk, gravel, mould, subsoil.

(Adjectives) Terrene, continental, earthy, terraqueous, terrestrial.

Littoral, riparian, alluvial, midland.

(Adverbs) Ashore, on shore, on land.

---

343 Gulf *(Substantives)*, bay, inlet, bight, estuary, roadstead, roads, arm of the sea, armlet, sound, frith, firth, fiord, lagoon, cove, creek, strait, belt, kyle, Euripus.

(Adjectives) Estuarine.

Lake *(Substantives)*, loch, lough, mere, tarn, linn, plash, broad, pond, dew-pond, pool, puddle, well, reservoir, standing water, dead water, a sheet of water, fish-pond, ditch, dike, backwater.

(Adjectives) Lacustrine (or lacustrian), lacuscular.

344 Plain *(Substantives)*, tableland, open country, the face of the country, champaign country, basin, downs, waste, wild, weald, steppe, pampas, savanna, llano, prairie, tundra, heath, common, wold, moor, moorland, the bush; plateau, flat (213).

Meadow, mead, haugh, pasturage, park, field, lawn, green, plot, plat, terrace, esplanade, sward, turf, sod, heather, lea, grounds, pleasuregrounds, playing-fields, campus.

(Phrase) A weary waste.

(Adjectives) Campestrian, champaign, lawny.

345 Marsh *(Substantives)*, marish, swamp, morass, moss, fen, bog, quag, quagmire, slough, sump, wash.

(Adjectives) Marshy, marish, swampy, boggy, quaggy, fenny, soft, plashy, poachy, paludal.

346 Island *(Substantives)*, isle, islet, ait, eyot, inch, holm, reef, atoll; archipelago.

(Adjectives) Insular, sea-girt.

---

3. FLUIDS IN MOTION

347 Fluid in motion.

Stream *(Substantives)*, flow, current, jet, undercurrent, course (348).

(Verb) To flow, stream, issue, run.

348 Water in motion.

River *(Substantives)*, running water, jet, spurt, squirt, spout, splash, rush, gush, water-spout, sluice, linn, waterfall, cascade, force, catadupe, cataract, debacle, cataclysm, inundation, deluge, avalanche, spate.

Rain, shower, scud, driving rain, downpour, drencher, soaker, cloudburst, mizzle, drizzle, Scotch mist, smirr, dripping, stillicidium; flux, flow, profluence, effluence, efflux, effluxion, defluxion.

Irrigation (337).

Spring, fountain, fount, rill, rivulet, gill, gullet, rillet, streamlet, runnel, sike, burn, beck, brooklet, brook, stream, reach, torrent, rapids, race, flush, flood, swash.

Tide, spring tide, high tide, tidal wave, bore, eagre, freshet, current, indraught, reflux, eddy, whirlpool, vortex, maelstrom, regurgitation.

Tributary, confluent, effluent, billabong; corrivation, confluence, effluence.

Wave, billow, surge, swell, chop, ripple, ground swell, surf, breaker, roller, comber, white caps, white horses.

Irrigation (337); sprinkler, sprayer, spray, atomizer, aspergillum, aspersorium, water-cart, watering-pot, watering-can, pump, syringe, hydrant.

Hydraulics, hydrodynamics, hydrography; rain-gauge.

(Verbs) To flow, run, meander, gush, spout, roll, billow, surge, jet, well, drop, drip, trickle, dribble, ooze (295), percolate, distil, transude,

349 Air in motion.

Wind *(Substantives)*, draught, current, breath, air, breath of air, puff, whiff, zephyr, blow, drift, aura.

Gust, blast, breeze, squall, gale, storm, tempest, hurricane, whirlwind, tornado, cyclone, typhoon, blizzard, simoom, samiel, harmattan, monsoon, trade wind, sirocco, mistral, *bise, tramontana, föhn*, pampero; windiness, ventosity.

Aeolus, Boreas, Auster, Euroclydon, the cave of Aeolus.

Bellows, blowpipe, fan, ventilator, punkah.

Anemometer, anemograph, windgauge, weathercock, vane.

Insufflation, sufflation, perflation, blowing, fanning, ventilation, blowing up, inflation, afflation; respiration, inspiration, expiration, sneezing, sternutation, cough, hiccup.

(Phrase) A capful of wind.

(Verbs) To blow, waft, blow hard, blow a hurricane, breathe, respire, inspire, expire, insufflate, puff, whiff, sough, whiffle, wheeze, gasp, snuffle, sniffle, sneeze, cough.

To fan, ventilate, inflate, perflate, blow up.

(Phrase) To blow great guns.

(Adjectives) Blowing, etc., rough, blowy, windy, breezy, gusty, squally, puffy, stormy, tempestuous, blustering.

stream, sweat, perspire (299), overflow, flow over, splash, swash, guggle, murmur, babble, bubble, purl, gurgle, sputter, spurt, regurgitate, surge.

To rain, rain hard, pour with rain, drizzle, spit, mizzle, set in.

To flow into, fall into, open into, drain into, discharge itself, disembogue, disgorge, debouch.

(Phrases) To rain cats and dogs; to rain in torrents.

To cause a flow, to pour, drop, distil, splash, squirt, spill, drain, empty, discharge, pour out, open the sluices or flood-gates; shower down, irrigate (337).

To stop a flow, to stanch, dam, dam up (261), intercept.

(Adjectives) Fluent, profluent, affluent, confluent, diffluent, tidal, flowing, etc., babbling, bubbling, gurgling, meandering, meandrous.

Fluviatile, fluvial, riverine, streamy, showery, drizzly, rainy, pluvial, pouring.

350 Channel for the passage of water.

Conduit *(Substantives)*, channel, duct, watercourse, watershed, race, adit, aqueduct, canal, sluice, dike, main, gully, moat, ditch, lode, leat, rhine, trough, gutter, drain, sewer, culvert, cloaca, sough, kennel, siphon, pipe (260), emunctory, gully-hole, artery, aorta, pore, spout, funnel, tap, faucet, scupper, adjutage (or ajutage), waste-pipe, hose, rose, gargoyle, artesian well.

Floodgate, dam, weir, levee, water-gate, lock, valve.

351 Channel for the passage of air.

Air-pipe *(Substantives)*, air-tube, shaft, flue, chimney, lum, funnel, smoke-stack, exhaust-pipe, exhaust, vent, blow-hole, nostril, nozzle, throat, weasand, trachea, larynx, windpipe, thrapple, spiracle, ventiduct.

Ventilator, louvre, register.

Tobacco-pipe, pipe, etc. (298A).

3°. *Imperfect Fluids*

352 Semiliquidity *(Substantives)*, pulpiness, viscidity, viscosity, ropiness, sliminess, gumminess, glutinosity, gummosity, siziness, clamminess, mucosity, spissitude, lentor, thickness, crassitude.

Inspissation, thickening, incrassation.

Jelly, mucilage, gelatine, mucus, chyme, phlegm, gum, glue, gluten, goo, colloid, albumen, size, milk, cream, emulsion, soup, broth, starch, treacle, squash, mud, clart, glaur, slush, slime, ooze, dope, glycerine; lava.

Pitch, tar, bitumen, asphalt, resin, rosin, varnish, copal, mastic, wax, amber.

(Verbs) To inspissate, thicken, incrassate, jelly, jellify, mash, squash, churn, beat up, pulp.

(Adjectives) Semi-fluid, semi-

353 Mixture of air and water.

Bubble *(Substantives)*, soda-water, aerated water, foam, froth, head, spume, lather, bleb, spray, spindrift, surf, yeast, barm, suds.

Cloud, vapour, fog, mist, smog, haze, steam, nebulosity (422); scud, rack, cumulus, cirrus, stratus, nimbus, mare's tail, mackerel sky.

Nephelology; Fido.

Effervescence, foaming, mantling, fermentation, frothing, etc.

(Verbs) To bubble, boil, foam, froth, mantle, sparkle, guggle, gurgle, effervesce, fizz, ferment.

(Adjectives) Bubbling, etc., frothy, yeasty, barmy, nappy, effervescent, fizzy, up, boiling, fermenting, sparkling, mantling, *mousseux*.

Cloudy, foggy, misty, vaporous, nebulous.

---

liquid, milky, emulsive, creamy, lacteal, lacteous, curdy, curdled, soupy, muddy, slushy, clarty, thick, succulent, squashy.

Gelatinous, albuminous, gummy, colloid, amylaceous, mucilaginous, glairy, slimy, ropy, stringy, clammy, glutinous (46), viscid, viscous, sticky, gooey, slab, slabby, sizy, lentous, tacky.

Tarry, pitchy, resinous, bituminous.

354 Pulpiness *(Substantives)*, pulp, paste, dough, curd, pap, pudding, poultice, soup, squash, mud, slush, grume, jam, preserve.

(Adjectives) Pulpy, pulpous, pultaceous, doughy, grumous.

355 Unctuousness *(Substantives)*, unctuosity, oiliness, greasiness, slipperiness, lubricity.

Lubrication (332), anointment, unction; ointment (356).

(Verbs) To oil, grease, anoint, wax, lubricate (332).

(Adjectives) Unctuous, oily, oleaginous, adipose, sebaceous, fat, fatty, greasy, waxy, butyraceous, soapy, saponaceous, pinguid, stearic, lardaceous.

356 Oil *(Substantives)*, fat, butter, margarine, cream, grease, tallow, suet, lard, dripping, blubber, pomatum, pomade, stearin, lanoline, soap, soft soap, wax, beeswax, sealing-wax, ambergris, spermaceti, adipocere, ointment, unguent, liniment, paraffin, kerosene, gasolene, petroleum, petrol, mineral oil, vegetable oil, olive oil, castor oil, linseed oil, train oil.

SECTION III—ORGANIC MATTER

1°. *Vitality*

1. VITALITY IN GENERAL

357 Organization *(Substantives)*, the organized world, organized nature, living nature, animated nature, living beings; protoplasm, protein.

Biology, ecology (or oecology), natural, history, organic chemistry, zoology (368), botany (369).

(Adjectives) Organic, animate.

358 Inorganization *(Substantives)*, the mineral world or kingdom; unorganized, inorganic, brute, or inanimate matter.

Mineralogy, geognosy, petrology, lithology, geology, metallurgy, inorganic chemistry.

(Adjectives) Inorganic, azoic, mineral, inanimate.

359 Life *(Substantives)*, vitality, animation, viability, the vital spark or flame or principle, the breath of life, life-blood; existence (1).

Vivification, revivification.

Physiology, biology; metabolism.

(Phrase) The breath of one's nostrils.

(Verbs) To be living, alive, etc., to live, subsist (1), breathe, fetch breath, respire, draw breath, to be born, be spared.

360 Death *(Substantives)*, decease, dissolution, demise, departure, obit, expiration; termination, close or extinction of life, existence, etc.; mortality, fall, doom, fate, release, rest, end, quietus, loss, bereavement, euthanasia, katabolism.

Last breath, last gasp, last agonies, the death-rattle, dying breath, agonies of death, dying agonies.

Necrology, death-roll, obituary.

(Phrases) The ebb of life; the king

To come to life, to revive, come to.

To give birth to (161); to bring, restore, or recall to life, to vivify, revive, revivify, quicken, reanimate, vitalize.

(Phrases) To see the light; to come into the world; to walk the earth; to draw breath.

To keep body and soul together; to support life.

(Adjectives) Living, alive, in life, above ground, breathing, animated, quick, viable.

Vital, vivifying, vivified, Promethean, metabolic.

(Phrases) Alive and kicking; in the land of the living; on this side of the grave.

---

of terrors; the jaws of death; the swan-song; the Stygian shore; the sleep that knows no waking; a watery grave.

(Verbs) To die, perish, expire.

(Phrases) Breathe one's last; cease to live; depart this life; end one's days; be no more; go off; drop off; pop off; peg out; lose one's life; drop down dead; resign, relinquish, lay down, or surrender one's life; drop or sink into the grave; close one's eyes; break one's neck.

To give up the ghost; to be all over with one; to pay the debt to nature; to make the great change; to take one's last sleep; to shuffle off this mortal coil; to go to one's last home; to go the way of all flesh; to kick the bucket; to hop the twig; to turn up one's toes; to slip one's cable; to cross the Stygian ferry.

To snuff out; to go off the hooks; to go to one's account; to go aloft; to join the majority; to go west; to have had it; to be numbered with the dead; to die a natural death; to hand in one's checks; to pass away or over.

(Adjectives) Dead, lifeless, deceased, demised, gone, departed, defunct, exanimate, inanimate, *kaput*, out of the world, mortuary; still-born.

Dying, expiring, moribund, *in articulo mortis, in extremis,* in the agony of death, etc., going, life ebbing, going off, life failing, *aux abois,* booked, having received one's death warrant.

(Phrases) Dead and gone; dead as a door-nail, as mutton, as a doorpost, as a herring; stone-dead; launched into eternity; gone to one's last home; gathered to one's fathers; gone to Davy Jones's locker; gone west; gone for a Burton; pushing up the daisies.

At death's door; on one's death-bed; in the jaws of death; death staring one in the face; one's hour being come; one's days being numbered; one's race being run; one foot in the grave; on one's last legs; life hanging by a thread; at one's last gasp.

(Adverbs) Post-mortem, post-obit.

361 Destruction of life, violent death.

Killing *(Substantives)*, homicide, parricide, matricide, fratricide, sororicide, infanticide, regicide, tyrannicide, vaticide, genocide, manslaughter, murder, assassination, blood, gore, bloodshed, slaughter, carnage, butchery, massacre, immolation, holocaust, fusillade, *noyade*, thuggee, thuggery, thuggism; casualty, fatality.

Death-blow, kiss of death, *coup de grâce*, grace-stroke, mercy killing, euthanasia.

Suicide, felo-de-se, hara-kiri, happy dispatch, suttee, martyrdom, execution.

Destruction of animals, slaughtering, battue, hecatomb.

Slaughter-house, shambles, abattoir.

A butcher, slayer, murderer, homicide, parricide, matricide, etc., assassin, cut-throat, bravo, thug, executioner (975).

(Verbs) To kill, put to death, do to death, slay, murder, assassinate, slaughter, butcher, immolate, massacre, decimate, take away or deprive of life, make away with, dispatch, burke, lynch, settle, do for, do in, bump off, brain, spiflicate.

To strangle, throttle, bowstring, choke, garrotte, stifle, suffocate, smother, asphyxiate, drown, hang, turn off, string up.

To cut down, sabre, cut to pieces, cut off, cut the throat, stab, knife, bayonet, shoot, behead, decapitate, stone, lapidate, execute (972).

To commit suicide, to make away with oneself.

(Phrases) To put to the sword; put to the edge of the sword; give no quarter to; run through the body; knock on the head; give one the works; put one on the spot; blow the brains out; give the death blow; the *coup de grâce*; put out of one's misery; launch into eternity; give a quietus to.

(Adjectives) Killing, etc., murderous, slaughterous, sanguinary, ensanguined, gory, bloody, blood-stained, blood-guilty, red-handed.

Mortal, fatal, deadly, lethal, internecine, suicidal, homicidal, fratricidal, etc.

362 Corpse *(Substantives)*, corse, carcass, bones, skeleton, carrion, defunct, relic, remains, ashes, earth, dust, clay, mummy.

Shade, ghost, *manes*; the dead, the majority, the great majority.

(Phrases) All that was mortal; this tenement of clay; food for worms or fishes.

(Adjectives) Cadaverous, corpse-like.

363 Interment *(Substantives)*, burial, sepulture, inhumation, obsequies, exequies, funeral, wake, lyke-wake, pyre, funeral pile, cremation.

Funeral rite or solemnity, knell, passing-bell, tolling, dirge, lament, coronach, keening (839), requiem, epicedium, obit, elegy, funeral oration, epitaph, death march, dead march, lying in state.

Grave-clothes, shroud, winding-sheet, cerecloth, cerement.

Coffin, casket, shell, sarcophagus, urn, pall, bier, hearse, catafalque.

Grave, pit, sepulchre, tomb, vault, catacomb, mausoleum, house of death, burial-place, cemetery, necropolis, churchyard, graveyard, God's acre, burial-ground, cromlech, dolmen, barrow, tumulus, cairn, ossuary, charnel-house, morgue, mortuary, crematorium, cinerator; Valhalla.

Monument, tombstone, gravestone, shrine, cenotaph.

Exhumation, disinterment; autopsy, necropsy, post-mortem.

Undertaker, mortician, mute, sexton, grave-digger.

(Verbs) To inter, bury, lay in the grave, consign to the grave or tomb, entomb, inhume, cremate, lay out, embalm, mummify.

To exhume, disinter.

(Adjectives) Buried, etc., burial, funereal, funebrial, funerary, mortuary, sepulchral, cinerary; elegiac.

(Phrases) Hic jacet; R.I.P.

2. SPECIAL VITALITY

364 Animality *(Substantives)*, animal life, animality, animation, breath, animalization.

Flesh, flesh and blood, physique.

(Verb) To animalize.

(Adjectives) Fleshly, corporal, carnal.

365 Vegetability *(Substantives)*, vegetable life, vegetation.

(Adjectives) Lush, rank, luxuriant.

366 Animal *(Substantives)*, the animal kingdom, brute creation, fauna, avifauna.

A beast, brute, creature, created being; creeping or living thing, dumb creature, flocks and herds, live-stock.

Cattle, kine, etc.

Game, *fera natura*, wild life.

Mammal, quadruped, bird, reptile, fish, mollusc, worm, insect, zoophyte, animalcule, etc.

(Phrases) The beasts of the field; fowls of the air; denizens of the deep.

(Adjectives) Animal, zoological, piscatory, fishy, molluscous, vermicular, etc., feral.

368 The science of animals.

Zoology *(Substantives)*, zoography, anatomy, zootomy, comparative anatomy, physiology, morphology.

Ornithology, ichthyology, herpetology, ophiology, malacology, helminthology, entomology, palaeontology.

370 The economy or management of animals.

Taming *(Substantives)*, domestication, domesticity; training, breaking-in, manège, breeding, pisciculture; veterinary art.

Menagerie, zoological garden, game reserve, aviary, apiary, vivarium, aquarium, fishery, fish-pond, duck-pond.

(Verbs) To tame, domesticate, train, tend, break in.

(Adjectives) Pastoral, bucolic.

367 Plant *(Substantives)*, vegetable, the vegetable kingdom, flora.

Tree, fruit-tree, shrub, bush, creeper, herb, herbage, grass, fern, fungus, lichen, moss, weed, seaweed, alga; annual, biennial, perennial; exotic.

Forest, wood, hurst, holt, greenwood, woodland, brake, grove, copse, coppice, hedgerow, boscage, plantation, thicket, spinney, underwood, undergrowth, brushwood, clump of trees, park, chase, weald, scrub, jungle, prairie.

Foliage, florescence, flower, blossom, branch, bough, spray, twig, leaf.

(Adjectives) Vegetable, vegetal, arboreal, herbaceous, herbal, botanic, sylvan, woodland, woody, wooded, well-wooded, shrubby, grassy, verdurous, verdant, floral, mossy.

369 The science of plants.

Botany *(Substantives)*, phytography, phytology, vegetable physiology, herborization, dendrology, mycology, Pomona, Flora, Ceres.

Herbarium, herbal, *hortus siccus*, vasculum.

(Verbs) To botanize, herborize.

371 The economy or management of plants.

Agriculture *(Substantives)*, cultivation, culture, intensive cultivation, husbandry, agronomy, geoponics, hydroponics, georgics, tillage, gardening, arboriculture, floriculture, the topiary art.

Vineyard, vinery, garden, kitchen garden, market garden, nursery, bed, plot, herbaceous border, parterre, hothouse, greenhouse, conservatory, espalier, shrubbery, orchard, rock garden, rockery, winter garden, pinery, arboretum, allotment.

A husbandman, horticulturist, gardener, florist, agriculturist, agriculturalist, woodcutter, backwoodsman, forester, land girl, farmer, yeoman, cultivator.

(Verbs) To cultivate, till, garden, farm; delve, dibble, dig, sow, plant, graft; plough, harrow, rake, reap, mow, cut, weed.

(Adjectives) Agricultural, agrarian, arable, rural, country, rustic, agrestic.

372 Mankind *(Substantives)*, the human race or species; man, human nature, humanity, mortality, flesh, generation; Everyman.

Anthropology, anthropography, ethnology, ethnography, demography, sociology, social economics; civics.

Anthropomorphism.

Human being, person, individual, type, creature, fellow creature, mortal, body, somebody, one, someone, a soul, living soul, earthling, party, personage, inhabitant; *dramatis personae*.

People, persons, folk, population, public, world, race, society, community, the million, commonalty (876), nation, state, realm, community, commonwealth, republic, commonweal, polity, nationality; civilized society, civilization.

Anthropologist, ethnologist, sociologist, etc.

(Phrases) The lords of creation; the body politic.

(Adjectives) National, civic, public, human, mortal, personal, individual, social, cosmopolitan, ethnic, racial; sociological, anthropological, ethnological, anthropomorphic, anthropomorphous, anthropoid, manlike.

---

373 Man *(Substantives)*, manhood, manliness, virility, he, menfolk.

A human being, man, male, mortal, person, body, soul, individual, fellow creature, one, someone, somebody, so-and-so.

Personage, a gentleman, sir, master, yeoman, citizen, denizen, burgess, burgher, cosmopolite, wight, swain, fellow, blade, bloke, beau, chap, guy, bod, type, cove, gossoon, buffer, gaffer, goodman; husband (903).

(Adjectives) Human, manly, male, masculine, manlike, mannish, virile, mannish, unwomanly, unfeminine.

(Phrase) The spear side.

---

374 Woman *(Substantives)*, female, feminality, femininity, womanhood, muliebrity, girlhood, she, womenfolk.

Womankind, the sex, the fair, the fair sex, the softer sex, the weaker vessel, a petticoat, skirt.

Dame, madam, madame, ma'am, mistress, lady, gentlewoman, donna, belle, matron, dowager, goody, gammer, good woman, goodwife; wife (903).

Damsel, girl, lass, lassie, maid (209), maiden, *demoiselle*, flapper, miss, missie, nymph, wench, bint, floosy, popsy, pusher, jade, dona, grisette, colleen.

(Adjectives) Female, feminine, womanly, ladylike, matronly, maidenly, girlish; womanish, effeminate, unmanly, pansy.

(Phrase) The distaff side.

2°. *Sensation*

1. SENSATION IN GENERAL

375 Physical Sensibility *(Substantives)*, sensitiveness, sensitivity, feeling, perceptivity, acuteness; allergy, idiosyncrasy; moral sensibility (822).

Sensation, impression consciousness (490).

The external senses.

(Verbs) To be sensible of, to feel, perceive, be conscious of, respond to, react to.

376 Physical Insensibility *(Substantives)*, obtuseness, dullness, paralysis, anaesthesia, analgesia, sleep, trance, stupor, coma, catalepsy; moral insensibility (823).

Anaesthetic, opium, ether, chloroform, chloral, cocaine, morphia, laudanum, nitrous oxide, laughing gas.

Anaesthetics.

(Verbs) To be insensible, etc. To

To render sensible, to sharpen, cultivate, train, tutor, condition.

To cause sensation; to impress, excite, or produce an impression.

(Adjectives) Sensible, conscious, sensitive, sensuous, aesthetic, perceptive.

Hypersensitive, thin-skinned, neurotic, hyperaesthetic, allergic.

Acute, sharp, keen, vivid, lively, impressive.

(Adverb) To the quick.

render insensible, to blunt, dull, obtund, benumb, deaden, stupefy, stun, paralyse, anaesthetize, dope, hocus, gas.

(Adjectives) Insensible, unfeeling, senseless, impercipient, impassable, thick-skinned, pachydermatous, hardened, proof, apathetic, obtuse, dull, anaesthetic, paralytic, palsied, numb, dead, unaffected, untouched.

(Phrase) Having a rhinoceros hide.

377 Physical Pleasure *(Substantives)*, bodily enjoyment, gratification, titillation, comfort, luxury, voluptuousness, sensuousness, sensuality; mental pleasure (827).

(Phrases) The flesh-pots of Egypt; creature comforts; a bed of roses; a bed of down; on velvet; in clover.

(Verbs) To feel, experience, receive, etc., pleasure, to enjoy, relish, luxuriate, revel, riot, bask, wallow in, feast on, gloat over, have oneself a ball.

To cause or give physical pleasure, to gratify, tickle, regale, etc. (829).

(Adjectives) Enjoying, etc., luxurious, sensual, voluptuous, comfortable, cosy, snug.

Pleasant, pleasing, agreeable, grateful, refreshing, comforting.

378 Physical Pain *(Substantives)*, bodily pain, suffering, sufferance, dolour, ache, aching, smart, smarting, shoot, shooting, twinge, twitch, gripe, headache, toothache, earache, sore, hurt, discomfort, malaise; mental pain (828).

Spasm, cramp, nightmare, crick, stitch, convulsion, throe.

Pang, anguish, agony, torment, torture, rack, cruciation, crucifixion, martyrdom.

(Verbs) To feel, experience, suffer, etc., pain; to suffer, ache, smart, bleed, tingle, shoot, twinge, lancinate, wince, writhe, twitch.

(Phrases) To sit on thorns; to sit on pins and needles.

To give or inflict pain; to pain, hurt, chafe, sting, bite, gnaw, pinch, tweak, grate, gall, fret, prick, pierce, gripe, etc., wring, torment, torture, rack, agonize, break on the wheel, put on the rack, convulse.

(Adjectives) In pain, in a state of pain; uncomfortable, pained, etc.

Painful, aching, etc., sore, raw, agonizing, excruciating.

---

2. SPECIAL SENSATION

(1) *Touch*

379 Sensation of pressure.

Touch *(Substantives)*, taction, tactility, feeling, palpation, manipulation, tangibility, palpability.

Organ of touch; hand, finger, forefinger, thumb, paw, feeler, antenna.

(Verbs) To touch, feel, handle, finger, thumb, paw, fumble, grope, grabble, scrabble; pass, or run the fingers over, manipulate.

(Phrase) To throw out a feeler.

(Adjectives) Tactual, tangible, palpable, tactile.

380 Sensations of Touch *(Substantives)*, itching, titillation, formication, etc., creeping, aura, tingling, thrilling.

(Verbs) To itch, tingle, creep, thrill; sting, prick, prickle, tickle, kittle, titillate.

(Adjectives) Itching, etc., ticklish, kittly.

381 Insensibility to touch.

Numbness *(Substantives)*, deadness, anaesthesia (376); pins and needles.

(Verbs) To benumb, paralyse, anaesthetize; to chloroform, inject with cocaine, etc. (376).

(Adjectives) Numb, benumbed; intangible, impalpable.

(2) *Heat*

382 Heat *(Substantives)*, caloric, temperature, warmth, fervour, calidity, incalescence, candescence, incandescence, glow, flush, hectic, fever, pyrexia, hyperpyrexia.

Fire, spark, scintillation, flash, flame, blaze, bonfire, firework, wildfire, pyrotechny, ignition (384).

Insolation, summer, dog-days, tropical heat, heat-wave, summer heat, blood heat, sirocco, simoom; isotherm.

Hot spring, thermal spring, geyser.

Pyrology, thermology, thermotics, calorimetry, thermodynamics; thermometer (389).

(Phrase) The devouring element.

(Verbs) To be hot, to glow, flush, sweat, swelter, bask, smoke, reek, stew, simmer, seethe, boil, burn, broil, bake, parch, fume, blaze, smoulder.

(Phrases) To be in a heat, in a glow, in a fever, in a blaze, etc.

(Adjectives) Hot, warm, mild, unfrozen, genial, tepid, lukewarm, blood-hot, thermal, thermotic, calorific, sunny, close, sweltering, stuffy, sultry, baking, boiling, broiling, torrid, tropical, aestival, canicular, glowing, piping, scalding, reeking, etc., on fire, afire, ablaze, alight, aglow, fervid, fervent, ardent, unquenched; isothermal, sotheral; feverish, pyretic, pyrexial, pyrexical.

Igneous, plutonic, fiery, candescent, incandescent, red-hot, white-hot, incalescent, smoking, blazing, unextinguished, smouldering.

(Phrases) Hot as fire; warm as toast; warm as wool; piping hot; like an oven; hot enough to roast an ox.

383 Cold *(Substantives)*, coldness, frigidity, coolness, coolth, gelidity, chill, chilliness, freshness, inclemency; cold storage.

Frost, ice, snow, snowflake, sleet, hail, hailstone, rime, hoar-frost, icicle, iceberg, ice-floe, glacier, winter.

Sensation of cold; chilliness, shivering, shuddering, goose-skin, goose-pimples, goose-flesh, rigor, horripilation, chattering of teeth.

(Verbs) To be cold, etc., to shiver, quake, shake, tremble, shudder, dither, quiver, starve.

(Adjectives) Cold, cool, chill, chilly, gelid, frigid, algid, bleak, raw, inclement, bitter, biting, cutting, nipping, piercing, pinching, clay-cold, fresh, keen; pinched, starved, perished, shivering, etc., aguish, frozen, frost-bitten, frost-nipped, frost-bound, unthawed, unwarmed; isocheimal, isochimenal.

Icy, glacial, frosty, freezing, wintry, brumal, hibernal, boreal, arctic, hiemal, hyperborean, icebound.

(Phrases) Cold as a stone; cold as marble; cold as a frog; cold as charity; cold as Christmas; cool as a cucumber; cool as a custard.

---

384 Calefaction *(Substantives)*, increase of temperature, heating, tepefaction.

Melting, fusion, liquefaction, thaw,

385 Refrigeration *(Substantives)*, infrigidation, reduction of temperature, cooling, freezing, congealing, congelation, glaciation.

liquescence (335), liquation, incandescence.

Burning, combustion, incension, accension, cremation, cautery, cauterization, roasting, broiling, frying, ustulation, torrefaction, scorification, branding, calcination, carbonization, incineration, cineration.

Boiling, coction, ebullition, simmering, scalding, decoction, smelting.

Ignition, inflammation, setting fire to, flagration, deflagration, conflagration, arson, incendiarism, fire-raising; *auto da fé*, suttee.

Inflammability, combustibility; incendiary, fire-bug, fire-ship, *pétroleur*.

Transmission of heat, diathermancy.

(Verbs) To heat, warm, mull, chafe, fire, set fire to, set on fire, kindle enkindle, light, ignite, relume, rekindle.

To melt, thaw, fuse, liquefy (335); defrost, de-ice.

To burn, inflame, roast, broil, fry, grill, brander, singe, parch, sweal, scorch, brand, scorify, torrify, bake, cauterize, sear, char, carbonize, calcine, incinerate, smelt.

To boil, stew, cook, seethe, scald, parboil, simmer.

To take fire, catch fire, kindle, light, ignite.

(Phrases) To stir the fire; blow the fire; fan the flame; apply a match to; make a bonfire of; to take the chill off.

To consign to the flames; to reduce to ashes; to burn to a cinder.

(Adjectives) Combustible, inflammable, heating, etc., heated, warmed, melted, molten, unfrozen, boiled, stewed, sodden, adust.

Fire-brigade, fire-extinguisher, fire-engine, fireman; incombustability.

(Verbs) To cool, refrigerate, congeal, freeze, glaciate, ice, benumb, refresh, damp, slack, quench, put out, blow out, extinguish, starve, pinch, pierce, cut.

To go out.

(Adjectives) Cooled, frozen, benumbed, etc., shivery, frigorific, refrigerant.

Incombustible, non-inflammable, fire-proof.

———

386 Furnace *(Substantives)*, fire, gas fire, electric fire, stove, kiln, oven, bakehouse, hothouse, conservatory, fire-place, grate, hearth, radiator, register, reverberatory, range, hob, hypocaust, crematorium, incinerator, forge, blast-furnace, brasier, salamander, geyser, heater, hot-plate, hot-water bottle, electric blanket, warming-pan, stew-pan, boiler, cauldron, kettle, pot, urn, chafing-dish, gridiron, saucepan, frying-pan; sudatorium, sudatory, Turkish bath, *hammam*, vapour bath.

387 Refrigeratory *(Substantives)*, refrigerator, frig, ice-pail, ice-bag, ice-house, freezing-mixture, cooler, freezer.

———

388 Fuel *(Substantives)*, firing, coal, anthracite, coke, charcoal, briquette, peat, combustible, log, tinder, touchwood.

Lucifer, ingle, brand, match, vesuvian, vesta, safety-match, fusee, lighter, spill, embers, faggot, firebrand, incendiary, port-fire, fire-ball, fire-barrel.

389 Thermometer *(Substantives)*, clinical thermometer, pyrometer, calorimeter, thermoscope, thermograph, thermostat, thermopile.

Fahrenheit, Centigrade, Celsius, Réaumur.

Thermometry, therm.

(3) *Taste*

390 Taste *(Substantives)*, flavour, gust, gusto, zest, savour, sapor, tang, twang, smack, relish, aftertaste, smatch, sapidity.

Tasting, gustation, degustation.

Palate, tongue, tooth, sweet tooth, stomach.

(Verbs) To taste, savour, smack, smatch, flavour, twang.

(Phrases) To tickle the palate; to smack the lips.

(Adjectives) Sapid, gustable, gustatory, saporific, strong, appetizing, palatable (394).

391 Insipidity *(Substantives)*, tastelessness, insipidness, vapidness, vapidity, mawkishness, wershness, mildness; wish-wash, milk and water, slops.

(Verbs) To be void of taste, tasteless, etc.

(Adjectives) Insipid, tasteless, savourless, mawkish, wersh, flat, vapid, *fade*, wishy-washy, watery, weak, mild; untasted.

———

392 Pungency *(Substantives)*, haut-goût, strong taste, twang, raciness, race, saltness, sharpness, roughness.

Ginger, caviare, cordial, condiment (393).

(Verbs) To be pungent, etc.

To render pungent, to season, spice, salt, pepper, pickle, brine, devil.

(Adjectives) Pungent, high-flavoured, high-tasted, high, sharp, strong, rough, stinging, piquant, racy, biting, mordant, spicy, seasoned, hot, peppery, gingery, high-seasoned, gamy, salt, saline, brackish.

(Phrases) Salt as brine; salt as a herring; salt as Lot's wife; hot as pepper.

393 Condiment *(Substantives)*, salt, mustard, pepper, cayenne, vinegar, curry, chutney, seasoning, spice, ginger, sauce, dressing, *sauce piquante*, caviare, potherbs, pickles, onion, garlic, sybo.

394 Savouriness *(Substantives)*, palatableness, toothsomeness, daintiness, delicacy, relish, zest.

A titbit, dainty, delicacy, ambrosia, nectar, *bonne-bouche*.

(Verbs) To be savoury, etc.

To render palatable, etc.

To relish, like, fancy, be partial to.

(Adjectives) Savoury, well-tasted, palatable, nice, good, dainty, delectable, toothsome, tasty, appetizing, delicate, delicious, exquisite, rich, luscious, ambrosial, meaty, fruity.

———

395 Unsavouriness *(Substantives)*, unpalatableness, bitterness, acridness, acridity, acrimony, roughness, acerbity, austerity; gall and wormwood, rue; sickener, scunner.

(Verbs) To be unpalatable, etc.

To sicken, disgust, nauseate, pall, turn the stomach.

(Adjectives) Unsavoury, unpalatable, ill-flavoured, bitter, acrid, acrimonious, unsweetened, rough, austere, uneatable, inedible.

Offensive, repulsive, nasty, fulsome, sickening, nauseous, nauseating, disgusting, loathsome, palling.

(Phrases) Bitter as gall; bitter as aloes.

396 Sweetness *(Substantives)*, dulcitude, dulcification, sweetening.

Sugar, saccharine, glucose, syrup, treacle, molasses, honey, manna, confection, confectionery, candy,

397 Sourness *(Substantives)*, acid, acidity, tartness, crabbedness, hardness, roughness, acetous fermentation.

Vinegar, verjuice, crab, alum.

(Verbs) To be sour, etc.

conserve, jam, jelly, marmalade, preserve, liquorice, julep, sugar-candy, toffee, caramel, butterscotch, plum, sugar-plum, lollipop, bonbon, jujube, lozenge, pastille, comfit, fudge, chocolate, sweet, sweetmeat, marzipan, marchpane, fondant, nougat; mead, nectar, hydromel, honeysuckle.

(Verbs) To be sweet, etc.

To render sweet, to sweeten, sugar, mull, edulcorate, candy, dulcify, saccharify.

To render or turn sour, to sour, acidify, acidulate.

(Phrase) To set the teeth on edge.

(Adjectives) Sour, acid, acidulous, acidulated, sourish, subacid, vinegary, tart, crabbed, acerb, acetic, acetous, acescent, acetose, styptic, hard, rough.

(Phrases) Sour as vinegar; sour as a crab.

———

(Adjectives) Sweet, saccharine, sacchariferous, sugary, dulcet, candied, honeyed, luscious, edulcorated, nectarous, nectareous, sweetish, sugary.

(Phrases) Sweet as a nut; sweet as honey.

(4) *Odour*

398 Odour *(Substantives)*, smell, scent, effluvium, emanation, fume, exhalation, essence; trail, nidor, redolence.

The sense of smell, act of smelling.

(Verbs) To have an odour, to smell of, to exhale, to give out a smell, etc.

To smell, scent, snuff, sniff, inhale, nose, snowk.

399 Inodorousness *(Substantives)*, absence, or want of smell; deodorization.

(Verbs) To be inodorous, etc., deodorize (652).

(Adjectives) Inodorous, odourless, scentless, smell-less, wanting smell.

———

(Adjectives) Odorous, odorant, odoriferous, smelling, strong-scented, graveolent, redolent, nidorous, pungent.

Relating to the sense of smell; olfactory, keen-scented.

400 Fragrance *(Substantives)*, aroma, redolence, perfume, savour, bouquet.

Incense, musk, myrrh, frankincense, ambrosia, attar (or otto), eau de-Cologne, civet, castor, ambergris, bergamot, lavender, sandalwood, orris root, balm, pot-pourri, pulvil; scent-bag, scent-bottle, sachet, nosegay.

(Phrase) 'All the perfumes of Arabia.'

(Verbs) To perfume, scent, embalm.

(Adjectives) Fragrant, aromatic, redolent, balmy, scented, sweet-smelling, sweet-scented, ambrosial, perfumed, musky.

———

401 Fetor *(Substantives)*, bad smell, empyreuma, stench, stink, mustiness, fustiness, frowziness, frowst, fug, rancidity, foulness, putrescence, putridity, mephitis.

A pole-cat, skunk, badger, teledu, asafoetida, cacodyl, stinkard, stink-bomb, stinkpot.

(Verbs) To smell, stink, hum, niff, pong.

(Phrase) To stink in the nostrils.

(Adjectives) Fetid, strong-smelling, smelly, whiffy, malodorous, noisome, offensive, rank, rancid, reasty, mouldy, fusty, musty, stuffy, frowsty, fuggy, foul, frowzy, olid, nidorous, stinking, rotten, putrescent, putrid, putrefying, tainted, high (653), mephitic, empyreumatic.

(5) *Sound*

(1) SOUND IN GENERAL

402 Sound *(Substantives)*, sonance, noise, strain, voice (580), accent, twang, intonation, tone, resonance (408); sonority, sonorousness, audibleness, audibility.

Acoustics, phonics, phonetics, phonology, diacoustics.

(Verbs) To produce sound; to sound, make a noise, give out or emit sound, to resound.

(Adjectives) Sonorous, sounding, soniferous, sonorific, sonoriferous, resonant, canorous, audible, distinct, phonic, phonetic.

------

403 Silence *(Substantives)*, stillness, quiet, peace, calm, hush, lull; muteness (581).

A silencer, mute, damper, sordine.

(Verbs) To be silent, etc.

To render silent, to silence, still, hush, stifle, muffle, stop, muzzle, mute, damp, gag.

(Phrases) To keep silence; to hold one's tongue; to hold one's peace.

(Adjectives) Silent, still, stilly, noiseless, soundless, inaudible, hushed, etc., mute, mum, mumchance (581), solemn, awful, deathlike.

(Phrases) Still as a mouse; deathlike silence; silent as the grave; one might hear a pin drop.

(Adverbs) Silently, softly, etc., *sub silentio.*

(Interjections) Hush! silence! soft! mum! whist! chut! *tace!*

404 Loudness *(Substantives)*, clatter, din, clangour, clang, roar, uproar, racket, hubbub, flourish of trumpets, tucket, tantara, taratantara, fanfare, blare, alarum, peal, swell, blast, boom, echo, fracas, shindy, row, rumpus, bobbery, clamour, hullaballoo, chorus, hue and cry, shout, yell, whoop, charivari, shivaree, vociferation; Stentor, Boanerges.

Speaking-trumpet, megaphone, loud-speaker, microphone, mike, amplifier, resonator.

Artillery, cannon, thunder.

(Verbs) To be loud, etc., to resound, echo, re-echo, peal, swell, clang, boom, blare, thunder, fulminate, roar, whoop, shout (411).

(Phrases) To din in the ear; to pierce, split, or rend the ears, or head; to shout, or thunder at the pitch of one's breath, or at the top of one's voice; to make the welkin ring; to rend the air; *faire le diable à quatre.*

(Adjectives) Loud, sonorous, resounding, etc., high-sounding, big-sounding, deep, full, swelling, clamorous, clangorous, multisonous, noisy, blatant, plangent, vocal, vociferous, stunning, piercing, splitting, rending, thundering, deafening, ear-deafening, ear-piercing, obstreperous,

405 Faintness *(Substantives)*, lowness, faint sounds, whisper, undertone, breath, underbreath, murmur, mutter, hum, susurration, tinkle, rustle.

Hoarseness, huskiness, raucity.

(Verbs) To whisper, breathe, murmur, mutter, mumble, purl, hum, croon, gurgle, ripple, babble, tinkle.

(Phrases) Steal on the ear; melt, float on the air.

(Adjectives) Inaudible, scarcely audible, low, dull, stifled, muffled, hoarse, husky, gentle, faint, breathed, etc., soft, floating, purling, etc., liquid, mellifluous, dulcet, flowing, soothing.

(Adverbs) In a whisper, with bated breath, under one's breath, *sotto voce*, between the teeth, from the side of one's mouth, aside, *piano, pianissimo, à la sourdine.*

------

blaring, deep-mouthed, open-mouthed, trumpet-tongued, uproarious, rackety, stentorian.

(Phrases) Enough to split the head or ears; enough to wake the dead; enough to wake the Seven Sleepers.

(Adverbs) Loudly, aloud, etc., *forte, fortissimo.*

(Phrases) At the top of one's voice; in full cry.

(2) SPECIFIC SOUNDS

406 Sudden and violent sounds.

Snap *(Substantives)*, knock, rap, tap, click, clash, slam, clack, crack, crackle, crackling, crepitation, decrepitation, report, pop, plop, bang, thud, thump, ping, zip, clap, burst, explosion, discharge, crash, detonation, firing, salvo, atmospherics.

Squib, cracker, gun, pop-gun.

(Verbs) To snap, knock, etc.

(Adjectives) Snapping, etc.

---

408 Resonance *(Substantives)*, ring, ringing, jingle, chink, tinkle, ting, tink, tintinnabulation, gurgle, chime, toot, tootle, clang, etc. (404).

Reflection, reverberation, echo.

(Verbs) To resound, reverberate, re-echo, ring, jingle, clink, chime, tinkle, etc.

(Adjectives) Resounding, resonant, tintinnabular, ringing, etc.

(Phrase) Clear as a bell.

Bass *(Substantives)*, low, flat or grave note, chest-note, baritone, contralto.

(Adjectives) Deep-toned, deep-sounding, deep-mouthed, hollow, sepulchral, *basso profondo.*

407 Repeated and protracted sounds.

Roll *(Substantives)*, rumble, rumbling, hum, humming, shake, trill, whirr, chime, tick, beat, toll, ticking, tick-tack, patter, tattoo, ding-dong, drumming, quaver, tremolo, ratatat, tantara, rataplan, rat-tat, clatter, clutter, rattle, racket, rub-a-dub; reverberation (408).

(Phrases) The devil's tattoo; tuck of drum.

(Verbs) To roll, beat, tick, toll, drum, etc., rattle, clatter, patter, shake, trill, whirr, chime, beat; to drum or din in the ear.

(Adjectives) Rolling, rumbling, etc.

409 Hissing sounds.

Sibilation *(Substantives)*, hiss, swish, buzz, whiz, rustle, fizz, fizzle, wheeze, whistle, snuffle, sneeze, sternutation.

(Verbs) To hiss, buzz, etc.

(Adjectives) Sibilant, hissing, buzzing, etc., wheezy.

Soprano *(Substantives)*, high note (410).

---

410 Harsh sounds.

Stridor *(Substantives)*, jar, grating, creak, clank, twang, jangle, jarring, creaking, rustling, roughness, gruffness, sharpness, cacophony.

High note, shrillness, acuteness, soprano, falsetto, treble, alto, counter-tenor, penny trumpet, head-note.

(Verbs) To creak, grate, jar, burr, pipe, twang, jangle, rustle, clank; to shrill, shriek, screech, squeal, skirl (411), stridulate.

(Phrases) To set the teeth on edge; to grate upon the ear.

(Adjectives) Strident, stridulous, jarring, etc., harsh, hoarse, horrisonous, discordant, scrannel (414), cacophonous, rough, gruff, sepulchral, grating.

Sharp, high, acute, shrill, piping, screaming.

411 Human sounds.

Cry *(Substantives)*, voice (580), vociferation, outcry, roar, shout, bawl, bellow, brawl, halloo, hullaballoo, hoop, whoop, yell, cheer, hoot, howl, chorus, scream, screech, screak, shriek, squeak, squawk, squeal, skirl, yawp, squall, whine, pule, pipe, grumble, plaint, groan, moan, snore, snort.

(Verbs) To vociferate, roar, shout, bawl, etc., sing out, thunder, raise or lift up the voice.

(Adjectives) Vociferating, etc., clamant, clamorous, vociferous, stertorous.

412 Animal sounds.

Ululation *(Substantives)*, latration, cry, roar, bellow, reboation, bark, yelp, howl, bay, baying, yap, growl, grunt, gruntle, snort, neigh, nicker, whinny, bray, croak, snarl, howl, caterwauling, mew, mewl, miaow, miaul, purr, pule, bleat, baa, low, moo, boo, caw, coo, croodle, cackle, gobble, quack, gaggle, squeak, squawk, squeal, chuckle, chuck, cluck, clack, chirp, chirrup, crow, woodnote, twitter, peep.

Insect cry, drone, buzz, hum.

Cuckoo, screech-owl.

(Verbs) To cry, bellow, rebellow, etc., bell, boom, trumpet, give tongue.

(Phrases) To bay the moon; to roar like a bull or lion.

(Adjectives) Crying, etc., blatant, latrant, remugient.

(3) MUSICAL SOUND

413 **Melody** *(Substantives)*, melodiousness, *melos*.

Pitch, note, interval, tone, intonation, timbre; high or low, acute or grave notes, treble, alto, tenor, bass, soprano, mezzo-soprano, contralto, countertenor, baritone, *basso profondo*.

Scale, gamut, diapason; diatonic, chromatic, enharmonic, whole-tone, etc., scales; key, clef; major, minor, Dorian, Phrygian, Lydian, etc., modes; tetrachord, hexachord, pentatonic scale; tuning, modulation, temperament; solmization, solfeggio, solfa.

Staff (or stave), lines, spaces, brace; bar, double bar, rest.

414 **Discord** *(Substantives)*, discordance, dissonance, jar, jarring, caterwauling, cocophony.

Hoarseness, croaking, etc. (410).

Confused sounds, babel, Dutch concert, cat's concert, marrow-bones and cleavers, charivari (404).

(Verbs) To be discordant, etc., to croak, jar (410).

(Adjectives) Discordant, dissonant, out of tune, sharp, flat, tuneless, absonant, unmusical, inharmonous, unmelodious, untuneful, untunable, singsong.

Cacophonous, harsh, hoarse, croaking, jarring, stridulous, etc. (410).

———

Notes of the scale: sharps, flats, naturals, accidentals; breve, semibreve, minim, crotchet, quaver, semiquaver, demisemiquaver, etc.

Tonic, keynote, supertonic, mediant, subdominant, dominant, submediant, leading note, octave; primes, seconds, triads, etc.

Harmonic, overtone, partial, fundamental, note, hum-note.

Harmony, harmoniousness, concord, concordance, unison, homophony, chord, chime, consonance, concert, euphony; counterpoint, polyphony; tonality, atonality; thorough-bass, figured bass.

Rhythm, time, tempo; common, duple, triple, six-eight, etc., time; *tempo rubato*, syncopation, ragtime, jazz, swing, jive, boogie-woogie, bebop, skiffle, rock-and-roll.

(Verbs) To harmonize, chime, be in unison; put in tune, tune, accord.

(Adjectives) Harmonious, harmonic, harmonical, in harmony, in

tune, etc., unisonant, unisonal, univocal, symphonic, homophonous; contrapuntal, chordal; diatonic, chromatic, enharmonic, tonal, atonal.

Measured, rhythmical, in time, on the beat, hot.

Melodious, musical, tuneful, tunable, sweet, dulcet, canorous, mellow, mellifluous, silver, toned, silvery, euphonious, euphonic, euphonical; enchanting, ravishing, etc., Orphean.

415 Music *(Substantives)*, tune, air, lilt, melody, refrain, burden, cadence, theme, motive, motif, *leit-motiv*, subject, counter-subject, episode, modulation, introduction, finale, etc.

Composition, work, opus, score, full score, vocal score, etc.

Solo, duet, trio, quartet, etc., concerted music, chorus, chamber music.

Instrumental music: Symphony, *sinfonietta*, symphonic poem, tone-poem, concerto, sonata, sonatina; *allegro, andante, largo,* scherzo, rondo, etc.; overture, prelude, intermezzo, postlude, voluntary; ballade, nocturne, serenade, aubade, barcarolle, *berceuse,* etc.; fugue, fugato, canon; variations, humoresque, rhapsody, caprice, *capriccio,* fantasia, impromptu; arrangement, pot-pourri; march, pibroch, minuet, gavotte, waltz, mazurka, etc. (840); accompaniment, *obbligato*; programme music.

Vocal music: Chant, plain-song, Gregorian music, neume, psalmody, psalm, hymn, anthem, motet, antiphon, canticle, introit, etc., service, song, ballad, *lied, chanson,* cavatina, canzonet, serenade, lullaby, ditty, chanty, folk-song, dithyramb; part-song, glee, catch, round, canon, madrigal, chorus, cantata, oratorio, etc.; opera (599).

Dirge, requiem, *nenia,* knell, lament, coronach, dead march.

Musical ornament; grace-note, appoggiatura, trill, shake, turn, beat, mordent, etc.; cadenza, roulade, bravura, colorature, *coloratura.*

Scale, run, arpeggio, chord; five-finger exercise, study, *étude,* toccata.

Performance, execution, technique, touch, expression, tone-colour, rendering, interpretation; voice-production, *bel canto; embouchure,* lipping, bowing.

Concert, recital, performance, ballad concert, etc., musicale, sing-song.

Minstrelsy, musicianship, musicality, musicalness, an ear for music; composition, composing, orchestration, scoring, filling in the parts.

Composer, harmonist, contrapuntist.

Apollo, the Muses, Erato, Euterpe, Terpsichore.

(Verbs) To play, fiddle, bow, strike, strike up, thrum, strum, grind, touch, tweedle, scrape, blow, pipe, tootle, blare, etc.; to execute, perform, render, interpret, conduct, accompany, vamp, arrange, prelude, improvise (612).

To sing, chant, vocalize, warble, carol, troll, lilt, hum, croon, chirp, chirrup, twitter, quaver, trill, shake, whistle, yodel.

To compose, set to music, score, harmonize, orchestrate.

To put in tune, tune, attune, accord, string, pitch.

(Adjectives) Musical, harmonious, etc. (413), instrumental, orchestral, pianistic, vocal, choral, operatic, etc.; musicianly, having a good ear.

(Phrase) Fanatico per la musica.

(Adverbs) Adagio, largo, larghetto, andante, andantino, maestoso, moderato, allegretto, con moto, vivace, veloce, allegro, presto, prestissimo, strepitoso, etc.; *scherzando, legato, staccato, crescendo, diminuendo, morendo, sostenuto, sforzando, accelerando, stringendo, più mosso, meno mosso, allargando, rallentando, ritenuto, a piacere,* etc.; *arpeggiando, pizzicato, glissando, martellato, da capo.*

416 Musician *(Substantives)*, minstrel, performer, player, soloist, virtuoso, maestro.

Organist, pianist, violinist, fiddler, cellist, harper, harpist, flautist, fifer, clarinettist, trombonist, etc., trumpeter, bugler, piper, bagpiper, drummer, timpanist; campanologist; band, orchestra, brass band, military band, string band, pipe band, waits; conductor, bandmaster, drum-major, leader, *chef d'orchestre*, etc., accompanist.

Vocalist, singer, songster, songstress, chanter, chantress, *cantatrice, lieder-singer*, ballad-singer, etc.; troubadour, minnesinger, gleeman; nightingale, Philomel, thrush, throstle, Orpheus.

Chorus, choir, chorister.

(Phrase) The tuneful Nine.

417 Musical Instruments.

1. Stringed instruments: Monochord, polycord, harp lyre, lute, theorbo, mandolin, guitar, gittern, cithern, banjo, ukelele, balalaika.

Violin, fiddle, Cremona, Stradivarius (or Strad), kit, viola (or tenor), violoncello (or cello), double-bass (or bass-viol), viol, viola d'amore, viola da gamba, violone, rebeck, psaltery.

Pianoforte (or piano), harpsichord, clavier, clavichord, clavicembalo, spinet, cembalo, virginal, zither, dulcimer.

2. Wind instruments: Organ, siren, pipe, pitch-pipe, Pan-pipes; piccolo, flute, bass-flute, oboe (or hautboy), oboe d'amore, cor anglais, clarinet, basset-horn, bass-clarinet, bassoon, double-bassoon, saxophone, horn, French horn, tuba, trumpet, cornet, cornet-à-piston, trombone, euphonium; fife, flageolot, whistle, penny-whistle, ocarina, bugle, serpent, ophicleide, clarion, bagpipe, musette; harmonium, American organ, seraphina, concertina, accordion, melodeon, mouth-organ, etc.; great, swell, choir, solo and echo organs.

3. Vibrating surfaces: Cymbal, bell, carillon, gong, tabor, tambourine, timbrel, drum, side-drum, bass-drum, kettle-drum, timpano, military drum, tom-tom, castanet; musical glasses, harmonica, glockenspiel; sounding-board.

4. Vibrating bars: Tuning-fork, triangle, xylophone, Jew's harp.

5. Mechanical instruments: Musical box, hurdy-gurdy, barrel-organ, piano-organ, orchestrion, piano-player, pianola, etc.; gramophone, phonograph, tape recorder, juke box, nickelodeon.

Key, string, bow, drumstick, bellows, sound-box, pedal, stop; loud or sustaining pedal, soft pedal, mute, sordine, sourdine, damper, swell-box; keyboard, finger-board, console; organ-loft, concert platform, orchestra, choir, singing-gallery, belfry, campanile.

(4) PERCEPTION OF SOUND

418 Sense of sound.

Hearing *(Substantives)*, audition, auscultation, listening, eavesdropping, audibility.

Acuteness, nicety, delicacy, of ear.

Ear, auricle, acoustic organs, auditory apparatus, lug, ear-drum, tympanum.

Telephone, speaking-tube, ear-trumpet, audiphone, audiometer, earphone, phone, gramophone, phonograph, dictaphone, intercom, receiver.

Wireless telephony, broadcasting, wireless, radio, transmitter, walkie-talkie, radiogram, microphone, mike.

419 Deafness *(Substantives)*, hardness of hearing, surdity; inaudibility.

(Verbs) To be deaf, to shut, stop, or close one's ears.

To render deaf, to stun, deafen.

(Phrase) To turn a deaf ear to.

(Adjectives) Deaf, stone deaf, tone deaf, hard of hearing, earless, surd, dull of hearing, deaf-mute, stunned, deafened, having no ear.

Inaudible, out of earshot.

(Phrases) Deaf as a post; deaf as a beetle; deaf as an adder.

A hearer, auditor, listener, eavesdropper, auditory, audience.

(Verbs) To hear, overhear, hark, listen, list, hearken, give or lend an ear, prick up one's ears, give a hearing or audience to, listen in.

To become audible, to catch the ear, to be heard.

(Phrases) To hang upon the lips of; to be all ears.

(Adjectives) Hearing, etc., auditory, auricular, acoustic.

(Interjections) Hark! list! hear! listen! oyez! (or oyes!)

(Adverbs) Arrectis auribus; with ears flapping.

(6) *Light*

(I) LIGHT IN GENERAL

420 Light *(Substantives)*, ray, beam, stream, gleam, streak, pencil, sunbeam, moonbeam, starbeam.

Day, daylight, sunshine, sunlight, moonlight, starlight, the light of day, the light of heaven, noontide, noonday, noontide light, broad daylight.

Glimmer, glimmering, glow, afterglow, phosphorescence, lambent flame, play of light.

Flush, halo, aureole, nimbus, glory, corona.

Spark, sparkle, scintilla, sparkling, scintillation, flame, flash, blaze, coruscation, fulguration, lightning, flood of light, glint.

Lustre, shine, sheen, gloss, tinsel, spangle, brightness, brilliancy, refulgence, dazzlement, splendour, resplendence, luminousness, luminosity, luminescence, lucidity, lucidness, incandescence, radiance, illumination, irradiation, glare, flare, flush, effulgence, fulgency, fluorescence, lucency, lambency.

Optics, photology, photometry, dioptrics, catoptrics.

Radioactivity, radiography, radiograph, radiometer, radioscopy, radiotherapy.

(Verbs) To shine, glow, glitter, glisten, glister, glint, twinkle, gleam, flicker, flare, glare, beam, radiate, shoot beams, shimmer, sparkle, scintillate, coruscate, flash, blaze, fizzle, daze, dazzle, bedazzle, to clear up, to brighten.

To illuminate, illume, illumine, lighten, enlighten, light, light up, irradiate, flush, shine upon, cast lustre upon; cast, throw, or shed a light upon; brighten, clear, relume.

421 Darkness *(Substantives)*, night, midnight, obscurity, dusk (422), duskiness, gloom, gloominess, murk, mirk, murkiness, shadow, shade, umbrage, shadiness, umbra, penumbra, Erebus.

Obscuration, adumbration, obumbration, obtenebration, obfuscation, black-out, extinction, eclipse, gathering of the clouds, dimness (422).

(Phrases) Dead of night; darkness visible; darkness that can be felt; blind man's holiday.

(Verbs) To be dark, etc.; to lour (or lower).

To darken, obscure, shade, shadow, dim, bedarken, overcast, overshadow, obfuscate, obumbrate, adumbrate, cast in the shade, becloud, overcloud, bedim, put out, snuff out, blow out, extinguish, dout, douse.

To cast, throw, spread a shade or gloom.

(Phrase) To douse the glim.

(Adjectives) Dark, obscure, darksome, darkling, tenebrous, tenebrific, rayless, beamless, sunless, moonless, starless, pitch-dark, pitchy; Stygian, Cimmerian.

Sombre, dusky, unilluminated, unillumined, unlit, unsunned, nocturnal, dingy, lurid, overcast, louring (or lowering), cloudy, murky, murksome, shady, shadowy, umbrageous.

Benighted, noctivagant, noctivagous.

(Phrases) Dark as pitch; dark as a pit; dark as Erebus; dark as a wolf's mouth; the palpable obscure.

422 Dimness *(Substantives)*, dim-

(Phrase) To strike a light.

(Adjectives) Luminous, luminiferous, shining, glowing, etc., lambent, glossy, lucid, lucent, luculent, lustrous, lucific, glassy, clear, bright, scintillant, light, lightsome, unclouded, sunny, orient, noonday, noontide, beaming, beamy, vivid, alight, splendent, radiant, radiating, cloudless, unobscured; radioactive, fluorescent, phosphorescent.

Garish, resplendent, refulgent, fulgent, effulgent, in a blaze, ablaze, relucent, splendid, blazing, rutilant, meteoric, burnished.

(Phrases) Bright as silver, as day, as noonday.

---

423 Source of light, self-luminous body.

Luminary *(Substantives)*, sun, Phoebus, star, orb, meteor, galaxy, constellation, blazing star, glowworm, firefly.

Meteor, northern lights, aurora borealis, aurora australis, fire-drake, ignis fatuus, jack-o'-lantern, will-o'-the-wisp, friar's lantern.

Artificial light, flame, gas-light, incandescent gas-light, electric light, limelight, acetylene, torch, candle, flash-lamp, flashlight, flambeau, link, light, taper, lamp, arc-lamp, mercury vapour lamp, neon lighting, lantern (or lanthorn), rushlight, farthing rushlight, night-light, firework, rocket, Very light, blue lights, fizgig, flare.

Chandelier, gaselier, electrolier, candelabra, girandole, lustre, sconce, gas-bracket, gas-jet, gas-burner, batswing; gas-mantle, electric bulb, filament.

Lighthouse, lightship, pharos, beacon, watch-fire, cresset, brand.

(Adjectives) Self-luminous, phosphoric, phosphorescent, radiant (420).

425 Transparency *(Substantives)*, transparence, diaphaneity, translucence, translucency, lucidity, pellucidity, limpidity, clarity.

Glass, crystal, mica, lymph, water.

(Verbs) To be transparent, etc., to transmit light.

(Adjectives) Transparent, pellucid,

-out, brown-out, paleness, glimmer, glimmering, owl-light, nebulousness, nebulosity, nebula, cloud, film, mist, haze, fog, brume, smog, smoke, haziness, eclipse, dusk, cloudiness, dawn, aurora, twilight, crepuscule, cockshut time, gloaming, daybreak, dawn, half-light, moonlight; moonshine, moonbeam, starlight, starshine, starbeam, candle-light.

(Verbs) To be dim, etc., to glimmer, loom, lour, twinkle.

To grow dim, to fade, to render dim, to dim, obscure, pale.

(Adjectives) Dim, dull, lack-lustre, dingy, darkish, glassy, faint, confused.

Cloudy, misty, hazy, foggy, brumous, muggy, fuliginous, nebulous, lowering, overcast, crepuscular, muddy, lurid, looming.

(Phrase) Shorn of its beams.

---

424 Shade *(Substantives)*, awning, parasol, sunshade, screen, curtain, veil, mantle, mask, gauze, blind, shutter, cloud, mist.

A shadow, chiaroscuro, umbrage, penumbra (421).

(Adjectives) Shady, umbrageous.

---

426 Opacity *(Substantives)*, thickness, opaqueness, turbidity, turbidness, muddiness.

Cloud, film, haze.

(Verbs) To be opaque, etc., to obfuscate, not to transmit, to obstruct the passage of light.

(Adjectives) Opaque, turbid, roily,

lucid, diaphanous, translucent, re-lucent, limpid, clear, crystalline, vit-reous, transpicuous, glassy, hyaline.

(Phrase) Clear as crystal.

————

(Adjectives) Semitransparent, escent, gauzy, pearly, milky.

thick, muddy, opacous, obfuscated, fuliginous, cloudy, hazy, misty, foggy, impervious to light.

427 Semitransparency, opa-lescence, pearliness, milkiness.

Film, gauze, muslin.

semi-diaphanous, semi-opaque, opal-

---

(2) SPECIFIC LIGHT

428 Colour *(Substantives)*, hue, tint, tinge, dye, complexion, shade, spectrum, tincture, blazonry, cast, livery, coloration, glow, flush, tone, key.

Pure or positive colour, primary colour.

Broken colour, secondary or tertiary colour.

Chromatics: prism, spectroscope.

A pigment, colouring matter, medium, paint, dye, wash, stain, distemper, mordant.

(Verbs) To colour, dye, tinge, stain, tinct, tincture, paint, wash, illuminate, blazon, emblazon, bedizen, imbue, distemper.

(Adjectives) Coloured, colorific, chromatic, prismatic, full-coloured, lush, dyed; tinctorial.

Bright, deep, vivid, florid, fresh, high-coloured, unfaded, gay, showy, gaudy, garish, flaunting, vivid, gor-geous, glaring, flaring, flashy, tawdry, meretricious, raw, intense, double-dyed, loud, noisy.

Mellow, harmonious, pearly, light, quiet, delicate, pastel.

429 Absence of colour.

Achromatism *(Substantives)*, de-coloration, discoloration, paleness, pallidity, pallidness, pallor, etiolation, anaemia, chlorosis, albinism, neutral tint, colourlessness; monochrome, black and white.

(Verbs) To lose colour, to fade, pale, blanch, become colourless.

To deprive of colour, discolour, bleach, tarnish, decolour, decolorate, decolorize, achromatize, tone down.

(Adjectives) Colourless, uncoloured, untinged, untinctured, achromatic, aplanatic, hueless, undyed, pale, pallid, pale-faced, pasty, etiolated, anaemic, chlorotic, faint, faded, dull, cold, muddy, wan, sallow, dead, dingy, ashy, ashen, cadaverous, glassy, lack-lustre, tarnished, bleached, discoloured.

(Phrases) Pale as death, as ashes, as a witch, as a ghost, as a corpse.

————

430 Whiteness *(Substantives)*, miliness, hoariness.

Albification, etiolation.

Snow, paper, chalk, milk, lily, sheet, ivory, silver, alabaster.

(Verbs) To be white, etc.

To render white, whiten, bleach, whitewash, blanch, etiolate.

(Adjectives) White, milk-white, snow-white, snowy, niveous, chalky, hoary, hoar, silvery, argent.

431 Blackness *(Substantives)*, darkness (421), swarthiness, dingi-ness, lividity, inkiness, pitchiness, nigritude.

Nigrification.

Jet, ink, ebony, coal, pitch, char-coal, soot, sloe, smut, raven, crow; negro, nigger, darkie, coon, blacka-moor.

(Verbs) To be black, etc.

To render black, to blacken, nigrify,

Whitish, off-white, cream-coloured, creamy, pearly, fair, blonde, etiolated, albescent.

(Phrases) White as the driven snow; white as a sheet.

———

denigrate, blot, blotch, smirch, smutch.

(Adjectives) Black, sable, swarthy, swart, sombre, inky, ebon, livid, coal-black, jet-black, pitch-black, fuliginous, dingy, dusky, Ethiopic, nigrescent.

(Phrases) Black as my hat; black as ink; black as coal; black as a crow; black as thunder.

432 Grey *(Substantives)*, neutral tint, dun.

(Adjectives) Grey, etc., drab, dingy, sombre, leaden, livid, ashen, mouse-coloured, slate-coloured, stone-coloured, cinereous, cineritious, grizzly, grizzled.

———

433 Brown *(Substantives)*, bistre, ochre, sepia.

(Adjectives) Brown, etc., bay, dapple, auburn, chestnut, nut-brown, umber, cinnamon, fawn, russet, olive, hazel, tawny, fuscous, chocolate, liver-coloured, tan, brunette, maroon, khaki, foxy, bronzed, sunburnt, tanned.

(Phrases) Brown as a berry, as mahogany, as a gipsy.

(Verbs) To render brown, embrown, to tan, bronze, etc.

Primitive Colours

434 Redness *(Substantives)*, red, scarlet, vermilion, crimson, carmine, pink, lake, maroon, carnation, damask, ruby, rose, blush colour, peach colour, flesh colour, gules, solferino.

Rust, cinnabar, cochineal, madder, red lead, ruddle; blood, lobster, cherry, pillar-box.

Erubescence, rubescence, rubefaction, rosiness, rufescence, ruddiness, rubicundity.

(Verbs) To become red, to blush, flush, mantle, redden, colour.

435 Greenness *(Substantives)*, verdure, viridescence, viridity.

Emerald, jasper, verd-antique, verdigris, beryl, aquamarine, malachite, grass.

(Adjectives) Green, verdant, pea-green, grass-green, apple-green, sea-green, turquoise-green, olive-green, bottle-green, glaucous, virescent, aeruginous, vert.

(Phrase) Green as grass.

———

To render red, redden, rouge, rubefy, rubricate, incarnadine.

(Adjectives) Red, scarlet, vermilion, carmine, rose, ruby, crimson, pink, etc., ruddy, rufous, florid, rosy, roseate, auroral, rose-coloured, blushing, mantling, etc., erubescent, blowzy, rubicund, stammel, blood-red, en-sanguined, rubiform, cardinal, cerise, *sang-de-boeuf,* murrey, carroty, sorrel, brick-coloured, brick-red, lateritic, cherry-coloured, salmon-coloured.

(Phrases) Red as fire, as blood, as scarlet, as a turkey-cock, as a cherry.

436 Yellowness *(Substantives)*, buff colour, orpiment, yellow ochre, gamboge, crocus, saffron, xanthin, topaz.

437 Purple *(Substantives)*, violet, plum, prune, lavender, lilac, peach colour, puce, gridelin, lividness, lividity, bishop's purple, magenta, mauve.

Lemon, mustard, jaundice, gold.

(Adjectives) Yellow, citron, gold, golden, aureate, citrine, fallow, tawny, flavous, fulvous, saffron, croceate, lemon, xanthic, xanthous, sulphur, amber, straw-coloured, sandy, lurid, Claude-tint, luteous, primrose-coloured, cream-coloured, buff, chrome.

(Phrases) Yellow as a quince, as a guinea, as a crow's foot.

Amethyst, murex.

(Verb) To empurple.

(Adjectives) Purple, violet, plum-coloured, lilac, mauve, livid, etc.

---

438 Blueness *(Substantives)*, bluishness, azure, indigo, ultramarine, Prussian blue, mazarine, bloom, bice.

Sky, sea, lapis lazuli, cobalt, sapphire, turquoise.

(Adjectives) Blue, cerulean, sky-blue, sky-coloured, sky-dyed, watchet, azure, bluish, sapphire, Garter-blue.

439 Orange *(Substantives)*, gold, flame, copper, brass, apricot colour; aureolin, nacarat.

Ochre, cadmium.

(Adjectives) Orange, golden, ochreous, etc., buff, flame-coloured.

---

440 Variegation *(Substantives)*, dichroism, trichroism, iridescence, play of colours, *reflet*, variegatedness, patchwork, check, plaid, chess-board, tartan, maculation, spottiness, pointillism, parquetry, marquetry, mosaic, inlay, buhl, striae, spectrum.

A rainbow, iris, tulip, peacock, chameleon, butterfly, tortoise-shell, leopard, zebra, harlequin, motley, mother-of-pearl, nacre, opal, marble.

(Verbs) To be variegated, etc.

To variegate, speckle, stripe, streak, chequer, bespeckle, fleck, freckle, inlay, stipple, spot, dot, damascene, embroider, tattoo.

(Adjectives) Variegated, varicoloured, many-coloured, versicolour, many-hued, divers-coloured, particoloured, polychromatic, bicolour, tricolour, dichromatic.

Iridescent, prismatic, opaline, nacreous, pearly, opalescent, shot, watered, *chatoyant, gorge de pigeon*, all manner of colours, pied, piebald, skewbald, daedal, motley, mottled, veined, marbled, paned, dappled, clouded, cymophanous.

Mosaic, inlaid, tessellated, chequered, tartan, tortoiseshell.

Dotted, spotted, bespotted, spotty, speckled, bespeckled, punctate, maculated, freckled, fleckered, flecked, flea-bitten, studded, tattooed.

Striped, striated, streaked, barred, veined, brinded, brindled, tabby, roan, grizzled, listed, stippled.

(Phrase) All the colours of the rainbow.

---

(3) PERCEPTIONS OF LIGHT

441 Vision *(Substantives)*, sight, optics, eyesight.

View, espial, glance, glimpse, peep, peek, look, squint, dekko, gander, the once-over, gaze, stare, leer, perlustration, contemplation, sight-seeing, regard, survey, reconnaissance, introspection, inspection, speculation,

442 Blindness *(Substantives)*, night-blindness, snow-blindness, cecity, amaurosis, cataract, ablepsy, nictitation, wink, blink.

A blinkard.

(Verbs) To be blind, etc., not to see, to lose sight of.

Not to look, to close or shut the

watch, *coup d'oeil*, oeillade, glad eye, bo-peep, ocular demonstration, autopsy, visualization, envisagement.

A point of view, gazebo, vista, loop-hole, peep-hole, look-out, belvedere, field of view, watch-tower, observation post, crow's nest, theatre, amphitheatre, horizon, arena, commanding view, bird's-eye view, coign of vantage, observatory, periscope.

The organ of vision, eye, the naked or unassisted eye, retina, pupil, iris, cornea, white, optics, peepers.

Perspicacity, penetration, discernment.

Cat, hawk, lynx, eagle, Argus.

Evil eye; cockatrice, basilisk.

(Verbs) To see, behold, discern, have in sight, descry, sight, catch a sight, glance, or glimpse of, spy, espy, to get a sight of.

eyes, to look another way, to turn away or avert the eyes, to wink, blink, nictitate.

To render blind, etc., to put out the eyes, to blind, blindfold, hoodwink, daze, dazzle.

(Phrase) To throw, dust in the eyes.

(Adjectives) Blind, eyeless, sightless, visionless, dark, stone-blind, sand-blind, stark-blind, mope-eyed, dazzled, hoodwinked, blindfolded, undiscerning.

(Phrases) Blind as a bat, as a buzzard, as a beetle, as a mole, as an owl.

(Adverbs) Blindly, etc., blindfold, darkly.

To look, view, eye, open one's eyes, glance on, cast or set one's eyes on, clap eyes on, look on or upon, turn or bend one's looks upon, turn the eyes to, envisage, visualize, peep, peer, peek, pry, scan, survey, reconnoitre, contemplate, regard, inspect, recognize, mark, discover, distinguish, see through, speculate; to see sights, lionize.

To look intently, strain one's eyes, be all eyes, look full in the face, look hard at, stare, gaze, pore over, gloat on, leer, to see with half an eye, to blink, goggle, ogle, make eyes at; to play at bo-peep.

(Phrases) To have an eye upon; keep in sight; look about one; glance round; run the eye over; lift up one's eyes; see at a glance, or with half an eye; keep a look-out for; to keep one's eyes skinned; to be a spectator of; to see with one's own eyes.

(Adjectives) Visual, ocular, optic, optical, ophthalmic.

Seeing, etc., the eyes being directed to, fixed, riveted upon.

Clear-sighted, sharp-sighted, quick-sighted, eagle-eyed, hawk-eyed, lynx-eyed, keen-eyed, Argus-eyed, piercing, penetrating.

(Phrase) The scales falling from one's eyes.

(Adverbs) Visibly, etc., at sight, in sight of, to one's face, before one's face, with one's eyes open, at a glance, at first sight, at sight.

(Interjections) Look! behold! see! lo! mark! observe! lo and behold!

443 Imperfect vision.

Dim-sightedness *(Substantives)*, purblindness, lippitude, confusion of vision, scotomy, failing sight, short-sightedness, near-sightedness, myopia, nictitation, long-sightedness, amblyopia, presbyopia, hypermetropia, nyctalopia (or nyctalopy), nystagmus, astigmatism, squint, strabismus, wall-eye, swivel-eye, cast of the eye, double sight; an albino, blinkard.

Fallacies of vision; *deceptio visus*, refraction, false light, phantasm, anamorphosis, distortion, looming, mirage, *fata morgana*, the spectre of the Brocken, ignis fatuus, phantasmagoria, dissolving views.

Colour-blindness, Daltonism.

Limitation of vision, blinker, screen.

(Verbs) To be dim-sighted, etc., to see double, to have a mote in the eye,

to squint, goggle, look askance (or askant), to see through a prism, wink, nictitate.
To glare, dazzle, loom.

(Adjectives) Dim-sighted, half-sighted, short-sighted, near-sighted, purblind, myopic, long-sighted, hypermetropic, presbyopic, moon-eyed, mope-eyed, blear-eyed, goggle-eyed, wall-eyed, one-eyed, nictitating, winking, monoculous, amblyopic, astigmatic.

444 Spectator *(Substantives)*, looker-on, onlooker, watcher, sightseer, bystander, *voyeur*, inspector, snooper, rubberneck (455), spy, beholder, witness, eye-witness, observer, star-gazer, etc., scout.

(Verbs) To witness, behold, look on at, spectate.

445 Optical Instruments *(Substantives)*, lens, meniscus, magnifier, reading-glass, microscope, megascope, spectacles, specs, glasses, barnacles, goggles, pince-nez, lorgnette, folders, eye-glass, monocle, contact lens, periscope, telescope, spy-glass, monocular, binoculars, field-glass, night-glass, opera-glass, glass, view-finder, range-finder.

Mirror, reflector, speculum, looking-glass, pier-glass, cheval-glass, kaleidoscope.

Prism, camera, cine-camera, cinematograph (448), camera lucida, camera obscura, magic lantern, phantasmagoria, thaumatrope, chromatrope, stereoscope, pseudoscope, bioscope.

Photometer, polariscope, spectroscope, collimator, polemoscope, eriometer, actinometer, exposure meter, lucimeter.

446 Visibility *(Substantives)*, perceptibility, conspicuousness, distinctness, conspicuity, appearance, exposure.

(Verbs) To be visible, etc., to appear, come in sight, come into view, heave in sight, open to the view, catch the eye, show its face, present itself, show itself, manifest itself, produce itself, discover itself, expose itself, come out, come to light, come forth, come forward, stand forth, stand out, arise, peep out, peer out, show up, turn up, crop up, start up, loom, burst forth, break through the clouds, glare, reveal itself, betray itself.

(Phrases) to show its colours; to see the light of day; to show one's face; to tell its own tale; to leap to the eye; *cela saute aux yeux*; to stare one in the face.

(Adjectives) Visible, perceptible, perceivable, discernible, in sight, apparent, plain, manifest, patent, obvious (525), clear, distinct, definite, well-defined, well-marked, recognizable, evident, unmistakable, palpable, naked, bare, barefaced, ostensible,

447 Invisibility *(Substantives)*, indistinctness, inconspicuousness, imperceptibility, nonappearance, delitescence, latency (526), concealment (528).

(Verbs) To be invisible, escape notice, etc., to lie hidden, concealed, etc. (528), to be in or under a cloud, in a mist, in a haze, etc.; to lurk, lie in ambush, skulk.

Not to see, etc., to be blind to.

To render invisible, to hide, conceal (528).

(Adjectives) Invisible, imperceptible, unseen, unbeheld, undiscerned, viewless, undiscernible, indiscernible, sightless, undescried, unespied, unapparent, non-apparent, inconspicuous, unconspicuous, hidden, concealed, etc. (528), covert, eclipsed.

Confused, dim, obscure, dark, misty, hazy, foggy, indistinct, ill-defined, indefinite, ill-marked, blurred, shadowy, nebulous, shaded, screened, veiled, masked.

(Phrases) Out of sight; not in sight; out of focus.

conspicuous, prominent, staring, glaring, notable, notorious, overt; periscopic, panoramic, stereoscopic.

(Phrases) Open as day; clear as day; plain as a pikestaff; there is no mistaking; plain as the nose on one's face; before one's eyes; above-board; exposed to view; under one's nose; in bold relief; in the limelight.

448 Appearance *(Substantives)*, phenomenon, sight, spectacle, show, premonstration, scene, species, view, *coup d'œil*, look-out, prospect, outlook, vista, perspective, bird's-eye view, scenery, landscape, seascape, streetscape, picture, tableau, *mise en scène*, display, exposure, exhibition, manifestation.

Pageant, pageantry, peep-show, raree-show, panorama, diorama, cosmorama, georama, *coup de théâtre, jeu de théâtre*.

Bioscope, biograph, magic lantern, epidiascope, cinematograph (or kinematograph).

Phantasm, phasma, phantom, spectrum, apparition, spectre, mirage, etc. (4, 443).

Aspect, phase, *phasis*, seeming, guise, look, complexion, shape, mien, air, cast, carriage, manner, bearing, deportment, port, demeanour, presence, expression.

Lineament, feature, trait, lines, outline, contour, face, countenance, physiognomy, visage, phiz, mug, dial, puss, pan, profile, *tournure*.

(Verbs) To seem, look, appear; to present, wear, carry, have, bear, exhibit, take, take on, or assume the appearance of; to play, to look like, to be visible, to reappear; to materialize.

To show, to manifest.

(Adjectives) Apparent, seeming, etc., ostensible.

(Adverbs) Apparently, to all appearance, etc., ostensibly, seemingly, on the face of it, *prima facie*, at the first blush, at first sight.

449 Disappearance *(Substantives)*, evanescence, eclipse, occultation.

Dissolving views, fade-out.

(Verbs) To disappear, vanish, dissolve, fade, melt away, pass, be gone, be lost, etc.

To efface, blot, blot out, erase, rub out, expunge (552).

(Phrase) To go off the stage.

(Adjectives) Disappearing, etc., lost, vanishing, evanescent, gone, missing.

Inconspicuous, unconspicuous (447).

(Phrases) Lost in the clouds; leaving no trace; out of sight.

(Interjections) Avaunt! vanish! disappear! (297).

CLASS IV

WORDS RELATING TO THE INTELLECTUAL FACULTIES

DIVISION I—FORMATION OF IDEAS

450 Intellect *(Substantives)*, mind, understanding, reason, thinking principle, nous, noesis, faculties, sense, common sense, consciousness, capacity, intelligence, percipience, intellection, intuition, instinct, conception, judgment, talent, genius, parts, wit, wits, shrewdness, intellectuality; the five senses; rationalism; ability, skill (698); wisdom (498).

Subconsciousness, subconscious mind, unconscious, id.

Soul, spirit, psyche, ghost, inner man, heart, breast, bosom.

Organ or seat of thought: *sensorium,* sensory, brain, head, headpiece, pate, noddle, nut, loaf, skull, brain-pan, grey matter, pericranium, cerebrum, cerebellum, cranium, upper storey, belfry.

Science of mind, phrenology, mental philosophy, metaphysics, psychology, psychics, psycho-analysis; ideology, idealism, ideality, pneumatology, immaterialism, intuitionism, realism; transcendentalism, spiritualism.

Metaphysician, psychologist, psychiatrist, psycho-analyst, psychotherapist.

(Verbs) Appreciate, realize, be aware of, be conscious of, take in, mark, note, notice.

(Adjectives) Intellectual, noetic, rational, reasoning, gnostic, mental, spiritual, subjective, metaphysical, psychical, psychological, noumenal, ghostly, immaterial (317), cerebral; subconscious, subliminal, Freudian.

450A Absence or want of intellect, imbecility (499), materialism.

(Adjectives) Material, objective, unreasoning.

———

451 Thought *(Substantives)*, reflection, cogitation, cerebration, consideration, meditation, study, lucubration, speculation, deliberation, pondering, head-work, brain-work, application, attention (457).

Abstraction, contemplation, musing, brown study, reverie (458); depth of thought, workings of the mind, inmost thoughts, self-counsel, self-communing, self-examination, introspection; succession, flow, train,

452 Absence or want of thought.

Incogitancy *(Substantives)*, vacancy, inanity, fatuity (499), thoughtlessness (458).

(Verbs) Not to think, to take no thought of, not to trouble oneself about, to put away thought; to inhibit, dismiss, discard, or discharge from one's thoughts, or from the mind; to drop the subject, set aside, turn aside, turn away from, turn

current, etc., of thought or of ideas, brain-wave.

Afterthought, second thoughts, hindsight, reconsideration, retrospection, retrospect (505), examination (461), imagination (515).

Thoughtfulness, pensiveness, intentness.

Telepathy, thought-transference, mind-reading, extra-sensory perception, retrocognition, telekinesis.

(Verbs) To think, reflect, cogitate, excogitate, consider, deliberate, speculate, contemplate, mediate, introspect, ponder, muse, ruminate, think over, brood over, reconsider, animadvert, con, con over, mull over, study, bend or apply the mind, digest, discuss, hammer at, puzzle out, weigh, perpend, fancy, trow, dream of.

To occur, present itself, pass in the mind, suggest itself, strike one.

To harbour, entertain, cherish, nurture, etc., an idea, a thought, a notion, a view, etc.

(Phrases) Take into account; take into consideration; to take counsel; to commune with oneself; to collect one's thoughts; to advise with one's pillow; to sleep on or over it; to chew the cud upon; revolve in the mind; turn over in the mind; to rack or cudgel one's brains; to put on one's thinking-cap.

To flash on the mind; to flit across the view; to enter the mind; come into the head; come uppermost; run in one's head.

To make an impression; to sink or penetrate into the mind; fasten itself on the mind; to engross one's thoughts.

(Adjectives) Thinking, etc., thoughtful, pensive, meditative, reflective, ruminant, introspective, wistful, contemplative, speculative, deliberative, studious, abstracted, introspective, sedate, philosophical, conceptual.

Close, active, diligent, mature, deliberate, laboured, steadfast, deep, profound, intense, etc., thought, study, reflection, etc.

Intent, engrossed, absorbed, deep-musing, rapt (or wrapt), abstracted; sedate.

(Phrases) Having the mind on the stretch; lost in thought; the mind or head running upon.

one's attention from, abstract oneself, dream.

To unbend, relax, divert the mind.

(Adjectives) Vacant, unintellectual (499), unoccupied, unthinking, inconsiderate, thoughtless, idealess, unidea'd, absent, *distrait*, abstracted, inattentive (458), diverted, distracted, distraught, unbent, relaxed.

Unthought-of, unconsidered, incogitable, undreamed-of, off one's mind.

(Phrase) In nubibus.

———

453 Object of thought.

Idea *(Substantives)*, notion, conception, apprehension, concept, thought, fancy, conceit, impression, perception, apperception, percept, ideation, image, eidolon, sentiment (484), fantasy, flight of fancy.

Point of view, light, aspect (448), field of view, standpoint; theory (514); fixed idea (481).

———

454 Subject of thought.

Topic *(Substantives)*, subject, matter, theme, motif, thesis, text, subject-matter, point, proposition, theorem, business, affair, case, matter in hand, question, argument, motion, resolution, moot point (461), head, chapter; nice or subtle point, quodlibet.

(Phrases) Food for thought; mental pabulum.

(Adverbs) In question, under consideration, on the carpet, *sur le tapis*, relative to, *re, in re* (9), concerning, touching.

455 The desire for knowlege.

Curiosity (*Substantives*), curiousness, inquisitiveness, an inquiring mind.

A quidnunc, busybody, eavesdropper, snooper, rubberneck, Peeping Tom, Nosy Parker, Paul Pry, newsmonger, gossip.

(*Verbs*) To be curious, etc., to take an interest in, to stare, gape, pry, snoop, rubber, lionize.

(*Adjectives*) Curious, inquisitive, inquiring, inquisitorial, all agog, staring, prying, snoopy, gaping, agape, over-curious, nosy.

(*Adverbs*) With open mouth, on tiptoe, with ears flapping, *arrectis auribus*.

456 Absence of curiosity.

Incuriosity (*Substantives*), incuriousness, insouciance, nonchalance, want of interest, indifference (866).

(*Verbs*) To be incurious, etc., to have no curiosity, take no interest in, not to care, not to mind; to mind one's own business.

(*Phrases*) Not to trouble oneself about; one couldn't care less; the devil may care; san fairy ann.

(*Adjectives*) Incurious, uninquisitive, indifferent, *sans souci*, insouciant, nonchalant, aloof, detached, apathetic, uninterested.

---

457 Attention (*Substantives*), advertence, advertency, observance, observation, interest, notice, heed, look, regard, view, remark, inspection, introspection, heedfulness, mindfulness, look-out, watch, vigilance, circumspection, surveillance, consideration, scrutiny, revision, revisal, recension, review, revise, particularity (459).

Close, intense, deep, profound, etc., attention, application, or study.

(*Verbs*) To be attentive, etc.; to attend, advert to, mind, observe, look, look at, see, view, look to, see to, remark, heed, notice, spot, twig, pipe, take heed, take notice, mark; give or pay attention to; give heed to, have an eye to; turn, apply, or direct the mind, the eye, or the attention to; look after, give a thought to, animadvert on, occupy oneself with, be interested in, devote oneself to, give oneself up to, see about.

To examine cursorily; to glance at, upon, or over; cast or pass the eyes over, run over, turn over the leaves, dip into, skim, perstringe.

To examine closely or intently, scrutinize, consider, give one's mind to, overhaul, pore over, perpend, note, mark, inspect, review, size up, take stock of, fix the eye, mind,

458 Inattention (*Substantives*) inconsideration, inconsiderateness, inadvertence, inadvertency, non-observance, inobservance, disregard, oversight, unmindfulness, giddiness, respectlessness, thoughtlessness (460), insouciance; wandering, distracted, etc., attention.

Absence of mind, abstraction, preoccupation, distraction, reverie, brown study, day-dream, day-dreaming, wool-gathering.

(*Phrases*) The wits going wool-gathering; the attention wandering; building castles in the air, or castles in Spain.

(*Verbs*) To be inattentive, etc., to overlook, disregard, pass by, slur over, pass over, gloss over, blink, miss, skim, skim the surface, *effleur* (460).

To call off, draw off, call away, divert, etc., the attention; to distract; to disconcert, put out, rattle, discompose, confuse, perplex, bewilder, bemuse, moider, bemuddle, muddle, dazzle, obfuscate, faze, fluster, flurry, flummox, befog.

(*Phrases*) To take no account of; to drop the subject; to turn a deaf ear to; to come in at one ear and go out of the other; to reckon without one's host.

thoughts, or attention on, keep in view, contemplate, revert to, etc. (451).

To fall under one's notice, observation, etc., to catch the eye; to catch, awaken, wake, invite, solicit, attract, claim, excite, engage, occupy, strike, arrest, fix, engross, monopolize, preoccupy, obsess, absorb, rivet, etc., the attention, mind, or thoughts; to interest.

To call attention to, point out, indicate (550).

(Phrases) To trouble one's head about; lend or incline an ear to; to take cognizance of; to prick up one's ears; to have one's eyes open; to keep one's eyes skinned.

To have one's wits about one; to bear in mind; to come to the point; to take into account; to read, mark, learn.

(Adjectives) Attentive, mindful, heedful, regardful, alive to, awake to, bearing in mind, occupied with, engaged, taken up with, interested, engrossed, wrapped in, absorbed, rapt.

Awake, watchful, on the watch (459), broad awake, wide awake, agape, intent on, with eyes fixed on, open-eyed, unwinking, undistracted, with bated breath, breathless, upon the stretch.

(Interjections) See! look! say! attention! hey! oy! mark! lo! behold! achtung! nota bene! N.B.

(Adjectives) Inattentive, mindless, unobservant, unmindful, uninterested, inadvertent, heedless, regardless, respectless, careless (460), insouciant, unwatchful, listless, cursory, blind, deaf, etc.

Absent, abstracted, *distrait,* absent-minded, lost, preoccupied, bemused, dreamy, moony, napping.

Disconcerted, put out, etc., dizzy, muzzy (460).

(Phrase) Caught napping.

(Adverbs) Inattentively, etc., cavalierly.

————

459 Care *(Substantives)*, caution, heed, heedfulness, attention (457), wariness, prudence, discretion, watch, watchfulness, alertness, vigil, vigilance, circumspection, watch and ward, deliberation, forethought (510), pre-deliberation, solicitude, precaution (673), scruple, scrupulousness, scrupulosity, particularity, surveillance.

(Phrases) The eyes of Argus; *l'œil du maître.*

(Verbs) To be careful, etc., to take care, have a care, beware, look to it, reck, heed, take heed, provide for, see to, see after, keep watch, keep watch and ward, look sharp, look about one, set watch, take precautions, take tent, see about.

(Phrases) To have all one's wits about one; to mind one's P's and Q's; to speak by the card; to pick one's steps; keep a sharp look out; keep one's weather eye open; to keep an eye on.

(Adjectives) Careful, cautious,

460 Neglect *(Substantives)*, negligence, omission, trifling, laches, heedlessness, carelessness, perfunctoriness, remissness, imprudence, secureness, indiscretion, *étourderie,* incautiousness, indiscrimination, rashness (863), recklessness, nonchalance, inattention (458); slovenliness, sluttishness.

Trifler, flibbertigibbet, Micawber; slattern, slut, sloven.

(Verbs) To be negligent, etc., to neglect, scamp, pass over, cut, omit, pretermit, set aside, cast or put aside.

To overlook, disregard, ignore, slight, pay no regard to, make light of, trifle with, blink, wink at, connive at; take or make no account of; gloss over, slur over, slip over, skip, skim, miss, shelve, sink, jump over, shirk (623), discount.

To waste time, trifle, frivol, fribble (683).

heedful, wary, canny, guarded, on one's guard, alert, on the alert, on the watch, watchful, on the look out, *aux aguets*, awake, vigilant, circumspect, broad awake, having the eyes open, Argus-eyed.

Discreet, prudent, sure-footed, provident, scrupulous, particular, meticulous.

(Phrase) On the *qui vive*.

(Adverbs) Carefully, etc., with care, etc., gingerly, considerately.

(Phrases) Let sleeping dogs lie; catching a weasel asleep.

(Interjections) Look out! mind your eye! watch! beware! cave! fore! heads!

To render neglectful, etc., to put or throw off one's guard.

(Phrases) To give to the winds; take no account of; turn a deaf ear to; shut one's eyes to; not to mind; think no more of; set at naught; give the go-by to.

(Adjectives) Neglecting, etc., unmindful, heedless, careless, *sans souci*, negligent, neglectful, slovenly, sluttish, remiss, perfunctory, thoughtless, unthoughtful, unheedful, off one's guard, unwary, incautious, unguarded, indiscreet, inconsiderate, imprudent, improvident, rash, headlong, reckless, heels over head, witless, hare-brained, giddy-brained, offhand, slapdash, happy-go-lucky, cursory, brain-sick, scatterbrained.

Neglected, missed, abandoned, shunted, shelved, unheeded, unperceived, unseen, unobserved, unnoticed, unnoted, unmarked, unattended to, untended, unwatched, unthought-of, overlooked, unmissed, unexamined, unsearched, unscanned, unweighed, unsifted, untested, unweeded, undetermined.

(Phrases) In an unguarded moment; buried in a napkin.

(Adverbs) Negligently, etc., anyhow, any old way.

(Interjections) Let it pass! never mind! no matter! I should worry! san fairy ann! *nichevo!*

---

461 Inquiry *(Substantives)*, search, research, quest, pursuit (622), examination, review, scrutiny, investigation, perquisition, perscrutation, referendum, straw vote, Gallup poll; discussion, symposium, inquest, inquisition, exploration, exploitation, sifting, screening, calculation, analysis, dissection, resolution, induction; the Baconian method.

Questioning, asking, interrogation, interpellation, interrogatory, the Socratic method, examination, cross-examination, cross-questioning, third degree, quiz, catechism.

Reconnoitring, reconnaissance, feeler, *ballon d'essai*, prying, spying, espionage, the lantern of Diogenes, searchlight.

Question, query, difficulty, problem, proposition, desideratum, point to be solved; point or matter in dispute; moot point, question at issue,

462 Answer *(Substantives)*. response, reply, replication, riposte, rejoinder, rebutter, surrejoinder, surrebutter, retort, come-back, repartee, rescript, antiphony, rescription, acknowledgment.

Explanation, solution, deduction, resolution, exposition, rationale, interpretation (522).

A key, master-key, open sesame, *passepartout*, clue.

Oedipus, oracle (513), solutionist.

(Verbs) To answer, respond, reply, rebut, retort, rejoin, return for answer, acknowledge, echo.

To explain, solve, resolve, expound, decipher, spell, interpret (522), to unriddle, unlock, cut the knot, unravel, fathom, pick or open the lock, discover, fish up, to find a clue to, to get to the bottom of.

(Phrases) To turn the tables upon; Q.E.D.

bone of contention, plain question, fair question, open question, knotty point, vexed question, crux.

Enigma, riddle, conundrum, crossword, bone to pick, quodlibet, Gordian knot.

(Adjectives) Answering, responding, etc., responsive, respondent.
(Adverb) On the right scent.
(Interjections) Eureka!

———

An inquirer, querist, questioner, heckler, inquisitor, scrutator, scrutineer, examiner, inspector, analyst, quidnunc, newsmonger, gossip (527, 532); investigator, detective, bloodhound, sleuth-hound, sleuth, inquiry agent, private eye, Sherlock Holmes, busy, dick, rozzer, flattie, G-men; secret police, Cheka, Ogpu, Gestapo.

(Verbs) To inquire, seek, search, look for, look about for, look out for, cast about for, beat up for, grope for, feel for, reconnoitre, explore, sound, rummage, fossick, ransack, pry, snoop, look round, look over, look through, scan, peruse.

To pursue, hunt, track, trail, mouse-dodge, trace, shadow, tail, dog (622), nose out, ferret out, unearth, hunt up.

To investigate; to take up, follow up, institute, pursue, conduct, carry on, prosecute, etc., an inquiry, etc.; to overhaul, examine, study, consider, fathom, take into consideration, dip into, look into, calculate, pre-examine, dive into, to delve into, rake, rake over, discuss, canvass, thrash out, probe, fathom, sound, scrutinize, analyse, anatomize, dissect, sift, screen, winnow, resolve, traverse, see into.

To ask, speer, question, query, demand; to put, propose, propound, moot, raise, stir, suggest, put forth, start, pop, etc., a question; to interrogate, catechize, pump, cross-question, cross-examine, grill, badger, heckle, dodge, require an answer.

(Phrases) To look, peer, or pry into every hole and corner, to beat the bushes; to leave no stone unturned; to seek a needle in a bundle of hay; to scratch the head.

To subject to examination; to grapple with a question; to put to the proof; pass in review; take into consideration; to ventilate a question; seek a clue; throw out a feeler.

To undergo examination; to be in course of inquiry; to be under consideration.

(Adjectives) Inquiring, etc., inquisitive, requisitive, requisitory, catechetical, inquisitorial, heuristic, analytic, in search of, in quest of, on the look out for, interrogative, zetetic.

Undetermined, untried, undecided, to be resolved, etc., in question, in dispute, under discussion, under consideration, *sub judice*, moot, proposed, doubtful.

(Adverbs) Why? wherefore? whence? *quaere?* how comes it? how happens it? how is it? what is the reason? what's in the wind? what's cooking?

463 Experiment *(Substantives)*, essay, trial, tryout, tentative method, *tâtonnement*, verification, probation, proof, criterion, test, acid test, reagent, check, control, touchstone, pyx, assay, ordeal; empiricism, rule of thumb method of trial and error.

A feeler, *ballon d'essai*, pilot-balloon, messenger-balloon; pilot-engine; straw to show the wind.

(Verbs) To experiment, essay, try, explore, grope, angle, cast about, beat the bushes; feel or grope one's way; to thread one's way; to make an experiment, make trial of.

To subject to trial, etc., to experiment upon, try over, rehearse, give a trial to, put, bring, or submit to the test or proof; to prove, verify, test, assay, touch, practise upon.

(Phrases) To see how the land lies; to see how the wind blows; to feel the pulse; to throw out a feeler; to have a try; to have a go.

(Adjectives) Experimental, crucial, tentative, probationary, empirical, *sub judice*, under probation, on trial, on approval.

(Adverb)A tâtons.

464 Comparison *(Substantives)*, collation, contrast, antithesis, identification.

A comparison, simile, similitude, analogy, parallel, parable, metaphor, allegory (521).

(Verbs) To compare to or with; to collate, confront, place side by side or in juxtaposition, to draw a parallel, institute a comparison, contrast, balance, identify.

(Adjectives) Comparative, metaphorical, figurative, allegorical, comparable, compared with, pitted against, placed by the side of.

465 Discrimination *(Substantives)*, distinction, differentiation, perception or appreciation of difference, nicety, refinement, taste (850), judgment, discernment, nice perception, tact, critique.

(Verbs) To discriminate, distinguish, differentiate, draw the line, sift, screen.

(Phrases) To split hairs; to cut blocks with a razor; to separate the chaff from the wheat or the sheep from the goats.

(Adjectives) Discriminating, etc., discriminative, distinctive, diagnostic, nice, judicial.

465A Indiscrimination *(Substantives)*, indistinctness, indistinction (460).

(Verbs) Not to distinguish or discriminate, to confound, confuse; to neglect, overlook, lose sight of a distinction.

(Adjectives) Indiscriminate, undistinguished, undistinguishable, unmeasured, sweeping, wholesale.

_____

466 Measurement *(Substantives)*, admeasurement, mensuration, triangulation, survey, valuation, appraisement, assessment, assize, estimation, reckoning, evaluation, gauging; mileage, voltage, horse power.

Geometry, geodetics, geodesy, orthometry, altimetry, sounding, surveying, weighing, ponderation, trutination, dead reckoning, metrology.

A measure, standard, rule, yardstick, compass, callipers, dividers, gauge, meter, line, rod, plumb-line, plummet, log, log-line, sound, sounding-rod, sounding-line, lead-line, index, flood-mark, Plimsoll line (or mark), check.

Scale, graduation, graduated scale, vernier, quadrant, theodolite, slide-rule, balance, spring balance, scales, steelyard, beam, weather-glass, barometer, aneroid, barograph, araeometer, altimeter, clinometer, graphometer, goniometer, thermometer, speedometer, tachometer, pedometer, ammeter, voltmeter, micrometer, etc.

A surveyor, geometer, leadsman, etc.

(Verbs) To measure, mete, value, assess, rate, appraise, estimate, form an estimate, set a value on, appreciate, span, pace, step; apply the compass, rule, scale, etc., gauge, plump, probe, sound, fathom, heave the log, survey, weigh, poise, balance, hold the scales, take an average, graduate, evaluate, size up, to place in the beam, to take into account, price.

(Adjectives) Measuring, etc., metrical, ponderable, measurable, mensurable.

SECTION III—MATERIALS FOR REASONING

467 Evidence, on one side *(Substantives)*, premises, data, grounds, *praecognita*, indication (550).

Oral, hearsay, internal, external, documentary, presumptive evidence.

Testimony, testimonial, deposition, declaration, attestation, testification, authority, warrant, warranty, guarantee, surety, handwriting, autograph, signature, endorsement, seal, sigil, signet (550), superscription, entry, finger-print.

Voucher, credential, certificate, deed, indenture, docket, dossier, probate, affidavit, diploma; admission, concession, allegation, deposition, citation, quotation, reference; admissibility.

Criterion, test, reagent, touchstone, check, control, prerogative, fact, argument, shibboleth.

A witness, eye-witness, indicator, ear-witness, deponent, telltale, informer, sponsor, special pleader.

Assumption, presumption, show of reason, postulation, postulate, lemma.

Reason, proof (478), circumstantial evidence.

Ex-parte evidence, one-sided view.

Secondary evidence, confirmation, corroboration, ratification, authentication, support, approval, compurgation.

(Phrases) A case in point; *ecce signum; ex pede Herculem.*

(Verbs) To be evidence, etc., to evidence, evince, show, indicate (550), imply, involve, entail, necessitate, argue, bespeak, admit, allow, concede, homologate, certify, testify, attest, bear testimony, depose, depone, witness, vouch for, sign, seal, set one's hand and seal to, endorse, confirm, ratify, corroborate, support, establish, uphold, bear upon, bear out, warrant, guarantee.

To adduce, cite, quote, refer to, appeal to, call, bring forward, produce, bring into court, confront witnesses, collect, bring together, rake up evidence, to make a case, make good, authenticate, substantiate, go bail for.

To allege, plead, assume, postulate, posit, presume; to beg the question.

468 Evidence on the other side, on the other hand.

Counter-evidence *(Substantives)*, disproof, contradiction, rejoinder, rebutter, answer (462), weak point, conflicting evidence, refutation (479), negation (536).

(Phrases) A *tu quoque* argument; the other side of the shield.

(Verbs) To countervail, oppose, rebut, check, weaken, invalidate, contradict, contravene.

(Phrases) To tell another story; to cut both ways.

(Adjectives) Countervailing, etc., contradictory; unauthenticated, unattested, unvouched-for.

(Adverbs) Although, though, albeit, but, *per contra*.

(Phrase) Audi alteram partem.

469 Qualification *(Substantives)*, limitation, modification, allowance, grains of allowance, consideration, extenuating circumstance, condition, proviso, saving clause, penalty clause, exception (83), assumption (514).

(Verbs) To qualify, limit, modify, tone down, colour, discount, allow for, make allowance for, take into account, introduce new conditions, admit exceptions, take exception.

(Adjectives) Qualifying, etc., conditional, exceptional (83), contingent, postulatory, hypothetical, supposititious (514).

(Adverbs) Provided, if, unless, but, yet, according as, conditionally, admitting, supposing, granted that; on the supposition, assumption, presumption, allegation, hypothesis, etc., of; with the understanding, even, although, for all that, at all events, after all.

(Phrases) With a grain of salt; *cum grano salis.*

(Phrases) To hold good, hold water; to speak volumes; to bring home to; to bring to book; to quote chapter and verse; to speak for itself; tell its own tale.

(Adjectives) Showing, etc., indicating, indicative, indicatory, evidential, evidentiary, following, deducible, consequential, collateral, corroborative, confirmatory, postulatory, presumptive.

Sound, logical, strong, valid, cogent, decisive, persuasive, persuasory, demonstrative, irrefragable, irresistible, etc. (578).

(Adverbs) According to, witness, admittedly, confessedly, *a fortiori,* still more, still less, all the more reason for.

Degrees of Evidence

470 Possibility *(Substantives)*, potentiality, contingency (156), what may be, what is possible, etc.

Practicability, feasibility (705), compatibility (23).

(Verbs) To be possible, etc., to admit of, to bear.

To render possible, etc., to put into the way of.

(Adjectives) Possible, contingent (475), conceivable, credible.

Practicable, feasible, achievable, performable, viable, accessible, surmountable, attainable, obtainable, compatible.

(Adverbs) Possibly, by possibility, maybe, perhaps, mayhap, haply, perchance, peradventure, *in posse* (156).

(Phrases) Wind and weather permitting; within the bounds of possibility; on the cards; D.V.

---

471 Impossibility *(Substantives)*, what cannot be, what can never be, imposs, no go, hopelessness (859).

Impracticability, incompatibility (704), incredibility.

(Verbs) To be impossible, etc., to have no chance whatever.

(Phrases) To make a silk purse out of a sow's ear; to wash a blackamoor white; to make bricks without straw; to get blood from a stone; to take the breeks off a highlandman; to square the circle; to eat one's cake and have it too.

(Adjectives) Impossible, contrary to reason, inconceivable, unreasonable, absurd, incredible, visionary, chimerical, prodigious (870), desperate, hopeless, unheard-of, unthinkable.

Impracticable, unattainable, unachievable, unfeasible, infeasible, beyond control, unobtainable, unprocurable, insuperable, unsurmountable, inaccessible, inextricable.

(Phrases) Out of the question; sour grapes; *non possumus.*

---

472 Probability *(Substantives)*, likelihood, *vraisemblance,* verisimilitude, plausibility, show of, colour of, credibility, reasonable chance, favourable chance, fair chance, hope, prospect, presumption, presumptive evidence, circumstantial evidence, the main chance, a *prima facie* case.

Probabilism, probabiliorism.

(Verbs) To be probable, likely, etc.; to think likely, dare say, expect (507).

(Phrases) To bid fair; to stand fair for; to stand a good chance; to stand to reason.

---

473 Improbability *(Substantives)*, unlikelihood, unfavourable chances, small chance, off-chance, bare possibility, long odds, incredibility.

(Verbs) To be improbable, etc., to have or stand a small, little, poor, remote, etc., chance; to whistle for.

(Adjectives) Improbable, unheard-of, incredible, unbelievable, unlikely.

(Phrases) Contrary to all reasonable expectation; having scarcely a chance; a chance in a thousand.

(Adjectives) Probable, likely, hopeful, well-founded.

Plausible, specious, ostensible, colourable, standing to reason, reasonable, credible, tenable, easy of belief, presumable, presumptive, *ben trovato*.

(Phrases) Likely to happen; in a fair way; appearances favouring; according to every reasonable expectation; the odds being in favour.

(Adverbs) Probably, etc., belike, in all probability, or likelihood, apparently, to all appearance, on the face of it, in the long run, *prima facie*, very likely, like enough, arguably, ten to one.

(Phrase) All Lombard Street to a china orange.

474 Certainty *(Substantives)*, certitude, positiveness, a dead certainty, dead cert, infallibleness, infallibility, gospel, scripture, surety, assurance, indisputableness, moral certainty.

Fact, matter of fact, *fait accompli*.

Bigotry, dogmatism, *ipse dixit*.

Bigot, dogmatist, Sir Oracle.

(Verbs) To be certain, etc., to believe (484).

To render certain, etc., to ensure, to assure, clinch, determine, decide.

To dogmatize, lay down the law.

(Phrases) To stand to reason; to make assurance doubly sure.

(Adjectives) Certain, sure, assured, solid, absolute, positive, flat, determinate, categorical, unequivocal, inevitable, unavoidable, avoidless, unerring, infallible, indubitable, indubious, indisputable, undisputed, uncontested, undeniable, incontestable, irrefutable, unimpeachable, incontrovertible, undoubted, doubtless, without doubt, beyond a doubt, past dispute, unanswerable, decided, unquestionable, beyond all question, unquestioned, questionless, irrefragable, evident, self-evident, axiomatic, demonstrable (478), authoritative, authentic, official, unerring, infallible, trustworthy (939).

(Phrases) Sure as fate; and no mistake; sure as a gun; clear as the sun at noonday; sure as death (and taxes); bet your life; you bet; *cela va sans dire*; it's in the bag; that's flat.

(Adverbs) Certainly, assuredly, etc., for certain, *in esse*, sure, surely, sure enough, to be sure, of course, as a matter of course, yes (488), depend upon it, that's so, by all manner of means, beyond a peradventure.

475 Uncertainty *(Substantives)*, incertitude, doubt (485), doubtfulness, dubiety, dubiousness, suspense, precariousness, indefiniteness, indetermination, slipperiness, fallibility, perplexity, embarrassment, dilemma, ambiguity (520), hesitation, vacillation (605), equivoque, vagueness, peradventure, touch-and-go.

(Phrases) A blind bargain; a pig in a poke; a leap in the dark; a moot point; an open question.

(Verbs) To be uncertain, etc.; to vacillate, hesitate, waver.

To render uncertain, etc., to perplex, embarrass, confuse, moider, confound, bewilder, disorientate.

(Phrases) To be in a state of uncertainty; not to know which way to turn; to be at a loss; to be at fault; to lose the scent.

To tremble in the balance; to hang by a thread.

(Adjectives) Uncertain, doubtful, dubious, precarious (665), chancy, casual, random, contingent, indecisive, dependent on circumstances, undecided, unsettled, undetermined, pending, pendent, vague, indeterminate, indefinite, ambiguous, undefined, equivocal, undefinable, puzzling, enigmatic, debatable, disputable, questionable, apocryphal, problematical, hypothetical, controvertible, fallible, fallacious, suspicious, fishy, slippery, ticklish.

Unauthentic, unconfirmed, undemonstrated, undemonstrable, unreliable, untrustworthy.

———

SECTION IV—REASONING PROCESSES

476 Reasoning (*Substantives*), ratiocination, dialectics, induction, deduction, generalization; inquiry (461).

Argumentation, discussion, *pourparler*, controversy, polemics, debate, wrangling, logomachy, apology, apologetics, ergotism, disputation, disceptation.

The art of reasoning, logic, process, train or chain of reasoning, analysis, synthesis, argument, lemma, proposition, terms, premises, postulate, data, starting-point, principle, inference, result, conclusion.

Syllogism, prosyllogism, enthymeme, sorites, dilemma, *perilepsis*, pros and cons, a comprehensive argument.

Correctness, soundness, force, validity, cogency, conclusiveness.

A thinker, a reasoner, disputant, controversialist, logician, dialectician, polemic, wrangler, arguer, debater.

(Phrases) A paper war; a war of words; a battle of the books; a full-dress debate.

The horns of a dilemma; *reductio ad absurdum; argumentum ad hominem; onus probandi.*

(Verbs) To reason, argue, discuss, debate, dispute, wrangle; bandy words or arguments; hold or carry on an argument, controvert, contravene (536), consider (461), comment upon, moralize upon, spiritualize.

(Phrases) To open a discussion or case; to moot; to join issue; to ventilate a question; to talk it over; to have it out; to take up a side or case.

To chop logic; to try conclusions; to impale on the horns of a dilemma; to cut the matter short; to hit the nail on the head; to take one's stand upon; to have the last word.

(Adjectives) Reasoning, etc., rational, rationalistic, ratiocinative, argumentative, controversial, dialectic, polemical, discursory, discursive, debatable, controvertible, disputatious; correct, just, fair, sound, valid,

477 The absence of reasoning.

Intuition (*Substantives*), instinct, association, presentiment, insight, second sight, sixth sense.

False or vicious reasoning, show of reason.

Misjudgment, miscalculation (481).

Sophistry (*Substantives*), paralogy, fallacy, perversion, casuistry, jesuitry, quibble, equivocation, evasion, chicanery, special pleading, quiddity, mystification; nonsense (497).

Sophism, solecism, paralogism, elenchus, fallacy, quodlibet, subterfuge, subtlety, quillet, inconsistency, antilogy.

Speciousness, plausibility, illusiveness, irrelevancy, invalidity; clap-trap, hot air.

Quibbler, casuist, *advocatus diaboli.*

(Phrases) Begging the question; *petitio principii; ignoratio elenchi;* reasoning in a circle; *post hoc, ergo propter hoc; ignotum per ignotius.*

The meshes or cobwebs of sophistry; a flaw in an argument; an argument falling to the ground.

(Verbs) To envisage, to judge intuitively, etc.

To reason ill, falsely, etc.; to pervert, quibble, equivocate, mystify, evade, elude, gloss over, varnish, misjudge, miscalculate (481).

To refine, subtilize, cavil, sophisticate, mislead.

(Phrases) To split hairs; to cut blocks with a razor; throw off the scent; to beg the question; reason in a circle; beat about the bush; prove that black is white; not have a leg to stand on; lose one's reckoning.

(Adjectives) Intuitive, instinctive, impulsive, unreasoning, independent of or anterior to reason.

Sophistical, unreasonable, irrational, illogical, false, unsound, not following, not pertinent, inconsequent, inconsequential, unwarranted, untenable, inconclusive, incorrect, fallacious, inconsistent, groundless, fallible, unproved, indecisive,

cogent, logical, demonstrative (478), relevant, pertinent (9, 23).

(Phrases) To the point; in point; to the purpose; *ad rem.*

(Adverbs) For, because, for that reason, forasmuch as, inasmuch as, since, hence, whence, whereas, considering, therefore, consequently, *ergo*, then, thus, accordingly, wherefore, *a fortiori, a priori, ex concesso.*

(Phrases) In consideration of; in conclusion; in fine; after all; *au bout du compte*; on the whole; taking one thing with another.

---

478 Demonstration *(Substantives)*, proof, conclusiveness, probation, comprobation, clincher, *experimentum crucis,* test, etc. (463), argument (476).

(Verbs) To demonstrate, prove, establish, show, evince, verify, substantiate; to follow.

(Phrases) Make good; set at rest; settle the question; reduce to demonstration; to make out a case; to prove one's point; to clinch an argument; bring home to; bear out.

(Adjectives) Demonstrating, etc., demonstrative, probative, demonstrable, unanswerable, conclusive, final, apodictic (or apodeictic), irrefutable, irrefragable, unimpeachable, categorical, decisive, crucial.

Demonstrated, proved, proven, etc., unconfuted, unrefuted; evident, self-evident, axiomatic (474); deducible, consequential, inferential.

(Phrases) Probatum est; it stands to reason; it holds good; there being nothing more to be said; Q.E.D.

(Adverbs) Of course, in consequence, consequently, as a matter of course, no wonder.

deceptive, illusive, illusory, specious, hollow, jesuitical, plausible, irrelevant.

Weak, feeble, poor, flimsy, trivial, trumpery, trashy, puerile, childish, irrational, silly, foolish, imbecile, absurd (499), extravagant, far-fetched, pettifogging, quibbling, fine-spun, hair-splitting.

(Phrases) Non constat; non sequitur; not holding water; away from the point; foreign to the purpose or subject; having nothing to do with the matter; not of the essence; *nihil ad rem*; not bearing upon the point in question; not the point; beside the mark.

479 Confutation *(Substantives)*, refutation, disproof, conviction, redargution, invalidation, exposure, exposition; demolition of an argument; answer, come-back, counter, retort.

(Phrases) Reductio ad absurdum; a knock-down argument; a *tu quoque* argument.

(Verbs) To confute, refute, disprove, redargue, expose, show the fallacy of, knock the bottom out of, rebut, parry, negative, defeat, overthrow, demolish, explode, riddle, overturn, invalidate, silence, reduce to silence, shut up, put down.

(Phrases) To cut the ground from one's feet; to give one a set-down.

(Adjectives) Confuting, etc., confuted, etc., capable of refutation, refutable, confutable, etc.; unproved, etc.

(Phrases) The argument falls to the ground; it won't hold water; that cock won't fight.

SECTION V—RESULTS OF REASONING

480 Judgment *(Substantives)*, conclusion, determination, deduction, inference, result, illation, corollary, rider, porism, consectary.

Estimation, valuation, appreciation, judication, adjudication, arbitrament, arbitration, assessment, award, ponderation.

Decision, sentence, verdict, moral, ruling, finding; detection, discovery, estimate; *chose jugée.*

Criticism, critique, review, report, notice; plebiscite, casting vote.

A judge, umpire, arbiter, arbitrator, assessor, censor, referee, critic, connoisseur, reviewer.

(Verbs) To judge, deduce, conclude, draw a conclusion, infer, make a deduction, draw an inference, put two and two together; come to, arrive or jump at a conclusion; to derive, gather, collect.

To estimate, appreciate, value, count, assess, rate, account, rank, regard, review, settle, decide, pronounce, arbitrate, perpend, size up.

(Phrases) To sit in judgment; to hold the scales; to pass an opinion; to pass judgment.

(Adjectives) Judging, etc., deducible (467); impartial, unbiased, unprejudiced, unwarped, unbigoted, equitable, fair, sound, rational, judicious, shrewd.

480ᴀ Detection *(Substantive)*, discovery.

(Verbs) To ascertain, determine, find, find out, make out, detect, discover, elicit, recognize, trace, get at; get or arrive at the truth; meet with, fall upon, light upon, hit upon, fall in with, stumble upon, lay the finger on, spot, solve, resolve, unravel, fish out, worm out, ferret out, root out, nose out, disinter, unearth, grub up, fish up, investigate (461).

To be near the truth, to get warm, to burn.

(Phrase) To smell a rat.

(Interjection) Eureka!

481 Misjudgment *(Substantives)*, obliquity of judgment, misconception, error (495), miscalculation, miscomputation, presumption.

Prejudgment, prejudication, prejudice, prenotion, *parti pris*, prevention, preconception, predilection, prepossession, preapprehension, presentiment, *esprit de corps,* clannishness, party spirit, partisanship, partiality.

Bias, warp, twist, fad, whim, crotchet, fike; narrow-mindedness, bigotry, dogmatism, intolerance, tenacity, obstinacy (606); blind side; one-sided, partial, narrow or confined views, ideas, conceptions, or notions; *idée fixe,* fixed idea, obsession, monomania, infatuation.

(Phrases) A bee in one's bonnet; a mote in the eye; a fool's paradise.

(Verbs) To misjudge, misestimate, misconceive, misreckon, etc. (495).

To prejudge, forejudge, prejudicate, dogmatize, have a bias, etc., presuppose, presume.

To produce a bias, twist, etc.; to bias, warp, twist, prejudice, obsess, infatuate, prepossess.

(Phrases) To have on the brain; to look only at one side of the shield; to view with jaundiced eye; to run away with the notion; to jump to a conclusion.

(Adjectives) Prejudging, misjudging, etc., prejudiced, jaundiced, narrow-minded, dogmatic, intolerant, illiberal, blimpish, besotted, infatuated, fanatical, *entêté,* positive, obstinate (606), tenacious, pig-headed, having a bias, twist, etc., warped, partial, one-sided, biased, bigoted, hide-bound, tendentious, opinionated, opinionative, opinioned, selfopinioned, selfopinionated, crotchety, pernickety, faddy, fussy, fiky.

(Phrases) Wedded to an opinion; the wish being father to the thought.

———

482 Overestimation (*Substantive*), exaggeration.

(*Phrases*) Much ado about nothing; much cry and little wool; a storm in a tea-cup.

(*Verbs*) To overestimate, estimate too highly, overrate, overvalue, overprize, overpraise, overweigh, outreckon; exaggerate, extol, puff, boost, make too much of, overstrain.

(*Phrases*) To set too high a value upon; to make a mountain out of a molehill; *parturiunt montes, nascetur ridiculus mus*; to make two bites of a cherry; all his geese are swans.

(*Adjectives*) Overestimated, etc.

————

483 Underestimation (*Substantives*), depreciation, disparagement, detraction (934), underrating, undervaluing, etc.

(*Verbs*) To depreciate, disparage, detract, underrate, underestimate, undervalue, underreckon, underprize, misprize, disprize, not to do justice to, make light of, slight, belittle, knock, slam, make little of, think nothing of, hold cheap, cheapen, disregard, to care nothing for, despise, set at naught, minimize, discount, deride, derogate, decry, cry down, crab, denigrate, smear, vilipend, run down (934).

To scout, deride, pooh-pooh, mock, scoff at, laugh at, whistle at, play with, trifle with, fribble, niggle, ridicule (856).

(*Phrases*) To snap one's fingers at; throw into the shade; not to care a pin, rush, hoot, tinker's cuss, etc., for; to damn with faint praise.

(*Adjectives*) Depreciating, etc., derogatory, cynical.

Depreciated, etc., unvalued, unprized.

484 Belief (*Substantives*), credence, faith, trust, troth, confidence, credit, dependence on, reliance, assurance.

Opinion, notion, idea (453), conception, apprehension, impression, conceit, mind, view, persuasion, conviction, convincement, sentiment, voice, conclusion, judgment (480), estimation, self-conviction.

System of opinions, creed, credo, religion (983, 987), doctrine, tenet, dogma, principle, school, ideology, articles of belief, way of thinking, popular belief, *vox populi*, public opinion, *esprit de corps*, partisanship; ism, doxy.

Change of opinion (607), proselytism, propagandism (537).

A convert, pervert, vert, proselyte.

(*Verbs*) To believe, credit, receive, give faith to, give credit to, rely upon, make no doubt, reckon, doubt not, confide in, count upon, depend upon, build upon, calculate upon, take upon trust, swallow, gulp down, take one's word for, take upon credit, swear by.

To be of opinion, to opine, presume;

485 Unbelief (*Substantives*), disbelief, misbelief, discredit, agnosticism, atheism (988), heresy (984), dissent (489).

Doubt, dubitation, scepticism, *diaporesis*, misgiving, demur, cliff-hanging, suspense; shade or shadow of doubt, distrust, mistrust, misdoubt, suspicion, shyness, embarrassment, hesitation, uncertainty (475), scruple, qualm, dilemma; casuistry, paradox; schism (489), incredulity (487).

Unbeliever, sceptic (487); Doubting Thomas.

(*Verbs*) To disbelieve, discredit, not to believe; refuse to admit or believe; misbelieve, controvert; put or set aside; join issue, dispute, etc.

To doubt, be doubtful, etc., diffide, distrust, mistrust, suspect, scent, jalouse; have, harbour, entertain, etc., doubts; demur, stick at, pause, hesitate, scruple, question, query, call in question, look askance (or askant).

To cause, raise, suggest, or start a doubt; to pose, stagger, floor, startle, embarrass, puzzle (704); shake or stagger one's faith or belief.

(*Phrases*) Not to know what to

to have, hold, possess, entertain, adopt, imbibe, embrace, foster, nurture, cherish, etc., a notion, idea, opinion, etc.; to think, look upon, view, consider, take, take it, hold, trow, ween, conceive, fancy, apprehend, regard, esteem, deem, account; meseems, methinks.

To cause to be believed, thought, or esteemed; to satisfy, persuade, assure, convince, convert, bring over, win over, indoctrinate, proselytize (537), evangelize; to vert.

(Phrases) To pin one's faith to; to take at one's word.

To take it into one's head; to run away with the notion; to come round to an opinion.

To cram down the throat; to bring home to; to find credence; to carry conviction; pass current; pass muster; to hold water; to go down.

make of; to smell a rat; to hang in doubt; to have one's doubts; to float in a sea of doubts.

(Adjectives) Unbelieving, doubting, etc., incredulous, scrupulous, suspicious, sceptical, shy of belief, at sea, at a loss (487).

Unworthy or undeserving of belief, hard to believe, doubtful (475), dubious, unreliable, fishy, questionable, suspect, staggering, puzzling, etc., paradoxical, incredible, inconceivable.

(Phrases) With a grain of salt; *cum grano salis; timeo Danaos et dona ferentes*; all is not gold that glitters; the cowl does not make the monk.

(Adjectives) Believing, etc., impressed with, imbued with, wedded to, unsuspecting, unsuspicious, void of suspicion, etc., credulous (486), convinced, positive, sure, assured, cocksure, certain, confident.

Believed, etc., credited, accredited, unsuspected, received, current, popular.

Worthy or deserving of belief, commanding belief, believable, persuasive, impressive, reliable, dependable, trustworthy (939), credible, probable (572), fiducial, fiduciary; relating to belief, doctrinal.

(Adverbs) In the opinion of, in the eyes of, on the strength of, to the best of one's belief, *me judice*.

486 Credulity *(Substantives)*, credulousness, gullibility, infatuation, self-delusion, self-deception, superstition, gross credulity, bigotry, dogmatism.

A credulous person, gull, gobemouche; dupe (547).

(Verbs) To be credulous, etc., to follow implicitly, swallow, take on trust, take for gospel.

To impose upon, practise upon, palm off upon, cajole, etc., deceive (545).

(Phrases) Credo quia absurdum; the wish being father to the thought.

(Adjectives) Credulous, gullible, confiding, trusting; easily deceived, cajoled, etc.; green, verdant, superstitious, simple, unsuspicious, etc. (484), soft, childish, silly, stupid, overcredulous, over-confident.

487 Incredulity *(Substantives)*, incredulousness, scepticism, pyrrhonism, nihilism, suspicion (485), suspiciousness, scrupulousness, scrupulosity.

An unbeliever, sceptic, misbeliever, pyrrhonist; nihilist.

(Verbs) To be incredulous, etc., to distrust (485).

(Adjectives) Incredulous, hard of belief, sceptical, unbelieving, inconvincible, shy of belief, doubting, distrustful, suspicious (485).

(Phrases) Oh yeah? says you! a likely story! rats! that be hanged for a tale; tell that to the marines; it won't wash; that cock won't fight; *credat Judaeus Apella*.

---

488 Assent (*Substantives*), acquiescence, admission, assentation, nod, consent, concession, accord, accordance, agreement (23), concord (714), concordance, concurrence, ratification, confirmation, corroboration, approval, recognition, acknowledgment, acceptance, granting, avowal, confession.

Unanimity, chorus; affirmation (535), common consent, acclamation, consensus.

Yes-man, sycophant, echo.

(*Verbs*) To assent, acquiesce, agree, yield assent, accord, concur, consent, nod assent, accept, coincide, go with, go along with, be at one with, chime in with, strike in with, close with, vote for, conform with, defer to; say yes, ay, ditto, amen, etc.

To acknowledge, own, avow, confess, concede, subscribe to, abide by, admit, allow, recognize, grant, endorse, ratify, countersign, O.K., okay, approve, carry.

(*Phrases*) To go or be solid for; to come to an understanding; to come to terms; one could not agree more.

(*Adjectives*) Assenting, etc., acquiescent, content, consentient, willing; approved, agreed, carried; uncontradicted, unchallenged, unquestioned, uncontroverted; unanimous.

(*Phrase*) Of one mind.

(*Adverbs*) Affirmatively, in the affirmative (535).

Yes, yea, yeah, yep, ay, aye, uh-huh, sure, very well, even so, just so, quite so, to be sure, all right, right oh! right you are, you said it, definitely, absolutely, exactly, precisely, truly, certainly, assuredly, no doubt, doubtless, verily, very true (494), *ex concesso*.

489 Dissent (*Substantives*), dissidence, discordance, denial (536), dissonance, disagreement; difference or diversity of opinion, recusancy, contradiction, nonconformity, schism (984), secession; protest.

A dissentient, dissenter, protestant, nonconformist, recusant, heretic; deviationist, nonjuror, schismatic, seceder.

(*Verbs*) To dissent, demur, deny, disagree, refuse assent, say no, differ, cavil, ignore, protest, contradict, secede, repudiate, refuse to admit.

(*Phrases*) To shake the head; to shrug the shoulders; to join issue; to give the lie; to differ *toto caelo*.

(*Adjectives*) Dissenting, etc., dissentient, dissident, discordant, protestant, nonconforming, recusant, nonjuring, non-content, schismatic, deviationist; unconvinced, unconverted, unavowed, unacknowledged.

Unwilling, reluctant, extorted, etc.

(*Adverbs*) Negatively, in the negative (536), at variance with.

No, nay, nope, nit, na, not, not so, not at all, nohow, nowise, not in the least, not a bit, not a whit, not a jot, by no means, by no manner of means, not for the world, on no account, in no respect.

(*Phrases*) Many men, many minds; *quot homines, tot sententiae; tant s'en faut*; the answer is in the negative; *il s'en faut bien*.

(*Interjections*) No sir! God forbid! I'll be hanged first! I'll see you far enough! not bloody likely! not on your nelly! not if I know it! over my dead body! pardon me! I beg your pardon!

Be it so, so be it, by all means, granted, O.K., okay, oke, okeydoke, by all manner of means, *à la bonne heure,* amen, willingly, etc. (602).

With one voice, with one accord, *una voce,* unanimously, in chorus, as one man, to a man, *nem. con.* or *nemine contradicente, nemine dissentiente, en bloc,* without a dissentient voice, one and all, on all hands.

---

490 Knowledge (*Substantives*), cognizance, cognition, cognoscence, awareness, gnosis, acquaintance, experience, ken, privity, insight,

491 Ignorance (*Substantives*), nescience, nescientness, unacquaintance, unconsciousness, darkness, blindness, incomprehension,

familiarity, apprehension, comprehension, understanding, recognition; discovery (480), appreciation; knowability.

Intuition, clairvoyance, consciousness, conscience, perception, precognition, light, enlightenment, glimpse, inkling, glimmer, dawn, scent, suspicion; conception, notion, idea (453).

Self-consciousness, self-knowledge, apperception.

System or body of knowledge, science, philosophy, pansophy, pandect, doctrine, ideology, theory, aetiology, literature, *belles-lettres*, *literae humaniores*, the humanities, humanism; ology.

Erudition, learning, lore, scholarship, letters, book-learning, bookishness, bibliomania, bibliolatry, education, instruction, information, acquisitions, acquirements, accomplishments, attainments, proficiency, cultivation, culture; a liberal education, encylopaedic knowledge, omniscience.

Elements, rudiments, abecedary (542), cyclopaedia, encyclopaedia, school, academy, etc.

Depth, extent, profoundness, profundity, stores, etc., solidity, accuracy, etc., of knowledge.

(Phrases) The march of intellect; the progress, advance, etc., of science; the schoolmaster being abroad.

(Verbs) To know, be aware of, savvy, ken, wot, ween, trow, have, possess, perceive, conceive, apprehend, ideate, understand, comprehend, make out, recognize, be master of, know full well, possess the knowledge of, experience, discern, perceive, see, see through, have in one's head.

(Phrases) To know what's what; to know how the wind blows; to know the ropes; to have at one's finger-tips or finger-ends.

(Adjectives) Knowing, aware of, etc., cognizant of, acquainted with, privy to, conscious of, no stranger to, *au fait, au courant*, versed in, hep,

incognizance, inexperience, emptiness.

Imperfect knowledge, smattering, sciolism, glimmering; bewilderment, perplexity (475); incapacity.

Affectation of knowledge, pedantry, charlatanry, quackery, dilettantism.

(Phrases) Crass ignorance; monumental ignorance.

A sealed book; unexplored ground; an unknown quantity; *terra incognita*.

(Verbs) To be ignorant, etc., not to know, to know nothing of, not to be aware of, to be at a loss, to be out of it, to be at fault, to ignore, to be blind to, etc., not to understand, etc.

(Phrases) To be caught tripping; not to know what to make of; to have no idea or notion; not to be able to make head or tail of; not to know a hawk from a handsaw; to lose one's bearings.

(Adjectives) Ignorant, unknowing, unconscious, unaware, unwitting, witless, a stranger to, unacquainted, unconversant, unenlightened, unilluminated, incognizant, unversed, uncultivated, clueless.

Uninformed, uninstructed, untaught, unapprised, untutored, unschooled, unguided.

Shallow, superficial, green, verdant, rude, half-learned, illiterate, unread, uneducated, unlearned, uncultured, Philistine, unlettered, empty-headed, having a smattering, etc., pedantic.

Confused, puzzled, bewildered, bemused, muddled, bemuddled, lost, benighted, belated, at sea, at fault, posed, blinded, abroad, distracted, in a maze, misinformed, hoodwinked, in the dark, at a loss, *désorienté*.

Unknown, novel, unapprehended, unexplained, unascertained, uninvestigated, unexplored, untravelled, uncharted, chartless, unheard-of, unperceived, unknowable.

(Phrases) Having a film over the eyes; wide of the mark; at cross purposes.

(Adverbs) Ignorantly, unwittingly,

up in, up to, alive to, wise to, conversant with, proficient in, read in, familiar with.

Apprised of, made acquainted with, informed of; undeceived.

Erudite, instructed, learned, well-read, lettered, literate, educated, cultivated, cultured, knowledgeable, enlightened, well-informed, shrewd, bookish, scholarly, scholastic, deep-read; self-taught, well-grounded, well-conned.

Known, etc., well-known, recognized, received, notorious, noted, proverbial, familiar; hackneyed, trite, commonplace; cognoscible, knowable; experiential.

(Phrases) Behind the scenes; in the know; at home in; the scales fallen from one's eyes.

(Adverbs) To one's knowledge, to the best of one's knowledge.

(Phrase) Experto crede.

unawares; for anything one knows; for aught one knows.

(Phrase) 'A little learning is a dangerous thing.'

---

492 Scholar *(Substantives),* student (541); savant, scientist, humanist, grammarian, intellectual, pundit, schoolman, don, professor, lecturer, reader, demonstrator, graduate, doctor, master of arts, licentiate, wrangler, gownsman, philosopher, philomath, clerk, encyclopaedist.

Linguist; *littérateur, literati, illuminati,* intelligentsia.

Pedant, pedagogue, bookworm, *helluo librorum,* bibliomaniac, bibliophile, blue-stocking, *bas-bleu,* highbrow, bigwig, bookman; swot, grind.

(Phrases) Man of letters; man of learning; at the feet of Gamaliel; a walking dictionary.

(Adjectives) Erudite, learned, scholarly (490).

493 Ignoramus *(Substantives),* sciolist, smatterer, novice, greenhorn, half-scholar, schoolboy, booby, dunce (501); bigot (481); quack, mountebank, charlatan, dilettante, low-brow, amateur, Philistine, obscurant, obscurantist.

(Phrase) The wooden spoon.

(Adjectives) Bookless, shallow (499), ignorant, etc. (491), prejudiced (481), obscurantist.

---

494 Object of knowledge.

Truth *(Substantives),* verity, actual existence (1), reality, fact, matter of fact, actuality, nature, principle, orthodoxy, gospel, holy writ, substantiality, genuineness, authenticity, realism.

Accuracy, exactness, exactitude, precision, preciseness, nicety, delicacy, fineness, strictness, rigour, punctuality.

(Phrases) The plain truth; the honest truth; the naked truth; the sober truth; the very thing; a stubborn fact; not a dream, fancy, illusion, etc.; the exact truth; 'the truth, the whole truth, and nothing but the

495 Untruth (546).

Error *(Substantives),* mistake, miss, fallacy, misconception, misapprehension, misunderstanding, inaccuracy, incorrectness, inexactness, misconstruction (523), miscomputation, miscalculation (481).

Fault, blunder, *faux pas,* bull, Irish bull, Irishism, bloomer, howler, floater, clanger, boner, lapse, slip of the tongue, *lapsus linguae,* Spoonerism, slip of the pen, malapropism, equivoque, cross purposes, oversight, flaw, misprint, erratum; heresy, misstatement, misreport, bad shot.

Illusion, delusion, self-deceit, self-deception, hallucination, monomania,

truth'; 'a round unvarnished tale'; *ipsissima verba*; the real Simon Pure.

(Verbs) To be true, real, etc., to hold good, to be the case.

To render true, legitimatize, legitimize, substantiate, realize, actualize, to make good, establish.

To get at the truth (480).

(Phrases) Vitam impendere vero; magna est veritas et praevalebit.

(Adjectives) True, real, veritable, veracious, actual, certain, positive, absolute, existing (1), substantial, categorical, realistic, factual; unrefuted, unconfuted, unideal, unimagined.

Exact, accurate, definite, precise, well-defined, just, correct, right, strict, hard-and-fast, literal, rigid, rigorous, scrupulous, conscientious, religious, punctilious, nice, mathematical, axiomatic, demonstrable, scientific, unerring, constant, faithful, bona fide, curious, delicate, meticulous.

Genuine, authentic, legitimate, pukka, orthodox, official, *ex officio*, pure, sound, sterling, hall-marked unsophisticated, unadulterated, unvarnished; solid, substantial, undistorted, undisguised, unaffected, unflattering, unexaggerated, unromantic.

(Phrases) Just the thing; neither more nor less; to a hair.

(Adverbs) Truly, verily, veritable, troth, certainly, certes, assuredly, in truth, in good truth, of a truth, really, indubitably, in sooth, for sooth, in reality, in fact, in point of fact, as a matter of fact, strictly speaking, *de facto*, indeed, in effect, actually, *ipso facto*, definitely, literally, positively, virtually, at bottom, *au fond*.

Precisely, accurately, *ad amussim*, etc., mathematically, to a nicety, to a hair, to a T, to an inch; to the letter, *au pied de la lettre*.

aberration; fable, dream, shadow, fancy, bubble, false light (443), the mists of error, will-o'-the wisp, jack-o'-lantern, ignis fatuus, chimera (515), *maya*.

(Verbs) To be erroneous, false, etc., to cause error, to mislead, lead astray, lead into error, delude, give a false impression or idea, to falsify, misstate, misrelate, misinform, misrepresent (544), deceive (545), beguile.

To err, be in error, to mistake, to receive a false impression; to lie or labour under an error, mistake, etc., to blunder, be in the wrong, be at fault, to misapprehend, misconceive, misunderstand, misremember, misreckon, miscalculate, miscount, misestimate, misjudge, misthink, flounder, trip.

(Phrases) To take the shadow for the substance; to go on a fool's errand; to have the wrong sow by the ear; to put one's foot in it; to pull a boner; to drop a brick.

(Adjectives) Erroneous, untrue, false, fallacious, duff, unreal, unsubstantial, baseless, groundless, less, ungrounded, unauthenticated, untrustworthy, heretical.

Inexact, incorrect, wrong, illogical, partial, one-sided, unreasonable, absonous, absonant, indefinite, unscientific, inaccurate, aberrant.

In error, mistaken, etc., tripping, floundering, etc.

Illusive, illusory, ideal, imaginary, fanciful, chimerical, visionary, shadowy, mock, futile.

Spurious, apocryphal, bogus, illegitimate, phoney, pseudo, bastard, meretricious, deceitful, sophisticated, adulterated.

(Phrases) Wide of the mark; on the wrong scent; barking up the wrong tree; out of it; without a leg to stand upon.

In every respect, in all respects, *sous tous les rapports,* at any rate, at all events, by all means.

(Phrases) Joking apart; in good earnest; in sober earnest; sooth to say.

496 Maxim *(Substantives),* aphorism, apophthegm, dictum, saying, *mot,* adage, gnome, saw, proverb, wisecrack, sentence, precept, rule, formula, tag, code, motto, slogan, catchword, word, byword, moral, sentiment, phylactery, conclusion, reflection, thought, golden rule, axiom, theorem, scholium, lemma, truism.

Catechism, creed (484), profession of faith.

(Adjectives) Aphoristic, gnomic, proverbial, phylacteric, axiomatic; hackneyed, trite.

(Phrases) 'Wise saws and modern instances'; as the saying is or goes.

---

497 Absurdity *(Substantives),* absurdness, nonsense, folly, paradox, inconsistency, quibble, sophism (477), stultiloquy, stultiloquence, Irish bull, Irishism, Hibernicism, sciamachy, imbecility (499).

Jargon, gibberish, rigmarole, double-Dutch, fustian, rant, bombast, bathos, amphigouri, rhapsody, extravagance, rodomontade, romance; nonsense verse, limerick, clerihew.

Twaddle, claptrap, flapdoodle, bunkum, blah, fudge, rubbish, piffle, verbiage, trash, truism, stuff, balderdash, slipslop, *bavardage,* palaver, *baragouin,* moonshine, fiddlestick, wish-wash, platitude, cliché, flummery, inanity, fiddle-faddle, rot, tommy-rot, bosh, tosh, hot air, havers, blethers, tripe, bilge, bull, hooey, hokum, boloney.

Vagary, foolery, tomfoolery, mummery, monkey-trick, monkey-shine, dido, *boutade,* lark, escapade, ploy, rag.

(Phrases) A cock-and-bull story; a mare's-nest; a wild-goose chase; talking through one's hat; 'a tale told by an idiot, full of sound and fury, signifying nothing'; clotted nonsense; arrant rot.

(Adjectives) Absurd, nonsensical, foolish, senseless, preposterous (499), sophistical, inconsistent, extravagant, ridiculous, cock-and-bull, quibbling, trashy, washy, wishy-washy, twaddling, etc.; topsy-turvy, Gilbertian.

498 Intelligence *(Substantives),* capacity, nous, parts, talent, sagacity, sagaciousness, wit, mother-wit, *esprit,* gumption, comprehension, understanding, quick parts, grasp of intellect.

Acuteness, acumen, shrewdness, astuteness, arguteness, sharpness, aptness, aptitude, quickness, receptiveness, subtlety, archness, penetration, perspicacity, perspicaciousness, clear-sightedness, discrimination, discernment, flair, refinement (850).

Head, brains, headpiece, a long head.

Wisdom, sapience, sense, good sense, common sense, plain sense, horse-sense, reason, reasonableness, rationality, judgment, judiciousness, solidity, depth, profoundness, catholicity, breadth of view, enlarged views, reach or compass of thoughts.

Genius, inspiration, the fire of genius.

499 Imbecility *(Substantives),* incapacity, vacancy of mind, poverty of intellect, shallowness, dullness, stupidity, asininity, obtuseness, stolidity, hebetude, doltishness, muddleheadedness, vacuity, short-sightedness, incompetence.

Silliness, simplicity, childishness, puerility, babyhood; dotage, second childhood, anility, fatuity, idiocy, idiotism (503).

Folly, unwisdom, absurdity, infatuation, irrationality, senselessness, foolishness, frivolity, inconsistency, lip-wisdom, conceit, vanity, irresponsibility, giddiness, extravagance, oddity, eccentricity (503), ridiculousness, desipience.

Act of folly (497), imprudence (699), rashness, fanaticism.

(Phrases) A fool's paradise; apartments to let; one's wits going woolgathering; the meanest capacity.

Wisdom in action, prudence, discretion, self-possession, aplomb (698), sobriety, tact, ballast.

(Phrase) Discretion being the better part of valour.

(Verbs) To be intelligent, wise, etc., to reason (476), to discern (441), discriminate (465), to penetrate, to see far into.

(Phrases) To have all one's wits about one; to see as far through a brick wall as anybody.

(Adjectives) Applied to persons: Intelligent, sagacious, receptive, quick, sharp, acute, fly, smart, shrewd, gumptious, canny, astute, sharp-sighted, quick-sighted, quick-eyed, keen, keen-eyed, keen-sighted, keen-witted, sharp-witted, quick-witted, needle-witted, penetrating, piercing, clear-sighted, perspicacious, discerning, discriminating, discriminative, clever (698), knowledgeable.

Wise, sage, sapient, sagacious, reasonable, rational, sound, commonsense, sane, sensible, judicious, judgmatic, enlightened, impartial, catholic, broad-minded, open-minded, unprejudiced, unbiased, unprepossessed, undazzled, unperplexed, judicial, impartial, fair, progressive.

Cool, cool-headed, long-headed, hard-headed, long-sighted, calculating, thoughtful, reflective, oracular, heaven-directed.

Prudent, discreet, sober, staid, deep, solid, considerate, provident, politic, diplomatic, tactful.

Applied to actions: Wise, sensible, reasonable, judicious, well-judged, well-advised, prudent, prudential, politic (646), expedient.

(Phrases) Wise as a serpent; wise in one's generation; not born yesterday; up to snuff; no flies on him; wise as Solomon.

(Verbs) To be imbecile, foolish, etc., to trifle, drivel, ramble, dote, *radoter,* blether, haver; to fool, to monkey, to footle.

(Phrases) To play the fool; to play the giddy goat; to make an ass of oneself; to go on a fool's errand; to pursue a wild-goose chase; *battre la campagne*; Homer nods.

(Adjectives) Applied to persons: Unintelligent, unintellectual, witless, reasonless, not bright, imbecile, shallow, *borné,* weak, soft, simple, sappy, spoony, weak-headed, weak-minded, feeble-minded, half-witted, short-witted, half-baked, not all there, deficient, wanting, shallow-pated, shallow-brained, dull, dumb, dense, crass, stupid, heavy, obtuse, stolid, doltish, asinine, addle-headed, dull-witted, blunt, dull-brained, dim-sighted, vacuous.

Childish, infantine, infantile, babyish, childlike, puerile, callow; anile.

Fatuous, idiotic, lack-brained, drivelling, blatant, brainless, blunt-witted, beef-witted, fat-witted, fat-headed, boneheaded, insulse, having no head or brains, thick-skulled, ivory-skulled, blockish, Boeotian.

Foolish, silly, senseless, irrational, insensate, nonsensical, blunder-headed, chuckle-headed, puzzle-headed, muddle-headed, muddy-headed, undiscerning, unenlightened, unphilosophical; prejudiced, bigoted, purblind, narrow-minded, wrong-headed, tactless, crotchety, conceited, self-opinionated, pig-headed, mulish, unprogressive, one-ideaed, stick-in-the-mud, reactionary, blimpish, besotted, infatuated, unreasoning.

Wild, giddy, dizzy, thoughtless, eccentric, odd, extravagant, quixotic, light-headed, rantipole, high-flying, crack-brained, cracked, cranky, hare-brained, scatter-brained, scatter-pated, unballasted, ridiculous, frivolous, balmy (or barmy), daft (503).

Applied to actions: Foolish, unwise, injudicious, improper, imprudent, unreasonable, nonsensical, absurd, ridiculous, silly, stupid, asinine, ill-imagined, ill-advised, ill-judged, ill-devised, tactless, inconsistent, irrational, unphilosophical, extravagant, preposterous, egregious, footling, imprudent, indiscreet, improvident, impolitic, improper (645, 647).

(Phrases) Dead from the neck up; concrete above the ears.
Without rhyme or reason; penny-wise and pound-foolish.

500 Sage *(Substantives)*, wise man, master-mind, thinker, *savant*, expert, luminary, adept, authority, egghead.

Oracle, a shining light, *esprit fort*, intellectual, high-brow, pundit, academist, academician, philomath, schoolman, magi, a Solomon, Nestor, Solon, Socrates, a second Daniel.

(Adjectives) Venerable, reverend, authoritative.

(Phrases) 'A Daniel come to judgment'; the wise men of the East.

(Ironically) Wiseacre, know-all, bigwig.

----

501 Fool *(Substantives)*, block-head, bonehead, idiot, tom-fool, lowbrow, simpleton, simp, sap, softy, sawney, witling, ass, donkey, goat, goose, ninny, dolt, booby, boob, noodle, muff, mug, muggins, juggins, owl, cuckoo, gowk, numskull, noddy, dumb-bell, gomeril, half-wit, imbecile, ninnyhammer, mutt, driveller, cretin, moron, natural, lackbrain, child, infant, baby, innocent, greenhorn, zany, zombie, gaby.

Dunce, lout, loon, oaf, dullard, duffer, calf, colt, buzzard, block, stick, stock, clod-poll, clot-poll, clodhopper, clod, lubber, bull-calf, bullhead, fat-head, thick-skull, dunderhead, addle-head, dizzard, hoddy-doddy, looby, Joe Soap, nincompoop, poop, put, *un sot à triple étage*, loggerhead, sot, shallow-brain, jobbernowl, changeling, dotard, driveller, moon-calf, giddy-head, gobemouche, rantipole, muddler, stick-in-the-mud, old woman, April fool.

(Phrases) One who is not likely to set the Thames on fire; one who did not invent gunpowder; one who is no conjurer; *qui n'a pas inventé la poudre*; who could not say 'Bo' to a goose; one with his upper storey to let; no fool like an old fool.

Men of Gotham; men of Boeotia.

502 Sanity *(Substantives)*, rationality; being in one's senses, in one's right mind, in one's sober senses; sobriety, lucidity, lucid interval, sound mind, *mens sana*.

(Verbs) To be sane, etc., to retain one's senses, reason, etc.

To become sane, come to one's senses, sober down.

To render sane, bring to one's senses, to sober.

(Adjectives) Sane, rational, reasonable, *compos*, in one's sober senses, in one's right mind, sober-minded.

(Phrase) In full possession of one's faculties.

(Adverbs) Sanely, soberly, etc.

----

503 Insanity *(Substantives)*, lunacy, madness, unsoundness, derangement, psychosis, neurosis, alienation, aberration, schizophrenia, split personality, dementia, paranoia, mania, melancholia, hypochondria, calenture, frenzy, phrenitis, raving, monomania, megalomania, kleptomania, dipsomania, etc., disordered intellect, incoherence, wandering, delirium, hallucination, lycanthropy, eccentricity (499), dementation; Bedlam.

(Phrases) The horrors; the jim-jams; pink spiders; snakes in the boots.

(Verbs) To be or become insane, etc., to lose one's senses, wits, reason, faculties, etc., to run mad, run amuck, go off one's head, rave, dote, ramble, wander, drivel.

To render or drive mad; to madden, dementate, turn the brain, addle the wits, turn one's head, befool, infatuate, craze.

(Phrases) Battre la campagne; avoir le diable au corps.

(Adjectives) Insane, mad, lunatic, crazy, crazed, *non compos*, cracked, cranky, loco, touched, deficient, wanting, out of one's mind, off one's head or nut or onion, bereft of reason, unsettled in one's mind, unhinged, insensate, reasonless, beside oneself.

Demented, daft, dotty, potty, dippy, scatty, loopy, batty, bats, wacky, crackers, cuckoo, haywire, bughouse, bugs, nuts, possessed, maddened, moon-struck, mad-brained, maniac, maniacal, delirious, incoherent, rambling, doting, doited, gaga.

Wandering, frantic, phrenetic, paranoiac, schizophrenic, megalomaniacal, kleptomaniacal, etc., raving, corybantic, dithyrambic, rabid, pixillated, light-headed, giddy, vertiginous, wild, haggard, flighty, neurotic, distracted, distraught, hag-ridden, *écervelé, tête montée.*

(Phrases) The head being turned; having a screw (or a tile) loose; far gone; stark staring mad; mad as a March hare; mad as a hatter; of unsound mind; up the pole; bats in the belfry; the devil being in one; dizzy as a goose; candidate for Bedlam; like one possessed.

The wits going wool-gathering or bird's-nesting.

504 Madman *(Substantives)*, lunatic, maniac, bedlamite, energumen, raver, monomaniac, paranoiac, schizophrenic, nut, screwball, crackpot, madcap, megalomaniac, dipsomaniac, kleptomaniac, psychopath, hypochondriac, *malade imaginaire*, crank, maenad.

SECTION VI—EXTENSION OF THOUGHT

1°. *To the Past*

505 Memory *(Substantives)*, remembrance, reminiscence, recognition, anamnesis, retention, retentiveness, readiness, tenacity.

Recurrence, recollection, retrospection, retrospect, flash-back, afterthought, hindsight.

Token of remembrance, reminder, memorial, memento, souvenir, keepsake, relic, reliquary, memorandum, aide-mémoire, remembrancer, prompter.

Things to be remembered, *memorabilia.*

Art of memory, artificial memory, *memoria technica*, mnemonics; Mnemosyne.

(Phrases) The tablets of the memory; *l'esprit de l'escalier.*

(Verbs) To remember, retain, mind, bear or keep in mind, have or carry in the memory, know by heart or by rote; recognize.

506 Oblivion *(Substantives)*, forgetfulness, amnesia, obliteration (552), a short memory; a lapse of memory; the memory failing, being in fault, or deserting one; the waters of Lethe, Nepenthe, *tabula rasa.*

(Verbs) To forget, lose, unlearn, efface, expunge, blot out, etc. (552); discharge from the memory.

To slip, escape, fade, die away from the memory, to sink into oblivion.

(Phrases) To cast behind one's back; to have a short memory; to put out of one's head; to apply the sponge; to think no more of; to consign to oblivion; to let bygones be bygones.

(Adjectives) Forgotten, etc., lost, effaced, blotted out, obliterated, discharged, sponged out, buried or sunk in oblivion, out of mind, clean out

To be deeply impressed, live, remain, or dwell in the memory; to be stored up, bottled up, to sink in the mind, to rankle, etc.

To recollect, call to mind, bethink oneself, recall, call up, retrace, carry one's thoughts back, review, look back, rake up, brush up, think upon, call to remembrance, tax the memory.

To suggest, prompt, hint, recall to mind, put in mind, remind, whisper, call up, summon up, renew, commend to.

To say by heart, by rote, say one's lesson, repeat as a parrot.

To commit to memory, get or learn by heart or rote, memorize, con, con over, repeat; to fix, imprint, impress, stamp, grave, engrave, store, treasure up, bottle up, embalm, enshrine, etc., in the memory; to load, store, stuff, or burden the memory with; to commemorate (883).

(Phrase) To have at one's fingers' ends.

To jog or refresh the memory; to pull by the sleeve; to bring back to the memory; to keep the memory alive; to keep the wound green; to reopen old sores; to put in remembrance.

(Adjectives) Remembering, etc., mindful, remembered, etc., fresh, green, unforgotten, present to the mind; living in, being in, or within one's memory; indelible, ineffaceable, green in remembrance, reminiscential, commemorative.

(Adverbs) By heart, by vote, *memoriter*, without book; in memory of, in memoriam.

of one's head or recollection, past recollection, unremembered.

Forgetful, oblivious, unmindful, mindless; Lethean.

———

2°. *To the Future*

507 Expectation *(Substantives)*, expectance, expectancy, anticipation, forestalling, foreseeing (510); reckoning, calculation.

Contemplation, prospect, look-out, outlook (121), perspective, horizon, vista, hope, trust (858), abeyance, waiting, suspense.

(Phrase) The torments of Tantalus.

(Verbs) To expect, look for, look out for, look forward to, anticipate, contemplate, flatter oneself, to dare to say, foresee (510), forestall, reckon upon, count upon, lay one's account to, to calculate upon, rely upon, build upon, make sure of, prepare oneself for, keep in view, not to wonder at.

To wait, tarry, lie in wait, watch for, abide, to bide one's time.

To hold out, raise, or excite expectation, to bid fair, to promise, to augur, etc. (511).

(Phrases) To count one's chickens before they are hatched.

508 Inexpectation *(Substantives)*, non-expectation; blow, shock, surprise (870).

False or vain expectation, miscalculation.

(Phrase) A bolt from the blue.

(Verbs) Not to expect, not to look for, etc., to be taken by surprise, to start, come upon, to fall upon, not to bargain for, to miscalculate.

To be unexpected, etc., to crop up, pop up, to come unawares, suddenly, abruptly, like a thunderbolt, creep upon, burst upon, bounce upon; surprise, take aback, stun, stagger, startle.

(Phrases) To reckon without one's host; to trust to a broken reed.

To drop from the clouds; you could have knocked me down with a feather.

(Adjectives) Non-expectant, surprised, taken by surprise, unwarned, unaware, startled, etc., taken aback.

Unexpected, unanticipated, unlooked-for, unhoped-for, unforeseen,

To have in store for; to have a rod in pickle.

(Adjectives) Expectant, expecting, etc., prepared for, gaping for, ready for, agog, anxious, ardent, eager, breathless, sanguine.

Expected, anticipated, foreseen, etc., long expected, impending, prospective, in prospect.

(Adverbs) With breathless expectation, on tenterhooks.

(Phrases) On the tiptoe of expectation; on edge; looming in the distance; the wish father to the thought; we shall see; *nous verrons.*

beyond expectation, abrupt, sudden, contrary to or against expectation, unannounced, unheralded backhanded.

(Adverbs) Suddenly, abruptly, unexpectedly, plump, pop, *à l'improviste*, unawares, without notice or warning (113).

(Phrases) Like a thief in the night; who would have thought it?

509 Failure of expectation.

Disappointment *(Substantives)*, vain expectation, blighted hope, surprise, astonishment (870); balk, afterclap, miscalculation.

(Phrase) 'There's many a slip 'twixt cup and lip.'

(Verbs) To be disappointed, etc., to miscalculate; to look blank, to look blue, to look or stand aghast.

To disappoint, balk, bilk, tantalize, let down, play false, stand up, dumbfound, dash one's hope (859), sell.

(Adjectives) Disappointed, disconcerted, aghast, blue, out of one's reckoning.

Happening, contrary to or against expectation.

(Phrase) Parturiunt montes, nascetur, ridiculus mus.

---

510 Foresight *(Substantives)*, prospiscience, prescience, foreknowledge, forethought, forecast, prevision, prognosis, precognition, second sight, clairvoyance.

Anticipation, foretaste, prenotion, presentiment, foregone conclusion, providence, discretion, prudence, sagacity.

Announcement, prospectus, programme, policy (626).

(Verbs) To foresee, foreknow, forejudge, forecast, predict (511), anticipate, look forwards or beyond; look, peep, or pry into the future.

(Phrases) To keep a sharp look out for; to have an eye to the future; *respice finem.*

(Adjectives) Foreseeing, etc., prescient, weather-wise, far-sighted, far-seeing; provident, prudent, rational, sagacious, perspicacious.

❦

511 Prediction *(Substantives)*, announcement, prognosis, forecast, weird, prophecy, vaticination, mantology, prognostication, astrology, horoscopy, haruspicy, auguration, auspices, bodement, omination, augury, foreboding, abodement, aboding, horoscope, nativity, genethliacs, fortune-telling, crystal-gazing, palmistry, chiromancy, oneiromancy, sortilege, *sortes Virgilianae*, soothsaying, ominousness, divination (992).

Place of prediction, adytum, tripod.

(Verbs) To predict, prognosticate, prophesy, vaticinate, presage, augur, bode, forebode, divine, foretell, croak, soothsay, auspicate, to cast a horoscope or nativity, tell one's fortune, read one's hand.

To foretoken, betoken, prefigure, portend, foreshadow, foreshow, usher in, herald, signify, premise, announce, point to, admonish, warn, forewarn, advise.

(Adjectives) Predicting, etc., predictive, prophetic, fatidical, vaticinal, oracular, Sibylline.

Ominous, portentous, augural, auspicious, monitory, premonitory, significant of, pregnant with, weatherwise, bodeful, big with fate.

(Phrase) 'Coming events cast their shadows before.'

512 Omen *(Substantives)*, portent, presage, prognostic, augury, auspice, sign, forerunner, precursor (64), harbinger, herald, monition, warning, avant-courier, pilot-balloon, handwriting on the wall, rise and fall of the barometer, a bird of ill omen, a sign of the times, gathering clouds.

(Phrases) Touch wood! *absit omen*.

513 Oracle *(Substantives)*, prophet, seer, soothsayer, haruspex, fortune-teller, spaewife, palmist, gipsy, wizard, witch, geomancer, Sibyl, Python, Pythoness, *Pythia*, Pythian oracle, Delphic oracle, Old Moore, Zadkiel, Mother Shipton, Witch of Endor, Sphinx, Tiresias, Cassandra, Oedipus, Sibylline leaves.

SECTION VII—CREATIVE THOUGHT

514 Supposition *(Substantives)*, conjecture, surmise, presurmise, speculation, inkling, guess, guess-work, shot, divination, conceit; assumption, postulation, hypothesis, presupposition, postulate, *postulatum*, presumption, theory, thesis; suggestion, proposition, motion, proposal, allusion, insinuation, innuendo.

(Phrases) A rough guess; a lucky shot.

(Verbs) To suppose, conjecture, surmise, guess, divine, theorize, give a guess, make a shot, hazard a conjecture, throw out a conjecture, etc., presuppose, fancy, wis, take it, dare to say, take it into one's head, assume, believe, postulate, posit, presume, presurmise.

To suggest, hint, insinuate, put forth, propound, propose, start, allude to, prompt, put a case, move, make a motion.

To suggest itself, occur to one, come into one's head; to run in the head; to haunt (505).

(Phrases) To put it into one's head; 'thereby hangs a tale.'

(Adjectives) Supposing, etc., supposed, supposititious, suppositious, suppositive, reputed, putative, suggestive, allusive, conjectural, presumptive, hypothetical, theoretical, warranted, authorized, mooted, conjecturable, supposable.

(Adverbs) If, if so be, an, gin, maybe, perhaps, on the supposition, in the event of, as if, *ex hypothesi, quasi*.

515 Imagination *(Substantives)*, fancy, conception, ideality, idealism, inspiration, afflatus, verve, dreaming, somnambulism, frenzy, ecstasy, excogitation, reverie, *Schwärmerei*, trance, imagery, vision; Pegasus.

Invention, inventiveness, originality, fertility, romanticism, utopianism, castle-building.

Conceit, maggot, figment, coinage, fiction, romance, novel (594), myth, Arabian Nights, fairyland, faerie, the man in the moon, dream, day-dream, pipe-dream, nightmare, vapour, chimera, phantom, phantasy, fantasia, whim, whimsy, vagary, rhapsody, extravaganza, air-drawn dagger, bugbear, men in buckram, castle in the air, air-built castle, castle in Spain, will-o'-the-wisp, ignis fatuus, jack-o'-lantern, Utopia, Atlantis, Shangri-la, land of Prester John, millennium, golden age, *fata morgana* (443).

A visionary, romancer, rhapsodist, high-flyer, enthusiast, idealist, energumen, dreamer, seer, fanatic, knight-errant, Don Quixote.

(Phrases) Flight of fancy; fumes of fancy; fine frenzy; thick-coming fancies; coinage of the brain; the mind's eye; a stretch of imagination; 'such stuff as dreams are made on.'

(Verbs) To imagine, fancy, conceive, ideate, idealize, realize, objectify; fancy or picture to oneself; create, originate, devise, invent, coin, fabricate, make up, mint, improvise, excogitate, conjure up.

(Phrases) To take into one's head; to figure to oneself; to strain or crack one's invention; to strike out something new; to give a loose to the fancy; to give the reins to the imagination; to set one's wits to work; to rack or cudgel one's brains.

(Adjectives) Imagining, imagined, etc.; ideal, unreal, unsubstantial, imaginary, *in nubibus*, fabulous, fictitious, legendary, mythological, chimerical, *ben trovato*, fanciful, faerie, fairylike, air-drawn, air-built, original, fantastic, fantastical, whimsical, high-flown.

Imaginative, inventive, creative, fertile, romantic, flighty, extravagant, high-flown, fanatic, enthusiastic, Utopian, Quixotic.

DIVISION II—COMMUNICATION OF IDEAS

SECTION I—NATURE OF IDEAS COMMUNICATED

516 Idea to be conveyed.

Meaning *(Substantives)*, signification, sense, import, purport, significance, drift, gist, acceptation, acceptance, bearing, interpretation (522), reading, tenor, allusion, spirit, colouring, expression.

Literal meaning, literality, obvious meaning, grammatical sense, first blush, *prima facie* meaning; after-acceptation.

Equivalent meaning, synonym, synonymity.

Thing signified: Matter, subject, substance, pith, marrow, argument, text; sum and substance.

(Verbs) To mean, signify, express, import, purport, convey, breathe, imply, bespeak, speak of, tell of, touch on, bear a sense, involve, declare (527), insinuate, allude to, point to, indicate, drive at; to come to the point, give vent to; to stand for.

To take, understand, receive, or accept in a particular sense.

(Adjectives) Meaning, etc., significant, significative, significatory, literal, expressive, explicit, suggestive, allusive; pithy, pointed, epigrammatic, telling, striking, full of meaning, pregnant with meaning.

517 Absence of meaning.

Unmeaningness *(Substantives)*, empty sound, a dead letter, scrabble, scribble; inexpressiveness, vagueness (519).

Nonsense, stuff, balderdash (497), jabber, gibberish, palaver, rigmarole, twaddle, tosh, bosh, bull, rubbish, rot, empty babble, empty sound, verbiage, *nugae*, truism, moonshine, inanity.

(Verbs) To mean nothing, to be unmeaning, etc.; to scribble, jabber, gibber, babble.

(Adjectives) Unmeaning, meaningless, nonsensical, void of meaning, of sense, etc., senseless, not significant, undefined, tacit, not expressed.

Inexpressible, indefinable, undefinable, unmeant, unconceived.

Trashy, trumpery, twaddling, etc.

(Phrases) Vox et praeterea nihil; 'a tale told by an idiot, full of sound and fury, signifying nothing'; 'sounding brass and tinkling cymbal.'

(Adverb) Tacitly.

Synonymous, equivalent, tantamount; the same thing as.

Implied, tacit, understood, implicit, inferred, latent.

(Adverbs) Meaningly, literally, etc., *videlicet* (522), viz., i.e.

(Phrases) Au pied de la lettre; so to speak; to that effect; so to express oneself; as it were; that is to say; *façon de parler.*

---

518 Intelligibility *(Substantives)*, clearness, lucidity, perspicuity, explicitness, distinctness, plain speaking, expressiveness, legibility, visibility (446); precision (494).

Intelligence, comprehension, understanding, learning (539).

(Phrases) A word to the wise; *verbum sapienti.*

(Verbs) To be intelligible, etc.

To render intelligible, etc., to simplify, clear up, throw light upon.

To understand, comprehend, follow, take, take in, catch, catch on to, twig, dig, get the hang of, get wise to, grasp, sense, make out, get, collect; master, tumble to, rumble.

(Phrases) It tells its own tale; he who runs may read; to stand to reason; to speak for itself.

To come to an understanding; to see with half an eye.

(Adjectives) Intelligible, clear, lucid, understandable, explicit, expressive, significant, express, distinct, precise, definite, well-defined, perspicuous, transpicuous, striking, plain, obvious, manifest, palpable, glaring, transparent, above-board, unambiguous, unmistakable, legible, open, positive, expressive (516), unconfused, unequivocal, pronounced, graphic, readable.

(Phrases) Clear as day; clear as crystal; clear as noonday; not to be mistaken; plain to the meanest capacity; plain as a pikestaff; in plain English.

---

519 Unintelligibility *(Substantives)*, incomprehensibility, inconceivability, darkness (421), imperspicuity, obscurity, confusion, perplexity, imbroglio, indistinctness, mistiness, indefiniteness, vagueness, ambiguity, looseness, uncertainty, mysteriousness (526), paradox, inexplicability, incommunicability, spinosity.

Jargon, gibberish, rigmarole, rodomontade, etc. (497); paradox, riddle, enigma, puzzle (533).

Double or High Dutch, Greek, Hebrew, etc.

(Verbs) To be unintelligible, etc., to pass comprehension.

To render unintelligible, etc., to perplex, confuse, confound, bewilder, darken, moither (475).

Not to understand, etc., to lose, miss, etc., to lose the clue.

(Phrases) Not to know what to make of; not to be able to make either head or tail of; to be all at sea; to play at cross purposes; to beat about the bush.

(Adjectives) Unintelligible, incognizable, inapprehensible, incomprehensible, inconceivable, unimaginable, unknowable, inexpressible, undefinable, incommunicable, above or past or beyond comprehension, inexplicable, illegible, undecipherable, inscrutable, unfathomable, beyond one's depth, paradoxical, insoluble, impenetrable.

Obscure, dark, confused, indistinct, indefinite, misty, nebulous, intricate, undefined, ill-defined, indeterminate, perplexed, loose, vague, ambiguous, disconnected, incoherent, unaccountable, puzzling, enigmatical, hieroglyphic, mysterious, mystic, mystical, at cross purposes.

Hidden, recondite, abstruse, crabbed, transcendental, far-fetched, *in nubibus,* searchless, unconceived, unimagined.

(Phrases) Greek to one; without rhyme or reason; *obscurum per obscurius; lucus a non lucendo.*

520 Having a double sense.

Equivocalness *(Substantives)*, double meaning, quibble, equivoque, equivocation, *double-entendre*, paragram, anagram, amphibology, amphiboly, ambiloquy, prevarication, white lie, mental reservation, tergiversation, slip of the tongue, *lapsus linguae*, a pun, play on words, homonym.

Having a doubtful meaning, ambiguity (475), homonymy.

Having a false meaning (544), *suggestio falsi*.

(Verbs) To be equivocal, etc., to have two senses, etc., to equivocate, prevaricate, tergiversate, palter to the understanding, to pun.

(Adjectives) Equivocal, ambiguous, amphibolous, amphibological, homonymous, double-tongued, double-edged, left-handed, equivocatory, paltering.

(Adverb) Over the left.

521 Metaphor *(Substantives)*, figure, metonymy, trope, catachresis, synecdoche, figure of speech, figurativeness, image, imagery, metalepsis, type (22), symbol, symbolism (550), tropology.

Personification, prosopopaeia, allegory, apologue, parable.

Implication, inference, allusion, application, adumbration, hidden meaning.

Allegorist, tropist, symbolist.

(Verbs) To employ metaphor, etc., to personify, allegorize, adumbrate, shadow forth, imply, understand, apply, allude to.

(Adjectives) Metaphorical, figurative, catachrestical, typical, tropical, parabolic, allegorical, allusive, symbolic (550), symbolistic, implied, inferential, implicit, understood.

(Adverbs) So to speak, as it were.

(Phrases) Where more is meant than meets the ear; in a manner of speaking; *façon de parler*; in a Pickwickian sense.

522 Interpretation *(Substantives)*, exegesis, explanation, meaning (516), explication, expounding, exposition, rendition, reddition.

Translation, version, rendering, construction, reading, spelling, restoration, metaphrase, literal translation, free translation, paraphrase.

Comment, commentary, inference, illustration, exemplification, definition, *éclaircissement*, elucidation, crib, cab, gloss, glossary, annotation, *scholium*, marginalia, note, clue, key, sidelight, master-key (631), rationale, denouement, solution, answer (462), object lesson.

Palaeography, dictionary, glossology, etc. (562), semantics, semasiology, oneirocritics, oneirocriticism, hermeneutics.

(Verbs) To interpret, expound, explain, clear up, construe, translate, render, English, do into, turn into, transfuse the sense of.

To read, spell, make out, decipher, decode, unfold, disentangle, elicit the

523 Misinterpretation *(Substantives)*, misapprehension, misunderstanding, misacceptation, misconstruction, misspelling, misapplication, catachresis, mistake (495), cross-reading, cross-purpose.

Misrepresentation, perversion, falsification, misquotation, garbling, exaggeration (549), false colouring, abuse of terms, parody, travesty, misstatement, etc. (544).

(Verbs) To misinterpret, misapprehend, misunderstand, misconceive, misdeem, misspell, mistranslate, misconstrue, misapply, mistake (495).

To misstate, etc. (544); to pervert, falsify, distort, misrepresent, torture, travesty; to stretch, strain, wring, or wrest the sense or meaning; to put a bad or false construction on; to misquote, garble, belie, explain away.

(Phrases) To give a false colouring to; to be or play at cross-purposes; to put a false construction on.

meaning of, make sense of, find the key of, unriddle, unravel, solve, resolve (480), restore.

To elucidate, throw light upon, illustrate, exemplify, expound, annotate, comment upon, define, unfold.

(Adjectives) Explanatory, expository, explicatory, explicative, exegetical, hermeneutic, constructive, inferential.

Paraphrastic, metaphrastic; literal, plain, simple, strict, synonymous; polyglot.

(Adverbs) That is to say, *id est* (or i.e.), *videlicet* (or viz.), in other words, in plain words, simply, in plain English.

Literally, word for word, verbatim, *au pied de la lettre,* strictly speaking (494).

(Adjectives) Misinterpreted, etc., untranslated, untranslatable.

(Phrase)Traduttori traditori.

———

524 Interpreter *(Substantives),* expositor, expounder, exponent, demonstrator, scholiast, commentator, annotator, metaphrast, paraphrast, palaeographer, spokesman, speaker, mouthpiece, guide, dragoman, cicerone, conductor, courier, showman, barker, oneirocritic; Oedipus (513).

SECTION II—MODES OF COMMUNICATION

525 Manifestation *(Substantives),* expression, showing, etc., disclosure (529), presentation, indication, exposition, demonstration, exhibition, production, display, showing off.

An exhibit, an exhibitor.

Openness, frankness, plain speaking (543), publication, publicity (531).

(Verbs) To manifest, make manifest, etc., show, express, indicate, point out, bring forth, bring forward, trot out, set forth, exhibit, expose, produce, present, bring into view, set before one, hold up to view, lay open, lay bare, expose to view, set before one's eyes, show up, shadow forth, bring to light, display, demonstrate, unroll, unveil, unmask, disclose (529).

To elicit, educe, draw out, bring out, unearth, disinter.

To be manifested, etc., to appear, transpire, come to light (446), to come out, to crop up, get wind.

(Phrases) Hold up the mirror; draw, lift up, raise, or remove the curtain; show one's true colours; throw off the mask.

To speak for itself; to stand to reason; to stare one in the face; to tell its own tale; to give vent to.

526 Latency *(Substantives),* secrecy, secretness, privacy, invisibility (447), mystery, occultness, darkness, reticence, silence (585), closeness, reserve, inexpression; a sealed book, a dark horse, an undercurrent.

Retirement, delitescence, seclusion (893).

(Phrases) More is meant than meets the ear (or eye).

(Verbs) To be latent, etc., to lurk, underlie, escape observation, smoulder; to keep back, reserve, suppress, keep close, etc. (528).

To render latent (528).

(Phrases) Hold one's tongue; hold one's peace; leave in the dark; to keep one's own counsel; to keep mum; to seal the lips; not to breathe a syllable about.

(Adjectives) Latent, lurking, secret, close, unapparent, unknown (491), dark, delitescent, in the background, occult, cryptic, snug, private, privy, *in petto,* anagogic, sequestered, dormant, smouldering.

Inconspicuous, unperceived, invisible (447), unseen, unwitnessed, impenetrable, unespied, unsuspected.

(Adjectives) Manifest, clear, apparent, evident, visible (446), prominent, in the foreground, salient, signal, striking, notable, conspicuous, palpable, patent, overt, flagrant, stark, glaring, open.

Manifested, shown, expressed, etc., disclosed (529), frank, capable of being shown, producible.

(Phrases) As plain as a pikestaff; as plain as the nose on one's face.

(Adverbs) Openly, before one's eyes, face to face, above-board, in open court, in open daylight, in the light of day, in the open streets, on the stage, on show.

Untold, unsaid, unwritten, unpublished, unmentioned, unbreathed, untalked of, unsung, unpronounced, unpromulgated, unreported, unexposed, unproclaimed, unexpressed, not expressed, tacit, implicit, implied, undeveloped, embryonic, unsolved, unexplained, undiscovered, untraced, untracked, unexplored.

(Phrase) No news being good news.

(Adverbs) Secretly, etc., *sub silentio.*

(Phrases) In the background; behind one's back; under the table; behind the scenes; between the lines.

---

527 Information *(Substantives)*, gen, pukka gen, low-down, enlightenment, communication, intimation, notice, notification, enunciation, announcement, annunciation, statement, specification, report, advice, monition, mention, acquaintance (490), acquainting, etc., outpouring, intercommunication, communicativeness.

An informant, teller, tipster, spy, nose, nark, stool-pigeon, intelligencer, correspondent, reporter, messenger, newsmonger, gossip (532).

Hint, suggestion (514), wrinkle, tip, pointer, insinuation, innuendo, wink, glance, leer, nod, shrug, gesture, whisper, implication, cue, office, byplay, eye-opener.

(Phrases) A word to the wise; *verbum sapienti*; a broad hint; a straight tip; a stage whisper.

(Verbs) To inform, acquaint, tell, mention, express, intimate, impart, communicate, apprise, post, make known, notify, signify to, let one know, advise, state, specify, give notice, announce, annunciate, publish, report, set forth, bring word, send word, leave word, write word, declare, certify, depose, pronounce, explain, undeceive, enlighten, put wise, set right, open the eyes of, convey the knowledge of, give an account of; instruct (537).

To hint, give an inkling of; give, throw out, or drop a hint, insinuate, allude to, glance at, touch on, make

528 Concealment *(Substantives)*, hiding, occultation, etc., secrecy, stealth, stealthiness, slyness (702), disguise, incognito, privacy, masquerade, camouflage, smoke screen, mystery, mystification, freemasonry, reservation, suppression, secretiveness, reticence, reserve, uncommunicativeness; secret path.

A mask, visor, ambush, etc. (530), enigma, etc. (533).

(Phrases) A needle in a bundle of hay; a nigger in the woodpile; a skeleton in the cupboard; a family skeleton.

(Verbs) To conceal, hide, put out of sight, secrete, cover, envelop, screen, cloak, veil, shroud, enshroud, shade, muffle, mask, disguise, camouflage, ensconce, eclipse.

To keep from, lock up, bury, cache, sink, suppress, stifle, withhold, reserve, burke, hush up, keep snug or close or dark.

To keep in ignorance, blind, hoodwink, mystify, pose, puzzle, perplex, embarrass, flummox, bewilder, bamboozle, etc. (545).

To be concealed, etc., to lurk, skulk, smoulder, lie hid, lie in ambush, lie perdu, lie low, lie doggo, sneak, slink, prowl, gumshoe, retire, steal into, steal along.

To conceal oneself, put on a veil, etc. (530), masquerade.

(Phrases) To draw or close the curtain; not breathe a word about;

allusion to, to wink, to tip the wink, glance, leer, nod, shrug, give the cue, give the office, give the tip, wave, whisper, suggest, prompt, whisper in the ear, give one to understand.

To be informed, etc., of, made acquainted with; to hear of, get a line on, understand.

To come to one's ears, to come to one's knowledge, to reach one's ears.

(Adjectives) Informed, etc., of, made acquainted with, in the know, hep; undeceived.

Reported, made known (531), bruited.

Expressive, significant, pregnant with meaning, etc. (516), declaratory, enunciative, nuncupatory, expository, communicatory, communicative, insinuative.

(Adverbs) Expressively, significantly, etc.

(Phrases) A little bird told me; *on dit*; from information received.

---

let it go no farther; keep it under your hat.

To play at bo-peep; to play at hide-and-seek; to hide under a bushel; to throw dust in the eyes.

(Adjectives) Concealed, hid, hidden, etc., secret, clandestine, perdu, close, private, privy, furtive, surreptitious, stealthy, feline, underhand, sly, sneaking, skulking, hole-and-corner, undivulged, unrevealed, undisclosed, incognito, incommunicado.

Mysterious, mystic, mystical, dark, enigmatical, problematical, anagogical, paradoxical, occult, cryptic, gnostic, cabbalistic, esoteric, recondite, abstruse, unexplained, impenetrable, undiscoverable, inexplicable, unknowable, bewildering, baffling.

Covered, closed, shrouded, veiled, masked, screened, shaded, disguised, under cover, under a cloud, veil, etc., in a fog, haze, mist, etc., under an eclipse; inviolate, inviolable, confidential, under wraps.

Reserved, uncommunicative, secretive, buttoned up, taciturn (585).

(Phrase) Close as wax.

(Adverbs) Secretly, clandestinely, incognito, privily, in secret, *in camera*, with closed doors, *à huis clos, à la dérobée*, under the rose, *sub rosa*, privately, in private, aside, on the sly, *sub silentio*, behind one's back, under the counter, behind the curtain, behind the scenes.

Confidentially, between ourselves, between you and me, *entre nous, inter nos*, in strict confidence, on the strict q.t., off the record, it must go no farther.

(Phrases) Like a thief in the night; under the seal of secrecy, of confession; between you and me and the gate-post; 'tell it not in Gath'; nobody any the wiser.

529 Disclosure *(Substantives)*, revealment, revelation, disinterment, exposition, show-down, exposure, effusion, outpouring.

Acknowledgment, avowal, confession; an *exposé*, denouement.

A telltale, talebearer, informer, stool-pigeon, nark, nose.

(Verbs) To disclose, open, lay open, divulge, reveal, bewray, discover, unfold, let drop, let fall, let out, let on, spill, lay open, acknowledge, allow, concede, grant, admit, own, own up, confess, avow, unseal, unveil, unmask, uncover, unkennel, unearth (525).

530 Ambush *(Substantives)*, hiding-place, hide, retreat, cover, lurking-hole, secret place, cubby-hole, recess, closet, priest's hole, crypt, cache, ambuscade, *guet-apens, adytum*, dungeon, oubliette.

A mask, veil, visor (or vizor), eye-shade, blinkers, cloak, screen, hoarding, curtain, shade, cover, disguise, masquerade dress, domino.

(Verbs) To lie in ambush, lurk, couch, lie in wait for, lay or set a trap for (545).

To blab, peach, squeal, let out, let fall, let on, betray, give away, tell tales, speak out, blurt out, vent, give vent to, come out with, round on, split; publish (531).

To make no secret of, to disabuse, unbeguile, undeceive, set right, correct.

To be disclosed, revealed, etc., to come out, to transpire, to ooze out, to leak out, to creep out, to get wind, to come to light.

(Phrases) To let into the secret; to let the cat out of the bag; to spill the beans; to unburden or disburden one's mind or conscience; to open one's mind; to unbosom oneself; to make a clean breast of it; to come clean; to give the show away; to own the soft impeachment; to tell tales out of school; to show one's hand; to turn Queen's (or King's or State's) evidence.

Murder will out.

(Adjectives) Disclosed, revealed, divulged, laid open, etc., unriddled, etc.; outspoken, etc. (543).

Open, public, exoteric.

(Interjection) Out with it!

531 Publication *(Substantives)*, announcement, notification, enunciation, annunciation, advertisement, promulgation, circulation, propagation, edition, redaction, proclamation, hue and cry, the Press, journalism, wireless, radio, broadcasting, television.

Publicity, notoriety, currency, cry, bruit, rumour, fame, report (532), on dit, flagrancy, limelight, town-talk, small talk, table-talk, puffery, bally-hoo, *réclame*, the light of day, daylight.

Notice, notification, manifesto, propaganda, advertisement, blurb, circular, placard, bill, *affiche*, poster, newspaper, journal, daily, periodical, weekly, gazette; personal column, agony column.

Publisher (593), publicity agent, advertising agent; tout, barker, town crier.

(Phrases) An open secret; *un secret de Polichinelle*.

(Verbs) To publish, make known, announce, notify, annunciate, gazette, set forth, give forth, give out, broach, voice, utter, advertise, circularize, placard, *afficher*, circulate, propagate, spread, spread abroad, broadcast, edit, redact, rumour, diffuse, disseminate, celebrate, blaze about; blaze or noise abroad; bruit, buzz, bandy, hawk about, trumpet, proclaim, herald, puff, boost, splash, plug, boom, give tongue, raise a cry, raise a hue and cry, tell the world, popularize; bring, lay or drag before the public, give currency to, ventilate, bring out.

(Phrases) To proclaim from the house-tops; to publish in the gazette; to send round the crier; with beat of drum.

To be published, etc., to become public, to go forth, get abroad, get about, get wind, take air, get afloat, acquire currency, get in the papers, spread, go the rounds, buzz about, blow about.

To pass from mouth to mouth; to spread like wildfire.

(Adjectives) Published, etc., made public, in circulation, exoteric, rumoured, rife, current, afloat, notorious, flagrant, whispered, buzzed about, in every one's mouth, reported, trumpet-tongued; encyclical.

(Phrases) As the story runs; to all whom it may concern.

(Interjections) Oyez! O yes! notice is hereby given!

532 News *(Substantives)*, piece of information, intelligence, tidings, budget of news, word, advice, message, communication, errand, embassy, dispatch, bulletin.

533 Secret *(Substantives)*, *arcanum, penetralia*, profound secret, mystery, crux, problem, enigma, teaser, poser, riddle, puzzle, conundrum, charade, rebus, logogriph,

Report, story, scoop, beat, rumour, canard, hearsay, *on dit*, fame, talk, gossip, tittle-tattle, *oui-dire*, scandal, buzz, bruit, *chronique scandaleuse*, town talk.

Letter, postcard, airgraph, telegram, wire, cable, wireless message, radiogram.

Newsmonger, scandalmonger, scaremonger, alarmist, talebearer, tattler, gossip (527), local correspondent, special correspondent, reporter (590).

anagram, acrostic, cross-word, cipher, code, cryptogram, monogram, paradox, maze, labyrinth, perplexity, chaos (528), the Hercynian wood; *terra incognita.*

Iron curtain, bamboo curtain, censorship, counter-intelligence.

(Phrases) The secrets of the prison-house; a sealed book.

(Adjectives) Secret, top secret, hush-hush, undercover, clandestine (528).

534 Messenger *(Substantives)*, envoy, nuncio, internuncio, intermediary, go-between, herald, ambassador, legate, emissary, *corps diplomatique.*

Marshal, crier, trumpeter, pursuivant, *parlementaire,* courier, runner, postman, telegraph-boy, errand-boy, bell-boy, bell-hop, Mercury, Hermes, Iris, Ariel, carrier pigeon.

Narrator, etc., talebearer, spy, secret-service agent, scout.

Mail, post (592), post office, telegraph, telephone, wireless, radio; grapevine, bush telegraph.

535 Affirmation *(Substantives)*, statement, predication, assertion, declaration, word, averment, asseveration, protestation, swearing, adjuration, protest, profession, deposition, avouchment, affirmance, assurance, allegation, acknowledgment, avowal, confession, confession of faith, oath, affidavit; vote, voice.

Remark, observation, position, thesis, proposition, saying, dictum, theorem, sentence.

Positiveness (474), dogmatism, *ipse dixit.*

A dogmatist, doctrinaire.

(Phrase) The big bow-wow style.

(Verbs) To assert, make an assertion, etc., say, affirm, predicate, enunciate, state, declare, profess, aver, avouch, put forth, advance, express, allege, pose, propose, propound, broach, set forth, maintain, contend, pronounce, pretend, pass an opinion, etc.; to reassert, reaffirm, reiterate; quoth, *dixit, dixi.*

To vouch, assure, vow, swear, take oath, depose, depone, recognize, avow, acknowledge, own, confess, announce, hazard or venture an opinion.

536 Negation *(Substantives)*, abnegation, denial, denegation, disavowal, disclaimer, abjuration, contradiction, *démenti,* contravention, recusation, retraction, retractation, recantation, renunciation, palinode, recusancy, protest.

Qualification, modification (469); rejection (610); refusal (764).

(Verbs) To deny, disown, contradict, negative, gainsay, contravene, disclaim, withdraw, recant, disavow, retract, revoke, abjure, negate.

(Phrases) To deny flatly; eat one's words; go back from, or upon one's word.

To dispute, impugn, controvert, confute (479), question, call in question, give the lie to, rebut, belie.

(Adjectives) Denying, etc., denied, etc., negative, contradictory, recusant.

(Adverbs) No, nay, not, nohow, not at all, by no means (489), far from it, anything but, on the contrary, quite the reverse.

To dogmatize, lay down, lay down the law; to call heaven to witness, protest, certify, warrant, posit, go bail for.

(Phrases) I doubt not; I warrant you; I'll engage; take my word for it; depend upon it; I'll be bound; I am sure; I have no doubt; sure enough; to be sure; what I have said, I have said; faith! that's flat.

To swear till one is black in the face; to swear by all the saints in the calendar; to call heaven to witness.

(Adjectives) Asserting, etc., dogmatic, positive, emphatic, declaratory, affirmative, predicable, pronounced, unretracted.

Positive, broad, round, express, explicit, marked, definitive, distinct, decided, formal, solemn, categorical, peremptory, absolute, fiat, pronounced.

(Adverbs) *Ex cathedra*, positively, avowedly, confessedly, broadly, roundly, etc.; ay, yes, indeed; by Jove, by George, by James, by jingo.

537 Teaching *(Substantives)*, instruction, direction, guidance, tuition, culture, inculcation, inoculation, indoctrination.

Education, co-education, initiation, preparation, practice, training, upbringing, schooling, discipline, exercise, drill, exercitation, breaking in, taming, drilling, etc., preachment, persuasion, edification, proselytism, propagandism.

A lesson, lecture, prolusion, prelection, exercise, task; curriculum, course.

Rudiments, ABC, elements, three Rs, grammar, text-book, vademecum, school-book (593).

Physical training, P.T., gymnastics, callisthenics.

(Verbs) To teach, instruct, enlighten, edify, inculcate, indoctrinate, instil, imbue, inoculate, infuse, impregnate, graft, infix, engraft, implant, sow the seeds of, infiltrate, give an idea of, cram, coach, put up to.

To explain, expound, lecture, hold forth, read a lecture or sermon, give a lesson, preach; sermonize, moralize, point a moral.

To educate, train, discipline, school, form, ground, tutor, prepare, qualify, prime, drill, exercise, practise, bring up, rear, nurture, dry-nurse, breed, break in, tame, domesticate, condition.

To direct, guide, initiate, put in the way of, proselytize, bring round to an opinion, bring over, win over, brainwash, re-educate, persuade, convince, convict, set right, enlighten, give one new ideas, put one up to, bring home to.

538 Misteaching *(Substantives)*, misdirection, misleading, misinformation, misguidance, perversion, false teaching, sophistry.

Indocility, incapacity, misintelligence, dullness, backwardness.

(Verbs) To misinform, misteach, mislead, misdirect, misguide, miscorrect, pervert, lead into error, bewilder, mystify (528), throw off the scent; to unteach.

(Phrases) To teach one's grandmother; *obscurum per obscurius*; the blind leading the blind.

(Adjectives) Misteaching, etc., unedifying.

539 Learning *(Substantives)*, acquisition of knowledge, acquirement, attainment, scholarship, erudition, instruction, study, etc. (490).

Docility (602), aptitude (698), aptness to be taught, teachableness, persuasibility, capacity.

(Verbs) to learn; to acquire, gain, catch, receive, imbibe, pick up, gather, collect, glean, etc., knowledge or information.

To hear, overhear, catch hold of, take in, fish up, drink in, run away with an idea, to make oneself acquainted with, master, read, spell, turn over the leaves, pore over, run through, peruse, study, grind, cram, mug, swot, go to school; to get up a subject; to serve one's time or apprenticeship.

To be taught, etc.

(Phrases) To teach the young idea how to shoot; to sharpen the wits; to enlarge the mind.

(Adjectives) Teaching, etc., taught, etc., educational.

Didactic, academic, doctrinal, disciplinal, disciplinary, instructive, scholastic, persuasive.

540 Teacher *(Substantives)*, instructor, apostle, master, director, tutor, preceptor, institutor, mentor, adviser, monitor, counsellor, expositor, dry-nurse, trainer, coach, crammer, grinder, governor, bear-leader, disciplinarian, martinet, guide, cicerone, pioneer, governess, duenna.

Orator, speaker, mouthpiece (582).

Professor, lecturer, reader, demonstrator, praelector, prolocutor, schoolmaster, schoolmistress, schoolmarm, usher, pedagogue, monitor, pupil-teacher, dominie, dame, moonshee; missionary, propagandist.

(Adjectives) Tutorial, professorial.

(Adjectives) Docile, apt, teachable, persuasible, studious, industrious, scholastic, scholarly.

(Phrase) To burn the midnight oil.

———

541 Learner *(Substantives)*, scholar, student, alumnus, disciple, pupil, *élève*, schoolboy, schoolgirl, beginner, tyro (or tiro), abecedarian, novice, neophyte, chela, inceptor, probationer, apprentice, tenderfoot, freshman, bejan (or bejant), undergraduate, undergraduette, sophomore.

Proselyte, convert, catechumen, sectator; class, form.

Pupilage, pupilarity, pupilship, tutelage, apprenticeship, novitiate, leading-strings, matriculation.

(Phrases) Freshwater sailor; *in statu pupillari*.

542 School *(Substantives)*, day school, boarding school, public school, council school, national school, board school, private school, preparatory school, elementary school, primary school, secondary school, senior school, grammar school, high school, academy, university, Alma Mater, university extension, correspondence school, college, seminary, lyceum, polytechnic, nursery, institute, institution, palaestra, gymnasium, class, form, standard; nursery school, infant school, kindergarten, crèche; reformatory, Borstal, approved school.

Horn-book, rudiments, vade-mecum, abecedary, manual, primer, school-book, text-book.

Professorship, lectureship, readership, chair; pulpit, ambo, theatre, amphitheatre, forum, stage, rostrum, platform.

(Adjectives) Scholastic, academic, collegiate.

543 Veracity *(Substantives)*, truthfulness, truth, sincerity, frankness, straightforwardness, ingenuousness, candour, honesty, fidelity, bona fides, openness, unreservedness, bluntness, plainness, plain speaking, plain dealing; simplicity, bonhomie, naïveté, artlessness (703), love of truth.

A plain-dealer, truth-teller, man of his word.

(Verbs) To speak the truth, speak one's mind, open out, think aloud.

(Phrases) Tell the truth and shame the devil; to deal faithfully with; to show oneself in one's true colours.

544 Falseness *(Substantives)*, falsehood, untruthfulness, untruth (546), falsity, mendacity, falsification, perversion of truth, perjury, fabrication, romance, forgery, prevarication, equivocation, shuffling, evasion, fencing, duplicity, double-dealing, unfairness, dishonesty, fraud, misrepresentation, *suggestio falsi, suppressio veri*, Punic faith, giving the go-by, disguise, disguisement, irony, understatement.

Insincerity, dissimulation, dissembling, deceit (545), shiftiness, hypocrisy, cant, humbug, gammon,

(Adjectives) Truthful, true, veracious, uncompromising, veridical, veridicious, sincere, candid, frank, open, outspoken, unreserved, free-spoken, open-hearted, honest, simple, simple-hearted, ingenuous, blunt, plain-spoken, true-blue, straightforward, straight, fair, fair-minded, single-minded, artless, guileless, natural, unaffected, simple-minded, undisguised, unfeigned, unflattering, warts and all.

(Adverbs) Truly, etc. (494), aboveboard, broadly.

(Phrases) In plain English; without mincing the matter; honour bright; honest Injun; bona fide; *sans phrase*.

———

jesuitry, pharisaism, mental reservation, lip-service, simulation, acting, sham, malingering, pretending, pretence, crocodile tears, false colouring, art, artfulness (702).

Deceiver (548).

(Verbs) To be false, etc., to play false, speak falsely, lie, fib, tell a lie or untruth, etc. (546), to mistake, misreport, misrepresent, misquote, belie, falsify, prevaricate, equivocate, quibble, palter, shuffle, fence, hedge, understate, mince the truth.

To forswear, swear false, perjure oneself, bear false witness.

To garble, gloss over, disguise, pervert, distort, twist, colour, varnish, cook, doctor, embroider, fiddle, wangle, gerrymander, put a false colouring or construction upon (523).

To invent, make up, fabricate, concoct, trump up, forge, fake, romance.

To dissemble, dissimulate, feign, pretend, assume, act or play a part, simulate, pass off for, counterfeit, sham, malinger, make believe, cant, put on.

(Phrases) To play the hypocrite; to give the go-by; to play fast and loose; to play a double game; to blow hot and cold; to lie like a conjurer; sham Abraham; to look as if butter would not melt in one's mouth; to sail under false colours; to ring false.

(Adjectives) False, dishonest, faithless, deceitful, mendacious, unveracious, truthless, trothless, unfair, uncandid, disingenuous, shady, shifty, underhand, underhanded, hollow, insincere, canting, hypocritical, jesuitical, sanctimonious, pharisaical, tartuffian, double, double-tongued, double-faced, smooth-spoken, smooth-tongued, plausible, mealy-mouthed, snide.

Artful, insidious, sly, designing, diplomatic, Machiavellian.

Untrue, unfounded, fictitious, invented, made up, *ben trovato*, forged, falsified, counterfeit, spurious, factitious, self-styled, bastard, sham, bogus, phoney, mock, pseudo, disguised, simulated, artificial, colourable, catchpenny, meretricious, tinsel, Brummagem, postiche, pinchbeck, illusory, elusory, supposititious, surreptitious, ironical, apocryphal.

(Phrase) All is not gold that glitters.

(Adverbs) Falsely, etc., slyly, stealthily, underhand.

545 Deception *(Substantives)*, falseness (544), fraud, deceit, imposition, artifice, juggle, juggling, sleight of hand, legerdemain, conjuration, hocus-pocus, jockeyship, trickery, coggery, fraudulence, imposture, *supercherie*, chicane, chicanery, covin, cozenage, circumvention, ingannation, prestidigitation, subreption, collusion, complicity, guile, gullery, hanky-panky, jiggery-pokery, rannygazoo.

Quackery, charlatanism, charlatanry, empiricism, humbug, hokum, eye-wash, hypocrisy, gammon, flapdoodle, bunkum, *blague*, bluff, mummery, borrowed plumes.

Stratagem, trick, cheat, wile, artifice, cross, deception, take-in, camouflage, make-believe, ruse, manœuvre, finesse, hoax, canard, hum, kid, chouse, bubble, fetch, catch, spoof, swindle, plant, sell, hocus, dodge, bite, forgery, counterfeit, sham, fake, fakement, rig, delusion, stalking-horse.

Snare, trap, pitfall, decoy, gin, spring, noose, hook, bait, net, meshes, mousetrap, trap-door, false bottom, ambush, ambuscade (530), masked battery, mine, mystery-ship, Q-boat.

(Phrases) A wolf in sheep's clothing; a whited (or painted) sepulchre; a pious fraud; a man of straw.

(Verbs) To deceive, mislead, cheat, impose upon, practise upon, circumvent, play upon, put upon, bluff, dupe, mystify, blind, hoodwink, best, outreach, trick, hoax, kid, gammon, spoof, hocus, bamboozle, hornswoggle, juggle, trepan, nick, entrap, beguile, lure, inveigle, decoy, lime, ensnare, entangle, lay a snare for, trip up, stuff the go-by.

To defraud, fiddle, take in, jockey, do, do brown, cozen, diddle, have, have on, chouse, welsh, bilk, bite, pluck, swindle, victimize, outwit, over-reach, nobble, palm upon, work off upon, foist upon, fob off, balk, trump up.

(Phrases) To throw dust in the eyes; to play a trick upon; to pull one's leg; to try it on; to cog the dice; to mark the cards; to live by one's wits; to play a part; to throw a tub to the whale.

(Adjectives) Deceiving, cheating, etc.; hypocritical, Pecksniffian; deceived, duped, done, had, etc., led astray.

Deceptive, deceitful, deceptious, illusive, illusory, delusory, prestigious, elusive, bogus, counterfeit, insidious, *ad captandum, ben trovato.*

(Phrase) Fronti nulla fides; timeo Danaos et dona ferentes.

546 Untruth *(Substantives)*, falsehood, lie, falsity, fiction, fabrication, fib, whopper, bouncer, cracker, crammer, tarradiddle, story, fable, novel, romance, flam, bull, gammon, flim-flam, *guet-apens*, white lie, pious fraud, canard, nursery tale, fairy-tale, tall story.

Falsification, perjury, forgery, false swearing, misstatement, misrepresentation, inexactitude.

Pretence, pretext, subterfuge, irony, evasion, blind, disguise, plea, claptrap, shuffle, make-believe, shift, mask, cloak, visor, veil, masquerade, gloss, cobweb.

(Phrases) A pack of lies; a tissue of falsehoods; a cock-and-bull story; a trumped-up story; all my eye and Betty Martin; a mare's-nest.

547 Dupe *(Substantives)*, gull (486), gudgeon, gobemouche, cully, victim, sucker, flat, greenhorn, puppet, cat's paw, April fool, simple Simon, Joe Soap, pushover, soft mark.

(Phrases) To be the goat; to hold the baby; to carry the can; *qui vult decipi, decipiatur.*

548 Deceiver *(Substantives)*, liar, hypocrite, tale-teller, shuffler, shammer, dissembler, serpent, cockatrice; Janus, Tartuffe, Pecksniff, Joseph Surface, Cagliostro.

Pretender, impostor, knave, cheat, rogue, trickster, swindler, spiv, adventurer, humbug, sharper, jockey, welsher, leg, blackleg, rook, shark, confidence man, con man, confidence trickster, decoy, decoy-duck, stool-pigeon, gipsy.

Quack, charlatan, mountebank, empiric, quacksalver, *saltimbanco*, medicaster, *soi-disant.*

Actor, player, mummer, tumbler, posture-master, jack-pudding; illusionist, conjurer (994).

(Phrases) A wolf in sheep's clothing; a snake in the grass; one who lives by his wits.

549 Exaggeration *(Substantives)*, hyperbole, overstatement, stretch, strain, colouring, bounce, flourish, vagary, bombast (884), yarn, figure of speech, flight of fancy, *façon de parler*, extravagance, rhodomontade, heroics, sensationalism, highfalutin; tale of Baron Munchausen, traveller's tale.

(Phrases) A storm in a teacup; much ado about nothing.

(Verbs) To exaggerate, amplify, magnify, heighten, overcharge, overstate, overcolour, overlay, overdo, strain, stretch, bounce, flourish, embroider; to hyperbolize, aggravate, to make the most of.

(Phrases) To make a song about; spin a long yarn; draw the long bow; deal in the marvellous; out-herod Herod; lay it on thick; pile it on; make a mountain of a molehill.

(Adjectives) Exaggerated, etc., hyperbolical, turgid, tumid, fabulous, extravagant, magniloquent, bombastic, *outré*, highly coloured, high-flying, high-flown, high-falutin, sensational, blood-and-thunder, lurid.

(Phrases) All his geese are swans; much cry and little wool.

SECTION III—MEANS OF COMMUNICATING IDEAS

1°. *Natural Means*

550 Indication *(Substantives)*, symbolization, symbolism, typification, notation, connotation, prefigurement, representation (554), exposition, notice (527), trace (551), name (564).

A sign, symbol, index, placard, exponent, indicator, pointer, mark, token, symptom, type, emblem, figure, cipher, code, device, epigraph, motto, posy.

Science of signs, sematology, semeiology, semeiotics.

Lineament, feature, line, stroke, dash, trait, characteristic, idiosyncrasy, score, stripe, streak, scratch, tick, dot, point, notch, nick, asterisk, red letter, rubric, italics, print, stamp, impress, imprint, sublineation, underlining, display, jotting.

For identification: Badge, criterion, check, countercheck, countersign, stub, counterfoil, duplicate, tally, label, book-plate, *ex-libris*, ticket, billet, card, visiting-card, *carte de visite*, identity-card, passport, bill, bill-head, facia, signboard, witness, voucher, coupon, trade mark, hall-mark, signature, handwriting, sign manual, monogram, seal, sigil, signet, chop, autograph, autography, superscription, endorsement, *visé*, title, heading, caption, docket, watchword, password, shibboleth, *mot du guet*, catchword; fingerprint.

Insignia: Banner, banneret, flag, colours, bunting, streamer, standard, eagle, ensign, pennon, pennant, pendant, burgee, jack, ancient, labarum, oriflamme; gonfalon, banderole, Union Jack, Royal Standard, Stars and Stripes, Tricolour, etc.; crest, arms, coat of arms, armorial bearings, shield, scutcheon, escutcheon, uniform, livery, cockade, epaulet, chevron, cordon, totem.

Indication of locality: Beacon, cairn, post, staff, flagstaff, hand, pointer, vane, guide-post, finger-post, signpost, landmark, sea-mark, lighthouse, lightship, pole-star, lodestar, cynosure, guide, address, direction, rocket, blue-light, watch-fire, blaze.

Indication of an event: Signal, nod, wink, glance, leer, shrug, beck, cue, gesture, gesticulation, deaf-and-dumb alphabet, by-play, dumb-show, pantomime, touch, nudge, freemasonry, telegraph, heliograph, semaphore.

Indication of time: Time-signal, clock (114), alarm-clock, hooter, blower, buzzer, siren; tattoo, reveille, last post, taps.

Indication of danger: Alarm, alarum, alarm-bell, alert, fog-signal, detonator, red light, tocsin, fire-hooter, maroon, S O S, beat of drum, fiery cross, sound of trumpet, war-cry, war-whoop, slogan.

Indication of safety; all-clear, green light.

(Verbs) To indicate, point out, be the sign, etc., of, denote, betoken, connote, connotate, represent, stand for, typify, symbolize, shadow forth, argue, bear the impress of, witness, attest, testify.

To put an indication, mark, etc.; to note, mark, stamp, impress, earmark, brand, label, ticket, docket, endorse, sign, countersign; put, append, or affix a seal or signature; dot, jot down, book, score, dash, trace, chalk, underline, italicize, print, imprint, engrave, stereotype, rubricate, star, obelize, initial.

To make a sign, signal, etc., signalize; give or hang out a signal; give notice, gesticulate, beckon, beck, nod, wink, nudge, tip the wink; give the cue, tip, or office; wave, unfurl, hoist, or hang out a banner, flag, etc., show one's colours, give or sound an alarm, beat the drum, sound the trumpets, raise a cry, etc.

(Adjectives) Indicating, etc., indicatory, indicative, sematic, semeiological, denotative, representative, typical, typic, symbolic, symbolical, diacritical, connotative, pathognomic, symptomatic, exponential, emblematic, pantomimic, attesting; armorial, totemistic.

Indicated, etc., typified, impressed, etc.

Capable of being denoted, denotable, indelible.

(Phrases) Ecce signum; in token of.

---

551 Record *(Substantives)*, trace, mark, tradition, vestige, footstep, footmark, footprint, footfall, wake, track, trail, slot, spoor, pug, scent.

Monument, relic, remains, trophy, hatchment, achievement, obelisk, monolith, pillar, stele, column, slab, tablet, medal, testimonial, memorial.

Note, minute, register, registry, index, inventory, catalogue, list (86), memorandum, jotting, document, account, score, tally, invoice, docket, voucher, protocol, inscription.

Paper, parchment, scroll, instrument, deed, indenture, debenture, roll, archive, schedule, file, dossier, cartulary, table, *procès verbal,* affidavit, certificate, attestation, entry, diploma, protest, round-robin, roster, rota, muster-roll, muster-book, notebook, commonplace-book, *adversaria,* portfolio.

552 Suppression of sign.

Obliteration *(Substantives)*, erasure, rasure, cancel, cancellation, circumduction, deletion.

(Verbs) To efface, obliterate, erase, raze, expunge, cancel, delete, blot out, take out, rub out, scratch out, strike out, elide, wipe out, wash out, black out, write off, render illegible.

To be effaced, etc., to leave no trace.

(Phrases) To draw the pen through; to apply the sponge.

(Adjectives) Obliterated, effaced, etc., printless, leaving no trace.

Unrecorded, unattested, unregistered, intestate.

(Interjections) Dele; out with it!

Chronicle, annals, gazette, Hansard, history (594), newspaper, magazine, gazetteer, blue-book, almanac, calendar, ephemeris, diary, log, journal, day-book, ledger.

Registration, tabulation, enrolment, booking.

(Verbs) To record, note, register, chronicle, calendar, make an entry of, enter, book, take a note of, post, enrol, jot down, take down, mark, sign, etc. (550), tabulate, catalogue, file, index, commemorate (883).

(Adjectives) Registered, etc.

(Adverbs) Under one's hand and seal, on record.

553 Recorder *(Substantives)*, notary, clerk, registrar, registrary, register, prothonotary, secretary, stenographer, amanuensis, scribe, remembrancer, journalist, historian, historiographer, annalist, chronicler, biographer, bookkeeper.

Recordership, secretaryship, secretariat, clerkship.

554 Representation *(Substantives)*, delineation, representment, reproduction, depictment, personification.

Art, the fine arts, the graphic arts, design, designing, illustration, imitation (19), copy (21), portraiture, iconography, photography.

A picture, drawing, tracing, photograph.

An image, likeness, icon, portrait, effigy, facsimile, autotype, imagery, figure, puppet, dummy, lay figure, figurehead, doll, manikin, *mannequin,* mammet, marionette, *fantoccini* (599) statue (557), waxwork.

Hieroglyphic, hieroglyph, inscription, diagram, monogram, draught (or draft), outline, scheme, *schema*, schedule.

Map, plan, chart, ground-plan, projection, elevation, ichnography, atlas; cartography, chorography.

(Verbs) To represent, present, depict, portray, photograph, delineate, design, figure, adumbrate, shadow forth, copy, draft, mould, diagrammatize, schematize, map.

To imitate, impersonate, personate, personify, act, take off, hit off, figure as; to paint (556); carve (557); engrave (558).

(Adjectives) Representing, etc.; artistic; imitative, representative, illustrative, figurative, hieroglyphic, hieroglyphical, diagrammatic, schematic.

555 Misrepresentation *(Substantives)*, distortion (243), caricature, burlesque (856), a bad likeness, daub, scratch, sign-painting, anamorphosis; misprint, *erratum*.

(Verbs) To misrepresent, distort, falsify, caricature, wrest the sense (or meaning).

———

556 Painting *(Substantives)*, depicting, drawing; perspective, composition, treatment.

Drawing in pencil, crayon, pastel, chalk, water-colour, etc.

Painting in oils, in distemper, in gouache, in fresco; encaustic painting, enamel painting, scene-painting; wash (428), body-colour, impasto.

A picture, drawing, painting, sketch, illustration, scratch, *graffito*, outline, tableau, cartoon, fresco, illumination; pencil, pen-and-ink, etc., drawing; oil, etc., painting; photograph; silver print; P.O.P.; bromide, gaslight, bromoil, platinotype, carbon print; autochrome, Kodachrome; daguerreotype, calotype; mosaic, tapestry, etc., picture-gallery.

Portrait, portraiture, likeness, full-length, etc., miniature, kitcat, shade, profile, silhouette, still, snapshot.

Landscape, seascape, nocturne, view, still-life, *genre*, panorama, diorama.

Pre-Raphaelitism, impressionism, etc. (559).

(Verbs) To paint, depict, portray, limn, draw, sketch, pencil, scratch, scrawl, block in, rough in, dash off, chalk out, shadow forth, adumbrate, outline, illustrate, illuminate; to take a portrait, take a likeness, to photograph, snap, pan.

(Phrases) Fecit, pinxit, delineavit.

(Adjectives) Painted, etc.; pictorial, graphic, picturesque, Giottesque, Raphaelesque, Turneresque, etc.; like, similar (17).

557 Sculpture *(Substantives)*, insculpture, carving, modelling.

A statue, statuary, statuette, figure, figurine, model, bust, image, high relief, low relief, alto-rilievo, mezzo-rilievo, basso-rilievo, bas-relief, cast, marble, bronze, intaglio, anaglyph; medallion, cameo.

(Verbs) To sculpture, sculp, carve, cut, chisel, model, mould, cast.

(Adjectives) Sculptured, etc., sculptural, sculpturesque, anaglyphic, cero-plastic, ceramic.

558 Engraving *(Substantives)*, etching, wood-engraving, process-engraving, xylography, chalcography, cerography, glyptography; poker-work.

A print, engraving, impression, plate, cut, wood-cut, steel-cut, linocut, vignette.

An etching, dry-point, stipple, roulette; copper-plate, mezzotint, aquatint, lithograph, chromolithograph, chromo, photo-lithograph, photogravure, anastatic-printing, collotype, electrotype, stereotype.

Matrix, flong.

(Verbs) To engrave, etc., lithograph, print, etc.

559 Artist *(Substantives)*, painter, limner, draughtsman, black-and-white artist, cartoonist, caricaturist, drawer, sketcher, pavement artist, screever, designer, engraver, copyist, photographer.

Academician; historical, landscape, portrait, miniature, scene, sign, etc., painter; an Apelles.

Primitive, Pre-Raphaelite, old master, quattrocentist, cinquecentist, impressionist, post-impressionist, futurist, vorticist, cubist, surrealist, Dadaist, pointillist.

A sculptor, carver, modeller, goldsmith, silversmith, *figuriste*; a Phidias, Praxiteles, Royal Academician, R.A.

Implements of art: pen, pencil, brush, charcoal, chalk, pastel, crayon; paint (428); stump, graver, style, burin; canvas, easel, palette, maul-stick, palette-knife; studio, *atelier*.

2°. *Conventional Means*

1. LANGUAGE GENERALLY

560 Language *(Substantives)*, tongue, speech, lingo, vernacular, mother-tongue, native tongue, standard English, King's (or Queen's) English, the genius of a language.

Dialect, local dialect, class dialect, provincialism, vulgarism, colloquialism, Americanism, Scotticism, Cockney speech, brogue, patois, patter, slang, cant, argot, Anglic, Basic English, broken English, pidgin English, lingua franca.

Universal languages: Esperanto, Volapük, Ido, Interglossa.

Philology, etymology (562), linguistics, glossology, dialectology, phonetics.

Literature, letters, polite literature, belles lettres, the muses, humanities, the republic of letters, dead languages, classics, *literae humaniores*.

Scholarship (490), linguist, scholar (492), writer (593), glossographer.

(Verbs) To express by words, to couch in terms, to clothe in language.

(Adjectives) Literary, belletristic, linguistic, dialectal, vernacular, colloquial, slang, current, polyglot, pantomimic.

(Adverbs) In plain terms, in common parlance, in household words.

561 Letter *(Substantives)*, alphabet, A B C, abecedary, spelling-book, horn-book, criss-cross-row; character (591), writing (590), hieroglyph, hieroglyphic; consonant, vowel, diphthong, triphthong; mute, liquid, labial, palatal, dental, guttural; spelling, orthography, phonetic spelling, misspelling; spelling-bee.

Syllable, monosyllable, dissyllable, trisyllable, polysyllable; anagram.

(Verbs) To spell, spell out.

(Adjectives) Literal, alphabetical, abecedarian, orthographic; syllabic, disyllabic, etc.

562 Word *(Substantives)*, term, vocable, terminology, part of speech (567), root, etymon.

Word similarly pronounced, homonym, homophone, paronym.

A dictionary, vocabulary, lexicon, index, polyglot, glossary, thesaurus, concordance, onomasticon, gradus; lexicography, lexicographer.

Derivation, etymology, glossology.

(Adjectives) Verbal, literal, titular, nominal, etymological, terminological.

Similarly derived, conjugate, paronymous.

(Adverbs) Nominally, etc., *verbatim*, word for word, in so many words, literally, *sic, totidem verbis, ipsissimis verbis, literatim*.

563 Neology *(Substantives)*, neologism, slang, cant, byword, hard word, jaw-breaker, dog Latin, monkish Latin, loan word, vogue word, nonce word, Gallicism.

A pun, play upon words, paronomasia, *jeu de mots, calembour,* palindrome, conundrum, acrostic, anagram (533).

Dialect (560).

Neologian, neologist.

(Verbs) To neologize, archaize, pun.

(Phrase) To coin or mint words.

(Adjectives) Neological, neologistic, paronomastic.

———

564 Nomenclature *(Substantives)*, nomination, naming, nuncupation.

A name, appellation, designation, appellative, denomination, term, expression, noun, byword, moniker, epithet, style, title, prenomen, forename, Christian name, baptismal name, given name, cognomen, agnomen, patronymic, surname, family name.

Synonym, namesake; euphemism, antonomasia, onomatopoeia.

Quotation, citation, chapter and verse.

(Verbs) To name, call, term, denominate, designate, style, clepe, entitle, dub, christen, baptize, characterize, specify, label (550).

To be called, etc., to take the name of, pass under the name of; to quote, cite.

(Phrases) To call a spade a spade; to rejoice in the name of.

(Adjectives) Named, called, etc., hight, yclept, known as; nuncupatory, nuncupative, cognominal, titular, nominal.

Literal, verbal, discriminative.

565 Misnomer *(Substantives)*, missaying, malaprop, malapropism, antiphrasis, nickname, sobriquet, byname, assumed name or title, alias, *nom de guerre, nom de plume*, pen-name, pseudonym, pet name, euphemism.

So-and-so, what's-his-name, thingummy, thingumbob, thingumajig, dingus, *Je ne sais quoi*.

A Mrs. Malaprop.

(Phrase) Lucus a non lucendo.

(Verbs) To misname, missay, miscall, misterm, nickname.

To assume a name.

(Adjectives) Misnamed, etc., malapropian, pseudonymous, *soi-disant*, self-called, self-styled, so-called.

Nameless, anonymous, without a name, having no name, innominate, unnamed.

———

566 Phrase *(Substantives)*, expression, phraseology, paraphrase, periphrasis, circumlocution (573), set phrase, round terms; mode or turn of expression; idiom, wording, *façon de parler*, mannerism, plain terms, plain English.

Sentence, paragraph, motto.

Figure, trope, metaphor (521), wisecrack, proverb (496).

(Verbs) To express, phrase, put; couch, clothe in words, give words to; to word.

(Adjectives) Expressed, etc., couched in, phraseological, idiomatic, paraphrastic, periphrastic, circumlocutory (573), proverbial.

(Phrase) As the saying is; in good set terms; *sans phrase*.

567 Grammar *(Substantives)*, accidence, syntax, parsing, analysis, praxis, punctuation, conjugation, declension, inflexion, case, voice, person, number; philology (560), parts of speech.

(Phrase) Jus et norma loquendi.

(Verbs) To parse, analyse, conjugate, decline, inflect, punctuate.

(Adjectives) Grammatical, syntatic, inflexional.

---

568 Solecism *(Substantives)*, bad or false grammar, slip of the pen or tongue, bull, howler, floater, clanger, *lapsus linguae*, barbarism, vulgarism; dog Latin.

(Verbs) To use bad or faulty grammar, to solecize, commit a solecism.

(Phrases) To murder the king's English; to break Priscian's head.

(Adjectives) Ungrammatical, barbarous, slipshod, incorrect, faulty, inaccurate.

569 Style *(Substantives)*, diction, phraseology, wording, turn of expression, idiom, manner, strain, composition, authorship; stylist.

(Adjectives) Stylistic, idiomatic, mannered.

(Phrases) Command of language; a ready pen; *le style, c'est l'homme même*.

Various Qualities of Style

570 Perspicuity *(Substantives)*, lucidity, lucidness, clearness, clarity, perspicacity, plain speaking, intelligibility (518).

(Adjectives), Perspicuous, clear (525), lucid, intelligible, plain, transparent, explicit.

571 Obscurity *(Substantives)*, ambiguity (520), unintelligibility (519), involution, involvedness, vagueness.

(Adjectives) Obscure, confused, crabbed, ambiguous, vague, unintelligible, etc., involved, wiredrawn, tortuous.

572 Conciseness *(Substantives)*, brevity, terseness, compression (195), condensation, concision, closeness, laconism, portmanteau word, telegraphese, pithiness, succinctness, quaintness, stiffness, ellipsis, ellipse, syncope.

Abridgment, epitome (596).

(Verbs) To be concise, etc., to condense, compress, abridge, abbreviate, cut short, curtail, abstract.

(Phrase) To cut the cackle and come to the horses.

573 Diffuseness *(Substantives)*, prolixity, verbosity, macrology, pleonasm, tautology, copiousness, exuberance, laxity, looseness, verbiage, flow, flow of words, fluency, *copia verborum*, loquacity (584), redundancy, redundance, digression, amplification, *longueur*, padding, circumlocution, ambages, periphrasis, officialese, commercialese, gobbledygook, episode, expletive.

(Verbs) To be diffuse, etc., to expatiate, enlarge, launch out, dilate, expand, pad out, spin out, run on,

(Adjectives) Concise, brief, crisp, curt, short, terse, laconic, sententious, gnomic, snappy, pithy, nervous, pregnant, succinct, *guindé*, stiff, compact, summary, compendious (596), close, cramped, elliptical, telegraphic, epigrammatic, lapidary.

(Adverbs) Concisely, briefly, etc., in a word, to the point, in short.

(Phrases) The long and short of it; *multum in parvo*; it comes to this; for shortness' sake; to make a long story short; to put it in a nutshell.

———

amplify, swell out, inflate, dwell on, harp on, descant, digress, ramble, maunder, rant.

(Phrases) To beat about the bush; to spin a long yarn; to make a long story of.

(Adjectives) Diffuse, wordy, verbose, prolix, copious, exuberant, flowing, fluent, bombastic, lengthy, long-winded, talkative (584), prosy, spun out, long-spun, loose, lax, slovenly, washy, slipslop, sloppy, frothy, flatulent, windy, digressive, discursive, excursive, tripping, rambling, ambagious, pleonastic, redundant, periphrastic, episodic, circumlocutory, roundabout.

Minute, detailed, particular, circumstantial.

(Adverbs) In detail, at great length, *in extenso*, about it and about, *currente calamo, usque ad nauseam.*

574 Vigour *(Substantives)*, energy, power, force, spirit, point, vim, snap, punch, ginger, *élan*, pep, go, raciness, liveliness, fire, glow, verve, piquancy, pungency, spice, boldness, gravity, warmth, sententiousness, elevation, loftiness, sublimity, eloquence, individuality, distinction, emphasis, virility.

(Phrase) 'Thoughts that glow and words that burn.'

(Adjectives) Vigorous, energetic, powerful, strong, forcible, nervous, spirited, vivid, virile, expressive, lively, glowing, sparkling, racy, bold, slashing, incisive, trenchant, snappy, mordant, poignant, piquant, pungent, spicy, meaty, pithy, juicy, pointed, antithetical, sententious, emphatic, individual, lofty, elevated, sublime, Miltonic, eloquent.

575 Feebleness *(Substantives)*, baldness, tameness, meagreness, coldness, frigidity, poverty, puerility, childishness, dullness, dryness, jejuneness, monotony.

(Adjectives) Feeble, bald, dry, flat, insipid, tame, meagre, invertebrate, weak, mealy-mouthed, wishy-washy, wersh, banal, uninteresting, jejune, vapid, cold, frigid, poor, dull (843), languid, anaemic, prosy, prosaic, pedestrian, platitudinous, conventional, mechanical, decadent, trashy, namby-pamby (866), puerile, childish, emasculate.

———

athletic, distinguished, original,

576 Plainness *(Substantives)*, simplicity, homeliness, chasteness, chastity, neatness, monotony, severity.

(Adjectives) Simple, unornamented, unvarnished, straightforward, artless, unaffected, downright, plain, unadorned, unvaried, monotonous, severe, chaste, blunt, homespun.

———

577 Ornament *(Substantives)*, floridness, floridity, flamboyance, richness, opulence, turgidity, tumidity, pomposity, inflation, altiloquence, spreadeagleism, pretension, fustian, affectation, euphuism, gongorism, mannerism, metaphor, preciosity, inversion, figurativeness, sesquipedalianism, *sesquipedalia verba*, rant, bombast, frothiness; flowers of speech, high-sounding words, well-rounded periods, purple patches.

A phrase-monger, euphuist.

(Verbs) To ornament, overcharge, overlay with ornament, lard or garnish with metaphors, lay the colours on thick, round a period, mouth.

(Adjectives) Ornamented, etc., ornate, florid, flamboyant, rich, opulent, golden-mouthed, figurative, metaphorical, pedantic, affected, pretentious, falsetto, euphuistic, Della Cruscan, pompous, fustian, high-sounding, mouthy, inflated, high-falutin (or high-faluting), bombastic, stilted, mannered, high-flowing, frothy, flowery, luscious, turgid, tumid, swelling, declamatory, rhapsodic, rhetorical, orotund, sententious, grandiose, grandiloquent, magniloquent, altiloquent, sesquipedalian, Johnsonian, ponderous.

(Adverb) Ore rotundo.

578 Elegance *(Substantives)*, grace, ease, naturalness, purity, concinnity, readiness, euphony; a purist.

(Phrases) A ready pen; flowing periods; *curiosa felicitas.*

(Adjectives) Elegant, graceful, Attic, Ciceronian, classical, natural, easy, felicitous, unaffected, unlaboured, chaste, pure, correct, flowing, mellifluous, euphonious, rhythmical, puristic, well-expressed, neatly put.

(Phrases) To round a period; 'to point a moral and adorn a tale.'

579 Inelegance *(Substantives)*, stiffness, uncouthness, barbarism, archaism, rudeness, crudeness, bluntness, brusquerie, ruggedness, abruptness, artificiality, cacophony.

(Phrases) Words that dislocate the jaw, that break the teeth.

(Verbs) To be inelegant, etc.

(Phrase) To smell of the lamp.

(Adjectives) Inelegant, ungraceful, stiff, forced, laboured, clumsy, contorted, tortuous, harsh, cramped, rude, rugged, dislocated, crude, crabbed, uncouth, barbarous, archaic, archaistic, affected (577), artificial, abrupt, blunt, brusque, incondite.

2. SPOKEN LANGUAGE

580 Voice *(Substantives)*, vocality, vocalization, utterance, cry, strain, articulate sound, prolation, articulation, enunciation, delivery, vocalism, pronunciation, orthoepy, euphony.

Cadence, accent, accentuation, emphasis, stress, tone, intonation, exclamation, ejaculation, vociferation, ventriloquism, polyphonism.

A ventriloquist, polyphonist.

Phonetics, phonology; voice-production.

(Verbs) To utter, breathe, cry, exclaim, shout, ejaculate, vociferate; raise, lift, strain the voice or lungs; to vocalize, prolate, articulate, enunciate, pronounce, accentuate, aspirate, deliver, mouth, rap out, speak out, speak up.

(Phrase) To whisper in the ear.

(Adjectives) Vocal, oral, phonetic, articulate.

Silvery, mellow, soft (413).

581 Aphony *(Substantives)*, obmutescence, absence or want of voice, dumbness, muteness, mutism, speechlessness, aphasia, hoarseness, raucity; silence (585).

A dummy, a mute, deaf-mute.

(Verbs) To render mute, to muzzle, muffle, suppress, smother, gag (585); to whisper (405).

(Phrases) To stick in the throat; to close one's lips; to shut up.

(Adjectives) Aphonous, dumb, speechless, mute, tongueless, muzzled, tongue-tied, inarticulate, inaudible, unspoken, unsaid, mum, mumchance, lips close or sealed, wordless; raucous, hoarse, husky, sepulchral.

(Phrases) Mute as a fish; hoarse as a raven; with bated breath; *sotto voce*; with the finger on the lips; mum's the word.

582 Speech (*Substantives*), locution, talk, parlance, verbal intercourse, oral communication word of mouth, palaver, prattle, effusion, narrative (594), tale, story, yarn, oration, recitation, delivery, say, harangue, formal speech, speechifying, sermon, homily, discourse (998), lecture, curtain lecture, pi-jaw, address, tirade, pep-talk, screed; preamble, peroration; soliloquy (589).

Oratory, elocution, rhetoric, declamation, eloquence, gift of the gab, *copia verborum*, grandiloquence, magniloquence.

A speaker, spokesman, prolocutor, mouthpiece, lecturer, orator, stumporator, speechifier; a Cicero, a Demosthenes.

(*Verbs*) To speak, break silence, say, tell, utter, pronounce (580), open one's lips, give tongue, hold forth, make or deliver a speech, speechify, harangue, talk, discourse, declaim, stump, flourish, spout, rant, recite, rattle off, intone, breathe, let fall, whisper in the ear, expatiate, run on; to lecture, preach, address, sermonize, preachify; to soliloquize (589); quoth he.

(*Phrases*) To have a tongue in one's head; to have on the tip of one's tongue; to have on one's lips; to pass one's lips; to find one's tongue.

(*Adjectives*) Speaking, etc., oral, spoken, unwritten, elocutionary, oratorical, rhetorical, declamatory, outspoken.

(*Adverbs*) Viva voce; *ore rotundo*; by word of mouth.

583 Imperfect speech.
Stammering (*Substantives*), inarticulateness, stuttering, impediment in one's speech, titubancy, faltering, hesitation, lisp, drawl, jabber, gibber, sputter, splutter, mumbling, mincing, muttering, mouthing, twang, a broken or cracked voice, broken accents or sentences, tardiloquence, falsetto, a whisper (405), mispronunciation.

(*Verbs*) to stammer, stutter, hesitate, falter, hem, haw, hum and ha, mumble, lisp, jabber, gibber, mutter, sputter, splutter, drawl, mouth, mince, lisp, croak, speak through the nose, snuffle, clip one's words, mispronounce, missay.

(*Phrases*) To clip the King's (or Queen's) English; *parler à tort et à travers*; not to be able to put two words together.

(*Adjectives*) Stammering, etc., inarticulate, guttural, nasal, tremulous.

---

584 Loquacity (*Substantives*), loquaciousness, talkativeness, garrulity, flow of words, prate, gas, jaw, gab, gabble, jabber, chatter, prattle, cackle, clack, clash, blether (or blather), patter, rattle, twaddle, bibble-babble, gibble-gabble, talkee-talkee, gossip.

Fluency, flippancy, volubility, verbosity, *cacoethes loquendi*, anecdotage.

A chatterer, chatterbox, blatherskite, babbler, wind-bag, gas-bag, rattle, ranter, tub-thumper, sermonizer, proser, driveller, gossip.

Magpie, jay, parrot, poll; Babel.

(*Phrases*) A twice (or thrice) told tale; a long yarn; the gift of the gab.

(*Verbs*) To be loquacious, etc., to

585 Taciturnity (*Substantives*), closeness, reserve, reticence (528), muteness, silence, curtness; aposiopesis; a clam, oyster.

(*Phrases*) A Quaker meeting; a man of few words.

(*Verbs*) To be silent, etc. (403), to hold one's tongue, keep silence, hold one's peace, say nothing, hold one's jaw, close one's mouth or lips, fall silent, dry up, shut up, stow it.

To render silent, silence, put to silence, seal one's lips, smother, suppress, stop one's mouth, gag, muffle, muzzle (581).

(*Adjectives*) Taciturn, silent, close, reserved, mute, sparing of words, buttoned up, curt, short-spoken, close-tongued, tight-lipped, reticent,

prate, palaver, chatter, prattle, jabber, jaw, rattle, twaddle, blether, babble, gabble, gas, out-talk, descant, dilate, dwell on, reel off, expatiate, prose, launch out, yarn, gossip, wag one's tongue, run on.

(Phrases) To din in the ears; to drum into the ear; to spin a long yarn; to talk at random; to bum one's chat; to talk oneself out of breath; to talk nineteen to the dozen.

(Adjectives) Loquacious, talkative, garulous, gassy, gabby, open-mouthed, chatty, chattering, etc.

Fluent, voluble, glib, flippant, long-tongued, long-winded, verbose, the tongue running fast.

(Adverb) Trippingly on the tongue.

secretive, uncommunicative, inconversable.

(Phrases) Not a word escaping one; not having a word to say.

(Interjections) Hush! silence! mum! *chut!* hist! whist! wheesht!

---

586 Allocution *(Substantives)*, address, apostrophe, interpellation, appeal, invocation, alloquialism, salutation, accost, greeting (894).

Feigned dialogue, imaginary conversation; inquiry (461).

(Phrase) A word in the ear.

(Verbs) To speak to, address, accost, buttonhole, apostrophize, appeal to, invoke, hail, make up to, take aside, call to, halloo (or hallo), salute.

(Phrases) To talk with one in private; to break the ice.

(Adjectives) Accosting, etc., alloquial, invocatory, apostrophic.

(Interjections) Hallo! hello! hullo! I say! hoy! oi! hey! what ho! psst!

587 Response *(Substantives)*, answer, reply (462).

(Verbs) To answer, respond, reply, etc.

(Phrase) To take up one's cue.

(Adjectives) Answering, responding, etc., responsive, respondent.

---

588 Interlocution *(Substantives)*, collocution, colloquy, conversation, converse, confabulation, confab, talk, discourse, verbal intercourse, dialogue, duologue, logomachy, communication, intercommunication, commerce, debate.

Chat, chit-chat, crack, small talk, table-talk, tattle, gossip, tittle-tattle, babblement, clack, prittle-prattle, idle talk, town-talk, bazaar talk, *on dit*, causerie, *chronique scandaleuse*.

589 Soliloquy *(Substantives)*, monologue, apostrophe, aside.

Soliloquist, monologist, monologuist.

(Verbs) To soliloquize, monologize; to say or talk to oneself, to say aside, to think aloud, to apostrophize.

(Adjectives) Soliloquizing, etc.

Conference, parley, interview, audience, tête-à-tête, reception, conversazione, palaver, pow-wow; council (686).

A talker, interlocutor, interviewer, gossip, tattler, chatterer, babbler (584), conversationalist, *causeur; dramatis personae*.

(Phrases) 'The feast of reason and the flow of soul'; a heart-to-heart talk.

(Verbs) To talk together, converse, collogue, commune, debate, discourse with, engage in conversation, interview; hold or carry on a conversation; chat, gossip, have a crack, put in a word, chip in, tattle, babble, prate, clack, prattle.

To confer with, hold conference, etc., to parley, palaver, commerce, hold intercourse with, be closeted with, commune with, have speech with, compare notes, intercommunicate.

(Adjectives) Conversing, etc., interlocutory, verbal, colloquial, discursive, chatty, gossiping, etc., conversable, conversational.

3. WRITTEN LANGUAGE

590 Writing *(Substantives)*, chirography, pencraft, penmanship, longhand, calligraphy, quill-driving, pen-pushing, typewriting, typing.

Scribble, scrawl, scratch, cacography, scribbling, etc., jotting, interlineation, palimpsest.

Uncial writing, court hand, cursive writing, picture writing, hieroglyphics, hieroglyph, cuneiform characters, demotic text, hieratic text, ogham, runes.

Pothooks and hangers.

Transcription, inscription, superscription, minute.

Shorthand, stenography, phonography, brachygraphy, tachygraphy, steganography.

Secret writing, writing in cipher, cryptography, polygraphy, stelography; cryptogram.

Automatic writing, planchette.

Composition, authorship, *cacoethes scribendi*.

Manuscript, MS., copy, transcript, rough copy, fair copy, carbon, black, duplicate, flimsy, handwriting, hand, fist, script, autograph, signature, sign-manual, monograph, holograph, endorsement, paraph.

A scribe, amanuensis, scrivener, secretary, clerk, penman, calligraphist, copyist, transcriber, stenographer, typist.

Writer, author, scribbler, quill-driver, ink-slinger, pamphleteer, essayist, critic, reviewer, novelist (593), journalist, editor, subeditor, reporter, pressman, penny-a-liner, hack, free-lance; Grub Street, Fleet Street.

Pen, quill, fountain-pen, stylograph, stylo, ball-point, Biro, pencil, stationery, paper, parchment, vellum, tablet, slate, marble, pillar, table, etc.

(Phrase) A dash or stroke of the pen.

(Verbs) To write, pen, typewrite, type, write out, copy, engross, write out fair, transcribe, scribble, scrawl, scratch, interline; to sign, undersign, countersign, endorse (497), set one's hand to.

To compose, indite, draw up, draft, minute, jot down, dash off, make or take a minute of, put or set down in writing; to inscribe, to dictate.

(Phrases) To take up the pen; to spill ink; to sling ink; set or put pen to paper; put on paper; commit to paper.

(Adjectives) Writing, etc., written, in writing, penned, etc., scriptorial; uncial, cursive, cuneiform, runic, hieroglyphical; editorial, journalistic, reportorial.

(Phrases) Under one's hand; in black and white; pen in hand; *currente calamo*.

591 Printing *(Substantives)*, print, letterpress, text, context, note, page, proof, pull, revise; presswork.

Typography, stereotypography, type, character, black-letter, fount (or font), capitals, majuscules, lower case letters, minuscules, etc.; roman, italic, type; braille.

Folio, quarto, octavo, etc. (593).

Printer, pressman, compositor, corrector of the press, proof-reader, copyholder; printer's devil.

Printing-press, linotype, monotype, etc.

(Verbs) To print, put to press, publish, edit, get out a work, etc.

(Adjectives) Printed, etc.

592 Correspondence *(Substantives)*, letter, epistle, note, line, airgraph, postcard, chit, billet, missive, circular, favour, *billet-doux*, dispatch, bulletin, memorial, rescript, rescription.

Letter-bag, mail, post; postage.

(Verbs) To correspond, write to, send a letter to.

(Phrase) To keep up a correspondence.

(Adjectives) Epistolary, postal.

593 Book *(Substantives)*, writing, work, volume, tome, codex, opuscule, tract, manual, pamphlet, chap-book, booklet, brochure, enchiridion, circular, publication, part, issue, number, journal, album, periodical, magazine, digest, serial, ephemeris, annual, yearbook.

Writer, author, publicist, scribbler, pamphleteer, poet, essayist, novelist, fabulist, editor (590).

Book-lover, bibliophile, bibliomaniac, paperback.

Bibliography, *incunabula,* Aldine, Elzevir, etc.; library.

Publisher, bookseller, bibliopole, bibliopolist, librarian.

Folio, quarto, octavo, duodecimo, sextodecimo, octodecimo.

Paper, bill, sheet, leaf, fly-leaf, page, title-page.

Chapter, section, paragraph, passage, clause.

(Adjectives) Auctorial, bookish, bibliographical, etc.

594 Description *(Substantives)*, account, statement, report, return, delineation, specification, particulars, sketch, representation (554), narration, narrative, yarn, relation, recital, rehearsal, annals, chronicle, saga, *adversaria*, journal (551), itinerary, log-book.

Historiography; historicity, historic muse, Clio.

Story, history, memoir, tale, tradition, legend, folk-tale, folk-lore, anecdote, ana, analects (596), fable, fiction, novel, novelette, thriller, whodunit, romance, short story, *conte, nouvelle*, apologue, parable; word-picture; local colour.

Biography, necrology, obituary, life, personal narrative, adventures, autobiography, confessions, reminiscences.

A historian, historiographer, narrator, *raconteur*, annalist, chronicler, biographer, fabulist, novelist, fictionist, story-teller.

(Verbs) To describe, state (535), set forth, sketch, delineate, represent (554), portray, depict, paint, shadow forth, adumbrate.

To relate, recite, recount, sum up, run over, recapitulate, narrate, chronicle, rehearse, tell, give or render an account of, report, draw up a statement, spin a yarn, unfold a tale, novelize, actualize.

To take up or handle a subject; to enter into particulars, detail, etc., to characterize, particularize, detail, retail, elaborate, write up; to descend to particulars; to Boswellize.

(Phrases) To plunge *in medias res*; to fight one's battles over again.

(Adjectives) Descriptive, narrative, graphic, realistic, naturalistic, novelistic, historic, traditional, traditionary, legendary, storied, romantic, anecdotic, Boswellian, described, etc.

595 Dissertation *(Substantives)*, treatise, tract, tractate, thesis, theme, monograph, essay, discourse, article, leading article, leader, leaderette, editorial, feuilleton, criticism, critique, review, memoir, prolusion, disquisition, exposition, exercitation, compilation, sermon, lecture, teach-in, homily, pandect, *causerie,* pamphlet (593).

Commentator, lecturer, critic, leader-writer, pamphleteer.

(Verbs) To dissert, descant, treat of, discuss, write, compile, touch upon ventilate, canvass; deal with, do justice to a subject.

(Adjectives) Discursive, disquisitional, expository, compiled.

596 Compendium *(Substantives)*, compend, summary, abstract, précis, epitome, *aperçu*, analysis, digest, sum and substance, *compte rendu, procès verbal*, draft, *exposé*, brief, recapitulation, résumé, conspectus, abridgment, abbreviation, minute, note, synopsis, argument, plot, syllabus, contents, heads, prospectus.

Scrap-book, album, note-book, commonplace-book, compilation, extracts, cuttings, clippings, text-book, analects, *analecta,* excerpts, flowers, anthology, *collectanea*, memorabilia.

(Verbs) To abridge, abstract, excerpt, abbreviate, recapitulate, run over, make or prepare an abstract, etc. (201), epitomize, sum up, summarize, boil down, anthologize.

(Adjectives) Compendious, etc., synoptic, abridged, etc., analectic.

(Phrase) In a nutshell; in substance; in short.

597 Poetry *(Substantives)*, poetics, poesy, the Muse, the Nine, Calliope, Parnassus, Helicon, the Pierian spring.

Verse, metre, measure, foot, numbers, strain, rhyme (or rime), head-rhyme, alliteration, rhythm, heroic verse, Alexandrine, octosyllables, *terza rima,* blank verse, free verse, *vers libre*, sprung rhythm, assonance, versification, macaronics, doggerel, jingle, prosody, orthometry, scansion.

Poem, epic, epopee, epic poem, ballad, ode, epode, idyll, lyric, eclogue, pastoral, bucolic, macaronic, dithyramb, anacreontic, sonnet, lay, roundelay, rondeau, rondel, ballade, villanelle, triolet, sestina, rhyme royal, madrigal, canzonet, libretto, posy, anthology; distich, stanza, stave, strophe, antistrophe, couplet, triplet, quatrain, cento, monody, elegy, *vers de société*.

Iambic (or iamb), trochee, spondee, dactyl, anapaest, amphibrach, amphimacer, tribrach, paeon, etc.

A poet, laureate, bard, scald, poetess, rhymer, rhymist, versifier, rhymester, sonneteer, poetaster, minor poet, minnesinger, meistersinger, troubadour, *trouvère*.

(Phrase) Genus irritabile vatum.

(Verbs) To rhyme, versify, sing, make verses, scan, poetize.

(Adjectives) Poetical, poetic, Castalian, Parnassian, Heliconian, lyric, lyrical, metrical, epic, heroic; catalectic, dithyrambic, doggerel, macaronic, leonine; Pindaric, Homeric, Virgilian, Shakespearian, Miltonic, Tennysonian, etc.

598 Prose *(Substantives)* prose-writer, proser, prosaist.

(Verb) To prose.

(Adjectives) Prosaic, prosaical, prosing, prosy, rhymeless, unrhymed, unpoetical, commonplace, humdrum.

---

599 The Drama *(Substantives)*, stage, theatre, the histrionic art, dramatic art, histrionics, acting; stage effect, *mise en scène*, stage production, setting, scenery; buskin, sock, cothurnus; Melpomene, Thalia, Thespis; play-writing, dramaturgy.

Play, stage-play, piece, tragedy, comedy, tragi-comedy, morality, mystery, melodrama, farce, knock-about farce, comedietta, curtain-raiser, interlude, afterpiece, vaudeville, extravaganza, *divertissement*, burletta, burlesque, variety show, revue; opera, grand opera, music-drama, comic opera, *opéra bouffe*, operetta, ballad opera, *singspiel*, musical comedy; ballet, pantomime, harlequinade, charade, wordless play, dumb-show, by-play; monodrama, monologue, duologue; masque, pageant, show; scenario, libretto, book of words, part, role; matinée, benefit; act, scene, prologue, epilogue.

Theatre, playhouse, music-hall, variety theatre; stage, the boards, the footlights, green-room, foyer, proscenium, flies, wings, stalls, box, pit, circle, dress-circle, balcony, amphitheatre, gallery.

An actor, player, stage-player, performer, artiste, comedian, comedienne, tragedian, tragedienne, Thespian, Roscius, clown, harlequin, pantaloon, *buffo*, buffoon, pierrot, pierrette, impersonator, entertainer, etc., strolling player; ballet dancer, *ballerina*, figurant, mime, star; prima donna, *primo tenore*, etc., leading lady, heavy lead, juvenile lead, *ingénue*, soubrette; supernumerary, super, walking, gentleman or lady, chorus girl; *dramatis personae*, cast, company, stock company, touring company, repertory company; a star turn.

Mummer, guiser, masquer; dancer, nautch-girl, bayadère, geisha.

Stage manager, impresario, producer, prompter, stage hands, call-boy, etc.

Dramatic writer, pantomimist, playwright, play-writer, dramatist, dramaturge, librettist.

(Phrase) The profession.

(Verbs) To act, enact, play, perform, personate (554), play or interpret a part, rehearse, spout, rant, gag, star, walk on.

To produce, present, stage, stage-manager.

(Phrases) To strut and fret one's hour on the stage; to tread the boards.

(Adjectives) Dramatic, theatre, theatrical, scenic, histrionic, comic, tragic, buskined, farcical, knock-about, slapstick, tragi-comic, melodramatic, transpontine, stagy, operatic.

599A Cinema *(Substantives)*, picture theatre, picturedrome, film, motion picture, pictures, movies, flicks, pix, silver screen; silent film, sound film, talkie, flattie; three-dimensional film, 3-D, wide-screen film, deepie; documentary, trailer.

Close-up, flash-back, fade-out.

Scenario, star, vamp; cinema-goer, cinemaddict, film fan.

(Verbs) To feature, screen; dub.

599B Radio *(Substantives)*, wireless, receiving set, transistor, walkie-talkie; broadcast, radio play; teleprompter.

Announcer, listener.

Television, TV., video, telly; telecast, telefilm, newscast, script.

Looker-in, televiewer, viewer.

(Verbs) To broadcast, televise, telecast.

To listen in, look in, view, teleview.

(Phrase) On the air.

(Adjective) Telegenic.

CLASS V

WORDS RELATING TO THE VOLUNTARY POWERS

DIVISION I—INDIVIDUAL VOLITION

SECTION I—VOLITION IN GENERAL

1°. *Acts of Volition*

600 Will *(Substantives)*, volition, voluntariness, velleity, conation, free-will, spontaneity, spontaneousness, freedom (748).

Pleasure, wish, mind, animus, breast, mood, bosom, *petto*, heart, discretion, accord.

Libertarianism.

Determination (604), predetermination (611), intention (620), choice (609).

(Verbs) To will, list, think fit, see fit, think proper, determine, etc. (604), settle, choose (609), to take upon oneself, to have one's will, to do as one likes, wishes, or chooses; to use or exercise one's own discretion, to volunteer, lend oneself to.

(Phrases) To have a will of one's own; *hoc volo, sic jubeo, stet pro ratione voluntas*; to take the will for the deed; to know one's own mind; to know what one is about; to see one's way; to have one's will; to take upon oneself; to take the law into one's own hands.

(Adjectives) Voluntary, volitional, willing, content, minded, spontaneous, free, left to oneself, unconstrained, unfettered, autocratic, bossy, unbidden, unasked, unurged, uncompelled, of one's own accord, gratuitous, of one's own head, prepense, advised, express, designed, intended, calculated, premeditated, preconcerted, predetermined, deliberate.

(Adverbs) At will, at pleasure, *à volonté, à discrétion, ad libitum, ad*

601 Necessity *(Substantives)*, instinct, blind impulse, necessitation, ἀνάγκη, fate, fatality, destiny, doom, kismet, weird (152), foredoom, destination, election, predestination, pre-ordination, fore-ordination, compulsion (744), subjection (749), inevitability, inevitableness.

Determinism, necessitarianism, fatalism, automatism.

A determinist, necessarian, necessitarian; robot, automaton.

The Fates, Parcae, the Three Sisters, fortune's wheel, the book of fate, the stars, astral influence, spell (152).

(Phrases) Hobson's choice; what must be; a blind bargain; a *pis aller*.

(Verbs) To lie under a necessity, to be fated, doomed, destined, etc. (152), to need be, have no alternative.

To necessitate, destine, doom, foredoom, predestine, preordain.

To compel, force, constrain, etc. (744), cast a spell, etc. (992).

(Phrases) To make a virtue of necessity; to be pushed to the wall; to dree one's weird.

(Adjectives) Necessitated, fated, destined, predestined, foreordained, doomed, elect, spellbound.

Compelled, forced, etc., unavoidable, inevitable, irresistible, irrevocable.

Compulsory, involuntary, unintentional, undesigned, unintended, instinctive, automatic, blind, mechanical, impulsive, unconscious, reflex, unwitting, unaware.

arbitrium, spontaneously, freely, of one's own accord, voluntarily, advisedly, designedly, intentionally, expressly, knowingly, determinately, deliberately, pointedly, in earnest, in good earnest, studiously, purposely, *proprio motu, suo motu, ex mero motu; quo animo.*

(Phrases) With one's eyes open; in cold blood.

---

602 Willingness *(Substantives),* voluntariness, disposition, inclination, leaning, *penchant,* humour, mood, vein, bent, bias, propensity, proclivity, aptitude, predisposition, predilection (865), proneness, docility, pliability (324), alacrity, earnestness, readiness, assent (448).

(Phrases) A labour of love; *labor ipse voluptas.*

(Verbs) to be willing, etc., to incline to, lean to, not mind (865), to propend; to volunteer.

(Phrases) To find in one's heart; to set one's heart upon; to make no bones of; have a mind to; have a great mind to; 'Barkis is willin'.'

(Adjectives) Willing, fain, disposed, inclined, minded, bent upon, set upon, forward, predisposed, content, favourable, hearty, ready, wholehearted, cordial, genial, keen, prepense, docile, persuadable, persuasible, facile, tractable, easy-going, easily led.

Free, spontaneous, voluntary, gratuitous, unforced, unasked, unsummoned, unbiased, unsolicited, unbesought, undriven.

(Adverbs) Willingly, freely, readily, lief, heartily, with a good grace, without reluctance, etc., as soon, of one's own accord (600), certainly, be it so (488).

(Phrases) With all one's heart, *con amore;* with heart and soul; with a right good will; with a good grace; *de bon cœur;* by all means; by all manner of means; nothing loth; *ex animo;* to one's heart's content.

Deterministic, necessitarian, fatalistic.

(Phrase) Unable to help it.

(Adverbs) Necessarily, needs, of necessity, perforce, forcibly, compulsorily; on or by compulsion or force, willy-nilly, *nolens volens;* involuntarily, etc., impulsively (612), unwittingly (491).

(Phrases) It must be; it needs must be; it is written; one's fate is sealed; *che sarà sarà;* there is no help for it; there is no alternative; nothing for it but; necessity knows no law; needs must when the devil drives.

603 Unwillingness *(Substantives),* indisposition, indisposedness, backwardness, disinclination, averseness, aversion, reluctance, repugnance, demur, renitence, remissness, slackness, lukewarmness, indifference, nonchalance.

Hesitation, shrinking, recoil, suspense, dislike (867), scrupulousness, scrupulosity, delicacy, demur, scruple, qualm.

A recusant, pococurante.

(Verbs) To be unwilling, etc., to demur, stick at, hesitate (605), waver, hang in suspense, scruple, stickle, boggle, falter, to hang back, hang fire, fight shy of, jib, grudge.

To decline, reject, refuse (764), refrain, keep from, abstain, recoil, shrink, reluct.

(Phrases) To stick in the throat; to set one's face against; to draw the line at; I'd rather not.

(Adjectives) Unwilling, unconsenting, disinclined, indisposed, averse, reluctant, not content, laggard, backward, shy, remiss, slack, indifferent, lukewarm, frigid, scrupulous, repugnant, disliking (867).

Demurring, wavering, etc., refusing (764), grudging.

(Adverbs) Unwillingly, etc., perforce.

(Phrases) Against the grain; *invita Minerva; malgré lui; bon gré, mal gré; nolens volens;* in spite of one's teeth; with a bad grace; not for the world; willy-nilly.

604 Resolution *(Substantives)*, determination, decision, resolve, resolvedness, fixedness, steadiness, constancy, indefatigability, unchangeableness, inflexibility, decision, finality, firmness, doggedness, tenacity of purpose, pertinacity, perseverance, constancy, solidity, stability.

Energy, manliness, vigour, spirit, spiritedness, pluck, bottom, backbone, stamina, gameness, guts, grit, sand, will, iron will; self-reliance; self-mastery; self-control.

A devotee, zealot, extremist, ultra, enthusiast, fanatic, fan; bulldog, British lion.

(Verbs) To be resolved, etc., to have resolution, etc., to resolve, decide, will, persevere, determine, conclude, make up one's mind; to stand, keep, or remain firm, etc., to come to a determination, to form a resolution, to take one's stand, to stand by, hold fast, stick to, abide by, adhere to, keep one's ground, persevere, keep one's course, hold on, hang on, not to fail.

To insist upon, to make a point of.

(Phrases) To determine once for all; to form a resolution; to steel oneself; to pass the Rubicon; take a decisive step; to burn one's boats; to nail one's colours to the mast; to screw one's courage to the sticking-place; to take the bull by the horns; to mean business; to set one's teeth; to keep a stiff upper lip; to keep one's chin up.

(Adjectives) Resolved, resolute, game, firm, steady, steadfast, staunch, constant; solid, manly, stout.

Decided, strong-willed, determined, uncompromising, purposive, self-possessed, fixed, unmoved, unshaken, unbending, unyielding, unflagging, unflinching, inflexible, unwavering, unfaltering, unshrinking, undiverted, undeterred, immovable, not to be moved, unhesitating, unswerving.

Peremptory, inexorable, indomitable, persevering, pertinacious, persistent, irrevocable, irreversible, reverseless, decisive, final.

Strenuous, bent upon, set upon, intent upon, proof against, master of oneself, steeled, staid, serious, stiff, stiff-necked, obstinate (606).

605 Irresolution *(Substantives)*, indecision, indetermination, demur, hesitation, suspense, uncertainty (475), hesitancy, vacillation, unsteadiness, inconstancy, wavering, fluctuation, flickering, changeableness, mutability, fickleness, caprice (608), levity, *légèreté*, trimming, softness, weakness, instability.

A weathercock, trimmer, timeserver, turncoat, shuttlecock, butterfly, harlequin, chameleon.

(Verbs) To be irresolute, etc., to hesitate, hang in suspense, demur, waver, vacillate, quaver, fluctuate, shuffle, boggle, flicker, falter, palter, debate, dilly-dally, shilly-shally, dally with, coquette with, swerve, etc.

(Phrases) To hang fire; to hum and ha; to blow hot and cold; not to know one's own mind; to leave *'ad referendum'*; letting 'I dare not' wait upon 'I would'.

(Adjectives) Irresolute, undecided, unresolved, undetermined, vacillating, wavering, hesitating, faltering, shuffling, etc., half-hearted, double-minded, indecisive.

Unsteady, unsteadfast, fickle, flighty, changing, changeable, versatile, variable, inconstant, mutable, protean, fluctuating, unstable, unsettled, unhinged, unfixed, weak-kneed, spineless.

Weak, feeble-minded, frail, soft, pliant, giddy, capricious, coquettish, volatile, fitful, frothy, freakish, lightsome, light-minded, invertebrate.

Revocable, reversible.

(Phrases) Infirm of purpose; without ballast; waiting to see which way the cat jumps, or the wind blows.

(Adverbs) Irresolutely, etc.; off and on.

(Phrases) Firm as a rock; game to the last; true to oneself; master of oneself; *in utrumque paratus.*

(Adverbs) Resolutely, etc., without fail.

(Phrases) Through thick and thin; through fire and water; at all hazards; sink or swim; *coûte que coûte; fortiter in re*; like grim death.

606 Obstinacy *(Substantives)*, obstinateness, wilfulness, self-will, pertinacity, pertinaciousness, pervicacity, pervicaciousness, tenacity, tenaciousness, inflexibility, immovability, doggedness, stubbornness, steadiness (604), restiveness, contumacy, cussedness, obduracy, obduration, unruliness.

Intolerance, dogmatism, bigotry, opinionatedness, opiniativeness, fanaticism, zealotry, infatuation, monomania, indocility, intractability, intractableness (481), pig-headedness.

An opinionist, *opiniâtre*, crank, diehard, blimp, stickler, enthusiast, monomaniac, zealot, dogmatist, fanatic, mule.

A fixed idea, rooted prejudice, blind side, obsession (481), King Charles's head.

(Phrase) A bee in one's bonnet.

(Verbs) To be obstinate, etc., to persist, stickle, opiniate.

(Phrases) To stick at nothing; to dig in one's heels; not yield an inch.

(Adjectives) Obstinate, opinionative, opinative, opinionated, opinioned, wedded to an opinion, self-opinioned, prejudiced (481), cranky, wilful, self-willed, positive, tenacious.

Stiff, stubborn, stark, rigid, stiff-necked, dogged, pertinacious, restive, pervicacious, dogmatic, arbitrary, bigoted, unpersuadable, mulish, unmoved, uninfluenced, hard-mouthed, unyielding, inflexible, immovable, pigheaded, wayward, intractable, hidebound, headstrong, restive, refractory, unruly, infatuated, *entêté*, wrong-headed, cross-grained, obdurate, contumacious, fanatical, rabid, inexorable, impracticable.

(Phrases) Obstinate as a mule; impervious to reason.

(Adverbs) Obstinately, etc.

(Phrases) *Non possumus; vestigia nulla retrorsum.*

607 Change of mind, intention, purpose, etc.

Tergiversation *(Substantives)*, retractation, recantation, revocation, revokement, reversal, palinode, volteface, renunciation, disavowal (536), abjuration, abjurement, apostasy, relinquishment (624), repentance (950), vacillation, etc. (605).

A turncoat, rat, Janus, renegade, apostate, pervert, backslider, recidivist, trimmer, time-server, opportunist, Vicar of Bray, deserter, weathercock, etc. (605), Proteus.

(Verbs) To change one's mind, etc., to retract, recant, revoke, forswear, unsay, take back, abjure, renounce, apostatize, relinquish, trim, straddle, veer round, change sides, rat, go over; pass, change, or skip from one side to another; back out, back down, swerve, flinch, balance.

(Phrases) To eat one's words; turn over a new leaf; think better of it; play fast and loose; blow hot and cold; box the compass; swallow the leek; eat dirt.

(Adjectives) Changeful, changeable, mobile, unsteady (605), trimming, double-faced, ambidexter, fast and loose, time-serving, facing both ways.

Fugacious, fleeting (111), revocatory.

608 Caprice *(Substantives)*, fancy, fantasy, humour, whim, crotchet, fad, fike, craze, *capriccio*, quirk, freak, maggot, vagary, whimsy, whim-wham, kink, prank, shenanigans, fit, flim-flam, escapade, ploy, dido, monkey-tricks, rag, monkey-shines, *boutade*, wildgoose chase, freakishness, skittishness, volatility, fancifulness, whimsicality, giddiness, inconsistency, contrariety; a madcap.

(Verb) To be capricious, etc.

(Phrases) To strain at a gnat and swallow a camel; to take it into one's head.

(Adjectives) Capricious, inconsistent, fanciful, fantastic, whimsical, full of whims, etc., erratic, crotchety, faddy, maggoty, fiky, perverse, humoursome, wayward, captious, contrary, contrarious, skittish, fitful.

(Phrases) The head being turned; the deuce being in him; by fits and starts.

609 Choice *(Substantives)*, option, election, arbitrament, adoption, selection, excerption, co-optation, gleaning, eclecticism, lief, preference, predilection, preoption, discretion (600), fancy.

Decision, determination, adjudication, award, vote, suffrage, ballot, poll, plebiscite, referendum, verdict, voice, plumper.

Alternative, dilemma (704).

Excerpt, extract, cuttings, clippings; pick, *élite*, cream (650).

Chooser, elector, voter, constituent; electorate, constituency.

(Verbs) To choose, decide, determine, elect, list, think fit, use one's discretion, fancy, shape one's course, prefer, have rather, have as lief, take one's choice, adopt, select, fix upon, pitch upon, pick out, single out, vote for, plump for, co-opt, pick up, take up, catch at, jump at, cull, glean, pick, winnow.

(Phrases) To winnow the chaff from the wheat; to indulge one's fancy; to pick and choose; to take a decided step; to pass the Rubicon (604); to hold out; offer for choice; commend me to; to swallow the bait; to gorge the hook; to yield to temptation.

(Adjectives) Optional, discretional, eclectic, choosing, etc., chosen, etc., decided, etc., choice, preferential; left to oneself.

(Adverbs) Discretionally, at pleasure, *à plaisir, a piacere*, at discretion, at will, *ad libitum*.

Decidedly, etc., rather; once for all, either the one or the other, for one's money, for choice.

610 Absence of Choice *(Substantives)*, Hobson's choice, necessity (601).

Indifference, indecision (605).

(Phrase) First come, first served.

(Adjectives) Neutral; indifferent, undecided.

(Phrase) To sit on the fence.

Rejection *(Substantives)*, refusal (764); declining, repudiation, exclusion.

(Verbs) To reject, refuse, etc., decline, give up, repudiate, exclude, lay aside, pigeon-hole, refrain, spare (678), abandon, turn down, black-ball; to fail, plough, pluck, spin, cast.

(Phrases) To lay on the shelf; to return to store; to throw overboard; to draw the line at.

(Adjectives) Rejecting, etc., rejected, etc., not chosen, etc.

(Phrases) Not to be thought of; out of the question.

(Adverbs) Neither; neither the one nor the other, nothing to choose between them.

———

611 Predetermination *(Substantives)*, premeditation, predeliberation, foregone conclusion, parti pris.

(Verbs) To predetermine, premeditate, preconcert, resolve beforehand.

(Adjectives) Prepense, premeditated, predetermined, advised, predesigned, aforethought, calculated, studied, designed (620).

612 Impulse *(Substantives)*, sudden thought, improvisation, inspiration, flash, spurt.

Improvisator, improvisatore, improvisatrice, creature of impulse.

(Verbs) To flash on the mind; to improvise, improvisate, make up, extemporize, vamp, ad-lib.

(Adjectives) Extemporaneous, ex-

(Adverbs) Advisedly, deliberately, etc., with the eyes open, in cold blood.

———

temporary, impulsive, unrehearsed, unpremeditated (674), improvised, improvisatorial, improvisatory, un-prompted, instinctive, spontaneous, natural, unguarded, unreflecting, pre-cipitate.

(Adverbs) Extempore, offhand, impromptu, *à l-improviste*, out of hand.
(Phrases) On the spur of the moment, or of the occasion.

613 Habit *(Substantives)*, habi-tude, wont, rule, routine, jog-trot, groove, rut.

Custom, consuetude, use, usage, practice, trick, run, run of things, way, form, prevalence, observance, fashion (852), etiquette, prescription, conven-tion, *convenances*, red tape, red-tapery, red-tapism, routinism, conventional-ism, vogue.

Seasoning, training, hardening, etc. (673), acclimatization, acclimation, acclimatation.

Second nature, *cacoethes*, taking root, diathesis.

A victim of habit, etc., an addict, junkie, *habitué*.

(Verbs) To be habitual, etc., to be in the habit of, be wont, be accustomed to, etc.

To follow, observe, conform to, obey, bend to, comply with, accom-modate oneself to, adapt oneself to; fall into a habit, convention, custom, or usage; to addict oneself to, take to, get the hang of.

To become a habit, to take root, to gain or grow upon one, to run in the blood.

To habituate, inure, harden, season, form, train, accustom, familiarize, naturalize, acclimatize, conventionalize, condition.

To acquire a habit, to get into the way of, to learn, etc.

(Phrases) To follow the multitude; go with the current, stream, etc.; run on in a groove; do in Rome as the Romans do.

(Adjectives) Habitual, accustomed, prescriptive, habituated, etc.; in the habit, etc., of; used to, addicted to, attuned to, wedded to, at home in; usual, wonted, customary, hackneyed, commonplace, trite, ordinary, set, stock, established, accepted, stereotyped, received, acknowledged, recognized; groovy, fixed, rooted, permanent, inveterate, ingrained, running in the blood, hereditary, congenital, innate, inborn, besetting, natural, instinctive, etc. (5).

Fashionable, in fashion, in vogue, according to use, routine, con-ventional, etc.

(Phrases) Bred in the bone; in the blood.

(Adverbs) Habitually; as usual, as the world goes, *more suo, pro more, pro forma*, according to custom, *de rigueur*.

614 Desuetude *(Substantives)*, disuse, want of habit or of practice, inusitation, newness to.

Non-observance (773), infraction, vilation, infringement.

(Phrase) 'A custom more honoured in the breach than the observance.'

(Verbs) To be unaccustomed, etc., to be new to; to leave off, wean oneself of, break off, break through, infringe, vilate, etc., a habit, usage, etc.; to disuse, to wear off.

(Adjectives) Unaccustomed, un-used, unusual, unwonted, unpractised, unprofessional, unfashionable, non-observant, lax, disused, weaned.

Unseasoned, uninured, untrained, green.

Unhackneyed, unconventional, Bohemian (83).

———

2°. Causes of Volition

615 Motive *(Substantives),* reason, ground, principle, mainspring, *primum mobile,* account, score, sake, consideration, calculation, *raison d'être.*

Inducement, recommendation, encouragement, attraction, allectation, temptation, enticement, bait, allurement, charm, witchery, bewitchment.

Persuasibility, softness, susceptibility, attractability, impressibility.

Influence, prompting, dictate, instance, impulse, impulsion, incitement, incitation, press, instigation, excitement, provocation, invitation, solicitation, advocacy, call, suasion, persuasion, hortation, exhortation, seduction, cajolery, tantalization, *agacerie,* seducement, fascination, blandishment, inspiration, honeyed words.

Incentive, stimulus, spur, fillip, urge, goad, rowel, provocative, whet, dram, cocktail, pick-me-up, appetizer.

Bribe, graft, sop, lure, decoy, charm, spell, magnetism, magnet, loadstone.

Prompter, tempter, seducer, seductor, siren, Circe, instigator, *agent provocateur.*

(Phrases) The pros and cons; the why and wherefore.

The golden apple; a red herring; a sop for Cerberus; the voice of the tempter; the song of the sirens.

(Verbs) To induce, move, lead, draw, draw over, carry, bring, to influence, to weigh with, bias, to operate, work upon, engage, incline, dispose, predispose, put up to, prompt, whisper, call, call upon, recommend, encourage, entice, invite, solicit, press, enjoin, entreat (765),

616 Absence of Motive, caprice (608).

(Adjectives) Aimless, motiveless, pointless, purposeless (621); uninduced, unmoved, unactuated, uninfluenced, unbiased, unimpelled, unswayed, impulsive, wanton, unprovoked, uninspired, untempted, unattracted.

(Phrase) Without rhyme or reason.

Dissuasion *(Substantives),* dehortation, discouragement, remonstrance, expostulation, deprecation (766).

Inhibition, check, restraint, curb (752), bridle, rein, stay, damper, chill; deterrent, disincentive.

Scruple, qualm, demur (867), reluctance, delicacy (868); counterattraction.

(Phrase) A wet blanket.

(Verbs) To dissuade, dehort, discourage, disincline, indispose, dispirit, damp, choke off, dishearten, disenchant, disillusion, deter, keep back, put off, render averse, etc.

To withhold, restrain, hold, hold back, check, bridle, curb, rein in, keep in, inhibit, censor, repel (751).

To cool, blunt, calm, quiet, quench slake, stagger, remonstrate, expostulate, warn, deprecate (766).

To scruple, refrain, abstain, etc. (603).

(Phrases) To throw cold water on; to turn a deaf ear to.

(Adjectives) Dissuading, etc., dissuasive, dehortatory, expostulatory, deprecatory.

Dissuaded, discouraged, etc.

Repugnant, averse, scrupulous, etc. (867), unpersuadable (606).

---

court, plead, advocate, exhort, enforce, dictate, tantalize, bait the hook, tempt, allure, lure, seduce, decoy, draw on, captivate, fascinate, charm, bewitch, conciliate, wheedle, coax, speak fair, carny (or carney), cajole, pat on the back or shoulder, talk over, inveigle, persuade, prevail upon, get to do, bring over, procure, lead by the nose, sway, over-persuade, come over, get round, turn the head, enlist, retain, kidnap, bribe, suborn, tamper with.

To act upon, to impel, excite, suscitate, stimulate, key up, motivate, incite, animate, instigate, provoke, set on, urge, pique, spirit, inspirit, inspire. awaken, buck up, give a fillip, light up, kindle, enkindle, rekindle, quicken, goad, spur, prick, edge, egg on, hurry on, stir up, work up, fan, fire, inflame, set on fire, fan the flame, blow the coals, stir the embers, put on one's mettle, set on, force, rouse, arouse, lash into fury, get a rise out of.

(Phrases) To grease the palm; to gild the pill; to work the oracle.

To follow the bent of; to follow the dictates of; to yield to temptation; to act on principle.

(Adjectives) Impulsive, motive, persuasive, hortative, hortatory, seductive. carnying, suasory, suasive, honey-tongued, attractive, tempting, alluring, piquant, exciting, inviting, tantalizing, etc.

Persuadable, persuasible, suasible, soft, yielding, facile, easily persuaded, etc.

Induced, moved, disposed, led, persuaded, etc., spellbound, instinct with or by.

(Adverbs) Because, for, since, on account of, out of, from; by reason of, for the sake of, on the score of.

As, forasmuch as, therefore, hence, why, wherefore; for all the world.

(Phrase) Hinc illae lacrimae.

617 Ostensible motive, or reason assigned.

Plea *(Substantives)*, allegation, pretext, pretence, excuse, alibi, cue, colour, gloss, salvo, loophole, handle, shift, quirk, guise, stalking-horse, makeshift, white lie, evasion, get-out, special pleading (477), claptrap, advocation, soft sawder, blarney (933), moonshine; a lame excuse or apology.

(Verbs) To make a pretext. etc., of; to use as a plea, etc.; to plead, allege, pretend, excuse, make a handle, etc., of, make capital of.

(Adjectives) Ostensible, colourable, pretended, alleged, etc.

(Phrases) Ad captandum; qui s'excuse s'accuse; playing to the gallery.

3°. Objects of Volition

618 Good *(Substantives)*, benefit, advantage, service, interest, weal, boot, gain, profit, velvet, good turn, blessing, boon; behoof, behalf.

Luck, piece of luck, windfall, strike, treasure trove, godsend, bonus, bunce, bonanza, prize; serendipity.

Goodness (648), utility (644), remedy (662).

(Phrases) The main chance; *summum bonum; cui bono?*

(Adjectives) Good, etc. (648), gainful (644).

(Adverbs) Aright, well, favourably, satisfactorily, for the best.

In behalf of, in favour of.

619 Evil *(Substantives)*, harm, ill, injury, wrong, scathe, curse, detriment, hurt, damage, disservice, ill-turn, bale, grievance, prejudice, loss, mischief, devilry (or deviltry), gravamen.

Disadvantage, drawback, trouble, vexation (828), annoyance, nuisance, molestation, oppression, persecution, plague, corruption (659).

Blow, dunt, knock (276), bruise, scratch, wound, mutilation, outrage, spoliation, mayhem, plunder, pillage, rapine, destruction (791), dilapidation, havoc, ravage, devastation, inroad, sweep, sack, foray (716), desolation, *razzia*, dragonnade.

Misfortune, mishap, woe, disaster, calamity, affliction, catastrophe, downfall, ruin (735), prostration, curse, wrack, blight, blast, Pandora's box; a plague-spot.

Cause of evil, bane (663).

(Phrases) Bad show; there's the devil to pay.

(Adjectives) Bad, hurtful, etc. (649).

(Adverbs) Amiss, wrong, evil, ill.

SECTION II—PROSPECTIVE VOLITION

1°. *Conceptional Volition*

620 Intention *(Substantives)*, intent, purpose, design, purport, mind, meaning, drift (516), animus, view, set purpose, point, bent, turn, proposal, study, scope, purview.

Final cause, object, aim, end, motive (615), *raison d'être*; destination, mark, point, butt, goal, target, prey, quarry, game, objective; the philosophers' stone.

Decision, determination, resolve, resolution (604), predetermination (611); set purpose.

A hobby, ambition, wish (865).

Study of final causes, teleology; study of final issues, eschatology.

(Verbs) To intend, purpose, plan (626), design, destine, mean, aim at, propose to oneself.

To be at, drive at, be after, point at, level at, take aim, aspire at or after, endeavour after.

To meditate, think of, dream of, premeditate (611), contemplate, compass.

To propose, project, devise, take into one's head.

(Phrases) To have in view; to have an eye to; to take upon oneself; to have to do; to see one's way; to find in one's heart.

(Adjectives) Intended, etc., intentional, deliberate, advised, studied, minded, express, prepense (611), aforethought; set upon, bent upon, intent upon, in view, *in petto*, in prospect; teleological, eschatological.

(Phrases) In the world; *sur le tapis*; on the stocks; in contemplation.

(Adverbs) Intentionally, etc., expressly, knowingly, wittingly, designedly, purposely, on purpose, with a view to, with an eye to, for the

621 Absence of purpose in the succession of events.

Chance *(Substantives)*, fortune, accident, hazard, hap, haphazard (156), lot, fate (601), chance-medley, hit, fluke, casualty, contingency, exigency, fate, adventure, random shot, off chance, toss-up, gamble.

A godsend, luck, a run of luck, a turn of the dice or cards, a break, windfall, etc. (618).

Drawing lots, sortilege, *sortes Virgilianae*.

Wager, bet, flutter, betting, gambling; pitch-and-toss, *roulette, rouge-et-noir*.

(Phrases) A blind bargain; a pig in a poke.

(Verbs) To chance, hap, turn up; to stand a chance.

To risk, venture, hazard, speculate, stake; incur or run the risk; bet, wager, punt, gamble, plunge, raffle.

(Phrases) To take one's chance; to chance it; to chance one's arm; try one's luck; shuffle the cards; put into a lottery; lay a wager; toss up; spin a coin; cast lots; draw lots; stand the hazard.

To buy a pig in a poke; *alea jacta est*; the die being cast; to go nap on; to put one's shirt on.

(Adjectives) Casual, fortuitous, accidental, inadvertent, fluky, contingent, random, hit-or-miss, happy-go-lucky, adventitious, incidental.

Unintentional, involuntary, aimless, driftless, undesigned, undirected; purposeless, causeless, without purpose, etc., unmeditated, unpurposed, indiscriminate, promiscuous.

On the cards, possible (470), at stake.

(Adverbs) Casually, etc., by chance,

purpose of, with the view of, in order to, to the end that, on account of, in pursuance of, pursuant to, with the intent, etc.

(Phrases) In good earnest; with one's eyes open; to all intents and purposes.

by accident, accidentally, etc., at haphazard, at a venture; heads or tails.

(Phrase) As luck would have it.

_____

622 Purpose in action.

Pursuit *(Substantives)*, pursuance, undertaking, enterprise (676), emprise, adventure, game, hobby, endeavour.

Prosecution, search, angling, chase, venery, quest, hunt, shikar, race, battue, drive, course, direction, wildgoose chase, steeplechase, point-to-point.

Pursuer, huntsman, hunter, Nimrod, shikari, hound, greyhound, foxhound, whippet, bloodhound, sleuthhound, beagle, harrier.

(Verbs) To pursue, undertake, engage in, take in hand, carry on, prosecute (461), endeavour.

To court, seek, angle, chase, give chase, course, dog, stalk, trail, hunt, drive, follow, run after, hound, bid for, aim at, take aim, make a leap at, rush upon, jump at, quest, shadow, tail, chivy.

(Phrases) Take or hold a course; tread a path; shape one's course; direct or bend one's steps or course; run a race; rush headlong; rush headforemost; make a plunge; snatch at, etc.; start game; follow the scent; to run or ride full tilt at.

(Adjectives) Pursuing, etc., in hot pursuit; in full cry.

(Adverbs) In order to, in order that, for the purpose of, with a view to, etc. (620); on the scent of.

(Interjections) Yoicks! tally-ho!

_____

623 Absence of pursuit.

Avoidance *(Substantives)*, forbearance, abstention, abstinence, sparing, refraining.

Flight, escape (671), evasion, elusion.

Motive for avoidance, counterattraction.

Shirker, slacker, quitter, truant, fugitive, runaway.

(Verbs) To avoid, refrain, abstain; to spare, hold, shun, fly, slope, flee, eschew, run away from, shrink, hold back, draw back (287), recoil from, flinch, blench, shy, elude, evade, shirk, blink, parry, dodge, let alone.

(Phrases) To give the slip or go-by; to part company; to beat a retreat; get out of the way; to give one a wide berth; steer clear of; fight shy of; to take to one's heels.

(Adjectives) Avoiding, etc., elusive, evasive, flying, fugitive, runaway, shy, retiring; unattempted, unsought.

(Adverbs) Lest, with a view to prevent.

(Phrases) *Sauve qui peut*; the devil take the hindmost.

624 **Relinquishment** *(Substantives)*, dereliction, abandonment (782), renunciation, desertion (607), discontinuance (142).

Dispensation, riddance.

(Verbs) To relinquish, give up (782); lay, set, or put aside; drop, yield, resign, abandon, renounce, discard, shelve, pigeon-hole, waive, desist from, desert, defect, leave, leave off, back out of, quit, throw up, chuck up, give over, forgo, give up, forsake, throw over, forswear, swerve from (279), put away, discontinue (681).

(Phrases) To drop all idea of; to think better of it; to wash one's hands of; to turn over a new leaf; to throw up the sponge; to have other fish to fry; to draw in one's horns; to lay on the shelf; to move the previous question.

To give warning; to give notice; to ask for one's books.

(Adjectives) Relinquishing, etc., relinquished, etc., unpursued.

(Interjections) Hands off! keep off! give over! chuck it!

625 Business *(Substantives)*, affair, concern, matter, task, work, job, job of work, assignment, darg, chore, stint, stunt, errand, agenda, commission, office, charge, part, duty, role; a press of business.

Province, department, beat, round, routine, mission, function, vocation, calling, avocation, profession, occupation, pursuit, cloth, faculty, trade, industry, commerce, art, craft, mystery, walk, race, career, walk of life, *métier*.

Place, post, orb, sphere, field, line, capacity, employment, engagement, exercise, occupation; situation, undertaking (676).

(Verbs) To carry on or run a business, ply one's trade, keep a shop, etc.; to officiate, serve, act, traffic.

(Phrases) To have to do with; have on one's hands; betake oneself to; occupy or concern oneself with; go in for; have on one's shoulders; make it one's business; go to do; act a part; perform the office of or functions of; to enter or take up a profession; spend time upon; busy oneself with, about, etc.

(Adjectives) Business-like, official, functional, professional, workaday, commercial, in hand.

(Adverbs) On hand, on foot, afoot, afloat, going.

(Phrase) In the swim.

626 Plan *(Substantives)*, scheme, device, design, project, proposal, proposition, suggestion.

Line of conduct, game, card course, tactics, strategy, policy, polity (692), craft, practice, campaign, platform, plank, ticket, agenda, orders of the day, gambit.

Intrigue, cabal, plot, conspiracy, complot, racket, machination, *coup d'état*.

Measure, step, precaution, proceeding, procedure, process, system, economy, set-up, organization, expedient, resource, contrivance, invention, artifice, shift, makeshift, gadget, stopgap, manœuvre, stratagem, fetch, trick, dodge, machination, intrigue, stroke, stroke of policy, masterstroke, great gun, trump card.

Alternative, loophole, counterplot, counter-project, side-wind, last resort, *dernier ressort, pis aller*.

Sketch, outline, blue-print, programme, draft (or draught), scenario, *ébauche*, rough draft, skeleton, forecast, prospectus, *carte du pays*, bill of fare, menu.

After-course, after-game, after-thought, *arrière-pensée,* under-plot.

A projector, designer, schemer, contriver, strategist, promoter, organizer, *entrepreneur,* artist, schematist, intriguant.

(Verbs) To plan, scheme, devise, imagine, design, frame, contrive, project, plot, conspire, cabal, intrigue (702), think out, invent, forecast, strike out, work out, chalk out, rough out, sketch, lay out, lay down, cut out, cast, recast, map out, countermine, hit upon, fall upon, arrange, mature, organize, systematize, concert, concoct, digest, pack, prepare, hatch, elaborate, make shift, make do, wangle.

(Phrases) To have many irons in the fire; to dig a mine; to lay a train; to spring a project; to take or adopt a course; to make the best of a bad job; to work the oracle.

(Adjectives) Planned, etc., strategic; planning, scheming, etc.

Well-laid, deep-laid, cunning, well-devised, etc., maturely considered, well-weighed, prepared, organized, etc.

(Adverbs) In course of preparation, under consideration, on the anvil, on the stocks, in the rough, *sur le tapis; faute de mieux*.

627 Way *(Substantives)*, method, manner, wise, form, mode, guise, fashion.

Path, road, gait, route, channel, walk, access, course, pass, ford, ferry, passage, line of way, trajectory, orbit, track, ride, avenue, approach, beaten track, pathway, highway, roadway, causeway, footway, pavement, sidewalk, *trottoir*, footpath, bridle path, corduroy road, cinder-path, turnpike road, high road, arterial road, *autobahn*, clearway, boulevard, the King's (or Queen's) highway, thoroughfare, street, lane, alley, gangway, hatchway, cross-road, crossway, flyover, cut, short cut, royal road, cross-cut, *carrefour*, promenade, subway.

Railway, railroad, tramway, tube, underground, elevated; canal.

Bridge, viaduct, stepping-stone, stair, corridor, aisle, lobby, staircase, moving staircase, escalator, companion-way, flight of stairs, ladder, step-ladder, stile, scaffold, scaffolding, lift, hoist, elevator; speedwalk, travolator.

Indirect way: By-path, by-way, by-walk, by-road, back door, backstairs.

Inlet, gate, door, gateway (260), portal, porch, doorway, adit, conduit, tunnel.

(Phrase) Modus operandi.

(Adverbs) How, in what way, in what manner, by what mode.

By the way, *en passant*, by the by, via, *in transitu, chemin faisant*.

One way or another, somehow, anyhow, by hook or by crook.

(Phrases) All roads lead to Rome; *hae tibi erunt artes*; where there's a will there's a way.

628 Mid-course *(Substantives)*, middle course, middle (68), mean (29), golden mean, *juste milieu, mezzo termine*.

Direct, straight, straightforward, course or path; great-circle sailing.

Neutrality, compromise.

(Verbs) To keep in a middle course, etc.; to compromise, go half-way.

(Adjectives) Undeviating, direct, straight, straightforward.

(Phrases) In medio tutissimus ibis; to sit on the fence.

629 Circuit *(Substantives)*, round-about way, zigzag, circuition, detour, circumbendibus (311), wandering, deviation (279), divergence (291).

(Verbs) To perform a circuit, etc., to deviate, wander, go round about, meander, etc. (279).

(Phrases) To beat about the bush; to make two bites of a cherry; to lead one a pretty dance.

(Adjectives) Circuitous, indirect, roundabout, tortuous, zigzag, etc.

(Adverbs) By a roundabout way, by an indirect course, etc.

630 Requirement *(Substantives)*, requisition, need, occasion, lack, wants, requisites, necessities, desideratum, exigency, pinch, *sine qua non*, the very thing, essential, must.

Needfulness, essentiality, necessity, indispensability, urgency, call for.

(Phrases) Just what the doctor ordered; a crying need; a long-felt want.

(Verbs) To require, need, want, have occasion for, stand in need of, lack, desire, be at a loss for, desiderate; not to be able to do without or dispense with; to want but little.

To render necessary, to necessitate, to create a necessity for, demand, call for.

(Adjectives) Requisite, required, etc., needful, necessary, imperative, exigent, essential, indispensable, irreplaceable, prerequisite, that cannot be spared or dispensed with, urgent.

2°. *Subservience to Ends*

1. ACTUAL SUBSERVIENCE

631 Instrumentality *(Substantives)*, medium, intermedium, vehicle, channel, intervention, mediation, dint, aid (707), agency (170).

Minister, handmaid; obstetrician, midwife, *accoucheur*.

Key, master-key, passport, safe-conduct, passe-partout, 'open sesame'; a go-between, middleman (758), a cat's-paw, jackal, pander, tool, ghost, mainstay, trump card.

(Phrase) Two strings to one's bow.

(Verbs) To subserve, minister, intervene, mediate, devil, pander to.

(Adjectives) Instrumental, intervening, intermediate, intermediary, subservient, auxiliary, ancillary.

(Adverbs) Through, by, with, by means of, by dint of, *à force de*, along with, thereby, through the medium, etc., of, wherewith, wherewithal.

632 Means *(Substantives)*, resources, wherewithal, appliances, ways and means, convenience, expedients, step, measure (626), aid (707), intermedium, medium.

Machinery, mechanism, mechanics, engineering, mechanical powers, automation, scaffolding, ladder, mainstay.

(Phrases) Wheels within wheels; a shot in the locker.

(Adjectives) Instrumental, accessory, subsidiary, mechanical.

(Adverbs) How, by what means, by all means, by all manner of means, by the aid of, by dint of.

(Phrases) By hook or by crook; somehow or other; for love or money; by fair means or foul; *quocumque modo*.

633 Instrument *(Substantives)*, tool, implement, appliance, contraption, apparatus, utensil, device, gadget, craft, machine, engine, motor, dynamo, generator, mill, lathe.

Equipment, gear, tackle, tackling, rigging, harness, trappings, fittings, accoutrements, paraphernalia, equipage, outfit, appointments, furniture, material, plant, appurtenances.

A wheel, jack, clockwork, wheel-work, spring, screw, turbine, wedge, flywheel, lever, bascule, pinion, crank, winch, crane, capstan, windlass, pulley, hammer, mallet, mattock, mall, bat, racket, sledge-hammer, mace, club, truncheon, pole, staff, bill, crow, crowbar, poleaxe, handspike, crutch, boom, bar, pitchfork, etc.

Organ, limb, arm, hand, finger, claw, paw, talons, tentacle, wing, oar, paddle, pincer, plier, forceps, thimble.

Handle, hilt, haft, shaft, shank, heft, blade, trigger, tiller, helm, treadle, pummel, peg (214, 215), key.

Edge-tool, hatchet, axe, pickaxe, etc. (253), axis (312).

634 Substitute *(Substantives)*, shift, makeshift, succedaneum (147), stop-gap, expedient, *pis aller*, surrogate, understudy, pinch-hitter, stand-in, locum tenens, proxy, deputy (759).

635 Materials *(Substantives)*, material, matter, stuff, constituent, ingredient (56), pabulum, fuel, grist, provender, provisions, food (298).

Supplies, munition, ammunition, reinforcement, relay, contingents.

Baggage, luggage, bag and baggage, effects, goods, chattels, household stuff, equipage, paraphernalia, impedimenta, stock-in-trade, cargo, lading (780).

Metal, stone, ore, brick, clay, wood, timber, composition, compo, plastic.

636 Store *(Substantives)*, stock, fund, supply, reserve, relay, budget, quiver, *corps de réserve*, reserve fund, mine, quarry, vein, lode, fountain, well, spring, milch cow.

Collection, accumulation, heap (72), hoard, cache, stockpile, magazine, pile, rick, nest-egg, savings, bank (802), treasury, reservoir, repository, repertory, repertoire, album, depot, depository, treasure, thesaurus, museum, storehouse, promptuary, reservatory, conservatory, menagerie, aviary, aquarium, receptacle, warehouse, godown, *entrepôt*, dock, larder, cellar, garner, granary, store-room, box-room, lumber-room, silo, cistern, well, tank, gasometer, mill-pond, armoury, arsenal, coffer (191).

(Verbs) To store, stock, stockpile, treasure up, lay in, lay by, lay up, file, garner, save, husband, hoard, deposit, amass, accumulate (72).

To reserve, keep back, hold back.

(Phrase) To husband one's resources.

(Adjectives) Stored, etc., in store, in reserve, spare, surplus, extra.

637 Provision *(Substantives)*, supply, providing, supplying, sustentation (707), purveyance, purveying, reinforcement, husbanding, commissariat, victualling.

Forage, pasture, food, provender (298).

A purveyor, caterer, contractor, commissary, quartermaster, sutler, victualler, *restaurateur*, feeder, batman; bum-boat.

(Verbs) To provide, supply, furnish, purvey, suppeditate, replenish, fill up, feed, stock with, recruit, victual, cater, find, fend, keep, lay in, lay in store, store, stockpile, forage, husband (636), upholster.

(Phrase) To bring grist to the mill.

638 Waste *(Substantives)*, consumption, expenditure, exhaustion, drain, leakage, wear and tear, dispersion (73), ebb, loss, misuse, prodigality (818), seepage, squandermania.

(Verbs) To waste, spend, expend, use, consume, spill, leak, run out, run to waste, disperse (73), ebb, dry up, impoverish, drain, empty, exhaust; to fritter away, squander.

(Phrases) to cast pearls before swine; to burn the candle at both ends; to employ a steam-hammer to crack nuts; to break a butterfly on a wheel; to pour water into a sieve.

(Adjectives) Wasted, spent, profuse, lavish, etc., at a low ebb.

(Phrase) Penny wise and pound foolish.

639 Sufficiency *(Substantives)*, adequacy, competence; enough, satiety.

Fullness, fill, plenitude, plenty, abundance, copiousness, amplitude, affluence, richness, fertility, luxuriance, uberty, foison.

Heaps, lots, bags, piles, lashings, oceans, oodles, mobs.

Impletion, repletion, saturation.

Riches (803), mine, store, fund, (636); a bumper, a brimmer, a bellyful, a cart-load, truck-load, ship-load; a plumper; a charge.

640 Insufficiency *(Substantives)*, inadequacy, inadequateness, incompetence.

Deficiency, stint, paucity, defect, defectiveness, default, defalcation, deficit, shortcoming, falling short (304), too little, what will not do, scantiness, slenderness, a mouthful, etc. (32).

Scarcity, dearth, shortage, want, need, lack, exigency, inanition, indigence, poverty, penury (804), destitution, dole, pittance, short allowance, short commons, a banian day,

A flood, draught, shower, rain (347), stream, tide, spring tide, flush.

(Phrases) The horn of plenty; the horn of Amalthea; cornucopia; the fat of the land.

(Verbs) To be sufficient, etc., to suffice, serve, pass muster, to do, satisfy, satiate, sate, saturate, make up.

To abound, teem, stream, flow, rain, shower down, pour, swarm, bristle with.

To render sufficient, etc., to make up, to fill, charge, replenish, pour in; swim in, wallow in, roll in.

(Adjectives) Sufficient, enough, adequate, commensurate, what will just do.

Moderate, measured.

Full, ample, plenty, copious, plentiful, plenteous, plenary, wantless, abundant, abounding, flush, replete, laden, charged, fraught; well stocked or provided, liberal, lavish, unstinted, to spare, unsparing, unmeasured; *ad libitum*, wholesale.

Brimful, to the brim, chock-full, saturated, crammed, up to the ears, fat, rich, affluent, full up, luxuriant, lush.

Unexhausted, unwasted, exhaustless, inexhaustible.

(Phrases) Enough and to spare; cut and come again; full as an egg; ready to burst; plentiful as blackberries; flowing with milk and honey; enough in all conscience; enough to go round; *quantum sufficit*.

(Adverbs) Amply, etc., galore.

fast (956), a mouthful, starvation, malnutrition, famine, drought, depletion, emptiness, vacancy, flaccidity, ebbtide, low water.

(Phrase) 'A beggarly account of empty boxes.'

(Verbs) To be insufficient, etc., not to suffice, to come short of, to fall short of, fail, run out of, stop short, to want, lack, need, require (630); caret.

To render insufficient, etc., to stint, grudge, hold back, withhold, starve, pinch, skimp, scrimp, famish.

(Phrase) To live from hand to mouth.

(Adjectives) Insufficient, inadequate, incompetent, too little, not enough, etc., scant, scanty, skimpy, scrimpy, deficient, defective, in default, scarce, empty, empty-headed, devoid, short of, out of, wanting, etc., hard up for.

Destitute, dry, drained, unprovided, unsupplied, unfurnished, unreplenished, unfed, unstored, untreasured, bare, meagre, poor, thin, spare, skimpy, stinted, starved, famished, pinched, fasting, starveling, jejune, without resources (735), shorthanded, undermanned, understaffed, etc.

(Phrases) In short supply; not to be had for love or money; at the end of one's tether; at one's last gasp.

———

641 Redundance *(Substantives)*, superabundance, superfluity, superfluence, glut, exuberance, profuseness, profusion, plethora, engorgement, congestion, surfeit, gorge, load, turgidity, turgescence, dropsy.

Excess, nimiety, overdose, oversupply, overplus, surplus, surplusage, over-flow, inundation, deluge, extravagance, prodigality (818), exorbitance, lavishness, immoderation.

An expletive (908), pleonasm.

(Phrases) *Satis superque*; a drug in the market; the lion's share.

(Verbs) To superabound, overabound, run over, overflow, flow over, roll in, wallow in.

To overstock, overdose, overlay, gorge, engorge, glut, sate, satiate, surfeit, cloy, load, overload, surcharge, overrun, choke, drown, drench, inundate, flood, whelm, deluge.

(Phrases) To go begging; it never rains but it pours; to paint the lily; to carry coals to Newcastle.

(Adjectives) Redundant, superfluous, exuberant, superabundant, immoderate, extravagant, excessive, in excess, *de trop*, needless, unnecessary, uncalled-for, over and above (40), more than enough, buckshee, running to waste, overflowing, running over.

Turgid, gorged, plethoric, dropsical, replete, profuse, lavish, prodigal, supervacaneous, extra, spare, duplicate, supernumerary, supererogatory, expletive, surcharged, overcharged, sodden, overloaded, overladen, overburdened, overrun, overfed, overfull.

(Phrase) Enough and to spare.

(Adverbs) Over, over and above, too much, overmuch, over and enough, too far, without measure, without stint.

(Phrase) Over head and ears.

2. DEGREE OF SUBSERVIENCE

642 Importance *(Substantives)*, consequence, moment, weight, gravity, seriousness, consideration, concern, significance, import, influence (175), pressure, urgency, instancy, stress, emphasis, interest, preponderance, prominence (250), greatness (31).

The substance, essence, quintessence, core, kernel, nub, gist, pith, marrow, soul, point, gravamen.

The principal, prominent, or essential part.

A notability, somebody, personage (875), V.I.P., bigwig, toff, big pot, big gun, his nibs; great doings, *notabilia*, a red-letter day.

(Phrases) A *sine qua non*; a matter of life and death; no laughing matter.

(Verbs) To be important, or of importance, etc., to signify, import, matter, boot, weigh, count, to be prominent, etc., to take the lead.

To attach, or ascribe importance to; to value, care for, etc. (897); overestimate, etc. (482), exaggerate (549).

To mark, underline, italicize, score, accentuate, emphasize, stress, rub in.

(Phrases) To be somebody; to fill the bill; to make much of; to make a stir, a fuss, a piece of work, a song and dance; set store upon; to lay stress upon; to take *au grand sérieux*.

(Adjectives) Important, of importance, etc., grave, serious, material, weighty, influential, significant, emphatic, momentous, earnest, pressing, critical, preponderating, pregnant, urgent, paramount, essential, vital.

643 Unimportance *(Substantives)*, indifference, insignificance, triflingness, triviality, triteness; paltriness, emptiness, nothingness, inanity, lightness, levity, frivolity, vanity, frivolousness, puerility, child's play.

Poverty, meagreness, meanness, shabbiness, etc. (804).

A trifle, small matter, minutiae, bagatelle, cipher, moonshine, molehill, joke, jest, snap of the fingers, flea-bite, pinch of snuff, old song, *nugae*, fiddlestick, fiddlestick end, bubble, bulrush, nonentity, lay figure, nobody.

A straw, pin, fig, button, rush, feather, farthing, brass farthing, red cent, dime, dam, doit, peppercorn, pebble, small fry.

Trumpery, trash, codswallop, stuff, *fatras*, frippery, chaff, drug, froth, smoke, cobweb.

Toy, plaything, knick-knack, gimcrack, gewgaw, thingumbob, bauble, kickshaw, bric-à-brac, fal-lal, whimwham, whigmaleerie, curio, bibelot.

Refuse, lumber, junk, litter, orts, tares, weeds, sweepings, scourings, offscourings; rubble, debris, dross, scoriae, dregs, scum, flue, dust (653).

(Phrases) 'Leather and prunella'; *peu de chose*; much ado about nothing; much cry and little wood; flotsam and jetsam; a man of straw; a stuffed shirt; a toom tabard.

(Verbs) To be unimportant, to be of little or no importance, etc.; not to signify, not to deserve, merit, or be

Great, considerable, etc. (31), capital, leading, principal, superior, chief, main, prime, primary, cardinal, prominent, salient, egregious, outstanding.

Signal, notable, memorable, remarkable, etc., grand, solemn, eventful, stirring, impressive; not to be despised, or overlooked, etc., unforgettable, worth while.

(Phrases) Being no joke; not to be sneezed at; no small beer.

worthy of notice, regard, consideration, etc.

(Phrases) To catch at straws; to make much ado about nothing; to cut no ice; *le jeu ne vaut pas la chandelle.*

(Adjectives) Unimportant, secondary, inferior, immaterial, inconsiderable, inappreciable, insignificant, unessential, non-essential, beneath notice, indifferent; of little or no account, importance, consequence, moment, interest, etc.; unimpressive, subordinate.

Trifling, trivial, trite, banal, mere, common, so-so, slight, slender, flimsy, trumpery, foolish, idle, puerile, childish, infantile, frothy, trashy, catchpenny, fiddling, frivolous, commonplace, contemptible, cheap.

Vain, empty, inane, poor, sorry, mean, meagre, shabby, scrannel, vile, miserable, scrubby, weedy, niggling, beggarly, piddling, peddling, pitiful, pitiable, despicable, paltry, ridiculous, farcical, finical, finicking, finicky, finikin, fiddle-faddle, wishy-washy, namby-pamby, gimcrack, twopenny, twopenny-halfpenny, two-by-four, one-horse, piffling, jerry, jerry built.

(Phrases) Not worth a straw; as light as air; not worth mentioning; not worth boasting about; no great shakes; nothing to write home about; small potatoes; neither here nor there.

(Interjections) No matter! pshaw! pooh! pooh-pooh! shucks! I should worry! fudge! fiddle-de-dee! nonsense! boloney! hooey! nuts! rats! stuff! *n'importe!*

(Adverbs) Meagrely, pitifully, vainly, etc.

---

644 Utility *(Substantives)*, service, use, function, office, sphere, capacity, part, role, task, work.

Usefulness, worth, stead, avail, advantageousness, profitableness, serviceableness, merit, *cui bono*, applicability, adequacy, subservience, subserviency, efficacy, efficiency, help, money's worth.

(Verbs) To be useful, etc., of use, of service.

To avail, serve, subserve, help (707), conduce, answer, profit, advantage, accrue, bedstead.

To render useful, to use (677), to turn to account, to utilize, to make the most of.

(Phrases) To stand in good stead; to do yeoman service; to perform a function; to serve a purpose; to serve a turn.

645 Inutility *(Substantives)*, uselessness, inefficacy, inefficiency, ineptness, ineptitude, inadequacy, inaptitude, unskilfulness, fecklessness, fruitlessness, inanity, worthlessness, unproductiveness, barrenness, sterility, vanity, futility, triviality, paltriness, unprofitableness, unfruitfulness, rustiness, obsoleteness, discommodity, supererogation, obsolescence.

Litter, rubbish, lumber, trash, junk, punk, job lot, orts, weeds (643), bilge, hog-wash.

A waste, desert, Sahara, wild, wilderness.

(Phrases) The labour of Sisyphus; the work of Penelope; a slaying of the slain; a dead loss; a work of supererogation.

(Verbs) To be useless, etc., to be of no avail, use, etc. (644).

(Adjectives) Useful, beneficial, advantageous, serviceable, helpful, gainful, profitable, lucrative, worth while.

Subservient, conducive, applicable, adequate, efficient, efficacious, effective, effectual, seaworthy.

Applicable, available, handy, ready.

(Adverbs) Usefully, etc.; *pro bono publico.*

To render useless, etc.; to dismantle, disable, disqualify, cripple.

(Phrases) To use vain efforts; to beat the air; to fish in the air; to lash the waves; to plough the sands.

(Adjectives) Useless, inutile, inefficient, inefficacious, unavailing, inadequate, inoperative, bootless, supervacaneous, unprofitable, unremunerative, unproductive, sterile, barren, unsubservient, supererogatory.

Worthless, valueless, at a discount, gainless, fruitless, profitless, unserviceable, rusty, effete, vain, empty, inane, wasted, nugatory, futile, feckless, inept, withered, good for nothing, wasteful, ill-spent, obsolete, obsolescent, stale, dud, punk, dear-bought, rubbishy.

Unneeded, unnecessary, uncalled-for, unwanted, incommodious, discommodious.

(Phrases) Not worth having; leading to no end; no good; not worth while; of no earthly use; a dead letter.

(Adverbs) Uselessly, etc., to no purpose.

646 Specific subservience.

Expedience *(Substantives)*, expediency, fitness, suitableness, suitability, aptness, aptitude, appropriateness, propriety, pertinence, seasonableness (134), adaptation, congruity, consonance (23), convenience, eligibility, applicability, desirability, seemliness, rightness.

An opportunist, time-server.

(Verbs) To be expedient, etc.

To suit, fit, square with, adapt itself to, agree with, consort with, accord with, tally with, confirm to, go with, do for.

(Adjectives) Expedient, fit, fitting, worth while, suitable, applicable, eligible, apt, appropriate, adapted, proper, advisable, politic, judicious, desirable, pertinent, congruous, seemly, consonant, becoming, meet, due, consentaneous, congenial, well-timed, pat, seasonable, opportune, apropos, befitting, happy, felicitous, auspicious, acceptable, etc., convenient, commodious, right.

(Phrases) Being just the thing; just as well.

648 Capability of producing good.

Goodness *(Substantives)*, excellence, integrity (939), virtue (944),

647 Inexpedience *(Substantives)*, inexpediency, disadvantageousness, unserviceableness, disservice, unfitness, inaptitude, ineptitude, ineligibility, inappropriateness, impropriety, undesirability, unseemliness, incongruity, impertinence, inopportuneness, unseasonableness.

Inconvenience, incommodiousness, incommodity, discommodity, disadvantage.

Inefficacy, inefficiency, inadequacy.

(Verbs) To be inexpedient, etc., to embarrass, cumber, lumber, handicap, be in the way, etc.

(Adjectives) Inexpedient, disadvantageous, unprofitable, unfit, unfitting, unsuitable, undesirable, amiss, improper, unapt, inept, impolitic, injudicious, ill-advised, unadvisable, ineligible, objectionable, inadmissible, unseemly, inopportune, unseasonable, inefficient, inefficacious, inadequate.

Inconvenient, incommodious, cumbrous, cumbersome, lumbering, unwieldy, unmanageable, awkward, clumsy.

649 Capability of producing evil.

Badness *(Substantives)*, hurtfulness, disserviceableness, injurious-

merit, value, worth, price, preciousness, estimation, rareness, exquisiteness.

Superexcellence, superiority, supereminence, transcendence, perfection (650).

Mediocrity (651), innocuousness, harmlessness, inoffensiveness.

Masterpiece, *chef d'œuvre,* flower, pick, cream, *crème de la crème, élite,* gem, jewel, treasure; a good man (948).

(Phrases) One in a thousand (or in a million); the salt of the earth.

(Verbs) To be good, beneficial, etc.; to be superior, etc., to excel, transcend, top, vie, emulate (708).

To be middling, etc. (651); to pass, to do.

To produce good, benefit, etc., to benefit, to be beneficial, etc., to confer a benefit, etc., to improve (658).

(Phrases) To challenge comparison; to pass muster; to speak well for.

(Adjectives) Good, beneficial, valuable, estimable, serviceable, advantageous, precious, favourable, palmary, felicitous, propitious.

Sound, sterling, standard, true, genuine, household, fresh, in good condition, unfaded, unspoiled, unimpaired, uninjured, undemolished, undamaged, unravaged, undecayed, natural, unsophisticated, unadulterated, unpolluted, unvitiated.

Choice, select, picked, nice, worthy, meritorious (944), fine, rare, unexceptionable, excellent, admirable, first-rate, splendid, swell, bully, wizard, priceless, smashing, super, topping, top-hole, clipping, ripping, nailing, prime, tiptop, crack, jake, cardinal, superlative, superfine, super-excellent, pukka, gradely, champion, exquisite, high-wrought, inestimable, invaluable, incomparable, transcendent, matchless, peerless, inimitable, unrivalled, *nulli secundus,* second to none, *facile princeps,* spotless, immaculate, perfect (650), *récherché,* first-class, first chop.

Moderately good (651).

Harmless, innocuous, innoxious,

ness, banefulness, mischievousness, noxiousness, malignancy, malignity, malevolence, tender mercies, venomousness, virulence, destructiveness, scathe, curse, pest, plague, bane (663), plague-spot, evil star, ill wind; evildoer (913).

Vileness, foulness, rankness, depravation, depravity; injury, outrage, ill treatment, annoyance, molestation, oppression; sabotage; deterioration (659).

(Phrases) A snake in the grass; a fly in the ointment; a nigger in the woodpile; a thorn in the side; a skeleton in the cupboard.

(Verbs) To be bad, etc.

To cause, produce, or inflict evil; to harm, hurt, injure, mar, damage, damnify, endamage, scathe, prejudice, stand in the light of, worsen.

To wrong, molest (830), annoy, harass, infest, grieve, aggrieve, trouble, oppress, persecute, weigh down, run down, overlay.

To maltreat, abuse, ill use, ill treat, bedevil, bruise, scratch, maul, mishandle, man-handle, strafe, knock about, strike, smite, scourge (972), wound, lame, maim, scotch, cripple, mutilate, hamstring, hough, stab, pierce, etc., crush, crumble, pulverize.

To corrupt, corrode, pollute, etc. (659).

To spoil, despoil, sweep, ravage, lay waste, devastate, dismantle, demolish, level, raze, consume, overrun, sack, plunder, destroy (162).

(Phrases) To play the deuce with; to break the back of; crush to pieces; crumble to dust; to grind to powder; to ravage with fire and sword; to knock the stuffing out of; to queer one's pitch; to let daylight into.

(Adjectives) Bad, evil, ill, wrong, prejudicial, disadvantageous, unprofitable, unlucky, sinister, left-handed, obnoxious, untoward, unadvisable, inauspicious, ill-omened.

Hurtful, harmful, injurious, grievous, detrimental, noxious, pernicious, mischievous, baneful, baleful.

Morbific, rank, peccant, malignant,

unoffending, inoffensive, unobjectionable.

(Phrases) The goods; the stuff to give them; a bit of all right; of the first water; precious as the apple of the eye; *ne plus ultra*; sound as a roach; worth its weight in gold; right as a trivet; up to the mark; an easy winner.

tabid, corroding, corrosive, virulent, cankering, mephitic, narcotic.

Deleterious, poisonous, venomous, envenomed, pestilent, pestilential, pestiferous, destructive, deadly, fatal, mortal, lethal, lethiferous, miasmal.

Vile, sad, wretched, sorry, shabby, scurvy, base, low, low-down (940), scrubby, lousy, stinking, horrid.

Hateful, abominable, loathsome, detestable, execrable, iniquitous, cursed, accursed, confounded, damnable, diabolic, devilish, demoniacal, infernal, hellish, Satanic, villainous, depraved, shocking (898).

(Adverbs) Wrong, wrongly, badly, to one's cost.

(Phrases) Corruptio optimi pessima; if the worst comes to the worst.

650 Perfection *(Substantives)*, perfectness, indefectibility, impeccability, infallibility, unimpeachability, *beau idéal*, summit (210).

Masterpiece, *chef d'œuvre, magnum opus*, classic, model, pattern, mirror, phoenix, *rara avis*, paragon, cream, nonsuch (or nonesuch), nonpareil, *élite*.

Gem, bijou, jewel, pearl, diamond, ruby, brilliant.

A Bayard, a Galahad, an Admirable Crichton.

(Phrases) The philosophers' stone; the flower of the flock; the cock of the roost; the peak or acme of perfection; the pick of the bunch; the *ne plus ultra*.

(Verbs) To be perfect, etc., to excel, transcend, overtop, etc. (33).

To bring to perfection, to perfect, to ripen, mature, etc. (52, 729).

(Phrases) To carry everything before it; to play first fiddle; bear away the bell; to sweep the board.

(Adjectives) Perfect, best, faultless, finished, indeficient, indefectible, immaculate, spotless, impeccable, transcendent, matchless, peerless, unparagoned, etc. (648), inimitable, unimpeachable, superlative, superhuman, divine, classical.

(Phrases) Right as a trivet; sound as a bell; *ad unguem factus; sans peur et sans reproche*.

651 Imperfection *(Substantives)*, imperfectness, unsoundness, faultiness, deficiency, disability, weak point, drawback, inadequacy, inadequateness (645), handicap.

Fault, defect, flaw, lacuna (198), crack, twist, taint, blemish, shortcoming (304), peccancy, vice.

Mediocrity, mean (29), indifference, inferiority.

(Verbs) To be imperfect, middling, etc., to fail, fall short, lie under a disadvantage, be handicapped.

(Phrases) To play second fiddle; barely to pass muster.

(Adjectives) Imperfect, deficient, defective, faulty, dud, inferior, inartistic, inadequate, wanting, unsound, vicious, cracked, warped, lame, feeble, frail, flimsy, sketchy, botched, gimcrack, gingerbread, tottering, wonky, decrepit, rickety, ramshackle, rattletrap, battered, worn out, threadbare, seedy, wormeaten, moth-eaten, played out, used up, decayed, mutilated, unrectified, uncorrected.

Indifferent, middling, mediocre, below par, so-so, *couci-couci*, secondary, second-rate, third-rate, etc., second-best, second-hand.

Tolerable, passable, bearable, pretty well, well enough, rather good, decent, fair, admissible, not bad, not amiss, not so dusty, unobjectionable, respectable, betwixt and between.

(Phrases) having a screw loose; out of order; out of kilter; no great catch; mill and water; no great shakes; nothing to boast of; on its last legs; no class.

652 Cleanness *(Substantives)*, cleanliness, asepsis, purity (960), neatness, tidiness, spotlessness, immaculateness.

Cleaning, purification, mundification, lustration, abstersion, depuration, expurgation, purgation, castration.

Washing, ablution, lavation, elutriation, lixiviation, clarification, defecation, edulcoration, filtration.

Fumigation, ventilation, antisepsis, decontamination, disinfection, soap; detergent, shampoo, antiseptic, disinfectant.

Washroom, wash-house, laundry; washerwoman, laundress, charwoman, cleaner, scavenger, dustman, sweep.

Brush, broom, besom, vacuum-cleaner, duster, handkerchief, napkin, face-cloth, towel, sponge, tooth-brush, nail-brush; mop, sieve, riddle, screen, filter.

(Verbs) To be clean, etc.

To render clean, etc., to clean, to mundify, cleanse, wipe, mop, sponge, scour, swab, scrub, brush, sweep, vacuum, dust, brush up.

To wash, lave, sluice, buck, launder, steep, rinse, absterge, deterge, descale, clear, purify, depurate, defecate, elutriate, lixiviate, edulcorate, clarify, drain, strain, filter, filtrate, fine, fine down.

To disinfect, deodorize, fumigate, delouse, ventilate, purge, expurgate, bowdlerize.

To sift, winnow, pick, screen, weed.

(Phrase) To make a clean sweep of.

(Adjectives) Clean, cleanly, pure, spotless, unspotted, immaculate, unstained, stainless, unsoiled, unsullied, taintless, untainted, sterile, aseptic, uninfected.

Cleansing, etc., detergent, detersive, abstersive, abstergent, purgatory, purificatory, etc., abluent, antiseptic.

Spruce, tidy, washed, swept, etc., cleaned, disinfected, purified, etc.

(Phrases) Clean as a whistle; clean as a new penny; neat as ninepence.

---

653 Uncleanness *(Substantives)*, immundicity, uncleanliness, soilure, sordidness, foulness, impurity (961), pollution, nastiness, offensiveness, beastliness, muckiness, defilement, contamination, abomination, taint, tainture, corruption, decomposition (49).

Slovenliness, slovenly, untidiness, sluttishness, coarseness, grossness, dregginess, squalor.

Dirt, filth, soil, slop, dust, flue, ooss, cobweb, smoke, soot, smudge, smut, stour, clart, glaur, grime, *sordes*, mess, muck.

Slut, slattern, sloven, frump, mudlark, riff-raff.

Dregs, grounds, sediment, lees, settlement, dross, drossiness, precipitate, scoriae, slag, clinker, scum, sweepings, off-scourings, garbage, *caput mortuum*, residuum, draff, fur, scurf, scurfiness, furfur, dandruff, vermin.

Mud, mire, slush, quagmire, slough, sludge, alluvium, silt, slime, spawn, offal, faeces, excrement, ordure, dung, droppings, guano, manure, compost, dunghill, midden, bog, laystall, sink, cesspool, sump, sough, *cloaca*, latrine, lavatory, water-closet, w.c., toilet, urinal, rear, convenience, privy, jakes, comfort station, heads, thunder-box, drain, sewer; hog-wash, bilge-water,

Sty, pigsty, dusthole, lair, den, slum.

Rottenness, corruption, decomposition, decay, putrefaction, putrescence, putridity, purulence, pus, matter, suppuration, feculence, rankness, rancidity, mouldiness, mustiness, mucidness, mould, mother, must, mildew, dry-rot, fetor (401).

Scatology, coprology.

(Phrases) A sink of corruption; an Augean stable.

(Verbs) To be unclean, dirty, etc., to rot, putrefy, corrupt, decompose, go bad, mould, moulder, fester, etc.

To render unclean, etc., to dirt, dirty, soil, tarnish, begrime, smear, besmear, mess, smirch, besmirch, smudge, besmudge, bemire, spatter, bespatter, splash, bedraggle, bedraggle, daub, bedaub, slobber, beslobber, beslime, to cover with dust.

To foul, befoul, sully, pollute, defile, debase, contaminate, taint, corrupt, deflower, rot.

(Adjectives) Unclean, dirty, soiled, filthy, grimy, clarty, dusty, dirtied, etc., smutty, sooty, smoky, reechy, thick, turbid, dreggy, slimy, filthy, mucky.

Slovenly, untidy, sluttish, blowzy, draggle-tailed, dowdy, frumpish, slipshod, unkempt, unscoured, unswept, unwiped, unwashed, unstrained, unpurified, squalid.

Nasty, foul, impure, offensive, abominable, beastly, lousy.

Mouldy, musty, mildewed, fusty, rusty, mouldering, moth-eaten, reasty, rotten, rotting, tainted, rancid, high, fly-blown, maggoty, putrescent, putrid, putrefied, bad, festering, purulent, feculent, fecal, stercoraceous, excrementitious.

(Phrases) Wallowing in the mire; rotten to the core.

654 Health *(Substantives)*, sanity, soundness, heartiness, haleness, vigour, freshness, bloom, healthfulness, euphoria, incorruption, incorruptibility.

(Phrases) Mens sana in corpore sano; a clean bill.

(Verbs) To be in health, etc., to flourish, thrive, bloom.

To return to health, to recover, convalesce, recruit, pull through, to get the better of.

To restore to health, to cure, recall to life, bring to.

(Phrases) To keep on one's legs; to take a new or fresh lease of life; to turn the corner.

(Adjectives) Healthy, in health, well, sound, healthful, hearty, hale, fresh, whole, florid, staunch, flush, hardy, vigorous, chipper, spry, bobbish, blooming, weather-proof, fit.

Unscathed, uninjured, unmaimed, unmarred, untainted.

(Phrases) Sitting up and taking nourishment; being on one's legs; sound as a bell, or roach; fresh as a daisy or rose; in fine or high feather; in good case; fit as a fiddle; in the pink of condition; in the pink; in good form.

655 Disease *(Substantives)*, illness, sickness, ailment, ailing, indisposition, complaint, disorder, malady, distemper.

Attack, visitation, seizure, stroke, fit.

Sickliness, sickishness, infirmity, diseasedness, tabescence, invalidation, delicacy, weakness, cachexy, witheredness, atrophy, marasmus, incurableness, incurability, palsy, paralysis, decline, consumption, prostration.

Taint, pollution, infection, septicity, epidemic, endemic, murrain, plague, pestilence, virus, pox.

A sore, ulcer, abscess, fester, boil, gathering, issue, rot, canker, cancer, carcinoma, sarcoma, caries, gangrene, mortification, eruption, rash, congestion, inflammation, fever.

A valetudinarian, invalid, patient, case, cripple.

Pathology, aetiology, nosology.

(Verbs) To be ill, etc., to ail, suffer, be affected with, etc., to complain of, to droop, flag, languish, halt, sicken, gasp; to malinger.

(Phrases) To be laid up; to keep one's bed.

(Adjectives) Diseased, ill, taken ill, seized, indisposed, unwell, sick, sickish, seedy, queer, crook, toutie, ailing, suffering, confined, bedridden, invalided.

Unsound, sickly, poorly, delicate, weakly, cranky, healthless, infirm, groggy, unbraced, drooping, flagging, withered, palsied, paralytic, paraplectic, decayed, decrepit, lame, crippled, battered, halting, worn out, used up, run down, off colour, moth-eaten, worm-eaten.

Morbid, tainted, vitiated, peccant, contaminated, tabid, tabescent, mangy, poisoned, immedicable, gasping, moribund (360).

(Phrases) Out of sorts; good for nothing; on the sick-list; on the danger list; in a bad way; *hors de combat*; on one's last legs; at one's last gasp.

656 Salubrity *(Substantives),* healthiness, wholesomeness, innoxiousness.

Preservation of health, prophylaxis, hygiene, sanitation.

A health resort, spa, hydropathic, sanatorium (662).

(Verbs) To be salubrious, etc., to agree with.

(Adjectives) Salubrious, wholesome, healthy, sanitary, hygienic, salutary, salutiferous, healthful, tonic, prophylactic, bracing, benign.

Innoxious, innocuous, harmless, uninjurious, innocent.

Remedial, restorative, sanatory (662), nutritious, alterative (660).

657 Insalubrity *(Substantives),* unhealthiness, unwholesomeness, deadliness, fatality.

Microbe, germ, virus, etc. (663).

(Adjectives) Insalubrious, insanitary, unsanitary, unhealthy, ungenial, uncongenial, unwholesome, morbific, mephitic, septic, deleterious, pestilent, pestiferous, pestilential, virulent, poisonous, toxic, contagious, infectious, catching, epidemic, epizootic, endemic, pandemic, zymotic, deadly, pathogenic, pathogenetic, lowering, relaxing; innutritious (645).

(Phrase) 'There is death in the pot.'

658 Improvement *(Substantives),* melioration, amelioration, betterment, mend, amendment, emendation, advance, advancement, progress, elevation, promotion, preferment, convalescence, recovery, recuperation, curability.

Repair, reparation, cicatrization, correction, reform, reformation, rectification, epuration, purification, etc. (652), refinement, relief, redress, second thoughts.

New edition; *réchauffé, rifacimento,* revision, revise, recension, rehash, redaction.

(Verbs) To be, become, or get better, etc., to improve, mend, advance, progress (282), to get on, make progress, gain ground, make way, go ahead, pick up, rally, recover, get the better of, get well, get over it, pull through, convalesce, recuperate.

To render better, improve, amend, better, meliorate, ameliorate, advance, push on, promote, prefer, forward, enhance.

To relieve, refresh, restore, renew, redintegrate, heal (660); to palliate, mitigate.

To repair, refit, cannibalize,

659 Deterioration *(Substantives),* wane, ebb, debasement, degeneracy, degeneration, degradation, degenerateness, demotion, relegation.

Impairment, injury, outrage, havoc, devastation, inroad, vitiation, adulteration, sophistication, debasement, perversion, degradation, demoralization, corruption, prostitution, pollution, contamination, alloy, venenation.

Decline, declension, declination, going downhill, recession, retrogression, retrogradation (283), caducity, decrepitude, decadence, falling off, pejoration.

Decay, disorganization, damage, scathe, wear and tear, mouldiness, rottenness, corrosion, moth and rust, dry-rot, blight, marasmus, atrophy, emaciation, falling to pieces, *délâbrement.*

(Verbs) To be, or become worse, to deteriorate, worsen, disimprove, wane, ebb, degenerate, fall off, decline, go downhill, sink, go down, lapse, droop, be the worse for, recede, retrograde, revert (283), fall into decay, fade, break, break up, break down, fall to pieces, wither, moulder,

retouch, revise, botch, vamp, tinker, cobble, clout, patch up, touch up, cicatrize, darn, fine-draw, rub up, do up, furbish, refurbish, polish, bolster up, caulk, careen; to stop a gap, to staunch.

To purify, depurate (652), defecate, strain, filter, rack, refine, disinfect, chasten.

To correct, rectify, redress, reform, review, remodel, prune, restore (660), mellow, set to rights, sort, fix, put straight, straighten out, revise.

(Phrases) To turn over a new leaf; to take a new lease of life; to make the most of; to infuse new blood into.

(Adjectives) Improving, etc., improved, etc., progressive, corrective, reparatory, emendatory, revisory, sanatory, advanced.

Curable, corrigible, capable of improvement.

———

rot, rust, crumble, totter, shake, tumble, fall, topple, perish, die (360).

To render less good; to weaken, vitiate, debase, alloy, pervert.

To spoil, embase, defile, taint, infect, contaminate, sophisticate, poison, canker, corrupt, tamper with, pollute, deprave, demoralize, envenom, debauch, prostitute, defile, degrade, downgrade, demote, adulterate, stain, spatter, bespatter, soil, tarnish (653), addle.

To corrode, erode, blight, rot, wear away, wear out, gnaw, gnaw at the root of, sap, mine, undermine, shake, break up, disorganize, dismantle, dismast, lay waste, do for, ruin, confound.

To embitter, acerbate, aggravate.

To wound, stab, maim, lame, cripple, mutilate, disfigure, deface.

To injure, harm, hurt, impair, dilapidate, damage, endamage, damnify, etc. (649).

(Phrases) To go to rack and ruin; to have seen better days; to go to the dogs; to go to pot; to go on from bad to worse; to go farther and fare worse; to run to seed; to play the deuce with; to sap the foundations of.

(Adjectives) Deteriorated, worse, impaired, etc., degenerate, *passé*, on the decline, on the down-grade, deciduous, unimproved, unrecovered, unrestored.

Decayed, etc., moth-eaten, worm-eaten, mildewed, rusty, time-worn, moss-grown, effete, wasted, worn, crumbling, tumbledown, dilapidated, overblown.

(Phrases) Out of the frying-pan into the fire; the worse for wear; worn to a thread; worn to a shadow; reduced to a skeleton; the ghost of oneself; a hopeless case.

660 Restoration *(Substantives)*, restoral, reinstatement, replacement, rehabilitation, instauration, re-establishment, rectification, revendication, redintegration, refection, reconstitution, cure, sanation, refitting, retrieval, refreshment.

Renovation, renewal, reanimation, recovery, resumption, reclamation, reconversion, recure, resuscitation, revivification, reviviscence, revival, renascence, renaissance, rejuvenation, rejuvenescence, regeneration, regeneracy, regenerateness, palingenesis, redemption; a Phoenix.

661 Relapse *(Substantives)*, lapse, falling back, backsliding, retrogression, reaction, set-back, recidivism, retrogradation, etc. (659).

Return to or recurrence of a bad state.

A recidivist, backslider, throw-back.

(Verbs) To relapse, lapse, backslide, fall back, slide back, sink back, go back, return, retrograde.

———

Réchauffé, *rifacimento* (658), recast.

(Phrases) A new lease of life; second youth; new birth; 'Richard's himself again.'

(Verbs) To return to the original state, to right itself, come to, come round, rally, revive, recover.

To restore, replace, re-establish, reinstate, reseat, replant, reconstitute, redintegrate, set right, set to rights, sort, fix, rectify, redress, reclaim, redeem, recover, recoup, recure, retrieve, cicatrize.

To refit, recruit, refresh, refocillate, rehabilitate, reconvert, renew, renovate, revitalize, revivify, reinvigorate, regenerate, rejuvenesce, rejuvenate, resuscitate, reanimate, recast, reconstruct, rebuild, reorganize.

To repair, retouch, revise (658).

To cure, heal, cicatrize, remedy, doctor, physic, medicate.

(Phrases) Recall to life; set on one's legs.

(Adjectives) Restoring, etc., restored, etc., restorative, recuperative, reparative, sanative, remedial, curative (662).

Restorable, sanable, remediable, retrievable, recoverable.

(Adverbs) In statu quo; as you were; Phoenix-like.

662 Remedy *(Substantives),* help, redress, cure, antidote, counter-poison, vaccine, antitoxin, antibiotic, antiseptic, specific, prophylactic, corrective, restorative, pick-me-up, bracer, sedative, anodyne, opiate, hypnotic, nepenthe, tranquillizer.

Febrifuge, diaphoretic, diuretic, carminative, purgative, laxative, emetic, palliative.

Physic, medicine, drug, tonic, medicament, nostrum, placebo, recipe, prescription, catholicon.

Panacea, elixir, *elixir vitae*, balm, balsam, cordial, cardiac, theriac, ptisan.

Pill, pilule, pellet, tablet, tabloid, pastille, lozenge, powder, draught, lincture, suppository.

Salve, ointment, plaster, epithem, embrocation, liniment, lotion, cataplasm, styptic, poultice, compress, pledget.

Treatment, diet, dieting, regimen.

663 Bane *(Substantives)*, scourge, curse, scathe, sting, fang, gall and wormwood.

Poison, virus, venom, toxin, microbe, germ, bacillus, miasma, mephitis, malaria, pest, rust, canker, cancer, canker-worm.

Hemlock, hellebore, nightshade, henbane, aconite, upas-tree.

Sirocco.

A viper, adder, serpent, cobra, rattlesnake, cockatrice, scorpion, wireworm, torpedo, hornet, vulture, vampire.

Science of poisons, toxicology.

(Adjectives) Poisonous, venomous, virulent, toxic, mephitic, pestilent, pestilential, miasmatic, baneful (649).

Pharmacy, pharmacology, materia medica, therapeutics, homoeopathy, allopathy, radiotherapy, actinotherapy, heliotherapy, thalassotherapy, hydrotherapy, hydropathy, osteopathy, dietetics, dietary, chirurgery, surgery, gynaecology, midwifery, obstetrics, paediatrics, geriatrics; psycho-analysis, psychiatry, psychotherapy; faith-healing.

A hospital, infirmary, pest-house, lazaretto, madhouse, asylum, lunatic asylum, mental hospital, *maison de santé*, ambulance, clinic, dispensary, sanatorium, spa, hydropathic, nursing home.

A doctor, physician, general practitioner, G.P., surgeon, anaesthetist, dentist, aurist, oculist, specialist, alienist, psycho-analyst, psychiatrist, psycho-therapist; apothecary, druggist; midwife, nurse.

(Verbs) To dose, physic, attend, doctor, nurse.

(Adjectives) Remedial, medical, medicinal, therapeutic, surgical, chirurgical, sanatory, sanative, curative, salutary, salutiferous, healing, paregoric, restorative, tonic, corroborant, analeptic, balsamic, anodyne, sedative, lenitive, demulcent, emollient, depuratory, detersive, detergent, abstersive, disinfectant, antiseptic, corrective, prophylactic, antitoxic, febrifuge, alterative, expectorant; veterinary.

Dietetic, alexipharmic, nutritious, nutritive, peptic, alimentary.

3. CONTINGENT SUBSERVIENCE

664 Safety *(Substantives),* security, surety, impregnability, invulnerability, invulnerableness, escape (671).

Safeguard, guard, guardianship, chaperonage, protection, tutelage, wardship, wardenship, safe-conduct, escort, convoy, garrison.

Watch, watch and ward, sentinel, sentry, scout, watchman, patrol, vedette, picket, bivouac.

Policeman, policewoman, police officer, constable, cop, copper, bobby, peeler, slop, bull, dick, rozzer.

Watch-dog, bandog, Cerberus.

Protector, guardian, guard (717), defender, warden, warder, preserver, chaperon, tutelary saint, guardian angel, palladium.

Custody, safe-keeping (751).

Isolation, segregation, quarantine; insurance, assurance; cover.

(Verbs) To be safe, etc.

To render safe, etc., to protect, guard, ward, shield, shelter, flank, cover, screen, shroud, ensonce, secure, fence, hedge in, entrench, house, nestle.

To defend, forfend, escort, convoy, garrison, mount guard, patrol, chaperon, picket.

(Phrases) To save one's bacon; to light upon one's feet; to weather the storm; to bear a charmed life; to make assurance doubly sure; to take no chances.

To play gooseberry.

(Adjectives) Safe, in safety, in security, secure, sure, protected, guarded, etc., snug, fireproof, waterproof, seaworthy, airworthy.

Defensible, tenable; insurable.

665 Danger *(Substantives),* peril, insecurity, jeopardy, risk, hazard, venture, precariousness, slipperiness.

Liability, exposure (177), vulnerability, vulnerable point, Achilles heel.

Hopelessness (859), forlorn hope, alarm (860), defencelessness.

(Phrases) The ground sliding from under one; breakers ahead; a storm brewing; the sword of Damocles.

(Verbs) To be in danger, etc., to be exposed to, to incur or encounter danger, run the danger of, run a risk.

To place or put in danger, etc., to endanger, expose to danger, imperil, jeopardize, compromise, adventure, risk, hazard, venture, stake.

(Phrases) To sit on a barrel of gunpowder; stand on a volcano; to engage in a forlorn hope.

(Adjectives) In danger, peril, jeopardy, etc., unsafe, insecure, unguarded, unscreened, unsheltered, unprotected, guardless, helpless, guideless, exposed, defenceless, vulnerable, at bay.

Unwarned, unadmonished, unadvised.

Dangerous, perilous, hazardous, parlous, risky, chancy, untrustworthy, fraught with danger, adventurous, precarious, critical, touch-and-go, breakneck, slippery, unsteady, shaky, tottering, top-heavy, harbourless, ticklish, dicky.

Threatening, ominous, alarming, minacious (909).

(Phrases) Not out of the wood; hanging by a thread; neck or nothing; in a tight place; between two fires; out of the frying-pan into the fire;

Invulnerable, unassailable, un-attackable, impregnable, inexpugnable.

Protecting, etc., guardian, tutelary.

Unthreatened, unmolested, unharmed, scatheless, unhazarded.

(Phrases) Out of harm's way; safe and sound; under lock and key; on sure ground; under cover; under the shadow of one's wing; the coast being clear; the danger being past; out of the wood; proof against.

(Interjections) All's well! *salva est res!* safety first!

between the devil and the deep sea; between Scylla and Charybdis; on the rocks; hard bested.

---

666 Means of safety.

Refuge *(Substantives)*, asylum, sanctuary, fastness, retreat, ark, hiding-place, dug-out, funk-hole, fox-hole, loophole, shelter, lee, cover.

Roadstead, anchorage, break-water, mole, groyne, port, haven, harbour, harbour of refuge, pier.

Fort, citadel, fortification, stronghold, strong point, keep, shield, etc. (717).

Screen, covert, wing, fence, rail, railing, wall, dike, ditch, etc. (232).

Anchor, kedge, grapnel, grappling-iron, sheet-anchor, prop, stay, main-stay, jury-mast, lifeboat, lifebuoy, lifebelt, plank, stepping-stone, umbrella, parachute, lightning-conductor, safety-valve, safety curtain, safety-lamp.

667 Source of danger.

Pitfall *(Substantives)*, rocks, reefs, sunken rocks, snags, sands, quick-sands, breakers, shoals, shallows, bank, shelf, flat, whirlpool, rapids, current, undertow, precipice, lee shore, air-pocket.

Trap, snare, gin, springe, deadfall, toils, noose, net, spring-net, spring-gun, masked battery, mine.

(Phrases) The sword of Damocles; a snake in the grass; trusting to a broken reed; a lion's den; a hornet's nest; an ugly customer.

---

668 Warning *(Substantives)*, caution, *caveat*, notice, premonition, premonishment, lesson, dehortation, monition, admonition (864); alarm (669).

Beacon, lighthouse, lightship, pharos, watch-tower, signal-post, guide-post (550).

Sentinel, sentry, watch, watchman, patrol, vedette (664); monitor, Cassandra.

(Phrases) The writing on the wall; the yellow flag; a red light; a stormy petrel; gathering clouds.

(Verbs) To warn, caution, forewarn, premonish, give notice, give warning, admonish, dehort, threaten, menace (909).

To take warning, to beware; to be on one's guard (864).

(Phrases) To put on one's guard; to sound the alarm.

(Adjectives) Warning, etc., monitory, premonitory, dehortatory, cautionary, admonitory.

Warned, etc., careful, on one's guard (459).

(Interjections) Beware! look out! mind what you are about! watch your step! let sleeping dogs lie! *foenum habet in cornu!* fore! heads! mind your back! cave!

669 Indication of danger.

Alarm *(Substantives)*, alert, alarum, alarm-bell, horn, siren, maroon, fog-signal, tocsin, tattoo, signal of distress, S O S, hue and cry.

False alarm, cry of wolf, bugbear, bugaboo, bogy.

(Verbs) To give, raise, or sound an alarm, to alarm, warn, ring the tocsin, dial 999; to cry wolf.

(Adjectives) Alarming, etc., threatening.

(Phrases) Each for himself; *sauve qui peut*.

670 Preservation *(Substantives)*, conservation, maintenance (141), support, upkeep, sustentation, deliverance, salvation, rescue, redemption, self-preservation, continuance (143).

Means of preservation, prophylaxis, preservative, preserver.

(Verbs) To preserve, maintain, support, keep, sustain, nurse, save, rescue, file (papers).

To embalm, mummify, dry, dehydrate, cure, kipper, smoke, salt, pickle, marinade, season, kyanize, bottle, pot, can, tin.

(Adjectives) Preserving, conservative, prophylactic, preservatory, hygienic.

Preserved, intact, unimpaired, uninjured, unhurt, unsinged, unmarred.

671 Escape *(Substantives)*, getaway, flight, elopement, evasion, retreat, reprieve, reprieval, deliverance, redemption, rescue.

Narrow escape, hair's-breadth, escape, close shave, close call, narrow squeak.

Means of escape: Bridge, drawbridge, loophole, ladder, plank, stepping-stone, trap-door, fire-escape, emergency exit.

A fugitive, runaway, refugee, evacuee.

(Verbs) To escape, elude, evade, wriggle out of, make or effect one's escape, make off, march off, pack off, skip, skip off, slip away, steal away, slink away, flit, decamp, run away, abscond, levant, skedaddle, scoot, fly, flee, bolt, bunk, scarper, scram, hop it, beat it, vamoose, elope, whip off, break loose, break away, get clear.

(Phrases) To take oneself off; play truant; to beat a retreat; to give one the slip; to slip the collar; to slip through the fingers; to make oneself scarce; to fly the coop; to take to one's heels; to show a clean pair of heels; to take French leave; to do a bunk; to do a guy; to cut one's lucky; to cut and run; to live to fight another day; to run for one's life; to make tracks.

(Interjections) *Sauve qui peut!* the devil take the hindmost!

(Adjectives) Escaping, etc., escaped, etc., runaway.

(Phrase) The bird having flown.

672 Deliverance *(Substantives)*, extrication, rescue, reprieve, respite, redemption, salvation, riddance, release, liberation (750); redeemableness, redeemability.

(Verbs) To deliver, extricate, rescue, save, redeem, ransom, help out, bring off, *tirer d'affaire*, to get rid, to work off, to rid.

(Phrases) To save one's bacon; to find a hole to creep out of.

(Adjectives) Delivered, saved, etc., scot-free, scatheless.

Extricable, redeemable, rescuable.

3°. *Precursory Measures*

673 Preparation *(Substantives)*, making ready, providing, provision, providence, anticipation, preconcertation, rehearsal, precaution; laying foundations, ploughing, sowing, semination, cooking, brewing, digestion,

674 Non-preparation *(Substantives)*, want or absence of preparation, inculture, inconcoction, improvidence.

Immaturity, crudeness, crudity, greenness, rawness, disqualification.

gestation, hatching, incubation, concoction, maturation, elaboration, predisposition, premeditation (611), acclimatization (613).

Physical preparation, training, drill, drilling, discipline, exercise, exercitation, gymnastics, callisthenics, eurhythmics, athletics, gymnasium, *palaestra*, prenticeship, apprenticeship, qualification, inurement, education, novitiate (537).

Putting or setting in order, putting to rights, clearance, arrangement, disposal, organization, adjustment, adaptation, disposition, accommodation, putting in tune, tuning, putting in trim, dressing, putting in harness, outfit, equipment, accoutrement, armament.

Groundwork, basis, foundation, pedestal, etc. (215), stepping-stone, first stone, scaffold, scaffolding, cradle, sketch (626).

State of being prepared, preparedness, ripeness, maturity, readiness, mellowness.

Preparer, pioneer, avant-courier, sappers and miners.

(Phrases) A stitch in time; clearing decks; a note of preparation; a breather; a trial bout; a practice swing.

(Verbs) To prepare, get ready, make ready, get up, anticipate, forecast, preestablish, preconcert, settle preliminaries, to found.

To arrange, set or put in order, set or put to rights, organize, dispose, cast the parts, mount, adjust, adapt, accommodate, trim, tidy, fit, predispose, inure, elaborate, mature, mellow, season, ripen, nurture, hatch, cook, concoct, brew, tune, put in tune, attune, set, temper, anneal, smelt, undermine, brush up, get up.

To provide, provide against, discount, make provision, keep on foot, take precautions, make sure, lie in wait for (507).

To equip, arm, man, fit out, fit up, furnish, rig, dress, dress up, furbish up, accoutre, array, fettle, vamp up, wind up.

To train, drill, discipline, break in, cradle, inure, habituate, harden, case-harden, season, acclimatize, qualify, educate, teach.

(Phrases) To take steps; prepare the ground; lay or fix the foundations,

Absence of art, state of nature, virgin soil.

An embryo, skeleton, rough copy, draft (626); germ, rudiment (153), raw material, rough diamond.

Tyro, beginner, novice, neophyte, greenhorn, new chum, pommy, recruit, sprog.

(Verbs) To be unprepared, etc., to want or lack preparation.

To improvise, extemporize (612).

To render unprepared, etc., to dismantle, dismount, dismast, disqualify, disable (645), unrig, undress (226).

(Phrases) To put *hors de combat*; to put out of gear; to spike the guns; to remove the sparking-plug.

(Adjectives) Unprepared, rudimentary, immature, embryonic, unripe, raw, green, crude, rough, roughcast, rough-hewn, unformed, unhatched, unfledged, unnurtured, uneducated, unlicked, unpolished, natural, in a state of nature, *au naturel*, unwrought, unconcocted, undigested, indigested, unrevised, unblown, unfashioned, unlaboured, unleavened, fallow, uncultivated, unsown, untilled, untrained, undrilled, unexercised, unseasoned, disqualified, unqualified, out of order, unseaworthy.

Unbegun, unready, unarranged, unorganized, unfurnished, unprovided, unequipped, undressed, in dishabille, dismantled, untrimmed.

Shiftless, improvident, unguarded, happy-go-lucky, feckless, thoughtless, unthrifty.

Unpremeditated, unseen, off-hand (612), from hand to mouth, extempore (111).

(Phrases) Caught on the hop; with their trousers down.

————

the basis, groundwork, etc.; to clear the ground or way or course; clear decks; clear for action; close one's ranks; plough the ground; dress the ground; till the soil; sow the seed; open the way; pave the way; lay a train; dig a mine; prepare a charge; erect the scaffolding; *reculer pour mieux sauter*.

Put in harness; sharpen one's tools; whet the knife; shoulder arms; put the horses to; oil up; crank up; warm up.

To prepare oneself; lay oneself out for; get into harvest; gird up one's loins; buckle on one's armour; serve one's time or apprenticeship; be at one's post; gather oneself together.

To set on foot; to lay the first stone; to break ground.

To erect the scaffold; to cut one's coat according to one's cloth; to keep one's powder dry; to beat up for recruits; to sound the note of preparation.

(Adjectives) Preparing, etc., in preparation, in course of preparation, in hand, in train, brewing, hatching, forthcoming, in embryo, afoot, afloat, on the anvil, on the carpet, on the stocks, *sur le tapis*.

Preparative, preparatory, provisional, in the rough, rough and ready (111).

Prepared, trained, drilled, etc., forearmed, ready, in readiness, ripe, mature, mellow, fledged, ready to one's hand, on tap, cut and dried, annealed, concocted, laboured, elaborated, planned (626).

(Phrases) Armed to the teeth; armed cap-à-pie; booted and spurred; in full feather; *in utrumque paratus*; in working order.

(Adverbs) In preparation, in anticipation of, etc., against.

675 Essay *(Substantives)*, endeavour, try, trial, experiment (463), probation, attempt (676), venture, adventure, tentative, *ballon d'essai*, *coup d'essai*, go crack, whack, slap, shot, speculation.

(Verbs) To try, essay, make trial of, try on, experiment, make an experiment, endeavour, strive, attempt, grope, feel one's way; to venture, adventure, speculate, take upon oneself.

(Phrases) To put out or throw out a feeler; to tempt fortune; to fly a kite; to send up a pilot balloon; to fish for information, compliments, etc.; to have a crack at; to try one's luck; to chance it; to risk it.

(Adjectives) Essaying, etc., experimental, tentative, empirical, on trial, probative, probatory, probationary.

(Adverbs) Experimentally, etc., at a venture.

676 Undertaking *(Substantives)*, enterprise, emprise, quest, mission, endeavour, attempt, move, first move, the initiative, first step.

(Verbs) To undertake, take in hand, set about, go about, set to, fall to, set to work, engage in, launch into, embark in, plunge into, take on, set one's hand to, tackle, grapple with, volunteer, take steps, launch out.

To endeavour, strive, use one's endeavours; to attempt, make an attempt, tempt.

To begin, set on foot, set agoing, take the first step.

(Phrases) To break the neck of the business; take the initiative; to get cracking; to break ground; break the ice; break cover; to pass the Rubicon; to take upon oneself; to take on one's shoulders; to put one's shoulder to the wheel; *ce n'est que le premier pas qui coûte*; well begun is half done.

To take the bull by the horns; to rush *in medias res*; to have too many irons in the fire; to attempt impossibilities.

(Adverbs) Undertaking, attempting, etc.

677 Use (*Substantives*), employment, employ, application, appliance, adhibition, disposal, exercise, exercitation.

Recourse, resort, avail, service, wear, usage, conversion to use, usufruct, utilization.

Agency (170); usefulness (644).

(*Verbs*) To use, make use of, utilize, exploit, employ (134), apply, adhibit, dispose of, work, wield, manipulate, handle, put to use; turn or convert to use; avail oneself of, resort to, have recourse to, take up with, betake oneself to.

To render useful, serviceable, available, etc.; to utilize, draw, call forth, tax, task, try, exert, exercise, practise, ply, work up, consume, absorb, expend.

To be useful, to serve one's turn (644).

(*Phrases*) To take advantage of; to turn to account; to make the most of; to make the best of; to bring to bear upon; to fall back upon; to press or enlist into the service; to make shift with; make a cat's-paw of.

To pull the strings or wires; put in action; set to work; set in motion; put in practice.

(*Adjectives*) Used, employed, etc., applied, exercised, tried, etc.

---

678 Disuse (*Substantives*), forbearance, abstinence, dispensation, desuetude (614), relinquishment, abandonment (624, 782).

(*Verbs*) To disuse, not to use, to do without, to dispense with, neglect, to let alone, to spare, waive.

To lay by; set, put, or lay aside, to discard, dismiss (756); cast off, throw off, turn off, turn out, turn away, throw away, scrap, dismantle, shelve (133), shunt, side-track, get rid of, do away with; to keep back (636).

(*Phrases*) To lay on the shelf; to lay up in a napkin; to consign to the scrapheap; to cast, heave, or throw overboard; to cast to the winds; to turn out neck and crop; to send to the right-about; to send packing.

(*Adjectives*) Disused, etc., not used, unused, unutilized, done with, unemployed, unapplied, unspent, unexercised, kept or held back.

Unessayed, untouched, uncalled-for, ungathered, unculled, untrodden.

679 Misuse (*Substantives*), misusage, misemployment, misapplication, misappropriation, abuse, profanation, prostitution, desecration.

Waste (818), wasting, spilling, exhaustion (638).

(*Verbs*) To misuse, misemploy, misapply, misappropriate, desecrate, abuse, profane, prostitute.

To waste, spill, fritter away, exhaust, throw or fling away, squander (818).

(*Phrases*) To waste powder and shot; cut blocks with a razor; cast pearls before swine.

(*Adjectives*) Misused, etc.

SECTION III—VOLUNTARY ACTION

1°. *Simple Voluntary Action*

680 Action (*Substantives*), performance, work, operation, execution, perpetration, proceeding, procedure, *démarche*, process, handiwork, handicraft, workmanship, manœuvre, evolution, transaction, bout, turn,

681 Inaction (*Substantives*), abstinence from action, inactivity (683), non-intervention, non-interference, neutrality, strike, Fabian tactics.

(*Verbs*) Not to do, to let be, abstain from doing; let or leave alone, refrain,

job, doings, dealings, business, affair.

Deed, act, overt act, touch, move, strike, blow, *coup*, feat, stunt, exploit, passage, measure, step, stroke of policy, *tour de force, coup de main, coup d'état*.

(Verbs) To act, do, work, operate, do or transact business, practise, prosecute, perpetrate, perform, execute (729), officiate, exercise, commit, inflict, strike a blow, handle, take in hand, put in hand, run.

To labour, drudge, toil, ply, set to work, pull the oar, serve, officiate, go about, turn one's hand to, dabble; to have in hand.

(Phrases) To have a finger in the pie; to take or play a part; to set to work; to put into execution (729); to lay one's hand to the plough; to ply one's task; to get on with the job; to discharge an office.

(Adjectives) Acting, etc., in action, in operation, etc., operative, in harness, in play, on duty, on foot, at work, red-handed.

(Interjection) Here goes!

desist, keep oneself from doing; let pass, lie by, let be, wait.

To undo, take down, take or pull to pieces, do away with.

(Phrases) To bide one's time; to let well alone; to cool one's heels; to stay one's hand; to wash one's hands of; to strike work; nothing doing; *nihil fit; dolce far niente*.

(Adjectives) Not doing, not done, let alone, undone, etc.; passive, neutral.

---

682 Activity *(Substantives)*, briskness, quickness, promptness, promptitude, expedition, dispatch, readiness, alertness, smartness, sharpness, nimbleness, agility (274).

Spirit, ardour, animation, life liveliness, vivacity, eagerness, *empressement, brio,* dash, *élan,* abandon, pep, go, alacrity, zeal, push, vim, energy (171), hustle, vigour, intentness.

Wakefulness, pervigilium, insomnia, sleeplessness.

Industry, assiduity, assiduousness, sedulity, sedulousness, diligence; perseverance, persistence, plodding, painstaking, drudgery, busyness, indefatigability, indefatigableness, patience, business habits.

Movement, bustle, commotion, stir, fuss, fluster, bother, pother, ado, fidget, restlessness, fidgetiness.

Officiousness, meddling, interference, interposition, intermeddling, tampering with, intrigue, *tripotage,* supererogation.

A man of action, busy bee, busybody, go-getter, zealot, devotee, meddler, hustler, whizz-kid.

(Phrases) The thick of the action; *in medias res*; too many cooks; new

683 Inactivity *(Substantives)*, inaction (681), idleness, sloth, laziness, indolence, inertness, inertia (172), lumpishness, supineness, sluggishness, segnitude, languor, torpor, quiescence, stagnation, lentor, limpness, listlessness, remissness, slackness.

Dilatoriness, cunctation, procrastination (133), relaxation, truancy, lagging, dawdling, rust, rustiness, want of occupation, resourcelessness.

Somnolence, drowsiness, doziness, nodding, oscitation, sleepiness, hypnosis.

Hypnology.

Sleep, nap, doze, slumber, shut-eye, bye-bye, snooze, dog-sleep, cat-nap, siesta, dream, faint, swoon, coma, trance, hypnotic state, snore, a wink of sleep, lethargy, hibernation, aestivation.

An idler, laggard, truant, do-nothing, lubber, sluggard, sleepy-head, slumberer, faineant, *flâneur,* loafer, drone, dormouse, slow-coach, stick-in-the-mud, lounger, slug, sundowner, bum, Weary Willie, lazybones, lotus-eater, slacker, trifler, dilettante.

brooms sweep clean; too many irons in the fire.

(Verbs) To be active, busy, stirring, etc., to busy oneself in, stir, bestir oneself, bustle, fuss, make a fuss, speed, hasten, push, make a push, go ahead, hustle; to industrialize.

To plod, drudge, keep on, hold on, persist, persevere, fag at, hammer at, peg away, stick to, buckle to, stick to work, take pains; to take or spend time in; to make progress.

To meddle, moil, intermeddle, interfere, interpose, kibitz, tamper with, fool with, get at, nobble, agitate, intrigue.

To overact, overdo, overlay, outdo, ride to death.

(Phrases) To look sharp; to lay about one; to have one's hands full; to kick up a dust; to stir one's stumps; to exert one's energies; to put one's best foot foremost; to do one's best; to do all one can; to leave no stone unturned; to have all one's eyes about one; make the best of one's time; not to let the grass grow under one's feet; to make short work of; to seize the opportunity; to come up to the scratch.

To take time by the forelock; to improve the shining hour; to make hay while the sun shines; to keep the pot boiling; to strike while the iron is hot; to kill two birds with one stone; to move heaven and earth; to go through fire and water; to do wonders; to go all lengths; to stick at nothing; to go the whole hog; to keep the ball rolling; to put one's back into it; to make things hum.

To have a hand in; to poke one's nose in; to put in one's oar; to have a finger in the pie; to mix oneself up with; steal a march upon.

(Adjectives) Active, brisk, quick, prompt, alert, on the alert, stirring, spry, sharp, smart, quick, nimble, agile, light-footed, tripping, ready, awake, broad awake, wide awake, alive, lively, live, animated, vivacious, frisky, forward, eager, strenuous, zealous, expeditious, enterprising, pushing, pushful, spirited, in earnest, up in arms, go-ahead.

Cause of inactivity (174), sedative, hypnotic, knock-out drops, hypnotism; lullaby.

(Phrases) The Castle of Indolence; *dolce far niente*; the Land of Nod; the Fabian policy; *laissez aller; laissez faire*; masterly inactivity; the thief of time.

Sleeping partner; waiter on Providence.

(Verbs) To be inactive, etc., to do nothing, let alone, lie by, lie idle, stagnate, lay to, keep quiet, hang fire, relax, slouch, loll, drawl, slug, dally, lag, dawdle, potter, lounge, loiter, laze, moon, moon about, loaf, hang about, stooge, mouch; to waste, lose, idle away, kill, trifle away, fritter away or fool away time; trifle, footle, dabble, fribble, peddle, fiddle-faddle.

To sleep, slumber, nod, close the eyes, close the eyelids, doze, drowse, fall asleep, take a nap, go off to sleep, hibernate, aestivate, vegetate.

To languish, expend itself, flag, hang fire.

To render idle, etc.; to sluggardize.

(Phrases) To fold one's arms; to let well alone; play truant; while away the time; to rest upon one's oars; to burn daylight; to take it easy; slack off.

To get one's head down; to hit the hay; to have forty winks; to sleep like a top or like a log; to sleep like a dormouse; to swing the lead; to eat the bread of idleness; to twiddle one's thumbs.

(Adjectives) Inactive, unoccupied, unemployed, unbusied, doing nothing (685), resourceless.

Indolent, easy-going, lazy, slothful, idle, thowless, fushionless, slack, inert, torpid, sluggish, languid, supine, heavy, dull, stagnant, lumpish, soulless, listless, moony, limp, languorous, exanimate.

Dilatory, laggard, lagging, tardigrade, drawling, creeping, dawdling, faddling, rusty, lackadaisical, fiddlefaddle, shilly-shally, unpractical, unbusiness-like.

Sleepy, dozy, dopy, dreamy, drowsy, somnolent, dormant, asleep,

Working, on duty, at work, hard at work, intent, industrious, up and coming, assiduous, diligent, sedulous, painstaking, business-like, practical, in harness, operose, plodding, toiling, hard-working, fagging, busy, bustling, restless, fussy, fidgety.

Persevering, indefatigable, untiring, unflagging, unremitting, unwearied, never-tiring, undrooping, unintermitting, unintermittent, unflinching, unsleeping, unslumbering, sleepless, persistent.

Meddling, meddlesome, pushing, intermeddling, tampering, etc., officious, over-officious, intriguing, managing.

(Phrases) Up and doing; up and stirring; busy as a bee; on the *qui vive*; nimble as a squirrel; the fingers itching; no sooner said than done; *nulla dies sine linea*; a rolling stone gathers no moss; the used key is always bright.

(Adverbs) Actively, etc. (684).

(Interjections) Look alive! look sharp! get a move on! get cracking! get busy! hump yourself! get weaving!

lethargic, comatose, napping, somniferous, soporific, soporous, soporose, somnific, hypnotic, narcotic, unawakened.

(Phrases) With folded arms; *les bras croisés*, with the hands in the pockets; at a loose end.

In the arms or lap of Morpheus.

---

684 Haste *(Substantives)*, dispatch, precipitancy, precipitation, precipitousness, impetuosity, post-haste, acceleration, spurt, quickness (274).

Hurry, flurry, drive, bustle, fuss, splutter, scramble, brusquerie, fidget, fidgetiness (682).

(Verbs) To haste, hasten, urge, press on, push on, bustle, hurry, hustle, buck up, precipitate, accelerate; to bustle, scramble, scuttle, scurry, scoot, plunge, rush, dash on, press on, scorch, speed.

(Phrases) To make the most of one's time; to lose not a moment; *festina lente*.

(Adjectives) Hasty, hurried, precipitate, scrambling, etc., headlong, boisterous, impetuous, brusque, abrupt, slapdash, cursory.

(Adverbs) Hastily, etc., headlong, in haste, slapdash, slap-bang, amain, hurry-scurry, helter-skelter, head and shoulders, head over heels, by fits and starts, by spurts.

(Phrases) No sooner said than done; a word and a blow.

685 Leisure *(Substantives)*, leisureliness, spare time, breathing-space, off-time, slack time, holiday, bank holiday, Sunday, sabbath, vacation, recess, red-letter day, relaxation, rest, repose, halt, pause (142), respite.

(Phrases) Otium cum dignitate; time to spare; time on one's hands.

(Verbs) To have leisure, take one's ease, repose (687), pause.

(Phrase) To shut up shop.

(Adjectives) Leisurely, undisturbed, quiet, deliberate, calm, slow (683).

(Adverbs) Leisurely, etc., at leisure.

---

686 Exertion *(Substantives)*, labour, work, toil, fag, exercise, travail, swink, sweat, exercitation, duty, trouble, pains, ado, drudgery, fagging, slavery, operoseness.

Effort, strain, grind, tug, stress,

687 Repose *(Substantives)*, rest, halt, pause, relaxation, breathing-space, respite (685).

Day of rest, *dies non*, sabbath, holiday.

(Verbs) To repose, rest, relax, take

tension, throw, stretch, struggle, spell, heft.

Gymnastics, gym, physical jerks, P.T.

(Phrases) A stroke of work; the sweat of one's brow.

(Verbs) To labour, work, exert oneself, toil, strive, use exertion, fag, strain, drudge, moil, take pains, take trouble, trouble oneself, slave, pull, tug, ply the oar, rough it, sweat, bestir oneself, get up steam, get a move on, fall to work, buckle to, stick to.

(Phrases) To set one's shoulder to the wheel; to strain every nerve; to spare no pains; to do one's utmost or damnedest; to work day and night; to work one's fingers to the bone; to do double duty; to work double tides; to put forth one's strength; to work like a nigger or a horse; to go through fire and water; to put one's best foot forward (682); to do one's level best, grub along; to lay oneself out, lean over backwards.

(Adjectives) Labouring, etc., laborious, toilsome, troublesome, operose, herculean, gymnastic, palaestric.

Hard-working, painstaking, energetic, strenuous (682).

(Adverbs) Laboriously, lustily, roundly.

(Phrases) By the sweat of the brow; with all one's might; *totis viribus*; with might and main; *vi et armis*; tooth and nail; hammer and tongs; through thick and thin; heart and soul.

rest, breathe, take breath, take one's ease, gather breath, recover one's breath, respire, pause, halt, stay one's hand, lay to, lie by, lie fallow, recline, lie down, go to rest, go to bed, go to sleep, etc., unbend, slacken.

(Phrases) To rest upon one's oars, to take a holiday; to shut up shop.

(Adjectives) Reposing, resting, etc., restful, unstrained; sabbatical.

---

688 Fatigue *(Substantives)*, lassitude, weariness (841), tiredness, exhaustion, sweat, collapse, prostration, swoon, faintness, faint, *deliquium,* syncope, yawning, anhelation; overstrain.

(Verbs) To be fatigued, etc., to droop, sink, flag, wilt, lose breath, lose wind, gasp, pant, pech, puff, yawn, drop, swoon, faint, succumb.

To fatigue, tire, weary, fag, irk, jade, harass, exhaust, knock up, prostrate, wear out, strain, overtask, overwork, overburden, overtax, overstrain, drive, sweat.

(Adjectives) Fatigued, tired, unrefreshed, weary, wearied, jaded; wayworn; overworked, hard-driven, toilworn, done up.

Breathless, out of breath, windless, out of wind, blown, winded, broken-winded.

Drooping, flagging, faint, fainting, done up, knocked up, exhausted, sinking, prostrate, spent, overspent, dead-beat, dog-tired, fagged out.

Worn out, played out, battered, shattered, weather-beaten, footsore, *hors de combat*, done for.

Fatiguing, etc., tiresome, irksome, wearisome, trying.

(Phrases) Ready to drop; tired to death; on one's last legs; run off one's legs; all in.

689 Refreshment *(Substantives)*, recovery of strength, recruiting, repair, refection, refocillation, relief, bracing, regalement, bait, restoration, revival; pick-up.

(Phrase) A giant refreshed.

(Verbs) To refresh, recruit, repair, refocillate, give tone, reinvigorate, reanimate, restore, recover.

To recover, regain, renew, etc., one's strength; perk up.

(Adjectives) Refreshing, etc., recuperative, tonic; refreshed, etc., untired, unwearied, etc. (682).

---

690 Agent *(Substantives)*, doer, performer, actor, perpetrator, practitioner, operator, hand, employee, commissionaire, executor, executrix, maker, effector, consignee, steward, broker, factor, middleman, jobber.

Artist, workman, workwoman, charwoman, worker, artisan, artificer, architect, craftsman, handicraftsman, mechanic, roustabout, machinist, machineman, manufacturer, operative, journeyman, labourer, navvy, stevedore, docker, smith, wright, day-labourer, co-worker; *dramatis personae*.

Drudge, hack, fag, man or maid of all work, hired man, hired girl, factotum, handy-man.

(Phrase) Hewers of wood and drawers of water.

691 Workshop *(Substantives)*, laboratory, manufactory, mill, shop, works, factory, mint, forge, smithy, loom, cabinet, office, bureau, studio, atelier, hive, hive of industry, workhouse, nursery, hothouse, hotbed, kitchen, dock, slip, yard, foundry.

Crucible, alembic, cauldron, matrix.

2°. *Complex Voluntary Action*

692 Conduct *(Substantives)*, course of action, practice, drill, procedure, business (625), transaction, dealing, ways, tactics, policy, polity, generalship, statesmanship, economy, strategy, husbandry, seamanship, stewardship, housekeeping, housewifery, *ménage*, regime, *modus operandi*, economy.

Execution, manipulation, handling, treatment, process, working-out, course, campaign, career, walk.

Behaviour, deportment, comportment, carriage, mien, air, demeanour, bearing, manner, observance.

(Verbs) To conduct, carry on, run, transact, execute, carry out, work out, get through, carry through, go through, dispatch, treat, deal with, proceed with, officiate, discharge, do duty, play a part or game, run a race.

To behave; to comport, acquit, demean, carry, hold, oneself.

(Phrases) To shape one's course; to paddle one's own canoe.

(Adjectives) Conducting, etc., strategical, business-like, practical, executive.

693 Direction *(Substantives)*, management, government, bureaucracy, statesmanship, conduct (692), regulation, charge, agency, senatorship, ministry, ministration, managery, directorate, directorship, chairmanship, guidance, steerage, pilotage, superintendence, stewardship, supervision, surveillance, proctorship, chair, portfolio, statecraft, politics, *haute politique*, kingcraft, cybernetics; council (696).

Helm, rudder, compass, needle, radar.

(Phrase) The reins of government.

(Verbs) To direct, manage, govern, guide, conduct, regulate, order, prescribe, brief, steer, con, pilot, have or take the direction, take the helm, have the charge of, administer, superintend, overlook, supervise, look after, see to, control, boss, run, preside, hold office, hold the portfolio.

To head, lead, show the way, etc.

(Phrase) To pull the wires.

(Adjectives) Directing, etc., managerial, gubernatorial, executive; dirigible.

694 Director *(Substantives)*, manager, executive, master (745), prime minister, premier, governor, statesman, legislator, controller, comptroller, intendent, superintendent, rector, matron, supervisor, president, preses, chairman, headman, supercargo, inspector, moderator, monitor, overseer, overlooker, shopwalker, taskmaster, leader, ringleader, demagogue, conductor, precentor, fugleman, official, jack-in-office, bureaucrat, minister, office-bearer. red-tapist, officer (726).

Conductor, steersman, helmsman, pilot, coxswain, guide, cicerone, guard, driver, engine-driver, motorman, whip, charioteer, coachman, Jehu, muleteer, teamster, chauffeur, postilion, *vetturino*.

Steward, factor, factotum, bailiff, landreeve, foreman, forewoman, gaffer, charge-hand, whipper-in, shepherd, proctor, procurator, housekeeper, major-domo, chef, master of ceremonies, M.C.

695 Advice *(Substantives)*, counsel, suggestion, recommendation, advocacy, hortation, exhortation, dehortation, instruction, charge, monition, admonition (668), admonishment, caution, warning, expostulation (616), obtestation, injunction, persuasion.

Guidance, guide, handbook, chart, compass, manual, itinerary, road-book, reference.

An adviser, senator, counsellor, counsel, consultant, specialist, monitor, mentor, Nestor, guide, teacher (540), physician, leech, doctor.

Referee, arbiter, arbitrator, referendary, assessor.

(Verbs) To advise, counsel, give advice, recommend, advocate, admonish, sub-monish, suggest, prompt, caution, warn, forewarn.

To persuade, dehort, exhort, enjoin, expostulate, charge, instruct.

To deliberate, consult together, hold a council, etc., confer, call in, refer to take advice, be closeted with.

(Phrases) To lay their heads together; to compare notes; to go into a huddle; to take counsel of one's pillow; to take one's cue from.

(Adjectives) Monitory, monitive, admonitory, recommendatory, hortatory, dehortatory, exhortatory, exhortative, warning, etc.

(Phrases) A word to the wise; *verb sap.*

(Interjection) Go to!

696 Council *(Substantives)*, conclave, court, chamber, cabinet, cabinet council, house, committee, subcommittee, board, bench, brains trust, *comitia*, staff.

Senate, *senatus*, parliament, synod, soviet, convocation, convention, congress, consistory, conventicle, chapter, chapel, witenagemot, junta, states-general, diet, Cortes, Riksdag, Thing, Storthing, Reichsrat, Reichstag, Duma, Politburo, Presidium, Comintern, Sobranje, Skupshtina, Tynewald, divan, durbar, kgotla, indala, Areopagus, sanhedrim, directory.

A meeting, assembly, sitting, session, séance, sederunt.

(Adjectives) Senatorial, curule.

697 Precept *(Substantives)*, direction, instruction, charge, prescript, prescription, recipe, receipt, order (741).

Rule, canon, code, formula, formulary, law, statute, act, rubric, maxim, apophthegm, etc. (496).

698 Skill *(Substantives)*, skilfulness, cleverness, ability, talent, genius, ingenuity, calibre, capacity, competence, shrewdness, sagacity, parts, endowment, faculty, gift, forte, strong point, turn, invention, headpiece.	**699 Unskilfulness** *(Substantives)*, inability, incompetence, incompetency, improficiency, improficiency, infelicity, inexpertness, indexterity, unaptness, ineptitude, lefthandedness, awkwardness, maladroitness, clumsiness, gaucherie, rawness,

Address, dexterity, adroitness, aptness, aptitude, facility, felicity, knack, expertness, quickness, sharpness, resourcefulness, smartness, readiness, excellence, habilitation, technique, virtuosity, artistry, ambidexterity, ambidextrousness, sleight of hand (545), know-how, knowingness.

Qualification, proficiency, panurgy, accomplishment, attainment, acquirement, craft, mastery, mastership.

Tact, knowledge of the world, *savoir faire*, discretion, finesse, worldly wisdom.

Prudence, discretion (864).

Art, science, management, tactics, manœuvring, sleight, trick, policy, strategy, jobbery, temporization, technology.

A masterstroke, *chef-d'œuvre*, a masterpiece, *tour de force*, a bold stroke, *coup de maître*, a good hit (650).

(Verbs) To be skilful, skilled, etc., to excel in, to specialize in, have the trick of, be master of; to temporize, manœuvre.

(Phrases) To play one's cards well; to stoop to conquer; to have all one's wits about one; to keep one's hand in; to know your stuff; to cut one's coat according to one's cloth; to know what one is about; to know what's what; to know the ropes.

(Adjectives) Skilled, skilful, etc., clever, able, accomplished, talented, versatile, many-sided, resourceful, ingenious, inventive, shrewd, gifted, hard-headed, sagacious, sharp-witted.

Expert, crack, dexterous, scientific, adroit, apt, sharp, handy, deft, fluent, facile, ready, quick, smart, slick, spry, yare, nimble, ambidextrous, neat-handed, fine-fingered.

Conversant, versed, proficient, efficient, capable, competent, qualified, good at, up to, master of, cut out for, at home in, knowing.

Experienced, practised, hackneyed, trained, initiated, prepared, primed, finished, schooled, thoroughbred, masterly, consummate.

slovenliness, greenness, inexperience, disability, disqualification.

Bungling, blundering, etc., blunder (495), *bêtise*; unteachableness, dumbness, dullness, stupidity (499).

Indiscretion, imprudence (863), thoughtlessness, giddiness, wildness, mismanagement, misconduct, maladministration, misrule, misgovernment, misapplication, misdirection.

(Phrases) Rule of thumb; a bad show.

(Verbs) To be unskilled, unskilful, etc.

To mismanage, bungle, blunder, botch, boggle, fumble, flounder, stumble, muff, foozle, miscue, muddle, murder, mistake, misapply, misdirect, misconduct; stultify.

(Phrases) To make a mess or hash of; to begin at the wrong end; to make sad work or a bad job of; to put one's foot in it; to lose or miss one's way; to lose one's balance; to stand in one's own light; to quarrel with one's bread and butter; to pay dear for one's whistle; to cut one's own throat; to kill the goose which lays the golden eggs; to reckon without one's host.

(Adjectives) Unskilled, etc., unskilful, bungling, etc., awkward, clumsy, unhandy, unworkmanlike, unscientific, shiftless, lubberly, *gauche*, maladroit, left-handed, hobbling, slovenly, sloppy, slatternly, giddy, gawky, dumb, dull, unteachable, at fault.

Unapt, unqualified, inhabile, incompetent, disqualified, untalented, ill-qualified, inapt, inept, inexpert, inartistic, raw, green, rusty.

Unaccustomed, unused, unhackneyed, unexercised, untrained, unpractised, undisciplined, uneducated, undrilled, uninitiated, unschooled, unconversant, unversed, inexperienced, unstatesmanlike, non-professional.

Unadvised, misadvised, ill-judged, ill-advised, unguided, misguided, foolish, wild, ill-devised, misconducted.

Technical, artistic, workmanlike, business-like, daedalian.

Discreet, politic, tactful, diplomatic, sure-footed, felicitous, strategic.

(Phrases) Up to snuff; sharp as a needle; no flies on him.

(Adverbs) Skilfully, etc., aright.

700 Proficient *(Substantives)*, adept, expert, specialist, genius, dab, crack, whiz, master, *maître*, masterhand, virtuoso, champion, first string, first fiddle, protagonist, ace, artist, tactician, marksman, old stager, veteran, top-sawyer, picked man, cunning man, conjurer, wizard, etc. (994); connoisseur (850); prodigy (872), an Admirable Crichton.

(Phrases) A man of the world; a practised hand; no slouch; a smart customer; an old file; an all-round man.

702 Cunning *(Substantives)*, craft, craftiness, wiliness, artfulness, subtlety, shrewdness, smartness, archness, insidiousness, slyness, opportunism, artificialness, artificiality.

Artifice, stratagem, wile, dodge, subterfuge, evasion, finesse, ruse, diplomacy, jobbery, backstairs influence.

Duplicity, guile, circumvention, chicane, chicanery, sharp practice, Machiavellism, legerdemain, trickery, etc. (545).

Net, toils, trap, etc. (667).

A slyboots, Ulysses, Machiavel, trickster, serpent, fox, intriguer, opportunist, time-server.

(Verbs) To be cunning, etc., to contrive, design, manœuvre, gerrymander, finesse, shuffle, wriggle, wangle, intrigue, temporize, overreach (545), circumvent, get round, nobble, undermine.

(Phrases) To play a deep game; to steal a march on; to know on which side one's bread is buttered.

(Phrases) His fingers are all thumbs; penny wise and pound foolish.

———

701 Bungler *(Substantives)*, blunderer, marplot, greenhorn, lubber, landlubber, fumbler, muddler, duffer, butter-fingers, novice, no conjurer, flat, muff, babe.

(Phrases) A poor hand at; no good at; a fish out of the water; a freshwater sailor; the awkward squad; not likely to set the Thames on fire.

———

703 Artlessness *(Substantives)*, nature, naturalness, simplicity, ingenuousness, *bonhomie*, frankness, naïveté, openness, *abandon*, candour, outspokenness, sincerity, straightforwardness, honesty (939), innocence (946).

(Phrases) Enfant terrible; a rough diamond, a mere babe.

(Verbs) To be artless, etc.

(Phrases) To call a spade a spade; not to mince one's words; to speak one's mind; to wear one's heart upon one's sleeve.

(Adjectives) Artless, natural, native, plain, simple-minded, ingenuous, candid, untutored, unsophisticated, simple, naïve, sincere, frank (543), open, frank-hearted, open-hearted, above-board, downright, unreserved, guileless, inartificial, undesigning, single-minded, honest, straightforward, outspoken, blunt, matter-of-fact.

———

(Adjectives) Cunning, crafty, artful, knowing, wily, sly, fly, pawky, smooth, sharp, smart, slim, feline, subtle, arch, designing, intriguing, contriving, insidious, canny, downy, leery, tricky, deceitful (545), artificial, deep, profound, diplomatic, vulpine, Machiavellian, time-serving.

(Phrases) Cunning as a fox; too clever by half; not born yesterday; not to be caught with chaff.

SECTION IV—ANTAGONISM

1°. *Conditional Antagonism*

704 Difficulty *(Substantives)*, hardness, toughness, hard work, uphill work, hard task, troublesomeness, laboriousness.

Impracticability, infeasibility, intractability, toughness, perverseness (471).

Embarrassment, awkwardness, perplexity, intricacy, intricateness, entanglement, knot, Gordian knot, labyrinth, net, meshes, maze, etc. (248).

Dilemma, nice point, delicate point, knotty point, stumbling-block, snag, vexed question, crux; *pons asinorum*, poser, puzzle, floorer, teaser, nonplus, quandary, strait, pass, critical situation, crisis, trial, pinch, emergency, exigency, scramble.

Scrape, hobble, fix, hole, lurch, contretemps, hitch, how-d'ye-do, slough, quagmire, hot water, pickle, stew, imbroglio, mess, ado, false position, stand, deadlock, encumbrance, cul-de-sac, impasse.

(Phrases) A Herculean task; a labour of Sisyphus; a difficult role to play; a sea of troubles; horns of a dilemma; a peck of troubles; a kettle of fish; a pretty state of things; a handful; 'Ay, there's the rub.'

(Verbs) To be difficult, etc.

To meet with, experience, labour under, get into, plunge into, be surrounded by, be encompassed with, be entangled by, struggle, contend against or grapple with difficulties.

To come to a stand, to stick fast, to be set fast, to boggle, flounder, get left.

To render difficult, etc., to embarrass, perplex, put one out, bother, pose, puzzle, floor, nonplus, ravel, entangle, gravel, faze, flummox, run hard.

(Phrases) To come to a deadlock; to be at a loss; to get into hot water; to get into a mess; to be bunkered; to weave a tangled web; to fish in troubled waters; to buffet the waves;

705 Facility *(Substantives)*, practicability, feasibility, practicableness (470).

Ease, easiness, smoothness, tractability, tractableness, ductility, flexibility, malleability, capability, disentanglement, freedom, advantage, vantage-ground.

A cinch, snap, cakewalk, walkover.

(Phrases) Plain sailing; smooth water; fair wind; a clear coast; a holiday task; a royal road; child's play; a soft job; a piece of cake.

(Verbs) To be easy, etc., to go, flow, swim, or drift with the tide or stream; to do with ease, to throw off.

To render easy, etc., to facilitate, popularize, smooth, ease, lighten, free, clear, disencumber, deobstruct, disembarrass, clear the way, smooth the way, disentangle, unclog, disengage, extricate, unravel, disburden, exonerate, emancipate, free from; to lubricate, etc. (332), relieve (834).

(Phrases) To have it all one's own way; to have a walk-over; to win in a canter; to make light (or nothing) of.

To leave a loophole; to open the door to; to pave the way to; to bridge over; to grease the wheels.

(Adjectives) Easy, facile, cushy, attainable, handy, practicable, feasible, achievable, performable, possible (470), superable, surmountable, accessible, come-at-able, get-at-able.

Easily managed or accomplished, etc., tractable, manageable, smooth, glib, pliant, yielding, malleable, ductile, flexible, plastic, submissive, docile.

At ease, free, light, unburdened, unencumbered, unloaded, disburdened, disencumbered, disembarrassed, exonerated, unrestrained, unobstructed, unimpeded, untrammelled, at home.

(Phrases) The coast being clear; as easy as falling off a log; like taking candy from a child.

to be put to one's shifts; not to know which way to turn; to skate over thin ice.

To lead one a pretty dance; to put a spoke in one's wheel; to leave in the lurch.

(Adjectives) Difficult, not easy, hard, stiff, troublesome, toilsome, formidable, laborious, onerous, operose, awkward, unwieldy, beset with or full of difficulties, Herculean, Sisyphean.

Unmanageable, tough, stubborn, hard to deal with, *difficile*, trying, provoking, ill-conditioned, refractory, perverse, crabbed, intractable, against the grain.

Embarrassing, perplexing, delicate, ticklish, pernickety, complicated, intricate, thorny, spiny, knotty, tricky, critical, pathless, trackless, labyrinthine.

Impracticable, not possible, impossible (471), not practicable, not feasible, unachievable, un-come-at-able, inextricable, impassable, innavigable, desperate, insuperable, insurmountable, unplayable.

In difficulty, perplexed, etc., beset, water-logged, put to it, hard put to it, run hard, hard pressed, thrown out, adrift, at fault, abroad, pushed.

Stranded, aground, stuck fast, at bay.

(Phrases) At a standstill; at a stand; up against it; up a gum-tree; out of one's depth; at the end of one's tether; in a cleft stick; on a wrong scent; driven from pillar to post; things being come to a pretty pass; at a pinch; between two stools; in the wrong box; in a fix; in a hole; in a tight place; in the cart; in the soup.

(Adverbs) With difficulty, hardly, etc., against the stream, against the grain, uphill.

Quite at home; in one's element; in smooth water; on velvet.

(Adverbs) Easily, etc., swimmingly.

2°. Active Antagonism

706 Hindrance *(Substantives)*, prevention, preclusion, impedance, retardment, retardation.

Obstruction, stoppage, interruption, interclusion, oppilation, interception, restriction, restraint, inhibition, embargo, blockade, embarrassment.

Interference, interposition, obtrusion, discouragement, chill.

An impediment, hindrance, obstacle, obstruction, bunker, hazard, let, stumbling-block, snag, check, impasse, countercheck, *contretemps*, set-back, hitch, bar, barrier, barrage, barricade, turnpike, dead wall, bulkhead, portcullis, etc. (717), dam, weir, broom, turnstile, tourniquet.

Drawback, objection.

An encumbrance, impedimenta, onus, clog, skid, drag, weight, dead weight, lumber, top-hamper, pack, millstone, incubus, nightmare; trammel, etc. (752).

707 Aid *(Substantives)*, assistance, help, succour, support, advocacy, relief, advance, furtherance, promotion.

Coadjuvancy, patronage, interest, championship, countenance, favour, helpfulness.

Sustentation, subvention, subsidy, alimentation, nutrition, nourishment, ministration, ministry, accommodation.

Supplies, reinforcements, succours, contingents, recruits; physical support (215); relief, rescue.

(Phrases) Corn in Egypt; a *deus ex machina.*

(Verbs) To aid, assist, help, succour, support, sustain, uphold, subscribe to, finance, promote, further, abet, advance, foster, cherish, foment; to give, bring, furnish, afford or supply support, etc., to reinforce, recruit, nourish, nurture.

A hinderer, marplot; killjoy, interloper, passenger; opponent (710).

(Phrases) A lion in the path; a millstone round one's neck; a wet blanket; the old man of the sea; *damnosa hereditas*; back to square one.

(Verbs) To hinder, impede, prevent, preclude, retard, slacken, obviate, forefend, avert, turn aside, ward off, draw off, cut off, counteract, undermine.

To obstruct, stop, stay, let, make against, bar, debar, inhibit, scotch, squash, cramp, restrain, check, stonewall, set back, discourage, discountenance, foreclose.

To thwart, traverse, contravene, interrupt, intercept, interclude, frustrate, defeat, disconcert, embarrass, baffle, undo, intercept; to balk, unsight, cushion, stymie, spoil, mar.

To interpose, interfere, intermeddle, obtrude (682).

To hamper, clog, cumber, encumber, saddle with, load with, overload, overlay, lumber, block up, incommode, hustle; to curb, shackle, fetter; to embog.

(Phrases) To lay under restraint; to tie the hands; to keep in swaddling-bands.

To stand in the way of; to take the wind out of one's sails; to break in upon; to run or fall foul of; to put a spoke in the wheel; to throw cold water on; to nip in the bud; to apply the closure.

(Adjectives) Hindering, etc., in the way of, impedimental, inimical, unfavourable, onerous, burdensome, cumbrous, intercipient, obstructive.

Hindered, etc., wind-bound, storm-stayed, water-logged, heavy-laden.

Unassisted, unaided, unhelped, unsupported, single-handed, unbefriended.

(Phrase) Prevention is better than cure.

To favour, countenance, befriend, smile upon, encourage, patronize, make interest for.

To second, stand by, relieve, rescue, back, back up, take part with, side with, to come or pass over to, to join, to rally round, play up to.

To serve, do service, minister to, oblige, humour, cheer, accommodate, work for, administer to, pander to; to tend, attend, take care of, wait on, nurse, dry-nurse, entertain.

To speed, expedite, forward, quicken, hasten, set forward.

(Phrases) To take the part of; consult the wishes of; to take up the cudgels for; to espouse the cause of; to enlist under the banners of; to lend or bear a hand; to hold out a helping hand; to give one a lift; to do one a good turn; to see one through; to take in tow; to pay the piper; to help a lame dog over the stile; to give a leg-up.

(Adjectives) Aiding, helping, assisting, etc., auxiliary, adjuvant, ancillary, accessory, ministrant, subservient, subsidiary, helpful.

Friendly, amicable, favourable, propitious, well-disposed, neighbourly.

(Adverbs) On or in behalf of; in the service of; under the auspices of; hand in hand.

(Interjections) Help! save us! *à moi!*

---

708 Opposition *(Substantives)*, antagonism, oppugnancy, oppugnation, counteraction (179), contravention, impugnment, control, clashing, collision, competition, conflict, rivalry, emulation.

Absence of aid, etc., counterplot (718).

(Phrase) A head wind.

709 Co-operation *(Substantives)*, coadjuvancy, collaboration, concert, collusion, participation, complicity, co-efficiency, concurrence (178).

Alliance, colleagueship, freemasonry, joint-stock, co-partnership, coalition, combine, syndicate (778), amalgamation, federation, confederation (712).

(Verbs) To oppose, antagonize, cross, counteract, control, contravene, countervail, counterwork, contradict, belie, controvert, oppugn, stultify, thwart, counter, countermine, run counter, go against, collide with, clash, rival, emulate, put against, militate against, beat against, stem, breast, encounter, compete with, withstand, to face, face down.

(Phrases) To set one's face against; to make a dead set against; to match (or pit) oneself against; to stand out against; to fly in the face of; to fall foul of; to come into collision with; to be or to play at cross-purposes; to kick against the pricks; to buffet the waves; to cut one another's throats; to join issue.

(Adjectives) Opposing, etc., adverse, antagonistic, opposed, conflicting, contrary, unfavourable, unfriendly, hostile, inimical; competitive, emulous.

(Phrases) Up in arms; at daggers drawn.

(Adverbs) Against, versus, counter to, against the grain; against the stream, tide, wind, etc., in the way of, in spite of, in despite of, in the teeth of, in the face of, *per contra*; single-handed.

Across, athwart, overthwart.

Though, although, (179), even, *quand même*, all the same.

(Phrases) In spite of one's teeth; with the wind in one's teeth.

(Phrases) A helping hand; a long pull.

(Verbs) To co-operate, combine, concur, conspire, concert, collaborate, draw or pull together, to join with, collude, unite one's efforts, club together, fraternize, be in league, etc., with, be a party to, to side with.

(Phrases) To make common cause; to be in the same boat; to stand shoulder to shoulder; to play into the hands of; to hunt in couples; to hit it off together; to lay their heads together; to play ball.

(Adjectives) Co-operating, etc., co-operative, co-operant, in co-operation, etc., in concert, allied, clannish; favourable (707).

Unopposed, unobstructed, unimpeded.

(Phrase) Wind and weather permitting.

(Adverbs) As one man (488).

---

710 Opponent *(Substantives)*, antagonist, adversary, adverse party, opposition, rival, competitor, pacemaker, enemy, foe (891), assailant; malcontent.

---

711 Auxiliary *(Substantives)*, assistant, adjuvant, adjunct, adjutant, help, helper, helpmate, helpmeet, colleague, partner, side-kick, *confrère*, coadjutor, co-operator collaborator, co-belligerent, ally, aide-de-camp, accomplice, accessory, stand-in, stooge.

Friend (890), confidant, champion, partisan, right hand, stand-by; adherent, *particeps criminis,* confederate, bottle-holder, second, candle-holder, servant (746); *fidus Achates.*

(Phrase) Deus ex machina.

---

712 Party *(Substantives)*, side, partnership, fraternity, sodality, company, society, firm, house, establishment, body, corporation, corporate body, union, association, syndicate, guild, tong, joint concern, combine, trust, cartel.

Fellowship, brotherhood, sisterhood, denomination, communion, community, clan, clanship, club, friendly society, clique, junto, coterie, faction, gang, ring, circle, *camarilla,* cabal, league, confederacy, confederation, federation; *esprit de corps;* alliance, partisanship.

Band, staff, crew, team, set, posse, phalanx, *dramatis personae.*

(Verbs) To unite, join, club together, join forces, federate, co-operate, befriend, aid, etc. (707), cement, form a party, league, etc., to be in the same boat.

(Adjectives) In partnership, alliance, etc., federal, federated, bounded, banded, linked, cemented, etc., together, embattled.

713 Discord *(Substantives)*, disagreement (24), variance, difference, divergence, dissent, dissension, misunderstanding, jar, jarring, clashing, friction, odds, dissonance, disaccord.

Disunion, schism, breach, falling out, division, split, rupture, disruption, open rupture, *brouillerie*, feud, vendetta, contentiousness, litigiousness, strife, contention (720); emnity (889).

Dispute, controversy, polemics, quarrel, tiff, spat, *tracasserie*, altercation, imbroglio, bickering, snip-snap, chicanery, squabble, row, shemozzle, rumpus, racket, fracas, brawl, bear garden, Donnybrook, debate (476).

Litigation, words, war of words, battle of the books, logomachy, wrangling, wrangle, jangle, breach of the peace, declaration of war (722).

Subject of dispute, ground of quarrel, disputed point, vexed question, bone of contention, apple of discord, *casus belli*.

(Verbs) To be discordant, etc., to differ, dissent, disagree, clash, jar, to misunderstand one another.

714 Concord *(Substantives)*, accord, agreement (23), unison, unity, union, good understanding, quiet, peace, conciliation, unanimity (488), harmony, amity, sympathy (897), *entente cordiale, rapprochement*, alliance.

(Phrases) The bonds of harmony; a happy family; kittens in a basket; a happy band of brothers.

(Verbs) To agree, accord, be in unison, etc., to harmonize with, fraternize, stand in with.

(Phrases) To understand one another; to see eye to eye with; to hit it off; to keep the peace; to pull together.

(Adjectives) Concordant, congenial, agreeing, etc., united, in unison, etc., harmonious, allied, cemented, friendly (888), amicable, fraternal, at peace, peaceful, pacific, tranquil.

(Phrases) At one with; with one voice.

To fall out, dispute, controvert, litigate, to quarrel, argue, wrangle, squabble, bicker, spar, jangle, nag, brawl; to break with; to declare war.

To embroil, entangle, disunite, set against, pit against; to sow dissension, disunion, discord, etc. among.

(Phrases) To be at odds with; to fall foul of; to have words with; to have a bone to pick with; to have a crow to pluck with; to have a chip on one's shoulder; to be at variance with; to be at cross purposes; to join issue; to pick a quarrel with; to part brass rags; to chew the fat or rag; to go to the mat with; to live like cat and dog.

To set by the ears; to put the cat among the pigeons; to sow or stir up contention.

(Adjectives) Discordant, disagreeing, differing, disunited, clashing, jarring, discrepant, divergent, dissentient, sectarian, at variance, controversial.

Quarrelsome, disputatious, litigious, litigant, factious, pettifogging, polemic, schismatic; unpacified, unreconciled.

(Phrases) At odds; on bad terms; in hot water; at daggers drawn; up in arms; out of tune; at sixes and sevens; at loggerheads; a house divided against itself; no love lost between them.

715 Defiance *(Substantives)*, challenge, dare, cartel, daring, war-cry, slogan, college yell, war-whoop.

(Verbs) To defy, challenge, dare, brave, beard, bluster, look big.

(Phrases) To set at naught; snap the fingers at; to cock a snook at; to bid defiance to; set at defiance; to hurl defiance at; to double the fist; to show a bold front; to brave it out; to show fight; to throw down the gauntlet or glove; to call out.

(Adjectives) Defying, etc., defiant.

(Adverbs) In defiance of; with arms akimbo.

(Interjections) Come on! let 'em all come! do your worst!

(Phrase) Nemo me impune lacessit.

716 Attack *(Substantives)*, aggression, offence, assault, charge, onset, onslaught, battue, brunt, thrust, pass, passado, cut, sally, inroad, invasion, irruption, incursion, excursion, sortie, camisade, storm, storming, boarding, escalade, foray, raid, air raid, razzia, dragonnade (619), siege, investment.

Fire, volley, cannonade, barrage, blitz, broadside, bombardment, stonk, hate, raking fire, platoon-fire, fusillade.

Kick, punch (276), lunge, a run at, a dead set at, carte and tierce, a back-hander.

An assailant, aggressor, invader.

(Verbs) To attack, assault, assail, go for, fall upon, close with, charge, bear down upon, set on, have at, strike at, run at, make a run at, butt, tilt at, poke at, make a pass at, thrust, pitch into, kick, buffet, bonnet, beat (972), lay about one, lift a hand against, come on, have a fling at, slap on the face, pelt, throw stones, etc., to round on.

To shoot, shoot at, fire at, fire upon, let fly at, brown, pepper, bombard, shell, bomb, dive-bomb, blitz, strafe, prang.

To beset, besiege, lay siege to, invest, beleaguer, open the trenches, invade, raid, storm, board, scale the walls.

To press one hard, be hard upon, drive one hard.

(Phrases) To draw the sword against; to launch an offensive; take the offensive; assume the aggressive; make a dead set at.

To give the cold steel to; to lay down a barrage; to pour in a broadside; to fire a volley.

717 Defence *(Substantives)*, self-defence, self-preservation, protection, ward, guard, guardianship, shielding, etc., resistance (719), safety (664).

Fence, wall, parapet, dike, ditch, fosse, moat (232), boom, mound, mole, outwork, trench, foxhole, dug-out, shelter, Anderson shelter, Morrison shelter, entrenchment, fortification, embankment, bulwark, barbican, battlement, stockade, laager, zareba, abattis, turret, barbette, casemate, muniment, vallum, circumvallation, contravallation, barbed-wire entanglement, sunk fence, ha-ha, buttress, abutment, breastwork, portcullis, glacis, bastion, redoubt, rampart.

Hold, stronghold, keep, donjon, palladium, fort, fortress, blockhouse, pillbox, hedgehog, sconce, citadel, tower, castle, capitol, fastness, asylum (666).

Anchor, sheet-anchor.

Shield, armour, buckler, aegis, breastplate, coat of mail, cuirass, hauberk, habergeon, chevaux de frise, screen, etc. (666), helmet, tin hat, battle bowler, casque, shako, bearskin, gas-mask, panoply; fender, torpedo-net, paravane, cow-catcher, buffer.

Defender, protector, guardian (664), champion, protagonist, knight errant; garrison, picket.

(Verbs) To defend, shield, fend, fence, entrench, guard (664), keep off, keep at bay, ward off, beat off, parry, repel, bear the brunt of, put to flight.

(Phrases) To act on the defensive; to maintain one's ground; to stand

(Adjectives) Attacking, etc., aggressive, offensive, up in arms.

———

at bay; to give a warm reception to.

(Adjectives) Defending, etc., defensive, defended, etc., armed, armoured, armour-plated, iron-clad, loopholed, sandbagged, castellated, panoplied, proof, bullet-proof, bomb-proof.

(Phrases) Armed cap-à-pie; armed to the teeth.

(Adverbs) Defensively, on the defence, on the defensive, at bay.

718 Retaliation *(Substantives)*, reprisal, retort, come-back, counter-stroke, reciprocation, *tu quoque*, re-crimination, retribution, counterplot, counterproject, counterblast, *lex talionis*, revenge (919), compensation (30).

(Phrases) Tit for tat; a *quid pro quo*; a Roland for an Oliver; diamond cut diamond; the biter bit; catching a Tartar; a game two can play at; hoist with his own petard.

(Verbs) To retaliate, retort, cap, reciprocate, recriminate, counter, get even with one, pay off.

(Phrases) To turn the tables; to return the compliment; to pay off old scores; to pay in one's own coin; to give as good as one got.

(Adjectives) Retaliating, retaliatory, retaliative, recriminatory, recriminative.

(Interjection) You're another!

719 Resistance *(Substantives)*, stand, oppugnation, reluctation, front, repulse, rebuff, opposition (708), disobedience (742), recalcitration.

Strike, industrial action, lockout, tumult, riot, pronunciamento, *émeute*, mutiny.

Revolt, rising, insurrection, re-bellion, *coup d'état, putsch*.

(Verbs) To resist, not to submit, etc., to withstand, stand against, stand firm, make a stand, repugn, reluct, reluctate, confront, grapple with, face down.

To kick, kick against, recalcitrate, lift the hand against (716), repel, repulse, rise, revolt, mutiny.

(Phrases) To show a bold front; to make head against; to stand one's ground; to stand the brunt of; to hold one's own; to keep at bay; to stem the torrent; to champ the bit; to sell one's life dearly.

To fly in the face of; to kick against the pricks; to take the bit between one's teeth.

———

(Adjectives) Resisting, etc., resistive, resistant, refractory, mutinous, recalcitrant, rebellious, up in arms, out.

Unyielding, unconquered, indomitable.

(Interjections) Hands off! keep off!

720 Contention *(Substantives)*, contest, struggle, contestation, debate (476), logomachy, paper war, litigation, high words, rivalry, corrivalry, corrivalship, competition, *concours*, gymkhana, race, heat, match, tie, bickering, strife (713).

Wrestling, jiu-jitsu, pugilism, boxing, fisticuffs, spar, prize-fighting, athletics, sports, gymnastics, set-to, round, fracas, row, shindy, scrap, dust, rumpus, shemozzle, stramash,

721 Peace *(Substantives)*, amity, truce, armistice, harmony (714), tranquillity.

(Phrases) Piping time of peace; a quiet life.

(Verbs) To be at peace, etc., to keep the peace, etc. (714), pacify (723).

(Adjectives) Pacific, peaceable, peaceful, tranquil, untroubled, blood-less, halcyon.

———

outbreak, clash, collision, shock, breach of the peace, brawl, Donnybrook (713).

Conflict, skirmish, rencounter, scuffle, encounter, velitation, tussle, scrimmage, scrummage, broil, fray, affray, *mêlée*, affair, brush, bout, fight, battle, combat, action, engagement, battle royal, running fight, free fight, joust, tournament, tourney, pitched battle, death struggle, Armageddon.

Naval engagement, naumachy, sea-fight; air duel, dogfight.

Duel, satisfaction, monomachy, single combat, passage of arms, affair of honour, a triangular duel.

(Verbs) To contend, contest, struggle, vie with, emulate, rival, race, race with, outvie, battle with, cope with, compete, join issue, bandy words with, try conclusions with, close with, square, buckle with, spar, box, tussle, fence, wrestle, joust, enter the lists, take up arms, take the field, encounter, struggle with, grapple, tackle, engage with, pitch into, strive with, fall to, encounter, collide with.

(Phrases) Join battle; fall foul of; have a brush with; break the peace; take up the cudgels; unsheathe the sword; break a lance; to run a tilt at; give satisfaction; measure swords; exchange shots; lay about one; cut and thrust; fight without the gloves; go on the warpath.

(Adjectives) Contending, etc., contentious, combative, bellicose (722); pugilistic, agonistic, competitive, rival, polemical (476), rough-and-tumble.

(Phrases) A word and a blow; pull devil, pull baker.

722 Warfare *(Substantives)*, war, hostilities, fighting, etc., arms, the sword, open war, *ultima ratio*, war to the knife.

Battle array, campaign, crusade, expedition, operation, mission, warpath.

Warlike spirit, military spirit, militarism, bellicosity.

The art of war, tactics, strategy, military evolutions, arms, service, campaigning, tented field; Mars, Bellona.

War-cry, slogan, fiery cross, trumpet, clarion, bugle, pibroch, warwhoop, beat of drum, tom-tom; mobilization.

(Phrases) The mailed fist; wager of battle.

(Verbs) To arm, fight, set to, spar, scrap, tussle, joust, tilt, box, skirmish, fight hand to hand, fence, measure swords, engage, combat, give battle, go to battle, join battle, engage in battle, raise or mobilize troops, declare war, wage war, go to war, come to blows, break a lance with, appeal to arms, appeal to the sword, give satisfaction, take the

723 Pacification *(Substantives)*, reconciliation, accommodation, arrangement, *modus vivendi*, adjustment, terms, amnesty.

Peace-offering, olive-branch, calumet or pipe of peace, preliminaries of peace.

Pacifism, pacificism, appeasement.

Truce, armistice, suspension of arms, of hostilities, etc., convention, *détente*.

Flag of truce, white flag, cartel.

(Phrases) Hollow truce; cold war; *pax in bello*.

(Verbs) To make peace, pacify, make it up, reconcile, conciliate, propitiate, appease, tranquillize, compose, allay, settle differences, restore harmony, heal the breach.

(Phrases) To put up the sword; to sheathe the sword; to beat swords into ploughshares; to bury the hatchet; to smoke the pipe of peace; to close the temple of Janus; to cry quits.

(Adjectives) Pacified, etc., pacific, conciliatory.

———

field, keep the field, fight it out, fight to a finish, spill blood, carry on war, carry on hostilities, to fight one's way, to serve, to fight like devils, to sell one's life dearly.

(Phrases) To see service; to smell powder; to go over the top.

(Adjectives) Contending, etc., unpeaceful, unpacific, contentious, belligerent, bellicose, jingo, chauvinistic, martial, warlike, military, militant, soldierly, soldierlike, gladiatorial, chivalrous, in arms, embattled.

(Phrases) Together by the ears; sword in hand.

(Adverbs) Pendente lite, the battle raging, in the cannon's mouth; in the thick of the fray.

(Interjections) To arms! the Philistines be upon thee!

724 Mediation *(Substantives)*, intervention, interposition, interference, intermeddling, intercession, parley, negotiation, arbitration, conciliation, mediatorship, good offices, diplomacy, peace-offering, eirenicon.

A mediator, intermediary, go-between, intercessor, peacemaker, diplomat, diplomatist, negotiator, troubleshooter, ombudsman.

(Verbs) To mediate, intermediate, intercede, interpose, interfere, intervene, negotiate, arbitrate, compromise, meet half-way.

(Phrase) To split the difference.

725 Submission *(Substantives)*, surrender, non-resistance, appeasement, deference, yielding, capitulation, cession.

Homage, obeisance, bow, curtsy, kneeling, genuflexion, prostration, kow-tow.

(Verbs) To surrender, succumb, submit, yield, give in, bend, cringe, crawl, truckle to, knuckle down or under, knock under, capitulate, lay down or deliver up one's arms, retreat, give way, cave in.

(Phrases) Beat a retreat; strike one's flag or colours; surrender at discretion; make a virtue of necessity; to come to terms.

To eat humble pie; to eat dirt; to swallow the pill; to kiss the rod; to turn the other cheek; to lick a person's boots.

(Adjectives) Surrendering, etc., non-resisting, unresisting, submissive, downtrodden.

Undefended, untenable, indefensible.

726 Combatant *(Substantives)*, belligerent, champion, disputant, controversialist, litigant, competitor, rival, corrival, assailant, bully, bruiser, fighter, duellist, fightingman, pugilist, pug, boxer, the fancy, prize-fighter, fighter, duellist, fighting-man, pugilist, buckler, fire-eater, berserker; swordsman, wrestler, Amazon, Paladin, son of Mars; staff, *état-major*, brass hats; militarist.

726A Non-combatant *(Substantives)*, civilian; passive resister, conscientious objector, conchy, Cuthbert, pacifist, pacificist; non-effective.

Quaker, Quirites.

(Adjectives) Non-effective.

Warrior, soldier, campaigner, veteran, man-at-arms, redcoat, man in khaki, Tommy Atkins, tommy, doughboy, G.I., *poilu*, trooper, dragoon, hussar, grenadier, fusilier, guardsman, lifeguard, lancer, cuirassier, spearman, musketeer, carabineer, rifleman, sniper, sharpshooter, *bersagliere*;

ensign, standard-bearer, halberdier; private, subaltern, conscript, recruit, cadet; effectives, line, rank and file, cannon fodder, P.B.I.

Engineer, artilleryman, gunner, cannoneer, bombardier, sapper, miner; archer, bowman.

Paratrooper, aircraftman, erk, pilot, observer, aircrew.

Marine, jolly, leatherneck; seaman, bluejacket, tar, A.B.

Guerrilla, Maquis, partisan, cossack, sepoy, gurkha, spahi, janizary, zouave, bashi-bazouk.

Armed force, the army, the military, regulars, soldiery, infantry, mounted infantry, fencibles, volunteers, territorials, yeomanry, cavalry, artillery, guns, tanks, armour, commando.

Militia, irregulars, *francs-tireurs*, Home Guard, train-band.

Legion, phalanx, myrmidons, squadron, wing, group, troop, cohort, regiment, corps, platoon, battalion, unit, mob, company (72), column, detachment, brigade, division, garrison, battle array, order of battle.

727 Arms *(Substantives)*, weapons, armament, armour, armoury, quiver, arsenal, magazine, armature.

Mail, chain-mail, lorication; ammunition, powder, gunpowder, gun-cotton, dynamite, gelignite, T.N.T., cordite, lyddite, cartridge, cartouche (635).

Artillery, park, ordnance piece, gun, cannon, swivel, howitzer, carronade, culverin, field-piece, machine-gun, Gatling, Maxim, submachine-gun, tommy-gun, mitrailleuse, pom-pom, mortar, grenade, petronel, petard, falconet.

Fire-arms, side-arms, stand of arms, musketry, musket, smooth-bore, muzzle-loader, firelock, match-lock, flint-lock, fowling-piece, rifle, revolver, six-shooter, carbine, blunderbuss, pistol, gat, rod, betsy, automatic pistol, derringer, Winchester, Lee-Metford, Mauser, Bren gun, Bofors, Sten gun, Lewis gun, bazooka.

Bow, arquebus (or harquebus), cross-bow, sling, catapult.

Missile, projectile, shot, round-shot, ball, shrapnel; grape, grape-shot, chain-shot, bullet, stone, shell, gas-shell, bomb, land-mine, block-buster, flying bomb, buzz-bomb, doodlebug, guided missile, V1, V2, atomic bomb, hydrogen bomb, torpedo, rocket, ballistics.

Pike, lance, spear, javelin, assagai, dart, arrow, reed, shaft, bolt, boomerang, harpoon.

Bayonet, sword, sabre, broadsword, cutlass, falchion, scimitar, rapier, skean, toledo, tuck, claymore, kris (or creese), dagger, dirk, hanger, poniard, stiletto, stylet, dudgeon, axe, bill, pole-axe, battle axe, halberd, tomahawk, bowie-knife, snickersnee, yataghan, kukri.

Club, mace, truncheon, staff, bludgeon, cudgel, knobkerrie, life-preserver, knuckle-duster, shillelagh, bat, cosh, sandbag, lathi.

Catapult, battering-ram; tank.

728 Arena *(Substantives)*, field, walk, battle-field, field of battle, lists, palaestra, campus, playing field, recreation ground, playground, course, cinder-track, dirt-track, gridiron, diamond, pitch, links, rink, court, platform, stage, boards, race-course, *corso*, circus, ring, cockpit, bear garden, scene of action, theatre of war, the enemy's camp, amphitheatre, hippodrome, coliseum (or colosseum), proscenium.

SECTION V—RESULTS OF VOLUNTARY ACTION

729 Completion *(Substantives)*, accomplishment, performance, fulfilment, fruition, execution, achievement, dispatch, work done, superstructure, finish, termination, denouement, catastrophe, conclusion, culmination, climax, consummation, *fait accompli*, winding up, the last stroke, finishing stroke, *coup de grâce*, last finish, final touch, crowning touch, coping-stone, end (67), arrival (292), completeness (52).

(Adjectives) To complete, effect, perform, do, execute, go through, accomplish, fulfil, discharge, achieve, compass, effectuate, dispatch, knock off, close, terminate, conclude, finish, end (67), consummate, elaborate, bring about, bring to bear, bring to pass, get through, carry through, bring through, bring off, pull off, work out, make good, carry out, wind up, dispose of, bring to a close, termination, conclusion, etc.

To perfect, bring to perfection, stamp, put the seal to, polish off, crown.

To reach, arrive (292), touch, reach, attain the goal; to run one's race.

(Phrases) To give the last finish or finishing touch; to be through with; to get it over; to deliver the goods; to shut up shop.

(Adjectives) Completing, final, terminal, concluding, conclusive, exhaustive, crowning, etc., done, completed, wrought.

(Phrases) It is all over; *finis coronat opus; actum est.*

(Adverbs) Completely, etc. (52), out of hand, effectually, with a vengeance, with a witness.

730 Non-completion *(Substantives)*, inexecution, shortcoming (304), non-fulfilment, non-performance, neglect; incompleteness (53); a drawn battle or game, a draw, a stalemate.

(Phrases) The web of Penelope; one swallow does not make a summer.

(Verbs) Not to complete, perform, etc., to fall short of, leave unfinished, let slip, lose sight of, neglect, leave undone, etc., draw.

(Phrases) To scotch the snake, not kill it; hang fire; do by halves.

(Adjectives) Not completed, etc., uncompleted, incomplete, unfinished, left undone (53), short, unaccomplished, unperformed, unexecuted.

In progress, in hand, proceeding, going on, on the stocks.

(Adverbs) Re infecta; nihil fit.

---

731 Success *(Substantives)*, successfulness, speed, thrift, advance, luck, good fortune (734), godsend, prize, windfall, trump card, hit, stroke, lucky strike, break; lucky or fortunate hit; bold stroke, master-stroke, *coup de maître*, knock-out blow (698), checkmate.

Continued success, run of luck, time well spent, tide, flood, high tide, heyday.

Advantage over, ascendancy, mastery, conquest, subdual, victory, subjugation, triumph, exultation (884).

732 Failure *(Substantives)*, unsuccess, non-success, disappointment, blow, frustration, inefficacy, discomfiture, abortion, miscarriage, lost trouble; vain, ineffectual, or abortive attempt or effort.

A mistake, error, blunder, fault, miss, oversight, blot, slip, trip, stumble, claudication, breakdown, false step, wrong step, howler, floater, clanger, boner, *faux pas, bêtise*, titubation, scrape, botch, bungle, foozle, mess, washout, stalemate, botchery, fiasco, flop, frost, sad work, bad job, bad show, want of skill.

A conqueror, victor, winner.

(Phrase) A feather in one's cap.

(Verbs) To succeed, to be successful, to come off successful, to be crowned with success, to come or go off well, catch on, to thrive, speed, prosper, bloom, blossom, flourish, go on well, be well off.

To gain, attain, carry, secure, or win a point or object; to triumph, be triumphant, etc.; to surmount, overcome, conquer, master, or get over a difficulty or obstacle; to score, make a hit.

To advance (282), come on, get on, gain ground, make one's way, make progress, progress, worry along, get by.

To bring to bear, to bring about, to effect, accomplish, complete (729), manage, contrive to, make sure; to reap, gather, etc., the benefit of.

To master, get the better of, conquer, subdue, subjugate, quell, reduce, overthrow, overpower, vanquish, get under; get or gain the ascendancy, obtain a victory; to worst, defeat, beat, lick, drub, trim, settle, floor, knock out, put down, trip up, beat hollow, checkmate, non-suit, trip up the heels of, capsize, shipwreck, ruin, kibosh, do for, victimize, put to flight, drown, etc.; to roll in the dust, to trample under foot, to wipe the floor with.

To baffle, disconcert, frustrate, confound, discomfit, dish, foil, outgeneral, outmanœuvre, outflank, outwit, overreach, balk, outvote, circumvent, score off, catch napping.

To answer, succeed, work well, turn out well.

(Phrases) to sail before the wind; to swim with the tide; to stem the torrent; to turn a corner; to weather a point; to fall on one's legs or feet; *se tirer d'affaire*; to take a favourable turn; to turn up trumps; to have the ball at one's feet; to come off with flying colours; to win or gain the day; to win the palm; to win one's spurs; to breast the tape; to bear away the bell.

To get the upper hand; to gain an

Mischance, mishap, misfortune, misadventure, disaster, bad or hard luck (735).

Repulse, rebuff, set-down, defeat, fall, downfall, rout, discomfiture, collapse, smash, crash, wreck, perdition, shipwreck, ruin, subjugation, overthrow, death-blow, quietus, knockout, destruction.

A victim, loser, bankrupt, insolvent (808).

(Phrases) A losing game; a flash in the pan; a wild-goose chase; a mare's-nest; a fool's errand.

(Verbs) To fail, to be unsuccessful etc., to come off badly, go badly, go amiss, abort, go wrong, fall flat, flop, fall through, fizzle out, turn out ill, work ill, lose ground, recede (283), fall short of (304), prang (162, 176).

To miss, miss one's aim; to labour, toil, etc., in vain; to lose one's labour, flounder, limp, miss one's footing, miscarry, abort; to make vain, ineffectual, or abortive efforts; to make a slip; to make or commit a mistake, commit a fault, make a mess of; to botch, make a botch of, bungle, foozle.

To be defeated, overthrown, foiled, worsted, let down, etc.; to break down, sink, drown, founder, go to ruin, etc., fall, slip, tumble, stumble, falter, be capsized, run aground, pack up, crock up, collapse.

(Phrases) To come to nothing; to end in smoke; to slip through one's fingers; to hang fire; to miss fire; to miss stays; to flash in the pan; to split upon a rock; to go to the wall; to have had it; to take a back seat; to get the worst of it; to go to the dogs; to go to pot; to be all up with; to be in the wrong box; to stand in one's own light; to catch a Tartar; to get hold of the wrong sow by the ear; to burn one's fingers; to shoot at a pigeon and kill a crow; to beat the air; to tilt against windmills; to roll the stone of Sisyphus; to fall between two stools; to pull a boner; to come a cropper or mucker.

(Adjectives) Unsuccessful, failing, etc., unfortunate, in a bad way,

advantage; to get the whip-hand of; to have on the hip; to get the start of; to have a run of luck; to make a hit; to make a killing; to score a success; to reap or gather the harvest; to strike oil; to give a good account of oneself; to carry all before one; to put to rout; to cook one's goose; to settle one's hash.

(Adjectives) Succeeding, etc., successful, home and dry, prosperous, felicitous, blooming, etc., set up, triumphant, victorious, cock-a-hoop.

Unfoiled, unbeaten, unsubdued, etc. Effective, well-spent.

(Phrases) Flushed with success; one's star being in the ascendant; the spoilt child of fortune.

(Adverbs) Successfully, etc., triumphantly, with flying colours, in triumph, *à merveille,* to good purpose.

(Phrase) Veni, vidi, vici.

———

unlucky, luckless, out of luck, ill-fated, ill-starred, disastrous.

Unavailing, abortive, addle, still-born, fruitless, bootless, ineffectual, stickit, unattained, lame, hobbling, impotent, futile.

Aground, grounded, swamped, stranded, cast away, wrecked, on the rocks, foundered, capsized, torpedoed, shipwrecked.

Defeated, overcome, overthrown, overpowered, mastered, worsted, vanquished, conquered, subjugated, routed, silenced, distanced, foiled, unhorsed, baffled, befooled, dished, tossed about, stultified, undone, done for, down and out, ruined, circumvented, planet-struck, nonplussed.

(Phrases) At a loss; wide of the mark; not having a leg to stand upon; ruined root and branch; the sport of fortune; bitched, bothered, and bewildered; hoist by one's own petard; left in the lurch; out of the running.

(Adverbs) Unsuccessfully, etc., in vain, to no purpose, all up with.
(Phrases) The game is up; all is lost.

733 Trophy *(Substantives),* laurel, palm, crown, bays, wreath, garland, chaplet, civic crown, medal, ribbon, cup, scalp, prize, award, oscar, triumphal arch, ovation, triumph (883), flourish of trumpets, flying colours.

(Phrase) A feather in one's cap.

734 Prosperity *(Substantives),* affluence (803), success (731), thrift, good fortune, welfare, well-being, felicity, luck, good luck, a run of luck, fair weather, sunshine, fair wind, a bed of roses, palmy days, the smiles of fortune, halcyon days, *Saturnia regna,* golden age.

An upstart, parvenu, *nouveau riche,* profiteer, skipjack, mushroom, self-made man.

A made man, a lucky dog.

(Phrase) A roaring trade.

(Verbs) To prosper, thrive, flourish, be well off; to flower, blow, blossom, bloom, fructify.

(Phrases) To feather one's nest; to line one's pockets; to make one's pile; to bask in the sunshine; to rise in the world; to make one's way; to better oneself; to light on one's feet.

735 Adversity *(Substantives),* bad, ill, evil, adverse, etc., fortune, hap, or luck, tough luck, hard lines, reverse, set-back, come-down, broken fortunes, falling or going down in the world, hard times, iron age, evil day, rainy day.

Fall, ruin, ruination, ruinousness, undoing, mishap, mischance, misadventure, misfortune, disaster, calamity, catastrophe (619), failure (732); a hard life; trouble, hardship, blight, curse, evil star, evil genius, evil dispensation.

(Phrases) The frowns of fortune; the ups and downs of life; a black look-out; the time being out of joint.

(Verbs) To be ill off; to decay, sink, go under, fall, decline, come down in the world, lose caste; to have had it.

(Adjectives) Prosperous, fortunate, lucky, well-off, well-to-do, bein, affluent, solvent (803), thriving, set up, prospering, etc., blooming, palmy, halcyon.

Auspicious, propitious, in a fair way.

(Phrases) Born with a silver spoon in one's mouth; the spoilt child of fortune; in clover; on velvet; in luck's way.

(Adverbs) Prosperously, etc., swimmingly.

(Adjectives) Unfortunate, unlucky, luckless, untoward, ill-off, badly off, decayed, ill-fated, ill-starred, impecunious, necessitous (804), bankrupt (808), unprosperous, adverse, untoward.

Disastrous, calamitous, ruinous, dire, deplorable, etc.

(Phrases) Down on one's luck; in a bad way; in poor shape; having seen better days; born with a wooden ladle in one's mouth; one's star on the wane; from bad to worse; down and out.

736 Mediocrity *(Substantives)*, the golden mean, *aurea mediocritas*, moderation (174), moderate circumstances; the middle classes, bourgeoisie.

(Adjectives) Tolerable, fair, middling, passable, average, so-so, ordinary, mediocre; middle-class, bourgeois.

(Verbs) To keep a middle course, jog on, get along, get by.

(Phrase) Medio tutissimus ibis.

DIVISION II—INTERSOCIAL VOLITION

SECTION I—GENERAL INTERSOCIAL VOLITION

737 Authority *(Substantives)*, influence, patronage, credit, power, prerogative, control, jurisdiction, censorship, authoritativeness, absoluteness, despotism, absolutism, tyranny.

Command, empire, sway, rule, dominion, domination, supremacy, sovereignty, suzerainty, lordship, headship, seigniory, seigniorship, mastery, mastership, office, government, administration, gubernation, empire, body politic, accession.

Hold, grasp, gripe, grip, reach, fang, clutches, talons, helm, reins.

Reign, dynasty, regime, directorship, proconsulship, prefecture, caliphate, seneschalship, magistrature, magistracy, presidency, presidentship, premiership.

Empire, autocracy, monarchy, kinghood, kingship, royalty, regality, kingcraft, aristocracy, oligarchy, feudalism, republic, republicanism, democracy, socialism, demagogy, ochlocracy, mobocracy, mob-rule, dictatorship of proletariat, ergatocracy, collectivism, communism,

738 Absence of authority.

Laxity *(Substantives)*, laxness, licence, licentiousness, relaxation, looseness, loosening, slackness, toleration, *laissez-faire*, remission, liberty (748).

Misrule, anarchy, interregnum.

Deprivation of power, dethronement, deposition, usurpation.

Denial of authority: anarchism, nihilism; insubordination, mutiny (742).

Anarchist, nihilist, usurper, mutineer.

(Phrases) A dead letter; *brutum fulmen.*

(Verbs) To be lax, etc., to hold a loose rein, tolerate, to relax, to misrule.

To dethrone.

(Phrases) To give a loose rein to; to give rope enough.

(Adjectives) Lax, permissive, loose, slack, remiss, relaxed, licensed, reinless, unbridled, anarchic, anarchical, nihilistic.

Unauthorized (925).

Bolshevism, bureaucracy, bumbledom, syndicalism, militarism, stratocracy, *imperium in imperio*, dictatorship, protectorate, protectorship, directorate, directory, executive, raj.

Limited monarchy, constitutional government, representative government, home rule, diarchy (or dyarchy), duumvirate, triumvirate.

Vicarious authority (755, 759).

Gynarchy, gynaecocracy, petticoat government, matriarchy; patriarchy, patriarchism.

(Verbs) To have, hold, possess, or exercise authority, etc.

To be master, etc.; to have the control, etc.; to overrule, override, overawe, dominate.

To rule, govern, sway, command, control, direct, administer, lead, preside over, boss; to dictate, reign, hold the reins; to possess or be seated on the throne; to ascend or mount the throne; to sway or wield the sceptre.

(Phrases) To have the upper hand; to have the whip-hand; to bend to one's will; to have one's own way; to rule the roast; to lay down the law; to be cock of the roost; to have under the thumb; to keep under; to lead by the nose; to wear the breeches; to have the ball at one's feet; to play first fiddle.

(Adjectives) Ruling, etc., regnant, dominant, paramount, supreme, authoritative, executive, gubernatorial, administrative, official.

Imperial, regal, sovereign, royal, royalist, kingly, monarchical, imperatorial, princely, baronial, feudal, seigneurial, seigniorial, aristocratic, democratic, etc.; totalitarian, ultramontane, absolutist.

Imperative, peremptory, arbitrary, absolute, overruling.

(Adverbs) In the name of, by the authority of, in virtue of, at one's command, under the auspices of, under the aegis of, *ex officio, ex cathedra*.

---

739 Severity *(Substantives)*, strictness, rigour, rigidity, rigidness, sternness, stringency, austerity, inclemency, harshness, acerbity, stiffness, rigorousness, inexorability.

Arbitrary power, absolutism, despotism, dictatorship, autocracy, domineering, tyranny; Moloch.

Assumption, usurpation.

A tyrant, disciplinarian, martinet, stickler, despot, oppressor, hard master; King Stork.

(Phrases) Iron rule; reign of terror; mailed fist; martial law; blood and iron; tender mercies; red tape.

740 Lenity *(Substantives)*, mildness, lenience, leniency, gentleness, indulgence, clemency, tolerance, forbearance.

(Verbs) To be lenient, etc., to tolerate, indulge, spoil, bear with, to allow to have one's own way, to let down gently.

(Adjectives) Lenient, mild, gentle, soft, indulgent, tolerant, easy-going, clement.

(Phrase) Live and let live.

(Verbs) To be severe, etc.; to assume, usurp, arrogate, take liberties; to hold or keep a tight hand; to bear or lay a heavy hand on; to be down on; to dictate; to domineer, bully, oppress, override, tyrannize.

(Phrases) To lord it over; to carry matters with a high hand; to ride roughshod over; to rule with a rod of iron; to put on the screw; to deal faithfully with; to keep a person's nose to the grindstone.

(Adjectives) Severe, strict, rigid, stern, stiff, dour, strait-laced, rigorous, exacting, stringent, hard and fast, peremptory, absolute, positive, uncompromising, harsh, austere, arbitrary, haughty, overbearing,

arrogant, autocratic, bossy, dictatorial, imperious, domineering, tyranni-
cal, masterful, obdurate, unyielding, inflexible, inexorable, exigent, inclement, Spartan, Rhadamanthine, Draconian.

(Adverbs) Severely, etc., with a heavy hand.

741 Command *(Substantives)*, order, fiat, bidding, dictum, hest, behest, call,
beck, nod, message, direction, injunction, charge, instructions, appointment,
demand, exaction, imposition, requisition, requirement, claim, reclamation, revendication.

Dictation, dictate, mandate, caveat, edict, decree, decretal, enactment, precept,
prescript, writ, rescript, law, ordinance, ordination, bull, regulation, prescription,
brevet, placet, ukase, firman, warrant, passport, mittimus, mandamus, summons,
subpoena, interpellation, citation, word of command.

(Verbs) To command, to issue a command, order, give order, bid, require,
enjoin, charge, claim, call for, demand, exact, insist on, make a point of, impose,
entail, set, tax, prescribe, direct, brief, appoint, dictate, ordain, decree, enact; to
issue or promulgate a decree, etc.

To cite, summon, call for, call up, send for, requisition, subpoena; to set or prescribe a task, to set to work, to give the word of command, to call to order.

(Phrase) The decree is gone forth.

(Adjectives) Commanding, etc., authoritative, peremptory, decretive, de-
cretory (737).

(Adverbs) By order, with a dash of the pen.

(Phrase) Le roy le veult.

742 Disobedience *(Substantives)*,
non-compliance, insubordination,
contumacy, defection, infringement,
infraction, violation; defiance (715),
resistance (719), non-observance
(773).

Rising, insurrection, revolt, *coup
d'état, putsch,* rebellion, turn-out,
strike, riot, riotousness, mutinous-
ness, mutiny, tumult, sedition, treason,
lese-majesty.

An insurgent, mutineer, rebel, rioter,
traitor, apostate, renegade, seceder,
quisling, fifth columnist; *carbonaro,*
sansculotte, *frondeur*; agitator,
demagogue, Jack Cade, Wat Tyler;
ringleader.

(Verbs) To disobey, violate, infringe,
resist (719), defy (715), turn restive,
shirk, kick, strike, mutiny, rise, rebel,
secede, lift the hand against, turn out,
come out, go on strike.

(Phrases) To champ the bit; to kick
over the traces; to unfurl the red
flag.

(Adjectives) Disobedient, resisting,
rebellious, unruly, unsubmissive, un-

743 Obedience *(Substantives)*, submission, non-resistance, passiveness,
resignation, cession, compliance, surrender (725), subordination, deference, loyalty, devotion, allegiance,
obeisance, homage, fealty, prostration,
kneeling, genuflexion, curtsy, kotow,
salaam, submissiveness, obsequiousness (886), servitorship, subjection (749).

(Verbs) To be obedient, etc.; to obey,
submit, succumb, give in, knock under,
cringe, yield (725), comply, surrender,
follow, give up, give way, resign, bend
to, bear obedience to.

To kneel, fall on one's knees, bend
the knee, curtsy, kowtow, salaam, bow,
pay homage to.

To attend upon, tend; to be under the
orders of, to serve.

(Phrases) To kiss the rod; to do one's
bidding; to play second fiddle; to take it
lying down; to dance attendance on.

(Adjectives) Obedient, submissive,
resigned, passive, complying, compliant, loyal, faithful, devoted, yielding, docile, tractable, amenable,

governable, uncomplying, uncompliant, restive, insubordinate, contumacious, mutinous, riotous, seditious, disaffected, recusant, recalcitrant, refractory, naughty.

Unbidden, unobeyed, a dead letter.

(Phrase) The grey mare being the better horse.

biddable, unresisting, henpecked; restrainable, unresisted.

---

744 Compulsion *(Substantives)*, coercion, coaction, force, constraint, enforcement, press, *corvée,* conscription, levy, duress, brute force, main force, *force majeure,* the sword, club law, *ultima ratio, argumentum baculinum.*

(Verbs) To compel, force, make, drive, coerce, constrain, steam-roller, enforce, put in force, oblige, force upon, press, conscribe, extort, put down, bind, pin down, bind over, impress, commandeer, requisition.

(Phrases) To cram down the throat; to take no denial; to insist upon; to make a point of.

(Adjectives) Compelling, etc., compulsory, compulsatory, obligatory, forcible, coercive, coactive, peremptory, rigorous, stringent, inexorable (739); being fain to do, having to do.

(Adverbs) By force, perforce, under compulsion, *vi et armis,* in spite of one's teeth; *bon gré, mal gré;* willy-nilly, *nolens volens; de rigueur.*

---

745 Master *(Substantives)*, lord, laird, chief, leader, captain, skipper, mate, protagonist, coryphaeus, head, chieftain, commander, commandant, director (694), captain of industry, ruler, potentate, dictator, liege, sovereign, monarch, autocrat, despot, tyrant, *führer, duce,* demagogue, ringleader, boss, big shot, fugleman.

Crowned head, emperor, king, majesty, tetrarch, *imperator,* protector, president, stadtholder, governor.

Caesar, czar, sultan, soldan, caliph, sophy, khan, cacique, inca, lama, mogul, imam, shah, khedive, pasha (or bashaw), dey, cham, judge, aga, hospodar, mikado, shogun, tycoon, exarch.

Prince, seignior, highness, archduke, duke, marquis, earl, viscount, baron (875), margrave, landgrave, palatine, elector, doge, satrap, rajah, maharajah, emir, bey, effendi, nizam, nawab, mandarin, sirdar, ameer, sachem, sagamore.

Empress, queen, czarina, sultana, princess, duchess, marchioness, countess, viscountess, baroness, infanta, ranee, maharanee, margravine, etc.

Military authorities, marshal, field-marshal, *maréchal,* generalissimo,

746 Servant *(Substantives)*, servitor, employee, attaché, secretary, subordinate, clerk, retainer, vassal, protégé, dependant, hanger-on, pensioner, client, emissary, *âme damnée.*

Retinue, cortège, staff, court, train, entourage, clientele, suite.

An attendant, squire, henchman, led captain, chamberlain, follower, usher, page, train-bearer, domestic, help, butler, footman, lackey, flunkey, parlour-man, valet, waiter, *garçon,* equerry, groom, jockey, ostler (or hostler), stable-boy, tiger, buttons, boot-boy, boots, livery servant, hireling, mercenary, underling, menial, gillie, under-strapper, journeyman, whipper-in, bailiff, castellan, seneschal, majordomo, cup-bearer, bottle-washer, scout, gyp.

Serf, villein, slave, galley-slave, thrall, peon, helot, bondsman, *adscriptus glebae,* wage-slave.

A maid, handmaid, abigail, chamber-maid, lady's maid, housekeeper, lady help, soubrette, *fille de chambre,* parlour-maid, housemaid, between-maid, kitchen-maid, nurse, *bonne,* scullion, laundress, bed-maker, skivvy, slavey, daily.

(Verbs) To serve, attend upon, dance attendance, wait upon, squire, valet.

commander-in-chief, admiral, com-
modore, general, lieutenant-general,
major-general, brigadier, colonel,
lieutenant-colonel, officer, captain,
major, lieutenant, adjutant, midship-
man, quartermaster, aide-de-camp, ensign, cornet, cadet, subaltern, non-
commissioned officer, drum-major, sergeant-major, sergeant, corporal, air-
marshal, group-captain, wing-commander, squadron-leader, flight-
lieutenant, centurion, *seraskier*, hetman, subahdar, *condottiere*.

Civil authorities, mayor, prefect, chancellor, provost, magistrate, syndic,
alcade (or alcayde), burgomaster, *corregidor*, sheik, seneschal, burgrave,
alderman, warden, constable (965), beadle, alguazil, kavass, tribune,
consul, proconsul, quaestor, praetor, aedile, archon, polemarch.

Statesman, politician, statist, legislator, lawgiver.

President, chairman, speaker, moderator, vice-president, comptroller,
director (694), monitor, monitress.

(Adverbs) In one's pay or employ, in
the train of.

---

747 Ensign, or badge of authority.

Sceptre *(Substantives)*, regalia, insigma (550), crown, coronet, rod of empire,
orb, mace, *fasces*, wand, baton, truncheon, staff, insignia (550), portfolio.

A throne, chair, divan, dais, woolsack.

Diadem, tiara, ermine, purple, signet, seals, keys, talisman, cap of maintenance, toga, robes of state, decoration.

748 Freedom *(Substantives)*, independence, liberty, licence (760), self-
government, autonomy, scope, range,
latitude, play, swing, free play, elbow-
room, *lebensraum*, margin.

Franchise, immunity, exemption,
emancipation (750), naturalization,
denizenship.

Freeland, freehold, allodium (780).

A freeman, freedman, denizen.

(Phrases) The four freedoms;
liberté, egalité, fraternité; a place in the
sun; Liberty Hall.

(Verbs) To be free, to have scope,
etc.

To render free, etc., to free, to
emancipate, enfranchise (750), naturalize.

(Phrases) To have the run of; to have
one's own way; to have one's fling; to
stand on one's own feet; to stand on
one's rights; to have a will of one's own;
to paddle one's own canoe; to play a
lone hand.

To take a liberty; to make free with;
to take the bit between one's teeth.

749 Subjection *(Substantives)*,
dependence, thrall, thraldom, subjugation, subordination, bondage,
serfdom, servitude, slavery, vassalage,
villeinage, service, clientship, liability
(177), enslavement, tutelage, constraint (751).

Yoke, harness, collar.

(Verbs) To be subject, dependent,
etc., to fall under, obey, serve (743).

To subject, subjugate, enthral,
enslave, keep under, control, etc. (751),
to reduce to slavery, mediatize, break
in.

(Phrases) To drag a chain; not dare
to call one's soul one's own; to be led by
the nose; to be or lie at the mercy of.

To keep in leading strings.

(Adjectives) Subject, subordinate,
dependent, subjected, in subjection to,
in thrall to, feudatory, feudal, enslaved,
a slave to, at the mercy of, downtrodden, overborne, henpecked, enthralled,
controlled, constrained (751).

(Phrases) Under the thumb of;
at the feet of; tied to the apron-

(Adjectives) Free, independent, loose, at large, unconstrained, unrestrained, unchecked, unobstructed, unconfined, unsubdued, unsubjugated, self-governed, autonomous, self-supporting, untrammelled, unbound, uncontrolled, unchained, unshackled, unfettered, uncurbed, unbridled, unrestricted, unmuzzled, unbuttoned, unforced, uncompelled, unbiased, spontaneous, unhindered, unthwarted, heart-whole, uncaught, unenslaved, unclaimed, ungoverned, resting.

Free and easy, at ease, *dégagé*, wanton, rampant, irrepressible, unprevented, unvanquished, exempt, freehold, allodial, enfranchised, emancipated, released, disengaged (750), out of hand.

(Phrases) Free as air; one's own master; *sui juris*; a law to oneself; on one's own; a cat may look at a king.

750 Liberation *(Substantives)*, disengagement, release, enlargement, emancipation, affranchisement, enfranchisement, manumission, discharge, dismissal.

Escape (671), deliverance (672), redemption, extrication, absolution, acquittance, acquittal (970).

Licence, toleration; parole, ticket of leave.

(Verbs) To gain, obtain, acquire, etc., one's liberty, freedom, etc., to get off, get clear, to deliver oneself from.

To break loose, escape, slip away, make one's escape, cut and run, slip the collar, bolt (671).

To liberate, free, set free, set at liberty, release, loose, let loose, loosen, relax, unloose, untie, unbind, unhand, unchain, unshackle, unfetter, unclog, disengage, unharness (44).

To enlarge, set clear, let go, let out, disenchain, disimprison, unbar, unbolt, uncage, unclose, uncork, discharge, disenthral, dismiss, deliver, extricate, let slip, enfranchise, affranchise, manumit, denizen, emancipate, assoil (748).

To clear, acquit, redeem, ransom, get off.

(Phrases) To throw off the yoke; to burst one's bonds; to break prison.

To give one one's head.

(Adjectives) Liberated, freed, etc.

strings of; the puppet, sport, plaything of.

————

751 Restraint *(Substantives)*, constraint, coercion, cohibition, repression, clamp down, control, discipline.

Confinement, durance, duress, detention, imprisonment, incarceration, prisonment, internment, blockade, quarantine, coarctation, mancipation, entombment, 'durance vile,' limbo, captivity, penal servitude.

Arrest, arrestation, custody, keep, care, charge, ward.

Prison, fetter (752); *lettre de cachet*.

(Verbs) To be under restraint or arrest, to be coerced, etc.

To restrain, constrain, coerce, check, trammel, curb, cramp, keep under, enthral, put under restraint, restrict, repress, cohibit, detain, debar; to chain, enchain, fasten, tie up (43), picket, fetter, shackle, manacle, handcuff, bridle, muzzle, gag, suppress, pinion, pin down, tether, hobble.

To confine, shut up, shut in, clap up, lock up, cage, encage, impound, pen, coop, hem in, jam in, enclose, bottle up, cork up, seal up, mew, wall in, rail in, cloister, bolt in, close the door upon, imprison, incarcerate, immure, entomb, seclude, corral.

To take prisoner, lead captive, send or commit to prison, give in charge or in custody, arrest, commit, run in, lag; recommit, remand.

(Phrases) To put in irons; to clap under hatches; to put in a straitwaistcoat.

(Adjectives) Restrained, coerced, etc., sewn up, pent up.

Held up, wind-bound, weather-bound, storm-stayed.

Coactive, stiff, restringent, strait-laced, hide-bound.

(Phrases) In limbo; under lock and key; laid by the heels; 'cabined, cribbed, confined'; in quod; in durance vile; doing time; bound hand and foot.

752 Means of restraint.

Prison *(Substantives)*, jail (or gaol), prison-house, house of detention, lock-up, the cells, clink, glasshouse, brig, jug, quod, cooler, choky, stir, calaboose, cage, coop, den, cell, stronghold, fortress, keep, dungeon, bastille, oubliette, bridewell, tollbooth, panopticon, hulks, galleys, penitentiary, guard-room, hold, round-house, blackhole, station, enclosure, concentration camp, pen, fold, pound, paddock, stocks, bilboes, nick.

Newgate, King's Bench, Fleet, Marshalsea, Pentonville, Holloway, Dartmoor, Portland, Peterhead, Broadmoor, Sing Sing, the Bastille.

Fetter, shackle, trammel, bond, chain, irons, collar, cangue, pinion, gyve, fetterlock, manacle, handcuff, darbies, strait waistcoat; yoke, halter, harness, muzzle, gag, bridle, curb, bit, snaffle, rein, martingale, leading-strings, swaddling-bands, tether, hobble, picket, band, brake.

Bolt, bar, lock, padlock, rail, wall, paling, palisade (232), fence, corral, barrier, barricade.

753 Keeper *(Substantives)*, custodian, *custos*, warder, jailer (or gaoler), turnkey, castellan, guard, ranger, gamekeeper, watch, watchman, watch and ward, sentry, sentinel, coastguard, convoy, escort, *concierge*, caretaker, watch-dog.

Guardian, duenna, nurse, ayah, chaperon.

754 Prisoner *(Substantives)*, prisoner-of-war, P.O.W., kriegie, captive, *détenu*, convict, jail-bird, lag; ticket-of-leave man.

(Adjectives) In custody, in charge, imprisoned, locked up, incarcerated, pent.

755 Vicarious authority.

Commission *(Substantives)*, delegation, consignment, assignment, devolution, procuration, deputation, legation, mission, agency, clerkship, agentship; power of attorney; errand, embassy, charge, brevet, diploma, exequatur, committal, commitment.

Appointment, nomination, ordination, installation, inauguration, return, accession, investiture, coronation.

Viceregency, regency, regentship.

Deputy (759).

(Verbs) To commission, delegate, depute, devolve, send out, assign, consign, charge, encharge, entrust with, commit to, enlist.

To appoint, name, nominate, accredit, engage, bespeak, ordain, install, induct, inaugurate, invest, crown, return, enrol.

756 Abrogation *(Substantives)*, annulment, cancel, cancellation, revocation, repeal, rescission, rescinding, deposal, deposition, dethronement, defeasance, dismissal, sack, *congé*, demission, disestablishment, disendowment.

Abolition, abolishment, counterorder, countermand, repudiation, nullification, recantation, palinode, retractation (607).

(Verbs) To abrogate, annul, cancel, revoke, repeal, rescind, reverse, override, overrule, abolish, disannul, dissolve, quash, repudiate, nullify, retract, recant, recall, countermand, counter-order, break off, disclaim, declare null and void, disestablish, disendow, deconsecrate, set aside, do away with.

To dismiss, send off, send away, discard, turn off, turn away, cashier,

Employ, empower, set over.
To be commissioned, to represent.
(Adverbs) Per procurationem, per pro., p.p.

sack, fire, bounce, oust, unseat, un-throne, dethrone, depose, uncrown, unfrock, disbar, disbench.

(Phrases) Send about one's busi-ness; put one's nose out of joint; give one the mitten, the chuck, the sack, the boot, the push.

To get one's books or cards; to get the key of the street.

(Adjectives) Abrogated, etc.; *functus officio.*

(Interjections) Get along with you! clear out! be off! beat it!

757 Resignation *(Substantives)*, retirement, abdication, renunciation, abjura-tion.

(Verbs) To resign, give up, throw up, retire, abdicate, lay down, abjure, renounce, forgo, disclaim, retract (756); to tender one's resignation, send in one's papers.

(Phrases) To swallow the anchor; to be given one's bowler.

(Adjective) Emeritus.

(Phrase) 'Othello's occupation's gone.'

758 Consignee *(Substantives)*, delegate, commissary, commissioner, vice-regent, legate, representative, secondary, nominee, surrogate, functionary, trustee, assignee.

Corps diplomatique, plenipotentiary, emissary, embassy, ambassador, diplomat(ist), consul, resident, nuncio, internuncio.

Agent, factor, attorney, broker, factotum, bailiff, man of business, go-between, intermediary, middleman, salesman, commission agent, commercial traveller, bagman, drummer, colporteur, commissionaire, employee, attaché, curator, clerk, placeman.

759 Deputy *(Substantives)*, substitute, vice, proxy, locum tenens, baby-sitter, *chargé d'affaires*, delegate, representative, *alter ego*, surrogate, understudy, stooge, stand-in, stopgap, pinch-hitter.

Regent, viceroy, viceregent, vicar, satrap, exarch, vizier, minister, premier, commissioner, chancellor, prefect, warden, lieutenant, proconsul, legate.

(Verbs) To deputize; to be deputy, etc., for; to appear for; to understudy; to take duty for.

(Phrase) To hold a watching brief for.

(Adjectives) Acting, deputizing, etc.

(Adverbs) In place of, vice.

SECTION II—SPECIAL INTERSOCIAL VOLITION

760 Permission *(Substantives)*, leave, allowance, sufferance, tolerance, toleration, liberty, law, licence, con-cession, grant, vouchsafement, authorization, sanction, accordance, admission, favour, dispensation, exemption, connivance.

A permit, warrant, brevet, precept, authority, firman, pass, passport,

761 Prohibition *(Substantives)*, inhibition, veto, disallowance, inter-diction, estoppage, hindrance (706), restriction, restraints (751), embargo, an interdict, ban, injunction, taboo, proscription; *index librorum pro-hibitorum.*

(Verbs) To prohibit, forbid, inhibit, disallow, bar, debar, interdict, ban,

furlough, ticket, licence, charter, patent, *carte blanche*, exeat.

(Verbs) To permit; to give leave or permission; to let, allow, admit, suffer, tolerate, concede, accord, vouchsafe, humour, indulge, to leave it to one; to leave alone; to grant, empower, charter, sanction, authorize, warrant, license; to give licence; to give a loose to.

To let off, absolve, exonerate, dispense with, favour, wink, connive at.

(Phrases) To give *carte blanche*; to give rein to; to stretch a point; leave the door open; to let one have a chance; to give one a fair show.

To take a liberty; to use a freedom; to make so bold; to beg leave.

(Adjectives) Permitting, etc., permissive, conceding, indulgent.

Allowable, permissible, lawful, legitimate, legal.

Unforbid, unforbidden, unconditional.

estop, veto, keep in, hinder, restrain (751), restrict, withhold, limit, circumscribe, keep within bounds.

To exclude, shut out, proscribe.

(Phrases) To clip the wings of; to forbid the banns.

(Adjectives) Prohibitive, restrictive, exclusive, prohibitory, forbidding, etc.

Not permitted, prohibited, etc., unlicensed, contraband, unauthorized.

(Phrases) Under the ban of; on the Index.

(Interjections) Hands off! keep off! God forbid!

---

762 Consent *(Substantives)*, compliance, acquiescence, assent (488), agreement, concession, yieldingness, acknowledgment, acceptance.

Settlement, ratification, confirmation.

(Verbs) To consent, give consent, assent, comply with, acquiesce, agree to, subscribe to, accede, accept.

To concede, yield, satisfy, grant, settle, acknowledge, confirm, homologate, ratify, deign, vouchsafe.

(Phrase) To take at one's word.

(Adjectives) Consenting, etc., having no objection, unconditional.

(Adverbs) Yes (488); if you please, as you please, by all means, by all manner of means, so be it, of course, certainly, sure, O.K.

(Phrases) Suits me; all right by me.

---

763 Offer *(Substantives)*, proffer, tender, present, overture, proposition, motion, proposal, invitation, candidature, presentation, offering, oblation, bid, bribe.

Sacrifice, immolation.

(Verbs) To offer, proffer, tender, present, invite, volunteer, propose, move, make a motion, start, press, bid, hold out, hawk about.

To sacrifice, immolate.

(Phrases) To be a candidate; to go a-begging.

(Adjectives) Offering, etc., in the market, for sale, on hire.

764 Refusal *(Substantives)*, rejection, declining, non-compliance, declension, dissent (489), denial, repulse, rebuff, discountenance.

Disclaimer, recusancy, abnegation, protest.

Revocation, violation, abrogation (756), flat refusal, peremptory denial.

(Verbs) To refuse, reject, deny, decline, disclaim, repudiate, protest, resist, repel, veto, refuse or withhold one's assent; to excuse oneself, to negative, turn down, rebuff, snub, spurn, resist, cross, grudge, begrudge.

To discard, set aside, rescind, revoke, discountenance, forswear.

(Phrases) To turn a deaf ear to; to shake the head; not to hear of;

to send to the right-about; to hang fire; to wash one's hands of; to declare off.

(Adjectives) Refusing, etc., recusant, restive, uncomplying, unconsenting.

Refused, etc., out of the question, not to be thought of.

(Adverbs) No, by no means, etc. (489).

(Phrases) Excuse me; nix on that; not on your life; nothing doing.

---

765 Request *(Substantives)*, requisition, asking, petition, demand, suit, solicitation, craving, entreaty, begging, postulation, adjuration, canvass, candidature, prayer, supplication, impetration, imploration, instance, obsecration, obtestation, importunity, application, address, appeal, motion, invitation, overture, invocation, interpellation, apostrophe, orison, incantation, imprecation, conjuration.

Mendicancy, begging letter, round robin.

Claim, reclamation, revendication.

766 Negative request.

Deprecation *(Substantives)*, expostulation, intercession, mediation.

(Verbs) To deprecate, protest, expostulate; to enter a protest; to intercede for.

(Adjectives) Deprecating, etc., deprecatory, expostulatory, intercessory; deprecated, protested.

Unsought, unbesought.

(Interjections) God forbid! forbid it heaven! *absit omen!*

(Verbs) To request, ask, sue, beg, cadge, crave, pray, petition, solicit, beg a boon, demand, prefer a request or petition, ply, apply to, make application, put to, make bold to ask, invite, beg leave, put up a prayer.

To beg hard, entreat, beseech, supplicate, implore, plead, conjure, adjure, invoke, evoke, kneel to, fall on one's knees, impetrate, imprecate, appeal to, apply to, put to, address, call for, press, urge, beset, importune, dun, tax, besiege, cry to, call on.

To bespeak, canvass, tout, make interest, court; to claim, reclaim.

(Phrases) To send the hat round; to beg from door to door.

(Adjectives) Requesting, asking, beseeching, etc., precatory, suppliant, supplicatory, postulant, importunate.

(Phrases) Cap in hand; on one's knees.

(Adverbs) Do, please, kindly, be good enough, pray, prithee, be so good as, have the goodness, vouchsafe.

For heaven's sake, for goodness' sake, for God's sake, for the love of Mike.

767 Petitioner *(Substantives)*, solicitor, applicant, suppliant, supplicant, mendicant, beggar, mumper, suitor, candidate, aspirant, claimant, postulant, canvasser, tout, cadger, sponger.

SECTION III—CONDITIONAL INTERSOCIAL VOLITION

768 Promise *(Substantives)*, word, troth, plight, profession, pledge, parole, word of honour, assurance, vow, oath.

Engagement, guarantee, undertaking, insurance, contract (769), obligation; affiance, betrothal, betrothment.

768A Release from engagement, disengagement, liberation (750).

(Adjectives) Absolute, unconditional, uncovenanted, unsecured.

(Verbs) To promise, give a promise, undertake, engage, assure; to give, pass, pledge or plight one's word, honour, credit, faith, etc.; to covenant, warrant, guarantee (467); to swear, vow, be sworn; take oath, make oath, kiss the book; to attest, adjure; to betroth, plight troth, affiance.

To answer for, be answerable for, secure, give security (771).

(Phrases) To enter on, make or form an engagement, take upon oneself; to bind, tie, commit, or pledge oneself; to be in for it; to contract an obligation; to be bound; to hold out an expectation.

To call heaven to witness; to swear by bell, book, and candle; to put on one's oath; to swear a witness.

(Adjectives) Promising, etc., promised, pledged, sworn, etc.; votive, promissory.

(Phrases) Under one's hand and seal; as one's head shall answer for.

(Interjection) So help me God!

769 Compact *(Substantives)*, contract, agreement, understanding, bargain, bond, deal, pact, paction, stipulation, covenant, settlement, convention, cartel, protocol, charter, treaty, indenture, concordat, *zollverein*.

Negotiation, transaction, bargaining, haggling, chaffering; diplomacy.

Ratification, settlement, signature, endorsement, seal, signet.

A negotiator, diplomatist, diplomat, agent, contractor, underwriter, attorney, broker (758).

(Verbs) To contract, covenant, agree for, strike a bargain, engage (768); to underwrite.

To treat, negotiate, bargain, stipulate, haggle (or higgle), chaffer, stick out for, insist upon, make a point of, compound for.

To conclude, close, confirm, ratify, endorse, clench, come to an understanding, take one at one's word, come to terms.

To subscribe, sign, seal, indent, put the seal to, sign and seal.

(Phrase) Caveat emptor.

770 Conditions *(Substantives)*, terms, articles, articles of agreement, clauses, proviso, provisions, salvo, covenant, stipulation, obligation, ultimatum, *sine qua non*.

(Verbs) To make it a condition, make terms; to stipulate, insist upon; to tie up.

(Adjectives) Conditional, provisional, guarded, fenced, hedged in.

(Adverbs) Conditionally, on the understanding; provided (469).

(Phrases) With a string tied to it; wind and weather permitting; God willing; D.V.; *Deo volente*.

771 Security *(Substantives)*, surety, guaranty, guarantee, mortgage, warranty, bond, debenture, pledge, tie, plight, pawn, lien, caution, sponsion, hostage, sponsor, bail, parole.

Deed, instrument, deed-poll, indenture, warrant, charter, cartel, protocol, recognizance; verification, acceptance, endorsement, signature, execution, seal, stamp, I O U.

Promissory note, bill of exchange, bill.

Stake, deposit, pool, kitty, jack-pot, earnest, handsel.

Docket, certificate, voucher, verification, authentication.

(Verbs) To give security, go bail, pawn (787); guarantee, warrant, accept, endorse, underwrite, insure; execute, stamp.

To hold in pledge.

772 Observance *(Substantives)*, performance, fulfilment, satisfaction, discharge, compliance, acquittance, quittance, acquittal, adhesion, acknowledgment, fidelity (939).

(Verbs) To observe, perform, keep, fulfil, discharge, comply with, make good, meet, satisfy, respect, abide by, adhere to, be faithful to, act up to, acquit oneself.

(Phrase) To redeem one's pledge.

(Adjectives) Observant, faithful, true, honourable (939), strict, rigid, punctilious.

(Adverb) Faithfully, etc., to the letter.

(Phrase) As good as one's word.

---

773 Non-observance *(Substantives)*, inobservance, evasion, omission, failure, neglect, laches, laxity, infringement, infraction, violation, forfeiture, transgression.

Retractation, repudiation, nullification, protest.

Informality, lawlessness, disobedience, bad faith (742).

(Verbs) To break, violate, fail, neglect, omit, skip, cut, forfeit, infringe, transgress.

To retract, discard, protest, go back upon or from one's word, repudiate, nullify, ignore, set at naught, wipe off, cancel, etc. (552), to fob off, palter, elude, evade.

(Phrases) To wash out; to shut one's eyes to; to drive a coach and six through.

(Adjectives) Violating, etc., elusive, evasive, transgressive, unfulfilled; compensatory (30).

774 Compromise *(Substantives)*, composition, middle term, *mezzo termine, modus vivendi*; bribe, hush-money.

(Verbs) To compromise, compound, commute, adjust, take the mean, split the difference, come to terms, come to an understanding, meet one half-way, give and take, submit to arbitration.

SECTION IV—POSSESSIVE RELATIONS

1°. *Property in general*

775 Acquisition *(Substantives)*, obtainment, gaining, earning, procuration, procuring, procurement, gathering, gleaning, picking, collecting, recovery, retrieval, totting, salvage, find.

Book-collecting, book-hunting, etc., philately, cartophily, phillumeny.

Gain, profit, benefit, emolument, the main chance, pelf, lucre, loaves and fishes, produce, product, proceeds, return, fruit, crop, harvest, scoop, takings, winnings.

Inheritance, bequest, legacy.

Fraudulent acquisition, subreption, stealing (791).

Profiteering, pot-hunting.

A collector, book-collector, etc., bird-fancier, etc., philatelist,

776 Loss *(Substantives)*, perdition, forfeiture, lapse.

Privation, bereavement, deprivation (789), dispossession, riddance.

(Verbs) To lose; incur, experience, or meet with a loss; to miss, mislay, throw away, forfeit, drop, let slip, allow to slip through the fingers; to get rid of (782), to waste (638, 679).

To be lost, lapse.

(Phrase) To throw good money after bad.

(Adjectives) Losing, etc., lost, etc.

Devoid of, not having, unobtained, unpossessed, unblest with.

Shorn of, deprived of, bereaved of, bereft of, rid of, quit of, dispossessed, denuded, out of pocket, minus, cut off.

cartophilist, phillumenist; a profiteer, money-grubber, pot-hunter.

(Verbs) To acquire, get, gain, win, earn, realize, regain, receive (785), take (789), obtain, procure, derive, secure, collect, reap, gather, glean, come in for, step into, inherit, come by, rake in, scrape together, get hold of, scoop, pouch.

To profit, make profit, turn to profit, make money by, obtain a return, make a fortune, coin money, profiteer.

To be profitable, to pay, to answer.

To fall to, come to, accrue.

(Phrases) To turn an honest penny; to earn an honest crust; to bring grist to the mill; to raise the wind; to line one's pockets; to feather one's nest; to reap or gain an advantage; to keep the wolf from the door; to keep the pot boiling.

(Adjectives) Acquisitive, acquiring, acquired, etc., profitable, lucrative, remunerative, paying.

(Phrase) On the make.

Irrecoverable, irretrievable, irremediable, irreparable.

(Interjections) Farewell to! adieu to!

777 Possession *(Substantives)*, ownership, proprietorship, tenure, tenancy, seisin, occupancy, hold, holding, preoccupancy.

Exclusive possession, impropriation, monopoly, inalienability.

Future possession, heritage, heirship, inheritance, reversion.

(Phrases) A bird in the hand; nine points of the law; the haves and the have-nots.

(Verbs) To possess, have, hold, own, be master of, be in possession of, enjoy, occupy, be seised of, be worth, to have in hand or on hand; to inherit (775).

To engross, monopolize, corner, forestall, absorb, preoccupy.

To be the property of, belong to, appertain to, pertain to, be in the hands of, be in the possession of.

(Adjectives) Possessing, etc., possessed of, seised of, worth, endowed with, instinct with, fraught, laden with, charged with.

Possessed, etc., proprietary, proprietorial; on hand, in hand, in store, in stock, unsold, unshared; inalienable.

778 Joint possession.

Participation *(Substantives)*, joint stock, common stock, partnership, copartnership, possession in common, communion, community of possessions or goods, socialism, collectivism, communism, syndicalism.

Bottle party, share-out, picnic.

A syndicate, ring, corner, combine, cartel, trust, monopoly, pool.

A partner, co-partner, shareholder; co-tenant, co-heir; a communist, socialist.

(Verbs) To participate, partake, share, communicate, go snacks, go halves, share and share alike; to have or possess, etc., in common; to come in for a share, to stand in with, to socialize, to pool.

(Adjectives) Partaking, etc.; socialist, socialistic, communist.

(Adverbs) Share and share alike, fifty-fifty, even Stephen.

779 Possessor *(Substantives)*, owner, holder, proprietor, proprietress, proprietary, master, mistress, heritor, occupier, occupant, landlord, landlady, landowner, lord of the manor, squire, laird, landed gentry; tenant, renter, lessee, lodger.

Future possessor, heir, heiress, inheritor.

780 Property (*Substantives*), possession, ownership, proprietorship, seisin, tenancy, tenure, lordship, title, claim, stake, legal estate, equitable estate, fee simple, fee tail, *meum et tuum*, occupancy.

Estate, effects, assets, resources, means, belongings, stock, goods, chattels, fixtures, plant, movables, furniture, things, traps, trappings, paraphernalia, luggage, baggage, bag and baggage, cargo, lading.

Lease, term, settlement, remainder, reversion, dower, jointure, apanage, heritage, inheritance, patrimony, heirloom.

Real property, land, landed estate, manor, demesne, domain, tenement, holding, hereditament, household, freehold, farm, ranch, *hacienda, estancia*, fief, feoff, seigniority, allodium.

Ground, acres, field, close.

State, realm, empire, kingdom, principality, territory, sphere of influence.

(Adjectives) Predial, manorial, freehold, etc., copyhold, leasehold.

781 Retention (*Substantives*), keep, holding, keeping, retaining, detention, custody, grasp, gripe, grip, tenacity.

Fangs, teeth, clutches, hooks, tentacles, claws, talons, nails.

Forceps, pincers, pliers, tongs, vice.

Incommunicableness, incommunicability.

(Phrase) A bird in the hand.

(Verbs) To retain, keep, keep in hand, secure, detain, hold fast, grasp, clutch, clench, cinch, gripe, grip, hug, withhold, keep back.

(Adjectives) Retaining, etc., retentive, tenacious.

Unforfeited, undeprived, undisposed, uncommunicated, incommunicable, inalienable, not transferable.

782 Relinquishment (*Substantives*), cession, abandonment (624), renunciation, surrender, dereliction, rendition, riddance (776), resignation (758).

(Verbs) To relinquish, give up, let go, lay aside, resign, forgo, drop, discard, dismiss, waive, renounce, surrender, part with, get rid of, lay down, abandon, cede, yield, dispose of, divest oneself of, spare, give away, throw away, cast away, fling away, maroon, jettison, chuck up, let slip, make away with, make way for.

(Phrases) To lay on the shelf; to throw overboard.

(Adjectives) Relinquished, etc., derelict, left, residuary (40), unculled.

2°. *Transfer of Property*

783 Transfer (*Substantives*), interchange, exchange, transmission, barter (794), conveyance, assignment, alienation, abalienation, demise, succession, reversion; metastasis.

(Verbs) To transfer, convey, assign, consign, make over, pass, transmit, interchange, exchange (148).

To change hands, change from one to another, alienate, devolve.

To dispossess, abalienate, disinherit.

(Adjectives) Alienable, negotiable, transferable.

784 Giving *(Substantives)*, bestowal, donation, accordance, presentation, oblation, presentment, delivery, award, investment, granting.

Cession, concession, consignment, dispensation, benefaction, charity, liberality, generosity, munificence, almsgiving.

Gift, donation, bonus, boon, present, testimonial, presentation, fairing, benefaction, grant, subsidy, subvention, offering, contribution, subscription, whip-round, donative, meed, tribute, gratuity, tip, Christmas box, handsel, trinkgeld, *douceur, pourboire,* baksheesh, cumshaw, dash, bribe, free gift, favour, bounty, largess, allowance, endowment, charity, alms, dole, peace-offering, payment (807).

Bequest, legacy, demise, dotation.

Giver, grantor, donor, benefactor.

(Phrase) Panem et circenses.

(Verbs) To give, bestow, accord, confer, grant, concede, present, give away, deliver, deliver over, make over, consign, entrust, hand, tip, render, impart, hand over, part with, fork out, yield, dispose of, put into the hands of, vest in, assign, put in possession, settle upon, endow, subsidize.

To bequeath, leave, demise, devise.

To give out, dispense, deal, deal out, dole out, mete out.

To contribute, subscribe, put up a purse, send round the hat, pay (807), spend (809).

To furnish, supply, administer, afford, spare, accommodate with, indulge with, shower upon, lavish.

To bribe, suborn, grease the palm, square.

(Adjectives) Giving, etc., given, etc., charitable, eleemosynary, tributary.

(Phrase) Bis dat qui cito dat.

785 Receiving *(Substantives)*, acquisition (775), reception, acceptance, admission.

A recipient, donee, assignee, legatee, grantee, stipendiary, beneficiary, pensioner, almsman.

(Verbs) To receive, take (789), accept, pocket, pouch, admit, catch, catch at, jump at, take in.

To be received, etc.; to accrue, come to hand.

(Adjectives) Receiving, etc., recipient, pensionary, stipendiary.

———

786 Apportionment *(Substantives)*, distribution, dispensation, allotment, assignment, consignment, partition, division, deal, share-out.

Dividend, portion, contingent, share, whack, meed, allotment, lot, measure, dole, pittance, quantum, ration, quota, modicum, allowance, appropriation.

(Phrase) Cutting up the melon.

(Verbs) To apportion, divide, distribute, administer, dispense, billet, allot, cast, share, mete, parcel out, serve out, deal, partition, appropriate, assign.

(Adjectives) Apportioning, etc., respective.

(Adverbs) Respectively, severally.

787 Lending *(Substantives)*, loan, advance, mortgage, accommodation, lease-lend, subsistence money, sub, pawn, pignoration, hypothecation, investment; pawnshop, *mont de piété.*

Lender, pawnbroker, uncle.

788 Borrowing *(Substantives)*, pledging, replevin, borrowed plumes, plagiarism, plagiary; a touch.

(Verbs) To borrow, hire, rent, farm, raise money, raise the wind; to plagiarize.

(Verbs) to lend, loan, advance, mortgage, invest, pawn, impawn, pop, hock, hypothecate, impignorate, place or put out to interest, entrust, accommodate with.

(Adjectives) Lending, etc., lent, etc., unborrowed.

(Adverb) In advance; up the spout.

(Adjectives) Borrowing, etc., borrowed, second-hand.

(Phrases) To borrow of Peter to pay Paul; to run into debt.

———

789 Taking *(Substantives)*, appropriation, prehension, capture, seizure, abduction, ablation, catching, seizing, apprehension, arrest, kidnapping, round-up.

Abstraction, subtraction, deduction, subduction.

Dispossession, deprivation, deprival, bereavement, divestment, sequestration, confiscation, disendowment.

Resumption, reprise, reprisal, recovery (775).

Clutch, swoop, wrench, catch, take, haul.

(Verbs) To take, capture, lay one's hands on; lay, take, or get hold of; to help oneself to; to possess oneself of, take possession of, make sure of, make free with.

To appropriate, impropriate, pocket, put into one's pocket, pouch, bag; to ease one of.

To pick up, gather, collect, round up, net, absorb (296), reap, glean, crop, get in the harvest, cull, pluck; intercept, tap.

To take away, carry away, carry off, bear off, hurry off with, abduct, kidnap, crimp, shanghai.

To lay violent hands on, fasten upon, pounce upon, catch, seize, snatch, nip up, whip up, jump at, snap at, hook, claw, clinch, grasp, gripe, grip, grab, clutch, wring, wrest, wrench, pluck, tear away, catch, nab, capture, collar, throttle.

To take from, deduct, subduct (38), subtract, curtail, retrench, abridge of, dispossess, expropriate, take away from, abstract, deprive of, bereave, divest, disendow, despoil, strip, fleece, shear, impoverish, levy, distrain, confiscate, sequester, sequestrate, commandeer, requisition, oust, extort, usurp, suck, squeeze, drain, bleed, milk, gut, dry, exhaust.

(Phrases) To suck like a leech; to be given an inch and take an ell; to sweep the board; to scoop the pool.

(Adjectives) Taking, etc., privative, prehensile, predatory, rapacious, raptorial, predial, ravenous.

790 Restitution *(Substantives)*, return, reddition, rendition, restoration, rehabilitation, remission, reinvestment, reparation, atonement.

Redemption, recovery, recuperation, release, replevin.

(Verbs) To return, restore, give back, bring back, derequisition, denationalize, render, refund, reimburse, recoup, remit, rehabilitate, repair, reinvest.

To let go, disgorge, regorge, regurgitate.

(Adjectives) Restoring, etc., recuperative.

(Phrase) Suum cuique.

———

791 Stealing *(Substantives)*, theft, thieving, thievery, abstraction, appropriation, plagiarism, depredation, pilfering, rape, larceny, robbery, shoplifting, burglary, house-breaking, abaction (of cattle), cattle-lifting, kidnapping.

Spoliation, plunder, pillage, sack, rapine, brigandage, foray, raid, hold-up, dragonnade, marauding.

Peculation, embezzlement, swindling (545), blackmail, *chantage*, smuggling, black market; thievishness, rapacity, kleptomania; den of thieves, Alsatia.

Licence to plunder, letter of marque.

(Verbs) To steal, thieve, rob, abstract, appropriate, filch, pilfer, purloin, nab, nim, prig, grab, bag, lift, pick, pinch, knock off.

To convey away, carry off, make off with, run or walk off with, abduct, spirit away, kidnap, crimp, seize, lay violent hands on, etc. (789), abact, rustle (of cattle), shanghai.

To scrounge, wangle, win, crib, sponge, rook, bilk, diddle, swindle (545), peculate, embezzle, fiddle, flog, poach, run, smuggle, hijack.

To plunder, pillage, rifle, sack, ransack, burgle, spoil, spoliate, despoil, hold up, stick up, bail up, strip, fleece, gut, loot, forage, levy blackmail, pirate, plagiarize.

(Phrases) To live by one's wits; to rob Peter to pay Paul; to obtain under false pretences; to set a thief to catch a thief.

(Adjectives) Stealing, etc., thievish, light-fingered, larcenous, stolen, furtive, piractical, predaceous.

792 Thief *(Substantives)*, robber, spoiler, pickpocket, cutpurse, dip, depredator, yegg, yeggman, footpad, highwayman, burglar, house-breaker, larcener, larcenist, pilferer, filcher, sneak-thief, shop-lifter, poacher, rustler; swell mob; the light-fingered gentry; kleptomaniac.

Swindler, crook, spiv, welsher, smuggler, bootlegger, hijacker, gangster, cracksman, magsman, mobsman, sharper, blackleg, shark, trickster, harpy, *chevalier d'industrie*, peculator, plagiarist, blackmailer; receiver, fence.

Brigand, freebooter, bandit, pirate, viking, corsair, buccaneer, thug, dacoit, picaroon, moss-trooper, rapparee, maurauder, filibuster, wrecker, bushranger; Autolycus, Turpin, Macheath, Bill Sikes, Jonathan Wild.

(Phrases) A snapper-up of unconsidered trifles; *homo triarum literarum*.

793 Booty *(Substantives)*, spoil, plunder, swag, loot, boodle, prey, pickings, grab, forage, blackmail, graft, prize.

3°. *Interchange of Property*

794 Barter *(Substantives)*, exchange, truck, swop (or swap), chop, interchange, commutation.

Traffic, trade, commerce, dealing, business, custom, negotiation, transaction, jobbing, agiotage, bargain, deal, package deal, commercial enterprise, speculation, brokery.

(Phrases) A Roland for an Oliver; a *quid pro quo*; payment in kind.

(Verbs) To barter, exchange, truck, interchange, commute, swap (or swop), traffic, trade, speculate, transact, or do business with, deal with, have dealings with; open or keep an account with; to carry on a trade; to rig the market.

To bargain; drive, make, or strike a bargain; negotiate, bid for, haggle (or higgle), chaffer, dicker, stickle, cheapen, compound for, beat down, outbid, underbid, outbargain, come to terms, do a deal, quote, underquote.

(Phrase) To throw a sprat to catch a whale.

(Adjectives) Commercial, mercantile, trading, interchangeable, marketable, negotiable; wholesale, retail.

795 Purchase *(Substantives)*, emption, buying, purchasing, shopping, hire-purchase, never-never; pre-emption, bribery, co-emption.

A buyer, purchaser, customer, emptor, shopper, patron, client, clientele.

(Verbs) To buy, purchase, procure, hire, rent, farm, pay, fee, repurchase, buy in, keep in one's pay; pre-empt; bribe, suborn, square, buy over; shop, market.

(Adjectives) Purchased, etc.

(Phrase) Caveat emptor.

---

796 Sale *(Substantives)*, disposal, custom.

Auction, Dutch auction, roup.

Lease, mortgage.

Vendibility, salability.

A vendor, seller (797).

To sell, vend, dispose of, retail, dispense, auction, auctioneer, hawk, peddle, undersell.

To let, sublet, lease, mortgage.

(Phrases) Put up to sale or auction; bring under the hammer.

(Adjectives) Vendible, marketable, salable; unpurchased, unbought, on one's hands, unsalable.

797 Merchant *(Substantives)*, trader, dealer, tradesman, buyer and seller, vendor, monger, chandler, shopkeeper, shopman, salesman, saleswoman, changer.

Retailer, chapman, hawker, huckster, regrater, higgler, pedlar, cadger, sutler, bumboatman, middleman, coster, costermonger; auctioneer, broker, money-broker, bill-broker, money-changer, jobber, factor, go-between, cambist, usurer, money-lender.

House, firm, concern, partnership, company, guild, syndicate.

798 Merchandise *(Substantives)*, ware, mercery, commodity, effects, goods, article, stock, stock-in-trade, cargo (190), produce, freight, lading, ship-load, staple commodity.

799 Mart *(Substantives)*, market, change (or 'change), exchange, bourse, market-place, fair, hall, staple, bazaar, guildhall, tollbooth (or tolbooth), custom-house.

Office, shop, counting-house, bureau, counter, stall, booth, chambers.

Warehouse, depot, store (636), *entrepôt*, emporium, godown.

4°. *Monetary Relations*

800 Money *(Substantives)*, funds, treasure, capital, stock, proceeds, assets, cash, bullion, ingot, nugget; sum, amount, balance.

Currency, soft currency, hard currency, circulating medium, legal tender, specie, coin, hard cash, sterling, pounds shillings and pence, L.S.D.

Ready, rhino, blunt, oof, lolly, splosh, chink, dibs, plunks, bucks, bones, siller, dust, tin, dough, jack, spondulicks, simoleons, mazuma, ducats, the needful, the wherewithal.

Gold, silver, copper, nickel, rouleau, dollar, etc.

Finance, gold standard, monometallism, bimetallism.

Pocket-money, pin money, chicken feed, petty cash, change, small coin; doit, farthing, bawbee, penny, shilling, stiver, mite, sou; plum, grand, monkey, pony, tenner, fiver, quid, wheel, bob, tanner, two bits.

Sum, amount, balance.

Paper money, note, bank-note, treasury note, greenback, note of hand, promissory note, I O U.

Cheque (or check), bill, draft (or draught), order, remittance, postal order, money order, warrant, coupon, debenture, bill of exchange, exchequer bill, treasury bill, assignat.

A drawer, a drawee.

False money, base coin, flash note, kite, stumer.

Science of coins, numismatics.

(Phrases) The sinews of war; the almighty dollar.

(Verbs) To draw, draw upon, endorse, issue, utter; to amount to, come to.

(Adjectives) Monetary, pecuniary, fiscal, financial, sumptuary; monometallic, bimetallic; numismatical.

(Phrases) To touch the pocket; *argumentum ad crumenam.*

801 Treasurer *(Substantives),* purse-bearer, purser, bursar, banker, moneyer, paymaster, cashier, teller, accountant, steward, trustee, almoner.

Chancellor of the Exchequer, minister of finance, Queen's Remembrancer.

802 Treasury *(Substantives),* bank, savings-bank, exchequer, coffer, chest, money-box, money-bag, strong-box, strong-room, safe, bursary, till, notecase, wallet, purse, *purse-monnaie,* purse-strings, pocket, fisc.

Consolidated fund, sinking fund, the funds, consols, government securities, war loan, savings certificates.

803 Wealth *(Substantives),* fortune, riches, opulence, affluence, independence, solvency, competence, easy circumstances, command of money; El Dorado, Golconda, plutocracy.

Means, provision, substance, resources, capital, revenue, income, alimony, livelihood, subsistence, loaves and fishes, pelf, mammon, lucre, dower (810), pension, superannuation, annuity, unearned increment, pin-money.

A rich man, capitalist, plutocrat, financier, money-bags, millionaire, a Nabob, Dives, Croesus, Midas; *rentier.*

(Phrases) The golden calf; a well-lined purse; the purse of Fortunatus; a mint or pot of money.

(Verbs) To be rich, etc., to afford.

To enrich, fill one's coffers, etc.; to capitalize.

(Phrases) To roll in riches; to wallow in wealth; to make one's pile; to feather one's nest; to line one's pockets; to keep one's head above water.

(Adjectives) Wealthy, rich, well-off, affluent, opulent, flush, oofy, solvent (734), moneyed, plutocratic.

(Phrases) Made of money; in

804 Poverty *(Substantives),* indigence, penury, pauperism, destitution, want, need, lack, necessity, privation, distress, an empty purse; bad, reduced, or straitened circumstances; narrow means, straits, insolvency, impecuniosity, beggary, mendicancy, mendicity.

A poor man, pauper, mendicant, beggar, tramp, bum, vagabond, gangrel, starveling; the proletariat; *un pauvre diable.*

Poorhouse, workhouse, the institution.

(Phrases) Res angusta domi; the wolf at the door.

(Verbs) To be poor, etc., to want, lack, starve.

To render poor, etc., to reduce, to impoverish, reduce to poverty, depauperate, ruin; to pauperize.

(Phrases) To live from hand to mouth; come upon the parish; not to have a penny; to have seen better days; to beg one's bread.

(Adjectives) Poor, indigent, penniless, moneyless, impecunious, short of money, out of money, out of dash, out of pocket, needy, destitute, necessitous, distressed, hard up, in need, in want, poverty-stricken,

funds; rich as Croesus; rolling in riches; one's ship come home.

———

badly off, in distress, pinched, straitened, dowerless, fortuneless, reduced, insolvent (806), bereft, bereaved, fleeced, stripped, stony broke, stony stumped.

(Phrases) Unable to make both ends meet; out at elbows; in reduced circumstances; not worth a sou; poor as Job; poor as a church mouse; down at heels; on one's uppers; on the rocks.

805   Credit *(Substantives)*, trust, tick, score, account.

Letter of credit, duplicate, traveller's cheque (or check); mortgage, lien, debenture.

A creditor, lender, lessor, mortgagee, debenture-holder; a dun, usurer, gombeen-man, Shylock.

(Verbs) To keep an account with, to credit, accredit.

To place to one's credit or account, give credit.

(Adjective) Crediting.

(Adverbs) On credit, on tick, on account, to pay, unpaid-for.

———

liable, chargeable, answerable for, insolvent, in the red.

Unrequited, unrewarded.

806   Debt *(Substantives)*, obligation, liability, debit, indebtment, arrears, deficit, default, insolvency.

Interest, usance, usury.

Floating debt, bad debt, floating capital, debentures; deferred payment, hire system, never-never system.

A debtor, debitor, borrower, lessee, mortgagor; a defaulter (808).

(Verbs) To be in debt, to owe, to answer for, to incur a debt, borrow (788).

(Phrases) To run up a bill; to go on tick; to outrun the constable.

(Adjectives) In debt, indebted, owing, due, unpaid, outstanding, in arrear, being minus, out of pocket, encumbered, involved, in difficulties,

807   Payment *(Substantives)*, defrayment, discharge, quittance, acquittance, settlement, clearance, liquidation, satisfaction, remittance, instalment, stake, reckoning, arrangement, composition, acknowledgment, release.

Repayment, reimbursement, retribution, reward (973).

Bill, cheque, cash, ready money (800).

(Phrase) A *quid pro quo*.

(Verbs) To pay, defray, discharge, settle, quit, acquit oneself of, reckon with, remit, clear, liquidate, release; repay, refund, reimburse.

(Phrases) To honour a bill; to strike a balance; to settle, balance, or square accounts with; to be even with; to wipe off old scores; to satisfy all demands; to pay one's way or shot; to pay in full.

808   Non-payment *(Substantives)*, default, defalcation, repudiation, protest.

Insolvency, bankruptcy, failure, whitewashing, application of the sponge.

Waste paper, dishonoured bills.

A defaulter, bankrupt, welsher, levanter, insolvent debtor, man of straw, lame duck.

(Verbs) Not to pay, to fail, break, become insolvent or bankrupt, default, defalcate.

To protest, dishonour, repudiate, nullify; hammer.

(Phrases) To run up bills; to tighten the purse-strings.

(Adjectives) Not paying, in debt, behindhand, in arrear, insolvent, bankrupt, gazetted.

(Phrases) Being minus or worse

(Adjectives) Paying, etc., paid, owing nothing, out of debt.

(Adverbs) On the nail, money down, C.O.D.

than nothing; plunged or over head and ears in debt; in the gazette; in Queer Street.

---

809 Expenditure *(Substantives)*, money going out; outgoings, expenses, disbursements, outlay.

Pay, payment, fee, hire, wages, perquisites, vails, allowance, stipend, salary, screw, dividend, tribute, subsidy, batta, bat-money, shot, scot.

Remuneration, recompense, reward (973), tips, *pourboire*, largess, honorarium, refresher, bribe, *douceur*, hush-money, extras, commission, rake-off.

Advance, subsistence money, sub, earnest, handsel, deposit, prepayment, entrance fee, entrance.

Contribution, donation, subscription, deposit, contingent, dole, quota.

Investment, purchase (795), alms (748).

(Verbs) To expend, spend, pay, disburse, lay out, lay or pay down, to cash, to come down with, brass up, shell out, fork out, bleed, make up a sum, to invest, sink money, prepay, tip.

(Phrases) To unloose the purse-strings; to pay the piper; to pay through the nose.

(Adjectives) Expending, etc., expended, etc., sumptuary.

810 Receipt *(Substantives)*, money coming in, incomings.

Income, revenue, earnings (775), rent, rental, rent-roll, rentage, return, proceeds, premium, bonus, gate-money, royalty.

Pension, annuity, tontine, jointure, dower, dowry, dot, alimony, compensation.

Emoluments, perquisites, recompense (809), sinecure.

(Verbs) To receive, pocket (789), to draw from, derive from.

To bring in, yield, return, afford, pay, accrue.

(Phrases) To get what will make the pot boil; keep the wolf from the door; bring grist to the mill.

(Adjectives) Receiving, etc., received, etc.

Gainful, profitable, remunerative, lucrative, advantageous (775).

---

811 Accounts *(Substantives)*, money matters, finance, budget, bill, score, reckoning, balance-sheet, books, account-books, ledger, day-book, cash-book, cash account, current account, deposit account, pass-book.

Book-keeping, audit, double entry.

An accountant, C.A., auditory, actuary, book-keeper.

(Verbs) To keep accounts, to enter, post, credit, debit, tot up, carry over; balance, make up accounts, take stock, audit.

To falsify, garble, cook, or doctor accounts.

812 Price *(Substantives)*, cost, expense, amount, figure, charge, demand, damage, fare, hire.

Dues, duty, toll, tax, supertax, pay-as-you-earn, P.A.Y.E., rate, impost, cess, levy, gabelle, octroi, assessment, benevolence, custom, tithe, exactment, ransom, salvage, excise, tariff, brokerage, demurrage.

Bill, account, score, reckoning.

Worth, rate, value, valuation,

813 Discount *(Substantives)*, abatement, reduction, deduction, depreciation, allowance, drawback, poundage, *agio*, percentage, rebate, set-off, backwardation, contango, tare and tret, salvage.

(Verbs) To discount, bate, abate, rebate, reduce, take off, allow, give, discount, tax.

(Adjectives) Discounting, etc.

(Adverb) At a discount.

evaluation, appraisement, market price, quotation; money's worth, pennyworth; price-current, price list.

(Verbs) To set or fix a price, appraise, assess, value, evaluate, price, charge, demand, ask, require, exact.

To fetch, sell for, cost, bring in, yield, make, change hands for, go for, realize, run into, stand one in; afford.

(Phrases) To run up a bill; to amount to; to set one back.

(Adjectives) Priced, charged, etc., to the tune of, *ad valorem*; mercenary, venal.

(Phrases) No penny, no paternoster; *point d'argent, point de Suisse.*

814 Dearness *(Substantives)*, costliness, high price, expensiveness, rise in price, overcharge, surcharge, extravagance, exorbitance, extortion.

(Phrase) A pretty penny.

(Verbs) To be dear, etc., to cost much, to come expensive; to overcharge, surcharge, bleed, fleece (791).

To pay too much, to pay through the nose.

(Adjectives) Dear, high, high-priced, expensive, costly, dear-bought, precious, unreasonable, extortionate, extravagant, exorbitant, steep, stiff.

(Adverbs) Dear, at great cost, at a premium.

-----

815 Cheapness *(Substantives)*, low price, inexpensiveness, drop in price, undercharge, bargain; absence of charge, gratuity, free admission.

(Phrases) A labour of love; the run of one's teeth; a drug in the market.

(Verbs) To be cheap, etc., to cost little, to come down or fall in price, to cut prices.

(Phrase) To have one's money's worth.

(Adjectives) Cheap, low, moderate, reasonable, inexpensive, unexpensive, low-priced, dirt-cheap, worth the money, half-price; catchpenny.

Gratuitous, gratis, free, for nothing, given away, free of cost, without charge, not charged, untaxed, scot-free, shot-free, expenseless, free of expense, free of all demands, honorary, unpaid.

(Phrases) Cheap as dirt; for a mere song; given away with a pound of tea; at cost price; at a reduction; at a sacrifice.

816 Liberality *(Substantives)*, generosity (942), bounty, munificence, bounteousness, bountifulness, charity (906), hospitality.

(Verbs) To be liberal, etc., spend freely, lavish, shower upon.

(Phrases) To loosen one's purse-strings; to give *carte blanche*; to spare no expense.

(Adjectives) Liberal, free, generous, charitable, hospitable, bountiful, bounteous, handsome, lavish, ungrudging, free-handed, open-handed, open-hearted, free-hearted, munificent, princely.

Overpaid.

-----

817 Economy *(Substantives)*, frugality, thrift, thriftiness, care, husbandry, good housewifery, austerity, retrenchment; parsimony (819).

(Verbs) To be economical, etc., to save, economize, skimp, scrimp, scrape, meet one's expenses, retrench; to lay by, put by, save up, invest, bank, hoard, accumulate.

(Phrases) To cut one's coat according to one's cloth; to make ends meet; to pay one's way; to look at both sides of a shilling; to provide for a rainy day.

(Adjectives) Economical, frugal, thrifty, canny, careful, saving, chary, spare, sparing, cheese-paring.

(Phrase) Take care of the pence and the pounds will take care of themselves.

818 Prodigality *(Substantives),* unthriftiness, thriftlessness, unthrift, waste, profusion, profuseness, extravagance, dissipation, squandering, squandermania, malversation.

A prodigal, spendthrift, squanderer, waster, wastrel.

(Verbs) To be prodigal, etc., to squander, lavish, waste, dissipate, exhaust, run through, spill, misspend, throw away money, drain.

(Phrases) To burn the candle at both ends; to make ducks and drakes of one's money; to spend money like water; to outrun the constable; to fool away, potter, muddle away, fritter away, etc., one's money; to pour water into a sieve; to go the pace.

(Adjectives) Prodigal, profuse, improvident, thriftless, unthrifty, wasteful, extravagant, lavish, dissipated.

(Phrases) Penny wise and pound foolish; money burning a hole in one's pocket.

---

819 Parsimony *(Substantives),* parsimoniousness, stint, stinginess, niggardliness, cheese-paring, extortion, illiberality, closeness, penuriousness, avarice, tenacity, covetousness, greediness, avidity, rapacity, venality, mercenariness, cupidity.

A miser, niggard, churl, screw, skinflint, money-grubber, codger, muckworm, hunks, curmudgeon, harpy.

(Phrase) Auri sacra fames.

(Verbs) To be parsimonious, etc., to grudge, begrudge, stint, pinch, screw, dole out.

(Phrases) To skin a flint; to drive a hard bargain; to tighten one's purse-strings.

(Adjectives) Parsimonious, stingy, miserly, mean, mingy, penurious, shabby, near, niggardly, cheese-paring, close, close-fisted, close-handed, chary, illiberal, ungenerous, churlish, sordid, mercenary, venal, covetous, avaricious, greedy, grasping, griping, pinching, extortionate, rapacious.

(Phrases) Having an itching palm; with a sparing hand.

CLASS VI

WORDS RELATING TO THE SENTIENT AND MORAL POWERS

SECTION I—AFFECTIONS IN GENERAL

820 Affections *(Substantives)*, character, qualities, disposition, nature, spirit, mood, tone, temper, temperament; cast or frame of mind or soul; turn, bent, idiosyncrasy, bias, turn of mind, predisposition, diathesis, predilection, propensity, proneness, proclivity, vein, humour, grain, mettle.

Soul, heart, breast, bosom, the inner man, inmost heart, heart's core, heart-strings, heart's-blood, heart of hearts, *penetralia mentis.*

Passion, pervading spirit, ruling passion, master-passion.

(Phrases) Flow of soul; fullness of the heart; the cockles of one's heart; flesh and blood.

(Verbs) To have or possess affections, etc.; be of a character, etc.; to breathe.

(Adjectives) Affected, characterized, formed, moulded, cast, tempered, attempered, framed, disposed, predisposed, prone, inclined, having a bias, etc., imbued or penetrated with; inbred, inborn, engrained (or ingrained).

821 Feeling *(Substantives)*, endurance, suffering, tolerance, sufferance, experience, sensibility (822), passion (825).

Impression, sensation, affection, response, emotion, pathos, warmth, glow, fervour, fervency, heartiness, effusiveness, effusion, gush, cordiality, ardour, exuberance, zeal, eagerness, *empressement, élan*, enthusiasm, verve, inspiration.

Blush, suffusion, flush, tingling, thrill, kick, excitement (824), turn, shock, agitation (315), heaving, flutter, flurry, fluster, twitter, stew, tremor, throb, throbbing, panting, palpitation, trepidation, perturbation, hurry of spirits, the heart swelling, throbbing, thumping, pulsating, melting, bursting; transport, rapture, ecstasy, ravishment (827).

(Verbs) To feel, receive, an impression, etc.; to be impressed with, affected with, moved with, touched with, keen on.

To bear, bear with, suffer, endure, brook, tolerate, stomach, stand, thole, experience, taste, meet with, go through, put up with, prove; to harbour, cherish, support, abide, undergo.

To blush, change colour, mantle, tingle, twitter, throb, heave, pant, palpitate, go pit-a-pat, agitate, thrill, tremble, shake, quiver, wince, simmer, burble.

To swell, glow, warm, flush, redden, look blue, look black, catch the flame, catch the infection, respond, enthuse.

To possess, pervade, penetrate, imbue, absorb, etc., the soul.

(Phrases) To bear the brunt of; to come home to one's feelings or bosom; to strike a chord.

(Adjectives) Feeling, suffering, enduring; sentient, emotive, emotional.

Impressed, moved, touched, affected with, etc., penetrated, imbued.

Warm, quick, lively, smart, strong, sharp, keen, acute, cutting, incisive, piercing, pungent, racy, piquant, poignant, caustic.

Deep, profound, indelible, ineffaceable, impressive, effective, deep-felt, home-felt, heart-felt, warm-hearted, hearty, cordial, swelling, thrilling, rapturous, ecstatic, soul-stirring, emotive, deep-mouthed, heart-expanding, electric.

Earnest, hearty, eager, exuberant, gushing, effusive, breathless, glowing, fervent, fervid, ardent, soulful, burning, red-hot, fiery, flaming, boiling, boiling over, zealous, pervading, penetrating, absorbing, hectic, rabid, fanatical; the heart being big, full, swelling, overflowing, bursting.

Wrought up, excited, passionate, enthusiastic (825).

(Phrase) Struck all of a heap.

(Adverbs) Heartily, cordially, earnestly, etc.

(Phrases) From the bottom of one's heart; *de profundis*; heart and soul; over head and ears.

---

822 Sensibility *(Substantives)*, impressibility, sensibleness, sensitiveness, hyperaesthesia (825), responsiveness, affectibility, susceptibleness, susceptibility, susceptivity, excitability, mobility, vivacity, vivaciousness, tenderness, softness, sentimentality, sentimentalism, schmalz.

Physical sensibility (375).

(Verbs) To be sensible, etc., to shrink, have a tender heart.

(Phrases) To be touched to the quick; to feel where the shoe pinches; to take it hard; to take to heart.

(Adjectives) Sensible, sensitive, impressible, impressionable, susceptive, susceptible, responsive, excitable, mobile, thin-skinned, touchy, alive, vivacious, lively, mettlesome, high-strung, intense, emotional, tender, soft, sentimental, maudlin, sloppy, romantic, enthusiastic, neurotic.

(Adverbs) Sensibly, etc., to the quick.

---

823 Insensibility *(Substantives)*, insensibleness, inertness, insensitivity, impassibility, impassibleness, impassivity, apathy, phlegm, dullness, hebetude, coolness, coldness, supineness, stoicism, insouciance, nonchalance, indifference, lukewarmness, frigidity, cold blood, sang-froid, dry eyes, cold heart, deadness, torpor, torpidity, ataraxia, pococurantism.

Lethargy, coma, trance, stupor, stupefaction, amnesia, paralysis, palsy, catalepsy, suspended animation, hebetation, anaesthesia (381), stock and stone, neutrality.

Physical insensibility (376).

(Verbs) To disregard, be insensible, not to be affected by, not to mind, to vegetate, *laisser aller*, not to care; to take it easy.

To render insensible (376), numb, benumb, paralyse, deaden, render callous, sear, inure, harden, steel, case-harden, stun, daze, stupefy, brutalize, hebetate.

(Phrases) To turn a deaf ear to; not care a straw (or a fig).

(Adjectives) Insensible, unconscious, impassive, unsusceptible, insusceptible, impassible, unimpressionable, unresponsive, unfeeling, blind to, deaf to, dead to, passionless, spiritless, soulless, apathetic, listless, phlegmatic, callous, hard-boiled, thick-skinned, pachydermatous, obtuse, proof against, case-hardened, inured, steeled against, stoical, dull, frigid, cold, cold-blooded, cold-hearted, flat, inert, bovine, supine, sluggish, torpid, languid, tame, tepid, numb, numbed, sleepy, yawning, comatose, anaesthetic.

Indifferent, insouciant, lukewarm, careless, mindless, regardless, disregarding, nonchalant, unconcerned, uninterested, pococurante; taking no interest in.

Unfelt, unaffected, unruffled, unimpressed, unmoved, unperturbed, uninspired, untouched, etc.; platonic, imperturbable, vegetative, automatic.

(Adverbs) Insensibly, etc., *aequo animo*, with dry eyes, with withers unwrung.

(Phrases) No matter; never mind; *n'importe*; it matters not; it does not signify; it is of no consequence or importance (643); it cannot be helped; nothing coming amiss; it is all the same or all one to; what's the odds? *nichevo*.

824 Excitation *(Substantives)*, of feeling, excitement, galvanism, stimulation, provocation, calling forth, infection, animation, inspiration, agitation, perturbation, subjugation, fascination, intoxication, enravishment, unction; a scene, sensation, tableau, shocker, thriller.

(Verbs) To excite, affect, touch, move, stir, wake, awaken, raise, raise up, evoke, call up, summon up, rake up.

To impress, strike, hit, quicken, swell, work upon.

To warm, kindle, stimulate, pique, whet, animate, hearten, inspire, impassion, inspirit, spirit, provoke, irritate, infuriate, sting, rouse, work up, hurry on, ginger up, commove.

To agitate, ruffle, flutter, fluster, flush, shake, thrill, penetrate, pierce, cut; to work oneself up, to simmer, bubble, burble.

To soften, subdue, overcome, master, overpower, overwhelm, bring under.

To shock, stagger, jar, jolt, stun, astound, electrify, galvanize, give one a shock, petrify.

To madden, intoxicate, fascinate, transport, ravish, enrapture, enravish, entrance, send.

(Phrases) To come home to one's feelings; to make a sensation; to prey on the mind; to give one a turn; to cut to the quick; to go through one; to strike one all of a heap; to make one's blood boil; to lash to a fury; to make one sit up.

(Adjectives) Excited, affected (825), wrought up, worked up, strung up, lost, *éperdu*, wild, haggard, feverish, febrile.

Exciting, etc., impressive, pathetic, sensational, provocative, piquant, aphrodisiac, dramatic, warm, glowing, fervid, swelling.

(Phrases) Being all of a twitter; all of a flutter; the head being turned.

825 Excess of sensitiveness.

Excitability *(Substantives)*, intolerance, impatience, wincing, perturbation, trepidation, disquiet, disquietude, restlessness, fidgets, fidgetiness, fuss, hurry, agitation, flurry, fluster, flutter, irritability (901), hypersensitiveness, hyperaesthesia.

Passion, excitement, vehemence, impetuosity, flush, heat, fever, fire, flame, fume, wildness, turbulence, boisterousness, tumult, effervescence, ebullition, boiling, boiling over, whiff, gust, storm, tempest, outbreak, outburst, burst, explosion, fit, paroxysm, brain-storm, the blood boiling.

Fierceness, rage, fury, furore, tantrum, hysteria, hysterics, raving, delirium, frenzy, intoxication, fascination, infection, infatuation, fanaticism, Quixotism, *la tête montée*.

826 Absence of excitability.

Inexcitability *(Substantives)*, hebetude, tolerance, patience.

Coolness, composure, calmness, imperturbability, sang-froid, collectedness, tranquillity, quiet, quietude, quietness, sedateness, soberness, poise, staidness, gravity, placidity, sobriety, philosophy, stoicism, demureness, meekness, gentleness, mildness.

Submission, resignation, sufferance, endurance, longanimity, long-sufferance, forbearance, fortitude, equanimity.

Repression, restraint (174), hebetation, tranquillization.

(Phrases) Patience of Job; even temper; cool head; Spartan endurance; a sober-sides.

(Verbs) To be composed, etc., to

(Verbs) To be intolerant, etc., not to bear, to bear ill, wince, chafe, fidget, fuss, not to be able to bear, stand, tolerate, etc.

To break out, fly out, burst out, explode, run riot, boil, boil over, fly off, flare up, fire, take fire, fume, rage, rampage, rave, run mad, run amuck, raise Cain.

(Phrases) To fly off at a tangent; to be out of all patience; to go off the deep end; to get the wind up; to make a scene; to go up in a blue flame.

(Adjectives) Excitable, etc., excited, etc.

Intolerant, impatient, unquiet, restless, restive, fidgety, irritable, mettlesome, chafing, wincing, etc.

Vehement, boisterous, impetuous, demonstrative, fierce, fiery, flaming, boiling, ebullient, over-zealous, passionate, impassioned, enthusiastic, rampant, mercurial, high-strung, skittish, overwrought, overstrung, hysterical, hot-headed, hurried, turbulent, furious, fuming, boiling, raging, raving, frantic, phrenetic, rampageous, wild, heady, delirious, intoxicated, demoniacal; hypersensitive.

Overpowering, overwhelming, uncontrolled, madcap, reckless, stanchless, irrepressible, ungovernable, uncontrollable, inextinguishable, volcanic.

(Phrases) More than flesh and blood can stand; stung to the quick; all hot and bothered.

(Interjections) Pish! pshaw! botheration!

bear, to bear well, tolerate, put up with, bear with, stand, bide, abide, aby, take easily, rub on, rub along, make the best of, acquiesce, submit, yield, bow to, resign oneself, suffer, endure, support, go through, reconcile oneself to, bend under; subside, calm down, pipe down.

To brook, digest, eat, swallow, pocket, stomach, brave, make light of.

To be borne, endured, etc., to go down.

To allay, compose, calm, still, lull, pacify, placate, quiet, tranquillize, hush, smooth, appease, assuage, mitigate, soothe, soften, temper, chasten, alleviate, moderate, sober down, mollify, lenify, tame, blunt, obtund, dull, deaden (823), slacken, damp, repress, restrain, check, curb, bridle, rein in, smother (174).

(Phrases) To take things as they come; to submit with a good grace; to shrug the shoulders.

To set one's heart at rest or at ease.

(Adjectives) Inexcitable, unexcited, calm, cool, temperate, composed, collected, placid, quiet, tranquil, unstirred, undisturbed, unruffled, serene, demure, sedate, staid, sober, dispassionate, unimpassioned, passionless, good-natured, easy-going, platonic, philosophic, stoical, imperturbable, cold-blooded, insensible (823).

Meek, tolerant, patient, submissive, unoffended, unresenting, content, resigned, subdued, bearing with, longsuffering, gentle, mild, sober-minded, cool-headed.

(Phrases) Gentle or meek as a lamb; mild as milk; patient as Job; armed with patience; cool as a cucumber.

SECTION II—PERSONAL AFFECTIONS

1°. *Passive Affections*

827 Pleasure *(Substantives)*, gratification, delectation, enjoyment, fruition, relish, zest, gusto, kick.

Well-being, satisfaction, complacency, content (831), ease, comfort, bed of roses, bed of down, velvet.

828 Pain *(Substantives)*, suffering; physical pain (378).

Displeasure, dissatisfaction, discontent, discomfort, discomposure, malaise.

Uneasiness, disquiet, inquietude,

Joy, gladness, delight, glee, cheer, sunshine.

Physical pleasure (377).

Treat, refreshment, feast, luxury, voluptuousness, clover.

Happiness, felicity, bliss, beatitude, beatification, enchantment, transport, rapture, ravishment, ecstasy, heaven, *summum bonum*, paradise, Eden, Arcadia, nirvana, elysium, empyrean (981).

Honeymoon, palmy days, halcyon days, golden age, *Saturnia regna*.

(Verbs) To be pleased, etc., to feel, receive, or derive pleasure, etc.; to take pleasure or delight in; to delight in, joy in, rejoice in, relish, like, enjoy, take to, take in good part.

To indulge in, treat oneself, solace oneself, revel, riot, luxuriate in, gloat over; to be on velvet, in clover, in heaven, etc.; to enjoy oneself; to congratulate oneself, hug oneself.

(Phrases) To slake the appetite; to bask in the sunshine; to tread on enchanted ground; to have a good time; to make whoopee.

(Adjectives) Pleased, enjoying, relishing, liking, gratified, glad, gladdened, rejoiced, delighted, overjoyed, charmed.

Cheered, enlivened, flattered, tickled, indulged, regaled, treated.

Comfortable, at ease, easy, cosy, satisfied, content (831), luxurious, on velvet, in clover, on a bed of roses, *sans souci*.

Happy, blest, blessed, blissful, overjoyed, enchanted, captivated, fascinated, transported, raptured, rapt, enraptured, in raptures, in ecstasies, in a transport, beatified, in heaven, in the seventh heaven, in paradise.

(Phrases) With a joyful face; with sparkling eyes; happy as a king; pleased as Punch; in the lap of luxury; happy as the day is long; *ter quaterque beatus*.

(Adverbs) Happily, etc.

———

weariness (841), dejection (837).

Annoyance, irritation, plague, bore, bother, botheration, worry, infliction, stew.

Care, anxiety, concern, mortification, vexation, chagrin, trouble, trial, solicitude, cark, dole, dule, load, burden, fret.

Grief, sorrow, distress, affliction, woe, bitterness, heartache, a heavy heart, a bleeding heart, a broken heart, heavy affliction.

Unhappiness, infelicity, misery, wretchedness, desolation, tribulation.

Dolour, sufferance, ache, aching, hurt, smart, cut, twitch, twinge, stitch, cramp, spasm, nightmare, convulsion, throe, angina.

Pang, anguish, agony, torture, torment, rack, crucifixion, martyrdom, purgatory, hell (982).

A sufferer, victim, prey, martyr.

(Phrases) Vexation of spirit; a peck of troubles; a sea of troubles; the ills that flesh is heir to; *mauvais quart d'heure*; the iron entering the soul.

(Verbs) To feel, suffer, or experience pain, etc.; to suffer, ache, smart, ail, bleed, twinge, tingle, gripe, wince, writhe.

To grieve, fret, pine, mourn, bleed, worry oneself, chafe, yearn, droop, sink, give way, despair (859).

(Phrases) To sit on thorns; to be on pins and needles; to labour under afflictions; to have a bad or thin time; to drain the cup of misery to the dregs; to fall on evil days.

(Adjectives) In pain; feeling, suffering, enduring, etc., pain; in a state of pain, of suffering, etc., sore, aching, suffering, ailing, etc., pained, hurt, stung (830).

Displeased, annoyed, dissatisfied, discontented, weary (832), uneasy, ungratified, uncomfortable, ill at ease.

Crushed, stricken, victimized, ill-used.

Concerned, afflicted, in affliction, sorry, sorrowful, in sorrow, cut up, bathed in tears (839).

Unhappy, unfortunate, hapless, unblest, luckless, unlucky, ill-fated, ill-starred, fretting, wretched, miserable, careworn, disconsolate, in-consolable, woebegone, poor, forlorn, comfortless, a prey to grief, etc., despairing, in despair (859), heart-broken, broken-hearted, the heart bleeding, doomed, devoted, accursed, undone.

829 Capability of giving pleasure.

Pleasurableness (*Substantives*), pleasantness, gratefulness, welcomeness, acceptableness, acceptability, agreeableness, delectability, deliciousness, daintiness, sweetness, luxuriousness, lusciousness, voluptuousness, eroticism.

Charm, attraction, attractiveness, sex-appeal, S.A., It, oomph, fascination, witchery, prestige, loveliness, takingness, winsomeness, likableness, invitingness, glamour.

A treat, dainty, titbit, bonbon, *bonne bouche*, sweet, sweetmeat, sugar-plum, nuts, *sauce piquante*.

(*Verbs*) To cause, produce, create, give, afford, procure, offer, present, yield, etc., pleasure, gratification, etc.

To please, take, gratify, satisfy, indulge, flatter, tickle, humour, regale, refresh, interest.

To charm, rejoice, cheer, gladden, delight, enliven (836), to transport, captivate, fascinate, enchant, entrance, bewitch, ravish, enrapture, enravish, beatify, enthral, imparadise.

(*Phrases*) To do one's heart good; to tickle one to death; to take one's fancy.

(*Adjectives*) Causing or giving pleasure, etc., pleasing, agreeable, grateful, gratifying, pleasant, pleasurable, acceptable, welcome, glad, gladsome, comfortable.

Sweet, delectable, nice, jolly, palatable, dainty, delicate, delicious, dulcet, savoury, toothsome, tasty, luscious, luxurious, voluptuous, genial, cordial, refreshing, comfortable, scrumptious.

Fair, lovely, favourite, attractive, engaging, winsome, winning, taking, prepossessing, inviting, captivating, bewitching, fascinating, magnetic, seductive, killing, stunning, ripping, smashing, likable.

Charming, delightful, exquisite, enchanting, enthralling, ravishing,

830 Capability of giving pain.

Painfulness (*Substantives*), disagreeableness, unpleasantness, irksomeness, displeasingness, unacceptableness, bitterness, vexatiousness, troublesomeness.

Trouble, care, cross, annoyance, burden, load, nuisance, pest, plague, bore, bother, botheration, vexation, sickener, pin-prick.

Scourge, bitter pill, worm, canker, cancer, ulcer, curse, gall and wormwood, sting, pricks, scorpion, thorn, brier, bramble, hornet, whip, lash, rack, wheel.

A mishap, misadventure, mischance, pressure, infestation, grievance, trial, crosses, hardship, blow, stroke, affliction, misfortune, reverse, infliction, dispensation, visitation, disaster, undoing, tragedy, calamity, catastrophe, adversity (735).

Provocation, infestation, affront, aggravation, indignity, outrage (900, 929).

(*Phrases*) A thorn in one's side; a fly in the ointment; a sorry sight; a bitter pill; a crumpled rose-leaf.

(*Verbs*) To cause, produce, give, etc., pain, uneasiness, suffering, etc.

To pain, hurt, wound, sting, pinch, grate upon, irk, gall, jar, chafe, gnaw, prick, lacerate, pierce, cut, cut up, stick, gravel, hurt one's feelings, mortify, horrify, shock, twinge, gripe.

To wring, harrow, torment, torture, rack, scarify, cruciate, crucify, convulse, agonize.

To displease, annoy, incommode, discompose, trouble, disquiet, grieve, cross, tease, rag, josh, bait, tire, vex, worry, try, plague, fash, faze, fret, haunt, obsess, bother, pester, bore, gravel, flummox, harass, importune, tantalize, aggravate.

To irritate, provoke, nettle, pique, rile, ruffle, aggrieve, enchafe, enrage.

rapturous, heart-felt, thrilling, beatific, heavenly, celestial, elysian, empyrean, seraphic, ideal.

Palmy, halcyon, Saturnian, Arcadian.

(Phrases) To one's heart's content; to one's taste.

———

To maltreat, bite, assail, badger, infest, harry, persecute, haze, roast.

To sicken, disgust, revolt, turn the stomach, nauseate, disenchant, repel, offend, shock.

To horrify, prostrate.

(Phrases) To barb the dart; to set the teeth on edge; to stink in the nostrils; to stick in one's throat; to add a nail to one's coffin; to plant a dagger in the breast; to freeze the blood; to make one's flesh creep; to make one's hair stand on end; to break or wring the heart.

(Adjectives) Causing, occasioning, giving, producing, creating, inflicting, etc., pain, etc., hurting, etc.

Painful, dolorific, dolorous, unpleasant, unpleasing, displeasing, unprepossessing, disagreeable, distasteful, uncomfortable, unwelcome, unsatisfactory, unpalatable, unacceptable, thankless, undesirable, untoward, unlucky, undesired, obnoxious.

Distressing, bitter, afflicting, afflictive, cheerless, joyless, comfortless, depressing, depressive, mournful, dreary, dismal, bleak, melancholy, grievous, pathetic, woeful, disastrous, calamitous, ruinous, sad, tragic, tragical, deplorable, dreadful, frightful, lamentable, ill-omened.

Irritating, provoking, provocative, stinging, biting, vexatious, annoying, unaccommodating, troublesome, fashious, wearisome, tiresome, irksome, plaguing, plaguy, teasing, pestering, bothering, bothersome, carking, mortifying, galling, harassing, worrying, tormenting, aggravating, racking, importunate, insistent.

Intolerable, insufferable, insupportable, unbearable, unendurable, shocking, frightful, terrific, grim, appalling, dire, heart-breaking, heart-rending, heart-wounding, heart-corroding, dreadful, horrid, harrowing, horrifying, horrific, execrable, accursed, damnable.

Odious, hateful, unpopular, repulsive, repellent, uninviting, offensive, nauseous, disgusting, sickening, nasty, execrable, revolting, shocking, vile, foul, abominable, loathsome, rotten.

Sharp, acute, sore, severe, grave, hard, harsh, bitter, cruel, biting, caustic, corroding, consuming, racking, excruciating, grinding, agonizing.

(Phrase) More than flesh and blood can bear.

(Adverbs) Painfully, etc.

---

831 Content *(Substantives)*, contentment, contentedness, satisfaction, peace of mind, complacency, serenity, sereneness, ease.

Comfort, snugness, well-being.

Moderation, patience (826), endurance, resignation, reconciliation.

(Verbs) To be content, etc.; to rest satisfied, to put up with; to take up with; to be reconciled to.

To render content, etc., to set at ease, to conciliate, reconcile, disarm, propitiate, win over, satisfy, indulge, slake, gratify.

832 Discontent *(Substantives)*, discontentment, dissatisfaction, disappointment, mortification.

Repining, taking on, inquietude, heart-burning, regret (833).

Nostalgia, home-sickness, *maladie du pays*.

Grumbler, grouser, croaker.

(Verbs) To be discontented, dissatisfied, etc.; to repine, regret (833), grumble (839).

To cause discontent, etc., to disappoint, dissatisfy, mortify.

(Phrases) To take in bad part; to

(Phrases) To make the best of; to let well alone; to take in good part; to set one's heart at ease or at rest.

(Adjectives) Content, contented, satisfied, at ease, easy, snug, comfortable, cosy.

Patient, resigned to, reconciled to, unrepining; disarming, conciliatory.

Unafflicted, unvexed, unmolested, unplagued, etc., serene, at rest, *sine cura, sans souci.*

(Phrases) To one's heart's content; like patience on a monument.

(Interjections) Very well, all right, suits me.

833 Regret *(Substantives)*, bitterness, repining; lamentation (839); self-reproach, penitence (950).

(Verbs) To regret, deplore, repine, lament, rue, repent (950).

(Phrase) To rue the day.

(Adjectives) Regretting, etc., regretful, regretted, regrettable, lamentable.

(Phrase) What a pity!

835 Aggravation *(Substantives)*, heightening, exacerbation, exasperation.

(Verbs) To aggravate, render worse, heighten, intensify, embitter, sour, acerbate, envenom, exacerbate, exasperate.

(Phrase) To add fuel to the flame.

(Adjectives) Aggravating, etc., aggravated, etc., unrelieved; aggravable.

(Phrases) Out of the frying-pan into the fire; from bad to worse.

836 Cheerfulness *(Substantives)*, gaiety, cheer, spirits, high spirits, high glee, light-heartedness, joyfulness, joyousness, good humour, geniality, hilarity, exhilaration, liveliness, sprightliness, briskness, vivacity, buoyancy, sunniness, jocundity, joviality, levity, sportiveness, playfulness, jocularity.

Mirth, merriment, merrymaking, laughter (838), amusement (840); nepenthe, Euphrosyne.

Gratulation, rejoicing, exultation,

have the hump; to quarrel with one's bread and butter.

(Adjectives) Discontented, dissatisfied, unsatisfied, malcontent, mortified, disappointed, cut up.

Repining, glum, grumbling, grousing, grouchy, exigent, *exigeant*, exacting; nostalgic, home-sick; disgruntled.

Disappointing, unsatisfactory.

(Phrases) Out of humour; in the dumps; in high dudgeon; down in the mouth.

————

834 Relief *(Substantives)*, easement, alleviation, mitigation, palliation, solace, consolation, comfort, encouragement, refreshment (689), lullaby; deliverance, delivery.

Lenitive, balm, oil, restorative, cataplasm (662); cushion, pillow, bolster (215).

(Phrases) A crumb of comfort; balm in Gilead.

(Verbs) To relieve, ease, alleviate, mitigate, palliate, soften, soothe, assuage, allay, cheer, comfort, console, encourage, bear up, refresh, restore, remedy, cure.

(Phrases) To dry the tears; to pour balm into; to lay the flattering unction to one's soul; to temper the wind to the shorn lamb; to breathe again; to breathe freely.

(Adjectives) Relieving, etc., consolatory; balmy, balsamic, soothing, lenitive, anodyne (662), remedial, curative; easeful.

837 Dejection *(Substantives)*, depression, low spirits, lowness or depression of spirits, dejectedness, sadness.

Heaviness, dullness, infestivity, joylessness, gloom, dolefulness, dolesomeness, weariness (841), heaviness of heart, heart-sickness.

Melancholy, melancholia, dismals, mumps, dumps, doldrums, blues, mulligrubs, blue devils, megrims, vapours, accidie, spleen, hypochondria; *taedium vitae; maladie du pays.*

jubilation, jubilee, triumph, paean, Te Deum, heyday; joy-bells.

(Verbs) To be cheerful, etc.; to be of good cheer, to cheer up, perk up, brighten up, light up; take heart, bear up.

To rejoice, make merry, exult, congratulate oneself, triumph, clap the hands, crow, sing, carol, lilt, frisk, prance, galumph, rollick, maffick, frivol.

To cheer, enliven, elate, exhilarate, entrance, inspirit, animate, gladden, buck up, liven up.

(Phrases) To drive dull care away; to make whoopee; to keep up one's spirits; care killed the cat; *ride si sapis*; laugh and grow fat.

(Adjectives) Cheerful, gay, blithe, cheery, jovial, genial, gleeful, of good cheer, in spirits, in good or high spirits, *allegro*, light, lightsome, buoyant, debonair, bright, glad, light-hearted, hearty, free and easy, airy, jaunty, canty, perky, spry, chipper, saucy, sprightly, lively, vivacious, sunny, breezy, chirpy, hopeful (858).

Merry, joyous, joyful, jocund, playful, waggish, frisky, frolicsome, sportive, gamesome, jokesome, joky, jocose, jocular, jolly, frivolous.

Rejoicing, elated, exulting, jubilant, hilarious, flushed, rollicking, cock-a-hoop.

(Phrases) In high feather; walking on air; with one's head in the clouds; gay as a lark; happy as a king or as the day is long; playful as a kitten; jolly as a sandboy; merry as a grig; full of beans.

(Adverbs) Cheerfully, cheerily, cheerly, etc.

(Interjections) Cheer up! never say die! hurrah! huzza!

Despondency, despair, pessimism, disconsolateness, prostration; the Slough of Despond (859).

Demureness, seriousness, gravity, solemnity, solemnness, sullenness.

A hypochondriac, self-tormentor, *malade imaginaire*, kill-joy, Job's comforter, wet blanket, pessimist, futilitarian.

(Verbs) To be dejected, sad, etc.; to grieve, take on, take to heart, give way, droop, sink, lour, look downcast, mope, mump, pout, brood over, fret, pine, yearn, frown, despond (859).

To depress, discourage, dishearten, dispirit, dull, deject, lower, sink, dash, unman, prostrate, over-cloud.

(Phrases) To look blue; to hang down the head; to wear the willow; to laugh on the wrong side of the mouth; to get the hump.

To prey on the mind or spirits; to dash one's hopes.

(Adjectives) Cheerless, unmirthful, mirthless, joyless, dull, glum, flat, dispirited, out of spirits, out of sorts, out of heart, in low spirits, spiritless, lowering, frowning, sulky.

Discouraged, disheartened, downhearted, downcast, cast down, depressed, chap-fallen, crest-fallen, dashed, drooping, sunk, heart-sick, dumpish, mumpish, desponding, pessimistic.

Dismal, melancholy, sombre, tristful, *triste*, pensive, *penseroso*, mournful, doleful, moping, splenetic, gloomy, lugubrious, funereal, woebegone, comfortless, forlorn, overcome, prostrate, cut up, care-worn, care-laden.

Melancholic, hipped, hypochondriacal, bilious, jaundiced, atrabilious, atrabiliar, saturnine, adust.

Disconsolate, inconsolable, despairing, in despair (859).

Grave, serious, sedate, staid, sober, solemn, grim, grim-faced, grim-visaged (846), rueful, sullen.

Depressing, preying upon the mind (830).

(Phrases) Down in the mouth; down on one's luck; sick at heart; with a long face; a prey to melancholy; dull as a beetle; dull as ditchwater; as melancholy as a gib-cat; grave as a judge.

838 Expression of pleasure.

Rejoicing (*Substantives*), exultation, heyday, triumph, jubilation, jubilee (840), paean (990).

Smile, simper, smirk, grin, broad grin.

Laughter, giggle, titter, snigger, crow, cheer, chuckle, guffaw, shout, hearty laugh, horse-laugh, cachinnation; a shout, burst, or peal of laughter. Derision, risibility (856).

Momus, Democritus the Abderite.

(*Verbs*) To rejoice, exult, triumph (884), hug oneself, sing, carol, dance with joy.

To smile, simper, smirk, grin, mock; to laugh, giggle, titter, snigger, chuckle, chortle, burble, crow, cackle; to burst out, shout, guffaw.

To cause, create, occasion, raise, excite, or produce laughter, etc.; to tickle, titillate.

(*Phrases*) To clap one's hands; to fling up one's cap; to laugh in one's sleeve; to shake one's sides; to hold both one's sides; to split one's sides; to die with laughter.

To tickle one's fancy; to set the table in a roar; to convulse with laughter; to be the death of one.

(*Adjectives*) Laughing, rejoicing, etc.; jubilant (836), triumphant.

Laughable, risible, ludicrous (853), side-splitting.

(*Phrases*) Ready to burst or split oneself; 'Laughter holding both his sides.'

(*Interjections*) Hurrah! three cheers!

---

839 Expression of pain.

Lamentation (*Substantives*), complaint, murmur, mutter, plaint, lament, wail, sigh, suspiration, heaving.

Cry, whine, whimper, sob, tear, moan, snivel, grumble, groan.

Outcry, scream, screech, howl, whoop, yell, roar (414).

Weeping, crying, etc.; lachrymation, complaining, frown, scowl, sardonic grin or laugh.

Dirge (363), elegy, requiem, monody, threnody, jeremiad; coronach, wake, keen, keening.

Plaintiveness, querimoniousness, languishment, querulousness.

Mourning, weeds, willow, cypress, crape, sackcloth and ashes.

A grumbler, grouser, croaker, drip; Heraclitus, Niobe.

(*Phrases*) The melting mood; wringing of hands; weeping and gnashing of teeth.

(*Verbs*) To lament, mourn, grieve, keen, complain, murmur, mutter, grumble, grouse, belly-ache, beef, squawk, sigh; give, fetch, or heave a sigh.

To cry, weep, sob, greet, blubber, blub; snivel, whimper; to shed tears; pule, take on, pine.

To grumble, groan, grunt, croak, whine, moan, bemoan, wail, bewail, frown, scowl.

To cry out, growl, mew, mewl, squeak, squeal, sing out, scream, cry out lustily, screech, skirl, bawl, howl, holloa, bellow, yell, roar, yammer.

(*Phrases*) To melt or burst into tears; to cry oneself blind; to cry one's eyes out; to beat one's breast; to wring one's hands; to gnash one's teeth; to tear one's hair; to cry before one is hurt; to laugh on the wrong side of one's mouth.

(*Adjectives*) Lamenting, complaining, etc.; mournful, doleful, sad, tearful, lachrymose, plaintive, plaintful, querulous, querimonious, elegiac.

(*Phrases*) With tears in one's eyes; bathed or dissolved in tears; the tears starting from the eyes.

(*Interjections*) O dear! ah me! alas! alack! heigh-ho! ochone! well-a-day! well-a-way! alas the day! woe worth the day! *O tempora, O mores!*

---

840 Amusement (*Substantives*), diversion, entertainment, sport, divertissement, recreation, relaxation, distraction, avocation, pastime.

841 Weariness (*Substantives*), tedium, ennui, boredom, lassitude, fatigue (688), dejection (837).

Disgust, nausea, loathing, sickness,

Fun, frolic, pleasantry, drollery, jollity, joviality, jovialness, jocoseness, laughter (838).

Play, game, gambol, romp, prank, quip, quirk, rig, lark, fling, bat, spree, burst, binge, razzle-dazzle, escapade, dido, monkey-shines, ploy, jamboree.

Dance (309), ball, ballet (599), hop, shindig, jig, fling, reel, strathspey, cotillion, quadrille, lancers, rigadoon, saraband, lavolta, pavane, galliard, hornpipe, can-can, tarantella, cachucha, fandango, bolero, minuet, gavotte, polka, mazurka, schottische, waltz (or valse), fox-trot, tango, maxixe, rumba, samba, blues, two-step, one-step; folk-dance, morris-dance, square dance, round dance, country dance, step-dance, clog-dance, sword-dance, egg-dance, cake-walk, break-down.

Festivity, festival, jubilee, party (892), merrymaking, rejoicing, fête, gala, ridotto, revelry, revels, carnival, corroboree, saturnalia, high jinks, night out.

Feast, banquet, entertainment, carousal, bean-feast, beano, wayz-goose, jollification, junketing, junket, wake, field-day, regatta, fair, kermess, fête champêtre, symposium, wassail.

Buffoonery, mummery, tomfoolery, raree-show, puppet-show, masquerade.

Bonfire, fireworks, feu de joie.

A holiday, gala day, red-letter day.

A place of amusement, theatre, music-hall, concert-hall, cinema, circus, hippodrome, ballroom, dance hall, arena, auditorium, recreation ground, playground, playing field, park.

Toy, plaything, bauble, doll, puppet, teddy-bear.

A master of ceremonies, or revels; a sportsman, sportswoman, gamester, reveller; devotee, votary, enthusiast, fan.

(Phrases) A round of pleasure; a short life and a merry one; high days and holidays.

(Verbs) To amuse, divert, entertain, rejoice, cheer, recreate, enliven, solace; to beguile or while away the time; to drown care.

To play, sport, disport, make merry, take one's pleasure, make holiday, keep holiday; to game, gambol, revel, frisk, frolic, romp, jollify, skylark, dally; to dance, hop, foot it, jump, caper, cut capers, skip.

To treat, feast, regale, carouse, banquet.

(Phrases) To play the fool; to jump over the moon; to make a night of it; to make whoopee; to go on the bust; to have one's fling; desipere in loco.

disgust of life, taedium vitae, Weltschmerz.

Wearisomeness, irksomeness, tiresomeness, monotony, sameness, treadmill, grind.

A bore, a buttonholer, proser, fossil, wet blanket.

(Phrases) A twice-told tale; time hanging heavily on one's hands; a thin time.

(Verbs) To tire, weary, fatigue, fag, jade, bore; set to sleep, send to sleep.

To sicken, disgust, nauseate.

(Phrases) To harp on the same string; to bore to tears; never hear the last of.

(Adjectives) Wearying, etc., wearisome, tiresome, irksome, uninteresting, devoid of interest, monotonous, humdrum, pedestrian, mortal, flat, tedious, prosy, prosing, slow, soporific, somniferous.

Disgusting, sickening, nauseating.

Weary, tired, etc.; aweary, uninterested, sick of, flagging, used up, blasé, bored, stale, fed up, browned off, brassed off, cheesed off, chokka, weary of life; drowsy, somnolent, sleepy (683).

(Adverbs) Wearily, etc.

(Phrase) Ad nauseam.

(Adjectives) Amusing, amusive, diverting, entertaining, etc., amused, etc.
Sportive, jovial, festive, jocose, tricksy, rompish.
(Phrases) On with the dance! *vogue la galère! vive la bagatelle!*

842 Wit *(Substantives)*, humour, comicality, imagination (515), fancy, fun, drollery, whim, jocularity, jocosity, facetiousness, waggery, waggishness, wittiness, salt, Atticism, Attic wit, Attic salt, *esprit*, smartness, banter, chaff, persiflage, badinage, farce, *espièglerie*.

Jest, joke, jape, conceit, quip, quirk, quiddity, crank, wheeze, side-splitter, *concetto*, witticism, gag, wisecrack, repartee, retort, comeback, *mot, bon mot*, pleasantry, funniment, flash of wit, happy thought, sally, point, dry joke, idle conceit, epigram, quibble, play upon words, pun (563), conundrum, anagram (533), quodlibet, *jeu d'esprit, facetiae*; a chestnut, a Joe Miller; an absurdity (497).

A practical joke, a rag.

(Phrases) The cream of the jest; the joke of it; *le mot pour rire*.

(Verbs) To joke, jest, jape, retort; to cut jokes, crack a joke, perpetrate a joke or pun.

To laugh at, banter, rally, chaff, josh, jolly, jeer (856), rag, guy, kid; to make fun of, make merry with.

(Phrase) To set the table in a roar.

(Adjectives) Witty, facetious, humorous, fanciful, quick-witted, ready-witted, nimble-witted, imaginative (515), sprightly, *spirituel*, smart, jocose, jocular, waggish, comic, comical, laughable, droll, ludicrous, side-splitting, killing, funny, risible, farcical, roguish, sportive, pleasant, playful, sparkling, entertaining, arch.

(Adverbs) In joke, in jest, in sport, for fun.

843 Dullness *(Substantives)*, heaviness, stolidness, stolidity, dumbness, stupidity (499), flatness, prosiness, gravity (837), solemnity; prose, matter of fact, platitude, commonplace, bromide.

(Verbs) To be dull, prose, fall flat.

To render dull, etc., damp, depress.

(Phrase) To throw cold water on.

(Adjectives) Dull, prosaic, prosing, prosy, unentertaining, dismal (837), uninteresting, boring, flat, pointless, stolid, humdrum (841), pedestrian, literal, unimaginative, matter-of-fact, commonplace.

Slow, stupid, dumb, plodding, Boeotian.

(Phrases) Dull as ditch-water; *Davus sum, non Oedipus; aliquando bonus dormitat Homerus.*

---

844 A Humorist *(Substantives)*, wag, wit, funny man, caricaturist, cartoonist, epigrammatist, *bel esprit*, jester, joker, punster, wise-cracker.

A buffoon (599), comedian, *farceur*, merry-andrew, jack-pudding, tumbler, mountebank, harlequin, punch, punchinello, scaramouch, clown, pantaloon.

(Phrase) The life and soul of the party.

2°. *Discriminative Affections*

845 Beauty *(Substantives)*, handsomeness, beauteousness, beautifulness, pulchritude, aesthetics.

Form, elegance, grace, symmetry, *belle tournure*; good looks.

846 Ugliness *(Substantives)*, deformity, inelegance, plainness, homeliness, uncomeliness, ungainliness, uncouthness, clumsiness, stiffness, disfigurement, distortion, contortion.

Comeliness, seemliness, shapeliness, fairness, prettiness, neatness, spruceness, attractiveness, loveliness, quaintness, speciousness, polish, gloss, nattiness; a good effect.

Bloom, brilliancy, radiance, splendour, magnificence, sublimity.

Concinnity, delicacy, refinement, charm, style.

A beautiful woman, belle, charmer, enchantress, goddess; Helen of Troy, Venus, Hebe, the Graces, Peri, Houri; Cupid, Apollo, Hyperion, Adonis, Antinous, Narcissus.

Peacock, butterfly, flower, rose, lily; the flower of, the pink of, etc.; a garden, a picture.

(Phrases) Je ne sais quoi; le beau idéal; a sight for sore eyes.

(Verbs) To be beautiful; to shine, beam, bloom.

To render beautiful, etc., to beautify, embellish, adorn, deck, bedeck, decorate, set out, set off, ornament (847), dight, bedight, array, garnish, furbish, smarten, trick out, rig out, fig out, dandify, dress up, prank, prink, perk, preen, trim, embroider, emblazon, adonize.

To polish, burnish, gild, varnish, japan, enamel, lacquer.

To powder, rouge, make up, doll up, titivate.

(Adjectives) Beautiful, handsome, good-looking, fine, pretty, lovely, graceful, elegant, delicate, refined, fair, personable, comely, seemly, bonny, braw, well-favoured, proper, shapely, well-made, well-formed, well-proportioned, symmetrical, sightly, becoming, goodly, neat, dapper, tight, trig, spruce, smart, stylish, chic, dashing, swagger, dandified, natty, sleek, quaint, jaunty, bright-eyed, attractive, seductive, stunning.

Blooming, rosy, brilliant, shining, beaming, splendid, resplendent, dazzling, gorgeous, superb, magnificent, sublime, grand.

Picturesque, statuesque, artistic, aesthetic, decorative, photogenic, well-composed, well-grouped.

malformation, monstrosity, misproportion, inconcinnity, want of symmetry, roughness, repulsiveness, squalor, hideousness, unsightliness, odiousness.

An eyesore, object, figure, sight, fright, guy, spectre, scarecrow, hag, harridan, satyr, sibyl, toad, baboon, monster, gorgon, Caliban, Hecate.

(Phrases) A forbidding countenance; a wry face; a blot on the landscape; no oil-painting; *'monstrum horrendum, informe, ingens, cui lumen ademptum.'*

(Verbs) To be ugly, etc.

To render ugly, etc., to deform, deface, distort, disfigure (241), disfeature, misshape, blemish, spot, stain, distain, soil, tarnish, discolour, sully, blot, daub, bedaub, begrime, blur, smear, besmear (653), bespatter, maculate, denigrate, uglify.

(Phrase) To make faces.

(Adjectives) Ugly, plain, homely, unsightly, unornamental, unshapely, unlovely, ill-looking, ordinary, unseemly, ill-favoured, hard-favoured, evil-favoured, hard-featured, hard-visaged, ungainly, uncouth, gawky, hulking, lumbering, slouching, ungraceful, clumsy, graceless, rude, rough, rugged, homespun, gaunt, raw-boned, haggard, scraggy.

Misshapen, shapeless, misproportioned, ill-proportioned, deformed, ill-made, ill-shaped, inelegant, disfigured, distorted, unshapen, unshapely, hump-backed, crooked, bandy, stumpy, dumpy, squat, stubby, bald, rickety.

Squalid, grim, grisly, gruesome, grooly, macabre, grim-faced, grim-visaged, ghastly, ghost-like, death-like, cadaverous, repellent, repulsive, forbidding, grotesque.

Frightful, odious, hideous, horrid, shocking, monstrous, unprepossessing.

Foul, soiled, tarnished, stained, distained, sullied, blurred, blotted, spotted, maculated, spotty, splashed, smeared, begrimed,

Passable, presentable, not amiss, undefaced, spotless, unspotted.

(Phrases) Easy to look at; dressed up to kill.

847 Ornament *(Substantives)*, ornamentation, adornment, decoration, embellishment, enrichment, illustration, illumination, ornature, ornateness, flamboyancy.

Garnish, polish, varnish, gilding, japanning, enamel, lacquer, ormolu.

Cosmetic, rouge, powder, lipstick, mascara, hair-oil, brilliantine.

Jewel, jewellery, bijouterie, spangle, trinket, locket, bracelet, bangle, anklet, necklace, earring, brooch, chain, chatelaine, carcanet, tiara, coronet, diadem.

Gem, precious stone, diamond, brilliant, emerald, sapphire, ruby, agate, garnet, beryl, onyx, topaz, amethyst, opal; pearl, coral.

Embroidery, broidery, brocade, galloon, lace, fringe, trapping, trimming, edging, border, chiffon, hanging, tapestry, arras.

Wreath, festoon, garland, lei, chaplet, tassel, knot, epaulette, frog, star, rosette, bow.

Feather, plume, *panache*, aigrette.

Nosegay, bouquet, posy, buttonhole.

Tracery, moulding, arabesque.

Frippery, finery, bravery, gewgaw, gaud, fal-lal, tinsel, spangle, clinquant, bric-à-brac, knick-knack.

Trope, flourish, flowers of rhetoric, purple patches (577).

Excess of ornament, tawdriness (851).

(Verbs) To ornament, embellish, illustrate, illuminate, enrich, decorate, adorn, beautify, garnish, polish, gild, varnish, enamel, paint, white-wash, stain, japan, lacquer, fume, grain; bespangle, bedeck, bedizen (845), embroider, work, chase, emboss, fret, tool; emblazon, illuminate.

(Adjectives) Ornamented, etc., beautified, rigged out, figged out, well-groomed, dolled up, ornate, showy, dressy, gaudy (851), garish, gorgeous, fine, gay, rich.

(Phrases) Fine as fivepence; in full fig; in one's Sunday best; dressed up to the nines.

850 Good taste.

Taste *(Substantives)*, delicacy, refinement, gust, gusto, *goût*, virtuosity, virtuosoship, nicety, finesse, grace, culture, virtu, τὸ πρέπον, polish, elegance.

spattered, bedaubed, besmeared; ungarnished.

(Phrases) Ugly as sin; not fit to be seen.

848 Blemish *(Substantives)*, disfigurement, defacement, deformity, eyesore, defect, fault, deficiency, flaw, fleck.

Stain, blot, spot, speck, mote, blur, macula, blotch, speckle, spottiness; soil, tarnish, smudge, smut, dirt, soot (653); freckle, birthmark.

Excrescence, pimple, pustule (250).

(Verbs) To blemish, disfigure, deface (846).

(Adjectives) Blemished, disfigured, etc.; spotted, speckled, freckled, pitted.

849 Simplicity *(Substantives)*, plainness, undress, chastity, chasteness; freedom from ornament or affectation, homeliness.

(Phrase) Simplex munditiis.

(Verbs) To be simple, etc., to render simple, etc., to simplify.

(Adjectives) Simple, plain, ordinary, household, homely, homespun, chaste, unaffected, severe, primitive.

Unadorned, unornamented, undecked, ungarnished, unarrayed, untrimmed, unsophisticated, in dishabille.

---

851 Bad taste.

Vulgarity *(Substantives)*, vulgarism, barbarism, Vandalism, Gothicism, *mauvais goût*, sensationalism, flamboyance.

Coarseness, grossness, indecorum,

Science of taste, aesthetics.

A man of taste, connoisseur, judge, critic, *cognoscente*, virtuoso, dilettante, amateur, aesthete, purist, precisian; an Aristarchus, Corinthian, *arbiter elegantiarum*.

(Phrase) Caviare to the general.

(Verbs) To appreciate, judge, discriminate, criticize (465).

(Adjectives) In good taste, tasteful, unaffected, pure, chaste, classical, attic, refined, aesthetic, cultivated, cultured, artistic, elegant.

(Adverb) Elegantly, etc.

(Phrases) To one's taste or mind; after one's fancy; *comme il faut*.

852 Fashion *(Substantives)*, style, tonishness, *ton, bon ton*, mode, vogue, craze, rage, fad.

Manners, breeding, politeness, gentlemanliness, courtesy (894), decorum, *bienséance, savoir faire, savoir vivre*, punctilio, convention, conventionality, propriety, the proprieties, Mrs. Grundy, form, formality, etiquette, custom, demeanour, air, port, carriage, presence.

Show, equipage, turn-out (882).

The world, the fashionable world, the smart set, the *beau monde*, high life, society, town, court, gentility (875), civilization, civilized life, the *élite*.

(Phrases) The height of fashion; *dernier cri*; the latest thing.

(Verbs) To be fashionable, etc.

(Phrases) To cut a dash; to be in the swim.

(Adjectives) Fashionable, in fashion, in vogue, *à la mode,* modish, tony, tonish, stylish, smart, courtly, *recherché*, genteel, aristocratic, conventional, punctilious, *comme il faut,* well-bred, well-mannered, polished, gentlemanlike, ladylike, well-spoken, civil, presentable, *distingué,* refined, thorough-bred, county, *dégagé,* jaunty, swell, swagger, posh, dashing, unembarrassed; trendy.

(Phrases) Having a run; all the go.

(Adverbs) Fashionably, in fashion.

lowness, low life, *mauvais ton*, bad form, ribaldry, clownishness, rusticity, boorishness, brutishness, brutality, rowdyism, ruffianism, awkwardness, *gaucherie*, want of tact, tactlessness.

Excess of ornament, false ornament, tawdriness, loudness, gaudiness, flashiness, ostentation.

A rough diamond, a hoyden, tomboy, slattern, sloven, dowdy, frump, cub, unlicked cub, clown, cad, guttersnipe, ragamuffin (876); a Goth, Vandal.

(Verbs) To be vulgar, etc., to misbehave.

(Adjectives) In bad taste, vulgar, coarse, unrefined, gross, ribald, heavy, rude, unpolished, indecorous, homespun, clownish, uncouth, awkward, *gauche*, ungraceful, slovenly, slatternly, dowdy, frumpish.

Ill-bred, ungenteel, impolite, ill-mannered, uncivil, tactless, underbred, caddish, ungentlemanly, unladylike, unfeminine, unmaidenly, unseemly, unpresentable, unkempt, uncombed.

Rustic, countrified, boorish, provincial, barbarous, barbaric, brutish, blackguardly, rowdy, raffish, Gothic, unclassical, heathenish, outlandish, untamed (876).

Obsolete, out of fashion, *démodé*, out of date, unfashionable, antiquated, fossil, old-fashioned, old-world, gone by.

New-fangled, odd, fantastic, grotesque, ridiculous (853), affected, meretricious, extravagant, sensational, monstrous, shocking, horrid, revolting.

Gaudy, tawdry, tinsel, bedizened, flamboyant, baroque, tricked out, gingerbread, loud, flashy, showy.

(Phrase) A back number.

853 Ridiculousness *(Substantives)*, ludicrousness, risibility.

Oddness, oddity, whimsicality, comicality, drollery, grotesqueness, fancifulness, quaintness, frippery, gawkiness, preposterousness, extravagance, monstrosity, absurdity (497).

Bombast, bathos, fustian, doggerel, nonsense verse, amphigouri, extravaganza, clerihew, bull, Irish bull, spoonerism.

(Adjectives) Ridiculous, absurd, extravagant, *outré*, monstrous, preposterous, irrational, nonsensical.

Odd, whimsical, quaint, queer, rum, droll, grotesque, fanciful, eccentric, bizarre, strange, out-of-the-way, outlandish, fantastic, baroque, rococo.

Laughable, risible, ludicrous, comic, serio-comic, mock-heroic, comical, funny, derisive, farcical, burlesque, *pour rire*, quizzical, bombastic, inflated, stilted.

Awkward, gawky, lumbering, lumpish, hulking, uncouth.

854 Fop *(Substantives)*, dandy, exquisite, swell, toff, dude, nut, masher, lady-killer, coxcomb, beau, macaroni, blade, blood, buck, spark, dog, popinjay, puppy, *petit-maître*, jackanapes, jack-a-dandy, tailor's dummy, man-milliner, man about town.

855 Affectation *(Substantives)*, mannerism, pretension, airs, dandyism, coxcombry, frills, side, swank, dog, conceit, foppery, affectedness, preciosity, euphuism, charlatanism, quackery, foppishness, pedantry, acting a part, pose, gush.

Prudery, Grundyism, demureness, coquetry, *minauderie*, sentimentality, lackadaisicalness, stiffness, formality, buckram, mock modesty, *mauvaise honte*.

Pedant, precisian, prig, square, bluestocking, *bas bleu*, formalist, *poseur*, mannerist, *précieuse ridicule*; prude, Mrs. Grundy.

(Phrases) A lump of affectation; prunes and prisms.

(Verbs) To affect, to give oneself airs, put on side or frills, to swank, simper, mince, to act a part, overact, attitudinize, gush, pose.

(Adjectives) Affected, conceited, precious, pretentious, stilted, pedantic, pragmatical, priggish, smug, puritanical, prim, prudish, starchy, up-stage, high-hat, stiff, formal, demure, goody-goody.

Foppish, namby-pamby, slip-slop, coxcombical, slipshod, simpering, mincing, niminy-piminy, la-di-da, sentimental, lackadaisical.

Exaggerated (549), overacted, overdone, high-falutin, gushing, stagy, theatrical.

856 Ridicule *(Substantives)*, derision, mockery, quiz, banter, chaff, badinage, irony, persiflage, raillery, send-up.

Jeer, gibe, quip, taunt, satire, scurrility, scoffing.

A parody, burlesque, travesty, skit, farce, comedy, tragi-comedy, doggerel, blunder, bull, *lapsus linguae*, slip of the tongue, malapropism, spoonerism, anticlimax.

Buffoonery, vagary, antic, mummery, tomfoolery, grimace, monkey-trick, escapade, prank, gambade, extravaganza, practical joke, booby-trap.

(Verbs) To ridicule, deride, laugh at (929), laugh down, scoff, mock, jeer, banter, quiz, rally, fleer, flout, rag, rot, chaff, josh, guy, rib, razz, roast, twit, taunt, point at, grin at.

To parody, caricature, burlesque, travesty, pillory, take off.

(Phrases) To raise a smile; to set the table in a roar; to make fun of; to poke fun at; to make merry with; to make a fool of; to make an ass of; to make game of; to make faces at; to make mouths at; to lead one a dance;

to run a rig upon; to make an April fool of; to laugh out of court; to laugh in one's sleeve; to take the micky out of.

(Adjectives) Derisory, derisive, sarcastic, ironical, quizzical, mock, scurrilous, burlesque, Hudibrastic.

857 Object and cause of ridicule.

Laughing-stock *(Substantives)*, gazing-stock, butt, stooge, target, quiz; an original, guy, oddity, card, crank, eccentric, monkey, buffoon, jester (844), mime, mimer (599), scaramouch, punch, punchinello, mountebank, golliwog.

(Phrases) A figure of fun; a queer fish; fair game.

3°. Prospective Affections

858 Hope *(Substantives)*, trust, confidence, reliance, faith, assurance, credit, security, expectation, affiance, promise, assumption, presumption.

Hopefulness, buoyancy, reassurance, optimism, enthusiasm, aspiration.

A reverie, day-dream, pipe-dream, Utopia, millennium.

Anchor, mainstay, sheet-anchor, staff (215).

(Phrases) Castles in the air; castles in Spain; a ray, gleam, or flash of hope; the silver lining of the cloud.

(Verbs) To hope; to feel, entertain, harbour, cherish, feed, nourish, encourage, foster, etc., hope or confidence; to promise oneself.

To trust, confide, rely on, build upon, feel or rest assured, confident, secure, etc.; to flatter oneself, expect, aspire, presume, be reassured.

To give or inspire hope; to augur well, shape well, bid fair, be in a fair way; to encourage, assure, promise, flatter, buoy up, reassure, embolden, raise expectations.

(Phrases) To see daylight; to live in hopes; to look on the bright side; to pin one's hope or faith upon; to catch at a straw; to hope against hope.

(Adjectives) Hoping, etc., in hopes, hopeful, confident, secure, buoyant, buoyed up, in good heart, sanguine, optimistic, enthusiastic, utopian.

Fearless, unsuspecting, unsuspicious; free or exempt from fear, suspicion, distrust, etc., undespairing.

Auspicious, promising, propitious, bright, rose-coloured, rosy, of good omen, reassuring.

859 Absence, want, or loss of hope.

Hopelessness *(Substantives)*, despair, desperation, despondency, pessimism (837); forlornness, a forlorn hope, the Slough of Despond.

(Phrases) A black look-out; a bad business.

(Verbs) To despair, despond, give up, be hopeless; to lose, give up, abandon, relinquish, etc., all hope; to yield to despair.

To inspire or drive to despair; to dash, crush, or destroy one's hopes.

(Phrases) To trust to a broken reed; *'lasciate ogni speranza voi ch'entrate.'*

(Adjectives) Hopeless, having lost or given up hope, losing, etc., hope, past hope, despondent, pessimistic, forlorn, desperate, despairing.

Incurable, irremediable, irreparable, irrevocable, incorrigible, beyond remedy.

Inauspicious, unpropitious, unpromising, threatening, ill-omened.

860 Fear *(Substantives)*, cowardice (862), timidity, diffidence, nervousness, restlessness, inquietude, disquietude, solicitude, anxiety, care, distrust, mistrust, hesitation, misgiving, suspicion, qualm, want of confidence, nerves.

Apprehension, flutter, trepidation, tremor, shaking, trembling, palpitation, jitters, the jumps, the creeps, the needle, ague-fit, fearfulness, despondency; stage fright, cold feet, wind up.

Fright, affright, alarm, dread, awe, terror, horror, dismay, obsession,

(Phrases) Nil desperandum; while there's life there's hope; *dum spiro spero*; never say die; all for the best.

———

(Phrases) Raw head and bloody bones; fee-faw-fum; butterflies in the stomach.

(Verbs) To fear, be afraid, etc., to distrust, hesitate, have qualms, misgiving, suspicions.

To apprehend, take alarm, start, wince, boggle, skulk, cower, crouch, tremble, shake, quake, quaver, quiver, shudder, quail, cringe, turn pale, blench, flutter, flinch, funk.

To excite fear, raise apprehensions, to give, raise, or sound an alarm, to intimidate, put in fear, frighten, fright, affright, alarm, startle, scare, haunt, obsess, strike terror, daunt, terrify, unman, awe, horrify, dismay, petrify, appal.

To overawe, abash, cow, browbeat, bully, deter, discourage.

(Phrases) To shake in one's shoes; to shake like an aspen leaf; to stand aghast; to eye askance.

To fright from one's propriety; to strike all of a heap; to make the flesh creep; to give one the creeps; to cause alarm and despondency.

(Adjectives) Fearing, timid, timorous, faint-hearted, tremulous, fearful, nervous, nervy, jumpy, funky, diffident, apprehensive, restless, haunted with the fear, apprehension, dread, etc., of.

Frightened, afraid, cowed, pale, alarmed, scared, terrified, petrified, aghast, awestruck, dismayed, horror-struck, horrified, appalled, panic-stricken.

Inspiring fear, fearsome, alarming, formidable, redoubtable, portentous, perilous (665), ugly, fearful, dreadful, dire, shocking, terrible, tremendous, horrid, horrible, horrific, ghastly, awful, awesome, horripilant, hair-raising, creepy, crawly.

(Phrases) White as a sheet; afraid of one's shadow; the hair standing on end; letting 'I dare not' wait upon 'I would'; more frightened than hurt; frightened out of one's senses or wits; in a blue funk.

panic, funk, flap, stampede, scare, consternation, despair (859).

Intimidation, terrorism, reign of terror; an alarmist, scaremonger.

Object of fear, bugbear, bugaboo, bogy, scarecrow, goblin (980), *bête noire*, nightmare, Gorgon, ogre.

861 Absence of fear.

Courage *(Substantives)*, bravery, value, boldness, spirit, moral fibre, spiritedness, daring, gallantry, intrepidity, contempt of danger, self-reliance, confidence, fearlessness, audacity.

Manhood, manliness, nerve, pluck, grit, guts, sand, mettle, gameness, heart, spunk, smeddum, virtue, hardihood, fortitude, firmness, resolution, sportsmanship.

Prowess, derring-do, heroism, chivalry.

A hero, heroine, ace, paladin, *preux chevalier,* Hector, Hotspur, Amazon, Joan of Arc, *beau sabreur,* fire-eater (863).

862 Excess of fear.

Cowardice *(Substantives)*, fear (860), pusillanimity, cowardliness, timidity, fearfulness, spiritlessness, faint-heartedness, softness, effeminacy, funk.

Poltroonery, baseness, dastardliness, yellow streak, a faint heart.

A coward, poltroon, dastard, recreant, funk, mollycoddle, milksop, cry-baby, 'fraid-cat, chicken, cowardy custard.

A runaway, fugitive, deserter, quitter.

(Verbs) To be cowardly, etc.; to quail (860), to flinch, fight shy, shy, turn tail, run away, cut and run, fly for one's life, stampede.

A lion, tiger, bulldog, gamecock, fighting-cock, sportsman.

(Verbs) To be courageous, etc., to face, front, affront, confront, despise, brave, defy, etc., danger; to take courage; to summon up, muster up, or pluck up courage; to rally.

To venture, make bold, face, dare, defy, brave (715), beard, hold out, bear up against, stand up to.

To give, infuse, or inspire courage; to encourage, embolden, inspirit, cheer, nerve.

(Phrases) To take the bull by the horns; to come up to the scratch; to face the music; to 'screw one's courage to the sticking-place'; to die game.

To pat on the back; to make a man of.

(Adjectives) Courageous, brave, valiant, valorous, gallant, intrepid.

Spirited, high-spirited, high-mettled, mettlesome, plucky, manly, manful, resolute, stout, stout-hearted, lion-hearted, heart of oak, firm, indomitable, game, sportsmanlike.

Bold, daring, audacious, fearless, unfearing, dauntless, undaunted, indomitable, unappalled, undismayed, unawed, unabashed, unalarmed, unflinching, unshrinking, unblenching, unblenched, unapprehensive, confident, self-reliant.

Enterprising, venturous, adventurous, venturesome, dashing, chivalrous, heroic, fierce, warlike (722).

Unfeared, undreaded, etc.

(Phrases) One's blood is up; brave as a lion; bold as brass; full of beans.

(Phrases) To show the white feather; to be in a sweat.

(Adjectives) Coward, cowardly, yellow, pusillanimous, shy, fearful, timid, skittish, timorous, poor-spirited, spiritless, weak-hearted, faint-hearted, chicken-hearted, white-livered.

Dastard, dastardly, base, craven, recreant, unwarlike, unheroic, unsoldierly, unmanly, womanish.

(Phrase) 'In face a lion, but in heart a deer.'

(Interjections) Sauve qui peut! the devil take the hindmost!

---

863 Rashness *(Substantives)*, temerity, audacity, presumption, precipitancy, precipitation, impetuosity, recklessness, overboldness, foolhardiness, desperation, knight-errantry, Quixotism; carelessness (460), want of caution, overconfidence.

Imprudence, indiscretion.

A desperado, madcap, bravo, daredevil, *enfant perdu*, gambler, adventurer, knight errant; Hotspur, Don Quixote, Icarus.

(Phrases) A leap in the dark; a blind bargain; a wild-cat scheme.

(Verbs) To be rash, incautious, etc.

(Phrases) To buy a pig in a poke; to go on a forlorn hope; to go at it baldheaded; to play with fire; to tempt providence.

(Adjectives) Rash, temerarious,

864 Caution *(Substantives)*, cautiousness, discretion, prudence, reserve, wariness, heed, circumspection, calculation, deliberation (459).

Coolness, self-possession, aplomb, presence of mind, sang-froid, self-command, steadiness, the Fabian policy.

(Phrases) The better part of valour; masterly inactivity.

(Verbs) To be cautious, etc., to beware, take care, have a care, take heed, ca' canny, be on one's guard, look about one, take no chances.

(Phrases) To look before one leaps; to think twice; to let sleeping dogs lie; to see which way the wind blows; to see how the land lies; to feel one's way; to count the cost; to be on the safe side; steady as she goes.

headstrong, insane, foolhardy, slap-dash, dare-devil, devil-may-care, overbold, wild, reckless, desperate, hot-headed, hare-brained, headlong, hot-blooded, over-confident, precipitate, impetuous, venturesome, impulsive, Quixotic.

Imprudent, indiscreet, uncalculating, incautious, improvident.

(Phrases) Without ballast; neck or nothing.

(Interjections) Vogue la galère! come what may!

865 Desire *(Substantives)*, wish, mind, inclination, leaning, bent, fancy, partiality, penchant, predilection, liking, love, fondness, relish.

Want, need, exigency.

Longing, hankering, solicitude, anxiety, yearning, yen, coveting, eagerness, zeal, ardour, aspiration, ambition, over-anxiety.

Appetite, appetence, appetency, the edge of appetite, keenness, hunger, stomach, thirst, thirstiness, drouth, mouth-watering, dipsomania, itch, itching, prurience, lickerishness, *cacoethes*, cupidity, lust, libido, concupiscence, greed.

Avidity, greediness, covetousness, craving, voracity, bulimia, rapacity.

Passion, rage, furore, mania, kleptomania, inextinguishable desire, vaulting ambition, impetuosity.

A gourmand, gourmet, glutton, cormorant (957).

An amateur, votary, devotee, fan, aspirant, solicitant, candidate.

Object of desire, desideratum, attraction, lure, allurement, fancy, temptation, magnet, loadstone, whim, whimsy (608), maggot, hobby, hobby-horse, pursuit.

(Phrases) The height of one's ambition; *hoc erat in votis*; the wish being father to the thought; the torments of Tantalus.

(Verbs) To desire, wish, long for, fancy, affect, like, have a mind to, be glad of, want, miss, need, feel the want of, would fain have, to care for.

To hunger, thirst, crave, lust after; to hanker after, itch for.

(Adjectives) Cautious, wary, careful, heedful, cautelous, chary, canny, cagey, circumspect, prudent, prudential, reserved, discreet, politic, noncommittal.

Unenterprising, unadventurous, cool, steady, self-possessed.

(Phrases) Safety first; better be sure than sorry.

———

866 Indifference *(Substantives)*, coldness, coolness, unconcern, nonchalance, insouciance, inappetency, listlessness, lukewarmness, neutrality, impartiality; apathy (823), supineness (683), disdain (930).

(Verbs) To be indifferent, etc.; to have no desire, wish, taste, or relish for; to care nothing about, take no interest in, not mind, make light of; to disdain, spurn (930).

(Phrase) Couldn't care less.

(Adjectives) Indifferent, undesirous, cool, cold, frigid, unconcerned, insouciant, unsolicitous, unattracted, lukewarm, half-hearted, listless, lackadaisical, unambitious, unaspiring, phlegmatic.

Unattractive, unalluring, uninviting, undesired, undesirable, uncared-for, unwished, uncoveted, unvalued.

Vapid, tasteless, insipid (391), wersh, unappetizing, mawkish, namby-pamby, flat, stale, vain.

(Phrases) Never mind; all one to Hippocleides.

867 Dislike *(Substantives)*, distaste, disrelish, disinclination, reluctance, backwardness, demur (603).

Repugnance, disgust, queasiness, turn, nausea, loathing, averseness, aversion, abomination, antipathy, abhorrence, horror, hatred, detestation (898), resentment (900); claustrophobia, agoraphobia, Anglophobia, Gallophobia.

(Verbs) To dislike, mislike, disrelish, mind, object to.

SATIETY

To desiderate; covet; to sigh, cry, gasp, pine, pant, languish, yearn for; to aspire after, catch at, jump at.

To woo, court, solicit, ogle, fish for.

To cause, create, raise, excite, or provoke, desire; to allure, attract, solicit, tempt, hold out temptation or allurement, to tantalize, appetize.

To gratify desire, slake, satiate (827).

(Phrases) To have at heart; to take a fancy to; to set one's heart upon; to make eyes at; to set one's cap at; to run mad after.

To whet the appetite; to make one's mouth water.

(Adjectives) Desirous, inclined, fain, keen, wishful, wishing, optative, desiring, wanting, needing, hankering after, dying for, partial to.

Craving, hungry, esurient, sharp-set, keen-set, peckish, thirsty, athirst, dry, drouthy.

Greedy, voracious, lickerish, open-mouthed, agog, covetous, ravenous, rapacious, extortionate; unsated, unslaked, insatiable, insatiate, omnivorous.

Eager, ardent, avid, fervent, bent on, intent on, aspiring, ambitious.

Desirable, desired, desiderated (829).

(Phrases) Pinched or perished with hunger; hungry as a hunter; parched with thirst; having a sweet tooth; nothing loth.

(Interjections) O for! would that!

To shun, avoid, eschew, withdraw from, shrink from, shrug the shoulders at, recoil from, shudder at.

To loathe, nauseate, abominate, detest, abhor, hate (898).

To cause or excite dislike; to disincline, repel, sicken, render sick, nauseate, disgust, shock, pall.

(Phrases) Not to be able to bear or endure or stand; to have no taste for; to turn up one's nose at; to look askance at.

To go against the grain; to turn one's stomach; to stink in the nostrils; to stick in one's throat; to make one's blood run cold.

(Adjectives) Disliking, disrelishing, etc., averse to, adverse, shy of, sick of, fed up with, queasy, disinclined.

Disliked, disagreeable, unpalatable, unpopular, offensive, loathsome, loathly, sickening, nauseous, nauseating, repulsive, disgusting, detestable, execrable, abhorrent, abhorred (830), disgustful.

(Adverbs) Disagreeably, etc.

(Phrase) Usque ad nauseam.

(Interjections) Faugh! Ugh!

868 Fastidiousness *(Substantives)*, nicety, daintiness, squeamishness, niceness, particularity, finicality, meticulosity, difficulty in being pleased, epicurism.

Excess of delicacy, prudery.

Epicure, gourmet, gourmand, *bon vivant*, gastronomer.

(Verbs) To be fastidious, etc., to discriminate, differentiate, disdain.

(Phrases) To split hairs; to mince one's words; to see spots in the sun.

(Adjectives) Fastidious, nice, difficult, dainty, delicate, finicky, lickerish, pernickety, squeamish, queasy, difficult to please, particular, choosy, punctilious, fussy, hypercriticial; prudish, strait-laced.

869 Satiety *(Substantives)*, fullness, repletion, glut, saturation, surfeit.

A spoilt child; too much of a good thing.

(Verbs) To sate, satiate, satisfy, saturate, quench, slake, pall, glut, overfeed, gorge, surfeit, cloy, tire, spoil, sicken.

(Adjectives) Satiated, sated, blasé, used up, fed up, browned off, brassed off, cheesed off, chokka, sick of.

(Phrases) Enough is enough; *Toujours perdrix*.

(Interjections) Enough! that'll do!

4°. Contemplative Affections

870 Wonder (*Substantives*), surprise, marvel, astonishment, amazement, amazedness, wonderment, admiration, awe, bewilderment, stupefaction, fascination, thaumaturgy (992).

(*Verbs*) To wonder, marvel, be surprised, admire; to stare, gape, start.

To surprise, astonish, amaze, astound, dumbfound, dumbfounder, strike, dazzle, startle, take by surprise, take aback, strike with wonder, electrify, stun, petrify, flabbergast, confound, stagger, stupefy, bewilder, fascinate, boggle.

To be wonderful, etc.

(*Phrases*) To open one's mouth or eyes; to look blank; to stand aghast; not to believe one's eyes; not to account for; not to know whether one stands on one's head or one's heels.

To make one sit up; to take one's breath away.

To beggar description; to stagger belief; imagination boggles at it.

(*Adjectives*) Surprised, astonished, amazed, astounded, struck, startled, taken by surprise, taken aback, struck dumb, awestruck, aghast, agape, dumbfounded, flabbergasted, thunder-struck, planet-struck, stupefied, open-mouthed, petrified.

Wondrous, wondrous, surprising, astonishing, amazing, astounding, startling, stunning, unexpected, unforeseen, strange, uncommon, unheard-of, unaccountable, incredible, inexplicable, indescribable, inexpressible, ineffable, unutterable, unspeakable, monstrous, prodigious, stupendous, marvellous, miraculous, passing strange, uncanny, weird, phenomenal.

(*Phrases*) Struck all of a heap; lost in wonder; like a dying duck in a thunder-storm; you could have knocked me down with a feather.

(*Adverbs*) Wonderingly, wonderfully, etc., with gaping mouth, all agog; *mirabile dictu*.

(*Interjections*) What! indeed! really! hallo! humph! you don't say so! my stars! good heavens! my goodness! good gracious! bless my soul! bless my heart! my word! O gemini! great Scott! gee! *wunderbar!* dear me! well, I'm damned! well, I never! lo! heyday! who'd have thought it!

871 Absence of wonder.

Expectance (*Substantives*), expectancy, expectation (507).

(*Verbs*) To expect, not to be surprised, not to wonder, etc., *nil admirari*.

(*Phrase*) To think nothing of.

(*Adjectives*) Expecting, etc., unamazed, astonished at nothing, blasé (841).

Common, ordinary (82); foreseen.

---

872 Prodigy (*Substantives*), phenomenon, wonder, cynosure, marvel, miracle, monster (83), unicorn, phoenix, gazing-stock, curiosity, *rara avis*, lion, sight, spectacle, wonderment, sign, portent (512), eye-opener; wonderland, fairyland.

Thunderclap, thunderbolt, bursting of a shell or bomb, volcanic eruption.

(*Phrases*) A nine days' wonder; *annus mirabilis*.

5°. Extrinsic Affections

873 Repute (*Substantives*), distinction, note, notability, name, mark, reputation, figure, *réclame*, *éclat*, celebrity, vogue, fame, famous-

874 Disrepute (*Substantives*), discredit, ingloriousness, derogation, abasement, degradation, odium, notoriety.

ness, popularity, renown, memory, immortality.

Glory, honour, credit, prestige, kudos, account, regard, respect, reputableness, respectability, respectableness, good name, illustriousness, gloriousness.

Dignity, stateliness, solemnity, grandeur, splendour, nobility, nobleness, lordliness, majesty, sublimity.

Greatness, highness, eminence, supereminence, pre-eminence, primacy, importance (642).

Elevation, ascent (305), exaltation, superexaltation, aggrandisement.

Rank, standing, condition, precedence, *pas*, station, place, status, order, degree, *locus standi*.

Dedication, consecration, enshrinement, glorification, beatification, canonization, deification, posthumous fame.

Chief, leader (745), hero, celebrity, notability, somebody, lion, cock of the roost, cock of the walk, man of mark, pillar of the state, prima donna.

A star, sun, constellation, galaxy, flower, pearl, paragon (650); honour, ornament, aureole.

(Phrases) A halo of glory; a name to conjure with; blushing honours; a feather in one's cap; the top of the tree; a niche in the temple of fame.

(Verbs) To glory in, to be proud of (878), to exult (884), to be vain of (880).

To be glorious, distinguished, etc., to shine, to figure, to make or cut a figure, dash, or splash; to rival, outrival, surpass, emulate, outvie, eclipse, outshine, overshadow, throw into the shade.

To live, flourish, glitter, flaunt.

To honour, lionize, dignify, glorify, ennoble, nobilitate, exalt, enthrone, signalize, immortalize, deify.

To consecrate, dedicate to, devote to, to enshrine.

To confer or reflect honour, etc., on; to do, pay, or render honour to; to redound to one's honour.

(Phrases) To acquire or gain honour, etc.; to bear the palm; to bear the bell; to take the cake; to

Dishonour, shame, disgrace, disfavour, disapprobation (932), slur, scandal, obloquy, opprobrium, ignominy, baseness, turpitude, vileness, infamy.

Tarnish, taint, defilement, pollution.

Stain, blot, spot, blur, stigma, brand, reproach, imputation, slur, black mark.

(Phrases) A burning shame; *scandalum magnatum*; a badge of infamy; the bar sinister; a blot on the scutcheon; a byword of reproach; a bad reputation.

(Verbs) To be conscious of shame, to feel shame, to blush, to be ashamed, humiliated, humbled (879, 881).

To cause shame, etc.; to shame, disgrace, put to shame, dishonour; to throw, cast, fling, or reflect shame, etc., upon; to be a reproach to, to derogate from.

To tarnish, stain, blot, sully, taint, discredit, degrade, debase, defile.

To impute shame to, to brand, stigmatize, vilify, defame, slur, run down, knock.

To abash, humiliate, humble, dishonour, discompose, disconcert, shame, show up, put out, put down, snub, confuse, mortify; to obscure, eclipse, outshine.

(Phrases) To feel disgrace; to cut a poor figure; to hide one's face; to look foolish; to hang one's head; to laugh on the wrong side of the mouth; not to dare to show one's face; to hide one's diminished head; to lose caste; to be in one's black books.

To put to the blush; to put out of countenance; to put one's nose out of joint; to cast into the shade; to take one down a peg; to take the shine out of; to tread or trample under foot; to drag through the mud.

(Adjectives) Feeling shame, disgrace, etc.; ashamed, abashed, disgraced, blown upon, branded, tarnished.

Inglorious, mean, base (940), shabby, nameless, unnoticed, unnoted, unhonoured.

Shameful, disgraceful, despicable, discreditable, unbecoming, degrading,

win laurels; to make a noise in the world; to go far; to make a sensation; to be all the rage; to have a run; to catch on.

To exalt one's horn; to leave one's mark; to exalt to the skies.

(Adjectives) Distinguished, *distingué*, noted, notable, respectable, reputable, celebrated, famous, famed, farfamed, honoured, renowned, popular, deathless, imperishable, immortal (112).

Illustrious, glorious, splendid, bright, brilliant, radiant, full-blown, heroic.

Eminent, prominent, conspicuous, kenspeckle, high, pre-eminent, peerless, signalized, exalted, dedicated, consecrated, enshrined.

Great, dignified, proud, noble, worshipful, lordly, grand, stately, august, imposing, transcendent, majestic, kingly, queenly, princely, sacred, sublime, commanding.

(Phrases) Redounding to one's honour; one's name living for ever; *sic itur ad astra*.

(Interjections) Hail! all hail! *vive! viva!* glory be to! honour be to!

humiliating, unworthy, disreputable, derogatory, vile, ribald, dishonourable, abject, scandalous, infamous, notorious.

(Phrases) Unwept, unhonoured, and unsung; shorn of its beams; unknown to fame; in bad odour; under a cloud; down in the world.

(Interjections) Fie! shame! for shame! *O tempora! O mores!*

---

875 Nobility *(Substantives)*, noblesse, aristocracy, peerage, gentry, gentility, quality, rank, blood, birth, donship, fashionable world (852), the *haute monde*, high life, the upper classes, the upper ten, the four hundred.

A personage, notability, celebrity, man of distinction, rank, etc.; a nobleman, noble, lord, peer, grandee, magnate, magnifico, hidalgo, don, gentleman, squire, patrician, lordling, nob, swell, dignitary, bigwig, big gun.

House of Lords, Lords Spiritual and Temporal.

Gentlefolk, landed proprietors, squirearchy, *optimates*.

Prince, duke, marquis, earl, viscount, baron, thane, banneret, baronet, knight, count, armiger, laird, esquire; nizam, maharajah, rajah, nawab, sultan, emir (or ameer), effendi, sheik, pasha.

Princess, duchess, marchioness, marquise, countess, viscountess, baroness, lady, dame, maharanee, ranee, sultana, begum.

(Verbs) To be noble, etc.

(Adjectives) Noble, exalted, titled,

876 Commonalty *(Substantives)*, the lower classes or orders, the vulgar herd, the crowd, the people, the commons, the proletariat, the multitude, Demos, οἱ πολλοί, the populace, the million, the masses, the mobility, the peasantry.

The middle classes, bourgeoisie.

The mob, rabble, rabble-rout, ruck, *canaille*, the underworld, riff-raff, *profanum vulgus*.

A commoner, one of the people, a proletarian, *roturier*, plebeian; peasant, yeoman, crofter, boor, carle, churl, serf, kern, tyke (or tike), chuff, ryot, fellah, cottar.

A swain, clown, hind, clodhopper, bog-trotter, chaw-bacon, hodge, joskin, yokel, bumpkin, hayseed, rube, hick, ploughman, plough-boy, gaffer, loon, looby, lout, *gamin*, street arab, guttersnipe, mudlark, slubberdegullion.

A beggar, tramp, vagrant, gangrel, gaberlunzie, bum, hobo, sundowner, panhandler, pariah, muckworm, sansculotte, raff, tatterdemalion, ragamuffin.

A Goth, Vandal, Hottentot, savage,

PRIDE—HUMILITY

patrician, aristocratic, high-born, well-born, genteel, *comme il faut*, gentlemanlike, ladylike, princely, courtly, fashionable (852).

(Phrases) Noblesse oblige; born in the purple.

877 Title *(Substantives)*, honour, princedom, principality, dukedom, marquisate, earldom, viscounty, baronetcy, lordship, knighthood.

Highness, excellency, grace, worship, reverence, esquire, sir, master, sahib, Mr., monsieur, signor, señor, Herr.

Decoration, laurel, palm, wreath, medal, gong, ribbon, cross, star, garter, feather, crest, epaulette, colours, cockade, livery; order, arms, shield, scutcheon.

(Phrase) A handle to one's name.

---

878 Pride *(Substantives)*, haughtiness, loftiness, hauteur, stateliness, pomposity, vainglory, superciliousness, assumption, lordliness, stiffness, primness, arrogance, *morgue*, starch, starchiness, side, swank, uppishness; self-respect, dignity.

A proud man, etc., a highflier.

(Verbs) To be proud, etc., to presume, assume, swagger, strut, prance, peacock, bridle.

To pride oneself on, glory in, pique oneself, plume oneself, preen oneself.

(Phrases) To look big; give oneself airs; to ride the high horse; to put on side; to put on dog; to hold up one's head; to get one's tail up.

To put a good face upon.

(Adjectives) Proud, haughty, lofty, high, mighty, high-flown, high-minded, high-mettled, puffed up, flushed, supercilious, patronizing, condescending, disdainful, overweening, consequential, on stilts, swollen, arrogant, pompous.

Stately, dignified, stiff, starchy, prim, perked up, buckram, strait-laced, vainglorious, lordly,

barbarian, yahoo, rough diamond, unlicked cub.

An upstart, parvenu, skipjack, *novus homo, nouveau riche,* outsider, vulgarian, snob, mushroom.

Barbarousness, barbarism.

(Phrases) The man in the street; the submerged tenth; ragtag and bobtail; the swinish multitude; hewers of wood and drawers of water; the great unwashed.

(Verbs) To be ignoble, etc.

(Adjectives) Ignoble, common, mean, low, plebeian, proletarian, vulgar, bourgeois, untitled, homespun, homely, Gorblimey.

Base, base-born, low-bred, beggarly, earth-born, rustic, agrestic, countrified, provincial, parochial; banausic, menial, sorry, scrubby, mushroom, dunghill, sordid, vile, uncivilized, loutish, boorish, churlish, rude, brutish, raffish, unlicked, barbarous, barbarian, barbaric.

879 Humility *(Substantives)*, humbleness, meekness, lowness, lowliness, abasement, self-abasement, self-contempt, humiliation, submission, resignation, verecundity, modesty (881).

(Verbs) To be humble, etc.; to deign; vouchsafe, condescend; to humble or demean oneself; stoop, submit, knuckle under, look foolish, feel small.

To render humble; to humble, humiliate, set down, abash, abase, shame, mortify, crush, take down, snub.

(Phrases) To sing small; to pipe down; to draw in one's horns; to hide one's diminished head; to eat humble-pie; to eat dirt; to kiss the rod; to pocket an affront; to stoop to conquer.

To throw into the shade; to put out of countenance; to put a person in his place; to put to the blush; to take down a peg, cut down to size; to send away with a flea in one's ear.

(Adjectives) Humble, lowly, meek, sober-minded, submissive (725), resigned, self-contemptuous, under correction.

magisterial, purse-proud, stand-offish, up-stage, toffee-nose.

Unabashed (880).

(Phrases) High and mighty; proud as a peacock; proud as Lucifer.

(Adverbs) Proudly, haughtily, arrogantly, etc.

Humbled, humiliated, abashed, ashamed, chapfallen, crestfallen.

(Phrases) Out of countenance; on one's bended knees; humbled in the dust; not having a word to say for oneself.

(Adverbs) Humbly, meekly, etc.

880 Vanity *(Substantives)*, conceit, conceitedness, self-conceit, self-confidence, self-sufficiency, self-esteem, self-approbation, self-importance, self-praise, self-laudation, self-admiration, complacency, self-complacency, swelled head, megalomania, *amour-propre*.

Pretensions, airs, mannerism, egotism, egoism, egomania, priggishness, coxcombry, gaudery, vainglory (943), elation, ostentation (882).

A coxcomb (854).

(Verbs) To be vain, etc., to egotize.

To render vain, etc., to puff up, to inspire with vanity, turn one's head.

(Phrases) To have a high or overweening opinion of oneself; to think no small beer of oneself; to thrust oneself forward; to give oneself airs; to show off; to fish for compliments.

(Adjectives) Vain, conceited, overweening, forward, vainglorious, puffed up, high-flown, inflated, flushed, stuck-up.

Self-satisfied, self-confident, self-sufficient, self-flattering, self-admiring, self-applauding, self-opinionated, self-centred, egocentric, egoistic, egoistical, egotistic, egotistical, complacent, self-complacent, pretentious, priggish.

Unabashed, unblushing, unconstrained, unceremonious, free and easy.

(Phrases) Vain as a peacock; wise in one's own conceit.

(Adverbs) Vainly, etc., ostentatiously (882).

881 Modesty *(Substantives)*, humility (879), diffidence, timidity, bashfulness, shyness, coyness, sheepishness, *mauvaise honte*, shamefacedness, verecundity, self-consciousness.

Reserve, constraint, demureness.

(Verbs) To be modest, humble, etc.; to retire, keep in the background, keep private, reserve oneself.

(Phrases) To hide one's light under a bushel; to take a back seat.

(Adjectives) Modest, diffident, humble (879), timid, bashful, timorous, shy, skittish, coy, sheepish, shamefaced, blushing, self-conscious.

Unpretending, unpretentious, unassuming, unostentatious, unboastful, unaspiring.

Abashed, ashamed, dashed, out of countenance, crestfallen (879).

Reserved, constrained, demure, undemonstrative.

(Adverbs) Modestly, diffidently, quietly, privately, unostentatiously.

————

882 Ostentation *(Substantives)*, display, show, flourish, parade, pomp, state, solemnity, pageantry, dash, splash, splurge, glitter, veneer, tinsel, magnificence, pomposity, showing off, swank, swagger, strut, *panache, coup de théâtre*, stage effect.

Flourish of trumpets, fanfare, salvo of artillery, salute, fireworks, *feu de joie*.

Pageant, spectacle, procession, march-past, review, promenade, turn-out, set-out, build-up, fête, gala, regatta, field-day.

Ceremony, ceremonial, mummery; formality, form, etiquette, ritual, protocol, punctilio, punctiliousness.

(Verbs) To be ostentatious, etc.; to display, exhibit, posture, attitudinize,

show off, swank, come forward, put oneself forward, flaunt, emblazon, prink, glitter; make or cut a figure, dash, or splash.

To observe or stand on ceremony, etiquette, etc.

(Adjectives) Ostentatious, showy, gaudy, garish, flashy, dashing, pretentious, flaunting, jaunty, glittering, sumptuous, spectacular, ceremonial, stagy, theatrical, histrionic.

Pompous, solemn, stately, high-sounding, formal, stiff, ritualistic, ceremonious, punctilious.

(Phrases) With flourish of trumpets; with beat of drum; with flying colours; in one's Sunday best; in one's best bib and tucker.

883 Celebration *(Substantives)*, jubilee, jubilation, commemoration, festival, feast, solemnization, ovation, paean, triumph.

Triumphal arch, bonfire, illuminations, fireworks, salute, salvo, *feu de joie*, flourish of trumpets, fanfare.

Inauguration, installation, presentation, coronation, fête (882).

Anniversary, silver wedding, golden wedding, diamond wedding, diamond jubilee, centenary, bicentenary, tercentenary, quatercentenary, quingentenary (or quincentenary), sexcentenary, etc., millenary.

(Verbs) To celebrate, keep, signalize, do honour to, pledge, drink to, toast, commemorate, solemnize.

To inaugurate, install.

(Phrase) To paint the town red.

(Adjectives) Celebrating, etc., in honour of, in commemoration of, in memoriam.

(Interjections) Hail! all hail! 'See the conquering hero comes.' 'For he's a jolly good fellow.'

884 Boasting *(Substantives)*, boast, vaunt, vaunting, brag, bounce, *blague*, swank, bluff, puff, puffing, puffery, flourish, fanfaronade, gasconade, braggadocio, bravado, tall talk, heroics, vapouring, rodomontade, bombast, exaggeration (549), self-advertisement, *réclame*; jingoism, Chauvinism, spread-eagleism.

Exultation, triumph, flourish of trumpets (883).

A boaster, braggart, braggadocio, Gascon, peacock; a pretender, charlatan.

(Verbs) To boast, make a boast of, brag, vaunt, puff, flourish, vapour, blow, strut, swagger, swank, skite, gas.

To exult, crow, chuckle, triumph, gloat, glory.

(Phrases) To talk big; to shoot a line; to blow one's own trumpet.

(Adjectives) Boasting, vaunting, etc., thrasonical, vainglorious, braggart, jingo, jingoistic, chauvinistic.

Elate, elated, flushed, jubilant.

(Phrases) On stilts; cock-a-hoop; in high feather.

885 Undue assumption of superiority.

Insolence *(Substantives)*, haughtiness, arrogance, imperiousness, contumeliousness, superciliousness, bumptiousness, bounce, swagger, swank.

Impertinence, sauciness, pertness, flippancy, petulance, malapertness.

Assumption, presumption, presumptuousness, forwardness, impudence, assurance, front, face, neck, cheek, lip, side, brass, shamelessness,

886 Servility *(Substantives)*, obsequiousness, suppleness, fawning, slavishness, abjectness, prostration, prosternation, genuflexion (900), abasement, subjection (749).

Fawning, mealy-mouthedness, sycophancy, flattery (833), humility (879).

A sycophant, parasite, gate-crasher, toad-eater, toady, spaniel, bootlicker, lickspittle, flunkey, sponger, snob, hanger-on, tuft-hunter, time-server, reptile, cur (941); Uriah Heep.

hardihood, a hardened front, effrontery, audacity, procacity, self-assertion, nerve, gall, crust.

(Verbs) To be insolent, etc.; to bluster, vapour, swagger, swank, swell, roister, arrogate, assume, bluff.

To domineer, bully, beard, snub, huff, outface, outlook, outstare, outbrazen, bear down, beat down, trample on, tread underfoot, outbrave, hector.

To presume, take liberties or freedoms.

(Phrases) to give oneself airs; to lay down the law; to put on side; to ride the high horse; to lord it over; *traiter, ou regarder de haut en bas*; to ride roughshod over; to carry with a high hand; to throw one's weight about; to carry it off; to brave it out.

(Adjectives) Insolent, etc.; haughty, arrogant, imperious, dictatorial, high-handed, contumelious, supercilious, snooty, uppish, self-assertive, bumptious, overbearing, intolerant, assumptive.

Flippant, pert, perky, cavalier, saucy, cheeky, fresh, forward, impertinent, malapert.

Blustering, swaggering, swanky, vapouring, bluff, roistering, rollicking, high-flown, assuming, presuming, presumptuous, self-assertive, impudent, free, brazen, brazen-faced, barefaced, shameless, unblushing, unabashed.

887 Blusterer *(Substantives)*, bully, swaggerer, braggart (884), fire-eater, daredevil, roisterer, puppy, sauce-box, hussy, minx, malapert, jackanapes, jack-in-office, jingo, Drawcansir, Captain Bobadil, Sir Lucius O'Trigger, Bombastes Furioso, Hector, Thraso, Bumble.

(Phrases) The great Panjandrum himself; a cool hand.

(Verbs) To cringe, bow, stoop, kneel, fall on one's knees, etc.

To sneak, crawl, crouch, cower, truckle to, grovel, fawn.

(Phrases) To pay court to; to dance attendance on; to do the dirty work of; to lick the boots of.

To go with the stream; to worship the rising sun; to run with the hare and hunt with the hounds.

(Adjectives) Servile, subservient, obsequious, sequacious, soapy, oily, unctuous, supple, mean, crouching, cringing, fawning, slavish, grovelling, snivelling, beggarly, sycophantic, parasitical, abject, prostrate.

(Adverb) Cap in hand.

SECTION III—SYMPATHETIC AFFECTIONS

1°. *Social Affections*

888 Friendship *(Substantives)*, amity, amicableness, amicability, friendliness, friendly regard, affection (897), goodwill, favour, brotherhood, fraternity, sodality, comradeship, *camaraderie*, confraternity, fraternization, cordiality, harmony, good understanding, concord (714), *entente cordiale*.

Acquaintance, introduction, intimacy, familiarity, fellowship, fellow-feeling, sympathy, welcomeness, partiality, favouritism.

889 Enmity *(Substantives)*, hostility, unfriendliness, antagonism, animosity, hate (898), dislike (867), malevolence (907), ill will, ill feeling, spite, bad blood, aversion, antipathy, alienation, estrangement; umbrage, pique.

(Verbs) To be inimical, etc.; to estrange, to fall out, alienate.

(Phrases) To keep at arm's length; to bear malice; to set by the ears.

(Adjectives) Inimical, unfriendly, hostile, antagonistic, adverse, at

(Verbs) To be friends, to be friendly, etc., to fraternize, sympathize with (897), to be well with, to be thick with, to befriend (707), to be in with, to keep in with.

To become friendly, to make friends with, to chum up with.

(Phrases) To take in good part; to hold out the right hand of fellowship; to break the ice; to scrape acquaintance with.

(Adjectives) Friendly, amical, amicable, brotherly, fraternal, harmonious, cordial, social, chummy, pally, neighbourly, on good terms, on a friendly footing, on friendly terms, well-affected, well-disposed, favourable.

Acquainted, familiar, intimate, thick, hand and glove, welcome.

Firm, staunch, intimate, familiar, bosom, cordial, devoted.

(Phrases) In one's good books; hail fellow well met.

(Adverbs) friendly, amicably, etc., *sans cérémonie*.

variance, at loggerheads, at daggers drawn, on bad terms.

Estranged, alienated, irreconcilable.

———

890 Friend *(Substantives)*, well-wisher, *amicus curiae, alter ego*, bosom friend, *fidus Achates*, partner (711); *persona grata*.

Partisan, sympathizer, ally, backer, patron, good genius, fairy godmother.

Neighbour, acquaintance, associate, compeer, comrade, companion, *confrère, camarade*, mate, messmate, shipmate, crony, cummer, confidant, chum, pal, buddy, side-kick, boon companion, pot-companion, schoolfellow, playfellow, playmate, bed-fellow, bed-mate, bunkie, room-mate.

Arcades ambo, Pylades and Orestes, Castor and Pollux, Nisus and Euryalus, Damon and Pythias, David and Jonathan, *par nobile fratrum*.

Host, guest, visitor, *habitué*, protégé.

891 Enemy *(Substantives)*, foe, opponent (710), antagonist.

Public enemy, enemy to society, anarchist, terrorist, Ishmael.

———

892 Sociality *(Substantives)*, sociability, sociableness, social intercourse, companionship, companionableness, consortship, intercommunication, intercommunion, consociation.

Conviviality, good fellowship, hospitality, heartiness, welcome, the glad hand, joviality, jollity, *savoir vivre*, festivity, merrymaking.

Society, association, union, co-partnership, fraternity, sodality, coterie, clan, club (72), circle, clique, knot.

Assembly-room, casino, clubhouse, common-room.

Esprit de corps, nepotism (11).

An entertainment, party, social gathering, reunion, gaudy, levee, soirée, conversazione, rout, *ridotto*,

893 Seclusion *(Substantives)*, privacy, retirement, withdrawal, reclusion, recess, retiredness, rustication.

Solitude, singleness, estrangement from the world, loneliness, lonesomeness, retiredness, isolation; hermitage, cloister, nunnery (1000); study, den; ivory tower, Shangri-la.

Wilderness, depopulation, desolation.

Agoraphobia, claustrophobia.

Exclusion *(Substantives)*, excommunication, banishment, expatriation, exile, ostracism, cut, cut direct, dead cut, inhospitality, inhospitableness, unsociability.

A recluse, hermit, cenobite, anchoret (or anchorite), stylite, santon,

at-home, house-warming, bee, tea-party, bunfight, picnic, garden-party, festival (840), interview, assignation, appointment, date, tryst, call, visit, visiting, reception (588).

A good fellow, good scout, boon companion, good mixer, *bon vivant*.

(Verbs) To be sociable, etc., to associate with, keep company with, to club together, sort with, hobnob with, consort, make advances, fraternize, make the acquaintance of.

To visit, pay a visit, interchange visits or cards, call upon, leave a card.

To entertain, give a party, dance, etc.; to keep open house; to receive, to welcome.

(Phrases) To make oneself at home; to crack a bottle with.

To be at home to; to do the honours; to receive with open arms; to give a warm reception to; to kill the fatted calf.

(Adjectives) Sociable, social, companionable, neighbourly, gregarious, clannish, clubbable, conversable, affable, accessible, familiar, on visiting terms, welcome, hospitable, convivial, jovial, festive.

(Phrases) Free and easy; hail fellow well met.

(Adverbs) En famille; in the family circle; in the social whirl; *sans façon; sans cérémonie; sans gêne*.

———

894 Courtesy *(Substantives)*, good manners, good breeding, good form, mannerliness, manners, *bienséance*, urbanity, civilization, polish, politeness, gentility, comity, civility, amenity, suavity, discretion, diplomacy, good temper, easy temper, gentleness, mansuetude, graciousness, gallantry, affability, obligingness, *prévenance*, amiability, good humour,

Compliment, fair words, soft words, sweet words, honeyed phrases, attentions, *petits soins,* salutation, reception, presentation, introduction, *accueil,* greeting, regards, remembrances, welcome, *abord,* respect, devoir.

troglodyte, solitary, ruralist; displaced person, outcast, pariah; foundling, waif, wastrel, castaway; Timon of Athens, Simon Stylites.

(Phrase) 'A lone lorn creetur.'

(Verbs) To be secluded, etc., to retire, to live retired, secluded, etc.; to keep aloof, keep snug, shut oneself up, deny oneself.

To cut, refuse to associate with or acknowledge; repel, cold-shoulder, blackball, outlaw, proscribe, excommunicate, boycott, exclude, banish, exile, ostracize, rusticate, send down, abandon, maroon.

To depopulate, dispeople, unpeople.

(Phrases) To retire from the world; to take the veil; to sport one's oak.

To send to Coventry; to turn one's back upon; to give one the cold shoulder.

(Adjectives) Secluded, sequestered, retired, private, snug, domestic, claustral.

Unsociable, unsocial, aloof, eremitical, offish, stand-offish, unclubbable, inhospitable, cynical, inconversible, retiring, unneighbourly, exclusive, unforthcoming.

Solitary, lonely, lonesome, isolated, single, estranged, unfrequented, uninhabited, unoccupied, tenantless.

Unvisited, cut, blackballed, uninvited, unwelcome, friendless, deserted, abandoned, derelict, lorn, forlorn, homeless, out of it.

(Phrase) Left to shift for oneself.

895 Discourtesy *(Substantives)*, ill-breeding; ill, bad, or ungainly manners; rusticity, inurbanity, impoliteness, ungraciousness, uncourtliness, insuavity, rudeness, incivility, tactlessness, disrespect, impertinence, impudence, cheek, barbarism, misbehaviour, *grossièreté*, brutality, blackguardism, roughness, ruggedness, brusqueness, brusquerie, bad form.

Bad or ill temper, churlishness, crabbedness, tartness, crossness, peevishness, moroseness, sullenness, sulkiness, grumpiness, grouchiness, acrimony, sternness, austerity, moodi-

Obeisance, reverence, bow, curtsy, scrape, salaam, kowtow, capping, shaking hands, embrace, hug, squeeze, accolade, salute, kiss, buss, kissing hands, genuflexion, prostration, obsequiousness.

Mark of recognition, nod, wave, valediction (293).

(Verbs) To be courteous, civil, etc., to show courtesy, civility, etc., to speak one fair; to make oneself agreeable; to unbend, thaw.

To visit, wait upon, present oneself, pay one's respects, kiss hands.

To receive, do the honours, greet, welcome, bid welcome, usher in, bid God speed; hold or stretch out the hand; shake, press, or squeeze the hand.

To salute, kiss, embrace, hug, drink to, pledge, hobnob; to wave to, nod to, smile upon, bow, curtsy, scrape, uncover, cap, present arms, take off the hat.

To pay homage or obeisance, kneel, bend the knee, prostrate oneself, etc.

To render polite, etc., to polish, civilize, humanize.

(Phrases) To mind one's p's and q's; to do the polite; to greet with open arms; to speed the parting guest.

(Adjectives) Courteous, courtly, civil, civilized, polite, Chesterfieldian, genteel, well-bred, well-mannered, mannerly, urbane, gentlemanly, lady-like, refined (850), polished, genial.

Gracious, affable, familiar, well-spoken, fair-spoken, soft-spoken, fine-spoken, suave, bland, mild, conciliatory, winning, obsequious, obliging, open-armed.

(Phrases) With a good grace; suaviter in modo; à bras ouverts.

(Interjections) Hail! welcome! good morning! good day! good afternoon! good evening! good night! well met! pax vobiscum!

ness, asperity, captiousness, sharpness, snappishness, perversity, cussedness, irascibility (901).

Sulks, dudgeon, mumps, scowl, frown, hard words, black looks.

A bear, brute, boor, blackguard, beast, cross-patch, grouch, sorehead.

(Verbs) To be rude, etc., frown, scowl, glower, lour, pout, snap, snarl, growl, nag; to cut, insult, etc.

To render rude, etc., to brutalize, decivilize, dehumanize.

(Phrases) To turn one's back upon; to turn on one's heel; to look black upon; to give one the cold shoulder, or the frozen face, or the frozen mitt; to take liberties with.

(Adjectives) Discourteous, uncourteous, uncourtly, ill-bred, ill-mannered, ill-behaved, unmannerly, mannerless, impolite, unpolished, ungenteel, ungentlemanly, unladylike, uncivilized.

Uncivil, rude, ungracious, cool, chilly, distant, stand-offish, offish, icy, repulsive, uncomplaisant, unaccommodating, ungainly, unceremonious, ungentle, rough, rugged, bluff, blunt, gruff, churlish, boorish, bearish, brutal, brusque, blackguardly, vulgar, stern, harsh, austere, cavalier.

Ill-tempered, out of temper or humour, cross, crusty, tart, sour, crabbed, sharp, short, snappish, testy, peevish, waspish, captious, grumpy, snarling, caustic, acrimonious, ungenial, petulant, pettish, pert.

Perverse, cross-grained, ill-conditioned, wayward, humoursome, naughty, cantankerous, intractable, curst, nagging, froward, sulky, glum, grim, morose, scowling, grouchy, glowering, surly, sullen, growling, splenetic, spleenful, spleeny, spleenish, moody, dogged, ugly.

(Phrases) Cross as two sticks; sour as a crab; surly as a bear.

(Adverbs) With a bad grace, grudgingly.

---

896 Congratulation (Substantives), felicitation, wishing joy, the compliments of the season, good wishes.

(Verbs) To congratulate, felicitate, give or wish joy, tender or offer one's congratulations.

(Adjectives) Congratulatory, etc.

(Phrases) Many happy returns of the day! merry Christmas! happy New Year!

897 Love *(Substantives)*, fondness, liking, inclination (865), regard, good graces, partiality, benevolence (906), admiration, fancy, tenderness, leaning, penchant, predilection; amativeness, amorousness.

Affection, sympathy, fellow-feeling, heart, affectionateness.

Attachment, yearning, amour, romance, gallantry, love-affair, *affaire de cœur*, passion, tender passion, *grande passion*, flame, pash, crush, rave, devotion, enthusiasm, fervour, enchantment, infatuation, adoration, idolatry, idolization.

Eros, Cupid, Aphrodite, Venus, Freya, the myrtle.

Maternal love, στοργή.

Attractiveness, etc., popularity.

Abode of love, love-nest, agapemone.

A lover, suitor, follower, admirer, adorer, wooer, beau, fiancé, gallant, young man, boy friend, sweetheart, flame, love, true-love, leman, paramour, amorist, *amoroso, cavaliere servente, cicisbeo*; turtle-doves.

Girl friend, lady-love, fiancée, sweetie, cutie, mistress, *inamorata*, idol, doxy, dona, Dulcinea, goddess.

Betrothed, affianced.

(Verbs) To love, like, affect, fancy, care for, regard, revere, cherish, admire, dote on, adore, idolize, fall for, hold dear, prize.

To bear love to; to take to; to be in love with; to be taken, smitten, etc., with; to have, entertain, harbour, cherish, etc., a liking, love, etc., for; to be fond of, be gone on.

To excite love; to win, gain, secure, etc., the love, affections, heart, etc.; to take the fancy of, to attract, attach, seduce, charm, fascinate, captivate, enamour, enrapture.

To get into favour; to ingratiate oneself, insinuate oneself, curry favour with, pay one's court to, *faire l'aimable*.

(Phrases) To take a fancy to; to

898 Hate *(Substantives)*, hatred, disaffection, disfavour, alienation, estrangement, odium, dislike (867), enmity (899), animus, animosity (900).

Umbrage, pique, grudge, dudgeon, spleen, bitterness, ill feeling, acrimony, acerbity, malice (907), implacability.

Disgust, repugnance, aversion, averseness, loathing, abomination, horror, detestation, antipathy, abhorrence.

Object of hatred, abomination, *bête noir*.

(Verbs) To hate, dislike, disrelish (867), loathe, nauseate, execrate, detest, abominate, shudder at, recoil at, abhor, shrink from.

To excite hatred, estrange, incense, envenom, antagonize, rile, alienate, disaffect, set against; to be hateful, etc.

(Phrases) To make one's blood run cold; to have a down on; to hate one's guts.

To sow dissension among; to set by the ears.

(Adjectives) Hating, etc., averse to, set against.

Unloved, disliked, unwept, unlamented, undeplored, unmourned, unbeloved, uncared-for, unvalued.

Crossed in love, forsaken, jilted, rejected, lovelorn.

Obnoxious, hateful, abhorrent, odious, repulsive, offensive, shocking, loathsome, sickening, nauseous, disgusting, abominable, horrid (830).

Invidious, spiteful, malicious (907), spleenful, disgustful.

Insulting, irritating, provoking.

(Phrases) Not on speaking terms; there being no love lost between them; at daggers drawn.

make a fuss of; to look sweet upon; to cast sheep's eyes at; to fall in love with; to set one's affections on; to lose one's heart to.

To set one's cap at; to turn one's head.

(Adjectives) Loving, liking, etc., attached to, fond of, taken with, struck with, gone on, sympathetic, sympathizing with, charmed, captivated, fascinated, smitten, bitten, *épris*, enamoured, lovesick, love-lorn.

Affectionate, tender, sweet upon, loving, lover-like, loverly, amorous, amatory, amative, spoony, erotic, uxorious, motherly, ardent, passionate, devoted, amatorial.

Loved, beloved, etc., dear, precious, darling, favourite (899), pet, popular.

Lovely, sweet, dear, charming, engaging, amiable, winning, winsome, lovesome, attractive, adorable, enchanting, captivating, fascinating, bewitching, taking, seductive (829).

(Phrases) Head over ears in love; to one's mind, taste, or fancy; in one's good graces; nearest to one's heart.

899 Favourite *(Substantives)*, pet, cosset, dear, darling, honey, duck, moppet, jewel, idol, minion, spoilt child, blue-eyed boy, *persona grata*.

(Phrases) The apple of one's eye; a man after one's own heart; the idol of the people; the answer to the maiden's prayer.

900 Resentment *(Substantives)*, displeasure, animus, animosity, anger, wrath, indignation.

Pique, umbrage, huff, miff, soreness, dudgeon, moodiness, acerbity, bitterness, asperity, spleen, gall, heart-burning, heart-swelling, rankling; temper (901), bad blood, ill blood, ill humour.

Excitement, irritation, exasperation, warmth, bile, choler, ire, fume, dander, passion, fit, tantrum, burst, explosion, paroxysm, storm, rage, wax, fury, desperation.

Temper, petulance, procacity, angry mood, taking, snappishness.

Cause of umbrage, affront, provocation, offence, indignity, insult (929).

The Furies; the Eumenides.

(Phrases) The blood being up or boiling; a towering passion; the vials of wrath; fire and fury.

A sore subject; a rap on the knuckles; *casus belli*.

(Verbs) To resent, take amiss, take offence, take umbrage, take huff, bridle up, bristle up, frown, scowl, lour, snarl, growl, gnash, snap.

To chafe, mantle, redden, colour, fume, froth up, kindle; get, fall, or fly into a passion, rage, etc.; fly out, take fire, fire up, flare up, boil, boil over, rage, storm, foam.

To cause or raise anger; to affront, offend, give offence or umbrage; hurt the feelings; discompose, fret, ruffle, nettle, excite, irritate, provoke, rile, chafe, wound, sting, incense, inflame, enrage, aggravate, embitter, exasperate, rankle, infuriate, peeve.

(Phrases) To take in bad part; to take it ill; to take exception to; to stick in one's gizzard; to take in dudgeon; to have a bone (or crow) to pick with one; to get up on one's hind legs; to show one's teeth; to lose one's temper; to stamp, quiver, swell, or foam with rage; to see red; to look as black as thunder; to breathe revenge; to cut up rough; to pour out the vials of one's wrath; to blaze up; to blow one's top; to go up in a blue flame; to go on the war-path; to raise Cain.

To put out of humour; to stir up one's bile; to raise one's dander or choler; to work up into a passion; to make one's blood boil; to lash into a fury; to drive one mad; to put one's monkey up; to get one's goat.

(Adjectives) Angry, wroth, irate, ireful, warm, boiling, fuming, raging, etc.,

nettled, sore, bitter, riled, ruffled, chafed, exasperated, wrought up, worked up, snappish.

Fierce, wild, rageful, furious, infuriate, mad, fiery, savage, rabid, waxy, shirty, boiling over, rankling, bitter, virulent, set against.

Relentless, ruthless, implacable, unpitying, pitiless (919), inexorable, remorseless, stony-hearted, immitigable.

(Phrases) One's back being up; up in arms; in a stew; the gorge rising; in the height of passion.

(Interjections) Hell's bells! zounds! damme! For crying out loud!

901 Irascibility *(Substantives)*, susceptibility, excitability, temper, bad temper, procacity, petulance, irritability, fretfulness, testiness, grouchiness, tetchiness, touchiness, frowardness, peevishness, snappishness, hastiness, tartness, huffiness, resentfulness, vindictiveness, acerbity, protervity, aggressiveness, pugnacity (895).

A shrew, vixen, termagant, virago, scold, spitfire, Xanthippe; a tartar, fire-eater, fury; *genus irritabile*.

(Verbs) To be irascible, etc.; to take fire, fire up, flare up (900).

(Adjectives) Irascible, susceptible, excitable, irritable, fretful, fretty, on the fret, fidgety, peevish, hasty, over-hasty, quick, warm, hot, huffish, huffy, touchy, testy, tetchy (or techy), grouchy, restive, pettish, waspish, snappish, petulant, peppery, fiery, passionate, choleric, short-tempered.

Ill-tempered, bad-tempered, cross, churlish, sour, crabbed, cross-grained, sullen, sulky, grumpy, fractious, splenetic, spleenful, froward, shrewish.

Quarrelsome, querulous, disputatious, contentious, cranky, cantankerous, sarcastic (932), resentful, vindictive, pugnacious, aggressive.

(Phrases) Like touchwood or tinder; a word and a blow; as cross as two sticks.

902 Expression of affection or love.

Endearment *(Substantives)*, caress, blandishment, fondling, billing and cooing, petting, necking, embrace, salute, kiss, buss, smack, osculation, deosculation.

Courtship, wooing, suit, addresses, attentions, *petits soins,* flirtation, coquetry, philandering, gallivanting, serenading, œillade, ogle, the glad eye, sheep's eyes, goo-goo eyes.

Love-tale, love-token, love-letter, *billet-doux,* valentine.

Flirt, coquette, gold digger, vamp; male flirt, masher, philanderer, lady killer, wolf, lounge lizard, cake eater, sheik.

(Verbs) To caress, fondle, wheedle, dandle, dally, cuddle, cockle, cosset, nestle, nuzzle, snuggle, clasp, hug, embrace, kiss, salute, bill and coo.

To court, woo, flirt, coquette, philander, spoon, canoodle, mash, spark, serenade.

(Phrases) To make much of; to smile upon; to make eyes at; to chuck under the chin; to pat on the cheek; to make love; to pay one's court or one's addresses to; to set one's cap at; to pop the question.

To win the heart, affections, love, etc., of

(Adjectives) Caressing, etc., caressed, etc., flirtatious, spoony.

903 Marriage *(Substantives)*, matrimony, wedlock, union, bridal, match, intermarriage, coverture, cohabitation, bed, the marriage bond, the nuptial tie.

Wedding, nuptials, Hymen, spousals, espousals; leading to the altar;

904 Celibacy *(Substantives)*, singleness, misogamy; bachelorhood, bachelorship; virginity, maidenhood, maidenhead.

An unmarried man, bachelor, celibate, misogamist, misogynist.

An unmarried woman, spinster,

the torch of Hymen; nuptial benediction, marriage song, epithalamium.

Bride, bridegroom, groom, bridesmaid, maid of honour, matron of honour, bridesman, groomsman, best man.

Honeymoon, honeymooner.

A married man, a husband, spouse, benedick (or benedict), consort, goodman, lord and master, hubby.

A married woman, a wife, lady, matron, mate, helpmate, helpmeet, rib, better half, *femme couverte* (or *feme coverte*), squaw.

A married couple, wedded pair, Darby and Joan, man and wife.

A monogamist, bigamist, polygamist, a much-married man, a Turk, a Bluebeard, a Mormon.

Monogamy, bigamy, digamy, deuterogamy, trigamy, polygamy, polygyny, polyandry, endogamy, exogamy.

A morganatic marriage, left-handed marriage, marriage of convenience, *mariage de convenance*, companionate marriage, trial marriage, misalliance, *mésalliance*.

(Verbs) To marry, wed, espouse, wive.

To join, give away, handfast, splice.

(Phrases) To lead to the altar; to take to oneself a wife; to take for better for worse; to give one's hand to; to get spliced.

To tie the nuptial knot; to give in marriage.

(Adjectives) Matrimonial, conjugal, connubial, nuptial, wedded, hymeneal, spousal, bridal, marital, epithalamic.

Monogamous, bigamous, polygamous, etc.

maid, maiden, old maid, virgin, *femme sole,* bachelor girl.

(Phrase) Single blessedness.

(Verb) To live single.

(Adjectives) Unwedded, unmarried, single, celibate, wifeless, spouseless, lone.

905 Divorce *(Substantives)*, dissolution of marriage, separation, divorcement.

A divorcee, co-respondent, cuckold.

(Verbs) To live separate, divorce, put away.

Widowhood, viduity, weeds.

Widow, relict, dowager, jointress, grass widow; widower, grass widower.

———

2°. Diffusive Sympathetic Affections

906 Benevolence *(Substantives)*, goodwill, good nature, kindness, kindliness, benignity, brotherly love, beneficence, charity, humanity, fellow-feeling, sympathy, good feeling, kind-heartedness, amiability, complaisance, loving-kindness; toleration, consideration, generosity.

Charitableness, bounty, bounteousness, bountifulness, almsgiving, philanthropy (910), unselfishness (942).

Acts of kindness, a good turn, good works, kind offices, attentions, good treatment.

(Phrases) The milk of human kindness; the good Samaritan.

(Verbs) To be benevolent, etc., to do good to, to benefit, confer a benefit, be of use, aid, assist (707),

907 Malevolence *(Substantives)*, ill will, unkindness, ill nature, malignity, malice, maliciousness, spite, spitefulness, despite, despitefulness.

Uncharitableness, venom, gall, rancour, rankling, bitterness, acerbity, harshness, mordacity, acridity, virulence, *acharnement*, misanthropy (911).

Cruelty, hardness of heart, obduracy, cruelness, brutality, brutishness, hooliganism, savageness, savagery, ferocity, barbarity, bloodthirstiness, immanity, pitilessness, truculence, devilry (or deviltry), devilment.

An ill turn, a bad turn, outrage, atrocity, affront (929).

(Phrases) A heart of stone; the evil eye; the cloven hoof.

render a service, treat well, to sympathize with.

(Phrases) To have one's heart in the right place; to enter into the feelings of others; to do a good turn to; to do as one would be done by.

(Adjectives) Benevolent, well-meaning, kind, obliging, accommodating, kind-hearted, tender-hearted, charitable, generous, beneficent, bounteous, bountiful, humane, clement, benignant, benign, considerate.

Good-natured, *bon enfant, bon diable,* a good sort, sympathizing, sympathetic, responsive, complaisant, accommodating, amiable, gracious.

Kindly, well-meant, well-intentioned, brotherly, fraternal, friendly (888).

(Adverbs) With a good intention, with the best intentions.

(Interjections) Good luck! God speed!

(Verbs) To be malevolent, etc.; to injure, hurt, harm, molest, disoblige, do harm to, ill treat, maltreat (649), do an ill office or turn to (830), to wrong.

To worry, harass, bait, oppress, grind, haze, persecute, hunt down, dragoon, hound.

(Phrases) To wreak one's malice on; to bear or harbour malice against; to do one's worst.

(Adjectives) Malevolent, malicious, ill-disposed, evil-minded, ill-intentioned, maleficent, malign, malignant.

Ill-natured, disobliging, inofficious, unfriendly, unsympathetic, unkind, uncandid, unaccommodating, uncharitable, ungracious, unamiable.

Surly, churlish (895), grim, spiteful, despiteful, ill-conditioned, foul-mouthed, acrid, rancorous, caustic, bitter, acrimonious, mordacious, vitriolic, venomous.

Cold, cold-blooded, cold-hearted, hard-hearted, iron-hearted, flint-hearted, marble-hearted, stony-hearted.

Pitiless, unpitying, uncompassionate, without bowels, ruthless, merciless, unmerciful, inexorable, relentless, unrelenting, virulent, dispiteous.

Cruel, brutal, savage, ferocious, atrocious, untamed, ferine, inhuman, barbarous, fell, Hunnish, bloody, blood-stained, bloodthirsty, bloody-minded, sanguinary, truculent (919), butcherly.

Fiendish, fiendlike, infernal, demoniacal, diabolical, devilish, hellish.

(Adverbs) Malevolently, etc., with bad intent or intention, despitefully.

908 Malediction *(Substantives),* curse, malison, imprecation, denunciation, execration, anathema, ban, proscription, excommunication, commination, fulmination, *maranatha.*

Cursing, scolding, revilement, vilification, vituperation, invective, flyting, railing, Billingsgate, expletive, oath, bad language, unparliamentary language, ribaldry, scurrility.

(Verbs) To censure, curse, imprecate, damn, scold, swear at, flyte on, rail at or against, execrate.

To denounce, proscribe, excommunicate, fulminate against, anathematize, blaspheme.

(Phrases) To devote to destruction; to invoke or call down curses on one's head; to swear like a trooper; to rap out an oath; to curse with bell, book and candle.

(Adjectives) Cursing, etc., accursed, cursed, etc., blue-pencil, asterisk; maledictory, imprecatory, blasphemous.

(Interjections) Curse! damn! blast! devil take it! hang! blow! confound! plague on it! woe to! beshrew! *ruat coelum!* ill betide!

909 Threat *(Substantives)*, menace, defiance (715), abuse, minacity, intimidation, commination.

(Verbs) To threaten, threat, menace, fulminate, thunder, bluster, defy, snarl; growl, gnarl, mutter; to intimidate (860).

(Phrases) To hurl defiance; to throw down the gauntlet; to look daggers; to show one's teeth; to shake the fist at.

(Adjectives) Threatening, menacing, minatory, comminatory, minacious, abusive, sinister, ominous, louring, defiant (715).

(Interjections) Let them beware! You have been warned!

910 Philanthropy *(Substantives)*, humanity, humanitarianism, altruism, public spirit.

Patriotism, civicism, nationality, nationalism, love of country, *amor patriae*, sociology, socialism, utilitarianism.

A philanthropist, humanitarian, utilitarian, Benthamite, socialist, cosmopolitan, cosmopolite, citizen of the world, patriot, nationalist, lover of mankind.

(Adjectives) Philanthropic, philanthropical, humanitarian, humane, utilitarian, patriotic, altruistic, public-spirited.

(Phrases) 'Humani nihil a me alienum puto'; pro bono publico; the greatest happiness of the greatest number.

911 Misanthropy *(Substantives)*, egotism, egoism, incivism, want of patriotism, moroseness, selfishness (943); misogynism.

A misanthrope, egotist, cynic, man-hater, Timon, Diogenes.

Woman-hater, misogynist.

(Adjectives) Misanthropic, misanthropical, antisocial, unpatriotic, fish, egotistical, morose, sullen, maladjusted.

_____

912 Benefactor *(Substantives)*, saviour, good genius, tutelary saint, guardian angel, fairy godmother, good Samaritan.

(Phrase) Deus ex machina.

_____

913 Maleficent being.

Evildoer *(Substantives)*, wrongdoer, mischief-maker, marplot, anarchist, nihilist, terrorist, firebrand, incendiary, evil genius (980).

Frankenstein's monster.

Savage, brute, ruffian, blackguard, villain, scoundrel, cutthroat, barbarian, caitiff, desperado, jail-bird, hooligan, tough, rough, teddy boy, larrikin, hoodlum, gangster, crook, yegg, apache (949).

Fiend, tiger, hyena, bloodhound, butcher, blood-sucker, vampire, ogre, ghoul, serpent, snake, adder, viper, rattlesnake, scorpion, hellhound, hag, hellbag, beldam, harpy, siren, fury, Jezebel.

Monster, demon, imp, devil (980), anthropophagi, Attila, vandal, Hun, Goth.

(Phrases) A snake in the grass; a scourge of the human race; a fiend in human shape; worker of iniquity.

3°. Special Sympathetic Affections

914 Pity *(Substantives)*, compassion, commiseration, sympathy, fellow-feeling, tenderness, yearning.

Forbearance, mercy, humanity, clemency, leniency, ruth, long-suffering, quarter.

(Phrases) The melting mood; *coup de grâce*; bowels of compassion; *argumentum ad misericordiam.*

(Verbs) To pity, commiserate, compassionate, sympathize, feel for, yearn for, console, enter into the feelings of, have or take pity; show or have mercy; to forbear, relent, thaw, spare, relax, give quarter.

To excite pity, touch, soften, melt, propitiate, disarm.

To ask for pity, mercy, etc.; to supplicate, implore, deprecate, appeal to, cry for quarter, etc.; beg one's life, kneel, fall on one's knees, etc.

(Phrase) To put one out of one's misery.

(Adjectives) Pitying, commiserating, etc.

Pitiful, compassionate, tender, clement, merciful, lenient, relenting, etc.; soft-hearted, sympathetic, touched, weak, soft, melting, unhardened (740).

Piteous, pitiable, sorry, miserable.

(Phrases) Tender as a woman; one's heart bleeding for.

(Interjections) For pity's sake! mercy! God help you! poor thing! poor fellow!

915 Condolence *(Substantives)*, lamentation, lament (839), sympathy, consolation.

(Verbs) To condole with, console, solace, sympathize; express, testify, etc., pity; to afford or supply consolation, grieve for, lament with, weep with (839).

4°. Retrospective Sympathetic Affections

916 Gratitude *(Substantives)*, gratefulness, thankfulness, feeling of obligation.

Acknowledgment, recognition, thanksgiving, giving thanks.

Thanks, praise, benediction, grace, paean, Te Deum (990).

Requital, thank-offering.

(Verbs) To be grateful, etc.; to thank, to give, render, return, offer, tender thanks, acknowledgments, etc.; to acknowledge, appreciate, requite.

To lie under an obligation, to be obliged, beholden, etc.

(Phrases) To overflow with gratitude; to thank one's stars; never to forget.

(Adjectives) Grateful, thankful, obliged, beholden, indebted to, under obligation.

(Interjections) Thanks! many thanks! ta! *merci!* gramercy! much obliged! thank heaven! heaven be praised!

917 Ingratitude *(Substantives)*, ungratefulness, thanklessness, oblivion of benefits.

(Phrases) 'Benefits forgot'; a thankless task.

(Verbs) To be ungrateful, etc.; to forget benefits.

(Phrases) To look a gift-horse in the mouth; to bite the hand that fed one.

(Adjectives) Ungrateful, unmindful, unthankful, thankless, ingrate, inappreciative.

Forgotten, unacknowledged, unthanked, unrequited, unrewarded, ill-requited.

(Phrase) Thank you for nothing.

———

918 Forgiveness *(Substantives)*, pardon, condonation, grace, remission, absolution, amnesty, indemnity, oblivion, indulgence, reprieve.

Reconcilement, reconciliation, appeasement, mollification, shaking of hands, pacification (723).

919 Revenge *(Substantives)*, vengeance, revengement, avengement, vendetta, feud, retaliation.

Rancour, vindictiveness, implacability.

Revenger, avenger, vindicator, Nemesis, Furies.

Excuse, exoneration, quittance, acquittal, propitiation, exculpation.

Longanimity, forbearance, placability.

(Verbs) To forgive, pardon, excuse, pass over, overlook, bear with, condone, absolve, pass, let off, remit, reprieve, exculpate, exonerate.

To allow for; to make allowance for.

To conciliate, propitiate, pacify, appease, placate, reconcile.

(Phrases) To make it up; to forgive and forget; to shake hands; to heal the breach; to kiss and be friends; to bury the hatchet; to wipe the slate clean; to let bygones be bygones.

(Verbs) To revenge, take revenge, avenge.

(Phrases) To wreak one's vengeance; to visit the sins on; to breathe vengeance; to have a bone to pick with; to have accounts to settle; to have a rod in pickle; to get one's knife into; to take one's change out of.

To harbour vindictive feelings; to rankle in the breast.

(Adjectives) Revengeful, revanchist, vindictive, vengeful, rancorous, unforgiving, pitiless, ruthless, remorseless, unrelenting, relentless, implacable, rigorous.

(Adjectives) Forgiving, etc., unreproachful, placable, conciliatory.

Forgiven, etc., unresented.

920 Jealousy *(Substantives)*, jealousness, heartburning.

(Phrases) A jaundiced eye; the green-eyed monster.

(Verbs) To be jealous, etc.; to view with jealousy.

(Adjectives) Jealous, jaundiced, yellow-eyed.

(Phrase) Eaten up with jealousy.

921 Envy *(Substantives)*, rivalry, emulation, covetousness; a Thersites, Zoilus.

(Verbs) To envy, rival, emulate, covet.

(Adjectives) Envious, invidious, covetous.

(Phrase) Bursting with envy.

SECTION IV—MORAL AFFECTIONS

1°. *Moral Obligation*

922 Right *(Substantives)*, what ought to be, what should be; goodness, virtue (944), rectitude, probity (939).

Justice, equity, equitableness, fitness, fairness, fair play, impartiality, reasonableness, propriety.

Astraea, Themis.

(Phrases) The scales of justice; even-handed justice; *suum cuique*; a fair field and no favour; *lex talionis; 'Fiat justitia, ruat coelum.'*

Morality, morals, ethics, duty (926).

(Verbs) To stand to reason; to be right, just, etc.

To deserve, merit; to be worthy of, to be entitled to (924).

923 Wrong *(Substantives)*, what ought not to be, badness, evil (945), turpitude, improbity (940).

Injustice, unfairness, inequity, foul play, partiality, favour, favouritism, leaning, bias, party spirit, undueness (925), unreasonableness, tort, unlawfulness (964), encroachment, imposition.

(Verbs) To be wrong, unjust, etc.; to favour, lean towards, show partiality, to encroach, impose upon.

(Phrase) To rob Peter to pay Paul.

(Adjectives) Wrong, wrongful, bad, unjust, unfair, undue, inequitable, unequal, partial, invidious, one-sided, improper, unreasonable, iniquitous, unfit, immoral (945).

(Phrases) To do justice to; to see justice done; to hold the scales even; to see fair play; to see one righted; to serve one right; to give the devil his due; to give and take; *audire alteram partem.*

(Adjectives) Right, just, equitable, fair, equal, even-handed, impartial, judicial, legitimate, justifiable, rightful, reasonable, fit, proper, becoming, decorous, decent (926).

Deserved, merited, condign (924).

(Adverbs) Rightly, in justice, in equity, fairly, etc., in reason, without distinction, without respect of persons.

(Phrases) En règle; de jure.

Unjustified, unjustifiable, unwarranted, unauthorized, unallowable, unwarrantable.

(Phrases) In the wrong; in the wrong box.

(Adverbs) Wrongly, unjustly, etc., amiss.

(Phrase) It won't do.

---

924 Dueness *(Substantives),* due.

Right, privilege, prerogative, title, claim, qualification, pretension, birthright, prescription, immunity, exemption, licence, liberty, franchise, enfranchisement, vested interest.

Sanction, authority, warranty, tenure, bond, security, lien, constitution, charter, warrant (760), patent, letters patent, copyright, *imprimatur.*

A claimant, pretender, appellant, plaintiff (938).

Women's rights, feminism; feminist, suffragist, suffragette.

(Verbs) To be due, etc., to.

To have a right to, to be entitled to, to be qualified for, to have a claim upon, a title to, etc.; to deserve, merit, be worthy of.

To demand, claim, call upon, exact, insist on, challenge, to come upon one for, to revendicate, make a point of, enforce, put in force, use a right.

To appertain to, belong to, etc. (777).

To lay claim to, assert, assume, arrogate, make good, substantiate; to vindicate a claim, etc., to make out a case.

To give or confer a right; to entitle, authorize, warrant, sanction, sanctify, privilege, enfranchise, license, legalize, ordain, prescribe, allot.

(Adjectives) Having a right to, a claim to, etc.; due to, entitled to, deserving, meriting, worthy of, claiming, qualified.

925 Absence of right.

Undueness *(Substantives),* unlawfulness, impropriety, unfitness, illegality (964).

Falseness, spuriousness, emptiness or invalidity of title, illegitimacy.

Loss of right, forfeiture, disfranchisement.

Usurpation, violation, breach, encroachment, stretch, imposition, relaxation.

(Verbs) Not to be due, etc., to; to be undue, etc.

To infringe, encroach, violate, do violence to; to stretch or strain a point; to trench on, usurp.

To disfranchise, disentitle, disfrock, unfrock; to disqualify, invalidate, relax.

To misbecome, misbehave (945).

(Adjectives) Undue, unlawful, illicit, unconstitutional.

Unauthorized, unwarranted, unsanctioned, unjustified, unprivileged, illegitimate, bastard, spurious, supposititious, false, usurped, unchartered, unfulfilled, unofficial, unauthorized.

Unentitled, disentitled, unqualified, underprivileged; disfranchised, forfeit.

Undeserved, unmerited, unearned.

Improper, unmeet, unbecoming, unfit, misbecoming, unseemly, preposterous.

(Phrases) Not the thing; out of the question; not to be thought of; out of court.

Privileged, allowed, sanctioned, warranted, authorized, permitted, licit, ordained, prescribed, chartered, enfranchised, constitutional, official.

Prescriptive, presumptive, absolute, indefeasible, unalienable, inalienable, imprescriptible, inviolable, unimpeachable, unchallenged, sacred, sacrosanct.

Condign, merited, deserved.

Allowable, permissible, lawful, legitimate, legal, legalized (963), proper, square, equitable, unexceptionable, reasonable (922), right, correct, meet, fitting (926).

(Adverbs) Duly, by right, by divine right, *ex officio, Dei gratia, de jure.*

---

926 Duty *(Substantives)*, what ought to be done; moral obligation, accountableness, accountability, liability, onus, responsibility, bounden duty; dueness (924).

Allegiance, fealty, tie, office, function, province, post, engagement (768).

Morality, morals, conscience, accountableness, conscientiousness; the Decalogue, the Ten Commandments.

Dueness, propriety, fitness, decency, seemliness, decorum.

Observance, fulfilment, discharge, performance, acquittal, satisfaction, redemption, good behaviour.

Science of morals, ethics, deontology; moral or ethical philosophy, casuistry.

(Phrases) The thing; the proper thing; a case of conscience; the still small voice.

(Verbs) To be the duty of, to be due to, to be up to; ought to be; to be incumbent on, to behove, befit, become, beseem, belong to, pertain to, devolve on, to be on one's head; to be, or stand, or lie under an obligation; to have to answer for, to be accountable for, to owe it to oneself, to be in duty bound, to be committed to, to be on one's good behaviour.

To impose a duty or obligation; to enjoin, require, exact, bind, pin down, saddle with, prescribe, assign, call upon, look to, oblige.

927 Dereliction of duty *(Substantives)*, guilt (947), sin (945), neglect, evasion, dead letter.

(Verbs) To violate, break, break through, infringe, set at naught, slight, neglect, trample on, evade, contravene, disregard, renounce, repudiate, quit, forswear, fail, transgress.

(Phrase) To wash one's hands of.

927A Exemption *(Substantives)*, freedom, irresponsibility, immunity, liberty, licence, release, exoneration, excuse, dispensation, absolution, franchise, renunciation, discharge.

(Verbs) To be exempt, free, at liberty, released, excused, exonerated, absolved, etc.

To exempt, release, excuse, exonerate, absolve, acquit, free, set at liberty, discharge, set aside, let off, remit, pass over, spare, excuse, license, dispense with; to give dispensation.

(Phrase) To stretch a point.

(Adjectives) Exempt, free, released, at liberty, absolved, exonerated, excused, let off, discharged, licensed, acquitted, unencumbered, dispensed, scot-free, immune.

Irresponsible, unaccountable, unanswerable, unbound.

To do one's duty, to enter upon a duty; to perform, observe, fulfil, discharge, adhere to; acquit oneself of an obligation.

(Phrases) To be at one's post; to redeem one's pledge; to toe the mark or line.

(Adjectives) Dutiful, duteous, docile, obedient, compliant, tractable.

Obligatory, binding, imperative, peremptory, mandatory, behoving, incumbent on, chargeable on, meet, due to.

Being under obligation, under obedience, obliged by, beholden to, bound by, tied by, saddled with, indebted to.

Amenable, liable, accountable, responsible, answerable.

Right, proper, fit, due, correct, seemly, fitting, befitting, decent, meet.

Moral, ethical, casuistical, conscientious.

(Adverbs) Conscientiously, with a safe conscience; as in duty bound; on one's own responsibility.

2°. *Moral Sentiments*

928 Respect *(Substantives)*, deference, reverence, regard, consideration, attention, honour, esteem, estimation, distance, decorum, veneration, admiration.

Homage, fealty, obeisance, genuflexion, kneeling, salaam, kowtow, presenting arms (896), prostration, obsequiousness, devotion, worship (990).

(Verbs) To respect, honour, reverence, regard, defer to, pay respect or deference to, render honour to, look up to, esteem, revere, think much of, think highly of, venerate, hallow.

To pay homage to, bow to, take off one's hat to, kneel to, bend the knee to, present arms, fall down before, prostrate oneself.

To command or inspire respect; to awe, overawe, dazzle.

(Phrases) To keep one's distance; to make way for; to observe due decorum.

(Adjectives) Respecting, etc., respectful, considerate, polite, attentive, reverential, obsequious, ceremonious, bare-headed, cap in hand, on one's knees, prostrate.

Respected, esteemed, honoured, hallowed, venerable, emeritus.

(Phrases) Saving your presence; begging your honour's pardon.

---

929 Disrespect *(Substantives)*, irreverence, dishonour, disparagement, slight, neglect, disesteem, disestimation, superciliousness, contumely, indignity, insult, rudeness.

Ridicule (856), sarcasm, derision, scurrility, mockery, scoffing, sibilation.

A jeer, gibe, taunt, scoff, sneer (930), hiss, hoot, fling, flout.

(Verbs) To treat with disrespect, etc., to disparage, dishonour, misprise, vilipend, slight, insult, affront, disregard, make light of, hold in no esteem, esteem of no account, set at naught, speak slightingly of, set down, pass by, overlook, look down upon, despise (930).

To deride, scoff, sneer at, laugh at, ridicule (856), roast, guy, rag, mock, jeer, taunt, twit, flout, gibe, hiss, hoot, boo.

(Phrases) To make game of; to point the finger at; to make a fool of; to turn into ridicule; to laugh to scorn; to turn one's back upon.

(Adjectives) Disrespectful, slighting, disparaging (934), dishonouring, scornful (940), irreverent, supercilious, contumelious, scurrilous, deriding, derisive, derisory.

Unrespected, unworshipped, unregarded, disregarded, ignored.

(Adverbs) Disrespectfully, cavalierly, etc.

930 Contempt *(Substantives)*, disdain, scorn, contumely, despisal, slight, sneer, spurn, sniff; a byword.

Scornfulness, disdainfulness, haughtiness, contemptuousness, superciliousness, derision (929).

The state of being despised, despisedness.

(Verbs) To despise, contemn, scorn, disdain, scout, spurn, look down upon,

disregard, slight, make light of, not mind, hold cheap, hold in contempt, pooh-pooh, sneeze at, sniff at, whistle at, hoot, flout, trample upon.

(Phrases) Not to care a straw, fig, button, etc., for (643); to turn up one's nose at; to shrug one's shoulders; to snap one's fingers at; to take no account of; to laugh to scorn; to make light of; to tread or trample under foot; to set at naught; to point the finger of scorn at.

(Adjectives) Contemptuous, disdainful, scornful, contumelious, cavalier, derisive, supercilious, toplofty, upstage, sniffy, sardonic.

Contemptible, despicable, poor, paltry (643), downtrodden, unenvied.

(Interjections) A fig for! hoots! bah! pshaw! pish! shucks! pooh-pooh! fiddlestick! fiddle-de-dee! tush! tut!

931 Approbation *(Substantives)*, approval, approvement, endorsement, sanction, esteem, admiration, estimation, good opinion, appreciation, regard, account, popularity, kudos.

Commendation, praise, laud, laudation, advocacy, good word; meed or tribute of praise, encomium, eulogium, eulogy, *éloge*, panegyric, puff, blurb, homage.

Applause, plaudit, cheer, clap, clapping, clapping of hands, acclamation; paean, benediction, blessing, benison, hosanna; claque.

(Phrases) A peal, shout, or chorus of applause; golden opinions; *succès d'estime*.

(Verbs) To approve, think well or highly of, esteem, appreciate, value, prize, admire, countenance, endorse.

To commend, speak well of, recommend, advocate, praise, laud, belaud, compliment, bepraise, clap, clap hands, applaud, cheer, panegyrize, celebrate, eulogize, cry up, root for, crack up, write up, extol, glorify, magnify, puff, boom, boost, exalt, swell, bless, give a blessing to.

To deserve praise, etc., to be praised, etc.

(Phrases) To set great store by; to sing the praises of; to extol to the skies; to applaud to the echo; to stick up for; to say a good word for; to pat on the back.

To redound to the honour or praise of; to do credit to.

To win golden opinions; to be in high favour; to bring down the house.

(Adjectives) Approving, etc., commendatory, complimentary, benedictory, laudatory, panegyrical, eulo-

932 Disapprobation *(Substantives)*, disapproval, dislike (867), blame, censure, reprobation, obloquy, dispraise, contumely, odium, disesteem, depreciation, detraction (934), condemnation, ostracism.

Reprobation, exprobation, insinuation, innuendo, animadversion, reflection, stricture, objection, exception, criticism, critique, correction, discommendation.

Satire, sneer, fling, gibe, skit, squib, quip, taunt, sarcasm, lampoon, cavil, pasquinade, recrimination, castigation.

Remonstrance, reprehension, reproof, admonition, expostulation, reproach, rebuke, reprimand, talking-to, telling-off.

Evil speaking, hard words, foul language, personalities, ribaldry, Billingsgate, unparliamentary language.

Upbraiding, abuse, invective, vituperation, scolding, wigging, dressing-down, objurgation, jaw, railing, jobation, nagging, reviling, contumely, execration (908).

A set-down, trimming, rating, slap, snub, frown, scowl, black look.

A lecture, curtain lecture, diatribe, jeremiad, tirade, philippic; clamour, outcry, hue and cry, hiss, hissing, sibilation, cat-call.

(Phrases) A rap on the knuckles; a slap in the face; a left-handed compliment.

(Verbs) To disapprove, dislike (867), dispraise, find fault with, criticize, glance at, insinuate, cut up, carp at, cavil, point at, peck at, nibble at, object to, take exception

gistic, encomiastic.

Approved, praised, uncensured, unimpeached, admired, popular, deserving or worthy of praise, praiseworthy, commendable, estimable, plausible, meritorious.

(Phrases) Lavish of praise; lost in admiration.

(Interjections) Well done! good man! stout fellow! good show! attaboy! bravo! bravissimo! *euge!* that's the stuff! hear, hear!

————

to, animadvert upon, protest against, frown upon, bar.

To disparage, depreciate, deprecate, crab, knock, traduce, smear, speak ill of, decry, vilify, vilipend, defame, detract (934), revile, satirize, sneer, gibe, lampoon, inveigh against, write down, scalp.

To blame; to lay or cast blame upon, reflect upon, cast a slur upon, censure, pass censure on, impugn, show up, denounce, censure, brand, stigmatize, reprobate, improbate.

To reprehend, reprimand, admonish, remonstrate, expostulate, reprove, pull up, take up, set down, snub, twit, taunt, reproach, load with reproaches, rebuke, come down upon, sit on, pitch into, get on to, tell off, tick off.

To chide, scold, wig, rate, objurgate, upbraid, vituperate, recriminate, anathematize, abuse, call names, exclaim against, jaw, mob, trounce, trim, rail at, nag, nag at, bark at, blackguard, revile, ballyrag, rag, natter, blow up, roast, lecture; castigate, chastise, correct, lash, flay; to fulminate against, fall foul of.

To cry out against, cry down, run down, clamour, hiss, hoot; to accuse (938), to find guilty, ostracize, blacklist, blackball.

To scandalize, shock, revolt, incur blame, excite disapprobation.

(Phrases) To set one's face against; to shake the head at; to take a poor or dim view of; to view with dark or jaundiced eyes; to pick holes in; to give a thing the bird; to damn with faint praise; to pluck a crow with; to have a fling at; to read a lecture; to put on the carpet (or mat); to take to task; to bring to book; to haul over the coals; to tear one off a strip; to shoot down in flames; to pull to pieces; to cut up; to cast in one's teeth; to abuse like a pickpocket; to speak or look daggers; to rail in good set terms; to give it one hot; to throw mud; to give a person the rough side of one's tongue.

To forfeit the good opinion of; to catch it; to be under a cloud; to carry the can; to stand corrected.

(Adjectives) Disapproving, disparaging, etc., condemnatory, damnatory, denunciatory, reproachful, abusive, objurgatory, clamorous, vituperative, dyslogistic.

Censorious, critical, carping, satirical, sarcastic, sardonic, cynical, dry, hypercritical, captious; sharp, cutting, mordant, biting, withering, trenchant, caustic, severe, scathing; squeamish, fastidious, strait-laced (868).

Disapproved, chid, unapproved, blown upon, unblest, unlamented, unbewailed.

Blameworthy, uncommendable, exceptionable (649, 945).

(Phrases) Hard upon one; weighed in the balance and found wanting; not to be thought of.

(Interjections) Bad show! shame!

————

933 Flattery *(Substantives)*, adulation, sycophancy, blandishment, cajolery, fawning, wheedling, coaxing,

934 Detraction *(Substantives)*, obloquy, scurrility, scandal, vilification, smear, defamation, aspersion,

flunkeyism, toad-eating, toadyism, tuft-hunting, back-scratching, blandiloquence, schmalz.

Incense, honeyed words, flummery, soft sawder, soft soap, butter, applesauce, blarney, malarkey; mouthhonour, lip-service.

(Verbs) To flatter, wheedle, cajole, fawn upon, coax (615), humour, gloze, butter, toady, sugar, bespatter, beslaver, earwig, jolly, flannel, truckle to, pander to, court, pay court to.

(Phrases) To curry favour with; to lay it on thick; to lay it on with a trowel; to ingratiate oneself with; to fool to the top of one's bent.

(Adjectives) Flattering, adulatory, mealy-mouthed, smooth, honeyed, candied, soapy, oily, unctuous, fairspoken, plausible, servile, sycophantic, fulsome; courtier-like.

935 Flatterer *(Substantives)*, adulator, eulogist, encomiast, whitewasher, toady, sycophant, toad-eater, *prôneur*, touter, booster, *claqueur*, spaniel, back-scratcher, flunkey, lickspittle, pick-thank, earwig, tuft-hunter, hanger-on, courtier, parasite, doer of dirty work, *âme damnée, Graeculus esuriens*.

937 Vindication *(Substantives)*, justification, exoneration, exculpation, acquittal, whitewashing.

Extenuation, palliation, mitigation, softening; extenuating circumstances.

Plea, excuse, apology, defence, gloss, varnish, salvo (617).

Vindicator, apologist, justifier, defender.

(Verbs) To vindicate, justify, warrant, exculpate, acquit, clear, set right, exonerate, disculpate, whitewash.

To extenuate, palliate, excuse, soften, apologize, varnish, slur, gloze, gloss over, bolster up.

To plead, advocate, defend, stand up for, stick up for, speak for, make good, bear out, say in defence, contend for.

traducement, slander, calumny, backbiting, criticism, slating, personality, evil-speaking, disparagement, depreciation (932).

Libel, lampoon, skit, squib, sarcasm.

(Verbs) To detract, criticize, asperse, depreciate, derogate, disparage, cheapen, blow upon, bespatter, blacken, denigrate, defame, brand, malign, decry, vilify, vilipend, backbite, libel, slate, lampoon, traduce, slander, calumniate, run down, write down.

(Phrases) To speak ill of one behind one's back; to damn with faint praise; to sell oneself short.

(Adjectives) Detracting, disparaging, libellous, scurrilous, abusive, cynical (932), foul-tongued, foulmouthed, slanderous, defamatory, calumnious, calumniatory.

936 Detractor *(Substantives)*, disapprover, critic, censor, caviller, carper, knocker, *frondeur*, defamer, backbiter, slanderer, traducer, libeller, calumniator, lampooner, satirist, candid friend, Thersites.

938 Accusation *(Substantives)*, charge, imputation, inculpation, exprobation, delation, crimination, recrimination, invective, jeremiad (932).

Denunciation, denouncement, challenge, indictment, libel, delation, citation, arraignment, impeachment, appeachment, bill of indictment, true bill, condemnation (971), scandal (934), *scandalum magnatum*.

Accuser, prosecutor, plaintiff, pursuer, informer, appellant, complainant.

Accused, defendant, prisoner, panel, respondent.

(Phrases) The gravamen of a charge; *argumentum ad hominem*.

(Verbs) To accuse, charge, tax, impute, twit, taunt with, slur, reproach, brand with, stigmatize, criminate,

(Phrases) To put in a good word for; to plead the cause of; to put a good face upon; to keep in countenance; to make allowance for.

(Adjectives) Vindicatory, vindicative, palliative, exculpatory; vindicating, etc.

Excusable, defensible, pardonable, venial, specious, plausible, justifiable, warrantable.

(Phrases) '*Honi soit qui mal y pense*'; *qui s'excuse s'accuse*.

---

incriminate, inculpate (932), implicate, saddle with.

To inform against; to indict, denounce, arraign, impeach, challenge, show up, pull up, cite, prosecute, summon.

(Phrases) To lay to one's door; to lay to one's charge; bring home to; to call to account; to bring to book; to take to task; to trump up a charge; to brand with reproach.

(Adjectives) Accusing, etc., accusatory, accusative, imputative, denunciatory, criminative, criminatory, incriminatory, accusable, imputable.

Indefensible, inexcusable, unpardonable, unjustifiable (945).

3°. Moral Conditions

939 Probity *(Substantives)*, integrity, uprightness, honesty, virtue (944), rectitude, faith, good faith, bona fides, fairness, honour, fair play, justice, principle, constancy, fidelity, incorruptibility.

Trustworthiness, trustiness, reliability, dependableness, grace, uncorruptedness, impartiality, equity, candour, veracity (545), straightforwardness, truth, equitableness, singleness of heart.

Conscientiousness, punctiliousness, nicety, scrupulosity, delicacy, sense of decency, strictness, punctuality.

Dignity, respectability, reputableness (873).

A man of honour, a gentleman, a man of his word, a sportsman, white man, trump, brick, *preux chevalier*.

(Phrases) The court of honour; a fair field and no favour; 'a verray parfit gentil knight.'

(Verbs) To be honourable, etc.; to keep one's word, to give and take, to deal honourably, squarely, impartially, fairly.

(Phrases) To hit straight from the shoulder; to play the game.

(Adjectives) Upright, honest, virtuous (944), honourable, fair, right, just, equitable, impartial, evenhanded, square, constant, faithful, loyal, staunch, straight.

940 Improbity *(Substantives)*, wickedness (945), bad faith, unfairness, infidelity, faithlessness, want of faith, dishonesty, disloyalty, falseness, falsity, one-sidedness, disingenuousness, shabbiness, littleness, meanness, caddishness, baseness, villainy, roguery, rascality, vileness, abjectness, turpitude, unreliability, untrustworthiness, insidiousness, knavery, knavishness, fraud (545), falsehood (544), shenanigans.

Disgrace, ignominy, infamy, tarnish, blot, stain, spot, slur, pollution, derogation, degradation (874).

Perfidy, perfidiousness, treason, high treason, perjury, apostasy (607), backsliding, breach of faith, defection, disloyalty, disaffection, foul play, sharp practice, graft, double-dealing, betrayal, treacherousness, treachery.

(Phrases) The kiss of Judas; divided allegiance; Punic faith.

(Verbs) To be of bad faith, dishonest, etc.; to play false, break one's word or faith, betray, forswear, shuffle (545).

To disgrace oneself, derogate, stoop, demean oneself, lose caste, dishonour oneself, sneak, crawl, grovel.

(Phrases) To seal one's infamy; to sell oneself; to go over to the enemy.

Trustworthy, trusty, reliable, dependable, tried, incorruptible, straightforward, ingenuous (703), frank, open-hearted, candid.

Conscientious, tender-conscienced, high-principled, high-minded, high-toned, scrupulous, strict, nice, punctilious, correct, punctual, inviolable, inviolate, unviolated, unbroken, unbetrayed.

Chivalrous, gentlemanlike, respectable, unbought, unbribed, unstained, stainless, untarnished, unsullied, untainted, unperjured, innocent (946).

(Phrases) Jealous of honour; as good as one's word; true to one's colours; *sans peur et sans reproche; integer vitae scelerisque purus.*

(Adverbs) Honourably, etc., bona fide; on the square; on the up and up.

(Adjectives) Dishonest, unfair, one-sided, fraudulent (545), bent, knavish, wicked (945), false, faithless, unfaithful, foul, disingenuous, trothless, trustless, untrustworthy, unreliable, slippery, double-faced, double-tongued, crooked, tortuous, unscrupulous, insidious, treacherous, perfidious, false-hearted, perjured, rascally.

Base, vile, grovelling, dirty, scurvy, scabby, low, low-down, abject, shabby, caddish, mean, paltry, pitiful, inglorious, scrubby, beggarly, putid, unworthy, disgraceful, dishonourable, derogatory, low-thoughted, disreputable, unhandsome, unbecoming (925), unbefitting, ungentlemanly, unmanly, unwomanly, undignified, base-minded, recreant, low-minded, blackguard, pettifogging, underhand, underhanded, unsportsmanlike.

(Phrases) Lost to shame; dead to honour.

(Adverbs) Dishonestly, etc., *mala fide,* on the crook.

941 Knave *(Substantives),* bad man (949), rogue, rascal, scoundrel, villain, spiv, sharper, shyster, blackleg, scab, trimmer, time-server, timist, turncoat, badmash, Vicar of Bray, Judas (607).

Apostate, renegade, pervert, black sheep, traitor, arch-traitor, quisling, fifth columnist, deviationist, betrayer, recreant, miscreant, cullion, outcast, mean wretch, slubberdegullion, snake in the grass, wolf in sheep's clothing.

942 Unselfishness *(Substantives),* selflessness, disinterestedness, generosity, highmindedness, nobleness, elevation, liberality, greatness, loftiness, exaltation, magnanimity, chivalry, chivalrous spirit, heroism, sublimity, altruism, self-forgetfulness, unworldliness.

Self-denial, self-abnegation, self-sacrifice, self-restraint, self-control, devotion, stoicism.

(Phrases) To put oneself in the background, in the place of others; to do as one would be done by.

(Adjectives) Unselfish, selfless, self-forgetful, handsome, generous, liberal, noble, princely, great, high, high-minded, elevated, lofty, exalted, spirited, stoical, self-denying, self-sacrificing, self-devoted, magnani-

943 Selfishness *(Substantives),* egotism, egoism, self-regard, self-love, self-indulgence, worldliness, worldly-mindedness, earthly-mindedness, self-interest, opportunism.

Illiberality, meanness, baseness.

A time-server, tuft-hunter, fortune-hunter, gold-digger, jobber, worldling, self-seeker, opportunist, hog, road-hog.

(Phrase) A dog in the manger.

(Verbs) To be selfish, etc., to indulge oneself, coddle oneself.

(Phrases) To look after one's own interest; to take care of number one; to have an eye for the main chance.

(Adjectives) Selfish, egotistical, egoistical, self-indulgent, apolaustic, self-regarding, self-centred, illiberal, self-seeking, mercenary, venal, mean, ungenerous, interested.

mous, chivalrous, heroic, sublime, unworldly.

Unbought, unbribed, pure, uncorrupted, incorruptible.

(Adverb) En prince.

Worldly, earthly, mundane, timeserving, worldly-minded.

(Phrases) To serve one's private ends; from interested motives; charity begins at home; I'm all right, Jack.

944 Virtue *(Substantives)*, virtuousness, goodness, righteousness, morals, morality (926), rectitude, correctness, dutifulness, conscientiousness, integrity, probity (939), uprightness, nobleness, nobility; innocence (946).

Merit, worth, worthiness, desert, excellence, credit, self-control, self-conquest, self-government, self-respect.

Well-doing, good actions, good behaviour, a well-spent life.

(Verbs) To be virtuous, etc.; to act well; to do, fulfil, perform, or discharge one's duty, to acquit oneself well, to practise virtue; to command or master one's passions (926).

(Phrases) To have one's heart in the right place; to keep in the right path; to fight the good fight; to set an example; to be on one's good behaviour.

(Adjectives) Virtuous, good, innocent (946), meritorious, deserving, worthy, correct, dutiful, duteous (926), moral, ethical, righteous, right-minded (939), laudable, well-intentioned, creditable, commendable, praiseworthy, excellent, admirable, sterling, pure, noble, well-conducted, well-behaved.

Exemplary, matchless, peerless, saintly, saint-like, heaven-born, angelic, seraphic, godlike.

(Phrase) Mens sibi conscia recti.

(Adverb) Virtuously, etc.

------

945 Vice *(Substantives)*, evildoing, wrongdoing, wickedness, sin, iniquity, unrighteousness, demerit, unworthiness, worthlessness, badness.

Immorality, impropriety, indecorum, laxity, looseness of morals, want of principle, obliquity, backsliding, recidivism, gracelessness, infamy, demoralization, pravity, depravity, depravation, obduracy, hardness of heart, brutality (907), corruption, pollution, dissoluteness, debauchery, grossness, baseness, knavery, roguery, rascality, villainy (940), profligacy, abandonment, flagrancy, atrocity, devilry (or deviltry), criminality, guilt (947).

Infirmity, weakness, feebleness, frailty, imperfection, error, weak side or point, blind side, foible, failing, failure, defect, deficiency, indiscretion, peccability.

(Phrases) The cloven hoof; the old Adam; the lowest dregs of vice; a sink of iniquity; the primrose path.

(Verbs) To be vicious, etc.; to sin, commit sin, do amiss, misdo, err, transgress, go astray, misdemean or misconduct oneself, misbehave; to fall, lapse, slip, trip, offend, trespass.

To render vicious, etc., to demoralize, corrupt, seduce, debauch, debase, vitiate.

(Phrases) To deviate from the line of duty or from the paths of virtue, rectitude, etc.; to blot one's copybook; to hug a sin or fault; to sow one's wild oats.

(Adjectives) Vicious, bad, sinful, wicked, evil, evil-minded, immoral, iniquitous, unprincipled, demoralized, unconscionable, worthless, unworthy, good for nothing, graceless, heartless, virtueless, undutiful, unrighteous, unmoral, amoral, guilty (947).

Wrong, culpable, naughty, incorrect, indictable, criminal, dissolute, debauched, disorderly, raffish, corrupt, profligate, depraved, degenerate, abandoned, graceless, shameless, recreant, villainous, sunk, lost, obdurate, reprobate, incorrigible, irreclaimable, ill-conditioned.

Weak, frail, lax, infirm, spineless, invertebrate, imperfect, indiscreet, erring, transgressing, sinning, etc., peccable, peccant.

Blamable, reprehensible, blameworthy, uncommendable, discreditable, disreputable, shady, exceptionable.

Indecorous, unseemly, improper, sinister, base, ignoble, scurvy, foul, gross, vile, black, felonious, nefarious, scandalous, infamous, villainous, heinous, grave, flagrant, flagitious, atrocious, satanic, satanical, diabolic, diabolical, hellish, infernal, stygian, fiendlike, fiendish, devilish, miscreatèd, misbegotten, hell-born, demoniacal.

Unpardonable, unforgivable, indefensible, inexcusable, irremissible, inexpiable.

(Phrases) Past praying for; of the deepest dye; not having a word to say for oneself; weighed in the balance and found wanting; *in flagrante delicto.*

(Adverbs) Wrongly, etc.; without excuse, too bad.

---

946 Innocence *(Substantives),* guiltlessness, harmlessness, innocuousness, incorruption, impeccability, inerrability, blamelessness, sinlessness.

A newborn babe, lamb, dove.

(Phrases) Clean hands; a clear conscience.

(Verbs) To be innocent, etc.

(Adjectives) Innocent, guiltless, not guilty, faultless, sinless, clear, spotless, stainless, immaculate, unspotted, innocuous, unblemished, untarnished, unsullied, undefiled.

Inculpable, unblamed, blameless, unblamable, clean-handed, irreproachable, unreproached, unimpeachable, unimpeached, unexceptionable, inerrable, unerring.

Harmless, inoffensive, unoffending, dovelike, lamblike, pure, uncorrupted, undefiled, undepraved, undebauched, chaste, unhardened, unsophisticated, unreproved.

(Phrases) Innocent as an unborn babe; in the clear; above suspicion; more sinned against than sinning.

(Adverbs) Innocently, etc.

947 Guilt *(Substantives),* sin, guiltiness, culpability, criminality, criminousness, sinfulness.

Misconduct, misbehaviour, misdoing, malpractice, malefaction, malfeasance, misprision, dereliction, *corpus delicti.*

Indiscretion, peccadillo, lapse, slip, trip, *faux pas,* fault, error, flaw, blot, omission, failure.

Misdeed, offence, trespass, transgression, misdemeanour, delinquency, felony, sin, crime, enormity, atrocity.

Science of crime, criminology.

(Phrases) Besetting sin; deviation from rectitude; a deed without a name.

---

948 Good man *(Substantives),* trump, brick, worthy, example, pattern, mirror, model, paragon, phoenix (650), superman, hero, demigod, seraph, angel, saint (987).

A good fellow, good sort, sportsman, white man.

(Phrases) One of the best; one in a million; the salt of the earth.

---

949 Bad man *(Substantives),* wrongdoer, evildoer, culprit, delinquent, criminal, recidivist, malefactor, outlaw, felon, convict, lag, outcast, sinner (988).

Knave, rogue, rascal, scoundrel, spiv, scamp, scapegrace, black sheep, scallywag, spalpeen, varlet, *vaurien,* blighter, rotter, good-for-nothing, twerp, heel, jerk, creep, goon, son of a gun, dastard, blackguard, sweep, loose fish, bad egg, bad lot, hard case, lost soul, vagabond, bum, *mauvais sujet*, cur, sad dog, rip, rascallion, rapscallion, slubberdegullion, cullion, roisterer.

Mohock, rowdy, hooligan, larrikin, teddy boy, apache, thug, reprobate, roué, recreant, jail-bird, crook, tough, rough, roughneck, gangster, gunman, hoodlum, yegg, villain, ruffian, miscreant, caitiff, wretch, *âme damnée*, castaway, monster, Jonathan Wilde, Jack Sheppard, Lazarillo de Tormes, Scapin (941).

Cur, dog, hound, skunk, swine, rat, viper, serpent, cockatrice, basilisk, reptile, urchin, tiger, imp, demon, devil, devil incarnate, Mephistopheles (978), hellhound, son of Belial, cut-throat, *particeps criminis*, incendiary.

Bad woman, hellcat, hellhag, bitch, witch, hag, harridan, trollop, jade, drab, hussy, minx, Jezebel.

Riff-raff, rabble, ragtag and bobtail, *canaille*.

(Phrases) A fiend in human shape; scum of the earth; poor white trash.

(Interjection) Sirrah!

---

950 Penitence *(Substantives)*, contrition, compunction, regret (833), repentance, remorse.

Self-reproach, self-reproof, self-accusation, self-condemnation.

Confession, acknowledgment, shrift, apology, recantation (607).

A penitent, prodigal, Magdalen.

(Phrases) The stool of repentance; the cutty-stool; sackcloth and ashes; qualms or prickings of conscience; a sadder and a wiser man.

(Verbs) To repent, regret, rue, repine, deplore, be sorry for.

To confess (529), acknowledge, apologize, shrive oneself, humble oneself, reclaim, turn from sin.

(Phrases) To have a weight on one's mind; to plead guilty; to sing small; to cry *peccavi*; to eat humble pie; to turn over a new leaf; to stand in a white sheet.

(Adjectives) Penitent, repentant, contrite, repenting, remorseful, regretful, sorry, compunctious, self-reproachful, self-accusing, self-convicted, conscience-stricken, conscience-smitten.

Not hardened, unhardened, reclaimed.

(Adverb) *Meâ culpâ*.

951 Impenitence *(Substantives)* obduracy, recusance, irrepentance, hardness of heart, a seared conscience, induration.

(Verbs) To be impenitent, etc.; to steel or harden the heart.

(Phrases) To make no sign; to die game.

(Adjectives) Impenitent, uncontrite, obdurate, hard, callous, unfeeling, hardened, seared, recusant, relentless, unrepentant, graceless, shiftless, lost, incorrigible, irreclaimable, irredeemable, unatoned, unreclaimed, unreformed, unrepented.

---

952 Atonement *(Substantives)*, reparation, compromise, composition, compensation (30), quittance, quits; propitiation, expiation, redemption, conciliation.

Amends, *amende honorable*, apology, satisfaction, peace-offering, olive branch, sin-offering, scapegoat, sacrifice, burnt-offering.

Penance, fasting, maceration, flagellation, sackcloth and ashes, white sheet, lustration, purgation, purgatory.

(Verbs) To atone, expiate, propitiate, make amends, redeem, make good, repair, ransom, absolve, do penance, apologize, purge, shrive, give satisfaction.

(Phrases) To purge one's offence; to pay the forfeit or penalty.

(Adjectives) Propitiatory, piacular, expiatory, expiational.

4°. *Moral Practice*

953 Temperance *(Substantives)*, moderation, forbearance, abnegation, self-denial, self-conquest, self-control, self-command, self-discipline, sobriety, frugality, vegetarianism.

Abstinence, abstemiousness, teetotalism, prohibition, asceticism (955), gymnosophy, system of Pythagoras.

An abstainer, ascetic, gymnosophist, vegetarian, teetotaller, Pythagorean.

(Phrases) The simple life; the blue ribbon.

(Verbs) To be temperate, etc.; to abstain, forbear, refrain, deny oneself, spare.

(Phrases) To sign the pledge; to go on the water wagon.

(Adjectives) Temperate, moderate, sober, frugal, sparing, abstemious, abstinent, Pythagorean, vegetarian, teetotal, dry.

954 Intemperance *(Substantives)*, excess, immoderation, unrestraint; epicurism, epicureanism, hedonism, sensuality, luxury, luxuriousness, animalism, carnality, effeminacy; the lap of pleasure or luxury; indulgence, self-indulgence, voluptuousness; drunkenness (959).

Dissipation, licentiousness, debauchery, dissoluteness, crapulence, brutishness.

Revels, revelry, carousal, orgy, spree, jag, toot, drinking bout, debauch, jollification, saturnalia.

A sensualist, epicure, epicurean, voluptuary, rake, rip, *roué*, sybarite, drug addict, dope fiend, hophead.

(Phrases) The Circean cup; a fast life; wine, women, and song.

(Verbs) To be intemperate, sensual, etc.

To indulge, exceed, revel, dissipate; give a loose to indulgence, live hard.

To debauch, pander to, sensualize, animalize, brutalize.

(Phrases) To wallow in voluptuousness, luxury, etc.; to plunge into dissipation; to paint the town red; to live on the fat of the land; to sow one's wild oats.

(Adjectives) Intemperate, sensual, pampered, self-indulgent, fleshly, inabstinent, licentious, wild, dissolute, dissipated, fast, rakish, debauched, brutish, crapulous, hedonistic, epicurean, sybaritical, Sardanapalian, voluptuous, apolaustic, orgiastic, swinish, piggish, hoggish; indulged, pampered.

955 Asceticism *(Substantives)*, austerity, puritanism, mortification, maceration, sackcloth and ashes, flagellation, martyrdom, yoga.

An ascetic, anchoret, yogi, martyr; a recluse, hermit (893); puritan, Cynic.

(Adjectives) Ascetic, ascetical, austere, puritanical.

956 Fasting *(Substantives)*, fast, spare diet, meagre diet, Lent, Quadragesima, a lenten entertainment, famishment, starvation, banian day, Ramadan.

(Phrases) A Barmecide feast; a hunger strike; short commons.

(Verbs) To fast, starve, clem, famish.

(Phrases) To dine with Duke Humphrey; to perish with hunger.

957 Gluttony *(Substantives)*, epicurism, greediness, good cheer, high living, edacity, voracity, gulosity, crapulence, hoggishness, piggishness.

Gastronomy; feast, banquet, good cheer, blow-out.

A glutton, epicure, *bon vivant*, cormorant, gourmand, gourmet, belly-god, pig, hog, Apicius, gastronome, gastronomer, gastronomist.

(Adjectives) Fasting, etc., unfed, famished, starved; lenten, Quadragesimal.

(Verbs) To gormandize, gorge, cram, stuff, guzzle, bolt, devour, gobble up, pamper.

(Phrases) To eat out of house and home; to have the stomach of an ostrich; to play a good knife and fork.

(Adjectives) Gluttonous, greedy, gormandizing, edacious, voracious, crapulent, swinish, piggish, hoggish, pampered, overfed; gastronomical.

---

958 Sobriety *(Substantives)*, teetotalism, total abstinence, temperance (953).

Compulsory sobriety, prohibition.

A water-drinker, teetaller, abstainer, total abstainer, blue-ribbonite, Rechabite, Band of Hope; prohibitionist.

(Verbs) To abstain, to take the pledge.

(Adjectives) Sober, abstemious, teetotal.

(Phrases) Sober as a judge; on the water wagon.

---

959 Drunkenness *(Substantives)*, insobriety, ebriety, inebriety, inebriation, intoxication, ebriosity, bibacity, drinking, toping, tippling, sottishness, tipsiness, bacchanals, compotation, intemperance (954); dipsomania, alcoholism, delirium tremens, D.T.

A drunkard, sot, toper, tippler, hard drinker, winebag, winebibber, dramdrinker, soak, soaker, sponge, tun, tosspot, pub-crawler, reveller, carouser, Bacchanal, Bacchanalian, Bacchant, a devotee to Bacchus; a dipsomaniac.

Drink, hard drinks, intoxicant, alcohol, liquor, spirits, booze, blue ruin, grog, cocktail, highball, dram, peg, stirrup-cup, doch-an-doris.

(Phrases) The flowing bowl; one for the road.

(Verbs) To drink, tipple, tope, booze; to guzzle, swill, soak, swig, get or be drunk, etc.; to take to drinking, drink hard, drink deep.

To inebriate, intoxicate, fuddle.

(Phrases) To liquor up; to wet one's whistle; to crack a bottle; to have a bucket; to look on the wine when it is red; to take a drop too much; to drink like a fish; to splice the main-brace; to crook or lift the elbow.

(Adjectives) Drunk, drunken, tipsy, intoxicated, in liquor, inebriated, fuddled, mellow, boozy, high, fou, boiled, tiddly, stinko, blotto, lit up, groggy, top-heavy, pot-valiant, glorious, overcome, overtaken, elevated, whiffled, sozzled, screwed, corned, raddled, sewed up, lushy, squiffy, muddled, oiled, canned, muzzy, maudlin, dead-drunk, disguised, tight, beery.

Bibacious, bibulous, sottish, Bacchanal, Bacchanalian.

(Phrases) In one's cups; *inter pocula*; the worse for liquor; half-seas-over; three sheets in the wind; under the table; drunk as a piper, as a fiddle, as a lord, as an owl, as David's sow; stewed to the eyebrows; pickled to the gills; one over the eight.

(Interjections) Cheers! here's to you! down the hatch! mud in your eye! skin off your nose! *prosit! slainte! skoal!*

---

960 Purity *(Substantives)*, modesty, decency, decorum, delicacy, continence, chastity, honesty, pudency, virtue, virginity.

961 Impurity *(Substantives)*, immodesty, grossness, coarseness, indelicacy, impropriety, impudicity, indecency, obscenity, obsceneness,

A virgin, maiden, maid, vestal; Joseph, Hippolytus, Lucrece.

(Phrase) The white flower of a blameless life.

(Adjectives) Pure, immaculate, undefiled, modest, delicate, decent, decorous.

Chaste, continent, honest, virtuous; Platonic.

———

ribaldry, smut, smuttiness, bawdiness, bawdry, *double entendre*, equivoque, pornography.

Concupiscence, lust, carnality, flesh, salacity, lewdness, prurience, lechery, lasciviousness, voluptuousness, lubricity.

Incontinence, intrigue, gallantry, debauchery, libertinism, libertinage, fornication, liaison, wenching, whoring, whoredom, concubinage, hetaerism.

Seduction, defloration, violation, rape, adultery, defilement, *crim. con.*, incest, harlotry, stupration, procuration, white slave traffic.

A seraglio, harem, brothel, bagnio, stew, bawdy-house, disorderly house, house of ill fame, red lamp district, Yoshiwara.

(Phrases) The morals of the farmyard; the oldest profession.

(Verbs) To intrigue, debauch, defile, seduce, abuse, violate, force, rape, ravish, deflower, ruin, prostitute, procure.

(Adjectives) Impure, immodest, indecorous, indelicate, unclean, unmentionable, unseemly, improper, suggestive, indecent, loose, coarse, gross, broad, equivocal, risky, *risqué*, high-seasoned, nasty, smutty, scabrous, ribald, obscene, bawdy, lewd, pornographic, Rabelaisian, Aristophanic.

Concupiscent, prurient, lickerish, rampant, carnal, fleshy, sensual, lustful, lascivious, lecherous, libidinous, goatish, erotic, ruttish, salacious.

Unchaste, light, wanton, debauched, dissolute, carnal-minded, licentious, frail, riggish, incontinent, meretricious, rakish, gallant, dissipated, adulterous, incestuous, bestial.

(Phrases) On the streets; of easy virtue; no better than she should be.

Near the knuckle; not for ears polite; four-letter words.

962 A Libertine *(Substantives)*, voluptuary, man of pleasure, sensualist (954), rip, rake, *roué*, debauchee, loose fish, intriguant, gallant, seducer, fornicator, lecher, satyr, whoremonger, *paillard*, adulterer, a gay deceiver, Lothario, Don Juan, Bluebeard.

A prostitute, courtesan, tart, call-girl, strumpet, harlot, whore, punk, *fille de joie*, *cocotte*, *lorette*, woman of the town, streetwalker, pick-up, piece, the frail sisterhood, the *demi-monde*, soiled dove, demirep, wench, trollop, trull, baggage, hussy, drab, jade, quean, slut, harridan, an unfortunate, Jezebel, Messalina, Delilah, Thais, Aspasia, Phryne, Lais.

Concubine, odalisque, mistress, doxy, kept woman, *petite amie*, hetaera.

Pimp, pander, ponce, *souteneur*, bawd, procuress.

5°. *Institutions*

963 Legality *(Substantives)*, legitimateness, legitimacy, justice (922).

Law, legislature, code, constitution, pandect, enactment, edict, statute, charter, rule, order, ordinance, injunction, institution, precept, regulation, by-law, decree, firman, bull, ukase, decretal.

964 Absence or violation of law.

Illegality *(Substantives)*, lawlessness, arbitrariness, antinomy, violence, brute force, despotism, outlawry.

Mob law, lynch law, club law, martial law.

Legal process, form, formula, formality, rite.

Science of law, jurisprudence, legislation, codification.

Equity, common law, *lex non scripta*, unwritten law, law of nations, international law, *jus gentium*, civil law, canon law, statute law, *lex mercatoria*, ecclesiastical law.

(Phrase) The arm of the law.

(Verbs) To legalize, enact, ordain, enjoin, prescribe, order, decree (741); to pass a law, issue an edict or decree; to legislate, codify.

(Adjectives) Legal, lawful, according to law, legitimate, constitutional, chartered, vested.

Legislative, statutable, statutory.

(Adverbs) Legally, etc.

(Phrases) In the eye of the law; *de jure*.

———

Camorra, Ku Klux Klan, Judge Lynch.

Informality, unlawfulness, illegitimacy, bastardy, the baton or bar sinister.

Smuggling, poaching, bootlegging; black market, grey market.

(Verbs) To smuggle, run, poach.

To invalidate, annul, illegalize, abrogate, void, nullify, quash.

(Phrases) To take the law into one's own hands; to set the law at defiance; to drive a coach and six through the law.

(Adjectives) Illegal, unlawful, illicit, illegitimate, injudicial, unofficial, lawless, unauthorized, unchartered, unconstitutional, informal, contraband, hot.

Arbitrary, extrajudicial, despotic, autocratic, irresponsible, unanswerable, unaccountable.

(Adverbs) Illegally, with a high hand.

965 Jurisdiction *(Substantives)*, judicature, soc (or soke), administration of justice.

Inquisition, inquest, coroner's inquest.

The executive, municipality, corporation, magistracy, police, police force, constabulary, posse, *gendarmerie*.

Lord lieutenant, sheriff, sheriff-substitute, deputy, officer, constable, policeman, state trooper, traffic warden, bailiff, tipstaff, bum-bailiff, catchpoll, beadle; *gendarme*, lictor, mace-bearer.

(Adjectives) Juridical, judicial, forensic, municipal, executive, administrative, inquisitorial, causidical.

(Phrases) Coram judice; ex cathedra.

966 Tribunal *(Substantives)*, court, guild, board, bench, judicatory, senate-house, court of law, court of justice, criminal court, police-court, Court of Chancery, of King's Bench; Probate, Divorce, Admiralty Court, court of appeal, justice-seat, judgment-seat, mercy-seat, Star Chamber, Judicial Committee of the Privy Council, U.S. Supreme Court, durbar.

City hall, town hall, theatre, bar, dock, forum, hustings, drum-head, woolsack, jury-box, witness-box.

Assize, sessions, quarter sessions, petty sessions, eyre, court-martial, wardmote.

967 Judge *(Substantives)*, justice, justiciar, justiciary, chancellor, magistrate, beak, recorder, common serjeant, stipendiary, coroner, arbiter, arbitrator, umpire, referee, jury, Justice of the Peace, J.P., Lord Chancellor, Lord Chief Justice, Master of the Rolls.

Mullah, ulema, mufti, cadi (or kadi), kavass.

Prosecutor, plaintiff, accuser, appellant, pursuer.

Defendant, panel, prisoner, the accused.

(Verbs) Judge, try, pass judgment, give verdict.

968 Lawyer *(Substantives)*, the bar, advocate, counsellor, counsel, queen's or king's counsel, Q.C., K.C., pleader, special pleader, conveyancer, bencher, proctor, civilian, barrister, barrister-at-law, jurist, jurisconsult, publicist, draughtsman, notary, notary public, scrivener, attorney, solicitor, legal adviser, writer to the signet, writer, marshal, pundit; pettifogger.

(Phrases) The gentlemen of the long robe; the learned in the law; a limb of the law.

(Verbs) To practise law, plead.

(Phrases) To be called to the bar; to take silk.

969 Lawsuit *(Substantives)*, suit, action, case, cause, trial, litigation.

Denunciation, citation, arraignment, prosecution, indictment, impeachment, apprehension, arrest, committal, imprisonment (751).

Pleadings, writ, summons, subpoena, plea, bill, affidavit, libel; answer, counterclaim, demurrer, rebutter, rejoinder, surrebutter, surrejoinder.

Verdict, sentence, judgment, finding, decree, arbitrament, adjudication, award, decision, precedent.

(Verbs) To denounce, cite, apprehend, sue, writ, arraign, summons, prosecute, indict, contest, impeach, attach, distrain; to commit.

To try, hear a cause, sit in judgment.

To pronounce, find, judge, adjudge, sentence, give judgment; bring in a verdict; to doom, arbitrate, adjudicate, award, report.

(Phrases) To go to law; to appeal to the law; to file a claim; to inform against; to lodge an information; to serve with a writ; to bring an action against; to bring to trial or the bar; to give in charge or custody; to throw into prison; to clap in jail.

(Adjectives) Litigious, litigant, litigatory.

(Adverbial phrase) Sub judice; pendente lite.

970 Acquittal *(Substantives)*, acquitment, absolution, exculpation, quietus, clearance, discharge, release, reprieve (918), respite, compurgation.

Exemption from punishment, impunity.

(Verbs) To acquit, absolve, whitewash, extenuate, exculpate, exonerate, clear, assoil, discharge, release, reprieve, respite.

(Adjectives) Acquitted, etc.

Uncondemned, unpunished, unchastised.

971 Condemnation *(Substantives)*, conviction, proscription, damnation, death-warrant.

Attainder, attainture, attaintment.

(Verbs) To condemn, convict, cast, find guilty, proscribe, ban, outlaw, attaint, damn, doom, sentence, confiscate, sequestrate, non-suit.

(Adjectives) Condemnatory, damnatory, condemned; self-convicted.

972 Punishment *(Substantives)*, punition, chastisement, castigation, correction, chastening, discipline, infliction.

Retribution, requital (973), penalty (974), reckoning, Nemesis.

Imprisonment (751), transportation, exile (297), cucking-stool, ducking-stool, treadmill, crank, hulks, galleys, penal servitude, preventive detention.

A blow, slap, spank, skelp, swish, hit, knock, rap, thump, bang, buffet, stripe, stroke, cuff, clout, kick, whack, thwack, box, punch, pummel.

Beating, lash, flagellation, flogging, etc., dressing, lacing, tanning, knock-out, fustigation, leathering, lathering, jacketing, strap-oil, gruelling, spiflication, bastinado, strappado, pillory (975), running the gauntlet, *coup de grâce, peine forte et dure.*

Execution, capital punishment, hanging, beheading, decollation, decapitation, electrocution, guillotine, garrotte, *auto da fé, noyade*, crucifixion, impalement, *hara-kiri*, martyrdom.

(Verbs) To punish, chastise, castigate, chasten, correct, inflict punishment, pay, do for, serve out, pay out, visit upon, give it to, strafe, spiflicate.

To strike, hit, smite, knock, slap, flap, rap, bang, thwack, whack, thump, kick, punch, pelt, beat, buffet, thrash, swinge, pummel, clapper-claw, drub, trounce, baste, belabour, lace, strap, comb, lash, lick, whip, flog, scourge, knout, swish, spank, skelp, birch, tan, larrup, lay into, knock out, wallop, leather, flagellate, horsewhip, bastinado, lapidate, stone.

To execute, hang, behead, decapitate, decollate, electrocute, guillotine, garrotte, shoot, gibbet; to hang, draw, and quarter; break on the wheel; crucify, impale, torture, flay, keelhaul; lynch.

To banish, exile, transport, deport, expel, drum out, disbar, disbench, unfrock.

To be hanged, etc., to be spread-eagled.

(Phrases) To make an example of; to serve one out; to give it one; to dust one's jacket; to tweak or pull the nose; to box the ears; to beat to a jelly; to tar and feather; to give a black eye; to lay it on.

To come to the gallows; to swing for it; to go to the chair; to die in one's shoes.

(Adjectives) Punishing, etc., punitory, punitive, inflictive, penal, disciplinary, castigatory, borstal.

(Interjection) A la lanterne!

---

973 Reward *(Substantives)*, recompense, remuneration, meed, guerdon, premium, indemnity, indemnification, compensation, reparation, requital, retribution, quittance, hush-money, acknowledgment, amends, solatium, sop, atonement, redress, consideration, return, tribute, honorarium, perquisite, tip, vail; salvage.

Prize, purse, crown, laurel, bays, cross, medal, ribbon, decoration (877).

(Verbs) To reward, recompense, repay, requite, recoup, remunerate, compensate, make amends, indemnify, atone, satisfy, acknowledge, acquit oneself.

(Phrase) To get for one's pains.

(Adjectives) Remunerative, munerary, compensatory, retributive, reparatory.

974 Penalty *(Substantives)*, punishment (972), pain, penance.

Fine, mulct, amercement, forfeit, forfeiture, escheat, damages, deodand, sequestration, confiscation.

(Phrases) Pains and penalties; the devil to pay.

(Verbs) To fine, mulct, amerce, sconce, confiscate, sequester, sequestrate, escheat, estreat.

975 Instrument of punishment.

Scourge *(Substantives)*, rod, cane, stick, rattan, switch, ferule, birch, cudgel.

Whip, lash, strap, thong, knout, cowhide, cat, cat-o'-nine-tails, sjambok, rope's end.

Pillory, stocks, cangue, whipping-post, ducking-stool, triangle, wooden horse, boot, thumbscrew, rack, wheel, treadmill.

Stake, tree, block, scaffold, gallows, halter, bowstring, gibbet, axe, maiden, guillotine, garrotte, electric chair, hot squat, lethal chamber.

Executioner, hangman, electrocutioner, firing squad, headsman, Jack Ketch.

SECTION V—RELIGIOUS AFFECTIONS

1°. *Superhuman Beings and Objects*

976 Deity *(Substantives)*, Divinity, Godhead, Omnipotence, Omniscience, Providence.

Quality of being divine, divineness, divinity.

God, Lord, Jehovah, The Almighty; The Supreme Being; The First Cause, *Ens Entium*; The Author of all things, The Infinite, The Eternal, The All-powerful, The All-wise, The All-merciful, The All-holy.

Attributes and perfections: infinite power, wisdom, goodness, justice, mercy, omnipotence, omniscience, omnipresence, unity, immutability, holiness, glory, majesty, sovereignty, infinity, eternity.

The Trinity, The Holy Trinity, The Trinity in Unity, The Triune God.

God the Father, The Maker, The Creator.

Functions: creation, preservation, divine government, theocracy, thearchy, providence; the ways, dispensations, visitations of Providence.

God the Son, Christ, Jesus, The Messiah, The Anointed, The Saviour, The Redeemer, The Mediator, The Intercessor, The Advocate, The Judge, The Son of Man, The Lamb of God, The Word, The Logos, Emmanuel, The King of Kings and Lord of Lords, The King of Glory, The Prince of Peace, The Good Shepherd, The Way of Truth and Life, The Bread of Life, The Light of the World, The Sun of Righteousness, the Incarnation, the Word made Flesh.

Functions: salvation, redemption, atonement, propitiation, mediation, intercession, judgment.

God the Holy Ghost, The Holy Spirit, Paraclete, The Comforter, The Spirit of Truth, The Dove.

Functions: inspiration, unction, regeneration, sanctification, consolation.

(Verbs) To create, uphold, preserve, govern.

To atone, redeem, save, propitiate, mediate.

To predestinate, elect, call, ordain, bless, justify, sanctify, glorify.

(Adjectives) Almighty, all-powerful, omnipotent, omnipresent, omniscient, all-wise, holy, hallowed, sacred, divine, heavenly, celestial.

Superhuman, ghostly, spiritual, supernatural, theocratic.

977 Beneficent spirits.

Angel *(Substantives)*, archangel.

The heavenly host; ministering spirits; the choir invisible.

Madonna, saint.

Seraphim, cherubim, thrones, principalities, powers, dominions.

(Adjectives) Angelic, angelical, seraphic, cherubic, celestial, heavenly, saintly.

978 Maleficent spirits.

Satan *(Substantives)*, the Devil, Lucifer, Beelzebub, Belial, Mephistopheles, Mephisto, Abaddon, Apollyon, the Prince of Devils.

His Satanic Majesty, the tempter, the evil one, the wicked one, the old Serpent, the Prince of darkness, the father of lies, the foul fiend, the archfiend, the common enemy, Old Harry, Old Nick, the Old Scratch, the Old Gentleman, Old Horny.

Diabolism, devilism, devilship; Satanism, the cloven hoof, the black mass.

Fallen angels, unclean spirits, devils, the powers of darkness, inhabitants of Pandemonium.

(Adjectives) Satanic, diabolic, devilish.

Gods of other Religions and Mythological Beings

979 Great spirit *(Substantives)*, deity, numen, god, goddess; Allah, Brahma, Vishnu, Siva, Krishna, Buddha, Mithra, Ormuzd, Isis, Osiris, Moloch, Baal, Asteroth.

Jupiter, Jove, Juno, Minerva, Apollo, Diana, Venus, Vulcan, Mars, Mercury, Neptune, Pluto; Zeus, Hera, Athena, Artemis, Aphrodite, Hephaestus, Ares, Hermes, Poseidon.

Odin or Woden, Frigga, Thor.

Good genius, demiurge, familiar; fairy, fay, sylph, peri, kelpie, nymph, nereid, dryad, hamadryad, naiad, merman, mermaid (341), undine; Oberon, Mab, Titania, Puck, Robin Goodfellow; the good folk, the little people.

(Adjectives) Fairy, faery, fairy-like, sylph-like, sylphine.

Mythical, mythological, fabulous, legendary.

980 Demon *(Substantives)*, evil genius, fiend, unclean spirit, caco-demon, incubus, succubus, succuba, flibbertigibbet; fury, harpy, siren, faun, satur, Eblis, Demogorgon.

Vampire, werewolf, ghoul, afreet (or afrite), ogre, ogress, gnome, djinn, imp, genie (or jinnee), lamia, bogy, bogle, nix, nixie, kobold, brownie, leprechaun, elf, pixy, troll, sprite, gremlin, spandule.

Supernatural appearance, ghost, spectre, apparition, shade, vision, goblin, hobgoblin, banshee, spook, wraith, *revenant, doppelgänger*, polter-geist.

(Phrase) The powers of darkness.

(Adjectives) Supernatural, ghostly, apparitional, elfin, elfish, unearthly, uncanny, eerie, weird, spectral, spook-ish, spooky, ghostlike, fiendish, fiend-like, impish, demoniacal, haunted.

981 Heaven *(Substantives)*, the kingdom of heaven; the kingdom of God, the heavenly kingdom; the throne of God, the presence of God.

Paradise, Eden, Zion, the Celestial City, the New Jerusalem, the abode of the blessed; celestial bliss or glory.

Mythological heaven, Olympus; mythological paradise, Elysium, the Elysian Fields, the garden of the Hesperides; Valhalla, Nirvana, happy hunting grounds.

Translation, apotheosis, deification, resurrection.

(Adjectives) Heavenly, celestial, supernal, unearthly, from on high, paradisaical, paradisical, paradisial, Elysian, beatific.

982 Hell *(Substantives)*, bottom-less pit, place of torment; the habita-tion of fallen angels, Pandemonium, Domdaniel.

Hell-fire, everlasting fire, the lake of fire and brimstone.

Purgatory, limbo, abyss.

Mythological hell, Tartarus, Hades, Pluto, Avernus, Styx, the Stygian creek, Acheron, Cocytus, Phlegethon, Lethe, Erebus, Tophet, Gehenna.

(Phrases) The fire that is never quenched; the worm that never dies.

The infernal or nether regions; the shades below; the realms of Pluto.

(Adjectives) Hellish, infernal, stygian, Tartarean, Plutonian.

2°. *Religious Doctrines*

983 Religious knowledge.

Theology (natural and revealed) *(Substantives)*, divinity, religion, monotheism, hagiology, hagiography, hierography, theosophy; comparative religion, compara-tive mythology.

Creed, belief, faith, persuasion, tenet, dogma, articles of faith, declaration, profession or confession of faith.

Theologian, divine, schoolman, the Fathers.

(Adjectives) Theological, religious, patristic, ecumenical, denominational, sectarian.

983ᴀ Christian Religion *(Substantives)*, true faith, Christianity, Christianism, Christendom, Catholicism, orthodoxy.

A Christian, a true believer.

The Church, the Catholic or Universal Church, the Church of Christ, the body of Christ, the Church Militant.

The members of Christ, the disciples or followers of Christ, the Christian community.

Protestant, Church of England, Anglican, Church of Scotland; Church of Rome, Roman Catholic; Greek Church, Orthodox Church.

(Adjectives) Christian, Catholic, orthodox, sound, faithful, true, scriptural, canonical, schismless.

984 Other religions *(Substantives)*, paganism, heathenism, ethnicism, polytheism, ditheism, tritheism, pantheism, hylotheism.

Judaism, Gentilism, Mohammedanism (or Mahometanism), Islam, Buddhism, Hinduism, Taoism, Confucianism, Shintoism, Sufism.

A pagan, heathen, paynim, infidel, unbeliever, pantheist, etc.

A Jew, Mohammedan (or Mahometan), Mussulman, Moslem, Brahmin (or Brahman), Parsee, Sufi, Magus, Gymnosophist, Fire-worshipper, Buddhist, Rosicrucian.

(Adjectives) Pagan, heathen, ethnic, gentile, pantheistic, etc.

Judaical, Mohammedan, Brahminical, Buddhistic.

984ᴀ Heresy *(Substantives)*, heterodoxy, false doctrine, schism, schismaticalness, latitudinarianism, recusancy, apostasy, backsliding, quietism, adiaphorism.

Bigotry, fanaticism, iconoclasm, bibliolatry, fundamentalism, puritanism, sabbatarianism.

Dissent, sectarianism, non-conformity, secularism, syncretism.

A heretic, deist, unitarian.

(Adjectives) Heretical, heterodox, unorthodox, unscriptural, uncanonical, schismatic, sectarian, nonconformist, recusant, latitudinarian.

Credulous, bigoted, fanatical, idolatrous, superstitious, visionary.

985 Christian revelation *(Substantives)*, Word, Word of God, Scripture, the Scriptures, Holy Writ, the Bible, the Holy Book.

Old Testament: Septuagint, Vulgate, Pentateuch, Hagiographa, the Law, the Prophets, the Apocrypha.

New Testament: the Gospel, the Evangelists, the Epistles, the Apocalypse, Revelation.

Talmud, Mishna, Masorah, Torah.

A prophet, seer, evangelist, apostle, disciple, saint, the Fathers.

(Adjectives) Scriptural, biblical, sacred, prophetic, evangelical, apostolic, apostolical, inspired, theopneustic, apocalyptic.

986 Other sacred books *(Substantives)*, the Koran (or Alcoran), Vedas, Upanishads, Puranas, Zend-Avesta.

Religious founders: Buddha (or Gautama), Zoroaster (or Zarathustra), Confucius, Lao-Tsze, Mohammed (or Mahomet).

Idols: Golden calf, Baal, Moloch, Dagon.

(Adjectives) Anti-scriptural, anti-christian, profane, idolatrous, pagan, heathen, heathenish.

3°. *Religious Sentiments*

987 Piety *(Substantives)*, religion, theism, faith, religiousness, godliness, reverence, humility, veneration, devoutness, devotion, spirituality, grace, unction, edification, unworldliness, other-worldliness; holiness, sanctity, sanctitude, sacredness, consecration; virtue (944).

Theopathy, beatification, adoption, regeneration, conversion, justification, salvation, inspiration.

A believer, convert, theist, Christian, saint, one of the elect, a devotee.

The good, righteous, faithful, godly, elect, just.

(Phrases) The odour of sanctity; the beauty of holiness; spiritual existence.

The children of God, of light.

(Verbs) To be pious, etc., to believe, have faith; to convert, edify, sanctify, hallow, beatify, regenerate, inspire; to consecrate, enshrine.

(Phrases) To work out one's salvation; to stand up for Jesus; to fight the good fight.

(Adjectives) Pious, religious, devout, reverent, reverential, godly, humble, heavenly-minded, pure, holy, spiritual, saintly, saint-like, unworldly, other-worldly.

Believing, faithful, Christian.

Sanctified, regenerated, born again, justified, adopted, elected, inspired, consecrated, converted, unearthly, sacred, solemn, not of the earth.

---

988 Impiety *(Substantives)*, irreverence, profaneness, profanity, blasphemy, desecration, sacrilege, sacrilegiousness, sin (945); scoffing, ribaldry, reviling.

Assumed piety, hyprocrisy, cant, pietism, lip-devotion, lip-service, lip-reverence, formalism, sanctimony, sanctimoniousness, pharisaism, precisianism, sabbatism, sabbatarianism, sacerdotalism, religiosity, religionism, *odium theologicum*.

Hardening, backsliding, declension, reprobation, perversion.

Sinner, outcast, castaway, lost sheep, reprobate.

A scoffer, hypocrite, pietist, pervert, religionist, precisian, formalist; son of darkness, son of Belial, blasphemer, Pharisee; bigot, devotee, fanatic, sabbatarian.

The wicked, unjust, ungodly, unrighteous.

(Phrase) The unco guid.

(Verbs) To be impious, etc., to profane, desecrate, blaspheme, revile, scoff, commit sacrilege.

To play the hypocrite, cant.

(Adjectives) Impious, profane, irreverent, sacrilegious, desecrating, blasphemous; unhallowed, unsanctified, hardened, perverted, reprobate.

Bigoted, priest-ridden, fanatical, churchy.

Hypocritical, canting, pietistical, sanctimonious, unctuous, pharisaical, over-righteous, righteous overmuch.

(Phrases) Under the mask, cloak, or pretence of religion.

---

989 Irreligion *(Substantives)*, ungodliness, unholiness, gracelessness, impiety (988).

Scepticism, doubt, unbelief, disbelief, incredulity, incredulousness, faithlessness, want of faith or belief (485, 487).

Atheism, hylotheism, materialism, positivism.

Deism, infidelity, freethinking, rationalism, agnosticism, unchristianness, antichristianity, antichristianism.

An atheist, sceptic, unbeliever, deist, freethinker, rationalist, agnostic, nullifidian, infidel, alien, giaour, heathen.

(Verbs) To be irreligious, disbelieve, lack faith, doubt.

To dechristianize, rationalize.

(Adjectives) Irreligious, undevout, godless, atheistic, atheistical, ungodly, unholy, unhallowed, unsanctified, graceless, without God, carnal-minded.

Sceptical, unbelieving, freethinking, agnostic, rationalistic, incredulous, unconverted, faithless, lacking faith.

Deistical, antichristian, unchristian, worldly-minded, mundane, carnal, earthly-minded.

(Adverbs) Irreligiously, etc.

4°. Acts of Religion

990 Worship *(Substantives)*, adoration, devotion, cult, homage, service, humiliation, kneeling, genuflexion, prostration.

Prayer, invocation, supplication, rogation, petition, orison, litany, the Lord's prayer, paternoster, collect.

Thanksgiving, giving or returning thanks, praise, glorification, benediction, doxology, hosanna, hallelujah, paean, Te Deum, Magnificat, Ave Maria, De Profundis, Nunc dimittis, Non nobis, Domine.

Psalmody, psalm, hymn, plainsong, chant, antiphon, response, anthem, motet.

Oblation, sacrifice, incense, libation, burnt-offering, votive offering; offertory, collection.

Discipline, self-discipline, self-examination, self-denial, fasting.

Divine service, religious service, office, duty, prime, terce, sext, matins, mass (998), angelus, nones, evensong, vespers, vigils, lauds, compline; prayer meeting, revival.

Worshipper, congregation, communicant, celebrant.

(Verbs) To worship, adore, reverence, venerate, do service, pay homage, humble oneself, bow down, kneel, bend the knee, prostrate oneself.

To pray, invoke, supplicate, petition, put up prayers or petitions; to ask, implore (765).

To return or give thanks; to say grace; to bless, praise, laud, glorify, magnify, sing praises, lead the choir, pronounce benediction.

To propitiate, offer sacrifice, fast, deny oneself; vow, offer vows, give alms.

(Phrases) To lift up the heart; to say one's prayers; to tell one's beads; to go to church; to attend divine service.

(Adjectives) Worshipping, etc., devout, solemn, devotional, reverent, pure, fervent, prayerful.

(Interjections) Hallelujah! alleluia! hosanna! glory be to God! *sursum corda!*

991 Idolatry *(Substantives)*, idol-worship, idolism, demonism, demonolatry, fire-worship, devil-worship, fetishism.

Sacrifices, hecatomb, holocaust; human sacrifices, immolation, mactation, infanticide, self-immolation, suttee.

Idol, image, fetish, ju-ju, Mumbo-Jumbo, Juggernaut, joss.

(Verbs) To worship idols, pictures, relics, etc.; to idolize, idolatrize.

(Adjectives) Idolatrous, fetishistic.

992 Occult arts *(Substantives)*, occultism, sorcery, magic, the black art, black magic, necromancy, theurgy, thaumaturgy, psychomancy, *diablerie*, bedevilment, witchcraft, witchery, bewitchment, wizardry, glamour, fetishism, vampirism, shamanism, voodooism, obeah (or obi), sortilege, conjuration, exorcism, fascination, mesmerism, hypnotism, animal magnetism, clairvoyance, telegnosis, telekinesis, psychokinesis, mediumship, spiritualism, extra-sensory perception, telepathy, parapsychology, second sight, spirit-rapping, table-turning, psychometry, crystal-gazing, divination, enchantment, hocus-pocus (545).

(Verbs) To practise sorcery, etc.; to conjure, exorcize, charm, enchant, bewitch, bedevil, hoodoo, entrance, mesmerize, hypnotize, fascinate; to taboo, wave a wand, cast a spell, call up spirits.

(Adjectives) Magic, magical, cabbalistic, talismanic, phylacteric, necromantic, incantatory, occult, mediumistic, charmed, exorcized, etc.

993 Spell *(Substantives)*, charm, fascination, incantation, exorcism, weird, cabbala, exsufflation, cantrip, runes, abracadabra, open sesame, mumbo-jumbo, taboo, counter-charm, evil eye, jinx, hoodoo, Indian sign.

Talisman, amulet, mascot, periapt, phylactery, philtre, fetish, wishbone, merrythought.

Wand, caduceus, rod, divining-rod, the lamp of Aladdin, magic ring, wishing-cap, seven-league boots.

994 Sorcerer *(Substantives)*, sorceress, magician, conjurer, necromancer, enchanter, enchantress, thaumaturgist, occultist, adept, Mahatma, seer, wizard, witch, warlock, charmer, exorcist, mage, archimage, soothsayer (513), shaman, medicine-man, witch-doctor, mesmerist, hypnotist, medium, spiritualist, clairvoyant; control.

(Phrase) Deus ex machina.

5°. Religious Institutions

995 Churchdom *(Substantives)*, ministry, apostleship, priesthood, prelacy, hierarchy, church government, Christendom, church; clericalism, sacerdotalism, priestcraft, theocracy, popery, papistry.

Monachism, monasticism, monkdom, monkhood, monkery.

Ecclesiastical offices and dignities: Pontificate, papacy, primacy, archbishopric, archiepiscopacy, bishopdom, episcopate, episcopacy, see, diocese, prelacy, deanery, stall, canonry, canonicate, prebend, prebendaryship; benefice, incumbency, advowson, living, cure, rectorship, vicarship, vicariate, deaconry, deaconship, curacy, chaplaincy, chaplainship; cardinalate, abbacy.

Holy orders, ordination, institution, consecration, induction, preferment, translation.

Council, conclave, sanhedrim, synod, presbytery, consistory, chapter, vestry (696).

(Verbs) To call, ordain, induct, install, prefer, translate, consecrate, canonize, beatify; to take the veil, to take vows.

(Adjectives) Ecclesiastical, clerical, sacerdotal, priestly, prelatical, hierarchical, pastoral, ministerial, capitular, theocratic.

Pontifical, papal, episcopal, archidiaconal, diaconal, canonical; monastic, monachal, monkish; levitical, rabbinical.

996 Clergy *(Substantives)*, ministry, priesthood, presbytery.

A clergyman, cleric, parson, divine, ecclesiastic, churchman, priest, presbyter, hierophant, pastor, father, shepherd, minister, father in Christ, patriarch, padre, abbé, curé; sky-pilot, holy Joe, devil-dodger.

Dignitaries of the church: Primate, archbishop, bishop, prelate,

997 Laity *(Substantives)*, flock, fold, congregation, assembly, brethren, people.

Temporality, secularization.

A layman, parishioner.

(Verb) To secularize.

(Adjectives) Secular, lay, laical, civil, temporal, profane.

diocesan, suffragan; dean, subdean, archdeacon, prebendary, canon, capitular, residentiary, beneficiary; rector, vicar, incumbent, chaplain, curate, deacon, sub-deacon, preacher, reader, evangelist, revivalist, missionary, missioner.

Churchwarden, sidesman; clerk, precentor, choir, chorister, almoner, verger, beadle, sexton, sacrist, sacristan, acolyte.

Roman Catholic priesthood: Pope, pontiff, cardinal, confessor, spiritual director.

Cenobite, conventual, abbot, prior, father superior, monk, oblate, friar, lay brother, mendicant, Franciscan (or Grey Friars, Friars minor, Minorites), Observant, Capuchin, Dominican (or Black Friars), Carmelite (or White Friars), Augustin (or Austin Friars), Crossed or Crutched Friars, Benedictine, Jesuit (or Society of Jesus).

Abbess, prioress, canoness, mother, mother superior, *religieuse*, nun, novice, postulant.

Greek Church: Patriarch, metropolitan, archimandrite, pope.

Under the Jewish dispensation: Prophet, priest, high-priest, Levite, rabbi (or rabbin), scribe.

Moslem: Imam, mullah, mufti, dervish, fakir, santon, hadji; muezzin.

Hindu: Brahmin, pundit, guru, yogi.

Buddhist: Lama, bonze.

(Phrase) The cloth.

(Adjectives) Reverend, ordained, in orders.

998 Rite *(Substantives)*, ceremony, ordinance, observance, cult, duty, form, formulary, ceremonial, solemnity, sacrament.

Baptism, immersion, christening, chrism, baptismal regeneration.

Confirmation, imposition or laying on of hands, ordination (995), consecration.

The Eucharist, the Lord's Supper, the communion, the sacrament, consubstantiation, celebration, consecrated elements, bread and wine.

Matrimony (903), burial (363), visitation of the sick, offertory.

Roman Catholic rites and ceremonies: Mass, high mass, low mass, dry mass; the seven sacraments, transubstantiation, impanation, extreme unction, viaticum, invocation of saints, canonization, transfiguration, auricular confession, maceration, flagellation, penance (952), telling of beads.

Relics, rosary, beads, reliquary, pyx (or pix), host, crucifix, *Agnus Dei*, thurible, censer, patera.

Liturgy, ritual, euchology, book of common prayer, litany, etc.; rubric, breviary, missal, ordinal; psalter, psalm book, hymn book, hymnal.

Service, worship (990), ministration, psalmody; preaching, predication; sermon, homily, lecture, discourse, exhortation, address.

Ritualism, ceremonialism, liturgics, liturgiology.

(Verbs) To perform service, do duty, minister, officiate; to baptize, dip, sprinkle; to confirm, lay hands on; to give or administer the sacrament; to take or receive the sacrament, communicate.

To preach, sermonize, predicate, lecture, harangue, hold forth, address the congregation.

(Adjectives) Ritual, ceremonial, baptismal, eucharistical, pastoral, liturgical.

999 Vestments *(Substantives)*, canonicals, robe, gown, pallium, surplice, cassock, alb, scapular (or scapulary), dalmatic, cope, soutane, chasuble, tonsure, cowl, hood, amice, calotte, bands, apron, biretta.

Mitre, tiara, triple crown, crosier.

1000 Place of worship, house of God.

Temple *(Substantives)*, cathedral, pro-cathedral, minster, church, kirk, chapel, meeting-house, tabernacle, conventicle, bethesda, little Bethel, basilica, fane, holy place, chantry, oratory.

Synagogue, mosque, pantheon, pagoda, joss-house, dagobah, tope.

Parsonage, rectory, vicarage, presbytery, deanery, bishop's palace, the Vatican.

Altar, shrine, sanctuary, *sanctum sanctorum,* the Holy of Holies, sacristy, communion table, holy table, table of the Lord; piscina, baptistery, font, aumbry.

Chancel, choir, nave, aisle, transept, vestry, crypt, apse, belfry, stall, pew, pulpit, ambo, lectern, reading-desk, confessional, prothesis, credence.

Monastery, priory, abbey, convent, nunnery, cloister.

(Adjectives) Claustral, monastic, monasterial, conventual.

INDEX

N.B. – The numbers refer to the headings under which the words occur. The headings or related words are given in italics, not to explain the meaning of the words, but to assist in the required reference. Words borrowed from another language have an asterisk prefixed to them.

Abominable, *painful*, 830
Abominate, *hate*, 898
  dislike, 867
Abomination, *foulness*, 653
*Abord, *courtesy*, 894
Aboriginal, *beginning*, 66
  native, 188
Aborigines, *inhabitants*, 188
Abortion, *failure*, 732
Abound, *sufficiency*, 639
About, *relative to*, 9
  near, 32, 197
  around, 227
Above, *height*, 206
  priority, 116
Above all, *greatness*, 31
Above-board, *visible*, 446
  plain, 518
  artless, 703
  true, 543
Above ground, *alive*, 359
Above par, *greatness*, 31
Abracadabra, *spell*, 993
Abrade, *subduct*, 38
Abrasion, *pulverulence*, 330
  friction, 331
Abreast, *lateral*, 236
  parallel, 216
Abridge, *shorten*, 201
  conciseness, 572
  lessen, 36
  deprive, 789
  in writing, 596
Abroach, *dispersion*, 73
Abroad, *extraneous*, 57
  exterior, 220
  distant, 196
  ignorant, 491
  perplexed, 704
Abrogation, *abrogation*, 756, 764
  illegality 964
Abrupt, *sudden*, 132
  hasty, 684
  violent, 173
  transient, 111
  steep, 217
  unexpected, 508
  style, 579
Abruption, *separation*, 44
Abscess, *disease*, 655
Abscission, *retrenchment*, 38
  division, 44
Abscond, *escape*, 671
  fly from, 287
Absence, *non-existence*, 2
  non-presence, 187
  inattention, 458
  thoughtlessness, 452
Absent-minded, *inattentive*, 458
Absentee, *absence*, 187
*Absit omen, *deprecation*, 766
Absolute, *not relative*, 1
  certain 474, 31
  positive, 535
  true, 494

Absolute, *unconditional*, 768A
  simple, 42
  authoritative, 737
  severe, 739
  due, 924
  complete, 52
Absolutely, *assent*, 488
Absolve, *forgive*, 918
  exempt, 927A
  liberate, 750
  permit, 760
  acquit, 970
Absonant, *unreasonable*, 495
  discordant, 414
Absorb, *combination*, 48
  take in, 296
  think, 451
  attend to, 457
  feel, 821
  possess, 777
  consume, 677
Absquatulate, *go away*, 287
Abstain, *refrain*, 603
  temperance, 953
  forbear, 623
Abstemious, *temperance*, 953,
                958
Absterge, *cleanness*, 652
Abstersive, *remedy*, 662
Abstinence, *disuse*, 678
  forbearance, 623, 953
Abstinent, *temperance*, 953
  sobriety, 958
Abstract, *separate*, 44
  deduct, 38
  idea, 451
  to abridge, 596, 572
  to take, 789
  to steal, 791
Abstraction, *inattention*, 458
  deduction, 38
  disjunction, 44
  unity, 87
Abstruse, *recondite*, 519
  hidden, 528
Absurd, *nonsensical*, 497, 499
  impossible, 471
  ridiculous, 853
Abundant, *copious*, 639
  great, 31
Abuse, *misuse*, 679
  ill treat, 649
  threat, 909
  upbraid, 932
  defame, 934
  debauch, 961
  deceive, 545
  of language, 523
Abut, *rest on*, 215
  touch, 199
Abyss, *depth*, 208
  space, 180
  hell, 982
Academic, *teaching*, 537
Academician, *artist*, 559

Academy, *school*, 542
Accede, *consent*, 762
Accelerate, *velocity*, 173, 274
  earliness, 132
  haste, 684
Accension, *calefaction*, 384
Accent, *tone of voice*, 580
  sound, 402
Accept, *receive*, 785
  consent, 762
  assent, 488
Acceptable, *agreeable*, 829
  expedient, 646
Acceptance, *security*, 771
Acceptation, *meaning*, 516
Accepted, *conformity*, 82
  habitual, 613
Access, *method*, 627
  approach, 286
Accessible, *facility*, 705
  possible, 470
  sociability, 892
Accession, *increase*, 35
  addition, 37
  commission, 755
  to power, 737
Accessory, *addition*, 37
  adjunct, 39
  means, 632
  auxiliary, 711
  aiding, 707
  accompanying, 88
Accidence, *grammar*, 567
Accident, *chance*, 156, 621
  event, 151
Accidental, *external*, 6
  music, 413
Accidie, *dejection*, 837
Acclamation, *approbation*, 931
  assent, 488
Acclimatize, *inure*, 613
  train, 673
Acclivity, *obliquity*, 217
Accolade, *courtesy*, 894
Accommodate, *suit*, 23
  equalize, 27
  reconcile, 723
  lend, 787
  prepare, 673
  aid, 707
  give, 784
Accommodating, *kind*, 906
Accommodation, *lodging*, 189
Accompaniment, *musical*, 415
  adjunct, 37, 39
Accompanist, *musician*, 416
Accompany, *coexist*, 88
  add, 37
Accomplice, *auxiliary*, 711
Accomplish, *execute*, 161
  finish, 729
Accomplishment, *talent*, 698
  learning, 490
Accord, *agree*, 23, 646
  assent, 488

Add, *numerically*, 85
Addendum, *adjunct*, 39
Adder, *viper*, 663
 maleficent being, 913
Addict, *habit*, 613
Addition, *adjunction*, 37
 thing added, 39
 arithmetical, 85
Addle, *barren*, 169
 abortive, 732
 to spoil, 659
Addle-headed, *imbecile*, 499
Address, *speak to*, 586
 skill, 698
 request, 765
 residence, 189
 direction, 550
 lecture, 582
 preach, 998
Addresses, *courtship*, 902
Adduce, *bring to*, 288
 evidence, 467
Adept, *proficient*, 700
 sorcerer, 994
Adequate, *sufficient*, 639
 power, 157
 strength, 159
 for a purpose, 644
Adhere, *stick*, 46
 fidelity, 772
 resoluteness, 604
Adherent, *follower*, 711
Adhesive, *coherence*, 46
 connective, 45
Adhibit, *use*, 677
Adiaphorism, *heresy*, 984A
Adieu, *departure*, 293
Adipose, *unctuous*, 355
Adiposity, *corpulence*, 192
Adit, *conduit*, 350
 orifice, 260
 way, 627
Adjacent, *nearness*, 197
Adjection, *addition*, 37
Adjective, *adjunct*, 39
Adjoin, *nearness*, 197
 contiguity, 199
Adjourn, *lateness*, 133
Adjudge, *lawsuit*, 969
Adjudication, *choice*, 609
 judgment, 480
 lawsuit, 969
Adjunct, *thing added*, 39
 accompaniment, 88
 aid, 707
Adjuration, *affirmation*, 535
Adjure, *request*, 765
 promise, 768
Adjust, *fit*, 27
 preface, 673
 settle, 723
 compromise, 774
Adjutage (or ajutage), *pipe*, 350
 opening, 260
Adjutant, *auxiliary*, 711

Adjutant, *military*, 745
Adjuvant, *helper*, 707, 711
Admeasurement, *measurement*, 466
Administer, *give*, 784
 apportion, 786
 manage, 693
 govern, 737
Administration, *of justice*, 965
Admirable, *excellent*, 648
 virtuous, 944
Admiral, *master*, 745
Admire, *approve*, 931
 love, 897
 wonder, 870
Admissible, *tolerable*, 651
Admission, *ingress*, 294, 296
 inclusion, 76
Admit, *let in*, 296
 accept, 785
 include, 76
 composition, 54
 concede in argument, 467
 disclose, 529
 allow, 760
 assent, 488
Admit of, *possibility*, 470
Admixture, *mixture*, 41
Admonish, *advise*, 695
 warn, 668
 reprove, 932
 predict, 511
Ado, *exertion*, 686
 activity, 682
 difficulty, 704
Adolescence, *youth*, 131
Adonis, *beauty*, 845
Adopt, *choice*, 609
Adore, *love*, 897
 worship, 990
Adorn, *beauty*, 845
Adown, *lowness*, 207
Adrift, *unrelated*, 10
 dispersed, 73
 at fault, 704
Adroit, *skill*, 698
Adscititious, *extrinsic*, 6
 added, 37
 supplementary, 52
*Adscriptus glebæ, *servant*, 746
Adulation, *flattery*, 933
Adulator, *flatterer*, 935
Adult, *adolescence*, 131
Adulterate, *mix*, 41
 deteriorate, 659
 falsify, 495
Adulterer, *libertine*, 962
Adultery, *impurity*, 961
Adumbrate, *sketch*, 594
 representation, 554
 painting, 556
 faint likeness, 21
 imitate, 19
 personify, 521
Adust, *burnt*, 384

Adust, *gloomy*, 837
Advance, *progress*, 282, 731
 to promote, 658
 forward, 707
 increase, 35
 lend, 787
 expenditure, 809
 assert, 535
Advanced, *progressive*, 658
 modern, 123
Advantage, *good*, 618
 utility, 644
 goodness, 648
 superiority, 33
 inequality, 28
 success, 705, 731
Advene, *addition*, 37
Advent, *arrival*, 292
 event, 151
 futurity, 121
Adventitious, *extrinsic*, 6
 casual, 156, 621
Adventure, *event*, 151
 chance, 156, 621
 pursuit, 622
 trial, 675
Adventurer, *deceiver*, 548
 rashness, 863
Adventurous, *courageous*, 861
 dangerous, 665
*Adversaria, *register*, 551
 chronicle, 594
Adversary, *opponent*, 710
Adverse, *opposed*, 708
 enmity, 889
 disliking, 867
 unprosperous, 735
Adversity, *adversity*, 735
Advert, *attention*, 457
Advertise, *publication*, 531
Advertisement, *preface*, 64
 information, 527
Advice, *counsel*, 695
 notice, 527; *news*, 532
Advisable, *expediency*, 646
Advise, *inform*, 527
 counsel, 695
 predict, 511
Advised, *voluntary*, 600
 intentional, 620
Adviser, *counsellor*, 695
 teacher, 540
Advocacy, *aid*, 707
Advocate, *counsellor*, 968
 advise, 695
 to prompt, 615
 commend, 931
 to vindicate, 937
 Saviour, 967
*Advocatus diaboli, *sophistry*, 477
Advowson, *churchdom*, 995
Adytum, *secret place*, 530
 room, 191
 prediction, 511

Aedile, *authority*, 745
Aegis, *defence*, 717
  patronage, 175
Aeolus, *wind*, 349
Aeon, *duration*, 106, 110
Aequiparate, *equate*, 27
*Aequo animo, *insensible*, 823
Aerate, *air*, 338
Aerial, *aeriform*, 334, 338
  elevated, 206
Aerie, *abode*, 189
  height, 206
Aeriform, *gaseity*, 334, 338
Aerodrome, *destination*, 292
Aeronautics, *navigation*, 267
Aeroplane, *aircraft*, 273A
Aerostat, *balloon*, 273A
Aerostatics, *gaseity*, 334
  navigation, 267
Aesthetic, *taste*, 850
  beauty, 845
  sensibility, 375
Aestival, *morning*, 125
Aestivate, *sleep*, 68
Aetiology, *knowledge*, 490
  attribution, 155
  disease, 655
Afar, *distance*, 196
Affable, *courteous*, 894
  sociable, 892
Affair, *business*, 625, 680
  event, 151
  topic, 454
  battle, 720
*Affaire de cœur, *love*, 897
Affect, *desire*, 865
  love, 897
  lend to, 176
  touch, 824
Affectability, *sensibility*, 822
Affectation, *pretension*, 855
  in style, 577
Affection, *disposition*, 820
  love, 897
  friendship, 888
Affiance, *trust*, 858
  promise, 768
*Affiche, *publication*, 531
Affidavit, *evidence*, 467
  affirmation, 535
  record, 551
Affiliation, *relation*, 9
  kindred, 11
  attribution, 155
Affinity, *relation*, 9
  similarity, 17
Affirm, *assert*, 535
  confirm, 488
Affirmatively, *assent*, 488
Affix, *to join*, 43
  add, 37
  sequel, 39
  addition, 37
Afflatus, *inspiration*, 515
Afflict, *painfulness*, 830

Affliction, *calamity*, 619
  pain, 828
Afflictive, *painfulness*, 830
Affluent, *flowing*, 348
  sufficient, 639
  prosperous, 734
  wealthy, 803
Afflux, *approach*, 286
Afford, *supply*, 134, 784
  wealth, 803
  accrue, 810
Affranchise, *liberation*, 750
Affray, *contention*, 720
Affright, *fear*, 880
Affront, *insult*, 900, 929
  courage, 861
  molest, 830
Affuse, *water*, 337
Afire, *heat*, 382
Afloat, *at sea*, 341
  on shipboard, 273
  unstable, 149
  public, 531
Afoot, *walking*, 266
  existing, 1
  business, 625
  in preparation, 673
Afore, *priority*, 116
Aforementioned, *precedence*, 62
Aforesaid, *repetition*, 104
  precedence, 62
  priority, 116
Aforethought, *intention*, 620
  premeditation, 611
Afraid, *fear*, 860
Afreet, *demon*, 980
Afresh, *new*, 123
  repeated, 104
  frequent, 136
Aft, *rear*, 235
After, *in order*, 63
  in time, 117
After all, *qualification*, 469
After-clap, *disappointment*, 509
After-course, *plan*, 626
After-game, *plan*, 626
After-life, *futurity*, 121
After-part, *sequel*, 65
After-piece, *drama*, 599
After-time, *futurity*, 121
Afterglow, *light*, 420
Aftermath, *sequel*, 65
  effect, 154
Afternoon, *evening*, 126
Aftertaste, *taste*, 390
Afterthought, *sequel*, 65
  thought, 451
  memory, 505
  plan, 626
Afterwards, *posteriority*, 117
Aga, *master*, 745
*Agacerie, *motive*, 615
Again, *repeated*, 104
  frequent, 136

Against, *physical opposition*, 179
  voluntary opposition, 708
  anteposition, 237
  provision, 673
Agape, *wonder*, 870
  curiosity, 455
Agate, *ornament*, 847
Age, *period*, 108
  oldness, 124
  duration, 106
  present time, 118
  advanced life, 128
Aged, *veteran*, 130
Ageless, *perpetual*, 112
Agency, *physical*, 170
  instrumentality, 157, 631, 755
  direction, 693
Agenda, *business*, 625
  plan, 626
Agent, *physical*, 153
  voluntary, 690
  consignee, 758, 769
Agentship, *commission*, 755
Agglomerate, *assemblage*, 72
  coherence, 46
Agglutinate, *coherence*, 46
Aggrandize, *in degree*, 35
  in bulk, 194
  honour, 873
Aggravate, *increase*, 35
  vehemence, 173
  distress, 835
  render worse, 659
  exasperate, 900
  exaggerate, 549
  provoke, 830
Aggregate, *whole*, 50
  collection, 72
Aggregation, *coherence*, 46
Aggression, *attack*, 716
Aggressive, *pugnacious*, 901
Aggrieve, *distress*, 830
  injure, 649
Aghast, *with wonder*, 870
  with fear, 860
  disappointed, 509
Agile, *swift*, 274
  active, 682
Agio, *discount*, 813
Agiotage, *barter*, 794
Agitate, *motion*, 315
  activity, 682
  to affect the mind, 821
  to excite, 824
Aglow, *hot*, 382
Agnation, *consanguinity*, 11
Agnomen, *nomenclature*, 564
Agnosticism, *unbelief*, 485, 989
*Agnus Dei, *rite*, 998
Ago, *preterition*, 122
Agog, *curiosity*, 455
  expectation, 507
  desire, 865
Agonistic, *contention*, 720
Agonize, *painfulness*, 830

Appearance, *sight*, 448
  probability, 472
Appease, *physically*, 174
  morally, 826
  conciliate, 918
Appeasement, *pacifism*, 723
  submission, 725
Appellant, *plaintiff*, 924, 938, 967
Appellation, *nomenclature*, 564
Append, *addition*, 37
  sequence, 63
  hang, 214
Appendage, *adjunct*, 39
Appendix, *sequel*, 65
Apperception, *knowledge*, 490
  conception, 453
Appertain, *belong*, 777
  related to, 9
  right, 922
  inclusion, 76
Appetence, *desire*, 865
Appetiser, *whet*, 298, 615
Appetite, *desire*, 865
Applaud, *approbation*, 931
Apple-green, *greenness*, 435
Apple of discord, *discord*, 713
Apple-sauce, *flattery*, 933
Appleton layer, *air*, 338
Appliance, *means*, 632
  instrument, 633
Applicable, *to use*, 644
  expedient, 646
  relative, 23
Applicant, *petitioner*, 767
Application, *use*, 677
  request, 765
  metaphor, 521
  study, 457
*Appoggiatura, *music*, 415
Appoint, *commission*, 755
  command, 741
Appointment, *salary*, 809
  equipment, 633
  interview, 892
Apportion, *allot*, 786
  arrange, 60
  portion, 51
Apportionment, *dispersion*, 73
Apposite, *agreeing*, 23
  relative, 9
Apposition, *agreement*, 23
  closeness, 199
Appraise, *value*, 812
  estimate, 466
Appreciate, *measure*, 466
  taste, 850
  realize, 450
  gratitude, 916
  judge, 480
  approve, 931
Apprehend, *know*, 490
  believe, 484
  fear, 860
  seize, 789, 969
Apprehension, *conception*, 453

Apprentice, *learner*, 541
Apprenticeship, *learning*, 539
  training, 673
Apprise, *information*, 527
Approach, *move*, 286
  nearness, 197
  path, 627
  of time, 121
Approbation, *approbation*, 931
Appropinquation, *approach*, 197,
  286
Appropriate, *fit*, 23, 646
  special, 79
  to assign, 786
  to take, 789
  to steal, 791
Appropriation, *stealing*, 791
Approve, *commend*, 931
  corroborate, 467
  assent, 488
Approximate, *approach*, 286
  nearness, 197
  in mathematics, 85
  resemble, 17
  related to, 9
Appulse, *convergence*, 286, 290
  collision, 276
Appurtenance, *part*, 51
  component, 56
Apricot, *colour*, 439
April fool, *fool*, 501
Apron, *dress*, 225
  vestments, 999
Apropos, *relation*, 9
  expedience, 646
  occasion, 134
Apse, *church*, 1000
Apt, *consonant*, 23
  clever, 698
  docile, 539
  willing, 539
  expedient, 646
  tendency, 176
Aptitude, *intelligence*, 498
  skill, 698
Aquarium, *domestication*, 370
  collection, 636
Aquatic, *water*, 337
Aquatint, *engraving*, 558
Aqueduct, *conduit*, 350
Aqueous, *water*, 337
Aquiline, *angularity*, 244
Arabesque, *ornament*, 847
Arable, *agriculture*, 371
Araeometer, *density*, 321
  measure, 466
Arbiter, *judge*, 480, 967
  adviser, 695
*Arbiter elegantiarum, *taste*,
  850
Arbitrament, *sentence*, 969
  judgment, 480
  choice, 609
Arbitrary, *without law*, 964
  authority, 737

Arbitrary, *obstinate*, 606
  severity, 739
  irregular, 83
  without relation, 10
Arbitrate, *mediate*, 724, 969
  judge, 480
Arbor, *support*, 215
Arborescence, *branching*, 205,
  242, 256
Arboretum, *agriculture*, 371
Arboriculture, *agriculture*, 371
Arbour, *abode*, 189
Arc, *curvature*, 245
Arc-lamp, *light*, 423
Arcade, *arch*, 245
  passage, 189
*Arcades ambo, *similarity*, 17
  friend, 890
Arcadian, *delightful*, 829
Arcanum, *secret*, 533
Arch, *curve*, 245
  great, 31
  cunning, 702
  roguish, 842
  greatness, 31
Archaeology, *preterition*, 122
Archaic, *oldness*, 124
Archaism, *inelegance*, 579
Archangel, *angel*, 977
Archbishop, *clergy*, 996
Archdeacon, *clergy*, 996
Archduke, *master*, 745
Archetype, *prototype*, 22
  model, 80
Arch-fiend, *Satan*, 978
Archiepiscopacy, *churchdom*, 995
Archimage, *sorcerer*, 994
Archimandrite, *clergy*, 996
Archipelago, *island*, 346
Architect, *constructor*, 164
  agent, 690
Architecture, *construction*, 161
  fabric, 329
Architrave, *summit*, 210
Archive, *record*, 551
Archness, *cunning*, 702
  cleverness, 498
  intelligence, 450
Archon, *master*, 745
Arch-traitor, *knave*, 941
Arctic, *polar*, 237
  cold, 383
Arcuation, *curvature*, 245
Ardent, *fiery*, 382
  feeling, 821
  desire, 865
  expectant, 507
Ardour, *activity*, 682
Arduous, *difficulty*, 704
Area, *region*, 181
  quantity, 25
Arefaction, *dryness*, 340
Arena, *field*, 181, 728
  amusement, 840
  workshop, 691

Aside, *disuse*, 678
Asinine, *imbecile*, 499
Ask, *inquire*, 461
   request, 765
   as price, 812
   supplicate, 990
Askance, *obliquity*, 217
   doubt, 485
Askew, *oblique*, 217
   distorted, 243
Aslant, *obliquity*, 217
Asleep, *inactivity*, 683
Aslope, *obliquity*, 217
Aspect, *appearance*, 448
   state, 7
   feature, 5
   situation, 183
   relation, 9
   of thought, 453
Asperge, *sprinkle*, 337
Aspergillum, *spray*, 348
Asperity, *roughness*, 256
   tartness, 895
   anger, 900
Asperse, *detraction*, 934
Aspersorium, *spray*, 348
Asphalt, *semiliquid*, 352
Asphyxiate, *killing*, 361
Aspirant, *petitioner*, 767
Aspirate, *voice*, 580
Aspire, *rise*, 305
   desire, 865
   hope, 858
   project, 620
Ass, *beast of burden*, 271
   fool, 501
Assagai, *arms*, 727
Assail, *attack*, 716
   plain, 830
Assailant, *opponent*, 710
   attacker, 716, 726
Assassinate, *killing*, 361
Assault, *attack*, 716
Assay, *experiment*, 463
Assemble, *assemblage*, 72
Assembly-room, *sociality*, 892
Assent, *agree*, 488
   consent, 762
Assert, *affirm*, 535
   claim as a right, 924
Assess, *measure*, 466
   judge, 480
   price, 812
Assessor, *adviser*, 695
Assets, *property*, 780
   money, 800
Asseverate, *affirm*, 535
Assiduous, *activity*, 682
Assign, *attribute*, 155
   transfer, 783
   give, 784
   commission, 755
   allot, 786
   duty, 926
Assignat, *money*, 800

Assignation, *sociality*, 892
Assignee, *receive*, 785
Assignment, *allotment*, 786
   business, 625
   commission, 755
Assimilate, *resemble*, 17, 144
   imitate, 19
   agree, 23
Assist, *aid*, 707
   benefit, 906
Assistant, *auxiliary*, 711
Assize, *measure*, 466
   tribunal, 966
Associate, *accompany*, 88
   concur, 178
   unite, 43
   mixture, 41
   assemble, 72
   friend, 890
   society, 892
Association, *relation*, 9
   intuition, 477
Assoil, *free*, 750
   acquit, 970
Assonance, *similarity*, 17
   poetry, 597
Assort, *arrange*, 60
Assortment, *class*, 75
   collection, 72
Assuage, *physically*, 174
   morally, 826
   relieve, 834
Assume, *suppose*, 514
   evidence, 467
   hope, 858
   right, 924
   insolence, 739, 885
   pride, 878
   falsehood, 544
Assumption, *qualification*, 469
   severity, 739
Assurance, *assertion*, 535
   promise, 768
   certainty, 474
   belief, 484
   hope, 858
   insolence, 885
Assuredly, *positively*, 31
   assert, 488
   safety, 664
Asterisk, *indication*, 550
   expletive, 908
Astern, *rear*, 235
Asteroid, *world*, 318
Asteroth, *deity*, 979
Asthenia, *weakness*, 160
Astigmatism, *dim-sightedness*,
                443
Astonish, *wonder*, 870
Astonishing, *great*, 31
Astound, *surprise*, 870
   excite, 824
Astraea, *right*, 922
Astral, *world*, 318
   immaterial, 317

Astray, *deviation*, 279
Astriction, *junction*, 43
Astride, *support*, 215
Astringent, *contraction*, 195
Astrology, *prediction*, 511
Astronaut, *navigator*, 269
Astronautics, *navigation*, 267
Astronomy, *world*, 318
Astrophysics, *world*, 318
Astute, *wisdom*, 498
Asunder, *separate*, 44
   distant, 196
   disjunction, 44
Asylum, *retreat*, 666
   hospital, 662
   defence, 717
Asymmetry, *disorder*, 59, 243
Asymptote, *converge*, 290
At-home, *sociality*, 892
At once, *transientness*, 111
At the end of the day, *finally*,
                67
Ataraxia, *insensibility*, 823
Atavism, *reversion*, 145
Atelier, *workshop*, 691
Atheism, *irreligion*, 989
   unbelief, 485
Athena, *goddess*, 979
Athirst, *desire*, 865
Athletic, *strength*, 159
Athletics, *training*, 673
   contention, 720
Athwart, *oblique*, 217
   crossing, 219
   opposing, 708
Atlantis, *visionary*, 515
Atlas, *support*, 215
   strength, 159; *maps*, 554
Atmosphere, *air*, 338
   circumstances, 227
Atoll, *island*, 346
Atom, *small in degree*, 32
   in size, 193
   particle, 330
Atomic bomb, *arms*, 727
Atomizer, *spray*, 348
Atonality, *melody*, 413
Atonement, *atonement*, 952
   religious, 976
   reward, 973
Atony, *weakness*, 160
Atrabilious, *dejection*, 837
Atrocious, *vice*, 945
   guilt, 947
   malevolence, 907
Atrophy, *shrinking*, 195
   disease, 655
   decay, 659
Attaboy, *approval*, 931
Attach, *join*, 43
   love, 897
   legal, 969
Attaché, *servant*, 746
   consignee, 758
Attaché-case, *receptacle*, 191

INDEX

Attachment, *see* Attach
Attack, *attack*, 716
   disease, 655
Attain, *arrive*, 292
   succeed, 731
Attainable, *possible*, 470
   easy, 705
Attainder, *condemnation*, 971
Attainment, *learning*, 539
   knowledge, 490
   skill, 698
Attar, *fragrance*, 400
Attemper, *mix*, 41
   moderate, 174
Attempt, *undertaking*, 676
   try, 675
Attend, *accompany*, 88
   follow, 281
   treat, 662
   apply the mind, 457
   frequent, 136
   be present, 186
Attendant, *servant*, 746
Attention, *attention*, 451, 457
   respect, 928
Attentions, *courtesy*, 894
   courtship, 902
   kindness, 906
Attenuate, *lessen*, 36
   rarefy, 322
   contract, 195
   narrow, 203
Attest, *bear testimony*, 467
   indicate, 550
   adjure, 768
Attestation, *record*, 551
Attic, *garret*, 191
   high, 206
   elegant, 578
   wit, 842
   taste, 850
Atticism, *wit*, 842
Attila, *evildoer*, 913
Attire, *vestment*, 225
Attitude, *posture*, 183, 240
   circumstance, 8
Attitudinize, *affectation*, 855
   ostentation, 882
Attorney, *consignee*, 758, 769
   in law, 968
Attract, *bring towards*, 288
   please, 829
   allure, 865
Attractability, *motive*, 615
Attractive, *beautiful*, 845
   pleasing, 829
   lovely, 897
   alluring, 615
Attrahent, *attraction*, 288
Attributable, *effect*, 154
Attribute, *power*, 157
Attribution, *attribution*, 155
Attrition, *friction*, 331
*Attroupement, *assemblage*, 72
Attune, *music*, 415

Attune, *prepare*, 673
*Au courant, *knowledge*, 490
*Au fait, *knowledge*, 490
*Au fond, *truth*, 494
   inbeing, 5
*Au pied de la lettre, *truth*, 494
   meaning, 516
*Au revoir, *departure*, 293
Aubade, *music*, 415
Auburn, *brown*, 433
Auction, *sale*, 796
Auctorial, *book*, 593
Audacity, *courage*, 861
   insolence, 863, 885
*Audi alteram partem, *evidence*,
                468
   right, 922
Audible, *sound*, 402
Audience, *hearing*, 418
   conversation, 588
Audiometer, *hearing*, 418
Audiphone, *hearing*, 418
Audit, *accounts*, 811
   numeration, 85
Audition, *hearing*, 418
Auditor, *hearer*, 418
   accounts, 811
Auditorium, *amusement*, 840
Auditory, *hearing*, 418
*Auf wiedersehen, *departure*, 293
Auger, *perforation*, 262
Augment, *to increase*, 35
   thing added, 39
Augmentation, *expansion*, 194
Augur, *predict*, 507, 511
   soothsayer, 513
Augury, *prediction*, 511, 512
August, *repute*, 873
Augustine, *clergy*, 996
Aura, *touch*, 380
   emanation, 295
Aureate, *yellowness*, 436
Aureole, *light*, 420
Aureolin, *orange*, 439
Auricular, *hearing*, 418
Aurist, *doctor*, 662
Aurora, *light*, 423
   dawn, 125
Auroral, *rosy*, 434
Auscultation, *hearing*, 418
Auspices, *patronage*, 175
   prediction, 511
Auspicious, *hopeful*, 858
   prosperous, 734
   expedient, 646
   opportune, 134
Auster, *wind*, 349
Austere, *harsh taste*, 395
   severe, 739
   discourteous, 895
   ascetic, 955
Austerity, *economy*, 817
Authentic, *truth*, 494
   certain, 474
   existence, 1

Authenticate, *record*, 551
   evidence, 467
   security, 771
Author, *producer*, 164
   cause, 153
   writer, 590
Authoritative, *certain*, 474
   peremptory, 741
Authority, *power*, 157, 737
   command, 741
   right, 924
   permission, 760
   testimony, 467
   sign, 500
*Auto da fé, *burning*, 384
   execution, 972
*Autobahn, *way*, 627
Autobiography, *description*, 594
Autobus, *vehicle*, 272
Autocar, *vehicle*, 272
Autochrome, *photograph*, 556
Autochthonous, *inhabitant*, 188
Autocracy, *severity*, 739
   authority, 737
Autocrat, *master*, 745
Autocrat, *arbitrary*, 739, 964
   will, 600
Autocycle, *vehicle*, 272
Autogiro, *aircraft*, 273A
Autograph, *warranty*, 467
   signature, 550
   writing, 590
Autolycus, *thief*, 792
Automatic, *mechanical*, 601
   insensible, 823
Automation, *means*, 632
Automobile, *vehicle*, 272
Autonomy, *freedom*, 748
Autopsy, *vision*, 441
   disinter, 363
Autotype, *copy*, 21
*Aux abois, *death*, 360
*Aux aguets, *care*, 459
Auxiliary, *aid*, 707
   helper, 711
   intermediary, 631
Avail, *use*, 677
   utility, 644
Avalanche, *fall*, 306
   debacle, 348
Avant-courier, *pioneer*, 673
   precursor, 64
Avant-garde, *go-ahead*, 282
Avarice, *parsimony*, 819
Avast, *quiescence*, 265
   cessation, 142
Avaunt, *disappear*, 449
   depart, 293
   repulse, 289
*Ave, *arrival*, 292
Avenge, *revenge*, 919
Avenue, *street*, 189
   method, 627
Aver, *affirmation*, 535
Average, *mean*, 29

Barricade, *obstacle*, 706
Barrier, *fence*, 232
   obstacle, 706
Barring, *except*, 83
   save, 38
Barrister, *lawyer*, 968
Barrow, *vehicle*, 272
   grave, 363
Barter, *exchange*, 794
*Bas bleu, *affectation*, 855
Bascule, *instrument*, 633
Base, *lowest part*, 211
   support, 215
   bad, 649
   dishonourable, 940
   shameful, 874
   vicious, 945
   cowardly, 862
   plebeian, 876
Base-minded, *improbity*, 940
Baseless, *unreal*, 2
   erroneous, 495
Basement, *base*, 211
Bashaw, *ruler*, 745
Bashful, *modesty*, 881
Basic, *support*, 215
Basic English, *language*, 560
Basilica, *temple*, 1000
Basilisk, *serpent*, 949
   monster, 83
   evil eye, 441
Basin, *hollow*, 252
   vessel, 191
   plain, 344
   dock, 189
Basis, *preparation*, 673
   foundation, 215
Bask, *warmth*, 382
   physical enjoyment, 377
   moral enjoyment, 827
   prosperity, 734
Basket, *receptacle*, 191
Basket-work, *plaiting*, 219
Basketry, *plaiting*, 219
Bas-relief, *convexity*, 250
Bass, *deep-sounding*, 408, 413
Bass-viol, *musical instrument*, 417
Bassinette, *vehicle*, 272
*Basso rilievo, *convexity*, 250
   sculpture, 557
Bassoon, *musical instrument*, 417
Bastard, *spurious*, 544, 925
   erroneous, 495
Bastardy, *illegitimacy*, 964
Baste, *beat*, 276
   punish, 972
Bastille, *prison*, 752
Bastinado, *punishment*, 972
Bastion, *defence*, 717
Bat, *club*, 727, 633
   spree, 840
Batch, *assemblage*, 72
   quantity, 25

Bate, *diminish*, 36, 38
   reduce price, 813
Bath, *immersion*, 300
   water, 337
Bath-chair, *vehicle*, 272
Bath-room, *room*, 191
Bathe, *immersion*, 300
   plunge, 310
Bathing-suit, *dress*, 225
Bathos, *depth*, 208
   anticlimax, 497
   ridiculous, 853
Bathymetry, *depth*, 208
Bathysphere, *depth*, 208
Baton, *sceptre*, 747
   impact, 276
Bats, *insane*, 503
Battalion, *troop*, 726
   assemblage, 72
Batten, *feed*, 296
Batter, *beat*, 276
   destroy, 162
Battered, *imperfect*, 651
Battering-ram, *weapon*, 276, 727
Battery, *instrument*, 633
Battle, *contention*, 720
Battle array, *warfare*, 722
   arrangement, 60
Battle-axe, *arms*, 727
Battle-bowler, *defence*, 717
Battle-cruiser, *ship*, 273
Battle-dress, *dress*, 225
Battle-field, *arena*, 728
Battlement, *bulwark*, 666
   defence, 717
   enclosure, 232
   embrasure, 257
Battleship, *ship*, 273
Battue, *pursuit*, 622
   killing, 361
Batty, *insane*, 503
Bauble, *trifle*, 643
   toy, 840
Baulk, *see* Balk
*Bavardage, *absurdity*, 497
Bawbee, *money*, 800
Bawd, *libertine*, 962
Bawdy, *impurity*, 961
Bawl, *cry*, 411, 839
Bay, *gulf*, 343
   brown, 433
   to howl, 412
Bay, at, *defence*, 717
Bayadère, *dancer*, 599
Bayard, *carrier*, 271
   perfection, 650
Bayonet, *arms*, 727
   attack, 716
   kill, 361
Bays, *trophy*, 733
   reward, 973
Bazaar, *mart*, 799
Bazooka, *gun*, 727
Be, *existence*, 1
Be of, *inclusion*, 76

Be off, *departure*, 293
   ejection, 297
Beach, *land*, 342
Beacon, *sign*, 423, 550
   warning, 668
Bead-roll, *list*, 86
Beadle, *janitor*, 263
   officer, 745
   law officer, 965
   church, 996
Beads, *rite*, 998
Beak, *front*, 234
   nose, 250
   judge, 967
Beaker, *receptacle*, 191
Beam, *support*, 215
   of a balance, 466
   of light, 420
   beauty, 845
Beamless, *darkness*, 421
Bean-feast, *pleasure*, 827, 840
   meal, 298
Bear, *sustain*, 215
   produce, 161
   carry, 270
   suffer, 821
   admit, 470
   brute, 895
Bear down upon, *attack*, 716
Bear-garden, *arena*, 728
   brawl, 713
Bear-leader, *teacher*, 540
Bear off, *taking*, 789
Bear out, *confirm*, 467
   vindicate, 937
Bear up, *cheerfulness*, 836
Bear upon, *influence*, 175
   evidence, 467
   to relate to, 9
Bear with, *indulge*, 740
Bearable, *tolerable*, 651
Beard, *spike*, 253
   rough, 256
   to defy, 715
   courage, 861
   insolence, 885
Beardless, *youth*, 127
Bearer, *carrier*, 271
Bearing, *support*, 215
   direction, 278
   meaning, 516
   appearance, 448
   demeanour, 692
   circumstance, 8
   situation, 183
Bearish, *discourtesy*, 895
Beast, *animal*, 366
   blackguard, 895
Beastly, *uncleanness*, 653
Beat, *strike*, 716, 972
   surpass, 33, 303
   periodic, 138
   oscillation, 314
   agitation, 315
   crush, 330; *sound*, 407

Beat, *succeed*, 731
   line of pursuit, 625
   news, 532
Beat down, *chaffer*, 794
   insolent, 885
Beat hollow, *superiority*, 33
Beat it, *go away*, 293, 287
   escape, 671
Beat off, *defence*, 717
Beat time, *chronometry*, 114
Beat up for, *seek*, 461
Beatify, *enrapture*, 829
   honour, 873
   sanctify, 987, 995
Beating, *impulse*, 276
Beatnik, *hippy*, 183
Beatitude, *pleasure*, 827
Beau, *fop*, 854
   man, 373; *admirer*, 897
*Beau idéal, *beauty*, 845
   perfection, 650
*Beau monde, *fashion*, 852
   nobility, 875
*Beau sabreur, *hero*, 861
Beauty, *beauty*, 845
   ornament, 847
   symmetry, 242
Beaver, *hat*, 225
Bebop, *melody*, 413
Becalm, *quiescence*, 265
Because, *attribution*, 155
   reasoning, 476
   motive, 615
Bechance, *eventuality*, 151
Beck, *rill*, 348
   signal, 550
   mandate, 741
Beckon, *signal*, 550
Becloud, *darkness*, 421
Become, *change to*, 144
   behove, 926
Become of, *event*, 151
Becoming, *proper*, 646
   beautiful, 845
   just, 922
   apt, 23
Bed, *layer*, 204
   support, 215
   lodgement, 191
Bed-maker, *servant*, 746
Bedabble, *splash*, 337
Bedarken, *darkness*, 421
Bedaub, *cover*, 222
   dirt, 653
   deface, 846
Bedazzle, *light*, 420
Bedeck, *beauty*, 845
   ornament, 847
Bedevil, *derange*, 61
   bewitch, 992
Bedew, *moisture*, 339
Bedfellow, *friend*, 890
Bedight, *beauty*, 845
Bedim, *darkness*, 421
Bedizen, *beautify*, 845

Bedizen, *ornament*, 851
Bedlam, *insanity*, 503
Bedlamite, *madman*, 504
Bedraggle, *soil*, 653
Bedridden, *disease*, 655
Bedstead, *support*, 215
Bedtime, *evening*, 126
Bee, *active*, 682
   party, 892
Bee-line, *direction*, 278
Bee-witted, *folly*, 499
Beef, *complain*, 839
Beefy, *corpulent*, 192
Beelzebub, *Satan*, 978
Beery, *drunken*, 959
Beeswax, *oil*, 356
Beetle, *high*, 206
   projecting, 250
   impact, 276
Befall, *eventuality*, 151
Befit, *agree*, 23
Befitting, *right*, 926
   expedient, 646
Befool, *deceive*, 503, 545
   baffle, 732
Before, *precedence*, 62
Before Christ, *period*, 108
Beforehand, *prior*, 116, 13
Befoul, *uncleanness*, 653
Beg, *request*, 765
Beg the question, *evidence*, 467
Beget, *produce*, 161
Begetter, *father*, 166
Beggar, *petitioner*, 767
   poor, 804
Beggarly, *mean*, 643
   vulgar, 876
   servile, 886
   vile, 940
Begilt, *ornament*, 847
Begin, *beginning*, 66
Begin again, *repetition*, 104
Beginner, *learner*, 541
   novice, 674
Beginning to end, from,
   whole, 50
   completeness, 52
   duration, 106
Begird, *encircle*, 227, 231
Begone, *depart*, 293
   repel, 289
Begrime, *soil*, 653
   deface, 846
Begrudge, *refusal*, 764
   parsimony, 819
Beguile, *deceive*, 545
   amuse, 840
Beguine, *nun*, 996
Begum, *nobility*, 875
Behalf, *advantage*, 618
   aid, 707
Behave, *conduct*, 692
Behead, *punish*, 972
   divide, 44
Behest, *command*, 741

Behind, *in order*, 63
   in space, 235
Behindhand, *late*, 133
   adversity, 735
   insolvent, 808
   shortcoming, 304
Behold, *vision*, 441
Beholden, *grateful*, 916
   obligatory, 926
Behoof, *good*, 618
Behove, *duty*, 926
Bein, *prosperous*, 734
Being, *abstract*, 1
   conduct, 3
Bejan, *learner*, 541
*Bel canto, *music*, 415
*Bel esprit, *humorist*, 844
Belabour, *thump*, 972
   buffet, 276
Belated, *late*, 133
   confused, 491
Belaud, *approbation*, 931
Belay, *junction*, 43
   stop, 265
Belch, *ejection*, 297
Beldam, *old woman*, 130
   hag, 913
Beleaguer, *attack*, 716
Belfry, *height*, 206
   church, 1000
   head, 450
Belie, *falsify*, 544
   misinterpret, 523
   deny, 536
   disagreement, 24
   oppose, 708
Belief, *credence*, 484
   supposition, 514
   religious creed, 983
Believer, *piety*, 987
Belike, *probability*, 472
Belittle, *disparage*, 483
Bell, *sound*, 417
   cry, 412
   funeral, 363
   alarm, 669
Bell-boy, *messenger*, 534
Bell-shaped, *globose*, 249
   concave, 252
Bell-washer, *precursor*, 64
Belle, *woman*, 374
   beauty, 845
Belles-lettres, *language*, 560
   knowledge, 490
Bellicose, *warlike*, 722
Belligerent, *warfare*, 722
Bellow, *cry*, 411, 412
   complain, 839
Bellows, *wind*, 349
Belly, *receptacle*, 191
   interior, 221
   to bulge, 250
Belly-ache, *complain*, 839
Belly-god, *glutton*, 957
Belly-timber, *food*, 298

Biannual, *periodic*, 138
Bias, *slope*, 217
  prepossession, 481
  unfairness, 923
  inclination, 602
  tendency, 176
  motive, 615
  disposition, 820
Bibacious, *drunkenness*, 959
Bibelot, *trifle*, 643
Bible, *revelation*, 985
Bibliography, *list*, 86
  book, 593
Bibliolatry, *heterodoxy*, 984A
  knowledge, 490
Bibliology, *book*, 593
Bibliomania, *erudition*, 490
  book, 593
Bibliophile, *book*, 593
  scholar, 492
Bibulous, *spongy*, 322
  drunken, 959
Bicentenary, *period*, 138
  celebration, 883
Bicentric, *duality*, 89
Bicker, *flutter*, 315
  discord, 713
  quarrel, 720
Bicuspid, *bisection*, 91
Bicycle, *travel*, 266
Bid, *order*, 741
  offer, 763
Bid for, *bargain*, 794
Biddable, *obedient*, 743
Bide, *tarry*, 133
  remain, 141
Bide one's time, *future*, 121
Biennial, *periodic*, 138
*Bienséance, *polish*, 852
  manners, 894
Bier, *interment*, 363
Bifacial, *duplication*, 90
Bifarious, *duality*, 89
Biff, *impact*, 276
Bifocal, *duality*, 89
Bifold, *duplication*, 90
Biform, *duplication*, 90
  bisection, 91
Biformity, *duality*, 89
Bifurcation, *bisection*, 91
  fork, 244
Big, *in degree*, 31
  in size, 192
Big pot, *importance*, 642
Bigamy, *marriage*, 903
Bight, *gulf*, 343
  bend, 245
Bigot, *impiety*, 989
Bigoted, *imbecile*, 499
  prejudiced, 481
  obstinate, 606
Bigotry, *prejudice*, 481
  credulity, 486
  certainty, 474
  obstinacy, 606

Bigotry, *heterodoxy*, 984A
Bigwig, *sage*, 500
  pedant, 492
  notability, 642, 875
Bijou, *gem*, 650
  little, 193
Bijouterie, *ornament*, 847
Bike, *bicycle*, 266
Bikini, *dress*, 225
Bilateral, *duplication*, 90
  side, 236
Bilbo, *arms*, 727
Bilboes, *prison*, 752
Bile, *resentment*, 900
Bilge, *trash*, 645
Bilge-water, *dirt*, 653
Bilious, *dejection*, 837
Bilk, *deception*, 545
  swindle, 791
  disappointment, 509
Bill, *money*, *account*, 811
  charge, 812
  money-order, 800
  security, 771
  in law, 969
  placard, 531
  ticket, 550
  instrument, 633
  weapon, 727
  sharpness, 253
Bill of fare, *food*, 298
  list, 86
  plan, 626
Billabong, *river*, 348
Billet, *epistle*, 592
  ticket, 550
  to apportion, 786
  to locate, 184
*Billet-doux, *epistle*, 592
  endearment, 902
Billiard-table, *level*, 213
Billingsgate, *scolding*, 932
  imprecatory, 908
Billion, *numbers*, 98
Billow, *wave*, 348
Billycock, *hat*, 225
Bimetallism, *money*, 800
Bimonthly, *periodical*, 138
Bin, *receptacle*, 191
Binary, *duality*, 89
Bind, *connect*, 43
  compel, 744
  obligation, 926
  condition, 770
Binge, *amusement*, 840
Bingle, *clip*, 201
Binoculars, *lens*, 445
Binomial, *duplication*, 90
Bint, *girl*, 374
Biograph, *spectacle*, 448
Biographer, *recorder*, 553
Biography, *description*, 594
Biology, *organization*, 357
  life, 359
Bioscope, *spectacle*, 448

Bipartition, *duplication*, 91
Biplane, *aircraft*, 273A
Birch, *scourge*, 975
  to punish, 972
Bird, *animal*, 366
Bird of passage, *traveller*, 268
Bird-fancier, *collector*, 775
Bird-lime, *vinculum*, 45
Bird's eye, *tobacco*, 298A
  general, 78
Bird's eye view, *sight*, 448
Birds of a feather, *inclusion*, 176
  conformity, 82
Bireme, *ship*, 273
Biretta, *cap*, 225
  vestments, 999
Biro, *pen*, 590
Birth, *beginning*, 66
  production, 161
  nobility, 875
Birthday, *anniversary*, 138
Birthmark, *blemish*, 848
Birthplace, *origin*, 153
Birthright, *dueness*, 924
*Bis, *duplication*, 89
  repetition, 104
*Bise, *wind*, 349
Bisection, *duality*, 91
Bishop, *clergy*, 996
Bishopric, *churchdom*, 995
Bissextile, *period*, 108
Bistoury, *sharpness*, 253
Bistre, *brown*, 433
Bisulcate, *fold*, 258, 259
Bit, *part*, 51
  mixture, 41
  small quantity, 32
  money, 800; *curb*, 752
Bit by bit, *part*, 51
  degree, 26
Bitch, *bad woman*, 949
Bite, *pain*, 378
  painful, 830
  cheat, 545
Biting, *cold*, 383
  pungent, 392
  painful, 830
Bitter, *taste*, 395
  cold, 383
  animosity, 898
  wrath, 900
  malevolence, 907
  regret, 833
  painful, 830
Bitumen, *semiliquid*, 352
Bivouac, *repose*, 265
  to encamp, 186
  camp, 189; *watch*, 664
Bizarre, *ridiculous*, 853
  unconformity, 83
Blab, *disclosure*, 529
Black, *colour*, 431
  crime, 945
  copy, 590
Black-and-white, *colourless*, 429

Bow, *ornament*, 847
  fore-part, 234
  shot, 284
  arms, 727
  to stoop, 308
  reverence, 894
  submission, 725
  obeisance, 743
  servility, 886
  respect, 928
  prominence, 250
Bow-legged, *curvature*, 245
  distortion, 243
Bowdlerize, *expurgate*, 652
Bowels, *interior*, 221
  of compassion, 914
Bower, *alcove*, 189
  chamber, 191
Bowie-knife, *arms*, 727
  sharpness, 253
Bowl, *vessel*, 191
  hollow, 252
  to propel, 284
Bowler, *hat*, 225
Bowling-green, *horizontality*, 213
Bowshot, *nearness*, 197
Bowstring, *scourge*, 975
Box, *chest*, 191
  house, 189
  theatre, 599
  to strike, 972
  to fight, 720
Boxer, *combatant*, 726
Boxing, *contention*, 720
Boy, *infant*, 129
Boy friend, *love*, 897
Boycott, *exclude*, 893
  eject, 297
Boyhood, *youth*, 127
Bra, *dress*, 225
Brace, *to tie*, 43
  fastening, 45
  two, 89
  to refresh, 689
  to strengthen, 159
Brace and bit, *perforator*, 262
Bracelet, *ornament*, 847
  circularity, 247
Bracer, *remedy*, 662
Brachygraphy, *writing*, 590
Bracing, *strengthening*, 159
  refreshing, 689
Bracket, *tie*, 43
  support, 215
  vinculum, 45
  couple, 89
Brackish, *pungent*, 392
Brad, *vinculum*, 45
Bradawl, *perforator*, 262
Brae, *height*, 206
Brag, *boasting*, 884
Braggadocio, *boasting*, 884
Braggart, *boasting*, 884
  bully, 887
Brahma, *god*, 979

Brahmin, *clergy*, 996
  religious, 984
Braid, *to tie*, 43
  ligature, 45
  intersection, 219
Braille, *printing*, 591
Brain, *intellect*, 450
  skill, 498
Brain-sick, *giddy*, 460
Brain-storm, *excitability*, 825
Brainless, *imbecile*, 499
Brains trust, *council*, 696
Brainwash, *teach*, 537
Brake, *copse*, 367
  curb, 752
  vehicle, 272
Bramble, *thorn*, 253
  painful, 830
Bran, *pulverulence*, 330
Bran-new, *see* Brand-new
Branch, *member*, 51
  plant, 367
  duality, 91
  posterity, 167
  ramification, 256
Branch off, *divergence*, 291
Branch out, *style*, 573
  divide, 91
Brand, *to burn*, 384
  fuel, 388
  to stigmatize, 932
  mark, 550
  to accuse, 938
  reproach, 874
Brand-new, *new*, 123
Brander, *roast*, 384
Brandish, *oscillate*, 314
  flourish, 315
*Bras croisés, *inactive*, 683
Brasier, *furnace*, 386
Brass, *insolence*, 885
  colour, 439
Brass up, *pay*, 809
Brassed off, *bored*, 641
  sated, 869
Brasserie, *food*, 298
Brassière, *dress*, 225
Brassy, *club*, 276
Brat, *infant*, 129
Bravado, *boasting*, 884
Brave, *courage*, 861
  to defy, 715
Bravery, *courage*, 861
  ornament, 847
Bravo, *assassin*, 361
  applause, 931
*Bravura, *music*, 415
Braw, *handsome*, 845
Brawl, *cry*, 411
  discord, 713
  contention, 720
Brawny, *strong*, 159
  stout, 192
Bray, *cry*, 412
  to grind, 330

Brazen-faced, *insolent*, 885
Breach, *crack*, 44
  quarrel, 713
  violation, 925
  exception, 83
Bread, *food*, 298
Breadstuffs, *food*, 298
Breadth, *thickness*, 202
  of mind, 498
Break, *fracture*, 44
  shatter, 162
  incompleteness, 53
  interval, 70, 106, 198
  opportunity, 134
  luck, 621, 731
  crumble, 328
  violation, 773
  bankruptcy, 808
  to infringe, 927
  to disclose, 529
  to tame, 749
  to decline, 659
  to swerve, 311
Break down, *fail*, 158, 732
Break ground, *undertaking*, 676
Break in, *teach*, 537
  train, 370, 673
Break loose, *escape*, 671
  liberate, 750
Break off, *a habit*, 614
  leave off, 142
  abrogate, 756
Break out, *fly out*, 825
Break the ranks, *derangement*, 61
Break the record, *superiority*, 33
Break up, *destroy*, 162
  deteriorate, 659
  decompose, 49
Break with, *discord*, 713
Breaker, *wave*, 348
  danger, 667
Breakfast, *food*, 298
Breakneck, *perilous*, 665
  precipitous, 217
Breakwater, *refuge*, 666
  enclosure, 232
Breast, *interior*, 221
  convexity, 250
  mind, 450
  will, 600
  soul, 820
  to oppose, 708
Breastplate, *defence*, 717
Breastwork, *defence*, 717
Breath, *air*, 349
  sound, 405
  life, 359, 364
Breathe, *exist*, 1
  live, 359
  blow, 349
  mean, 516
  utter, 580, 582
  repose, 687

Brush, *to clean*, 652
  painting, 559
  fight, 720
  rough, 256
Brush up, *memory*, 505
Brushwood, *plant*, 367
Brusque, *discourteous*, 895
  inelegant, 579
  rough, 173
Brutal, *vicious*, 945
  ill-bred, 895
  savage, 907
Brutalize, *harden*, 823, 895
Brute, *animal*, 366
  rude, 895
  maleficent, 913
Brute force, *illegality*, 964
Brute matter, *materiality*, 316
  inanimate matter, 358
Brutish, *vulgar*, 851, 876
  intemperate, 954
*Brutum fulmen, *impotence*,
                              158
  laxity, 738
Bubble, *air*, 353
  light, 320
  trifle, 643
  error, 495
  vision, 515
  deceit, 545
  excitement, 824
  flow, 348
Buccaneer, *thief*, 792
Buck, *leap*, 309
  to wash, 652
  fop, 854
  money, 800
Buck up, *hasten*, 274
  stimulate, 615
  cheer, 836
Bucket, *receptacle*, 191
Bucketful, *quantity*, 25
Buckle, *to tie*, 43
  vinculum, 45
  distort, 243
Buckle to, *apply oneself*, 682
Buckle with, *grapple*, 720
Buckler, *defence*, 666, 717
Buckram, *hardness*, 323
  affectation, 855
Buckshee, *superfluous*, 641
Bucolic, *domestication*, 370
  poem, 597
Bud, *beginning*, 66
  to expand, 194
  effect, 154
  graft, 300
Buddha, *deity*, 979
  religious founder, 986
Buddhism, *religions*, 984
Buddy, *friend*, 891
  associate, 88
Budge, *move*, 264
Budget, *heap*, 72
  store, 636

Budget, *news*, 523
  accounts, 811
Buff, *yellow*, 436
  grindstone, 331
Buffer, *defence*, 717
  fellow, 373
Buffet, *cupboard*, 191
  beat, 276, 972
Buffet car, *vehicle*, 272
*Buffo, *the drama*, 599
Buffoon, *humorist*, 844
  butt, 857
  actor, 599
Buffoonery, *amusement*, 840
  ridiculous, 856
Bugaboo, *fear*, 860
Bugbear, *fear*, 860
  alarm, 669
  imaginary, 515
Buggy, *vehicle*, 272
Bughouse, *insane*, 503
Bugle, *instrument*, 417
  war-cry, 722
Bugs, *insane*, 503
Buhl, *variegation*, 440
Build, *construct*, 161
  compose, 54
Build-up, *display*, 882
Build upon, *expect*, 507, 858
  count upon, 484
Builder, *producer*, 164
Building, *abode*, 189
Bulb, *knob*, 249, 250
Bulbous, *swollen*, 194
  rotund, 249
Bulge, *convexity*, 250
Bulimia, *desire*, 865
Bulk, *whole*, 50
  size, 192
Bulkhead, *hindrance*, 706
Bulky, *size*, 192
Bull, *absurdity*, 497, 853
  error, 495
  solecism, 568
  nonsense, 497, 517
  law, 963
  ordinance, 741
  police, 664
Bull-calf, *fool*, 501
Bulldog, *courage*, 861
  resolution, 604
Bullet, *ball*, 249
  missile, 284
  arms, 727
  swiftness, 274
Bullet-proof, *defence*, 717
Bulletin, *message*, 532
Bullion, *money*, 800
Bull's-eye, *middle*, 68
Bully, *bluster*, 885
  blusterer, 887
  fight, 726
  domineer, 739
  frighten, 860
  good, 648

Bulrush, *unimportance*, 643
Bulwark, *defence*, 717
  refuge, 666
Bum, *tramp*, 268, 876
  loafer, 683
  pauper, 804
  rascal, 949
Bumbledom, *authority*, 737
Bumboat, *ship*, 273
  provision, 637
Bumboatman, *trader*, 797
Bump, *projection*, 250
  thump, 276
Bump off, *kill*, 361
Bumper, *sufficiency*, 639
  fullness, 52
Bumpkin, *commonalty*, 876
Bumptious, *insolent*, 885
Bun-fight, *party*, 892
Bunce, *profit*, 618
Bunch, *protuberance*, 250
  collection, 72
Bundle, *packet*, 72
  to move, 275
Bung, *stopper*, 263
  throw, 284
Bung-ho, *departure*, 293
Bungalow, *abode*, 189
Bungle, *unskilfulness*, 699
  failure, 732
Bungler, *unskilful*, 701
Bunion, *swelling*, 250
Bunk, *bed*, 191, 215
  escape, 671
Bunker, *receptacle*, 191
  obstruction, 706
Bunkie, *friend*, 891
Bunkum, *humbug*, 545
  nonsense, 497
Bunt, *inversion*, 218
  deviate, 279
Bunting, *flag*, 550
Buoy, *float*, 320
  to raise, 307
  to hope, 858
Buoyant, *floating*, 305
  levity, 320
  elastic, 325
  hopeful, 858
  cheerful, 836
Bur, *rough*, 256
  clinging, 46
Burberry, *dress*, 225
Burden, *weight*, 319
  clog, 706
  chorus, 104, 415
  frequency, 136
  lading, 190
  care, 830
  oppression, 828
Bureau, *cabinet*, 691
  office, 799
Bureaucracy, *direction*, 693
  authority, 737
Burgee, *flag*, 550

Burgeon, *expansion*, 194
   increase, 35
Burgess, *citizen*, 188, 373
Burgher, *man*, 373
Burglar, *thief*, 792
Burglary, *stealing*, 791
Burgomaster, *master*, 745
Burgrave, *master*, 745
Burial, *corpse*, 362
Buried, *depth*, 208
Burin, *engraving*, 559
Burke, *kill*, 361
   destroy, 162
   suppress, 528
Burlesque, *imitation*, 19
   travesty, 21
   drama, 599
   ridicule, 856
   ridiculous, 853
Burletta, *the drama*, 599
Burly, *size*, 192
Burn, *heat*, 382
   consume, 384
   detection, 480
   passions, 821
   rivulet, 348
Burnish, *polish*, 255
   beautify, 845
   shine, 420
Burnous, *dress*, 225
Burp, *belch*, 297
Burrow, *excavate*, 252
   lodge, 186
Bursar, *treasurer*, 801
Bursary, *treasury*, 802
Burst, *explosion*, 173
   sound, 406
   of anger, 900
   paroxysm, 825
   spree, 840
   separate, 44
Burst forth, *appear*, 446
   sprout, 194
Burst out, *ejaculate*, 580
Burst upon, *inexpectation*, 508
Bury, *inter*, 363
   conceal, 528
Bus, *vehicle*, 272
Busby, *hat*, 225
Bush, *branch*, 51
   shrub, 367
Bushel, *receptacle*, 191
Bushy, *roughness*, 256
Business, *occupation*, 625
   event, 151
   topic, 454
   action, 680
   barter, 794
Business-like, *activity*, 682
   skilful, 698
   order, 58
Buskin, *dress*, 225
   drama, 599
Buss, *ship*, 272
   kiss, 902

Bustle, *activity*, 682
   agitation, 315
   haste, 684
   energy, 171
   earliness, 132
Busy, *activity*, 682
Busybody, *activity*, 682
   curiosity, 455
But, *exception*, 83, 179
   counter-evidence, 468
Butcher, *evildoer*, 913
Butchery, *killing*, 361
Butler, *servant*, 746
Butt, *aim*, 620
   laughing-stock, 857
   remnant, 40
   part, 51; *to push*, 276
   to attack, 716
Butt-end, *end*, 67
Butt in, *intervene*, 228
Butte, *height*, 206
Butter, *softness*, 324
   oiliness, 356
   to flatter, 933
Butter-fingers, *bungler*, 701
Butterfly, *beauty*, 845
   fickleness, 605
   fear, 860
Butterscotch, *sweet*, 396
Button, *knob*, 250
   to fasten, 43
   fastening, 45
   hanging, 214
   trifle, 643
Buttoned up, *reserved*, 528
   taciturn, 585
Buttonhole, *ornament*, 847
   accost, 586
Buttonholer, *weariness*, 841
Buttons, *servant*, 746
Buttress, *support*, 215
   defence, 717
   strengthen, 159
Buxom, *plump*, 192
   cheerful, 836
Buy, *purchase*, 795
Buzz, *sound*, 409, 412
   to publish, 531
   news, 532
Buzz-bomb, *arms*, 727
Buzz off, *depart*, 293
Buzzard, *fool*, 501
By and by, *transientness*, 111
By fits and starts, *disorder*, 59
   irregularity, 139
By jingo, *affirmation*, 535
By-law, *legality*, 963
By-name, *misnomer*, 565
By the by, *opportunity*, 134
Bye-bye, *departure*, 293
   sleep, 683
Bygone, *former*, 122
   forgotten, 506
Bypath, *road*, 627
Byplay, *gesture*, 550

Byssus, *roughness*, 256
Bystander, *spectator*, 444
   near, 197
Byway, *road*, 627
Byword, *maxim*, 496
   cant term, 563
   contempt, 930

C

C.A., *accounts*, 811
C.O.D., *payment*, 807
Ca' canny, *caution*, 864
Cab, *vehicle*, 272
   translation, 522
Cabal, *confederacy*, 712
   plan, 626
Cabbage, *purloin*, 791
Cabbala, *spell*, 993
Cabbalistic, *mysterious*, 528
Caber, *missile*, 284
Cabin, *room*, 189
   receptacle, 191
Cabin cruiser, *ship*, 273
Cabinet, *receptacle*, 191
   workshop, 691
   council, 696
Cable, *vinculum*, 45
Cabriolet, *vehicle*, 272
Cache, *hiding-place*, 530
   conceal, 528
   store, 636
Cachexy, *disease*, 655
   weakness, 160
Cachinnation, *rejoicing*, 838
Cachucha, *dance*, 840
Cacique, *master*, 745
Cackle, *of geese*, 412
   talk, 588
   laughter, 838
Cacodemon, *demon*, 980
Cacodyl, *fetor*, 401
*Cacoethes, *habit*, 613
   itch, 865
   writing, 590
*Cacoethes loquendi,
   loquacity, 584
*Cacoethes scribendi,
   writing, 590
Cacography, *writing*, 590
Cacophony, *stridor*, 410
   discord, 414
   style, 579
Cad, *vulgarity*, 851
Cadastre, *list*, 86
Cadaverous, *corpse*, 362
   pale, 429
   thin, 203
   hideous, 846
Caddish, *mean*, 940
Caddy, *receptacle*, 191
Cadence, *accent*, 580
   music, 415
   descent, 306
Cadenza, *music*, 415

Catastrophe, *convulsion*, 146
Catch, *take*, 134, 789
   receive, 785
   learn, 539
   gather meaning, 518
   cheat, 545
   vinculum, 45
Catch at, *receiving*, 785
Catch on, *success*, 731
Catch up, *overtake*, 292
Catching, *infectious*, 657
Catchpenny, *trumpery*, 643
   cheap, 815
   false, 544
Catchpoll, *jurisprudence*, 965
Catchword, *formula*, 80
   maxim, 496
Catechetical, *inquiry*, 461
Catechize, *inquiry*, 461
Catechumen, *learner*, 541
Categorical, *true*, 494
   positive, 474
   demonstrative, 478
   affirmative, 535
Category, *class*, 75
   arrangement, 60
   state, 7
Catenary, *curve*, 245
Catenation, *continuity*, 69
Cater, *provision*, 637
Caterwauling, *cry*, 412
   discord, 414
Cates, *food*, 298
Cathedral, *temple*, 1000
Catholic, *universal*, 78
   Christian, 983A
   broad-minded, 498
Catholicity, *generality*, 78
   broad-mindedness, 498
Catholicon, *remedy*, 662
Cat's-cradle, *crossing*, 219
Cat's-paw, *instrument*, 631
   dupe, 547
Cattle-lifting, *stealing*, 791
Cattle-truck, *vehicle*, 272
Caucus, *assemblage*, 72
Caudal, *end*, 67
Caudate, *pendency*, 214
Cauldron, *mixture*, 41
   vessel, 191
   heating, 386
   laboratory, 691
Caulk, *repair*, 658
Causality, *cause*, 153
   power, 157
Causation, *cause*, 153
   agency, 170
Cause, *source*, 153
   final, 620
   lawsuit, 969
Causeless, *casual*, 156
   aimless, 621
Causerie, *chat*, 588
*Causeur, *talker*, 588
Causeway, *road*, 627

Causidical, *juridical*, 965
Caustic, *feeling*, 821
   painful, 830
   gruff, 895
   disapproving, 932
   malevolent, 907
Cautelous, *caution*, 864
Cauterize, *calefaction*, 384
Caution, *care*, 459
   warning, 668
   prudence, 864
   advice, 695
   security, 771
Cavalcade, *continuity*, 69
Cavalier, *horseman*, 268
   insolent, 885
   discourteous, 895
   contemptuous, 930
*Cavaliere servente, *lover*, 897
Cavalierly, *inattention*, 458
Cavalry, *combatant*, 726
*Cavatina, *music*, 415
Cave, *cavity*, 252
   cell, 191
   dwelling, 189
   warning, 668
   care, 459
Cave in, *submit*, 729
Caveat, *warning*, 668
Cavendish, *tobacco*, 298A
Cavern, *hollow*, 252
   cell, 191
   dwelling, 189
Cavernous, *hollow*, 252
   porous, 322
Caviare, *pungent*, 171, 392
Cavil, *censure*, 932
   dissent, 489
   split hairs, 477
Caviller, *detractor*, 936
Cavity, *concavity*, 252
Cavort, *prance*, 315
Caw, *animal cry*, 412
Cayenne, *condiment*, 393
   pungent, 171
Cease, *cessation*, 142
Ceaseless, *perpetuity*, 112
Cecity, *blindness*, 442
Cede, *relinquish*, 782
Ceiling, *height*, 206
   summit, 210
   covering, 222
*Cela va sans dire, *conformity*,
                  82
   effect, 154
Celebrant, *worship*, 990
Celebrate, *solemnize*, 883
   publish, 531
   praise, 931
Celebration, *fête*, 883
   rite, 998
. Celebrity, *repute*, 873
   nobility, 875
Celerity, *velocity*, 274
Celestial, *physical*, 318

Celestial, *moral*, 829
   religious, 976, 981
   angelic, 977
Celibacy, *bachelor*, 904
Cell, *cavity*, 252
   receptacle, 191
   abode, 189
   prison, 752
Cellar, *room*, 191
   store, 636
   lowness, 207
Cellaret, *receptacle*, 191
Cellular, *concavity*, 252
Cellule, *receptacle*, 191
Celsius, *thermometer*, 389
Cembalo, *musical instrument*,
                 417
Cement, *connective*, 45
   to unite, 46
   concord, 714
Cemetery, *interment*, 363
Cenobite, *recluse*, 893
   anchoret, 996
Cenotaph, *interment*, 363
Censer, *temple*, 1000
Censor, *detractor*, 936
   inhibit, 616
Censorious, *disapprobation*, 932
Censorship, *authority*, 737
   secret, 533
Censure, *disapprobation*, 932
Census, *counting*, 85
   list, 86
Centaur, *unconformity*, 83
Centenary, *numbers*, 98
   celebration, 883
Centennial, *numbers*, 98
   period, 108, 138
Centesimal, *hundred*, 98
Centigrade, *thermometer*, 389
Cento, *poetry*, 597
Central, *centrality*, 223
Centralize, *combine*, 48
   focus, 72
   concentrate, 223
Centre, *in order*, 68
   in space, 223
Centre in, *convergence*, 290
Centrifugal, *divergence*, 291
Centripetal, *convergence*, 290
Centuple, *number*, 98
Centurion, *master*, 745
Century, *period*, 108
   duration, 106
Ceramic, *sculpture*, 557
Cerberus, *janitor*, 263
   custodian, 664
Cerebration, *thought*, 451
Cerebrum, *intellect*, 450
Cerement, *interment*, 363
Ceremonious, *respect*, 928
Ceremony, *parade*, 882
   religious, 998
Ceres, *botany*, 369
Cerise, *red*, 434

Charter, *compact*, 769
   security, 771
   commission, 755
Charwoman, *clean*, 652
Chary, *economical*, 817
   cautious, 864
Chase, *pursue*, 622
   follow, 281
   shape, 240
   adorn, 847
   convexity, 250
   wood, 367
Chasm, *discontinuity*, 4, 70
   interval, 198
Chassis, *framework*, 215
Chaste, *simple*, 576, 849
   good taste, 850
   symmetry, 242
   pure, 960
   innocent, 946
   style, 576
Chasten, *punish*, 972
   refine, 658
   moderate, 826
Chastise, *punish*, 932, 972
Chasuble, *vestments*, 999
Chat, *interlocution*, 588
Château, *abode*, 189
Chatelaine, *ornament*, 847
*Chatoyant, *variegation*, 440
Chattels, *goods*, 635
   property, 780
Chatter, *talk*, 584
   cold, 383
Chatterbox, *loquacity*, 584
Chauffeur, *driver*, 694
Chauvinistic, *bellicose*, 722
   boasting, 884
Chaw, *food*, 298
Chaw-bacon, *boor*, 876
Cheap, *low price*, 815
   worthless, 643
Cheapen, *barter*, 794
   depreciate, 483
Cheat, *deceiver*, 548
   to deceive, 545
Check, *restrain*, 174, 751
   pacify, 826
   slacken, 275
   counteract, 179
   hinder, 706
   impediment, 135
   dissuade, 616
   test, 463
   evidence, 467
   ticket, 550
   money order, 800
   numerical, 85
   variegate, 440
Checkmate, *success*, 731
Cheek, *side*, 236
   insolence, 885
   discourtesy, 895
Cheer, *mirth*, 836
   rejoicing, 838

Cheer, *amusement*, 840
   pleasure, 827
   to give pleasure, 829
   relief, 834
   cry, 411
   repast, 298
   applaud, 931
   aid, 707
   inspirit, 861
Cheered, *pleasure*, 827
Cheerful, *pleasurable*, 836
Cheerio, *departure*, 293
Cheerless, *dejection*, 830, 837
Cheers, *drink*, 959
Cheese-parings, *remainder*, 40
   parsimony, 819
Cheesed off, *bored*, 841
   sated, 869
Chef, *director*, 694
*Chef-d'œuvre, *masterpiece*, 650
   capability, 648
   master-stroke, 698
Cheka, *detective*, 461
Chela, *novice*, 541
Chemise, *dress*, 225
Chemistry, *conversion*, 144
Cheque, *money*, 800
Chequer, *variegation*, 440
Cherish, *love*, 897
   aid, 707
   entertain, 820
Cheroot, *tobacco*, 298A
Cherry, *red*, 434
Cherub, *angel*, 977
Chessboard, *variegated*, 440
Chest, *box*, 191
   money-box, 802
Chest-note, *resonance*, 408
Chesterfield, *seat*, 215
Chesterfieldian, *courtesy*, 894
Chestnut, *brown*, 433
   joke, 842
Cheval-glass, *mirror*, 445
*Chevalier d'industrie, *thief*, 792
Chevaux-de-frise, *defence*, 717
   spikes, 253
*Chevelure, *hair*, 256
Chevron, *indication*, 550
Chew, *eat*, 296
   tobacco, 298A
Chew the cud, *thought*, 451
*Chez soi, *at home*, 221
Chiaroscuro, *shade*, 424
Chibouque, *tobacco-pipe*, 298A
Chic, *beauty*, 845
Chicane, *cunning*, 702
   deception, 545
Chicanery, *sophistry*, 477
   deception, 545
   wrangling, 713
Chicken, *youth*, 127
   weakness, 160
   cowardice, 862
Chicken feed, *money*, 800
Chicken-hearted, *cowardice*, 862

Chide, *disapprobation*, 932
Chief, *principal*, 642
   master, 745
Chieftain, *master*, 745
Chiffon, *ornament*, 847
Chignon, *head-dress*, 225
Chilblain, *swelling*, 250
Child, *youth*, 129
   fool, 501
   offspring, 167
Childish, *foolish*, 499
   banal, 575
   trifling, 643
Child's play, *unimportance*, 643
   easy, 705
Chiliad, *numbers*, 98
   duration, 106
Chill, *cold*, 383
   discouragement, 616, 706
Chilly, *ungracious*, 895
Chime, *resonance*, 408
   roll, 407
   repetition, 104
   to harmonize, 413
Chime in with, *agree*, 23
   conformity, 82
   assent, 488
Chimera, *monster*, 83
   error, 495
   imaginary, 515
Chimerical, *impossible*, 471
Chimney, *air-pipe*, 351
   fissure, 198
   opening, 260
   egress, 295
Chin-chin, *departure*, 293
Chink, *gap*, 198
   opening, 260
   sound, 408
   money, 800
Chip, *bit*, 51
   small part, 193
   to detach, 44
   to reduce, 195
Chip in, *interpose*, 228
   conversation, 588
Chip of the old block, *similarity*,
   17
Chipper, *gay*, 836
   healthy, 654
Chirography, *writing*, 590
Chiromancy, *prediction*, 511
Chirp, *bird cry*, 412
   sing, 415
Chirpy, *cheerful*, 836
Chirrup, *see* Chirp
Chisel, *sculpture*, 557
   sharpness, 253
   form, 240
   fabricate, 161
Chit, *infant*, 129
   small, 193
   letter, 592
Chit-chat, *colloquy*, 588
Chivalrous, *martial*, 722

Chivalrous, *honourable*, 939
  bold, 861
  generous, 942
Chivy, *chase*, 622
Chloral, *anaesthetic*, 376
Chlorosis, *achromatism*, 429
Chlorotic, *achromatism*, 429
Chock-full, *sufficiency*, 639
  fullness, 52
Chocolate, *brown*, 433
  sweet, 396
Choice, *election*, 609
  excellent, 648
Choir, *music*, 415
  orchestra, 416
  church, 1000
Choke, *close*, 261
  hinder, 706
  surfeit, 641
  suffocate, 361
Choke off, *dissuade*, 616
Chokka, *bored*, 841
  sated, 869
Choky, *prison*, 752
Choler, *resentment*, 900
Choleric, *irascible*, 901
Choose, *choice*, 609
  will, 600
Choosy, *particular*, 868
Chop, *disjoin*, 44
  change, 140
  barter, 794
  wave, 348
  sign, 550
Chop logic, *reasoning*, 476
Chopping, *large*, 192
Chops, *orifice*, 66
Choral, *music*, 415
Chord, *harmony*, 413
Chore, *business*, 625
Choreography, *dance*, 840
Chorister, *musician*, 416
  clergy, 996
Chorography, *situation*, 183, 554
Chortle, *to laugh*, 838
Chorus, *sound*, 404
  voices, 411
  musicians, 416
  unanimity, 488
*Chose jugée, *judgment*, 480
*Chota hazri, *food*, 298
Chouse, *deception*, 545
Chrism, *rite*, 998
CHRIST, *Deity*, 976
Christen, *nomenclature*, 564
Christendom, *Christianity*, 983A
Christian, *piety*, 987
  Christianity, 983A
Christianity, *Christian religion*,
  983A
Christmas box, *gift*, 784
Chromatic, *colour*, 428
  musical scale, 413
Chromatrope, *optical instrument*,
  445

Chromolithograph, *engraving*,
  558
Chronic, *diuturnity*, 110
Chronicle, *annals*, 551
  measure of time, 114
  account, 594
Chronicler, *recorder*, 553
*Chronique scandaleuse,
  gossip, 532, 588
Chronology, *time measurement*,
  114
Chronometry, *time measurement*,
  114
Chrysalis, *youth*, 127, 129
Chubby, *size*, 192
Chuck, *throw*, 284
  desist, 142
  cry, 412
  food, 298
Chuck out, *expel*, 297
Chuck up, *abandon*, 624
Chucker-out, *doorkeeper*, 263
Chuckle, *laugh*, 838
  exult, 884
Chuckle-head, *fool*, 501
Chum, *friend*, 890
Chummy, *friendly*, 888
Chunk, *size*, 192
  part, 51
Chunky, *short*, 201
  broad, 202
Church, *Christian religion*, 983A
  temple, 1000
Churchdom, *churchdom*, 995
Churchman, *clergy*, 996
Churchwarden, *clergy*, 996
  tobacco-pipe, 298A
Churchy, *bigoted*, 988
Churchyard, *interment*, 363
Churl, *boor*, 876
  rude, 895
  irascible, 901
  niggard, 819
Churn, *agitation*, 315, 352
Chute, *obliquity*, 217
Chutney, *condiment*, 393
Chyle, *fluid*, 333
Chyme, *semiliquid*, 352
Cicatrize, *improvement*, 658
Cicerone, *teacher*, 540
  director, 694
*Cicisbeo, *love*, 897
*Ci-devant, *preterition*, 122
Cigar, *tobacco*, 298A
Cigar-case, *receptacle*, 191
Cigar-shaped, *rotund*, 249
Cigarette, *tobacco*, 298A
Cigarette-case, *receptacle*, 191
Ciliated, *roughness*, 256
Cimmerian, *darkness*, 421
Cinch, *grip*, 781
  connection, 45
  easy, 705
Cincture, *circularity*, 247
Cinders, *remainder*, 40

Cine-camera, *lens*, 445
Cinema, *theatre*, 599A
  amusement, 840
Cinemaddict, *cinema*, 599A
Cinematograph, *show*, 448
Cinerary, *burial*, 363
Cineration, *calefaction*, 384
Cinerator, *furnace*, 386
Cinereous, *grey*, 432
Cingulum, *belt*, 229
Cinnabar, *red*, 434
Cinque, *numbers*, 98
Cipher, *zero*, 101
  number, 84
  to compute, 85
  secret, 533
  mark, 550
  writing, 590
  unimportant, 643
Circe, *seductor*, 615
  sensuality, 954
Circle, *form*, 247
  curvature, 245
  space, 181
  theatre, 599
  party, 712
  social, 892
Circuit, *deviation*, 279
  indirect path, 629
  winding, 248
  turn, 311
  tour, 266
  space, 181
Circuitous, *devious*, 279
  turning, 311
  indirect, 629
Circular, *round*, 247
  curved, 245
  advertisement, 531
  letter, 592
Circulate, *rotate*, 312
  publish, 531
Circumambient, *circumjacence*,
  227
Circumambulate, *move*, 266
  wind, 311
Circumbendibus, *winding*, 248
  circuit, 629
  circuition, 311
Circumference, *outline*, 229
Circumfluent, *circuition*, 311
Circumfuse, *dispersion*, 73
Circumgyration, *rotation*, 312
Circumjacence, *surrounding*, 227
Circumlocution, *phrase*, 566, 573
Circumnavigation, *navigation*,
  267
  circuition, 311
Circumrotation, *rotation*, 312
Circumscribe, *surround*, 231
  limit, 761
Circumspect, *attentive*, 457
  careful, 459
  cautious, 864
Circumstance, *phrase*, 8

Circumstance, *event*, 151
Circumstantial, *diffuse*, 573
   evidence, 472
Circumvallation, *enclosure*, 232
   defence, 717
Circumvent, *cheat*, 545
   defeat, 731
   cunning, 702
Circumvolution, *rotation*, 312
Circus, *arena*, 728
   amusement, 840
   edifice, 189
Cistern, *receptacle*, 191
   store, 636
Citadel, *fort*, 666
   defence, 717
Cite, *quote as example*, 82, 564
   as evidence, 467
   summon, 741
   accuse, 938
   arraign, 969
Cithern, *musical instrument*, 417
Citizen, *inhabitant*, 188
   man, 373
Citrine, *yellow*, 436
City, *abode*, 189
Civet, *fragrance*, 400
Civic, *urban*, 189
   public, 372
Civicism, *patriotism*, 910
Civil, *courteous*, 894
   laity, 997
Civilian, *lawyer*, 968
   non-combatant, 726A
Civilization, *courtesy*, 894
   mankind, 372
Civvies, *dress*, 225
Clachan, *village*, 189
Clack, *talk*, 588
   snap, 406
   animal cry, 412
Clad, *dressed*, 225
Claim, *demand*, 741, 765
   property, 780
   right, 924
Claimant, *dueness*, 924
   petitioner, 767
Clairvoyance, *occult arts*, 992
   insight, 490
   foresight, 510
Clam, *taciturn*, 585
Clamant, *cry*, 411
Clamber, *ascent*, 305
Clammy, *semiliquid*, 352
Clamour, *loudness*, 404, 411
Clamp, *to fasten*, 43
   fastening, 45
Clamp down, *restrict*, 751
Clan, *class*, 75; *kindred*, 11
   clique, 892
Clandestine, *concealment*, 528
   secret, 534
Clang, *loudness*, 404
   resonance, 408
Clanger, *error*, 495, 732

Clanger, *solecism*, 568
Clank, *harsh sound*, 410
Clannishness, *prejudice*, 481
   co-operation, 709
Clap, *explosion*, 406
   to applaud, 931
Clap on, *addition*, 37
Clap up, *restraint*, 751
Clapperclaw, *beat*, 972
Claptrap, *plea*, 617
   pretence, 546
   sophistry, 477
   nonsense, 492
*Claqueur, *flatterer*, 935
Clarence, *vehicle*, 272
Clarify, *cleanness*, 652
Clarinet, *musical instrument*,
   417
Clarion, *musical instrument*, 417
Clarity, *transparency*, 425
   perspicuity, 570
Clart, *mud*, 352
   dirt, 653
Clash, *oppose*, 708
   disagree, 24
   discord, 713
   contest, 720
   concussion, 276
   sound, 406
   chatter, 584
Clasp, *to unite*, 43
   fastening, 45
   entrance, 903
   come close, 197
Clasp-knife, *sharpness*, 253
Class, *category*, 75
   to arrange, 60
   learner, 541
Classic, *masterpiece*, 650
   symmetry, 242
   ancient, 124
Classical, *taste*, 578, 580
Classify, *arrangement*, 60
   class, 75
Clatter, *roll*, 407
   din, 404
Clause, *part*, 51
   passage, 593
   condition, 770
Claustral, *secluded*, 893
Claustrophobia, *dislike*, 867
   seclusion, 893
Clavichord, *musical*, 417
Claw, *hook*, 633
   to grasp, 789
Clay, *earth*, 342
   corpse, 362
   tobacco-pipe, 298A
Clay-cold, *cold*, 383
Claymore, *arms*, 727
Clean, *unstained*, 652
   entirely, 31
Clean-handed, *innocence*, 946
Cleanse, *purge*, 652
Clear, *transparent*, 425

Clear, *light*, 420
   visible, 446
   intelligible, 518
   perspicuous style, 570
   to prepare, 673
   to free, 750
   to vindicate, 937
   to acquit, 970
   innocent, 946
   simple, 42
   easy, 705
   to pay, 807
   to pass, 302
Clear decks, *prepare*, 673
Clear of, *distant*, 196
Clear out, *eject*, 297
   depart, 203
Clear-sighted, *vision*, 441
   shrewd, 498
Clear up, *interpret*, 518, 522
Clearance, *payment*, 807
Clearway, *way*, 627
Cleave, *adhere*, 46
   sunder, 44, 91
Cleek, *club*, 276
Clef, *music*, 413
Cleft, *chink*, 198
Clem, *starve*, 956
Clement, *lenient*, 740
   kind, 906
   pitiful, 914
Clench, see Clinch
Clepsydra, *chronometry*, 114
Clergy, *clergy*, 996
Clerical, *churchdom*, 995
Clerihew, *drollery*, 853
   absurdity, 497
Clerk, *scholar*, 492
   recorder, 553
   writer, 590
   servant, 746
   agent, 758; *church*, 996
Clerkship, *commission*, 755
Clever, *skill*, 698
Cliché, *platitude*, 497
Click, *snap*, 406
Client, *dependant*, 746
   buyer, 795
   frequenter, 136
Clientship, *subjection*, 749
Cliff, *height*, 206
   verticality, 212, 217
Cliff-hanging, *suspense*, 485
Climacteric, *age*, 128
Climate, *region*, 181
   weather, 338
Climax, *summit*, 210
   completion, 729
   increase, 35
   in degree, 33
Climb, *ascent*, 305
Clime, *region*, 181
Clinch, *snatch*, 789
   fasten, 43
   close, 261

*Cocotte, *prostitute*, 962
Coction, *calefaction*, 384
Cocytus, *hell*, 982
Coda, *end*, 67
Code, *law*, 963
   precept, 697
   secret, 533
   signal, 550
Codex, *book*, 593
Codger, *parsimony*, 819
Codicil, *adjunct*, 39
   sequel, 65
Codify, *legality*, 963
Codswallop, *nonsense*, 643
Coefficient, *co-operating*, 709
   accompanying, 88
   factor, 84
Coemption, *purchase*, 795
Coenobite, *seclusion*, 893
Coequal, *equality*, 27
Coerce, *restrain*, 751
   compel, 744
   dissuade, 616
Coessential, *identity*, 13
Coetaneous, *synchronism*, 120
Coeternal, *perpetuity*, 112
Coeval, *synchronism*, 120
Coexist, *synchronism*, 120
   accompany, 88
   contiguity, 199
Coextension, *equality*, 27
   parallelism, 216
Coffee-house, *food*, 298
Coffer, *chest*, 191
   money-chest, 802
   store, 636
Coffin, *interment*, 363
Coffin-nail, *tobacco*, 298A
Cog, *tooth*, 253; *ship*, 273
   deceive, 545
   flatter, 933
Cogent, *powerful*, 157
   argument, 467, 476
Cogitate, *thought*, 451
Cognate, *rule*, 80
   relation, 9
Cognation, *relation*, 9
Cognition, *knowledge*, 490
Cognizance, *knowledge*, 490
Cognomen, *nomenclature*, 564
Cognoscence, *knowledge*, 490
*Cognoscente, *taste*, 850
Cognoscible, *knowledge*, 490
Cohabitation, *marriage*, 903
Co-heir, *partner*, 778
Cohere, *unite*, 46
   dense, 321
Cohesive, *uniting*, 46
   dense, 321
   tenacious, 327
Cohibition, *restraint*, 751
Cohort, *combatant*, 726
Coif, *dress*, 225
Coiffure, *dress*, 225
Coil, *convolution*, 248

Coil, *circuition*, 311
   disorder, 59
Coin, *money*, 800
   to fabricate, 161
   to imagine, 515
Coincidence, *identity*, 13
   in time, 120
   in place, 199
   in opinion, 488
Coinstantaneity, *synchronism*, 120
Coke, *fuel*, 388
Colander, *opening*, 260
Cold, *frigidity*, 383
   style, 575
   insensible, 823
   indifferent, 866
Cold-blooded, *malevolent*, 907
   dispassionate, 823, 826
Cold-hearted, *enmity*, 889
Cold-shoulder, *exclusion*, 893
   repulsion, 289
Cold war, *truce*, 723
Coliseum, *arena*, 728
Collaborate, *accompany*, 88
   co-operate, 178, 709
Collapse, *contraction*, 195
   prostration, 160
   fatigue, 688
   incapacity, 158
   failure, 732
Collar, *dress*, 225
   shackle, 749, 752
   seize, 789
Collate, *compare*, 464
Collateral, *relation*, 11
   lateral, 236
   consequential, 467
Collation, *food*, 299
   comparison, 464
Colleague, *auxiliary*, 711
   co-operating, 709
Collect, *assemble*, 72
   take, 789
   acquire, 775
   learn, 539
   opine, 480
   understand, 518
   prayer, 990
Collectanea, *assemblage*, 72
   compendium, 596
Collected, *calm*, 826
Collection, *store*, 636
   offering, 990
   assemblage, 72
Collectiveness, *whole*, 50
Collectivism, *participation*, 780
   authority, 737
Collector, *assemblage*, 72
Colleen, *woman*, 374
   girl, 129
College, *school*, 542
Collide, *see* Collision
Collier, *ship*, 273
   man, 373

Colligate, *assemblage*, 72
Colligation, *junction*, 43
Collimation, *direction*, 278
Collimator, *optical instrument*, 445
Collision, *approach*, 286
   percussion, 276
   clashing, 179
   opposition, 708
   encounter, 720
Collocate, *arrange*, 60
   assemble, 72
Collocution, *interlocution*, 588
Collogue, *confer*, 588
Colloid, *semiliquid*, 352
Collop, *part*, 51
Colloquialism, *language*, 560
Colloquy, *interlocution*, 588
Collotype, *engraving*, 558
Collusion, *deceit*, 545
   concurrence, 178
   conspiring, 709
Colon, *stop*, 142
Colonel, *master*, 745
Colonize, *location*, 184, 188
Colonnade, *continuity*, 69
Colony, *region*, 181
   settlement, 184, 188
Colophon, *end*, 67
   sequel, 65
Coloration, *colour*, 428
*Coloratura, *music*, 415
Colossal, *size*, 192
   height, 206
Colour, *hue*, 428
   plea, 617
   disguise, 545
   qualify, 469
   to blush, 434
Colourable, *deceptive*, 545
   ostensible, 472
Colouring, *meaning*, 516
   exaggeration, 549
Colourless, *achromatism*, 429
Colours, *standard*, 550
   decoration, 877
Colporteur, *agent*, 758
Colt, *fool*, 501
   horse, 271
Column, *series*, 69
   height, 206
   monument, 551
   cylinder, 249
   procession, 266
   troop, 726
Colure, *universe*, 318
Coma, *insensibility*, 376, 823
   inactivity, 683
Comb, *sharpness*, 253
Combat, *contention*, 720, 722
Combatant, *contention*, 726
Comber, *wave*, 348
Combination, *union*, 48
Combinations, *arithmetical*, 84
   dress, 225

Crucify, *painfulness*, 830
  execution, 972
Crude, *unprepared*, 674
  inelegant, 579
Cruel, *painful*, 830
  inhuman, 907
Cruet, *receptacle*, 191
Cruise, *navigation*, 267
Cruiser, *ship*, 273
Crumb, *small part*, 51
  grain, 193
  powder, 330
  bit, 32
Crumble, *pulverize*, 330
  destroy, 162
  diminish, 36
  spoil, 659
  brittleness, 328
Crumple, *ruffle*, 256
  crease, 258
  contract, 195
Crunch, *bruise*, 44
  masticate, 297
  pulverize, 330
Crupper, *rear*, 235
Crusade, *warfare*, 722
Cruse, *vessel*, 191
Crush, *pulverize*, 330
  destroy, 162
  injure, 649
  humiliate, 879
  pain, 828
  contract, 195
  love, 897
Crust, *covering*, 222
  insolence, 885
Crusty, *discourtesy*, 895
Crutch, *support*, 215
  angle, 244
  instrument, 633
Crux, *question*, 461
  mystery, 533
Cry, *animal*, 412
  human, 411
  loudness, 404
  voice, 580
  publish, 531
  weep, 839
Cry down, *disapprove*, 932
Cry for, *desire*, 865
Cry to, *beseech*, 765
Cry up, *praise*, 931
Crypt, *cell*, 191
  hide, 530
  grave, 363
  altar, 1000
Cryptic, *latent*, 526, 528
Cryptogram, *cipher*, 533
Cryptography, *writing*, 590
Crystal-gazing, *prediction*, 511
Crystalline, *dense*, 321
  transparent, 425
Cub, *young*, 129
  clown, 876
Cube, *triality*, 92

Cube, *angularity*, 244
Cubist, *artist*, 559
Cuckold, *divorce*, 905
Cuckoo, *repetition*, 104
  imitation, 19
  cry, 412
  fool, 501
  insane, 503
Cuddle, *caress*, 902
Cuddy, *carrier*, 271
Cudgel, *beat*, 975
  bludgeon, 276, 727
Cue, *hint*, 527
  watchword, 550
  plea, 617
Cuff, *beat*, 276, 972
  dress, 225
*Cui bono, *utility*, 644
Cuirass, *defence*, 717
Cuirassier, *combatant*, 726
Cuisine, *food*, 298
*Cul-de-lampe, *tail-piece*, 67
Cul-de-sac, *concavity*, 252
  closure, 261
  difficulty, 704
*Culbute, *inversion*, 218
  descent, 306
Culinary, *food*, 298
Cull, *choice*, 609
  take, 789
Cullender, *sieve*, 260
Cullion, *wretch*, 941, 949
Cully, *dupe*, 547
Culminate, *maximum*, 33
  height, 206, 210
Culmination, *completion*, 729
Culpability, *guilt*, 947
Culpable, *vice*, 945
Culprit, *sinner*, 949
Cult, *worship*, 990
  rite, 998
Cultivate, *improve*, 658
  sensitiveness, 375
  taste, 850
  till, 371
Culture, *tillage*, 371
  taste, 850
  teaching, 537
  knowledge, 490
Culverin, *arms*, 727
Culvert, *conduit*, 350
*Cum grano salis, *qualify*, 469
  unbelief, 485
Cumber, *load*, 319
  to incommode, 647
  to obstruct, 706
Cummer, *friend*, 891
Cummerbund, *girdle*, 247
Cumshaw, *gift*, 784
Cumulation, *assemblage*, 72
Cumulative, *increase*, 35
  addition, 37
Cumulus, *cloud*, 353
Cunctation, *delay*, 133
  inactivity, 683

Cuneiform, *angular*, 244
  writing, 590
Cunning, *art*, 702
  sagacity, 698
  well-planned, 626
Cup, *hollow*, 252
  vessel, 191
Cupboard, *receptacle*, 191
Cupid, *beauty*, 845
  love, 897
Cupidity, *avarice*, 819
  desire, 865
Cupola, *dome*, 250
  height, 206
Cur, *knave*, 949
Curable, *improvement*, 658
Curacy, *churchdom*, 995
Curate, *clergy*, 996
Curative, *remedial*, 834
Curator, *consignee*, 758
Curb, *restrain*, 751
  hinder, 706
  shackle, 752
  moderate, 174
  check, 826
  dissuade, 616
  counteract, 179
  slacken, 275
Curd, *mass*, 46
  density, 321
  pulp, 354
Curdle, *condense*, 321
  coagulate, 46, 352
Cure, *remedy*, 662, 834
  reinstate, 660
  religious, 995
  preserve, 670
  improve, 656
 *Curé, *priest*, 996
Curfew, *evening*, 126
Curio, *toy*, 643
*Curiosa felicitas, *elegance*, 578
Curiosity, *curiosity*, 455
  phenomenon, 872
Curious, *true*, 494
  exceptional, 83
Curl, *bend*, 245, 248
  cockle up, 258
Curlicue, *convolution*, 248
Curliewurlie, *convolution*, 248
Curmudgeon, *parsimony*, 819
Currency, *publicity*, 531
  money, 800
Current, *existing*, 1
  present, 118
  happening, 151
  stream, 347
  river, 348
  wind, 349
  course, 109
  danger, 667
  opinion, 484
  public, 531
  prevailing, 82
*Currente calamo, *diffuseness*, 573

Debacle, *destruction*, 162

Debag, *divest*, 226

Debar, *prohibit*, 761
  hinder, 751
  exclude, 77

Debark, *arrive*, 292

Debase, *depress*, 308
  deteriorate, 659
  foul, 653
  vicious, 945

Debatable, *uncertain*, 475

Debate, *reason*, 476
  dispute, 713, 720
  hesitate, 605
  talk, 508

Debauch, *spoil*, 659
  vice, 945
  intemperance, 954
  impurity, 961

Debenture, *certificate*, 551
  security, 771
  credit, 805

Debility, *weakness*, 160

Debit, *debt*, 806
  accounts, 811

Debonair, *cheerfulness*, 836

Debouch, *march out*, 292
  flow out, 295, 348

Debrett, *list*, 86

Debris, *part*, 51
  pulverulence, 330
  unimportance, 643

Debt, *debt*, 806

Debtor, *debt*, 806

Debus, *arrival*, 292

Début, *beginning*, 66

Decade, *number*, 98
  period, 108
  duration, 106

Decadence, *deterioration*, 659

Decadent, *feeble*, 575

Decagon, *number*, 98
  angularity, 244

Decahedron, *ten*, 98

Decalogue, *duty*, 926

Decamp, *move off*, 287, 293
  escape, 671

Decant, *transfer to*, 270

Decanter, *receptacle*, 191

Decapitate, *kill*, 361, 972

Decay, *spoil*, 659
  disease, 655
  shrivel, 195
  decrease, 36

Decayed, *imperfect*, 651
  old, 124
  adversity, 735

Decease, *death*, 360

Deceit, *deception*, 544, 545

Deceiver, *deceiver*, 548

Decent, *modest*, 960
  tolerable, 651
  seemly, 926
  right, 922

Decentralize, *disperse*, 73

Deception, *deception*, 545
  sophistry, 477

Decide, *judge*, 480
  choose, 609
  make certain, 474
  cause, 153

Decided, *resolved*, 604
  positive, 535
  certain, 475
  great, 31

Deciduous, *transitory*, 111
  falling, 306
  spoiled, 659

Decimal, *number*, 84, 98

Decimate, *subduct*, 38, 103
  kill, 361

Decipher, *interpret*, 522
  solve, 462

Decision, *intention*, 620
  conclusion, 480
  resolution, 604
  verdict, 969

Decisive, *final*, 67
  evidence, 467
  resolution, 604
  demonstration, 478

Decivilize, *brutalize*, 895

Deck, *floor*, 211
  to beautify, 845

Declaim, *speech*, 582

Declamatory, *florid*, 577

Declare, *assert*, 535
  inform, 516, 527

Declension, *descent*, 306
  deterioration, 659
  grammar, 567
  intrinsicality, 5

Decline, *decrease*, 36
  descent, 306
  weaken, 160
  decay, 735
  disease, 655
  become worse, 659
  reject, 610
  refuse, 764
  be unwilling, 603
  grammar, 567

Declivity, *obliquity*, 217

Decoction, *calefaction*, 384

Decode, *interpret*, 522

Decollate, *punishment*, 972

Decoloration, *achromatism*, 429

Decompose, *decomposition*,
          49, 653

Decomposite, *combination*, 48

Decompound, *combination*, 48

Deconsecrate, *cancel*, 756

Decontamination, *cleanness*,
          652

Decorate, *embellish*, 845, 847

Decoration, *repute*, 873
  title, 877
  insignia, 747

Decorous, *decent*, 960
  befitting, 922

Decorticate, *divest*, 226

Decorum, *politeness*, 852
  respect, 928
  purity, 960

Decoy, *entice*, 615
  deceive, 545
  deceiver, 548

Decrease, *in degree*, 36
  in size, 195

Decree, *law*, 963
  judgment, 969
  order, 741

Decrement, *deduction*, 38

Decrepit, *old*, 124, 128
  weak, 160
  frail, 651

Decrepitude, *age*, 128
  feebleness, 160

*Decrescendo, *decrease*, 36, 415

Decretal, *law*, 963
  order, 741

Decry, *depreciate*, 483
  censure, 932
  defame, 934

Decumbent, *horizontality*, 213

Decuple, *number*, 98

Decurrent, *descent*, 306

Decursive, *descent*, 306

Decussation, *crossing*, 219

Dedicate, *consecrate*, 873

Deduce, *infer*, 480
  retrench, 38

Deducible, *evidence*, 467,
        478, 480

Deduct, *retrench*, 38
  deprive, 789

Deduction, *abatement*, 813
  decrease, 36
  reasoning, 476

Deed, *act*, 680
  record, 467, 551
  security, 771

Deem, *belief*, 484

Deep, *profound*, 208, 451
  the sea, 341
  cunning, 702
  prudent, 498
  feeling, 821
  sound, 404; *colour*, 428
  greatness, 31

Deep-mouthed, *loud*, 404

Deep-rooted, *fixed*, 150

Deep-seated, *interior*, 221
  deep, 208

Deep-toned, *resonant*, 408

Deepie, *cinema*, 599A

Deface, *render ugly*, 846
  injure, 659
  destroy form, 241

Defacement, *blemish*, 848

Defalcation, *default*, 304
  contraction, 195
  incompleteness, 53
  insufficiency, 640
  non-payment, 808

Defame, *detract*, 934
   shame, 874; *censure*, 932
Defamer, *detractor*, 936
Default, *insufficiency*, 640
   shortcoming, 304
   non-payment, 806, 808
Defaulter, *debtor*, 806
Defeat, *to confute*, 479
   master, 731; *failure*, 732
Defecate, *clean*, 652
   improve, 658
Defect, *incomplete*, 53
   imperfect, 651
   failing, 945
   to desert, 124
Defection, *disobedience*, 742
   disloyalty, 940
Defective, *incomplete*, 53
   imperfect, 651
   insufficient, 640
Defence, *resistance*, 717
   vindication, 937
   safety, 664
Defenceless, *weak*, 158, 160
   exposed, 665
Defendant, *judge*, 967
   accusation, 938
Defer, *put off*, 133
Defer to, *respect*, 928
   assent, 488
Deference, *subordination*, 743
   submission, 725
   respect, 928
Defiance, *daring*, 715
   threat, 909
Deficiency, *inferiority*, 34
   blemish, 848
   frailty, 945
Deficient, *incomplete*, 53
   imperfect, 651
   insufficient, 640
   inferior, 34
   witless, 499
   insane, 502
Deficit, *debt*, 806
Defile, *ravine*, 198, 203
   march, 266
   dirt, 653
   spoil, 659
   shame, 874
   debauch, 961
Define, *name*, 564
   explain, 522
Definite, *exact*, 494
   special, 79
   visible, 446
   limited, 233
   intelligible, 518
Definitely, *assent*, 488
Definitive, *decided*, 535
   final, 67
Deflagration, *calefaction*, 384
Deflate, *contract*, 195
Deflection, *curvature*, 245
   deviation, 279

Defloration, *impurity*, 961
   soil, 653
Defluxion, *river*, 348
Deform, *deface*, 241, 846
Deformity, *blemish*, 848
Defraud, *cheat*, 545
   non-payment, 808
Defray, *pay*, 807
Defrost, *melt*, 384
Deft, *clever*, 698
   suitable, 23
Defunct, *dead*, 360
Defy, *dare*, 715
   disobey, 742
   threaten, 909
Dégagé, freedom, 748
   fashion, 825
Degenerate, *deterioration*, 659
   vice, 945
Deglutition, *swallowing*, 296
Degradation, *shame*, 874
   dishonour, 940
   deterioration, 659
Degree, *quantity*, 26
   term, 71
   honour, 873
Degustation, *taste*, 390
Dehortation, *dissuasion*, 616
   advice, 695
   warning, 668
Dehumanize, *brutalize*, 895
Dehydrate, *dry*, 340
   preserve, 670
De-ice, *melt*, 384
Dei gratiâ, dueness, 924
Deification, *heaven*, 981
   idolatory, 991
   honour, 873
Deign, *condescend*, 879
   consent, 762
Deiseal, *rotation*, 312
Deism, *irreligion*, 989
   heresy, 984A
Deity, *deity*, 976
   great spirit, 979
Dejection, *sadness*, 828, 837, 841
Déjeuner, food, 298
Dekko, *look*, 441
Délâbrement, deterioration,
             659
Delation, *accusation*, 938
Delay, *lateness*, 133
   protraction, 110
   slowness, 275
Dele, *obliteration*, 552
Delectable, *savoury*, 394
   agreeable, 829
Delectation, *pleasure*, 827
Delegate, *consignee*, 758, 759
   to commission, 755
Deleterious, *pernicious*, 649
   unwholesome, 657
Deletion, *obliteration*, 552
Deliberate, *think*, 451
   cautious, 864

Deliberate, *slow*, 275
   leisurely, 685
   advised, 620, 695
Deliberately, *slowly*, 133
   designedly, 600, 611
Delicacy, *of texture*, 329
   slenderness, 203
   weak, 160
   sickly, 655
   savoury, 394
   dainty, 298
   of taste, 850
   fastidiousness, 868
   exactness, 494
   pleasing, 829
   beauty, 845
   honour, 939
   purity, 960
   difficulty, 704
   scruple, 603, 616
Delicatessen, *food*, 298
Delicious, *taste*, 394
   pleasing, 829
Delight, *pleasure*, 827
Delightful, *pleasureableness*, 829
Delilah, *temptress*, 615
Delimit, *circumscribe*, 231
Delineate, *describe*, 594
   represent, 554
Delineavit, painting, 556
Delinquency, *guilt*, 947
Delinquent, *sinner*, 949
Deliquescent, *liquid*, 333
Deliquium, weakness, 160
   fatigue, 688
Delirium, *raving*, 503
   passion, 825
Delirium tremens, *drunken-
   ness*, 959
Delitescence, *latency*, 526
Deliver, *transfer*, 270
   give, 784
   liberate, 750
   relieve, 834
   utter, 582
   rescue, 672
   escape, 671
Dell, *concavity*, 252
Delouse, *disinfect*, 652
Delta, *land*, 342
Delude, *deceive*, 495, 545
Deluge, *flow*, 337, 348
   redundance, 641
   multitude, 72
Delusion, *error*, 495
   deceit, 545
Delve, *dig*, 252
   cultivate, 371
   depth, 208
Demagogue, *leader*, 745
   director, 694
   agitator, 742
Demagogy, *authority*, 737
Demand, *claim*, 924
   ask, 765

Demand, *require*, 630
   inquire, 461
   order, 741
   price, 812
Demarcation, *limit*, 199, 233
*Démarche, *procedure*, 680
Dematerialize, *immateriality*,
               317
Demean, *humble*, 879
   dishonour, 940
Demeanour, *conduct*, 692
   air, 448
   fashion, 852
Dementation, *insanity*, 503
*Démenti, *contradiction*, 536
Demerit, *vice*, 945
   inutility, 645
Demesne, *property*, 780
Demi, *bisection*, 91
Demigod, *hero*, 948
Demijohn, *receptacle*, 191
Demi-rep, *libertine*, 962
Demise, *death*, 360
   to transfer, 783
   to give, 784
Demiurge, *deity*, 979
Demivolt, *leap*, 309
Demobilize, *disperse*, 73
Democracy, *authority*, 737
*Démodé, *obsolete*, 851
Demogorgon, *demon*, 980
Demoiselle, *woman*, 374
Demolish, *destroy*, 162
   confute, 479
   damage, 649
Demolisher, *destroyer*, 165
Demon, *devil*, 980
   wretch, 913
   violent, 173
Demoniacal, *wicked*, 945
   furious, 825
   diabolic, 649, 980
Demonism, *idolatry*, 991
Demonolatry, *idolatry*, 991
Demonstrate, *prove*, 85, 478
   manifest, 525
Demonstrative, *evidential*,
              467, 478
   excitable, 825
Demonstrator, *scholar*, 492
   teacher, 540
Demoralize, *vice*, 945
   degrade, 659
Demos, *commonalty*, 876
Demote, *abase*, 308
   degrade, 659
Demotic, *writing*, 590
Demulcent, *mild*, 174
   soothing, 662
Demur, *unwillingness*, 603
   hesitation, 605
   to disbelieve, 485
   dissent, 489
   dislike, 867
Demure, *grave*, 826

Demure, *modest*, 881
   affected, 855
Demurrage, *charge*, 812
Demurrer, *lawsuit*, 969
Den, *lair*, 189
   room, 191, 893
   prison, 752
   sty, 653
Denary, *number*, 98
Denationalize, *restore*, 790
Denaturalized, *unconformity*, 83
Dendriform, *rough*, 256
Denegation, *negation*, 536
Denial, *negation*, 536
Denigrate, *blacken*, 431
   decry, 483, 934
Denization, *liberation*, 750
Denizen, *inhabitant*, 188
   man, 373
Denominate, *nomenclature*, 564
Denomination, *class*, 75
   party, 712
Denominational, *theology*, 983
Denominator, *number*, 84
Denote, *indication*, 550
Denouement, *result*, 154
   end, 67
   elucidation, 522
   completion, 729
Denounce, accuse, 297
   blame, 932
   cite, 965
Dense, *close*, 321
   crowded, 72
   stupid, 499
Density, *closeness*, 46, 321
Dent, *notch*, 257
   hollow, 252
Dental, *letter*, 561
Denticle, *sharpness*, 253
Denticulated, *sharp*, 253
Dentist, *doctor*, 662
Denude, *divest*, 226
   deprive, 776
Denunciation, *see* Denounce
Deny, *negative*, 536
   dissent, 489
   refuse, 764
*Deo volente, *conditions*, 770
Deodand, *penalty*, 974
Deodorize, *disinfect*, 652
Deontology, *duty*, 926
Depart, *set out*, 293
   die, 360
Departed, *gone*, 2
Department, *class*, 75
   part, 51; *region*, 181
   business, 625
Depauperate, *impoverish*, 804
Depend, *hang*, 214
   be contingent, 475
Depend upon, *trust*, 484
   be the effect of, 154
   affirm, 535
Dependable, *belief*, 484

Dependable, *probity*, 939
Dependant, *servant*, 746
Dependence, *subjection*, 749
Dependent, *liable*, 177
Depict, *paint*, 556
   represent, 554
   describe, 594
Depletion, *insufficiency*, 640
Deplorable, *bad*, 649
   disastrous, 735
   painful, 830
Deplore, *regret*, 833
   complain, 839
   remorse, 950
Deploy, *expansion*, 194
Depone, *affirm*, 535
Deponent, *evidence*, 467
Depopulate, *displace*, 185
   desert, 893
Deportation, *displace*, 185
   exclusion, 55
   transfer, 270
   emigration, 297
   punishment, 972
Deportment, *conduct*, 692
   appearance, 448
Depose, *evidence*, 467
   tell, 527
   record, 551
   dethrone, 738, 756
   declare, 535
Deposit, *place*, 184
   secure, 771
   store, 636
   expenditure, 809
   solidify, 321
Depository, *store*, 636
Depot, *store*, 636
   focus, 74
   mart, 799
Deprave, *spoil*, 659
Depraved, *bad*, 649
   vicious, 945
Deprecate, *deprecation*, 766
   dissuade, 616
   disapproval, 932
   pity, 914
Depreciate, *detract*, 483
   censure, 932
   decrease, 36
Depreciation, *discount*, 813
   stealing, 791
Depredator, *thief*, 792
Depression, *lowering*, 308
   lowness, 207
   depth, 208
   concavity, 252
   dejection, 837
Deprive, *take*, 789
   subduct, 38
   lose, 776
Depth, *physical*, 208
   mental, 450, 490
Depurate, *clean*, 652
   improve, 658

Depuratory, *remedy*, 662
Depute, *commission*, 755
Deputy, *substitute*, 147, 634, 759
   jurisdiction, 965
Derangement, *mental*, 503
   physical, 61
   disorder, 59
Derelict, *solitary*, 893
Dereliction, *relinquishment*,
            624, 782
   guilt, 947
Derequisition, *restore*, 790
Deride, *ridicule*, 856
   disrespect, 929
   contempt, 930
   trifle with, 643
   scoff, 483
Derisive, *ridiculous*, 853
Derivation, *origin*, 153
   verbal, 562
Derivative, *effect*, 154
Derive, *attribute*, 155
   receive, 785
   acquire, 775
   income, 810
Dermal, *covering*, 222
*Dernier cri, *fashion*, 852
   newness, 123
*Dernier ressort, *plan*, 626
Derogate, *detract*, 483, 934
   demean, 940
   shame, 874
Derrick, *raise*, 307
Derring-do, *courage*, 861
Derringer, *arms*, 727
Dervish, *clergy*, 996
Descale, *clean*, 652
Descant, *dissert*, 595
   dwell upon, 584
   diffuseness, 573
Descendant, *posterity*, 167
Descent, *slope*, 217
   motion downwards, 306
   order, 58
Describe, *set forth*, 594
Description, *kind*, 75
   narration, 594
Descry, *vision*, 441
Desecrate, *misuse*, 679
   profane, 988
Desert, *solitude*, 101, 893
   waste, 645
   merit, 944
   to relinquish, 624
   to escape, 671
Deserter, *apostate*, 607
   coward, 862
Desertless, *vice*, 945
Deserve, *merit*, 944
   right, 922, 924
*Déshabillé, *see* Dishabille
Desiccate, *dryness*, 340
Desiderate, *desire*, 865
   require, 630
Desideratum, *desire*, 865

Desideratum, *inquiry*, 461
   requirement, 630
Design, *intention*, 620
   cunning, 702
   plan, 626
   delineation, 554
   prototype, 22
Designate, *specify*, 79, 564
Designation, *kind*, 75
Designed, *intended*, 600
Designer, *artist*, 559, 626
Designing, *false*, 544
   artful, 702
Desirable, *expedient*, 646
Desire, *longing*, 865
Desist, *discontinue*, 142
   relinquish, 624
   inaction, 681
Desk, *support*, 215
   receptacle, 191
Desolate, *alone*, 87
   secluded, 893
   afflicted, 828
   to ravage, 162
Desolation, *evil*, 619
Despair, *hopelessness*, 859
   dejection, 837
Despatch, *see* Dispatch
Desperado, *rashness*, 863
Desperate, *great*, 31
   violent, 173
   rash, 863
   difficult, 704
   impossible, 471
Desperation, *hopelessness*, 859
Despicable, *shameful*, 874
   contemptible, 930
   trifling, 643
Despise, *contemn*, 930
   deride, 483, 929
Despite, *notwithstanding*,
            179, 708
   malevolence, 907
Despoil, *take*, 789
   rob, 791
   hurt, 649
Despondency, *sadness*, 837
   fear, 860
   despair, 859
Despot, *master*, 745
Despotism, *arbitrariness*, 964
   authority, 737
   severity, 739
Desquamation, *divestment*, 226
Dessert, *food*, 298
Destination, *fate*, 152, 601
   arrival, 292
   intention, 620
Destiny, *fate*, 601
   chance, 152
Destitute, *insufficient*, 640
   poor, 804
Destrier, *carrier*, 271
Destroy, *demolish*, 162

Destroy, *injure*, 649
   deface, 241
Destroyed, *inexistence*, 2
Destroyer, *ship*, 273
Destruction, *demolition*,
            162, 732
   evil, 619
Destructive, *hurtful*, 649
Desuetude, *disuse*, 614, 678
Desultory, *discontinuous*, 70
   irregular in time, 139
   disordered, 59
   multiform, 81
   deviating, 149, 279
   agitated, 315
Detach, *separate*, 10, 44, 47
Detached, *irrelated*, 10, 47
   indifferent, 456
   unity, 87
Detachment, *part*, 51
   army, 726
Detail, *to describe*, 594
   special portion, 79
Detain, *retention*, 781
Detection, *discovery*, 480A
Detective, *inquiry*, 461
Detention, *retention*, 781
   imprisonment, 751
*Détenu, *prisoner*, 754
Deter, *dissuasion*, 616
   fear, 860
Detergent, *remedy*, 662
   remedial, 656
   cleanness, 652
Deteriorate, *deterioration*, 659
Determinate, *special*, 79
   exact, 474
   resolute, 604
Determination, *resolution*, 604
   will, 600
   judgment, 480
Determine, *find out*, 480A
   intend, 620
   direction, 278
   make certain, 474
   cause, 153
   resolve, 604
   designate, 79
Determinism, *necessity*, 601
Deterrent, *restraint*, 616
Detersive, *cleanness*, 652
Detest, *hate*, 867, 898
Detestable, *bad*, 649, 867
Dethrone, *abrogation*, 756
Dethronement, *anarchy*, 738
Detonate, *sound*, 406
   explode, 173
Detonator, *signal*, 550
Detour, *circuit*, 629
   curvature, 245
   deviation, 279
Detract, *subduct*, 38
   depreciate, 483
   censure, 932
   slander, 934

Detractor, *slanderer*, 936
Detrain, *arrival*, 292
Detriment, *evil*, 619
Detrimental, *hurtful*, 649
Detritus, *part*, 51
  pulverulence, 330
Detrude, *cast out*, 297
  cast down, 308
Detruncation, *subduction*, 38
  disjunction, 44
Deuce, *duality*, 89
  demon, 980
Deuced, *great*, 31
*Deus ex machina, *helper*,
                707, 711
  wonder-worker, 994
Deuterogamy, *marriage*, 903
Devastate, *destroy*, 162
  injure, 649
Devastation, *havoc*, 659
Develop, *cause*, 153
  produce, 161
  increase, 35
  expand, 194
  evolve, 313
Development, *effect*, 154
Deviate, *differ*, 15
  vary, 20
  change, 140
  turn, 279
  diverge, 291
  circuit, 629
  bend, 245
Deviationist, *revolutionary*, 146
  dissent, 489
Device, *expedient*, 626
  instrument, 633
  motto, 550
Devices, *inclination*, 602
Devil, *Satan*, 978
  maleficent being, 913
  mediate, 631
  culprit, 949
  seasoned food, 392
Devil-may-care, *rash*, 863
Devilish, *great*, 31
  bad, 649
  hell, 982
Devilry, (or Deviltry), *evil*, 619
  cruelty, 907
  wickedness, 945
  sorcery, 992
Devious, *deviating*, 245, 279
  different, 15
Devise, *plan*, 620, 626
  imagine, 515
  bequeath, 784
Devitalize, *empty*, 640
  absent, 187
  not having, 776
*Devoir, *courtesy*, 894
Devolution, *delegation*, 755
Devolve, *transfer*, 783
Devolve on, *duty*, 926
Devote, *attention*, 457

Devote, *curse*, 908
  employ, 677
  consecrate, 873
Devoted, *loving*, 897
  friendly, 888
  doomed, 152, 735, 828
Devotee, *pious*, 987
  resolute, 604
  enthusiast, 682, 840
Devotion, *piety*, 987
  worship, 990
  respect, 928
  love, 897
  obedience, 743
  disinterestedness, 942
Devour, *eat*, 296
  gluttony, 957
  destroy, 162
Devout, *pious*, 897
Dew, *moisture*, 339
Dew-pond, *lake*, 343
Dexter, *right*, 238
Dexterous, *skill*, 698
Dey, *master*, 745
Dhow, *ship*, 273
Diablerie, *sorcery*, 992
Diabolic, *malevolent*, 907
  wicked, 945
  bad, 649
  satanic, 978
Diacoustics, *sound*, 402
Diacritical, *distinctive*, 550
Diadem, *regalia*, 747
  ornament, 847
Diagnostic, *intrinsicality*, 5
  speciality, 79
  discrimination, 465
Diagonal, *oblique*, 217
Diagram, *representation*, 554
Diagraph, *imitation*, 19
Dial, *clock*, 114
  face, 234, 448
Dialect, *neology*, 563
Dialectic, *argumentation*, 476
  language, 560
Dialogue, *interlocution*, 588
Diameter, *breadth*, 202
Diamond, *lozenge*, 244
  arena, 728
  gem, 650
  ornament, 847
  hardness, 323
Diana, *goddess*, 979
Diapason, *melody*, 413
Diaper, *reticulation*, 219
Diaphanous, *transparent*, 425
Diaphoresis, *excretion*, 298
Diaphoretic,*remedy*, 662
Diaphragm, *partition*, 228
  middle, 68
Diarchy, *authority*, 737
Diary, *record*, 551
  journal, 114
Diastole, *expansion*, 194
  pulse, 314

Diathermancy, *calefaction*, 384
Diathesis, *state*, 7
  habit, 613
  affections, 820
Diatonic, *harmony*, 413
Diatribe, *disapprobation*, 932
Dibble, *perforator*, 262
  cultivate, 371
Dibs, *money*, 800
Dice, *chance*, 156
Dichotomy, *bisection*, 91
  angularity, 244
Dichroism, *variegation*, 440
Dick, *detective*, 461
  police, 664
Dicker, *barter*, 794
  interchange, 148
Dicky, *seat*, 215
Dictaphone, *hearing*, 418
Dictate, *command*, 741
  authority, 737
  enjoin, 615
  write, 590
Dictator, *master*, 745
Dictatorial, *severe*, 739
  insolent, 885
Dictatorship, *authority*, 737
Diction, *style*, 569
Dictionary, *word*, 562
Dictum, *maxim*, 496
  affirmation, 535
  command, 741
Didactic, *teaching*, 537
Diddle, *deception*, 545
  swindle, 791
Dido, *leap*, 309
  prank, 840
  foolery, 497
  caprice, 608
Die, *chance*, 156
  mould, 22
  expire, 2, 360
  cease, 142
Die for, *desire*, 865
Die-hard, *obstinacy*, 606
*Dies non, *never*, 107
  repose, 687
Diet, *food*, 298
  remedy, 662
  council, 696
Dietetics, *remedy*, 662
Differ, *dissent*, 489
Difference, *difference*, 15
  inequality, 28
  dissimilarity, 18
  discord, 713
  numerical, 84
Differential, *number*, 84
Differentiation, *numeration*, 85
  difference, 15
  discrimination, 465
  fastidiousness, 868
*Difficile, *troublesome*, 704
Difficult, *fastidious*, 868
Difficulty, *hardness*, 704

Disfigure, *deform*, 846
 blemish, 848
Disfranchise, *disentitle*, 925
Disgorge, *emit*, 297
 restore, 790
 flow out, 348
Disgrace, *shame*, 874
 dishonour, 940
Disguise, *conceal*, 528
 falsify, 544
 deceive, 545
 mask, 530
 untruth, 546
Disguised, *in liquor*, 959
Disgust, *dislike*, 867
 hatred, 898
 offensive, 830
 weary, 841
 taste, 395
Dish, *plate*, 191
 food, 299
 upset, 162
 to foil, 731
Dishabille, *undress*, 225
 unprepared, 674
 simplicity, 849
Dishearten, *dissuade*, 616
 deject, 837
Dished, *failure*, 732
Dishevelled, *loose*, 47
 disordered, 61
 intermixed, 219
 twisted, 248
Dishonest, *false*, 544
 faithless, 940
Dishonour, *baseness*, 940
 to repudiate a bill, 808
 disrespect, 929
 disrepute, 874
Disillusion, *dissuasion*, 616
Disimprove, *deteriorate*, 659
Disincentive, *check*, 616
Disincline, *dissuade*, 616
Disinclined, *unwilling*, 603
 disliking, 867
Disinfect, *purify*, 652
 improve, 658
Disinfectant, *remedy*, 662
Disingenuous, *false*, 544
 dishonourable, 940
Disinherit, *transfer*, 783
Disintegrate, *separate*, 44
 decompose, 49
 pulverize, 330
Disinter, *exhume*, 363
 discover, 480A, 525
Disinterested, *unselfish*, 942
Disjoin, *loosen*, 44
Disjointed, *loosened*, 44
 in disorder, 59
Disjunction, *incoherence*, 47
 decomposition, 49
Disk, *face*, 234
 exterior, 220
Dislike, *distaste*, 867

Dislike, *disapproval*, 932
 hate, 898
 enmity, 889
 reluctance, 603
Dislocate, *loosen*, 44
 derange, 61
Dislodge, *displace*, 185
Disloyal, *improbity*, 940
Dismal, *dejection*, 837
 dullness, 843
Dismantle, *destroy*, 162
 disuse, 678
 despoil, 649
 injure, 659
 divest, 226
Dismast, *disuse*, 678
 dismantle, 659, 674
Dismay, *fear*, 860
Dismember, *loosen*, 44
Dismiss, *discard*, 678, 756, 782
 eject, 297
 liberate, 750
Dismount, *descend*, 306
 arrive, 292
 disable, 674
Disobey, *disobedience*, 742
Disobliging, *malevolent*, 907
Disorder, *confusion*, 59
 to derange, 61
 disease, 655
Disorderly, *violent*, 173
Disorganize, *derange*, 61
 destroy, 162
 spoil, 659
Disown, *negation*, 536
Disparage, *depreciate*, 483
 disrespect, 929
 censure, 932
Disparate, *different*, 15
 dissimilar, 18
 single, 87
 disagreeing, 24
 unequal, 28
Disparity, *dissimilarity*, 18
Dispart, *disjoin*, 44
Dispassionate, *calm*, 826
Dispatch, *speed*, 274
 activity, 682
 haste, 684
 earliness, 132
 to conduct, 692
 complete, 729
 kill, 162, 361
 eat, 296
 epistle, 592
 intelligence, 532
Dispatch-box, *receptacle*, 191
Dispatch-case, *receptacle*, 191
Dispel, *destroy*, 162
 scatter, 73
Dispensable, *disuse*, 678
Dispensation, *licence*, 760
 calamity, 830
Dispense, *exempt*, 927A
 permit, 760

Dispense, *disuse*, 678
 relinquish, 624
 give, 784
 allot, 786
 disperse, 73
 retail, 796
Dispeople, *seclusion*, 893
Disperse, *scatter*, 73, 638
 separate, 44
 diverge, 291
Dispersion, *removal*, 270
Dispirit, *sadden*, 837
 discourage, 616
Displace, *remove*, 185
 transfer, 270
 derange, 61
Display, *show*, 525
 appear, 448
 parade, 882
Displease, *painfulness*, 830
Displeasure, *pain*, 828
 anger, 900
Displosion, *violence*, 173
Disport, *amusement*, 840
Dispose, *arrange*, 60
 prepare, 673
 tend, 176
 induce, 615
Dispose of, *sell*, 796
 give, 784
 relinquish, 782
 use, 677
Disposition, *order*, 58
 arrangement, 60
 inclination, 602
 mind, 820
Dispossess, *take away*, 789
 transfer, 783
Dispossessed, *deprived*, 776
Dispraise, *disapprove*, 932
Disprize, *depreciate*, 483
Disproof, *counter-evidence*, 468
 confutation, 479
Disproportion, *irrelation*, 10
 disagreement, 24
Disprove, *confute*, 479
Disputant, *debater*, 476
 combatant, 726
Disputatious, *irritable*, 901
Dispute, *discord*, 713
 denial, 485, 536
 discussion, 476
Disqualified, *incapacitated*, 158
 incompetent, 699
Disqualify, *incapacitate*, 158
 weaken, 160
 disentitle, 925
 unprepared, 674
Disquiet, *excitement*, 825
 uneasiness, 149, 828
 to give pain, 830
Disquietude, *apprehension*, 860
Disquisition, *dissertation*, 595
Disregard, *overlook*, 458
 neglect, 460, 927

Disregard, *indifferent*, 823
   slight, 483
Disrelish, *dislike*, 867
   hate, 898
Disreputable, *vicious*, 945
Disrepute, *disgrace*, 874
Disrespect, *irreverence*, 929
   discourtesy, 895
Disrobe, *divestment*, 226
Disruption, *disjunction*, 44
   breaking up, 162
   schism, 713
Dissatisfaction, *discontent*, 832
   sorrow, 828
Dissect, *anatomize*, 44, 49
   investigate, 461
Dissemble, *falsehood*, 544
Dissembler, *liar*, 548
Disseminate, *scatter*, 73
   diverge, 291
   publish, 531
   pervade, 186
Dissension, *discord*, 713
Dissent, *disagree*, 489
   refuse, 764
   heterodoxy, 984A
   discord, 713
Dissertation, *disquisition*, 595
Disservice, *disadvantage*, 619
   inexpedience, 647
Dissever, *disjoin*, 44
Dissidence, *disagreement*, 24
   dissent, 489
Dissilience, *violent*, 173
Dissimilar, *unlike*, 18
Dissimulate, *falsehood*, 544
Dissipate, *scatter*, 73
   waste, 638
   prodigality, 818
   dissolute, 961
   licentiousness, 954
Dissociation, *irrelation*, 10
   separation, 44
Dissolute, *intemperate*, 954
   profligate, 945
   debauched, 961
Dissolution, *decomposition*, 49
   liquefaction, 335
   death, 360
Dissolve, *vanish*, 2, 4
   disappear, 449
   abrogate, 756
   liquefy, 335
Dissonance, *disagreement*, 24
   discord, 414
Dissuade, *dissuasion*, 616
Distain, *ugliness*, 846
Distance, *longinquity*, 196
   swiftness, 274
   to overtake, 282
   to leave behind, 303, 732
   respect, 928
   of time, 110
Distant, *far*, 196
   discourteous, 895

Distaste, *dislike*, 867
Distasteful, *disagreeable*, 830
Distemper, *disease*, 655
   painting, 556
Distend, *expansion*, 194
Distended, *swollen*, 194
Distich, *poetry*, 597
Distil, *evaporate*, 336
   flow, 348
   drop, 295
Distinct, *visible*, 446
   audible, 402
   intelligible, 518, 535
   disjoined, 44
Distinction, *difference*, 15
   discrimination, 465
   fame, 873
   style, 574
Distinctive, *special*, 75
*Distingué, *repute*, 873
   fashionable, 852
Distinguish, *perceive*, 441
Distortion, *obliquity*, 217
   twist, 243, 555
   falsehood, 554
   of vision, 443
   perversion, 523
   ugliness, 846
Distracted, *insane*, 503
   unthinking, 452
   confused, 491
Distraction, *inattention*, 458
   amusement, 840
Distrain, *seize*, 789, 969
*Distrait, *incogitancy*, 452
   inattention, 458
Distraught, *see* Distracted
Distress, *affliction*, 828
   cause of pain, 830
   poor, 804
Distribute, *disperse*, 73
   arrange, 60
   allot, 786
   diverge, 291
District, *region*, 181
Distrust, *disbelief*, 485
   fear, 860
Disturb, *derange*, 61
   alter, 140
   agitate, 315
Disunion, *separation*, 44
   discord, 713
Disuse, *unemployment*, 678
   desuetude, 614
Ditch, *conduit*, 350
   hollow, 252
   trench, 259, 343
   defence, 717
   upset, 162
   sea, 341
Ditheism, *heathen*, 984
Dither, *shiver*, 315, 383
Dithyrambic, *poetry*, 597
Ditto, *repetition*, 104, 136
Ditty, *music*, 415

Diuretic, *remedy*, 662
Diurnal, *period*, 108, 138
Diuturnal, *diuturnity*, 110
Divan, *sofa*, 215
   council, 696
Divarication, *divergence*, 291
   deviation, 279
   difference, 15
Dive, *plunge*, 310
   descent, 306
   depth, 208
Divellicate, *disjoin*, 44
Divergence, *variation*, 20
   dissimilarity, 18
   difference, 15
   discord, 713
   dispersion, 73
   separation, 291
   disagreement, 24
   deviation, 279
Divers, *many*, 102
   different, 15
   multiform, 81
Diversified, *varied*,
        15, 16A, 18, 20, 81
Diversion, *amusement*, 840
   change, 140
Diversity, *difference*, 15
   dissimilarity, 18
   multiform, 16A, 81
Divert, *turn*, 279
   amuse, 840
   abstract, 452
*Divertissement, *drama*, 599
Dives, *wealth*, 803
Divest, *denude*, 226
   take, 789
Divest oneself of, *leave*, 782
Divide, *separate*, 44
   part, 51, 91
   apportion, 786
Dividend, *part*, 51
   number, 84
   portion, 786
Dividers, *measure*, 466
Divination, *prediction*, 511
   occult arts, 992
Divine, *Deity*, 976
   clergyman, 996
   theologian, 983
   to guess, 514
   predict, 510, 511
   perfect, 650
Diving-bell, *depth*, 208
Divining-rod, *spell*, 993
Divinity, *Deity*, 976
   theology, 983
Division, *separation*, 44
   part, 51; *class*, 75
   troop, 72, 726
   arithmetical, 85
   discord, 713
   distribution, 786
Divisor, *number*, 84
Divorce, *matrimonial*, 905

Dudgeon, *club*, 727
Duds, *clothes*, 225
Due, *proper*, 924, 926
　owing, 806
　effect, 154
　expedient, 646
Duel, *contention*, 720
Duellist, *combatant*, 726
Dueness, *right*, 924
Duenna, *teacher*, 540
　accompaniment, 88
　keeper, 753
Dues, *price*, 812
Duet, *music*, 815
Duff, *false*, 495
Duffer, *fool*, 501
　bungler, 700
Duffle coat, *dress*, 225
Dug, *convexity*, 250
Dug-out, *refuge*, 666, 717
　canoe, 273
Duke, *noble*, 875
　ruler, 745
Dukedom, *title*, 877
Dulcet, *sound*, 405
　melodious, 413
　agreeable, 829
Dulcify, *sweeten*, 396
Dulcimer, *musical instrument*,
417
Dulcinea, *favourite*, 899
Dull, *inert*, 172
　insensible, 376
　tame, 575
　callous, 823
　blunt, 254
　weak, 160
　moderate, 174
　colourless, 429
　dejected, 837
　inexcitable, 826
　stolid, 699
　prosing, 843
　unapt, 499
Dull-brained, *folly*, 499
Dull-witted, *folly*, 499
Dullard, *fool*, 501
Duma, *council*, 696
Dumb, *aphony*, 581
　stupid, 499, 843
　unskilful, 699
Dumb-bell, *fool*, 501
Dumb show, *the drama*, 599
Dumbfound, *astonish*, 870
　disappoint, 509
Dummy, *aphony*, 581
　effigy, 554
Dump, *deposit*, 184
Dumps, *sadness*, 837
　mortification, 832
Dumpy, *broad*, 202
　short, 200
　ugly, 846
Dun, *colour*, 432
　to importune, 765

Dun, *creditor*, 805
Dunce, *ignoramus*, 493
　fool, 501
Dunderhead, *fool*, 501
Dundreary, *whisker*, 256
Dune, *hillock*, 206
Dung, *uncleanness*, 653
Dungarees, *dress*, 225
Dungeon, *prison*, 752
　hide, 530
Dunghill, *vulgar*, 876
Dunt, *blow*, 619
Duodecimal, *twelve*, 98
Duodecimo, *littleness*, 193
　book, 593
Duodenary, *numbers*, 98
Duologue, *interlocution*, 588
　drama, 599
Dupe, *to deceive*, 545
　deceived, 547
　credulous, 486
Duplex, *double*, 89, 90
Duplicate, *double*, 89, 90
　superfluous, 641
　copy, 21, 590
　pledge, 550, 805
Duplication, *imitation*, 19
Duplicity, false, 544, 702
Durable, lasting, 110
　stable, 150
Durance, *restraint*, 751
Duration, *period*, 106
Durbar, *tribunal*, 966
　assembly, 696
Duress, *restraint*, 751
　compulsion, 744
During, *lasting*, 106
During pleasure, *contingent
　duration*, 108A
Durity, *hardness*, 323
Dusk, *evening*, 126
　obscurity, 422
Dusky, *darkness*, 421
Dust, *powder*, 330
　corpse, 362
　levity, 320
　dirt, 653
　trash, 643
　to clean, 652
　contest, 720
　money, 800
Dustman, *cleaner*, 652
Duteous, *virtue*, 944
Dutiful, *virtue*, 944
　filial, 167
Duty, *obligation*, 926
　business, 625
　work, 686
　tax, 812
　rite, 990, 998
Duumvirate, *authority*, 737
Dwarf, *small*, 193
　low, 207
　to lessen, 36
Dwell, *tarry*, 265

Dwell, *reside*, 186
Dwell on, *descant*, 573, 584
Dweller, *inhabitant*, 188
Dwelling, *location*, 189
　residence, 184
Dwindle, *diminish*, 32, 195
　lessen, 36
Dyad, *duality*, 89
Dyarchy, *authority*, 737
Dye, *colour*, 428
Dying, *death*, 360
Dyke, see Dike
Dynamic, *powerful*, 157
Dynamics, *force*, 159, 276
Dynamite, *arms*, 727
Dynams, *instrument*, 633
Dynasty, *authority*, 737
Dyslogistic, *disapproving*, 932

E

Each, *speciality*, 79
Eager, *ardent*, 507, 821
　desirous, 865
　active, 682
Eagle, *swift*, 274
　sight, 441
　standard, 550
Eagre, *tide*, 348
Ear, *hearing*, 418
Ear-deafening, *loudness*, 404
Ear-phone, *hearing*, 418
Ear-piercing, *loud*, 404
Ear-trumpet, *hearing*, 418
Ear-witness, *evidence*, 467
Earache, *pain*, 378
Earl, *nobility*, 875
　master, 745
Earldom, *title*, 877
Earless, *deaf*, 419
Early, *earliness*, 132
Earmark, *sign*, 550
Earn, *acquire*, 775
Earnest, *intention*, 620
　strenuous, 682
　emphatic, 642
　pledge, 771
　pay in advance, 809
　eager, 821
Earring, *pendant*, 214
　ornament, 847
Earshot, *nearness*, 197
Earth, *land*, 342
　ground, 211
　world, 318
　den, 189
Earth-born, *commonalty*, 876
Earthly-minded, *selfish*, 943
　worldly, 989
Earthquake, *violence*, 146, 173
Earwig, *to flatter*, 933
　flatterer, 935
Ease, *facility*, 705
　relief, 834
　content, 831

Essay, *try*, 463
  endeavour, 675
  dissertation, 595
Essayist, *writing*, 590
Essence, *nature*, 5
  existence, 1
  odour, 398
  pith, 642
Essential, *great*, 31
  requisite, 630
Establish, *fix*, 184
  demonstrate, 478
  evidence, 467
  create, 161
  substantiate, 494
  settle, 150
Established, *received*, 82
  habitual, 613
Establishment, *fixture*, 141
  party, 712
  location, 184
*Estancia, *property*, 780
Estate, *condition*, 7
  property, 780
Esteem, *judge*, 480
  believe, 484
  approve, 931
Estimable, *good*, 648
  commendable, 931
Estimate, *measure*, 466
  judge, 480
  count, 85
Estimation, *opinion*, 484
  respect, 928
  good, 648
Estoppage, *prohibition*, 761
Estrade, *horizontal*, 213
Estrange, *alienate*, 449
  hate, 898
  seclude, 893
Estreat, *penalty*, 974
Estuary, *gulf*, 343
Esurient, *hungry*, 865
*État-major, *combatant*, 726
Etcetera, *addition*, 37
  inclusion, 76
  plurality, 100
Etch, *engraving*, 558
Eternal, *perpetuity*, 112
Ether, *sky*, 313, 338
  void, 4
  vapour, 334
Ethical, *virtue*, 944
Ethics, *duty*, 926
Ethiopic, *blackness*. 431
Ethnic, *heathen*, 984
  racial, 372
Ethnology, *mankind*, 372
Ethos, *nature*, 5
Etiolate, *bleach*, 429, 430
Etiquette. *fashion*, 852
  custom, 613
  ceremony, 882
*Étude, *music*, 415
Etymology, *word*, 562

Etymology, *language*, 560
Etymon, *origin*, 153
  verbal, 562
Eucharist, *rite*, 998
Euchology, *rite*, 998
Eugenics, *production*, 161
Eulogy, *approval*, 931
Euphemism, *misnomer*, 565
Euphonious, *musical*, 413
  style, 578
Euphony, *harmony*, 413
Euphoria, *health*, 654
Euphuism, *ornament*, 577
  affectation, 855
Eurasian, *mixture*, 41
Eureka, *judgment*, 480
  answer, 462
Eurhythmics, *training*, 673
Eurhythmy, *symmetry*, 242
Euroclydon, *wind*, 349
Euterpe, *music*, 415
Euthanasia, *death*, 360
  killing, 361
Evacuate, *emit*, 297
  excrete, 299
Evacuee, *escape*, 671
Evade, *avoid*, 623
  escape, 671
  sophistry, 477
  dereliction, 927
Evaluate, *appraise*, 466, 812
Evanescent, *transient*, 111
  minute, 32, 193
  disappearing, 449
Evangelist, *revelation*, 985
Evangelize, *convert*, 484
Evaporate, *vapour*, 336
  gas, 334
  unsubstantiality, 4
Evasion, *escape*, 623, 671
  sophistry, 477
  plea, 617
  falsehood, 544
  untruth, 546
  cunning, 702
  dereliction, 927
Eve, *evening*, 126
  priority, 116
Even, *equal*, 27
  uniform, 16
  level, 213; *flat*, 251
  smooth, 265
  straight, 246
  although, 179, 469
Even-handed, *equitable*, 922
  honourable, 939
Even so, *assent*, 488
Evening, *evening*, 126
  worship, 990
  evening, 126
Event, *eventuality*, 151
Eventful, *stirring*, 151
  remarkable, 642
Eventide, *evening*, 126
Eventual, *futurity*, 121

Eventuate, *occur*, 1
Ever, *always*, 112
  seldom, 137
Ever and anon, *repetition*, 104
Ever-changing, *mutability*, 149
Ever-recurring, *repetition*, 104
Evergreen, *newness*, 123
  diuturnity, 110
  continuous, 69
  perpetuity, 112
Everlasting, *perpetual*, 112, 136
Evermore, *perpetual*, 112
Every, *generality*, 78
Everyday, *conformity*, 82
  perpetuity, 112
Everyman, *mankind*, 372
Everywhere, *space*, 180, 186
Eviction, *displacement*, 185
Evidence, *evidence*, 467
Evident, *visible*, 446
  certain, 474
  demonstrable, 478
  manifest, 525
Evil, *harm*, 619
  wrong, 923
  vice, 945
  producing evil, 649
Evil day, *adversity*, 735
Evil eye, *malevolence*, 907
  glance, 441
Evil-minded, *malevolent*, 907
  vicious, 945
Evil-speaking, *detraction*, 934
Evildoer, *maleficent*, 913
  badness, 649
  culprit, 949
Evince, *show*, 467
  prove, 478
Eviscerate, *extract*, 301
  divide, 44
  mutilate, 38
Evoke, *call upon*, 765
  excite, 824
Evolution, *numerical*, 85
  effect, 154
  development, 161
  turning out, 313
  circuition, 311
Evulsión, *extraction*, 301
Ewer, *receptacle*, 191
*Ex cathedra, *affirmation*, 535
  insolence, 885
*Ex concesso, *reasoning*, 476
  assent, 488
*Ex-libris, *label*, 550
*Ex mero motu, *will*, 600
*Ex necessitate rei, *destiny*, 152
*Ex officio, *truth*, 494
  authority, 737
  dueness, 924
*Ex parte, *evidence*, 467
*Ex post facto, *preterition*, 122
Exacerbate, *increase*, 35
  aggravate, 835
  exasperate, 173

Exonerate, *acquit*, 970
  disburden, 705
  absolve, 760
  release, 756
Exorbitant, *enormous*, 31
  redundant, 641
  dear, 814
Exorcise, *conjure*, 992
Exorcism, *theology*, 993
Exorcist, *heterodoxy*, 994
Exordium, *beginning*, 66
Exosmosis, *passage*, 302
Exoteric, *disclosed*, 531
  public, 529
Exotic, *alien*, 10
  exceptional, 83
Expand, *swell*, 194
  increase, 35
  in breadth, 202
  rarefy, 322
  in writing, 573
Expanse, *space*, 180, 202
  size, 192
Expansion, *space*, 180
Expatiate, *in writing*, 573
  in discourse, 582, 584
Expatriate, *deport*, 295
  displace, 185
  exclude, 55, 893
Expect, *look for*, 121, 507
  not wonder, 871
  hope, 858
Expectorant, *remedy*, 662
Expectorate, *eject*, 296
Expedience, *utility*, 646
Expedient, *means*, 632
  substitute, 634
  plan, 626
Expedite, *accelerate*, 274
  earliness, 132
  aid, 707
Expedition, *speed*, 274
  activity, 682
  warfare, 722
  march, 266
Expel, *displace*, 185
  eject, 297
  drive from, 289
  punish, 972
Expend, *use*, 677
  waste, 638
  pay, 809
Expense, *price*, 812
Expensive, *dear*, 814
Experience, *knowledge*, 490
  undergo, 821
  event, 151
Experienced, *skilled*, 698
Experiment, *trial*, 463
  endeavour, 675
*Experimentum crucis,
  demonstration, 478
Expert, *skill*, 698
  adept, 700
*Experto crede, *knowledge*, 490

Expiate, *atonement*, 952
Expire, *death*, 360
  end, 67
  breathe out, 349
Explain, *expound*, 522
  inform, 527
  teach, 537
  answer, 462
Explain away, *misinterpret*, 523
Expletive, *redundance*, 573, 641
  malediction, 908
Explication, *interpret*, 522
Explicit, *distinct*, 516, 518, 535
Explode, *burst*, 173
  sound, 406
  refute, 479
  passion, 825
  anger, 900
Exploit, *action*, 680
  to use, 677
Explore, *investigate*, 461
  experiment, 463
Explosion, *see* Explode
Exponent, *index*, 550
  numerical, 84
  interpreter, 522
Export, *transfer*, 270
  send out, 297
  thing sent, 295
*Exposé, *account*, 596
  disclosure, 529
Expose, *show*, 525
  interpret, 522
  confute, 479
  denude, 226
  endanger, 665
Exposition, *answer*, 462
  disclosure, 529
Expositor, *interpreter*, 524
  teacher, 540
Expository, *information*, 527, 595
Expostulate, *deprecate*, 766
  reprehend, 932
  dissuade, 616
  advise, 695
Exposure, *disclosure*, 529
Exposure meter, *optical instrument*, 445
Exposure to, *liability*, 177
Expound, *interpret*, 522
  teach, 537
  answer, 462
Expounder, *interpreter*, 524
Express, *voluntary*, 600
  intentional, 620
  declare, 525
  mean, 516
  inform, 527
  phrase, 566
  intelligible, 518
  name, 564
  squeeze out, 301
  rapid, 274
Expression, *aspect*, 448
Expressive, *style*, 574

Exprobation, *disapproval*, 932
  accusation, 938
Expropriate, *take*, 789
Expulsion, *see* Expel
Expunge, *efface*, 506, 552
  destroy, 162
  disappear, 449
Expurgation, *cleanness*, 652
Exquisite, *excellent*, 648
  pleasurable, 829
  savoury, 394
  fop, 854
Exquisitely, *great*, 31
Exsiccate, *dryness*, 340
Exsufflation, *sorcery*, 992
Extant, *being*, 1
Extempore, *instantly*, 113
  early, 132
  off-hand, 612
  unprepared, 674
Extend, *prolong*, 200
  expand, 194
  reach, 196
  increase, 35
Extensile, *pliable*, 324
Extension, *space*, 180
Extensive, *spacious*, 180
  considerable, 31
Extent, *degree*, 26
  space, 180
Extenuate, *decrease*, 36
  diminish, 192
  excuse, 937
  acquit, 970
Exterior, *exteriority*, 220
Exterminate, *destruction*, 162
Exterminator, *destroyer*, 165
External, *exteriority*, 220
Externalize, *materialize*, 316
Extinction, *destruction*, 162
  non-existence, 2
  of life, 360
Extinguish, *destroy*, 162
  darken, 421
  blow out, 385
Extinguisher, *destroyer*, 165
Extirpate, *destruction*, 162
  extraction, 301
Extol, *praise*, 931
  over-estimate, 482
Extort, *despoil*, 789
  extract, 301
  compel, 744
Extortionate, *greedy*, 865
  dear, 814
  parsimonious, 819
Extra, *additional*, 37, 39
  supernumerary, 641
  store, 636
*Extra muros, *exteriority*, 220
Extra-sensory, *occult*, 992
  thought, 451
  immaterial, 317
Extract, *take out*, 301
  part, 51

Fair sex, *woman,* 374
Fair-spoken, *courteous,* 894
   flattering, 933
Fairing, *gift,* 784
Fairly, *great,* 31
Fairy, *fabulous being,* 979
Fairy-cycle, *bicycle,* 266
Fairy godmother, *friend,* 891
   benefactor, 912
Fairy-tale, *lie,* 546
*Fait accompli, *completion,* 729
Faith, *belief,* 484
   hope, 858
   honour, 939
   creed, 983
   piety, 987
Faithful, *likeness,* 17
   true, 494
   obedient, 743
   observant, 772·
   Christian, 983A
   godly, 987
Faithless, *false,* 544
   dishonourable, 940
   sceptical, 989
Fake, *imitation,* 19
   deception, 545
   to forge, 544
Fakir, *clergy,* 996
Falcated, *curved,* 245
   sharp, 244
Falchion, *arms,* 727
Falciform, *angularity,* 244
   curvature, 245
Fall, *descend,* 306
   destruction, 162
   slope, 217
   fail, 732
   die, 360
   adversity, 735
   decline, 659
   happen, 151
   vice, 945
   autumn, 126
Fall away, *decrease,* 36
   shrink, 195
Fall back, *recede,* 283, 287
   relapse, 661
Fall behind, *sequence,* 281
Fall down, *descend,* 306
   worship, 990
Fall for, *love,* 897
Fall foul of, *oppose,* 708
   encounter, 720
   reprimand, 932
Fall in, *marshal,* 58, 60
   happen, 151
Fall in with, *find,* 480A
   uniformity, 16
   agree, 23
Fall off, *deterioration,* 659
   decrease, 36
   disjunction, 44
Fall out, *happen,* 151
   drop, 297

Fall short, *shortcoming,* 304, 730
   fail, 53
   insufficiency, 640
Fall through, *failure,* 732
Fall to, *work,* 686
   devour, 296
   fight, 722
Fall to pieces, *disjunction,* 44
Fall under, *inclusion,* 76
Fall upon, *attack,* 716
   discover, 480A
   devise, 626
Fallacy, *error,* 495
   uncertainty, 475
   sophistry, 477
Fal-lal, *ornament,* 847
   rifle, 643
Fallible, *uncertain,* 475, 477
Fallow, *yellow,* 436
   unproductive, 169
   unready, 674
False, *untrue,* 544
   error, 495
   sophistry, 477
   spurious, 925
   dishonourable, 940
False-hearted, *improbity,* 940
Falsehood, *lie,* 546
Falsetto, *music,* 413
   affected, 577
Falsify, *misinterpret,* 523
   accounts, 811
   deceive, 495
   lie, 544
Falstaffian, *fat,* 192
Falter, *stammer,* 583
   hesitate, 605
   demur, 603
   slowness, 275
Fame, *renown,* 873
   rumour, 531
   news, 532
Familiar, *common,* 82
   habit, 613
   known, 490
   friendly, 888
   affable, 894, 892
   spirit, 979
Family, *class,* 75
   consanguinity, 11
   paternity, 166
   posterity, 167
Famine, *insufficiency,* 640
Famished, *fasting,* 956
Famous, *repute,* 873
   greatness, 31
Fan, *blow,* 349
   excite, 615
   enthusiast, 840, 865
   frequenter, 136
Fanatic, *extravagant,* 515
Fanatical, *feeling,* 821
Fanaticism, *folly,* 499
   obstinacy, 606
   religious, 984A

Fanciful, *capricious,* 608
   imaginative, 515
   mistaken, 495
   unreal, 2
Fancy, *think,* 451
   believe, 484
   wit, 842
   idea, 453
   suppose, 514
   imagine, 515
   caprice, 608
   choice, 609
   desire, 865
   like, 394
   love, 897
   pugilism, 726
Fandango, *dance,* 840
Fane, *temple,* 1000
Fanfare, *loudness,* 404
   ostentation, 882
Fanfaronade, *boasting,* 884
Fang, *bane,* 663
Fanlight, *opening,* 260
Fantasia, *music,* 415
   imagination, 515
Fantastic, *odd,* 83
   imaginary, 515
   capricious, 608
   ridiculous, 853
Fantasy, *caprice,* 608
   imagination, 515
   idea, 453
*Fantoccini, *marionettes,*
             554, 599
Far, *distant,* 196
Far-fetched, *irrelation,* 10
   irrelevant, 24
   irrational, 477
   obscure, 519
Far from it, *dissimilarity,* 18
Far-seeing, *foresight,* 510
Farce, *drama,* 599
   ridiculous, 856
*Farceur, *humorist,* 844
Farcical, *ridiculous,* 856
   witty, 842
   trifling, 643
Fardel, *assemblage,* 72
Fare, *circumstance,* 8
   event, 151
   to eat, 296
   food, 298
   price, 812
Farewell, *departure,* 293
Farm, *house,* 189
   property, 780
   to rent, 788, 795
Farrago, *mixture,* 41
   confusion, 59
Farthing, *coin,* 800
   worthless, 643
Farthingale, *dress,* 225
Fasces, *sceptre,* 747
Fascia, *band,* 205
   circle, 247

Fascicle, *assemblage*, 72
Fascinate, *please*, 829
  excite, 824, 825
  astonish, 870
  love, 897
  conjure, 992
Fascination, *spell*, 993
  motive, 615
  occult arts, 992
Fash, *worry*, 830
Fashion, *form*, 144, 240
  custom, 613
  mould, 140
  mode, 627, 852
  nobility, 875
Fast, *rapid*, 274
  steadfast, 150
  stuck, 265
  joined, 43
  dissolute, 954
  not to eat, 640, 956
Fast and loose, *false*, 544
  changeful, 607
Fasten, *join*, 45, 214
  fix, 150
  restrain, 751
Fastener, *hanging*, 214
Fastening, *vinculum*, 45
Fastidious, *dainty*, 868
  squeamish, 932
Fasting, *abstinence*, 956
  atonement, 952
  insufficient, 640
Fastness, *asylum*, 666
  defence, 717
Fat, *oleaginous*, 356
  unctuous, 355
  broad, 202
  big, 192
Fat-head, *fool*, 501
Fat-witted, *folly*, 499
*Fata morgana, *phantasm*, 4
  dim sight, 443
  imagination, 515
Fatal, *lethal*, 361
  pernicious, 649
Fatalism, *destiny*, 152
  necessity, 601
Fatality, *killing*, 361
Fate, *necessity*, 601
  chance, 152, 621
  end, 67, 360
Father, *paternity*, 166
  priest, 996
  theologian, 983
Father upon, *attribute*, 155
Fatherland, *home*, 189
Fatherless, *unsustained*, 160
Fathom, *measure*, 466
  investigate, 461
  answer, 462
Fathomless, *depth*, 208
Fatidical, *prediction*, 511
Fatigue, *lassitude*, 688
  weariness, 841

*Fatras, *unimportance*, 643
Fatten on, *feeding*, 296
Fatuity, *folly*, 499
*Faubourg, *suburb*, 227
Fauces, *beginning*, 66
Faucet, *opening*, 260
  channel, 350
  outlet, 295
Faugh! *dislike*, 867
Fault, *imperfection*, 651
  blemish, 848
  break, 70
  vice, 945
  guilt, 947
  error, 495
  failure, 732
  ignorance, 491
Faultless, *perfect*, 650
  innocent, 946
Fauna, *animal*, 366
*Faute de mieux, *shift*, 147, 626
*Fauteuil, *support*, 215
*Faux pas, *failure*, 732
  error, 495
  vice, 945
Favour, *aid*, 707
  permit, 760
  friendship, 888
  partiality, 923
  gift, 784
  letter, 592
  to resemble, 17
Favourable, *good*, 648
  willing, 602
  friendly, 707, 888
  co-operating, 709
Favourite, *pleasing*, 829
  beloved, 897, 899
Favouritism, *wrong*, 923
Fawn, *colour*, 433
  cringe, 886
  flatter, 933
Fay, *fairy*, 979
Faze, *worry*, 830
  discompose, 458
  perplex, 704
Fealty, *duty*, 926
  respect, 928
  obedience, 743
Fear, *fear*, 860
  cowardice, 862
Fearful, *great*, 31
Fearless, *hopeful*, 858
  courageous, 861
Feasible, *possible*, 470
  easy, 705
Feast, *repast*, 298
  to devour, 296
  gluttony, 957
  revel, 840
  enjoyment, 827
  celebration, 883
  anniversary, 138
Feast on, *enjoy*, 377
Feat, *action*, 680

Feather, *tuft*, 256
  lightness, 320
  trifle, 643
  class, 75
  ornament, 847
  decoration, 877
Feather-bed, *softness*, 324
Feathery, *roughness*, 256
Feature, *character*, 5
  form, 240
  appearance, 448
  lineament, 550
  component, 56
  to resemble, 17
  cinema, 599A
Febrifuge, *remedy*, 662
*Fecit, *painting*, 556
Feckless, *feeble*, 160
  improvident, 674
  useless, 645
Feculence, *uncleanness*, 653
Fecund, *productive*, 168
Fecundation, *production*, 161
Fed up, *weariness*, 841
  dislike, 867
  satiety, 869
Federation, *co-operation*, 709
  party, 712
Fee, *expenditure*, 795, 809
Fee simple, *property*, 780
Feeble, *weak*, 160
  imperfect, 651
  scanty, 32
  silly, 477
  style, 575
Feeble-minded, *foolish*, 499
  irresolute, 605
Feed, *eat*, 296
  supply, 637
  meal, 298
Feel, *touch*, 379
  sensibility, 375
  moral, 821
Feel for, *seek*, 461
  sympathize, 914
Feeler, *inquiry*, 461
Feet, *journey*, 266
Feign, *falsehood*, 544
Feint, *deception*, 545
Felicitate, *congratulate*, 896
Felicitous, *expedient*, 646
  favourable, 648
  skilful, 698
  successful, 731
  happy, 827
  elegant, 578
  apt, 23
Felicity, *happiness*, 827
  prosperity, 734
  skill, 698
Feline, *stealthy*, 528
  sly, 702
Fell, *mountain*, 206
  cut down, 308
  knock down, 213

Fell, *dire*, 162
    wicked, 907
Fellah, *commonalty*, 876
Fellow, *similar*, 17
    equal, 27
    companion, 88
    man, 373
    dual, 89
Fellow creature, *man*, 372, 373
Fellow-feeling, *love*, 897
    friendship, 888
    sympathy, 906, 914
Fellowship, *sociality*, 892
    partnership, 712
    friendship, 888
Felo-de-se, *killing*, 361
Felon, *sinner*, 949
Felonious, *vice*, 945
Felony, *guilt*, 947
Felt, *matted*, 219
Felucca, *ship*, 273
Female, *woman*, 374
Feminality, *feebleness*, 160
Feminine, *woman*, 374
Feminism, *rights*, 924
Femme couverte, marriage,
    903
Femme de chambre, servant,
    746
Fen, *marsh*, 345
Fence, *circumscribe*, 231
    enclose, 232
    defence, 717
    fight, 720, 722
    safety, 664
    refuge, 666
    prison, 752
    to evade, 544
Fencible, *combatant*, 726
Fend, *defence*, 717
    provision, 637
Fenestrated, *windowed*, 260
Feoff, *property*, 780
Ferine, *malevolence*, 907
Ferment, *disorder*, 59
    energy, 171
    violence, 173
    agitation, 315
    effervesce, 353
Fern, *plant*, 367
Ferocity, *brutality*, 907
    violence, 173
Ferret, *tape*, 45
Ferret out, *inquiry*, 461
    discover, 480A
Ferry, *transference*, 270
    way, 627
Fertile *productive*, 168
    abundant, 639
Ferule, *scourge*, 975
Fervent, *devout*, 990
Fervour, *heat*, 382
    animation, 821
    desire, 865
    love, 897

Fester, *disease*, 655
    corruption, 653
Festina lente, haste, 684
Festival, *celebration*, 883
    anniversary, 138
Festive, *amusement*, 840
    sociality, 892
Festoon, *ornament*, 847
    curvature, 245
Fetch, *bring*, 270
    arrive, 292
    stratagem, 626
    evasion, 545
    price, 812
Fête, *amusement*, 840
    ostentation, 882
    celebration, 883
    convivial, 892
Fête champêtre, amusement,
    840
Fetid, *fetor*, 401
Fetish, *spell*, 993
Fetishism, *idolatry*, 991
    sorcery, 992
Fetter, *hinder*, 706
    restrain, 751
    shackle, 752
    join, 43
Fettle, *preparation*, 673
Fetus, *see* Foetus
Feud, *discord*, 713
    revenge, 919
Feudal, *authority*, 737
Feudatory, *subjection*, 749
Feu de joie, firework, 840
    salute, 882
Feuilleton, *essay*, 595
Fever, *heat*, 382
    disease, 655
    excitement, 825
Few, *fewness*, 103
    plurality, 100
Fez, *cap*, 225
Fiancée, *love*, 897
Fiasco, *failure*, 732
Fiat, *command*, 741
Fib, *falsehood*, 544, 546
Fibre, *link*, 45
    filament, 205
Fibrous, *thin*, 203
Fichu, *dress*, 225
Fickle, *irresolute*, 605
Fictile, *form*, 240
Fiction, *untruth*, 546
    fancy, 515
    story, 594
Fictitious, *false*, 544
Fiddle, *to play*, 415
    violin, 417
    deceive, 545
    swindle, 791
    falsify, 544
Fiddle-de-dee, *trifling*, 643
    contemptible, 930
Fiddle-faddle, *trifle*, 643

Fiddle-faddle, *dawdle*, 683
Fiddler, *musician*, 416
Fiddlestick, *contemptible*, 930
    absurd, 497
    trifling, 643
Fiddling, *trifling*, 643
Fidelity, *honour*, 939
    observance, 772
Fidget, *excitability*, 825
    irascibility, 901
    agitation, 315
    activity, 682
Fidgety, *changeable*, 149
Fido, *mist*, 353
Fiducial, *belief*, 484
Fidus Achates, auxiliary, 711
Fie! *disrepute*, 874
Fief, *property*, 780
Field, *plain*, 344
    arena, 728
    scope, 180
    business, 625
    property, 780
Field-day, *pageant*, 882
    festivity, 840
Field-marshal, *master*, 745
Field of view, *vista*, 441
    idea, 453
Field-piece, *arms*, 727
Fiend, *demon*, 980
    ruffian, 913
Fiendish, *malevolent*, 907
    wicked, 945
Fierce, *violent*, 173
    passion, 825
    daring, 861
    angry, 900
Fiery, *violent*, 173
    excitable, 825
    hot, 382
    fervent, 821
Fiery cross, *warfare*, 722
Fife, *musical instrument*, 417
Fifth columnist, *traitor*, 742
Fig, *unimportant*, 643
    dress, 225
    adorn, 845, 847
Fight, *contention*, 720, 722
Fighter, *combatant*, 726
    aircraft, 273A
Fighter-bomber, *aircraft*, 273A
Figment, *imagination*, 515
Figurante, the drama, 599
Figuration, *form*, 240
Figurative, *metaphorical*, 521
    style, 577
    comparison, 464
Figure, *state*, 7
    number, 84
    price, 812
    form, 240
    metaphor, 521, 566
    imagine, 515
    represent, 550, 554
    reputation, 873

Figure, *ugliness*, 846
  parade, 882
Figurehead, *effigy*, 554
  inaction, 683
Figurine, *sculpture*, 557
Fike, *whim*, 481
Filament, *slender*, 205
  ligature, 45
  light, 423
Filamentous, *thin*, 203
Filch, *steal*, 791, 792
File, *to smooth*, 255
  to pulverize, 330
  to string together, 60
  row, 69
  duality, 89
  collection, 72
  list, 86
  store, 636
  register, 551
File off, *march*, 266
  diverge, 291
Filial, *posterity*, 167
Filiation, *consanguinity*, 11
  posterity, 167
  derivation, 155
Filibeg, *dress*, 225
Filibuster, *thief*, 792
  delay, 133
Filigree, *crossing*, 219
Filings, *pulverulence*, 330
Fill, *occupy*, 186
  fullness, 52
Fill out, *expand*, 194
Fill up, *complete*, 52
  close, 261
  satisfy, 639
  composition, 54
  compensate, 30
*Fille de joie, *libertine*, 962
Fillet, *band*, 45
  circle, 247
  gut, 297
Filling, *contents*, 190
Fillip, *stimulus*, 615
  impulse, 276
  propulsion, 284
Filly, *horse*, 271
  young, 129
Film, *layer*, 204
  dimness, 421, 426
  semitransparency, 427
  cinema, 599A
Filmy, *texture*, 329
Filter, *clean*, 652
  percolate, 295
  amend, 658
Filth, *uncleanness*, 653
Filtration, *passage*, 302
Fimbriated, *rough*, 256
Fin, *instrument*, 267, 633
Final, *end*, 67
  conclusive, 478
  resolved, 604
Finale, *music*, 415

Finance, *money*, 800
  accounts, 811
Find, *discover*, 480A
  term, 71
  provide, 637
  sentence, 969
  acquisition, 775
Fine, *rare*, 322
  textural, 329
  good, 648
  beautiful, 845
  adorned, 847
  thin, 203
  mulct, 974
  to clarify, 652
Fine-draw, *improve*, 658
Fine-spoken, *courtesy*, 894
Fine-spun, *thinness*, 203
Finery, *ornament*, 847
Finesse, *cunning*, 702
  manoeuvre, 545
  tact, 698
  taste, 850
Finger, *touch*, 379
  instrument, 633
Finger-post, *indication*, 550
Finger-print, *evidence*, 467
  sign, 550
Finical, *unimportant*, 643
Finicky, *fastidious*, 868
Finikin, *unimportant*, 643
Finis, *end*, 67
Finish, *complete*, 52
  achieve, 729
  end, 67
  symmetry, 242
Finished, *perfect*, 242, 650
  accomplished, 698
  greatness, 31
Finite, *smallness*, 32
Fiord, *gulf*, 343
Fire, *heat*, 382, 384
  furnace, 386
  vigour, 574
  energy, 171
  to excite, 825
  to urge, 615
  dismiss, 756
Fire at, *attack*, 716
Fire away, *begin*, 66
Fire-brigade, *cooling*, 385
Fire-bug, *incendiary*, 384
Fire-drake, *light*, 423
Fire-eater, *blusterer*, 887
  fury, 173, 901
Fire-engine, *cooling*, 385
Fire-escape, *escape*, 671
Fire off, *propulsion*, 284
Fire-place, *furnace*, 386
Fire-ship, *ship*, 273
  burning, 384
Fire up, *resentment*, 900
Fire-worshipper, *heathen*, 984
Firebrand, *brand*, 388

Firebrand, *incendiary*, 913
Firefly, *luminary*, 423
Firelock, *arms*, 727
Fireman, *cooling*, 385
Fireproof, *incombustible*, 385
  safe, 664
Fireside, *abode*, 189
Firework, *fire*, 382
  light, 423
  display, 882
  celebration, 883
Firing, *fuel*, 388
  explosion, 406
Firkin, *receptacle*, 191
Firm, *hard*, 323
  junction, 43
  stable, 150
  resolute, 604
  brave, 861
  party, 712
  partnership, 797
  friendship, 888
Firmament, *world*, 318
Firman, *order*, 741
  permit, 760
  decree, 963
First, *beginning*, 66
First-born, *age*, 124, 128
First-rate, *ship*, 273
  excellent, 648
  superiority, 33
First-string, *proficient*, 700
First to last, from, *whole*, 50
  completeness, 52
  duration, 106
Firth, *gulf*, 343
Fisc, *treasury*, 802
Fiscal, *money*, 800
Fish, *animal*, 366
Fish for, *desire*, 865
Fish out, *discover*, 480A
Fish out of water,
        disagreement, 24
Fish up, *elevation*, 307
Fishery, *domestication*, 370
Fishy, *dubious*, 475, 478
Fissile, *brittle*, 328
Fission, *disjunction*, 44
Fissure, *chink*, 198
Fist, *writing*, 590
Fistula, *opening*, 260
Fit, *state*, 7
  paroxysm, 173
  disease, 655
  caprice, 608
  to prepare, 673
  equalize, 27
  excitement, 825
  anger, 900
  duty, 926
  agreement, 23
  expedient, 646
  right, 922
Fit out, *preparation*, 673
Fitful, *capricious*, 608

Fitful, *irresolute*, 605
   discontinuous, 70
   irregular, 139
Fitness, *agreement*, 23
Fitting, *expedient*, 646
   right, 922, 926
   due, 924
   instrument, 633
Five, *number*, 98
Fiver, *money*, 800
Fix, *place*, 150, 184
   rectify, 658, 660
   solidify, 321
   arrangement, 60
   situation, 8
   difficulty, 704
Fix together, *junction*, 43
Fix upon, *choose*, 609
Fixed, *determined*, 604
   permanent, 141, 150
   quiescent, 265
Fixture, *property*, 780
   stability, 150
Fizgig, *firework*, 423
Fizz, *sibilation*, 409
   bubble, 353
Fizzle, *hiss*, 409
Fizzle out, *failure*, 158, 732
Fjord, *see* Fiord
Flabbergast, *astound*, 870
Flabby, *soft*, 324
Flaccid, *shrivelled*, 172, 193
   soft, 324
   empty, 640
Flag, *streamer*, 550
   flat stone, 204
   weakness, 160
   floor, 211
   droop, 688
   inactive, 683
   infirm, 160, 655
   slowness, 275
Flagellation, *flogging*, 972
   atonement, 952
   asceticism, 955
Flageolet, *musical*, 417
Flagitious, *vice*, 945
Flagrant, *notorious*, 531
   manifest, 525
   great, 31
   atrocious, 945
Flagstaff, *sign*, 550
   high, 206
Flail, *impulse*, 276
Flair, *intelligence*, 498
Flake, *layer*, 204
Flam, *untruth*, 546
Flambeau, *luminary*, 423
Flamboyant, *vulgar*, 851
   ornamented, 577, 847
Flame, *light*, 420
   fire, 382
   luminary, 423
   passion, 825
   love, 897

Flame, *favourable*, 899
Flame-coloured, *orange*, 439
Flaming, *excited*, 821, 825
*Flâneur, *idler*, 683
Flange, *support*, 215
Flank, *side*, 236
   safety, 664
Flannel, *flattery*, 933
Flannels, *dress*, 225
Flap, *adjunct*, 39
   hanging, 214
   move about, 315
   beat, 972
   fear, 860
Flapdoodle, *deception*, 546
   nonsense, 497
Flapjack, *receptacle*, 191
Flapper, *girl*, 129, 374
Flapping, *loose*, 47
Flare, *glare*, 420
   violence, 173
Flare up, *kindle*, 825
   anger, 900
Flaring, *colour*, 428
Flash, *instant*, 113
   fire, 382
   light, 420
   thought, 451
   sudden act, 612
   violence, 173
Flash-lamp, *light*, 423
Flash note, *money*, 800
Flashback, *memory*, 505
   cinema, 599A
Flashy, *gaudy colour*, 428
   bad taste, 851
   ostentatious, 882
Flask, *receptacle*, 191
Flat, *level*, 251
   uniform, 16
   horizontal, 213
   novice, 701
   dupe, 547
   low, 207
   vapid, 391
   inert, 172, 823
   dull, 841, 843
   insipid, 575
   dejected, 837
   sound, 408
   indifferent, 866
   positive, 535
   abode, 189
   apartment, 191
Flatlet, *abode*, 189
Flatter, *pleasure*, 829
   encourage, 858
   adulation, 933
   servility, 886
Flatterer, *eulogist*, 935
Flattie, *detective*, 461
   cinema, 599A
Flatulent, *windy*, 338
   gaseous, 334
   style, 573

Flaunt, *display*, 873, 882
   gaudy, 428
   ornament, 847
Flautist, *musician*, 416
Flavour, *taste*, 390
Flavous, *yellow*, 436
Flaw, *crack*, 198
   error, 495
   imperfection, 651
   blemish, 848
   fault, 947
Flay, *divest*, 226
   punish, 972
Flea-bag, *bed*, 215
Flea-bite, *trifle*, 643
Flea-bitten, *variegated*, 440
Fleckered, *variegation*, 440
Fledged, *preparation*, 673
Flee, *escape*, 671
   avoid, 623
Fleece, *tegument*, 222
   to rob, 791
   to strip, 789
   impoverish, 804
Fleer, *ridicule*, 956
Fleet, *swift*, 274
   ships, 273
Fleeting, *transient*, 111
   changeful, 607
Flesh, *mankind*, 372
   carnality, 961
Flesh colour, *redness*, 434
Flesh-pots, *food*, 298
Fleshly, *sensual*, 954, 961
Fleshy, *corpulent*, 192
Flexible, *pliant*, 324
   tractable, 705
Flexion, *bending*, 245
   deviation, 279
   fold, 258
Flexuous, *convolution*, 248
Flexure, *bending*, 245
   fold, 258
Flibbertigibbet, *trifler*, 460
Flick, *propel*, 284
   cinema, 599A
Flicker, *flutter*, 315
   oscillate, 314
   waver, 149, 605
   shine, 420
Flickering, *irregular*, 139
Flight, *departure*, 287, 293
   escape, 671
   volitation, 267
   swiftness, 174
   multitude, 102
Flight-lieutenant, *master*, 745
Flight of Fancy, *imagination*, 515
   idea, 453
Flighty, *insane*, 503
   fickle, 605
Flim-flam, *lie*, 546
   caprice, 608
Flimsy, *texture*, 329

Galaxy, *luminary*, 423
   multitude, 102
   glory, 873
Gale, *wind*, 349
Gall, *bitterness*, 395
   pain, 378
   to pain, 830
   insolence, 885
   malevolence, 907
   anger, 900
Gallant, *brave*, 861
   courteous, 894
   lover, 897
   licentious, 961, 962
Gallantry, *love*, 897
Galleon, *ship*, 273
Gallery, *room*, 191
   theatre, 599
   passage, 260
Galley, *ship*, 273
   prison, 752
Galliard, *dance*, 840
Gallicism, *neology*, 563
Galligaskins, *dress*, 225
Gallimaufry, *mixture*, 41
Galliot, *ship*, 273
Gallipot, *receptacle*, 191
Gallivant, *travel*, 266
Gallop, *ride*, 266
   scamper, 274
Gallophobia, *dislike*, 867
Galloway, *carrier*, 271
Gallows, *scourge*, 975
Gallup poll, *inquiry*, 461
Galore, *multitude*, 102
   sufficiency, 639
Galosh, *dress*, 225
Galumph, *exult*, 836
Galvanic, *violent*, 173
Galvanism, *excitation*, 824
Galvanize, *energize*, 171
*Gambade, *leap*, 309
   prank, 856
Gamble, *chance*, 156, 621
Gambler, *rashness*, 863
Gambol, *amusement*, 840
Game, *chance*, 156
   pursuit, 622
   plan, 626
   intent, 620
   amusement, 840
   resolute, 604
   brave, 861
Game-cock, *courage*, 861
Game-reserve, *menagerie*, 370
Gamekeeper, *keeper*, 753
Gamesome, *cheerful*, 836
*Gamin, *commonalty*, 876
Gammon, *untruth*, 544, 546
   to hoax, 545
Gamut, *harmony*, 413
Gamy, *pungent*, 392
Gander, *look*, 441
Gang, *party*, 712
   knot, 72

Gangling, *lank*, 203
Gangrel, *tramp*, 876
   pauper, 804
Gangrene, *disease*, 655
Gangster, *evildoer*, 913, 949
   swindler, 792
Gangway, *way*, 627
   opening, 260
Gaol, *see* Jail
Gap, *discontinuity*, 70
   chasm, 4, 198
Gape, *open*, 260
   wonder, 870
   curiosity, 455
   desire, 865
Garage, *house*, 189
Garb, *dress*, 225
Garbage, *unclean*, 653
Garble, *retrench*, 38
   misinterpret, 523
   falsify, 544
Garbled, *incomplete*, 53
*Garçon, *servant*, 746
Garden, *beauty*, 845
Gardening, *agriculture*, 371
Gargantuan, *size*, 192
Gargle, *water*, 337
Gargoyle, *spout*, 350
Garish, *colour*, 428
   light, 420
   ornament, 847
   display, 882
Garland, *ornament*, 847
   trophy, 733
Garlic, *condiment*, 393
Garment, *dress*, 225
Garner, *collect*, 72
   store, 636
Garnet, *ornament*, 847
Garnish, *adorn*, 845
   ornament, 847
   addition, 39
Garret, *room*, 191
   high, 206
Garrison, *combatant*, 726
   defend, 664, 717
Garrotte, *killing*, 361
   punishment, 972
   gallows, 975
Garrulity, *loquacity*, 584
Gas, *rarity*, 322
   gaseity, 334
   to chatter, 584
   to boast, 884
Gas-bag, *loquacity*, 584
Gas-mantle, *light*, 423
Gasconade, *boasting*, 884
Gaselier, *light*, 423
Gash, *disjunction*, 44, 198
Gaslight print, *photograph*, 556
Gasoline, *oil*, 356
Gasometer, *gas*, 334
   store, 636
Gasp, *pant*, 349, 688
   desire, 865

Gasp, *droop*, 655
Gastronomy, *gluttony*, 957
   epicurism, 868
Gat, *gun*, 727
Gate, *beginning*, 66
   way, 627
   mouth, 260
   barrier, 232
Gate-crasher, *parasite*, 886
Gather, *collect*, 72, 789
   acquire, 775
   enlarge, 194
   learn, 539
   conclude, 480
   fold, 258
   unite in a focus, 74
Gathering, *disease*, 655
Gatling, *gun*, 727
*Gauche, *unskilful*, 699
   ill-mannered, 851
Gaud, *ornament*, 847
Gaudery, *vanity*, 880
Gaudy, *colouring*, 428
   ornamental, 847
   vulgar, 851
   flaunting, 882
   party, 72, 892
Gauge, *measure*, 466
Gaunt, *spare*, 203
   ugliness, 846
Gauntlet, *defiance*, 715
   punishment, 972
   glove, 225
   anger, 909
Gautama, *religious founder*,
         986
Gauze, *shade*, 424
Gauzy, *filmy*, 329
Gavotte, *dance*, 840
   music, 415
Gawky, *awkward*, 699
   ridiculous, 853
   ugly, 846
Gay, *cheerful*, 836
   adorned, 847
   colour, 428
Gaze, *vision*, 441
Gazebo, *look-out*, 441
   building, 189
Gazelle, *velocity*, 274
Gazette, *publication*, 531
   record, 551
Gazetted, *bankrupt*, 808
Gazetteer, *list*, 86
Gazing-stock, *prodigy*, 872
Gear, *clothes*, 225
   harness, 633
Gee! *wonder*, 870
Gee-gee, *carrier*, 271
Geezer, *veteran*, 130
Gehenna, *hell*, 982
Geisha, *dancer*, 599
Gelatine, *pulpiness*, 354
Gelatinous, *semiliquid*, 352
Gelding, *carrier*, 271

Gelid, *cold*, 383
Gelignite, *arms*, 727
Gem, *jewel*, 650
   ornament, 847
   goodness, 648
Gemination, *duplicate*, 90
Gemini, *duality*, 89
Gen, *information*, 527
*Gendarme, *police*, 965
Gender, *class*, 75
Genealogy, *continuity*, 69
   filiation, 155
General, *generic*, 78
   officer, 745
Generalissimo, *master*, 745
Generality, *generic*, 78
Generalship, *conduct*, 692
Generate, *produce*, 161, 168
Generation, *mankind*, 372
   period, 108
Generic, *general*, 78
Generous, *liberal*, 816
   benevolent, 906
   giving, 784
   unselfish, 942
Genesis, *production*, 161
Genial, *warm*, 382
   cordial, 602, 829
   courteous, 894
   cheerful, 836
Geniculated, *angular*, 244
Genie, *demon*, 980
Genius, *talent*, 498
   intellect, 450
   skill, 698
   spirit, 979
   proficient, 700
*Genius loci, *location*, 184
Genocide, *killing*, 361
*Genre, *class*, 75
   style, 7
   painting, 556
Genteel, *fashionable*, 852
Gentile, *heathen*, 984
Gentility, *rank*, 875
   politeness, 852, 894
Gentle, *moderate*, 174
   slow, 275
   meek, 826
   lenient, 740
   courteous, 894
   sound, 405
Gentleman, *person*, 373
   squire, 875
   man of honour, 939
Gentlemanly, *polite*, 852
   noble, 875
   courteous, 894
Gentlewoman, *woman*, 374
Gently, *slowly*, 174, 275
Gentry, *nobility*, 875
Genuflexion, *bow*, 308
   homage, 725, 743
   respect, 928
   servility, 886

Genuflexion, *worship*, 990
Genuine, *true*, 494
   real, 1
   good, 648
Genus, *class*, 75
Geodesy, *measurement*, 466
Geography, *place*, 183
Geology, *mineral*, 358
Geometry, *measurement*, 466
Geriatrics, *remedy*, 662
Germ, *rudiment*, 153, 674
   beginning, 66
   bane, 663
   insalubrity, 657
Germane, *relation*, 23
Germinate, *sprout*, 154, 194
   produce, 153
Gerrymander, *garble*, 544
   cunning, 702
Gestapo, *detective*, 461
Gestation, *pregnancy*, 168
   production, 161
   preparation, 673
Gesticulate, *sign*, 550
Gesture, *hint*, 527
   indication, 550
Get, *acquire*, 775
   understand, 518
   become, 144
Get about, *publication*, 531
Get among, *mixture* 41
Get at, *tamper with*, 682
   find out, 480A
Get-at-able, *attainable*, 705
Get back, *arrival*, 292
Get before, *precedency*, 62
Get by, *succeed*, 731
Get down, *descend*, 306
Get home, *arrive*, 292
Get off, *depart*, 293
   liberate, 750
   escape, 927
Get on, *advance*, 282
   succeed, 731
   improve, 658
Get on to, *blame*, 932
Get out, *repulsion*, 289
   ejection, 297
Get-out, *plea*, 617
Get round, *circumvent*, 702
Get the start, *precede*, 62
Get to, *arrive*, 292
Get together, *assemble*, 72
Get up, *rise*, 305
   prepare, 673
   style, 7
Get wind, *come to light*, 525
Getaway, *escape*, 671
Gewgaw, *trifle*, 643
   ornament, 847
Geyser, *heat*, 382
   furnace, 386
Ghastly, *tedious*, 846
   frightful, 860
Ghost, *soul*, 450

Ghost, *apparition*, 980
   shade, 362
   emaciated, 193
   Deity, 976
   instrumentality, 631
Ghoul, *demon*, 980
   evildoer, 913
Giant, *tall*, 206
   large, 192
Gibber, *stammer*, 583
   unmeaning, 517
Gibberish, *jargon*, 519
   nonsense, 517
   absurdity, 497
Gibbet, *gallows*, 975
   to execute, 972
Gibbous, *globose*, 249
   convex, 250
   distorted, 244
Gibe, *jeer*, 856, 932
   taunt, 929
Giddiness, *caprice*, 608
   inattention, 458
   bungling, 699
Giddy, *careless*, 460
   irresolute, 605
   bungling, 699
   light-headed, 503
Gift, *given*, 784
   power, 157
   talent, 698
Gig, *vehicle*, 272
   ship, 273
Gigantic, *large*, 192
   tall, 206
Giggle, *laugh*, 838
Gild, *adorn*, 845
   ornament, 847
   coat, 222
Gill, *river*, 348
Gillie, *servant*, 746
Gimbals, *rotation*, 312
Gimble, *rotate*, 312
Gimcrack, *brittle*, 328
   weak, 160
   valueless, 645
   imperfect, 651
   ornament, 847
   whim, 865
Gimlet, *perforator*, 262
Gimmick, *speciality*, 79
Gin, *trap*, 667
Ginger, *pungency*, 392
   condiment, 393
   vigour, 574
Ginger up, *excite*, 824
Gingerbread, *flimsy*, 651
   ornament, 847
Gingerly, *carefully*, 459
   slowly, 275
Gipsy, *deceiver*, 548
   fortune-teller, 513
Girandole, *luminary*, 423
Gird, *bind*, 43
   surround, 227

Go, *try*, 675
Go about, *undertake*, 676
Go across, *passage*, 302
Go ahead, *advance*, 282
    improve, 658
    activity, 682
Go-ahead, *energetic*, 171
Go bail, *security*, 771
Go-between, *intermedium*,
                    228, 631
    messenger, 534
    agent, 758
Go by, *pass*, 303
Go-by, *evasion*, 623
Go down, *sink*, 306
    decline, 659
Go forth, *depart*, 293
    publish, 531
Go-getter, *activity*, 682
Go halves, *divide*, 91
Go hand in hand with,
    accompany, 88
Go in for, *business*, 625
Go near, *approach*, 286
Go off, *cease*, 142
    explode, 173
    die, 360
    fare, 151
Go on, *continue*, 143
Go over, *change sides*, 607
Go round, *circuition*, 311
Go through, *pass*, 302
    complete, 729
    endure, 821
Go to, *direction*, 278
    remonstrance, 695
Go under, *name*, 564
    sink, 310
    ruin, 735
Go up, *ascent*, 305
Go with, *assent*, 488
    suit, 646
Goad, *motive*, 615
Goal, *object*, 620
    reach, 292
Goat, *fool*, 501
Goatish, *impure*, 961
Gobbet, *piece*, 51
Gobble, *devour*, 296
    gluttony, 957
    cry, 412
Gobbledygook, *verbiage*, 573
*Gobemouche, *credulous*, 486
    fool, 501
    dupe, 547
Goblin, *ghost*, 980
    bugbear, 860
God, *Deity*, 976
Goddess, *great spirit*, 979
    favourite, 899
    beauty, 845
Godless, *irreligion*, 989
Godlike, *virtue*, 944
Godliness, *piety*, 987
Godown, *store*, 636, 799

Godsend, *luck*, 621
    advantage, 618
    success, 731
Goer, *horse*, 271
Goggle, *optical instrument*, 445
    to stare, 441
Goggle-eyed, *dimsighted*, 443
Golconda, *wealth*, 803
Gold, *money*, 800
Gold-digger, *flirt*, 902
    selfishness, 943
Golden, *yellow*, 436
Golden age, *pleasure*, 827
    prosperity, 734
    imagination, 515
Golden calf, *idols*, 986
Golden-mouthed, *ornament*,
                            577
Golden wedding, *celebration*,
                            883
    anniversary, 138
Goldsmith, *artist*, 559
Goliath, *strength*, 159
    giant, 192
Gombeen-man, *usurer*, 805
Gomeril, *fool*, 501
Gondola, *ship*, 273
Gondolier, *mariner*, 269
Gone, *non-extant*, 2
    absent, 187
    dead, 360
Gone by, *past*, 123
Gone on, *loving*, 897
Gonfalon, *flag*, 550
Gong, *resonance*, 417
    decoration, 877
Goniometer, *angle*, 244
    measure, 466
Goo, *adhesive*, 45
    viscid, 352
Good, *advantage*, 618
    advantageous, 648
    virtuous, 944
    right, 922
    tasty, 394
Good-bye, *departure*, 293
Good day, *arrival*, 292
    salute, 894
Good-fellowship, 892
Good-for-nothing, *rascal*, 949
Good humour, *cheerfulness*,
                            836
Good-looking, *beauty*, 845
Good manners, *courtesy*, 894
Good morning, *salute*, 894
Good nature, *benevolence*, 906
    inexcitability, 826
Good show, *approval*, 931
Goodly, *large*, 192
    beautiful, 845
Goods, *effects*, 780
Goods train, *vehicle*, 272
Goodwill, *benevolence*, 906
    friendship, 888
    merchandise, 798

Goodwill, *materials*, 635
Goody, *woman*, 374
Gooey, *sticky*, 46
Goo-goo eyes, *ogle*, 902
Goon, *rascal*, 949
Goose, *fool*, 501
Goose-skin, *cold*, 383
Gorblimey, *vulgar*, 876
Gordian knot, *problem*, 461
    difficulty, 704
Gore, *opening*, 260
    angularity, 244
Gorge, *ravine*, 198
    narrowness, 203
    to devour, 296
    full, 641; *satiety*, 869
    gluttony, 957
Gorgeous, *colour*, 428
    splendid, 845
    ornamented, 847
Gorgon, *fear*, 860
    ugliness, 846
Gormandize, *gluttony*, 957
    reception, 296
Gory, *killing*, 361
Gospel, *scripture*, 985
    truth, 494
    certainty, 474
Gossamer, *texture*, 329
    slender, 205
    light, 320
Gossip, *conversation*, 588
    chatterer, 584
    news, 532
Gossoon, *boy*, 129, 373
Goth, *barbarian*, 876
    evildoer, 913
Gothic, *vulgarity*, 851
    defacement, 241
*Gouache, *painting*, 556
Gouge, *concavity*, 252
Gourmand, *gluttony*, 957
    epicure, 868
Gourmet, *desire*, 865
    epicure, 868
    gluttony, 957
*Goût, *taste*, 850
Govern, *direct*, 693
    authority, 737
Governess, *teacher*, 540
Governess-cart, *vehicle*, 272
Governor, *director*, 694
    master, 745
    tutor, 540
Gowk, *fool*, 501
Gown, *dress*, 225
Grab, *snatch*, 789
    steal, 791
    booty, 793
Grabble, *fumble*, 379
Grace, *elegance*, 845
    polish, 850
    forgiveness, 918
    honour, 939
    title, 877

Grey-headed, *age*, 128
　veteran, 130
Grey market, *illegality*, 964
Grey matter, *brain*, 450
Greybeard, *veteran*, 130
Greyhound, *swift*, 274
Grid, *lattice*, 219
Gridelin, *purple*, 437
Gridiron, *lattice*, 219
　arena, 728
Grief, *dejection*, 837
Grievance, *injury*, 619
　pain, 830
Grieve, *complain*, 828, 839
　afflict, 830
　injure, 649
Griffin, *unconformity*, 83
　keeper, 753
Grig, *cheerful*, 836
Grill, *calefaction*, 384
　question, 461
Grille, *lattice*, 219
Grim, *ugly*, 846
　frightful, 828
　discourteous, 895
　ferocious, 907
Grim-visaged, *grave*, 837
Grimace, *ridicule*, 856
Grime, *unclean*, 653
Grin, *laugh*, 838
　ridicule, 856
　scorn, 929
Grind, *pulverize*, 330
　an organ, 415
　oppress, 907
　learn, 539
　sharpen, 253
　scholar, 492
Grinder, *teacher*, 540
Grinding, *painful*, 831
Grip, *power*, 737
　bag, 191
Grip-sack, *bag*, 191
Gripe, *seize*, 789
　retain, 781
　pain, 378, 828
　to give pain, 830
　power, 737
Griping, *avaricious*, 819
*Grisette, *woman*, 374
Grisly, *ugliness*, 846
Grist, *provision*, 637
　materials, 635
Gristle, *toughness*, 327
Grit, *pulverulence*, 330
　determination, 604
　courage, 861
Gritty, *hard*, 323
Grizzled, *variegation*, 440
Grizzly, *grey*, 432
Groan, *cry*, 411
　lament, 839
Groggy, *drunk*, 959
　ill, 655
Groin, *angular*, 244

Grooly, *ugly*, 845
Groom, *servant*, 746
　marriage, 903
Groomsman, *marriage*, 903
Groove, *furrow*, 259
　habit, 613
Grope, *feel*, 379
　experience, 463
　inquire, 461
　try, 675
Gross, *whole*, 51
　greatness, 31
　vulgar, 851
　vicious, 945
　impure, 961
*Grossièreté, *rudeness*, 895
Grot, *see* Grotto
Grotesque, *deformed*, 846
　ridiculous, 851, 853
　outlandish, 83
Grotto, *alcove*, 189
　hollow, 252
Grouchy, *discourteous*, 895
　bad-tempered, 901
Ground, *land*, 342
　support, 215
　base, 211
　region, 181
　cause, 153
　motive, 615
　plea, 617
　property, 780
　arena, 728
　teach, 537
Ground swell, *surge*, 348
　agitation, 315
Grounded, *knowing*, 490
　wrecked, 732
Groundless, *erroneous*, 495
　sophistical, 477
Groundling, *commonalty*, 876
Grounds, *lees*, 653
Groundwork, *basis*, 211
　support, 215
　cause, 153
　precursor, 64
　preparation, 673
Group, *cluster*, 72
　troop, 726
　to marshal, 58
Group-captain, *master*, 745
Grouse, *grumble*, 832, 839
Grout, *vinculum*, 45
Grove, *wood*, 367
　house, 189
Grovel, *move slowly*, 275
　be low, 207
　cringe, 886
　base, 940
Grow, *increase*, 35
　expand, 194
Grow from, *effect*, 154
Growl, *cry*, 412
　complain, 839
　threaten, 909

Growl, *be rude*, 895
　anger, 900
Growler, *vehicle*, 272
Growth, *in degree*, 35
　in size, 194
Groyne, *refuge*, 666
Grub, *little*, 193
　food, 298
Grub up, *extract*, 301
　destroy, 162
　discover, 480A
Grudge, *hate*, 898
　stingy, 640, 819
　unwilling, 603
Gruelling, *punishment*, 972
Gruesome, *ugly*, 846
Gruff, *morose*, 895
　sound, 410
Grumble, *sound*, 411
　complain, 832, 839
Grumous, *dense*, 321
　pulpy, 354
Grumpy, *discourteous*, 895
　bad-tempered, 901
Grundyism, *prudery*, 855
Grunt, *cry*, 412
　complain, 839
Guano, *manure*, 653
Guarantee, *security*, 771
　evidence, 467
　promise, 768
Guard, *defend*, 717
　safety, 664
Guard-room, *prison*, 752
Guarded, *circumspect*, 459
　conditional, 770
Guardian, *safety*, 664, 717
　keeper, 753
Guardless, *danger*, 665
Guardsman, *combatant*, 726
Gubernatorial, *directing*, 693
　authority, 737
Gudgeon, *dupe*, 547
Guerdon, *reward*, 973
Guerrilla, *combatant*, 726
Guess, *suppose*, 514
Guest, *friend*, 890
　arrival, 292
*Guet-apens, *untruth*, 546
　ambush, 530
Guffaw, *laughter*, 834
Guggle, *see* Gurgle
Guide, *direct*, 693
　director, 694
　advice, 695
　teach, 537
　teacher, 540
　road-book, 266
Guide-post, *indicator*, 550
　warning, 668
Guideless, *danger*, 665
Guild, *corporation*, 712
　tribunal, 966
　partnership, 797
Guildhall, *mart*, 799

Hallucination, *delusion*, 503
Halo. *light*, 420
   glory, 873
Halt. *stop*, 142, 265
   flag, 655
   rest, 685, 687
   limp, 275
Halter. *rope*, 45
   fetter, 752
   punishment, 975
Halting. *lame*, 160
Halve, *bisect*, 91
Halyard, *rope*, 45
Hamadryad, *nymph*, 979
Hamlet. *abode*, 189
*Hammal. *carrier*, 271
Hammam. *furnace*, 386
Hammer, *to knock*, 276
   instrument, 633
   auction, 796
   repetition, 104
   bankrupt, 808
Hammer at, *thought*, 583
   action, 682
Hammock, *support*, 215
Hamper, *basket*, 191
   obstruct, 706
Hamstring, *injure*, 649
   weaken, 160
   incapacitate, 158
Hand, *instrument*, 633
   indicator, 550
   agent, 690
   side, 236
   writing, 590
   to give, 784
   agency, 170
Hand-barrow, *vehicle*, 272
Hand-gallop, *velocity*, 274
Hand in hand, *accompaniment*,
   88
Hand over, *transfer*, 270
Handbook, *advice*, 695
Handcuff, *tie together*, 43
   manacle, 751, 752
Handfast, *marriage*, 903
Handful, *quantity*, 25, 103
   smallness, 32
Handicap, *inequality*, 28
   disadvantage, 651
Handicraft, *action*, 680
Handicraftsman, *agent*, 690
Handiwork, *action*, 680
   effect, 154
Handkerchief, *dress*, 225
   clean, 652
Handle, *instrument*, 633
   plea, 617
   touch, 379
   use, 677
   describe, 594
   dissert, 595
   work, 680
Handling, *treatment*, 692
Handmaid, *servant*, 746

Handmaid, *instrumentality*, 631
Hands off! *resist*, 719
   prohibit, 761
Handsel, *security*, 771
   give, 784
   pay, 809
   begin, 66
Handsome, *beautiful*, 845
   liberal, 816
   disinterested, 942
Handspike, *instrument*, 633
Handwriting, *omen*, 512
   signature, 550
   autograph, 590
Handy, *near*, 197
   skilful, 698
   useful, 644
   attainable, 705
Hang, *pendency*, 214
   kill, 361
   execute, 972
   expletive, 908
Hang about, *loiter*, 275
Hang back, *hesitate*, 603
Hang fire, *reluctance*, 603
   vacillation, 605
   stop, 142
   refuse, 764
   lateness, 133
   slowness, 275
   inactivity, 683
Hang out, *reside*, 188
Hang over, *futurity*, 121
   destiny, 152
   height, 206
Hang together, *junction*, 43
Hang up, *defer*, 133
Hangar, *building*, 189
Hanger, *arms*, 727
Hanger-on, *servant*, 746
   accompany, 88
   follow, 281
   parasite, 886
   flatterer, 935
Hangings, *ornaments*, 847
Hangman, *executioner*, 975
Hank, *skein*, 219
Hanker, *desire*, 865
Hanky-panky, *fraud*, 545
Hansard, *record*, 551
Hansel, *see* Handsel
Hansom, *vehicle*, 272
Hap, *chance*, 156, 621
Haphazard, *chance*, 156, 621
Hapless, *hopeless*, 859
   miserable, 828
Haply, *chance*, 156
   possibly, 470
Happen, *event*, 151
Happy, *glad*, 827
   expedient, 646
   agreement, 23
Happy-go-lucky, *careless*, 460
   aimless, 621
   improvident, 674

Happy medium, *middle*, 68
Happy thought, *wit*, 842
Hara-kiri, *suicide*, 361
   execution, 972
Harangue, *speech*, 582
   preach, 998
Harass, *worry*, 907
   fatigue, 688
   vex, 830
Harbinger, *omen*, 512
   precursor, 64, 116
Harbour, *anchorage*, 189
   refuge, 666
   haven, 292
   to cherish, 821
Harbourless, *exposed*, 665
Hard, *dense*, 323
   difficult, 704
   grievous, 830
   strong, 159
   obdurate, 951
   sour, 397
Hard-and-fast, *exact*, 494
   strict, 739
Hard-boiled, *callous*, 823
Hard case, *bad man*, 949
Hard currency, *money*, 800
Hard-favoured, *ugly*, 846
Hard-headed, *skill*, 698
   wise, 498
Hard-hearted, *cruel*, 907
Hard lines, *adversity*, 735
Hard-mouthed, *obstinacy*, 606
Hard up, *poverty*, 804
Hard-working, *exertion*, 682, 68
Harden, *accustom*, 613
   train, 673
   render callous, 376, 823
   impious, 988
   impenitent, 951
Hardihood, *courage*, 861
   insolence, 885
Hardly, *scarcely*, 32
   infrequency, 137
Hardness of heart, *vice*, 945
Hardship, *pain*, 830
   adversity, 735
Hardy, *strong*, 159
   healthy, 654
Hare, *velocity*, 274
Hare-brained, *rash*, 460, 863
Harem, *apartment*, 191
   impurity, 961
Hark, *hearing*, 418
Hark back, *regression*, 283
Harlequin, *motley*, 440
   pantomimic, 599
   humorist, 844
Harlot, *libertine*, 962
Harlotry, *impurity*, 961
Harm, *evil*, 619
   badness, 649
   malevolence, 907
Harmattan, *wind*, 349
Harmless, *innocent*, 946

Harmless, *innocuous*, 648
   impotent, 158
Harmonic, *music*, 413
Harmonica, *musical instrument*,
   417
Harmonium, *musical instrument*,
   417
Harmonize, *uniformity*, 16
Harmony, *agreement*, 23
   melody, 413; *concord*, 714
   peace, 721
   conformity, 82
   friendship, 888
Harness, *fasten*, 43
   fastening, 45; *bond*, 752
   accoutrement, 225
   instrument, 633
   subjection, 749
Harp, *musical instrument*, 417
   to repeat, 104
   to weary, 841
Harper, *musician*, 416
Harpoon, *arms*, 727
Harpsichord, *musical instrument*,
   417
Harpy, *demon*, 980
   evildoer, 913
   thief, 792
   miser, 819
Harquebus, *arms*, 727
Harridan, *hag*, 846
   trollop, 962
   bad woman, 949
Harrow, *pain*, 830
   cultivate, 371
Harry, *pain*, 830
Harsh, *severe*, 739
   morose, 895
   disagreeable, 830
   malevolent, 907
   sound, 410
Harum-scarum, *disorder*, 59
*Haruspex, *oracle*, 513
Harvest, *acquisition*, 775
   effect, 154
Hash, *mixture*, 41
   disorder, 59
   to cut, 44
Hasp, *lock*, 45
   to lock, 43
Hassock, *support*, 215
*Hasta la vista, *departure*, 293
Haste, *in time*, 132
   in motion, 274
   in action, 684
   activity, 682
Hasten, *to promote*, 707
Hasty, *transient*, 111
   irritable, 901
Hat, *dress*, 225
Hatch, *produce*, 161
   plan, 626; *prepare*, 673
   door, 66; *opening*, 260
Hatchet, *instrument*, 633
   sharpness, 253

Hatchet-faced, *thin*, 203
Hatchment, *record*, 551
Hatchway, *way*, 627
   opening, 260
Hate, *hate*, 898
   enmity, 889
   bombardment, 716
Hateful, *noxious*, 649
   painful, 830
Hatter, *dress*, 225
Hauberk, *arms*, 717
Haughty, *proud*, 878
   severe, 739
   insolent, 885
Haul, *traction*, 285
   catch, 789
Haunch, *side*, 236
Haunt, *presence*, 186
   alarm, 860; *abode*, 189
   resort, 74
   frequent, 136
   trouble, 830
*Haut-goût, *pungency*, 392
Hautboy, *musical instrument*,
   417
*Haute monde, *noble*, 875
*Haute politique, *government*,
   693
Hauteur, *pride*, 878
Have, *possession*, 777
   deceive, 545
Have it, *belief*, 484
Have oneself a ball, *enjoy*, 377
Haven, *anchorage*, 189
   refuge, 292, 666
Havers, *nonsense*, 497
   folly, 499
Haversack, *receptacle*, 191
Havoc, *evil*, 162, 619
Haw, *stammering*, 583
Hawk, *sell*, 796
   publish, 531
Hawk-eyed, *vision*, 441
Hawker, *merchant*, 797
Hawser, *rope*, 45
Hay-cock, *bundle*, 72
Hayseed, *peasant*, 876
Haywire, *insane*, 503
Hazard, *chance*, 156, 621
   danger, 665
   obstacle, 706
Haze, *mist*, 353
   dimness, 422
   opacity, 426
   to harass, 830, 907
Hazel, *brown*, 433
Hazy, *indistinct*, 447
Head, *beginning*, 66
   class, 75
   summit, 210
   front, 234
   to lead, 280
   froth, 353
   intellect, 450
   wisdom, 498

Head, *master*, 745
   direction, 693
   director, 694
   topic, 454
Head and shoulders, *whole*, 50
Head-foremost, *rash*, 863
Head-rhyme, *similarity*, 17
   poetry, 597
Head-work, *thought*, 451
Headache, *pain*, 378
Header, *plunge*, 310
Headgear, *dress*, 225
Heading, *title*, 550
   precursor, 64
   beginning, 66
Headlong, *projection*, 250
   cape, 342
   height, 206
Headlong, *rashly*, 460, 863
   hastily, 684
   swiftly, 274
Headpiece, *intellect*, 450, 498
   skill, 698
Headquarters, *focus*, 74
   abode, 189
Heads, *compendium*, 596
   warning, 668
   care, 459
   toilet, 191, 653
Headship, *authority*, 737
Headstrong, *rash*, 863
   obstinate, 606
   violent, 173
Headway, *space*, 180
   progress, 282
   navigation, 267
Heal, *repair*, 658
   forgive, 918
Health, *health*, 654
Healthy, *salubrity*, 656
Heap, *collection*, 72
   store, 636
   plenty, 639
   much, 31, 50
Hear, *audition*, 418
   learn, 539
Hearken, *audition*, 418
Hearsay, *news*, 532
Hearse, *interment*, 363
Heart, *interior*, 221
   centre, 223
   mind, 450
   will, 600
   affections, 820
   courage, 861
   love, 897
Heart-breaking, *painful*, 830
Heart-broken, *pain*, 828
Heart-felt, *feeling*, 821
Heart-rending, *painful*, 830
Heart-sick, *dejected*, 837
Heart-strings, *affections*, 820
Heart-swelling, *resentment*, 900
Heart-whole, *free*, 748
Heartache, *pain*, 828

Hullabaloo, *noise*, 404
   cry, 411
Hullo, *see* Hallo
Hum, *faint sound*, 405
   continued sound, 407, 412
   to sing, 415
   deceive, 545
   stink, 401
Hum and ha, *hesitate*, 583
   demur, 605
Hum-note, *melody*, 413
Human, *mankind*, 372
Humane, *benevolent*, 906
   philanthropic, 910
Humanism, *knowledge*, 490
Humanist, *scholar*, 492
Humanitarian, *philanthropist*,
         906
Humanities, *letters*, 560
Humanity, *human nature*, 372
   benevolence, 906
Humanize, *courtesy*, 894
Humble, *meek*, 879
   modest, 881
   to abash, 874
   pious, 987
Humbug, *deception*, 545
   falsehood, 544
Humdrum, *dull*, 843
Humectate, *moisten*, 339
Humid, *moist*, 339
Humiliate, *humble*, 879
   shame, 874
   worship, 990
Humility, *piety*, 987
Humming-top, *musical*, 417
Hummock, *height*, 206, 250
Humoresque, *music*, 415
Humorist, *humorist*, 844
Humour, *essence*, 5
   liquid, 333
   disposition, 602
   tendency, 176
   caprice, 608
   indulge, 760
   affections, 820
   to please, 829
   wit, 842
Humoursome, *capricious*, 608
   discourteous, 895
Hump, *convexity*, 250
Hump bluey, *journey*, 266
Hump yourself, *activity*, 682
Humpbacked, *distortion*, 243
   ugliness, 846
Humph! *wonder*, 870
Humus, *soil*, 342
Hun, *evildoer*, 913
Hunch, *convexity*, 250
Hundred, *number*, 99
   region, 181
Hunger, *desire*, 865
Hunks, *parsimony*, 819
Hunnish, *malevolent*, 907
Hunt, *follow*, 281

Hunt, *pursue*, 622
   inquire, 461
Hunter, *carrier*, 271
Hunting grounds, *heaven*, 981
Hurdle, *fence*, 232
Hurdy-gurdy, *musical*, 417
Hurl, *propel*, 284
Hurly-burly, *confusion*, 59
   turmoil, 315
Hurrah! *cheerfulness*, 836
   rejoicing, 838
Hurricane, *tempest*, 349
   violence, 173
Hurried, *excitability*, 825
Hurry, *haste*, 684
   swiftness, 274
   earliness, 132
   to urge, 615
   to excite, 824
Hurst, *plant*, 367
Hurt, *evil*, 619
   physical pain, 378
   moral pain, 828
   to injure, 649, 907
   to molest, 830
Hurtful, *badness*, 649
Hurtle, *impulse*, 276
Husband, *spouse*, 903
   to store, 636
Husbandman, *agriculture*, 371
Husbandry, *agriculture*, 371
   conduct, 692
   economy, 817
Hush, *silence*, 403
   latent, 526
   moderate, 174
   assuage, 723
   pacify, 723
Hush-hush, *secret*, 534
Hush-money, *bribe*, 809
   compensation, 30
Hush up, *conceal*, 526, 528
Husk, *covering*, 222
   to strip, 226
Husky, *dry*, 340
   big, 192
   strong, 159
   faint sound, 405, 501
Hussar, *combatant*, 726
Hussy, *libertine*, 962
   bad woman, 949
   impertinent, 887
Hustings, *tribunal*, 966
   platform, 542
Hustle, *push*, 276
   disarrange, 61
   agitate, 315
   bustle, 171, 682
   haste, 684
Hut, *abode*, 189
Hutch, *abode*, 189
Huzza! *cheerfulness*, 836
Hyaline, *transparency*, 425
Hybrid, *mixture*, 41
   nondescript, 83

Hydra, *unconformity*, 83
Hydra-headed, *reproduction*,
         163
Hydrant, *spray*, 348
Hydraulics, *fluids*, 348
Hydrogen bomb, *arms*, 727
Hydrographic, *sea*, 341
Hydrology, *water*, 333
Hydromel, *sweetness*, 396
Hydrometer, *density*, 321
Hydropathic, *salubrity*, 656
   remedy, 662
Hydropathy, *remedy*, 662
Hydrophobia, *dislike*, 867
Hydroplane, *aircraft*, 273A
Hydroponics, *agriculture*, 371
Hydrostatics, *water*, 333
Hydrotherapy, *remedy*, 662
Hyena, *evildoer*, 913
Hygiene, *salubrity*, 656
Hygrology, *moisture*, 339
Hygrometer, *moisture*, 339
Hylotheism, *heathen*, 984
Hymen, *marriage*, 903
Hymn, *worship*, 990
Hymnal, *rite*, 998
Hyperaesthesia, *excitability*, 825
   sensibility, 376, 822
Hyperbole, *exaggeration*, 549
Hyperborean, *cold*, 383
Hypercritical, *disapprobation*,
         932
   fastidious, 868
Hyperion, *beauty*, 845
Hypermetropia, *vision*, 443
Hyperpyrexia, *heat*, 382
Hypersensitive, *sensitive*, 375,
         825
Hypertrophy, *expansion*, 194
Hyphen, *vinculum*, 45
Hypnology, *inactivity*, 683
Hypnosis, *inactivity*, 683
Hypnotic, *remedy*, 662
   sedative, 683
Hypnotize, *occult*, 992, 994
Hypocaust, *furnace*, 386
Hypochondriac, *dejection*, 837
   insanity, 503, 504
Hypocrisy, *deception*, 545
   religious, 988
Hyprocite, *deceiver*, 548
Hypocritical, *falsehood*, 544
Hypostasis, *substantiality*, 3
Hypostatic, *Deity*, 976
Hypothecation, *lending*, 787
Hypothesis, *supposition*, 514
Hysterical, *violence*, 173
   excitement, 825
Hysteron proteron, *inversion*,
         218

I

Inexplicable, *unintelligible*, 519
   wonderful, 870
Inexpressible, *unmeaning*, 517
   wonder, 870
   great degree, 31
Inexpressive, *unmeaning*, 517,
       510
Inexpugnable, *safety*, 664
Inextinguishable, *immutable*,
       150
   uncontrollable, 825
   energetic, 157
Inextricable, *difficult*, 704
   impossible, 471
   disorder, 59
   coherence, 46
Infallible, *certainty*, 474
   perfect, 650
Infamy, *dishonour*, 940
   shame, 874
   vice, 945
Infancy, *beginning*, 66
   youth, 127
Infant, *infant*, 129
Infanta, *master*, 745
Infanticide, *killing*, 361
Infantile, *puerile*, 643
   foolish, 499
Infantry, *combatant*, 726
Infatuation, *folly*, 499
   misjudgment, 481
   obstinacy, 606
   credulity, 486
   passion, 825
   love, 897
Infeasible, *impossible*, 471
   difficult, 704
Infect, *mix*, 41
Infection, *disease*, 655
   contamination, 659
   excitation, 824
Infectious, *insalubrity*, 657
Infecund, *unproductiveness*, 169
Infelicity, *unhappiness*, 828
   inexpertness, 699
Infer, *judgment*, 480
Inference, *judgment*, 480
   interpretation, 522
Inferential, *deducible*, 478
Inferior, *less*, 34
   imperfect, 651
Infernal, *bad*, 649
   wicked, 945
   malevolent, 907
Infertility, *unproductiveness*,
       169
Infest, *annoy*, 649, 830
   frequent, 136
Infibulation, *junction*, 43
Infidel, *heathen*, 984
Infidelity, *dishonour*, 940
   irreligion, 989
Infiltrate, *intervene*, 228
   influence, 175
   imbue, 339

Infiltrate, *teach*, 537
   mixture, 41
Infiltration, *ingress*, 294
   passage, 302
   presence, 186
Infinite, *in quantity*, 105
   in degree, 31
   in size, 192
Infinitesimal, *in degree*, 32
   in quantity, 193
Infinity, *infinitude*, 105
   space, 180
Infirm, *weak*, 160
   irresolute, 605
   vicious, 945
Infirmary, *remedy*, 662
Infirmity, *weakness*, 160
   disease, 655
   failing, 945
Infix, *teaching*, 537
Inflame, *burn*, 384
   stir up, 173
   incense, 900
   incite, 615
Inflammation, *disease*, 655
Inflate, *expend*, 194
   rarefy, 322
   blow, 349
   style, 573, 577
   ridiculous, 853
   vanity, 880
Inflect, *curvature*, 245
   grammar, 567
Inflexible, *hard*, 323
   resolved, 604
   obstinate, 606
   stern, 739
Inflexion, *curvature*, 245
   change, 140
   appendage, 39
   grammar, 567
Inflict, *condemn*, 971
   act upon, 680
   give pain, 830
Infliction, *pain*, 828
Influence, *physical*, 175
   authority, 737
   inducement, 615
   importance, 642
Influential, *important*, 642
Influx, *ingress*, 294
Inform, *information*, 527
Inform against, *accusation*, 938
Informal, *irregular*, 83
   lawless, 964
Information, *knowledge*, 490
   communication, 527
Informer, *witness*, 467
*Infra, *posterior*, 117
*Infra dignitatem, *disrepute*,
       874
Infra-microscopic, *little*, 193
Infraction, *non-observance*, 773
   unconformity, 83
   exemption, 927

Infraction, *disobedience*, 742
   violation, 614
Infrangible, *coherence*, 46, 321
Infrastructure, *base*, 211
Infrequency, *infrequency*, 137
   fewness, 103
Infringe, *transgress*, 303
   violate, 742, 773, 925, 927
   break through, 614
Infundibular, *concavity*, 252
Infuriate, *wrathful*, 900
   excite, 824
   violent, 173
Infuse, *mix*, 41
   insert, 300
   teach, 537
Infusible, *solid*, 321
Ingeminate, *duplication*, 90
Ingenious, *skill*, 698
*Ingénue, *actress*, 599
Ingenuous, *artless*, 703
   sincere, 543
   guileless, 939
Ingest, *absorb*, 296
Ingle, *fuel*, 388
Inglorious, *disrepute*, 874
   base, 940
Ingoing, *ingress*, 294
Ingot, *money*, 800
Ingraft, see Engraft
Ingrate, *ingratitude*, 917
Ingratiate, *love*, 897
Ingratitude, *ingratitude*, 917
Ingredient, *component*, 56
Ingress, *ingress*, 294
Ingrowing, *insertion*, 300
Ingurgitate, *reception*, 296
Inhabile, *unskilfulness*, 699
Inhabit, *presence*, 186
Inhabitant, *inhabitant*, 188
Inhale, *reception*, 296
   sniff, 398
Inharmonious, *discordant*, 414
   incongruity, 24
Inherence, *intrinsicality*, 5
Inherit, *acquire*, 775
   possess, 777
Inheritance, *property*, 780
Inhesion, *intrinsicality*, 5
Inhibit, *prohibit*, 761
   not think of, 452
   dissuade, 616
   hinder, 706
Inhospitable, *seclusion*, 893
Inhuman, *malevolence*, 907
Inhume, *interment*, 363
Inimical, *hostile*, 708, 889
   unfavourable, 706
Inimitable, *perfect*, 650
   good, 648
Iniquitous, *bad*, 649
Iniquity, *wrong*, 923
   vice, 945
Initiate, *begin*, 66
   teach, 537

Instruct, *teach*, 537
   advise, 695
   precept, 697
   command, 741
Instructor, *teacher*, 540
Instrument, *implement*, 633
   record, 551
   security, 771
Instrumental, *means*, 632
   music, 415
   subservient, 631
Instrumentality, *medium*, 631
Insubordinate, *disobedience*, 742
   anarchy, 738
Insubstantiality, *nothingness*, 4
Insufferable, *painfulness*, 830
Insufficient, *insufficiency*, 640
   shortcoming, 304
Insufflation, *wind*, 349
Insular, *island*, 346
   detach, 44
   single, 87
Insulate, *separate*, 44
Insult, *rudeness*, 895
   disrespect, 929
   offence, 900
Insuperable, *difficulty*, 704
   impossible, 471
Insupportable, *painfulness*, 830
Insuppressible, *violence*, 173
Insurance, *promise*, 768
   security, 771
   precaution, 664
Insurgent, *disobedience*, 742
Insurmountable, *difficulty*, 704
   impossible, 471
Insurrection, *disobedience*, 742
   resistance, 719
Insusceptible, *insensibility*, 823
Intact, *permanence*, 141
   preserve, 669
Intaglio, *concavity*, 252
   sculpture, 557
Intake, *inlet*, 260
Intangible, *numbness*, 381
   immaterial, 317
Integer, *whole*, 50
Integral calculus, *number*, 84
Integral part, *component*, 56
Integrate, *consolidate*, 50
   complete, 52
Integration, *number*, 84
Integrity, *whole*, 50
   virtue, 944
   probity, 939
Integument, *covering*, 222
Intellect, *intellect*, 450
Intelligence, *mind*, 450
   news, 532
   wisdom, 498
Intelligible, *intelligibility*, 518, 570
Intemperate, *intemperance*, 954
   drunkenness, 957

Intempestivity, *unseasonableness*, 135
Intend, *design*, 620
Intendant, *director*, 694
Intended, *will*, 600
Intensify, *energize*, 171
   aggravate, 835
Intensity, *degree*, 26
   greatness, 31
   energy, 171
Intent, *active*, 682
   thoughtful, 451, 457
Intention, *design*, 620
Intentional, *will*, 600
Intentness, *attention*, 457
   thought, 451
Inter, *bury*, 363
   insert, 300
*Inter alia, *conformity*, 82
Interaction, *reciprocal*, 12
Interblend, *mix*, 41
Interbreed, *mix*, 41
Intercalate, *insert*, 300
   intervene, 228
Intercede, *mediate*, 724
   deprecate, 766
Intercept, *hinder*, 706
   take, 789
Intercession, *deprecation*, 766
Interchange, *interchange*, 148
   reciprocate, 12
   barter, 794
   transfer, 783
Intercipient, *hinder*, 706
Interclude, *hindrance*, 706
Intercom, *hearing*, 418
Intercommunicate, *interlocution*, 588
   information, 527
Intercommunion, *society*, 892
Intercostal, *interiority*, 221
Intercourse, *converse*, 588
Intercross, *mix*, 41
Intercurrence, *passage*, 302
Interdict, *prohibition*, 761
Interdigitate, *intervene*, 228
   intersect, 219
Interest, *advantage*, 618
   concern, 9
   importance, 642
   curiosity, 455
   attention, 457
   aid, 707
   to please, 829; *debt*, 806
Interested, *selfish*, 943
Interesting, *style*, 574
Interfere, *intervene*, 228
   meddle, 682
   disagree, 24
   counteract, 179
   thwart, 706
   mediate, 724
   activity, 682
Interglossa, *language*, 560
Interim, *duration*, 106

Interim, *synchronism*, 120
Interior, *interiority*, 221
Interjacence, *coming between*, 228
   middle, 68
Interject, *insert*, 300
   interpose, 228
Interlace, *twine*, 219
   join, 43
Interlard, *interpose*, 228
   mix, 41
   insert, 300
Interleave, *interjacence*, 228
   addition, 37
Interline, *insert*, 228
   write, 590
Interlink, *junction*, 43
Interlocation, *interjacence*, 228
Interlock, *cross*, 219
   join, 43
Interlocution, *interlocution*, 588
Interloper, *intervene*, 228
   obstruct, 706
   extraneous, 57
Interlude, *dramatic*, 599
   time, 106
   interjacence, 228
   interruption, 70
Intermarriage, *marriage*, 903
Intermeddle, *hinder*, 706
   interfere, 682
Intermeddling, *mediation*, 724
Intermediary, *messenger*, 534
Intermediate, *mean*, 29
   middle, 68
   intervening, 228
Intermedium, *link*, 45
   instrument, 631
   intervention, 228
Interment, *interment*, 300, 363
Intermezzo, *interlude*, 106
   music, 415
Interminable, *infinite*, 105
   eternal, 112
   long, 200
Intermingle, *mixture*, 41
Intermission, *discontinuance*, 142
Intermit, *interrupt*, 70
   discontinue, 142
   recur, 138
   suspend, 265
   in time, 106
Intermix, *mixture*, 41
Intermutation, *interchange*, 148
Intern, *restrain*, 751
Internal, *interior*, 221
   intrinsic, 5
International, *reciprocal*, 12
   law, 963
Internecine, *slaughter*, 361
   war, 722
Internuncio, *messenger*, 534
   consignee, 758
Interpellation, *inquiry*, 461

L

L.S.D., *money*, 800
Laager, *defence*, 717
Labarum, *flag*, 550
Label, *indication*, 550
Labial, *letter*, 561
Laboratory, *workshop*, 691
Labour, *exertion*, 686
  work, 680
  difficulty, 704
Labourer, *agent*, 690
Labyrinth, *secret*, 533
  difficulty, 704
  disorder, 59
  convolution, 248
Lace, *tie*, 43
  net, 219
  to beat, 972
Lacerable, *fragile*, 328
Lacerate, *disjunction*, 44
  pain, 830
Laches, *neglect*, 460
  omission, 773
Lachrymation, *lamentation*, 839
Lack, *insufficiency*, 640
  destitution, 804
  requisition, 630
  number, 98
Lack-brain, *fool*, 501
Lack-lustre, *dim*, 423
  discoloured, 429
Lackadaisical, *affected*, 855
  indifferent, 866
Lacker, *see* Lacquer
Lackey, *servant*, 746
Laconic, *conciseness*, 572
  shortness, 201
Lacquer, *varnish*, 22
  adorn, 845, 847
Lacteal, *semiliquid*, 352
Lacuna, *orifice*, 260
  pit, 252
  deficiency, 53
  interval, 198
  break, 70
Lacuscular, *lake*, 343
Lacustrine, *lake*, 343
Lad, *infant*, 129
Ladder, *method*, 627
Lade, *transfer*, 270
Laden, *charged*, 639
La-di-da, *foppish*, 855
Lading, *cargo*, 190, 635
  baggage, 780
Ladle, *spoon*, 272
  vessel, 191
Lady, *woman*, 374
  wife, 903
  noble, 875
Lady help, *servant*, 746
Lady-killer, *fop*, 854
  philanderer, 902
Lady-love, *sweetheart*, 897
Ladylike, *fashion*, 852

Ladylike, *courteous*, 894
  noble, 875
Lag, *linger*, 275
  follow, 281
  dawdle, 683
  lateness, 133
  imprison, 751
  prisoner, 754
Laggard, *slack*, 603, 683
Lagoon, *lake*, 343
Laical, *laity*, 997
Lair, *den*, 189
  sty, 653
Laird, *nobility*, 875
  possessor, 779
*Laissez aller, *inactivity*, 683
*Laissez faire, *laxity*, 738
  inactivity, 683
  permanence, 141
Laity, *laity*, 997
Lake, *lake*, 343
Lama, *priest*, 996
  master, 745
Lamarckism, *causation*, 153
Lamb, *innocent*, 946
  nursling, 129
  Saviour, 976
  saint, 948
Lambent flame, *light*, 420
Lamblike, *innocent*, 946
Lame, *weak*, 160
  bad, 649
  imperfect, 650
  failing, 732
  laxity, 738
Lamella, *layer*, 204
Lament, *complain*, 839
  regret, 833
  funeral, 363
  pity, 914
Lamentable, *greatness*, 31
  painful, 830
  regret, 833
Lamia, *demon*, 980
Lamina, *layer*, 204
  part, 51
Lamp, *luminary*, 423
Lampoon, *disparage*, 932
  libel, 934
Lance, *perforate*, 260
  javelin, 727
Lancer, *combatant*, 726
Lancet, *perforator*, 262
  sharpness, 253
Lancinate, *pain*, 378
Land, *ground*, 342
  to arrive, 292
  to stop, 265
  estate, 780
Land girl, *agriculture*, 371
Land-mine, *arms*, 727
Landau, *vehicle*, 272
Landaulette, *vehicle*, 272
Landgrave, *master*, 745
Landing-ground, *arrival*, 292

Landing-place, *support*, 215
  destination, 292
Landing-stage, *arrival*, 292
Landlocked, *circumscribed*, 231
Landlord, *possessor*, 779
Landlubber, *bungler*, 701
Landmark, *indicate*, 550
Landowner, *possessor*, 779
Landscape, *view*, 448
  delineation, 556
Landslide, *fall*, 306
Landslip, *fall*, 306
Lane, *street*, 189
  way, 627
Language, *words*, 560
Languid, *weak*, 160
  slow, 275
  torpid, 683, 823
  style, 575
Languish, *desire*, 865
  illness, 655
  decline, 36
Languor, *weakness*, 160
  inactivity, 683
Lank, *little*, 193
Lanolin, *oil*, 356
Lantern, *light*, 423
Lantern-jawed, *lean*, 193
Lao-Tsze, *religious founder*, 986
Lap, *support*, 215
  interior, 221
  to wrap, 222
  encompass, 227
  speed, 274
  surpass, 303
  drink, 296
Lapel, *fold*, 258
Lapidary, *concise*, 572
Lapidate, *kill*, 361
Lapis lazuli, *blue*, 438
Lappet, *adjunct*, 39
Lapse, *of time*, 109, 135
  past time, 122
  fall, 306
  be lost, 776
  degeneracy, 659
  guilt, 947
  error, 495
*Lapsus linguae, *solecism*, 568
  ridicule, 856
  error, 495
  equivocal, 520
Larboard, *left*, 239
Larcener, *thief*, 792
Larceny, *theft*, 791
Lard, *unctuousness*, 353, 256
Larder, *store*, 636
  food, 298
Lares and Penates, *abode*, 189
Large, *in quantity*, 31
  in size, 192
Largess, *giving*, 784, 809
*Largo, *slowness*, 275, 415
Lariat, *vinculum*, 45
Lark, *mount*, 305

Libel, *lawsuit*, 969
Liberal, *generous*, 816
   disinterested, 942
   ample, 639
   giving, 784
Liberate, *release*, 672, 750
   disjoin, 44
Libertarianism, *will*, 600
Libertinage, *impurity*, 961
Libertine, *libertine*, 962
Libertinism, *impurity*, 961
Liberty, *freedom*, 748
   right, 924
   exemption, 927A
   permission, 760
Libidinous, *impurity*, 961
Libido, *desire*, 865
Library, *book*, 593
   room, 191
Librate, *oscillation*, 314
Libretto, *poetry*, 597
Licence, *permission*, 760
   laxity, 738
   right, 924
   exemption, 927
   toleration, 750
License, *permit*, 760
   exempt, 927A
Licentiate, *scholar*, 492
Licentious, *dissolute*, 954
   debauched, 961
Lich-gate, see Lych-gate
Lichen, *plant*, 367
Licit, *dueness*, 924
Lick, *beat*, 972
Lickerish, *fastidious*, 868
   greedy, 865
   licentious, 961
Lickspittle, *flatterer*, 935
   servile, 886
Lictor, *law*, 965
Lid, *cover*, 263
   integument, 22
Lie, *place*, 186
   position, 183
   exist, 1
   recline, 213, 215
   descend, 306
   to deceive, 545
   untruth, 546
   contradict, 489
Lie by, *inaction*, 681
Lie doggo, *conceal*, 528
Lie in wait, *ambush*, 530
Lie low, *lowness*, 207
   concealment, 528
Lie over, *postpone*, 133
   future, 121
Lie to, *quiescence*, 265
*Lied, *music*, 415
Lief, *willingness*, 602
Liege, *master*, 745
Lien, *dueness*, 924
   security, 771
   credit, 805

Lieutenant, *officer*, 745
   deputy, 759
Life, *vitality*, 359
   activity, 682
   existence, 1
   events, 151
Life and death, *important*, 642
Life-preserver, *impact*, 276
Lifeblood, *life*, 359
   inbeing, 5
Lifeboat, *boat*, 273
   safety, 666
Lifeless, *dead*, 360
   inert, 172
Lifelike, *similarity*, 17
Lift, *raise*, 307
   way, 627
   aid, 707
   steal, 791
Ligament, *vinculum*, 45
Ligation, *junction*, 43
Ligature, *vinculum*, 45
Light, *luminosity*, 420
   opening, 260
   levity, 320
   colour, 428
   to kindle, 384
   luminary, 423
   small, 32
   trifling, 643
   gay, 836
   idea, 453
   knowledge, 490
   descent, 306
   to arrive, 292
   loose, 961
Light-fingered, *stealing*, 791
Light-footed, *swift*, 274
   active, 682
Light-headed, *delirious*, 503
   foolish, 499
Light-hearted, *cheerful*, 836
Light-legged, *velocity*, 274
Light-minded, *irresolution*, 605
Light up, *illuminate*, 420
   cheer, 836
   awaken, 615
Light upon, *find*, 480A
   arrive, 292
Lighten, *render easy*, 705
Lighter, *ship*, 273
   fuel, 388
Lighterman, *mariner*, 269
Lighthouse, *beacon*, 668
   luminary, 423
Lightness, see Light
Lightning, *velocity*, 274
   luminousness, 420
Lightship, *light*, 423
   warning, 668
Lightsome, *cheerful*, 836
   fickle, 605
Likable, *attractive*, 829
Like, *similar*, 17
   to relish, 394

Like, *will*, 600
   enjoy, 827
Likely, *probable*, 472
Likeness, *similitude*, 17
   copy, 21
   representation, 554
   portrait, 556
Likewise, *addition*, 37
Liking, *love*, 897
   desire, 865
Lilac, *purple*, 437
Lilliputian, *little*, 193
   low, 207
Lilt, *music*, 415
   rhythm, 138
   cheerful, 836
Lily, *whiteness*, 430
   beauty, 845
Limature, *pulverulence*,
          330, 331
Limb, *member*, 51
   component, 56
   instrument, 633
Limber, *flexible*, 324
Limbo, *incarceration*, 751
   purgatory, 982
Lime, *deception*, 545
Limelight, *publicity*, 531
Limerick, *absurdity*, 497
Limit, *boundary*, 233
   end, 67
   to circumscribe, 231
   qualify, 469
   prohibit, 761
Limitless, *infinity*, 105
   space, 180
Limn, *painting*, 556
Limner, *artist*, 559
Limousine, *vehicle*, 272
Limp, *halt*, 275
   fail, 732
   weak, 160
   inert, 172, 683
   soft, 324
Limpid, *transparent*, 425
Lincture, *remedy*, 662
Line, *length*, 200
   filament, 205
   to coat, 224
   band, 45
   order, 58
   contour, 229
   continuity, 69
   direction, 278
   business, 625
   soldier, 726
   feature, 550
   appearance, 448
   posterity, 167
   epistle, 592
Lineage, *posterity*, 167
   series, 69
   kindred, 11
Lineament, *appearance*, 448
   mark, 550

Man, *to arm*, 673
Man-handle, *maltreat*, 649
Man of straw, *defaulter*, 808
Man-of-war, *ship*, 273
Manacle, *shackle*, 751, 752
  to fetter, 43
Manage, *direction*, 693
  succeed, 731
Manageable, *facility*, 705
Management, *skill*, 698
Manager, *director*, 694
Managing, *active*, 682
Mancipation, *restraint*, 751
Mandamus, *command*, 741
Mandarin, *master*, 745
Mandate, *command*, 741
  region, 181
Mandatory, *obligatory*, 926
Mandolin, *musical instrument*, 417
Mandrel, *rotation*, 312
Manducation, *feeding*, 296
Mane, *rought*, 256
Manège, *training*, 370
*Manes, *corpse*, 362
Manful, *strong*, 159
  brave, 861
Mangle, *disjunction*, 44
  smooth, 255
Mangy, *disease*, 655
Manhood, *virility*, 131, 373
  bravery, 861
Mania, *insanity*, 503
  desire, 865
Maniac, *mad*, 504
Manifest, *visible*, 446
  obvious, 518
  to show, 525
  to appear, 448
Manifesto, *publication*, 531
Manifold, *multitude*, 102
Manikin, *image*, 554
  dwarf, 193
Manila, *tobacco*, 298A
Manipulate, *handle*, 379
  use, 677
  conduct, 692
Mankind, *man*, 372
Manlike, *strength*, 159
Manly, *adolescent*, 131
  resolute, 604
  brave, 861
Manna, *sweetness*, 396
Mannequin, *image*, 554
Manner, *intrinsic*, 5
  way, 627
  appearance, 448
  conduct, 692
  kind, 75
Mannerism, *singularity*, 79, 83
  phrase, 566
  ornament, 577
  affectation, 855
  vanity, 880
Mannerly, *courtesy*, 894

Manners, *breeding*, 852
  politeness, 894
Manoeuvre, *scheme*, 626
  operation, 680
  skill, 698
  stratagem, 545, 702
Manor, *property*, 780
Manse, *temple*, 1000
Mansion, *abode*, 189
Mansuetude, *courtesy*, 894
Mantel, *support*, 215
Mantilla, *dress*, 225
Mantle, *cloak*, 225
  kindle, 900
  flush, 821
  spread, 194
Mantlet, *dress*, 225
Mantology, *prediction*, 511
Manual, *book*, 542, 593
  reference, 695
Manufactory, *workshop*, 691
Manufacture, *production*, 161
Manufacturer, *agent*, 690
  producer, 164
Manumit, *liberate*, 750
Manure, *unclean*, 653
Manuscript, *writing*, 590
Many, *multitude*, 102
Many-coloured, *variegation*, 440
Many-sided, *accomplished*, 698
Map, *representation*, 554
  journey, 266
Maquis, *fighter*, 726
Mar, *spoil*, 649
  obstruct, 706
*Maranatha, *malediction*, 908
Marasmus, *atrophy*, 655
  shrinking, 195
Marauder, *thief*, 792
Marauding, *stealing*, 791
Marble, *ball*, 249
  hard, 323
  sculpture, 557
Marble-hearted, *malevolence*, 907
Marbled, *variegated*, 440
March, *journey*, 226
  progression, 282
March-past, *display*, 882
March with, *contiguity*, 199
Marches, *limit*, 233
Marchioness, *noble*, 875
  chief, 745
Marchpane, *sweet*, 396
Marconigram, *message*, 532
Mare, *carrier*, 271
*Maréchal, *master*, 745
Mare's nest, *absurdity*, 497
  failure, 732
Mare's tail, *cloud*, 353
Margin, *edge*, 230
  space, 180
  latitude, 748
Marginalia, *commentary*, 522

Margrave, *master*, 745
Marinade, *pickle*, 670
Marine, *oceanic*, 341
  fleet, 273
  soldier, 726
Marish, *marsh*, 345
Marital, *marriage*, 903
Maritime, *oceanic*, 341
Mark, *indication*, 550
  record, 551
  repute, 873
  object, 620
  degree, 26, 71
  observe, 441, 450
  attend to, 457
Marked, *great*, 31
Market, *mart*, 799
  buy, 795
Market garden, *agriculture*, 371
Marketable, *trade*, 794, 796
Marksman, *proficient*, 700
Marl, *land*, 342
Marmalade, *sweet*, 396
Maroon, *seclusion*, 893
  abandon, 782
  signal, 550, 669
Marplot, *bungler*, 701
  obstacle, 706
  malicious, 913
Marquee, *tent*, 189
Marquetry, *mixture*, 41
  variegation, 440
Marquis, *noble*, 875
  master, 745
Marquisate, *title*, 877
Marriage, *marry*, 903
  union, 41
Marriageable, *adolescence*, 131
Marrow, *essence*, 5
  interior, 221
  central, 223
  gist, 516
  essential, 642
Mars, *god*, 979
Marsh, *marsh*, 345
  moisture, 339
Marshal, *arrange*, 60
  officer, 745
  in law, 968
  messenger, 534
Mart, *mart*, 799
*Martellato, *music*, 415
Martial, *contention*, 720
Martinet, *tyrant*, 739
  teacher, 540
Martingale, *bridle*, 752
Martyr, *pain*, 828
Martyrdom, *torture*, 378
  agony, 828
  killing, 361
  asceticism, 955
Marvel, *wonder*, 870
  prodigy, 872
Marvellous, *great*, 31

Mean, *shabby*, 874
  base, 940
  humble, 879
  sneaking, 886
  selfish, 943
  stingy, 819
  intend, 620
  to signify, 516
Meander, *circulation*, 311
  convolution, 248
  river, 348
  wander, 279, 629
Meaningless, *nonsense*, 517
Means, *appliances*, 632
  fortune, 803
  property, 780
Meantime, *period*, 106, 120
Meanwhile, *duration*, 106, 120
Measure, *extent*, 25
  degree, 26
  moderation, 174, 639
  to compute, 466
  proceeding, 626, 680
  to apportion, 786
  in music, 413
  in poetry, 597
Measure, in a great, *greatness*, 31
Measure for measure, *compensation*, 30
Meat, *food*, 298
Meaty, *savoury*, 394
Mechanic, *agent*, 690
Mechanical, *automatic*, 601
  style, 575
  imitative, 19
Mechanics, *force*, 159
  machinery, 632
Mechanism, *means*, 632
Medal, *reward*, 973
  record, 551
  palm, 733
  decoration, 877
Medallion, *sculpture*, 557
Meddle, *interpose*, 682
  act, 680
Meddlesome, *interpose*, 682
Medial, *middle*, 68
Median, *mean*, 29
Mediation, *mediation*, 724
  deprecation, 766
Mediator, *Saviour*, 976
Medicament, *remedy*, 662
Medicaster, *deceiver*, 548
Medicate, *heal*, 660
  compound, 41
Medicine, *remedy*, 662
Medieval, *oldness*, 124
  past, 122
Mediocrity, *moderate*, 32
  mean, 29
  of fortune, 736
  imperfect, 648, 651
Meditate, *think*, 451
  purpose, 620

Mediterranean, *middle*, 68
  interjacent, 228
Medium, *mean*, 29
  pigment, 428
  instrument, 631
  spiritualist, 994
Medley, *mixture*, 41
Meed, *reward*, 973
  gift, 784
  share, 786
  praise, 931
Meek, *humble*, 879
  gentle, 826
Meerschaum, *tobacco-pipe*, 298 A
Meet, *contact*, 199, 292
  agreement, 23
  converge, 290
  assemble, 72
  expedient, 646
  proper, 926, 924
  fulfil, 772
Meet with, *find*, 480 A
  happen, 151
Meeting-place, *focus*, 74
Megalomania, *insanity*, 503
  vanity, 880
Megalomaniac, *madman*, 504
Megaphone, *loudness*, 404
Megascope, *optical instrument*, 445
Megrims, *dejection*, 837
Melancholia, *insanity*, 503
Melancholy, *distressing*, 830
  dejection, 837
*Mélange, *mixture*, 41
*Mêlée, *contention*, 720
  disorder, 59
Meliorate, *improve*, 658
Mellifluous, *sound*, 405
  melody, 413
  style, 578
Mellow, *sound*, 413, 580
  mature, 144, 673
  old, 124
  soft, 324
  tipsy, 959
Melodeon, *wind instrument*, 417
Melodrama, *the drama*, 599
Melody, *music*, 413
Melpomene, *the drama*, 599
Melt, *liquefy*, 335
  fuse, 384
  change, 144
  disappear, 449
  pity, 914
Melt away, *disappear*, 2, 449
Member, *part*, 51
  component, 56
Membrane, *layer*, 204
Memento, *memory*, 505
*Memento mori, *interment*, 363
Memoir, *description*, 594
  dissertation, 595

*Memorabilia, *memory*, 505
Memorable, *importance*, 642
Memorandum, *memory*, 505
  record, 551
Memorial, *record*, 551
  epistle, 592
*Memoriter, *memory*, 505
Memory, *reminiscence*, 505
  fame, 873
Menace, *threat*, 908
*Ménage, *conduct*, 692
Menagerie, *taming*, 370
  collection, 72
  store, 636
Mend, *improve*, 658
Mendacity, *falsehood*, 544
Mendelism, *production*, 161
Mendicant, *beggar*, 767
  monk, 996
Mendicity, *beggar*, 804
Menial, *servant*, 746
  servile, 876
Menstrual, *period*, 108
Mensuration, *measure*, 466
Mental, *intellect*, 450
Mention, *information*, 527
Mentor, *adviser*, 695
  teacher, 540
Menu, *list*, 86
  food, 298
  plan, 626
Mephistopheles, *Satan*, 978
  miscreant, 949
Mephitic, *fetid*, 401
  pernicious, 649
  deleterious, 657
  poison, 663
Mercantile, *merchant*, 794
Mercenary, *parsimonious*, 819
  price, 812
  servant, 746
  self-seeking, 943
Merchandise, *goods*, 798
Merchant, *merchant*, 797
Merchantman, *ship*, 273
*Merci, *thanks*, 917
Merciful, *pity*, 914
Merciless, *malevolence*, 907
Mercurial, *excitable*, 825
  mobile, 264
  quick, 274
Mercury, *god*, 979
  messenger, 534
Mercy, *mercy*, 914
Mercy-seat, *tribunal*, 966
Mere, *simple*, 32
  unimportant, 643
  lake, 343
Meretricious, *false*, 495, 544
  vulgar, 851
  licentious, 961
  colour, 428
Merge, *plunge*, 337
  insert, 300
  include, 76

Misrepresentation, *perversion*, 523
 falsehood, 544
 caricature, 555
Misrule, *misconduct*, 699
 laxity, 738
Miss, *lose*, 776
 fail, 732
 inattention, 458, 460
 want, 865
 girl, 374
Missal, *rite*, 998
Missay, *stammer*, 583
 misnomer, 565
Misshapen, *ugliness*, 846
 distortion, 243
Missile, *thing thrown*, 284
 arms, 727
Missing, *absence*, 187
Mission, *commission*, 755
 undertaking, 676
 business, 625
 warfare, 722
Missionary, *clergy*, 996
Missive, *correspond*, 592
Misspell, *misinterpret*, 523
Misspend, *prodigal*, 818
Misstate, *misinterpret*, 523
 falsify, 544
Misstatement, *error*, 495
 falsehood, 544
 untruth, 546
 perversion, 523
Mist, *dimness*, 422
Mistake, *error*, 495
 failure, 732
 mismanagement, 699
 misconstrue, 523
Misteach, *misteach*, 538
Misterm, *misnomer*, 565
Misthink, *error*, 495
Mistime, *intempestivity*, 135
Mistral, *wind*, 349
Mistranslate, *misinterpret*, 523
Mistress, *lady*, 374
 sweetheart, 897
 concubine, 962
Mistrust, *doubt*, 485
Misty, *opaque*, 426
 dim, 422
 invisible, 447
Misunderstanding, *error*, 495
 misinterpretation, 523
 discord, 713
Misuse, *misuse*, 679
 waste, 638
Mite, *small*, 193
 bit, 32
 money, 800
Mitigate, *abate*, 36, 174
 relieve, 834
 calm, 826
 improve, 658
 extenuate, 937
*Mitrailleuse, *gun*, 727

Mitre, *canonicals*, 999
 joint, 43
Mitten, *dress*, 225
Mittimus, *command*, 741
Mix, *mix*, 41
Mixed, *disorder*, 59
Mixture, *mix*, 41
Mizzle, *rain*, 348
Mnemonics, *memory*, 505
Mnemosyne, *memory*, 505
Moan, *lamentation*, 839, 411
Moat, *enclosure*, 232
 ditch, 350
 defence, 717
Mob, *crowd*, 72, 31
 multitude, 102
 troop, 726
 plenty, 639
 vulgar, 876
 to scold, 932
Mob law, *illegal*, 964
Mobile, *movable*, 264
 sensible, 822
 inconstant, 607
Mobilization, *warfare*, 722
 move, 264
Mobility, *commonalty*, 876
Mobocracy, *authority*, 737
Mobsman, *thief*, 792
Moccasin, *dress*, 225
Mock, *imitate*, 17
 repeat, 104
 erroneous, 495
 false, 544
 to ridicule, 483, 856
 laugh at, 838
Mock-heroic, *ridiculous*, 853
Modal, *extrinsic*, 6
 state, 7
 circumstance, 8
Mode, *fashion*, 852
 method, 627
Model, *prototype*, 22
 to change, 140, 144
 rule, 80
 example, 82
 to copy, 19
 sculpture, 557
 perfection, 650
 saint, 948
Modeller, *artist*, 559
Moderate, *small*, 32
 allay, 174
 to assuage, 826
 temperate, 953
 cheap, 815
Moderation, *temperateness*, 174
 mediocrity, 736
*Moderato, *music*, 415
Moderator, *master*, 745
 director, 694
Modern, *newness*, 123
Modernize, *change*, 140
Modesty, *humility*, 881
 purity, 960

Modicum, *little*, 33
 allotment, 786
Modification, *difference*, 15
 variation, 20
 change, 140
 qualification, 469
Modify, *convert*, 144
Modish, *fashion*, 852
Modulation, *change*, 140
 harmony, 413
*Modus operandi, *method*, 627
 conduct, 692
*Modus vivendi, *arrangement*, 723
 compromise, 774
Mogul, *master*, 745
Mohammed, *religious founder*, 986
Mohammedanism, *religions*, 984
Mohock, *roisterer*, 949
Moider, *bewilder*, 475
 inattention, 458
Moiety, *bisection*, 91
Moil, *action*, 680
 work, 686
Moist, *wet*, 337
 humid, 339
Moke, *carrier*, 271
Molasses, *sweetness*, 396
Mole, *mound*, 206
 defence, 717
 refuge, 666
Molecule, *small*, 32, 193
Molehill, *lowness*, 207
 trifling, 643
Molestation, *evil*, 619
 .*damage*, 649
 malevolence, 907
Mollify, *allay*, 174
 soften, 324
 conciliate, 918
 assuage, 826
Mollusc, *animal*, 366
Mollycoddle, *cowardice*, 862
Moloch, *tyranny*, 739
 divinity, 979
 idol, 986
Molten, *liquid*, 335
Moment, *of time*, 113
 importance, 642
Momentary, *transient*, 111
Momentum, *impulse*, 276
Momus, *rejoicing*, 838
Monachism, *church*, 995
Monad, *littleness*, 193
 unity, 87
Monarch, *master*, 745
Monarchy, *authority*, 737
Monastery, *temple*, 1000
Monastic, *churchdom*, 995
Monetary, *money*, 800
Money, *money*, 800
Money-bag, *treasury*, 802
Money-changer, *merchant*, 797

Multiple, *product,* 84
Multiplicand, *number,* 84
Multiplication, *arithmetical,*
    85
    reproduction, 163
Multiplicator, *number,* 84
Multiplicity, *multitude,* 102
Multiplier, *number,* 84
Multisonous, *loud,* 404
Multitude, *number,* 102
    greatness, 31; *mob,* 876
    assemblage, 72
Multitudinous, *multitude,* 102
*Multum in parvo, *contraction,*
    195
    conciseness, 572
Mum, *silence,* 403
    aphony, 581
    mother, 166
Mumble, *eat,* 296
    mutter, 405, 583
Mumbo Jumbo, *idol,* 991
    spell, 993
Mumchance, *silent,* 403
    mute, 581
Mummer, *the drama,* 599
Mummery, *absurdity,* 497
    ridicule, 856
    parade, 882
    imposture, 545
    masquerade, 840
Mummify, *preserve,* 670
    bury, 363
Mummy, *corpse,* 362
    dryness, 340
    mother, 166
Mump, *dejection,* 837
Mumper, *beggar,* 767
Mumps, *sullenness,* 895
Munch, *eat,* 296
Munchausen, *exaggerate,* 549
Mundane, *world,* 318
    selfishness, 943
    irreligion, 989
Munerary, *reward,* 973
Municipal, *law,* 965
    distinct, 189
Munificent, *liberality,* 816
    giving, 784
Muniment, *record,* 551
    defence, 717
    refuge, 666
Munition, *material,* 635
Murder, *killing,* 361
    to bungle, 699
Murex, *purple,* 437
Muricate, *sharpness,* 253
Murky, *darkness,* 421
Murmur, *sound,* 405
    complaint, 839
    flow, 348
Murrain, *disease,* 655
Murrey, *redness,* 434
Muscle, *strength,* 159
Muse, *to reflect,* 451

Muse, *poetry,* 597
    language, 560
Musette, *musical instrument,*
    415
Museum, *store,* 636
    collection, 72
    focus, 74
Mushroom, *small,* 193
    newness, 123
    low-born, 876
    upstart, 734; *increase,* 35
Music, *music,* 415
Music-hall, *theatre,* 599
    amusement, 840
Musical, *melodious,* 413
Musician, *musician,* 416
Musk, *fragrance,* 400
Musket, *arms,* 727
Musketeer, *combatant,* 726
Muslin, *semitransparent,* 427
Muss, *dishevel,* 61
Mussulman, *religions,* 984
Must, *mucor,* 653
    necessity, 152
    obligation, 926
    compulsion, 744
    essential, 630
Mustard, *condiment,* 393
    yellow, 436
Mustard-seed, *little,* 193
Muster, *collect,* 72
    numeration, 85
Muster-roll, *record,* 551
    list, 86
Musty, *foul,* 653
    rank, 401
Mutable, *changeable,* 149
    irresolute, 605
Mutation, *change,* 140
*Mutatis mutandis, *recip-
    rocalness,* 12
    substitution, 147
*Mutato nomine, *substitution,*
    147
Mute, *silent,* 403
    letter, 561
    silencer, 417
    speechless, 581
    taciturn, 585
    interment, 363
Mutilate, *retrench,* 38
    deform, 241
    garble, 651
    incomplete, 53
    injure, 649, 659
    spoliation, 619
Mutineer, *disobey,* 742
Mutiny, *disobey,* 742
    misrule, 738
    revolt, 719
Mutt, *fool,* 501
Mutter, *speak,* 583
    murmur, 405
    threaten, 909
Mutual, *reciprocal,* 12, 148

Muzzle, *opening,* 260
    edge, 230
    to silence, 403, 581
    taciturn, 585
    to incapacitate, 158
    restrain, 751
    imprison, 752
Muzzle-loader, *gun,* 727
Muzzy, *confused,* 458
    in liquor, 959
Myopic, *dim sight,* 443
Myriad, *number,* 98
    multitude, 102
Myrmidon, *troop,* 726
Myrrh, *fragrance,* 400
Myrtle, *love,* 897
Mysterious, *concealed,* 528
    obscure, 519
Mystery, *secret,* 533
    latency, 526
    concealment, 528
    craft, 625
    drama, 599
Mystery-ship, *deception,* 545
Mystic, *concealed,* 528
    obscure, 519
Mystify, *to deceive,* 545
    hide, 528
    falsify, 477
    misteach, 538
Myth, *imagination,* 515
Mythological, *god,* 979
    imaginary, 515

N

N.B., *attention,* 457
N or M, *generality,* 78
Na, *dissent,* 489
Nab, *seize,* 789
Nabob, *wealth,* 803
Nacreous, *variegation,* 440
Nadir, *base,* 211
Naffy, *food,* 298
Nag, *carrier,* 271
    be rude, 895
    discord, 713
    to scold, 932
Naiad, *mythological,* 979
Nail, *to fasten,* 43
    fastening, 45
Nail-brush, *clean,* 652
Nailing, *good,* 648
Naïveté, *artless,* 703
Naked, *denuded,* 226
    visible, 446
Namby-pamby, *affected,* 855
    insipid, 866
    trifling, 643
    style, 575
Name, *appellation,* 564
    fame, 873
    to appoint, 755
Nameless, *anonymous,* 565
    obscure, 874

Nugget, *lump*, 321
Nuisance, *annoyance*, 830
  evil, 619
Null, *unsubstantiality*, 4
Nullah, *gap*, 198
*Nulli secundus, *superiority*,
                   33
  goodness, 648
Nullifidian, *atheist*, 988
Nullify, *counteract*, 179
  repudiate, 773
  invalidate, 964
  compensate, 30
Numb, *morally*, 823
  physically, 376, 381
Number, *abstract*, 84
  plurality, 100
  grammar, 568
  publication, 593
  to count, 85
Numberless, *infinity*, 105
Numbers, *poetry*, 597
Numbness, *physical*, 381
  moral, 823
Numen, *great spirit*, 979
Numeral, *number*, 84
Numeration, *numeration*, 85
Numerator, *number*, 84
Numerous, *multitude*, 102
Numismatics, *money*, 800
Numskull, *fool*, 501
Nun, *clergy*, 996
*Nunc dimittis, *worship*, 990
Nuncio, *messenger*, 534
  consignee, 758
Nuncupatory, *naming*, 564
  informing, 527
Nunnery, *temple*, 1000
  seclusion, 893
Nuptials, *marriage*, 903
Nurse, *servant*, 746
  treat, 662
  to help, 707
  preserve, 670
Nursery, *room*, 191
  school, 542
  workshop, 691
  for plants, 367
Nurseryman, *horticulture*, 371
Nursling, *infant*, 129
Nurture, *food*, 298
  to support, 707
  prepare, 673
Nut, *head*, 450
  fop, 854
  madman, 504
Nut-brown, *brown*, 433
Nutation, *oscillation*, 314
Nutmeg-grater, *rough*, 256
Nutriment, *food*, 298
Nutrition, *aid*, 707
Nuts, *insane*, 503
  rubbish, 643
Nutshell, *littleness*, 193
  compendium, 596

Nuzzle, *endearment*, 902
Nyctalopia, *dim-sighted*, 443
Nylons, *dress*, 225
Nymph, *woman*, 374
  goddess, 979
Nystagmus, *dim-sighted*, 443

O

O.K., *assent*, 488
  consent, 762
Oaf, *fool*, 501
Oak, *strength*, 159
Oar, *instrument*, 633
  paddle, 267
Oasis, *land*, 342
Oath, *promise*, 768
  assertion, 535
  expletive, 908
*Obbligato, *music*, 415
Obduracy, *sin*, 945
  impenitence, 931
  obstinacy, 606
  severity, 739
  malevolence, 907
Obeah, *occult arts*, 992
Obedience, *obedience*, 743
  duty, 926
Obeisance, *bow*, 894
  reverence, 928
  submission, 725
  worship, 990
  fealty, 743
Obelisk, *monument*, 551
  tall, 206
Obelize, *indicate*, 550
Oberon, *sprite*, 980
Obesity, *size*, 192
Obey, *obedience*, 743, 749
Obfuscate, *darken*, 421, 426
  bewilder, 458
Obit, *death*, 360
*Obiter dictum, *irrelation*, 10
Obituary, *description*, 594
  death, 360
Object, *thing*, 3, 316
  intention, 620
  ugly, 846
  to disapprove, 932
Object lesson, *explanation*, 522
Object to, *dislike*, 867
Objectify, *existence*, 1
Objective, *extrinsic*, 6
  material, 316, 450A
Objurgate, *disapprobation*, 932
Oblate, *shortness*, 201
  monk, 996
Oblation, *gift*, 789
  proffer, 763
  worship, 990
Obligation, *duty*, 926
  promise, 768
  conditions, 770
  debt, 806
  gratitude, 916

Oblige, *compel*, 744
  benefit, 707
Obliging, *kind*, 906
  courteous, 894
Oblique, *obliquity*, 217
Obliquity, *vice*, 945
Obliterate, *efface*, 552
Oblivion, *oblivion*, 506
Oblong, *length*, 200
Obloquy, *censure*, 932
  disgrace, 874
Obmutescence, *aphony*, 581
Obnoxious, *hateful*, 898
  unpleasing, 830
  pernicious, 649
Oboe, *musical instrument*, 417
Obscene, *impurity*, 961
Obscurantist, *ignoramus*, 493
Obscure, *dark*, 421
  unseen, 447
  unintelligible, 519
  style, 571
  to eclipse, 874
*Obscurum per obscurius,
  unintelligibility, 519
  misteaching, 538
Obsecration, *request*, 765
Obsequies, *interment*, 363
Obsequious, *respectful*, 928
  courteous, 894
  servile, 886
Observance, *fulfilment*, 772
  rule, 82
  habit, 613
  practice, 692
  rites, 998
Observatory, *universe*, 318
Observe, *note*, 457
  conform, 926
  remark, 535
Observer, *spectator*, 444
  fighter, 726
Obsess, *preoccupy*, 457
  worry, 830
  haunt, 860
Obsession, *misjudgment*, 481
  fixed idea, 606
Obsolete, *old*, 124
  effete, 645
  vulgar, 851
Obstacle, *physical*, 179
  moral, 706
Obstetrician, *instrumentality*,
                631
Obstinate, *stubborn*, 606
  resolute, 604
  prejudiced, 481
Obstreperous, *violent*, 173
  loud, 404
Obstruct, *hinder*, 706
  close, 261
Obtain, *exist*, 1
  acquire, 775
Obtainable, *possibility*, 470
Obtestation, *entreaty*, 765

Pelf, *materials*, 635
  gain, 775
Pellet, *rotundity*, 249
  remedy, 662
Pellicle, *film*, 205
  skin, 222
Pell-mell, *disorder*, 59
Pellucid, *transparency*, 425
Pelt, *skin*, 222
  throw, 276
  attack, 716
  beat, 972
Pen, *surround*, 231
  enclose, 232
  restrain, 751
  imprison, 752
  draw, 559
  write, 590
Pen-and-ink, *drawing*, 556
Pen-name, *misnomer*, 565
Penal, *punishment*, 972
Penalty, *penalty*, 974
Penance, *atonement*, 952
  rite, 998
  penalty, 974
*Penchant, *inclination*, 865
  love, 897
Pencil, *bundle*, 72
  of light, 420
  artist, 556, 559, 590
Pencraft, *writing*, 590
Pendant, *adjunct*, 39
  flag, 550
  pendency, 214
  match, 17
Pendent, *during*, 106
  hanging, 214
  uncertain, 485
*Pendente lite, *warfare*, 722
  lawsuit, 969
Pending, *duration*, 106
  lateness, 133
  uncertain, 475
Pendulous, *pendency*, 214
Pendulum, *clock*, 114
  oscillation, 314
Penetralia, *interiority*, 221
  secret, 533
Penetrate, *fill*, 186
  influence, 175
Penetrating, *affecting*, 821
Penetration, *ingress*, 294
  passage, 302
  discernment, 441
  sagacity, 498
Penfold, *enclosure*, 232
Peninsula, *land*, 342
Penitent, *penitence*, 950
Penitentiary, *prison*, 752
Penmanship, *writing*, 590
Penniless, *poverty*, 804
Pennon, *indication*, 550
Penny-a-liner, *writer*, 590
Penny-farthing, *bicycle*, 266
Pennyworth, *price*, 812

*Penseroso, *dejection*, 837
Pensile, *pendency*, 214
Pension, *wealth*, 803, 810
Pensioner, *servant*, 746
  recipient, 785
Pensive, *thoughtful*, 451
  sad, 837
Pent, *imprisoned*, 754
Pentad, *five*, 98
Pentagon, *angularity*, 244
  five, 98
Pentahedron, *angularity*, 244
  five, 98
Pentatonic, *melody*, 413
Penthouse, *building*, 189
Penultimate, *end*, 67
Penumbra, *darkness*, 421, 424
Penurious, *parsimony*, 819
Penury, *poverty*, 804
  scantiness, 640
People, *man*, 373
  inhabitant, 188
  commonalty, 876
  to colonize, 184
Pep, *energy*, 171, 682
  vigour, 574
Pep-talk, *speech*, 582
Pepper, *hot*, 171
  pungent, 392
  condiment, 393
  attack, 716
Peppercorn, *unimportance*, 643
Peppery, *irascibility*, 901
Peptic, *remedy*, 662
*Per contra, *contrariety*, 14
  opposition, 708
*Per procurationem, *commission*, 755
*Per saltum, *discontinuity*, 70
  transientness, 111
  instantaneity, 113
*Per se, *unity*, 87
Peradventure, *change*, 156
  possibly, 470
  uncertainty, 475
Perambulate, *journey*, 266
Perceivable, *visible*, 446
Percentage, *proportion*, 84
  discount, 813
Perceptible, *visibility*, 446
Perception, *idea*, 453
  of touch, 380
Perceptivity, *sensibility*, 375
Perch, *support*, 215
  to alight, 186
  tall, 206
  habitation, 189
Perchance, *chance*, 156
  possibly, 470
Percipience, *intellect*, 450
Percolate, *distil*, 295
Percolation, *passage*, 302
Percussion, *impulse*, 276
Perdition, *ruin*, 732
  loss, 776

Perdu, *concealment*, 528
Perdurable, *permanence*, 141
Peregrination, *journey*, 266
Peremptory, *assertion*, 535
  denial, 536
  firm, 604
  rigorous, 739
  authoritative, 737
  compulsory, 744
  obligatory, 926
  order, 740, 741
Perennial, *diuturnity*, 110, 150
Perfect, *entire*, 52
  complete, 729
  excellent, 650
Perfectly, *greatness*, 31
Perfidy, *improbity*, 940
Perforate, *opening*, 260
Perforator, *perforator*, 263
Perforce, *compulsion*, 744
Perform, *do*, 170, 680
  achieve, 729
  produce, 161
  act, 599
  fulfil, 772
  duty, 926
Performable, *facility*, 705
  possible, 470
Performance, *effect*, 154
Performer, *musician*, 416
  actor, 599
  workman, 164
  agent, 690
Perfume, *fragrance*, 400
Perfunctory, *neglect*, 460
  incomplete, 53
Perhaps, *possibly*, 470
  chance, 156
  supposition, 514
Peri, *fairy*, 979
Periapt, *spell*, 993
Perigee, *nearness*, 197
Perihelion, *nearness*, 197
Peril, *danger*, 665
Perimeter, *outline*, 229
Period, *end*, 67
  of time, 106, 108
  stop, 142
  point, 71
  recurrence, 138
Periodical, *book*, 593
  publication, 531
Peripatetic, *traveller*, 268
  ambulatory, 266
Periphery, *outline*, 229
Periphrasis, *phrase*, 566
  diffuseness, 573
Perique, *tobacco*, 298A
Periscope, *vision*, 441
  optical instrument, 445
Perish, *vanish*, 2
  be destroyed, 162
  die, 360; *decay*, 659
Peristaltic, *convolution*, 248
Periwig, *dress*, 225

Posthumous, *subsequent*, 117
Postiche, *artificial*, 544
Postilion, *director*, 694
Postlude, *music*, 415
   posterior, 117
Postman, *messenger*, 534
Postpone, *lateness*, 133
Postscript, *sequel*, 65
   appendix, 39
Postulant, *petitioner*, 767
   request, 765
   nun, 997
Postulate, *supposition*, 514
   evidence, 467
   reasoning, 476
Postulation, *request*, 765
Posture, *circumstance*, 8
   attitude, 240
   display, 882
Posy, *motto*, 550
   poem, 597
   flowers, 847
Pot, *mug*, 191
   stove, 386
   greatness, 31
   ruin, 732
Pot-companion, *friend*, 890
Pot-hooks, *writing*, 590
Pot-hunting, *acquisition*, 775
Pot-luck, *food*, 298
Pot-pourri, *mixture*, 41
   fragrance, 400
   music, 415
Pot-valiant, *drunk*, 959
Potable, *drinkable*, 298
Potation, *drink*, 296
Potency, *power*, 157
Potentate, *master*, 745
Potential, *virtual*, 2
   possible, 470
   power, 157
Pother, *to worry*, 830
   fuss, 682
   confusion, 59
Pottage, *food*, 298
Potter, *idle*, 683
Pottle, *receptacle*, 191
Potty, *mad*, 503
*Pou sto, *influence*, 175
Pouch, *receptacle*, 191
   insert, 184
   receive, 785
   take, 789
   acquire, 775
Pouffe, *support*, 215
Poultice, *soft* , 354
   remedy, 662
Pounce upon, *taking*, 789
Pound, *bruise*, 330
   mix, 41
   enclose, 232
   imprison, 752
Poundage, *discount*, 813
Pounds, *money*, 800
Pour, *egress*, 295

Pour out, *eject*, 185, 297, 248
*Pour rire, *ridicule*, 853
*Pourboire, *giving*, 784
   expenditure, 809
*Pourparler, *discussion*, 476
Pout, *sullen*, 895
   sad, 837
Poverty, *indigence*, 804
   scantiness, 640
   trifle, 643
Powder, *pulverulence*, 330
   ornament, 845, 847
Powder-box, *receptacle*, 191
Power, *efficacy*, 157
   physical energy, 171
   authority, 737
   spirit, 977
   much, 31
   multitude, 102
   numerical, 84
   of style, 574
Powerful, *strength*, 159
Powerless, *weakness*, 160
Pow-wow, *conference*, 588
Pox, *disease*, 655
   expletive, 908
Praam, *ship*, 273
Practicable, *possible*, 470
   easy, 705
Practical, *activity*, 672
   agency, 170
Practice, *act*, 680
   conduct, 692
   use, 677; *habit*, 613
   teaching, 537; *rule*, 80
   proceeding, 626
Practise, *deceive*, 645
Practised, *skill*, 698
Practitioner, *agent*, 690
*Praecognita, *evidence*, 467
Praenomen, *name*, 564
Praetor, *master*, 745
Pragmatical, *pedantic*, 855
   vain, 880
Prairie, *plain*, 344
   plaint, 367
Praise, *commendation*, 931
   thanks, 916
   worship, 990
Praiseworthy, *commendable*, 931
   virtuous, 944
Prance, *dance*, 315
   swagger, 878
   move, 266
Prang, *bomb*, 162, 716, 732
Prank, *caprice*, 608
   amusement, 840
   vagary, 856
   to adorn, 845
Prate, *babble*, 584, 588
Prattle, *talk*, 582, 588
Pravity, *badness*, 649
Pray, *request*, 765
Prayer, *request*, 765
   worship, 990

Preach, *teach*, 537
   speech, 582
   predication, 998
Preacher, *clergy*, 996
Preachify, *speech*, 582
Preamble, *precursor*, 64
   speech, 582
Preapprehension, *misjudgment*, 481
Prebendary, *clergy*, 996
Prebendaryship, *churchdom*, 995
Precarious, *uncertain*, 475
   perilous, 665
Precatory, *request*, 764
Precaution, *care*, 459
   expedient, 626
   preparation, 673
Precede, *in order*, 62
   in time, 116
   lead, 280
Precedence, *rank*, 873
Precedent, *rule*, 80
   verdict, 969
Precentor, *clergy*, 996
   director, 694
Precept, *maxim*, 697
   order, 741
   rule, 80
   permit, 760
   decree, 963
Preceptor, *teacher*, 540
Precession, *in order*, 62
   in motion, 280
*Précieuse ridicule, *affectation*, 855
   style, 577
Precincts, *environs*, 227
   boundary, 233
   region, 181
   place, 182
Preciosity, *affectation*, 855
Precious, *excellent*, 648
   valuable, 814
   beloved, 897
Precipice, *slope*, 217
   vertical, 212
   danger, 667
Precipitancy, *haste*, 274, 684
Precipitate, *rash*, 863
   impulse, 612
   early, 132
   transient, 111
   to sink, 308
   refuse, 653
   consolidate, 321
   swift, 274
Precipitous, *obliquity*, 217
Précis, *compendium*, 596
Precise, *exact*, 494
   definite, 518
Precisely, *assent*, 488
Precisian, *formalist*, 855
   taste, 850
Preclude, *hindrance*, 706

Precocious, *early*, 132
    immature, 674
Precognition, *foresight*, 510
    knowledge, 490
Preconception, *misjudgment*,
    481
Preconcert, *preparation*, 673
    predetermine, 611
Preconcerted, *will*, 600
Precursor, *forerunner*, 64
    precession, 280
    harbinger, 512
Precursory, *in order*, 62
    in time, 116
Predacious, *stealing*, 791
Predatory, *stealing*, 791
Predecessor, *in order*, 64
    in time, 116
Predeliberation, *care*, 459
Predestination, *fate*, 152
    necessity, 601
Predetermination, *predeter-
    mination*, 611
Predetermined, *will*, 600
    predetermination, 611
Predial, *property*, 780
Predicament, *situation*, 8
    class, 75
Predicate, *affirmation*, 535
Predication, *rite*, 998
Prediction, *prediction*, 511
Predilection, *love*, 897
    desire, 865
    choice, 609
    prejudice, 481
    inclination, 602
    affections, 820
Predisposition, *proneness*, 602
    tendency, 176
    motive, 615
    affection, 820
    preparation, 673
Predominance, *influence*, 175
    inequality, 28
    superiority, 33
Pre-eminent, *famed*, 873
    superior, 31, 33
Pre-emption, *purchase*, 795
Pre-emptive, *early*, 132
Preen, *adorn*, 845
Pre-establish, *preparation*, 673
Pre-examine, *inquiry*, 461
Pre-exist, *priority*, 116
    past, 122
Prefab, *abode*, 189
Preface, *precedence*, 62
    precursor, 64
    front, 234
Prefatory, *in order*, 62, 64
    in time, 106
Prefect, *ruler*, 745
    deputy, 759
Prefecture, *authority*, 737
Prefer, *choose*, 609
    a petition, 765

Preferment, *improvement*, 658
    ecclesiastical, 995
Prefiguration, *indication*, 550
    prediction, 510
Prefix, *precedence*, 62
    precursor, 64
Pregnant, *productive*, 161, 168
    predicting, 511
    important, 642
    concise, 572
Prehension, *taking*, 789
Prehistoric, *preterition*, 122
    old, 124
Prejudge, *misjudgment*, 481
Prejudice, *evil*, 619
    detriment, 649
Prelacy, *churchdom*, 995
Prelate, *clergy*, 996
Prelection, *teaching*, 537
Prelector, *teacher*, 540
Preliminary, *preceding*, 62
    precursor, 64
    priority, 116
Prelude, *preceding*, 62
    precursor, 64
    priority, 116
    music, 415
Prelusory, *preceding*, 62
    precursor, 64
    priority, 116
Premature, *earliness*, 132
Premeditate, *intend*, 630
    predetermine, 611
Premeditated, *will*, 600
Premier, *director*, 694, 759
Premiership, *authority*, 737
Premise, *prefix*, 62
    precursor, 64
    announce, 511
Premises, *ground*, 182
    evidence, 467
Premisses, *see* Premises
Premium, *reward*, 973
    receipt, 810
Premonition, *warning*, 668
Prenticeship, *preparation*, 673
Preoccupied, *inattentive*, 458
Preoccupy, *possess*, 777
    the attention, 457
Preoption, *choice*, 609
Preordain, *necessity*, 601
Preordination, *destiny*, 152
Preparatory. *precedence*, 62
Prepare, *mature*, 673
    plan, 626
    instruct, 537
Prepared, *ready*, 698
Prepay, *expenditure*, 809
Prepense, *advised*, 611
    spontaneous, 600
    intended, 620
Prepollence, *power*, 157
Preponderant, *unequal*, 28
    superior, 33
    important, 642

Preponderant, *influential*, 175
Prepossessing, *pleasurableness*,
    829
Prepossession, *misjudgment*,
    481
Preposterous, *in degree*, 31
    ridiculous, 853
    absurd, 497, 499
Prepotency, *power*, 157
Pre-Raphaelite, *artist*, 559
Prerequisite, *requirement*, 630
Prerogative, *right*, 924
    authority, 737,
Presage, *omen*, 512
    to predict, 511
Presbyopic, *dim-sightedness*,
    443
Presbytery, *parsonage*, 1000
Prescient, *foresight*, 510
Prescribe, *order*, 741
    direct, 693
    entitle, 924
    duty, 926
Prescript, *decree*, 741
    preceipt, 697
    law, 963
Prescription, *remedy*, 662
    convention, 613
Prescriptive, *dueness*, 924
Presence, *in space*, 186
    existence, 1
    appearance, 448
    carriage, 852
Presence of mind, *caution*, 864
Present, *in time*, 118
    in place, 186
    in memory, 505
    give, 784
    offer, 763
    show, 525
    represent, 554
    introduce, 894
    to the mind, 451
Presentable, *fashion*, 852
    beauty, 845
Presentation, *offer*, 763
    manifestation, 525
    gift, 784
    celebration, 883
Presentiment, *prejudgment*, 481
    instinct, 477
    foresight, 510
Presently, *soon*, 111, 132
Preservation, *continuance*, 141
    conservation, 670
Preserve, *sweet*, 396
Preses, *director*, 694
Preside, *command*, 737
    direct, 693
Presidency, *authority*, 737
President, *master*, 694, 745
Presidium *council*, 696
Press, *hasten*, 132, 684
    beg, 765
    compel, 744

Prototype, *thing copied*, 22
Protract, *time*, 110, 133
   length, 200
Protractor, *angularity*, 244
Protrude, *convexity*, 250
Protuberance, *convexity*, 250
Proud, *lofty*, 878
   dignified, 873
Prove, *demonstrate*, 85, 478
   try, 463
   turn out, 151
   affect, 821
Provenance, *cause*, 153
Provender, *food*, 298
   materials, 635
   provision, 637
Proverb, *maxim*, 496
Proverbial, *knowledge*, 490
Provide, *furnish*, 637
   prepare, 673
Provided, *qualification*, 469
   condition, 770
   conditionally, 8
Providence, *foresight*, 510
   divine government, 976
Provident, *careful*, 459
   foresight, 510
   wise, 498
   prepared, 673
Providential, *opportune*, 134
Province, *region*, 181
   department, 75
   office, 625
   duty, 926
Provincialism, *language*, 560
   vulgarity, 851, 876
Provision, *supply*, 637
   materials, 635
   preparation, 673
   wealth, 803
   food, 298
Provisional, *preparing*, 673
   substituted, 147
   temporary, 111
   conditional, 8
Proviso, *qualification*, 469
   condition, 770
Provoke, *incite*, 615
   cause, 153
   excite, 824
   vex, 830
   hatred, 898
   anger, 900
Provoking, *difficult*, 704
Provost, *master*, 745
Prow, *front*, 234
Prowess, *courage*, 861
Prowl, *journey*, 266
   conceal, 528
Proximity, *nearness*, 197
   contiguity, 199
Proximo, *futurity*, 121
   posterior, 117
Proxy, *deputy*, 759
   substitute, 634

Prude, *affectation*, 855
Prudent, *cautious*, 864
   foresight, 510
   careful, 459
   wise, 498
   discreet, 698
Prudery, *affectation*, 855
Prune, *shorten*, 201
   correct, 658
   purple, 437
Prunella, *unimportance*, 643
Prurient, *desire*, 865
   lust, 961
Pry, *inquire*, 461
   curiosity, 455
   look, 441
Psalm, *worship*, 990
Psalmody, *music*, 415
Psalter, *rite*, 998
Pseudo, *spurious*, 495
   sham, 544
Pseudonym, *misnomer*, 565
Pseudoscope, *optical*, 445
Pshaw, *contempt*, 930
Psst, *accost*, 586
Psyche, *soul*, 450
Psychiatrist, *mind*, 450
   remedy, 662
Psychical, *immaterial*, 317
   intellectual, 450
Psycho-analysis, *remedy*, 662
Psychokinesis, *occult*, 992
Psychology, *intellect*, 450
Psychomancy, *divination*, 992
Psychopath, *madman*, 504
Psychosis, *insanity*, 503
Psycho-therapist, *intellect*, 450
   remedy, 662
Ptisan, *remedy*, 662
Pub-crawler, *drunkard*, 959
Puberty, *youth*, 127
Public, *people*, 373
   open, 529, 531
Public-house, *drink*, 298
Public-spirited, *philanthropy*, 910
Publication, *promulgation*, 531
   showing, 525
   printing, 591
   book, 593
Publicist, *writer*, 593
   lawyer, 968
Publicity, *publication*, 531
Publish, *inform*, 527
Puce, *purple*, 437
Puck, *imp*, 980
Pucker, *fold*, 258
Pudder, *disorder*, 59
Pudding, *food*, 298
Puddle, *lakelet*, 343
   lining, 224
Pudency, *purity*, 960
Puerile, *boyish*, 127, 129
   trifling, 643
   foolish, 499

Puerile, *weak*, 477, 575
Puff, *wind*, 349
   vapour, 334
   tobacco, 298A
   inflate, 194
   commendation, 931
   advertisement, 531
   boast, 884; *pant*, 688
Puffed up, *vain*, 770
   proud, 878
Puffy, *swollen*, 194
   wind, 349
Pug, *shortness*, 201
   footprint, 551
   boxer, 726
Pugilism, *contention*, 720
Pugilist, *combatant*, 726
Pugnacity, *anger*, 901
Puisne, *posterior*, 117
Puissant, *strong*, 157, 159
Puke, *ejection*, 297
Pukka, *true*, 494
   goodness, 648
Pulchritude, *beauty*, 845
Pule, *cry*, 411, 412
   weep, 839
Pull, *draw*, 285
   attract, 288
   row, 267
   swerve, 279
   advantage, 33
   proof, 21, 591
Pull down, *destroy*, 162
   lay low, 308
Pull off, *accomplish*, 729
Pull out, *extract*, 301
Pull through, *recover*, 658
Pull together, *concord*, 714
Pull up, *stop*, 142, 265
   accuse, 938
Pullet, *infant*, 129
Pulley, *instrument*, 633
Pullman car, *vehicle*, 272
Pullover, *dress*, 225
Pullulate, *grow*, 194
   multiply, 168
Pulp, *pulpiness*, 354
   soften, 324
   semiliquid, 352
Pulpit, *rostrum*, 542
   church, 1000
Pulsate, *see Pulse*
Pulse, *oscillate*, 314
   agitate, 315
   periodically, 138
Pultaceous, *pulpy*, 354
Pulverize, *maltreat*, 649
Pulverulence, *powder*, 330
Pulvil, *fragrance*, 400
Pummel, *handle*, 633
   beat, 276, 972
Pump, *inquire*, 461
   spray, 348
   reservoir, 636
Pun, *verbal*, 520, 563

Raze, *level*, 308
    obliterate, 552
    demolish, 649
Razor, *sharp*, 253
Razz, *ridicule*, 856
Razzle-dazzle, *frolic*, 840
*Re, *concerning*, 454
Reabsorb, *reception*, 296
Reach, *length*, 200
    river, 348
    degree, 26
    distance, 196
    fetch, 270
    arrive at, 292
    grasp, 737
React, *recoil*, 277
    revert, 145
    counteract, 179
    sensibility, 375
    relapse, 661
Reactionary, *mulish*, 499
    reversion, 145
Read, *interpret*, 522
    learn, 539
Readable, *intelligible*, 518
Reader, *teacher*, 492, 540
    clergy, 996
Reading, *meaning*, 516
Reading-glass, *lens*, 445
Readjust, *equality*, 27
Readmit, *reception*, 296
Ready, *prepared*, 673
    capable, 157
    willing, 602
    useful, 644
    eager, 682
    dexterous, 698
    early, 132
    cash, 800
Ready money, *payment*, 807
Reagent, *criterion*, 467
    test, 463
Real, *existing*, 1
    substantial, 3
    true, 494
Realism, *truth*, 494
Realistic, *description*, 594
Reality, *existence*, 1
Realize, *attribute*, 155
    produce, 161
    substantiate, 494
    be aware of, 450
    imagine, 515
    price, 812
Really, *very*, 31
    indeed, 870
Realm, *region*, 181
    property, 780
    land, 372
Reanimate, *revivify*, 163
    refresh, 689
    reinstate, 660
Reap, *cultivate*, 371
    acquire, 775
    succeed, 731

Reap, *take*, 789
Reaping-hook, *sharpness*, 253
Reappear, *repetition*, 104, 163
    frequency, 136
Rear, *back*, 67, 235
    erect, 161, 307
    sequel, 65
    bring up, 537
    room, 191
    privy, 653
Rearrange, *arrangement*, 60
Reason, *cause*, 153
    motive, 615
    intellect, 450
    evidence, 467
    argue, 476
    wisdom, 498
    moderation, 174
Reasonable, *judicious*, 498
    right, 922
    equitable, 924
    probable, 472
    sane, 502
    moderate, 174
    cheap, 815
Reasoning, *logic*, 476
Reasonless, *fool*, 499
Reassemble, *gather*, 72
Reassure, *hope*, 858
Reasty, *foul*, 653
    fetid, 401
Réaumur, *thermometer*, 389
Rebate, *moderate*, 174, 813
Rebeck, *musical instrument*, 417
Rebel, *disobey*, 742
Rebellion, *resistance*, 719
    revolution, 146
Rebellow, *ululation*, 412
Rebound, *recoil*, 277, 283
    revert, 144
    react, 179
*Rebours, *regression*, 283
Rebuff, *refuse*, 764
    repulse, 732
    resist, 719
    recoil, 277, 325
Rebuild, *reconstruct*, 163
    restore, 660
Rebuke, *disapprove*, 932
Rebus, *secret*, 533
Rebut, *answer*, 462
    confute, 479
    deny, 536
    counter-evidence, 468
Rebutter, *lawsuit*, 969
Recalcitrant, *disobedient*, 742
Recalcitrate, *resist*, 276, 719
    counteract, 179
Recall, *recollect*, 505
    cancel, 756
Recant, *retract*, 607
    repent, 950
    deny, 536
    resign, 757

Recapitulate, *summary*, 596
    describe, 594
    repeat, 104
    enumerate, 85
Recast, *plan*, 626, 660
    refashion, 146
Recede, *move back*, 283
    move from, 287
    decline, 659
Receipt, *money*, 810
    recipe, 697
Receive, *admit*, 296
    take in, 785
    include, 76
    acquire, 775
    learn, 539
    believe, 484
    welcome, 892, 894
    money, 810
Received, *ordinary*, 82
    habitual, 613
Recension, *revision*, 457
    improvement, 658
Recent, *past*, 122
    new, 123
Receptacle, *recipient*, 191
    store, 636
Reception, *arrival*, 292
    comprehension, 54
    inclusion, 76
    ingestion, 296
    conference, 588
    admission, 785
    visit, 892, 894
Receptive, *intelligent*, 498
Recess, *place*, 182
    regression, 283
    ambush, 530
    holiday, 685
    interval, 106
    retirement, 893
Recession, *motion from*, 287
    motion backwards, 283
*Réchauffé, *copy*, 21
    improve, 658
*Recherché, *goodness*, 648
Recidivism, *relapse*, 661
    reversion, 145
    vice, 945
Recidivist, *criminal*, 949
    turncoat, 607
Recipe, *remedy*, 662
    precept, 697
Recipient, *receptacle*, 191
    receiving, 785
Reciprocal, *mutual*, 12
    quantity, 84
    interchange, 148
Reciprocation, *retaliation*, 718
Recital, *music*, 415
Recitative, *music*, 415
Recite, *narrate*, 594
    speak, 582
    enumerate, 85
Reck, *care*, 459

Re-establishment, *restoration,*
    145, 660
Refashion, *remodel,* 146
Refection, *refreshment,* 689
    meal, 298
Refectory, *room,* 191
Refer, *attribute,* 155
    relate, 9
Referee, *judge,* 480, 967
    adviser, 695
Referendum, *vote,* 609
    inquiry, 461
Refinement, *elegance,* 845
    fashion, 852
    taste, 850
    discrimination, 465
    improvement, 658
    wisdom, 498
    sophistry, 477
Refit, *repair,* 658
    reinstate, 660
Reflect, *think,* 451
    imitation, 19
Reflect upon, *blame,* 932
Reflecting, *thoughtful,* 498
Reflection, *maxim,* 496
    likeness, 21
    imitation, 19
    blame, 932
Reflector, *optical instrument,*
    445
Reflet, variegation, 440
Reflex, *regress,* 283
    recoil, 277
Reflux, *regress,* 283
    recoil, 277
Refocillate, *refresh,* 689
    restore, 660
Reform, *improve,* 658
    change, 140
Reformatory, *school,* 542
Refraction, *deviation,* 279
    angularity, 244
Refractor, *optical instrument,*
    445
Refractory, *resisting,* 719
    obstinate, 606
    disobedient, 742
    difficult, 704
Refrain, *avoid,* 623
    reject, 610
    unwilling, 603
    abstain, 616, 681
    temperance, 953
    repetition, 104, 415
Refresh, *cool,* 385
    relieve, 834
    refit, 658
    restore, 660
    strengthen, 159
Refresher, *fee,* 809
Refreshing, *pleasing,* 377, 829
Refreshment, *food,* 298
    pleasure, 827
    recruiting, 689

Refrigeration, *refrigerate,* 385
Refrigeratory, *cold,* 387
Reft, *disjoin,* 44
Refuge, *refuge,* 666
Refugee, *escape,* 671
Refulgence, *light,* 420
Refund, *restore,* 790
    pay, 807
Refurbish, *improve,* 658
Refuse, *decline,* 764
    reject, 610
    remains, 40
    offscourings, 643
Refute, *confute,* 479
Regain, *acquisition,* 775
Regal, *authority,* 737
Regale, *feast,* 298
    pleasing, 377, 829
Regalia, *sceptre,* 747
Regard, *esteem,* 931
    respect, 928
    love, 897
    compliment, 894
    view, 441
    judge, 480
    conceive, 484
    credit, 873
Regarding, *relation,* 9
Regardless, *inattention,* 458
Regatta, *amusement,* 840
Regency, *commission,* 755
Regenerate, *reproduce,* 163
    restore, 660
    piety, 987
Regent, *deputy,* 759
    governor, 745
Regicide, *killing,* 361
Regime, *authority,* 737
    circumstance, 8
    conduct, 692
Regimen, *diet,* 298
    remedy, 662
Regiment, *army,* 726
    assemblage, 72
Regimentals, *dress,* 225
Region, *region,* 181
Register, *record,* 551
    list, 86
    to arrange, 60
    range, 26
    to coincide, 199
    ventilator, 351
    fire-place, 386
Registrar, *recorder,* 553
Regorge, *restitution,* 790
Regrater, *merchant,* 797
Regress, *regression,* 283
Regressive, *reversion,* 145
Regret, *sorrow,* 833
    penitence, 950
Regular, *orderly,* 58
    complete, 52
    rule, 80, 82
    symmetric, 242
    periodic, 138

Regular, *soldier,* 726
Regulation, *arrangement,* 60
    direction, 693
    usage, 80
    order, 741
    law, 963
Regurgitate, *return,* 283
    flow, 348
    restore, 790
Rehabilitate, *reinstate,* 660
    restore, 790
Rehash, *repetition,* 104
    improvement, 658
Rehearse, *repeat,* 104
    trial, 463
    describe, 594
    prepare, 673
    dramatic, 599
Reify, *materialize,* 3
Reign, *authority,* 175, 737
Reimburse, *restore,* 790
    pay, 807
Rein, *moderate,* 174
    check, 179
    slacken, 275
    restrain, 616
    hold, 737
Reincarnation, *reproduction,*
    163
Reindeer, *carrier,* 271
Reinforce, *strengthen,* 159
    aid, 707
    add, 37, 39
Reinforcement, *supplies,*
    635, 637
Reinstate, *restore,* 660
Reinvigorate, *restore,* 660
    refresh, 689
Reiterate, *frequent,* 136
    repeat, 104, 535
    multitude, 102
Reject, *decline,* 610
    refuse, 764
    exclude, 55
    eject, 297
Rejoice, *exult,* 838
    gratify, 829
    cheer, 836
    amuse, 840
Rejoinder, *answer,* 462
    evidence, 468
    lawsuit, 969
Rejuvenate, *restore,* 660
Rekindle, *ignite,* 384
    motive, 615
Relapse, *reversion,* 145
    retrogression, 661
Relate, *narrate,* 594
    refer, 9
Relation, *relation,* 9
Relative, *consanguinity,* 11
Relax, *weaken,* 160
    soften, 324
    slacken, 275
    unbend the mind, 452

Repellent, *unpleasant*, 830
  ugly, 846
Repent, *penitence*, 950
Repercussion, *recoil*, 277
  counteraction, 179
Repertoire, *store*, 636
Repertory, *store*, 636
  theatre, 599
Repetend, *iteration*, 104
  arithmetical, 84
Repetition, *iteration*, 90, 104
  copy, 21
  imitation, 19
Repine, *discontent*, 832
  regret, 833
  repent, 950
Replace, *restore*, 660
  supersede, 147
Replant, *restore*, 660
Replenish, *fill*, 637
  complete, 52
Repletion, *filling*, 637
  satiety, 641, 869
Replevin, *restore*, 790
  borrow, 788
Replica, *copy*, 21
Reply, *answer*, 462
Report, *noise*, 406
  record, 551
  inform, 527
  publish, 531
  rumour, 532
  statement, 594
  judgment, 480
  law, 969
Repose, *quiescence*, 265
  rest, 685, 687
Repose on, *support*, 215
Reposit, *location*, 184
Repository, *store*, 636
  focus, 74
Repoussé, *convexity*, 250
Reprehend, *disapprove*, 932
Represent, *delineate*, 554
  imitate, 19
  simulate, 17
  describe, 594
  denote, 550
  commission, 755
Representative, *consignee*, 758
  typical, 82
Repress, *quiet*, 174
  calm, 826
  restrain, 751
  control, 179
Reprieve, *pardon*, 918
  deliverance, 671, 672
  respite, 970
Reprimand, *disapprove*, 932
Reprint, *copy*, 21
Reprisal, *retaliation*, 718
Reproach, *blame*, 932
  disgrace, 874
Reprobate, *blame*, 932
  sinner, 949

Reprobate, *vicious*, 945
  impious, 988
Reproduce, *repeat*, 104
  represent, 554
  copy, 19
  renovate, 163
Reprove, *disapprove*, 932
Reptile, *animal*, 366
  servile, 886
  base, 940
  apostate, 941
  miscreant, 949
Republic, *man*, 373
  authority, 737
Repudiate, *exclude*, 55
  reject, 610
  dissent, 489
  refuse, 764
  violate, 773
  evade, 927
  non-payment, 808
Repugn, *resistance*, 719
Repugnance, *dislike*, 876
  reluctance, 603
  hate, 898
  incongruity, 24
Repulse, *repel*, 289
  resist, 719
Repulsive, *disagreeable*,
              830, 898
  nauseous, 395
  ugly, 846
Repurchase, *purchase*, 795
Reputable, *repute*, 873
Request, *request*, 765
Requiem, *funereal*, 363
  dirge, 415
  lamentation, 839
Require, *need*, 630
  insufficient, 640
  to exact, 741
  charge, 812
Requisition, *command*, 741
  take, 789
  request, 765
  requirement, 630
Requital, *reward*, 973
  gratitude, 916
  punishment, 972
Rescind, *cut off*, 44
  abrogate, 756
  refuse, 764
Rescission, *see* Rescind
Rescript, *order*, 741
  letter, 592
  answer, 462
Rescue, *deliver*, 672
  preserve, 670
  aid, 707
Research, *inquiry*, 461
Reseat, *restore*, 660
Resection, *disjunction*, 44
Resemblance, *similarity*, 17
Resent, *resentment*, 900
Reservation, *concealment*, 528

Reservation, *silence*, 585
  shyness, 881
  store, 636
Reserve, *concealment*, 528
  silence, 585
  shyness, 881
  caution, 864
  store, 636
Reservoir, *store*, 636
  receptacle, 191
  lake, 343
Reside, *inhabit*, 184, 186
Residence, *abode*, 189
  location, 184
Resident, *inhabitant*, 188
  emissary, 758
Residue, *remainder*, 40
Resign, *give up*, 757
  relinquish, 624, 782
  submit, 743
Resignation, *endurance*, 826
  content, 831
  abdication, 757
  humility, 743, 879
  renunciation, 872
Resilient, *elasticity*, 325
  rebound, 283
Resin, *semiliquid*, 352
Resist, *withstand*, 719
  disobey, 742
  refuse, 764
  oppose, 179
  tenacity, 327
Resistant, *tough*, 327
Resistless, *strength*, 159
Resolute, *determined*, 604
  brave, 861
Resolution, *decomposition*, 49
  investigation, 461
  solution, 462
  topic, 454
  determination, 604
  courage, 861
Resolve, *purpose*, 620
  to liquefy, 335
  decompose, 49
  investigate, 461
  discover, 480A
  interpret, 522
Resonant, *sonorous*, 402
  ringing, 408
Resorb, *reception*, 296
Resort, *employ*, 677
  converge, 290
  focus, 74
  assemble, 72
  frequent, 136
  move, 266
  dwell, 189
Resound, *be loud*, 402, 404
  ring, 408
  praises, 931
Resourceful, *skill*, 698
Resourceless, *inactive*, 683
Resources, *means*, 632, 780

Reverberatory, *fire*, 386
Reverence, *respect*, 928
   salutation, 894
   piety, 987
   worship, 990
   title, 877
Reverend, *clergy*, 996
Reverie, *train of thought*, 451
   imagination, 515
Reversal, *inversion*, 218
Reverse, *antiposition*, 237
   contrary, 14
   change, 140
   cancel, 756
   evolution, 313
   inversion, 218
   misfortune, 830
   adversity, 735
Reversion, *possession*, 777
   property, 780
   transfer, 783
Revert, *recur*, 104, 136
   go back, 283
   deteriorate, 659
Review, *consider*, 457
   memory, 505
   judge, 480
   criticism, 595
   rectify, 658
   display, 882
Reviewer, *writer*, 590
Revile, *abuse*, 932
   blaspheme, 988
Revise, *consider*, 457
   improve, 658
   restore, 660
   proof, 21, 591
Revisit, *presence*, 186
Revitalize, *restore*, 660
Revival, *worship*, 990
Revivalist, *clergy*, 996
Revive, *live*, 359
   restore, 660
   refresh, 689
Revivify, *reproduction*, 163
   restore, 660
Revoke, *recant*, 607
   deny, 536
   cancel, 756
   refuse, 754
Revolt, *resist*, 719
   revolution, 146
   disobey, 742
   shock, 830, 932
Revolting, *vulgar*, 851
Revolution, *rotation*, 312
   change, 140, 146
   periodicity, 138
Revolve, *meditate*, 451
Revolver, *arms*, 727
Revue, *drama*, 599
Revulsion, *recoil*, 277
Reward, *reward*, 973
Rhadamanthine, *severe*, 739
Rhapsody, *discontinuity*, 70

Rhapsody, *nonsense*, 497
   fancy, 515
   music, 415
Rhetoric, *speech*, 582
Rhetorical, *ornament*, 577
Rheum, *humour*, 333
   water, 337
Rhine, *ditch*, 350
Rhino, *money*, 800
Rhomb, *angularity*, 244
Rhombohedron, *angularity*, 244
Rhomboid, *angularity*, 244
Rhombus, *angularity*, 244
Rhumb, *direction*, 278
Rhyme, *poetry*, 597
   similarity, 17
Rhymeless, *prose*, 598
Rhythm, *harmony*, 413
   regularity, 138
   poetry, 597
Rib, *ridge*, 250
   banter, 256
   wife, 903
Ribald, *vile*, 874, 961
   vulgar, 851
   maledictory, 908
   impious, 988
   abuse, 932
Ribbed, *furrow*, 259
Ribbon, *filament*, 205
   tie, 45
   trophy, 733
   decoration, 877
Rich, *wealthy*, 803
   abundant, 639
   savoury, 394
   adorned, 847
   style, 577
Richly, *great*, 31
Rick, *store*, 636
   accumulation, 72
Rickety, *weak*, 160
   imperfect, 651
   ugly, 846
Rickshaw, *vehicle*, 272
Ricochet, *recoil*, 277
   reversion, 145
Rid, *loss*, 776
   relinquish, 782
   abandon, 624
   deliver, 672
Riddle, *enigma*, 533
   obscurity, 519
   question, 461
   confute, 479
   sieve, 260
   arrange, 60
Ride, *move*, 266
   get above, 206
   road, 627
Rider, *equestrian*, 268
   corollary, 480
   appendix, 39
Ridge, *narrowness*, 203
   projection, 250

Ridicule, *deride*, 856
   depreciate, 483
   disrespect, 929
Ridiculous, *grotesque*, 853
   vulgar, 851
   absurd, 497
   silly, 499
   trifling, 643
Riding, *region*, 181
*Ridotto, *gala*, 840
   rout, 892
*Rifacimento, *recast*, 660
Rife, *ordinary*, 82
   frequent, 136
   prevailing, 175
Riff-raff, *rabble*, 876, 949
   dirt, 653
Rifle, *to plunder*, 791
   arms, 727
Rifleman, *combatant*, 726
Rift, *separation*, 44
   fissure, 198
Rig, *dress*, 225
   prepare, 673
   frolic, 840
   deception, 545
   adorn, 845
Rigadoon, *dance*, 840
Rigescence, *hardness*, 323
Rigging, *gear*, 225
   cordage, 45
Right, *just*, 922
   privilege, 924
   duty, 926
   honour, 939
   straight, 246
   true, 494
   suitable, 646
Righteous, *virtuous*, 944
   just, 922
Rigid, *hard*, 323
   exact, 494
   strict, 772
   severe, 739
   stubborn, 606
   regular, 82
Rigmarole, *nonsense*, 497, 517
   unintelligible, 519
Rigour, *severity*, 739
   compulsion, 744
   exactness, 494
Rile, *irritate*, 830, 900
   alienate, 898
Rill, *river*, 348
Rim, *edge*, 230
Rime, *cold*, 383
Rind, *covering*, 222
Ring, *circle*, 247
   sound, 408
   arena, 728
   party, 712
   syndicate, 778
Ring-fence, *enclosure*, 232
Ringleader, *master*, 745
   director, 694

Saline, *pungent*, 392
Saliva, *excretion*, 299
   lubricant, 332
Sallow, *yellow*, 436
   pale, 429
Sally, *issue*, 293
   attack, 716
   wit, 842
Salmagundi, *mixture*, 41
Salmon-coloured, *red*, 434
*Salon, *room*, 191
Saloon, *room*, 191
   vehicle, 272
Salt, *pungent*, 392
   condiment, 393
   wit, 842
   preserve, 670
Saltation, *dancing*, 309
Saltatory, *leap*, 309
   agitation, 351
*Saltimbanco, *quack*, 548
Salubrity, *health*, 656
Salutary, *salubrious*, 656
   remedial, 662
Salute, *compliment*, 894
   kiss, 902
   address, 586
   firing, 882, 883
Salvage, *tax*, 812
   discount, 813
   reward, 973
   acquisition, 775
   to save, 672
Salvation, *deliverance*, 672
   preservation, 670
   religious, 976
Salve, *to relieve*, 834
   remedy, 662
Salver, *dish*, 191
Salvo, *exception*, 83
   condition, 770
   excuse, 937
   plea, 617
   explosion, 406
   salute, 882
Samaritan, *benefactor*, 912
Samba, *dance*, 840
Sambo, *mixture*, 41
Same, *identity*, 13
Sameness, *monotony*, 841
Samiel, *wind*, 349
Samovar, *vessel*, 191
Sampan, *ship*, 273
Sample, *specimen*, 82
San fairy ann, *indifference*, 456
   neglect, 460
Sanatorium, *salubrity*, 656
Sanatory, *improvement*, 658
   remedy, 662
Sanctify, *authorize*, 924
   piety, 987
Sanctimony, *hypocrisy*, 988
   falsehood, 544
Sanction, *authority*, 924
   approbation, 931

Sanction, *permission*, 760
Sanctity, *piety*, 987
Sanctuary, *refuge*, 666
   altar, 1000
Sanctum, *holy*, 1000
   room, 191
Sand, *pulverulence*, 330
   manliness, 604
   courage, 861
Sand-blind, *dim-sighted*, 443
Sand-shoe, *dress*, 225
Sandal, *dress*, 225
Sandalwood, *fragrance*, 400
Sandbag, *defence*, 717
   arms, 727
Sandpaper, *smooth*, 255
Sands, *pitfall*, 667
Sandwich, *interpose*, 228
Sandy, *pulverulence*, 330
Sane, *intelligent*, 498
   rational, 502
Sang-froid, *insensibility*, 823
   inexcitability, 826
   caution, 864
Sanguinary, *brutal*, 907
Sanguine, *expectant*, 507
   hopeful, 858
Sanhedrim, *tribunal*, 696
Sanies, *fluidity*, 333
Sanitary, *salubrity*, 656
Sanity, *rationality*, 502
   health, 654
Sans, *absence*, 187
*Sans cérémonie, *modesty*, 881
   sociality, 892
   friendship, 888
*Sans façon, *modesty*, 881
   sociality, 892
*Sans pareil, *superiority*, 33
*Sans phrase, *frankness*,
            543, 566
*Sans souci, *pleasure*, 827
   content, 831
Sansculotte, *rebel*, 742
   commonalty, 876
Santon, *hermit*, 893
   priest, 996
Sap, *juice*, 333
   inbeing, 5
   to destroy, 162
   damage, 659
   fool, 501
Sapid, *tasty*, 390
Sapient, *wisdom*, 498
Sapless, *dry*, 340
Sapling, *youth*, 129
Saponaceous, *soapy*, 355
Sapor, *flavour*, 390
Sapphire, *ornament*, 847
Sappy, *juicy*, 333
   foolish, 499
Saraband, *dance*, 840
Sarcasm, *satire*, 932
   disrespect, 929
Sarcastic, *irascible*, 901

Sarcastic, *derisory*, 856
Sarcoma, *disease*, 655
Sarcophagus, *interment*, 363
Sardonic, *contempt*, 838
Sartorial, *dress*, 225
Sash, *central*, 247
Satan, *devil*, 978
Satanic, *evil*, 649
   hellish, 982
   vicious, 945
Satchel, *bag*, 191
Sate, *see* Satiate
Satellite, *follower*, 281
   companion, 88
   space ship, 273A
Satiate, *sufficient*, 639
   redundant, 641
   cloy, 869
Satiety, *see* Satiate
Satin, *smooth*, 255
Satire, *ridicule*, 856
   censure, 932
Satirist, *detractor*, 936
Satisfaction, *duel*, 720
   reward, 973
Satisfactorily, *well*, 618
Satisfy, *content*, 831
   gratify, 827, 829
   convince, 484
   fulfil a duty, 926
   an obligation, 772
   reward, 973
   pay, 807; *suffice*, 639
   satiate, 869
   grant, 762
Satrap, *ruler*, 745
   deputy, 759
Satrapy, *province*, 181
Saturate, *fill*, 52, 639
   soak, 337
   moisten, 339
   satiate, 869
Saturated, *greatness*, 31
Saturnalia, *amusement*, 840
   intemperance, 954
   disorder, 59
Saturnian, *halcyon*, 734, 829
Saturnine, *grim*, 837
Satyr, *ugly*, 846
   demon, 980
   rake, 961
Sauce, *mixture*, 41
   adjunct, 39
   abuse, 832
Sauce-box, *impudence*, 887
Saucepan, *stove*, 386
Saucer, *receptacle*, 191
Saucy, *insolent*, 885
   flippant, 895
   cheerful, 836
Saunter, *ramble*, 266
   dawdle, 275
*Sauve qui peut, *speed*, 274
   recession, 287
   avoidance, 623

Smitten, *love*, 897

Smock, *dress*, 225

Smog, *mist*, 353
   dimness, 422

Smoke, *cloud*, 334
   dimness, 422
   heat, 382
   trifle, 643
   dirt, 653
   preserve, 670

Smoke-stack, *funnel*, 351

Smooth, *not rough*, 16, 255
   to calm, 174
   lubricate, 332
   easy, 705
   to flatter, 933
   cunning, 702

Smooth-bore, *gun*, 727

Smooth-faced, *falsehood*, 544

Smooth-spoken, *falsehood*, 544

Smooth-tongued, *falsehood*, 544

Smother, *kill*, 361
   repress, 174
   calm, 826
   silence, 581
   suppress, 528, 585

Smoulder, *burn*, 382
   inert, 172
   latent, 528

Smout, *littleness*, 193

Smudge, *dirt*, 653
   blemish, 848

Smug, *affected*, 855

Smuggle, *contraband*, 791
   introduce, 294

Smuggler, *thief*, 792

Smut, *dirt*, 653
   black, 431
   blemish, 848
   impurity, 961

Smutch, *blacken*, 431

Snack, *participate*, 778
   food, 298

Snaffle, *restraint*, 752

Snag, *danger*, 667
   difficulty, 704
   hindrance, 706
   sharp, 253
   projection, 250

Snail, *slow*, 275

Snake, *miscreant*, 913

Snaky, *winding*, 248

Snap, *noise*, 406
   brittle, 328; *break*, 44
   be rude, 895, 900
   seize, 789
   vigour, 574
   easy, 705

Snappy, *concise*, 572

Snare, *trap*, 667

Snarl, *growl*, 412
   angry, 900; *rude*, 895
   threaten, 909
   disorder, 59

Snatch, *to seize*, 789

Snatch, *opportunity*, 134
   part, 51

Sneak, *servility*, 886
   basement, 940
   to hide, 528
   retire, 287

Sneakers, *shoes*, 225

Sneer, *contempt*, 930
   blame, 932
   disparage, 929

Sneeze, *snuffle*, 409
   blow, 349

Snick, *part*, 51

Snickersnee, *weapon*, 727

Snide, *false*, 544

Sniff, *odour*, 398

Sniff at, *despise*, 930

Sniffy, *contemptuous*, 930

Snigger, *laugh*, 838

Snip, *cut*, 44

Snip-snap, *discord*, 713

Sniper, *fighter*, 727

Snippet, *smallness*, 32

Snivel, *cry*, 839

Snivelling, *servile*, 886

Snob, *commonalty*, 876
   sycophant, 886

Snood, *dress*, 225
   fastening, 45

Snooper, *spectator*, 444
   curiosity, 455
   inquire, 461

Snooty, *insolence*, 885

Snooze, *sleep*, 683

Snore, *noise*, 411
   sleep, 683

Snort, *noise*, 411
   sleep, 683
   drink, 298

Snout, *prominence*, 250

Snow, *ice*, 383
   white, 430

Snow-shoe, *locomotion*, 266

Snowball, *collection*, 72

Snowk, *sniff*, 398

Snub, *bluster*, 885
   blame, 932
   refuse, 764
   abash, 874
   short, 201

Snuff, *odour*, 398
   tobacco, 298A

Snuff-box, *receptacle*, 191

Snuff out, *die*, 360

Snuff up, *inhale*, 296

Snuffle, *hiss*, 409
   blow, 349
   stammer, 583

Snug, *comfortable*, 377, 831
   safe, 664
   latent, 526
   secluded, 893

Snuggery, *room*, 189

Snuggle, *draw near*, 286
   cuddle, 902

So-and-so, *euphemism*, 565

So-called, *miscall*, 565

So long, *departure*, 293

So-so, *unimportant*, 643
   imperfection, 651
   smallness, 32
   tolerable, 736

Soak, *immerse*, 300
   water, 337
   moisture, 339

Soaker, *drunkenness*, 959

Soap, *oil*, 356
   cleanness, 652

Soapy, *unctuous*, 355
   servile, 886
   flattering, 933

Soar, *rise*, 305
   height, 206
   great, 31
   fly, 267

Sob, *weep*, 839

Sober, *moderate*, 174
   temperate, 953
   abstinent, 958
   sane, 502
   wise, 498
   calm, 826
   grave, 837

Sober-minded, *wise*, 502
   calm, 826

Sobranje, *council*, 696

Sobriquet, *misnomer*, 565

Sociable, *friendly*, 892

Social, *friendly*, 888, 892

Socialism, *participation*, 778
   philanthropy, 910
   authority, 737

Society, *man*, 372
   friendly, 892
   party, 712
   fashion, 852

Sociology, *mankind*, 372
   philanthropy, 910

Sock, *stocking*, 225
   drama, 599

Socket, *receptacle*, 191, 252

Socrates, *sage*, 500

Socratic method, *quiz*, 461

Sod, *turf*, 344

Soda-water, *bubble*, 353

Sodality, *fraternity*, 712
   association, 892
   friendship, 888

Sodden, *wet*, 339
   overcharged, 641

Sofa, *support*, 215

Soft, *not hard*, 324
   marshy, 345
   moderate, 174
   sound, 405
   smooth, 255
   weak, 160
   silly, 499
   irresolute, 605
   timid, 862

Soft, *lenient*, 740
   compassionate, 914
   tender, 822
Soft currency, *money*, 800
Soft mark, *dupe*, 547
Soften, *soothe*, 826
   mitigate, 834
   palliate, 937
   subdue, 824
Softy, *fool*, 501
Soggy, *wet*, 337
*Soi-disant, *deceiver*, 548
   misnomer, 565
   boaster, 884
Soil, *land*, 342
   dirt, 653
   spoil, 659
   deface, 846
   tarnish, 848
Soiled dove, *courtesan*, 962
Soirée, *assemblage*, 72
   reception, 892
Sojourn, *abode*, 189
   inhabit, 186
   settle, 265
Sol-fa, *melody*, 413
Solace, *relief*, 834
   comfort, 827
   condolence, 915
   recreation, 840
Solar, *world*, 318
Solatium, *recompense*, 973
Soldan, *master*, 745
Solder, *cohere*, 46
   join, 43
   cement, 45
Soldier, *combatant*, 726
   warfare, 722
Sole, *alone*, 87
   base, 211
Solecism, *ungrammatical*, 568
   sophistry, 477
Solemn, *awful*, 873
   sacred, 987
   grave, 837
   pompous, 882
   positive, 535
   important, 642
Solemnity, *parade*, 882
   rite, 998
   dullness, 843
Solemnize, *celebrate*, 883
*Solfeggio, *melody*, 413
Solicit, *induce*, 615
   request, 765
   desire, 865
Solicitor, *law*, 968
Solicitude, *anxiety*, 860
   care, 459
   desire, 865
Solid, *complete*, 52
   dense, 321
   certain, 474
   true, 494
   firm, 604

Solid, *wise*, 498
Solidify, *coherence*, 46
   density, 321
Soliloquy, *speech*, 589
Solitary, *alone*, 87
   secluded, 893
Solitude, *see* Solitary
Solmization, *melody*, 413
Solo, *music*, 415
Soloist, *musician*, 416
Solomon, *sage*, 500
Solon, *sage*, 500
   wise, 498
Soluble, *dissolve*, 335
Solution, *dissolving*, 335
   explanation, 462
   interpretation, 522
Solve, *explain*, 462
   discover, 480A
Solvency, *wealth*, 803
Somatics, *material*, 316
Sombre, *dark*, 421
   grey, 432
   black, 431
   melancholy, 837
Some, *a few*, 100
Somebody, *one*, 87
   man, 373
   celebrity, 873
Somehow, *manner*, 155
Somersault, *inversion*, 218
Somerset, *inversion*, 218
Something, *thing*, 3
   small degree, 32
Sometimes, *frequency*, 136
Somewhat, *small*, 32
Somewhere, *place*, 182
Somnambulism, *imagination*,
                           515
Somniferous, *sleepy*, 683
   weary, 841
Somnolence, *sleepy*, 683
   weary, 841
Son, *relation*, 167
Sonance, *sound*, 402
Sonata, *music*, 415
Song, *music*, 415
Song, old, *unimportant*, 643
Songster, *musician*, 416
Soniferous, *sound*, 402
Sonnet, *poetry*, 597
Sonorous, *sound*, 402
   loud, 404
Sonsy, *fat*, 102
Soon, *early*, 132
   transient, 111
Soot, *black*, 431
   dirt, 653
   blemish, 846
Sooth, *truth*, 494
Soothe, *allay*, 174
   calm, 826
   relieve, 834
Soothsay, *predict*, 511
Soothsayer, *omen*, 513

Soothsayer, *magician*, 994
Sop, *bribe*, 615
   reward, 973
   wet, 337
Sophism, *bad logic*, 477
   absurdity, 497
Sophisticate, *mix*, 41
   mislead, 477
   debase, 659
Sophistry, *false reasoning*, 477
   misteaching, 538
Sophomore, *learner*, 541
Sophy, *ruler*, 745
Soporific, *sleepy*, 683
   boring, 841
Sopping, *moist*, 339
Soprano, *music*, 413
   high note, 409, 410
Sorcerer, *sorcerer*, 994
Sorcery, *occult arts*, 992
*Sordes, *uncleanness*, 653
Sordid, *mean*, 819
   base, 876
Sordine, *silencer*, 417
   damper, 403
Sore, *pain*, 378
   grievance, 828
   painful, 830
   angry, 900
Sorehead, *discourtesy*, 895
Sorely, *greatness*, 31
Sorites, *reasoning*, 476
Sororicide, *killing*, 361
Sorrel, *redness*, 434
Sorrow, *pain*, 828
Sorry, *grieved*, 828
   penitent, 950
   pitiful, 914
   bad, 649
   mean, 876
   trifling, 643
   smallness, 32
Sort, *kind*, 75
   degree, 26
   rectify, 658, 660
   to arrange, 60
   simplify, 42
*Sortes, *chance*, 156, 621
   prediction, 511
Sortie, *attack*, 716
Sortilege, *sorcery*, 992
   prediction, 511
   chance, 621
Sorting, *arrangement*, 60
*Sostenuto, *music*, 415
Sot, *fool*, 501
   drunkard, 959
*Sotto voce, *faintness*, 405
   aphony, 581
   stammering, 583
Sou, *money*, 800
Soubrette, *actress*, 599
   servant, 746
Sough, *conduit*, 350
   cloaca, 653

Sough, *wind*, 349
Soul, *intrinsic*, 5
  intellect, 450
  affections, 820
  man, 373
  important part, 50, 642
Soulful, *feeling*, 821
Soulless, *insensible*, 823
Sound, *noise*, 402
  healthy, 654
  perfect, 650
  good, 648
  great, 31
  to measure, 466
  to investigate, 461
  true, 494
  wise, 498
  orthodox, 983A
  bay, 343
  gap, 198
Sounder, *herd*, 72
Sounding-rod, *depth*, 208
Soundings, *deep*, 208
Soundless, *deep*, 208
  silent, 403
Soundly, *great*, 31
Soup, *food*, 298
  pulp, 354
Soup-and-fish, *dress*, 225
*Soupçon, *little*, 32, 193
  mixture, 41
Sour, *acid*, 397
  uncivil, 895
  misanthropic, 901
  to embitter, 835
Source, *origin*, 66, 153
Sourdine, *silencer*, 417
Souse, *immerse*, 300
  water, 337
Soutane, *canonicals*, 999
*Souteneur, *libertine*, 962
South, *opposite*, 237
Souvenir, *memory*, 505
Sou'wester, *dress*, 225
Sovereign, *great*, 31
  superiority, 33
  strong, 157
  ruler, 745
Sovereignty, *authority*, 73
Soviet, *council*, 696
Sow, *scatter*, 73
  cultivate, 371
  prepare, 673
Sozzled, *drunk*, 959
Spa, *salubrity*, 656
  remedy, 662
Space, *room*, 180
  separate, 44
Space ship, *aircraft*, 273A
Space travel, *voyage*, 267
Spacious, *roomy*, 180
Spade, *sharpness*, 253
Spaewife, *oracle*, 513
Spahi, *combatant*, 726
Spalpeen, *bad man*, 949

Span, *distance*, 196
  nearness, 197
  length, 200
  measure, 466
  time, 106
  duality, 89
Spandule, *demon*, 980
Spangle, *spark*, 420
  ornament, 847
Spaniel, *servile*, 886
  flatterer, 935
Spank, *impact*, 276
  beat, 972
Spanking, *size*, 192
Spar, *discord*, 713
  contention, 720, 722
Spare, *meagre*, 203
  scanty, 640
  to give, 784
  relinquish, 782
  disuse, 678
  exempt, 927A
  refrain, 623
  pity, 914
  frugal, 953
  economic, 817
  superfluous, 641
  in reserve, 636
Spare time, *leisure*, 685
Sparge, *sprinkle*, 73
Sparing, *temperate*, 953
  small, 32
  economic, 817
Spark, *light*, 420
  fire, 382
  fop, 854
  court, 902
Sparkle, *glisten*, 420
  bubble, 353
Sparkling, *vigorous*, 574
Sparse, *scattered*, 73
  tenuous, 322
  few, 103
*Sparsim, *non-assemblage*, 73
Spartan, *severe*, 739
Spasm, *fit*, 173
  throe, 146
  pain, 378, 828
Spasmodic, *fitful*, 139
Spat, *quarrel*, 713
Spatial, *space*, 99
Spatter, *dirt*, 653
  damage, 659
Spatterdash, *dress*, 225
Spatula, *layer*, 204
  trowel, 191
Spawn, *dirt*, 653
  offspring, 167
Spay, *sterilize*, 169
Speak, *speech*, 582
Speak fair, *conciliate*, 615
Speak of, *mean*, 516
Speak to, *allocution*, 586
Speak out, *disclose*, 529
Speaker, *speech*, 582

Speaker, *teacher*, 540
  interpreter, 524
  president, 745
Spear, *lance*, 727
  to pierce, 260
  pass through, 302
Spearman, *combatant*, 726
Special, *particular*, 79
  peculiar, 5
Special pleading, *sophistry*, 477
Specialist, *adviser*, 695
  doctor, 662
  proficient, 700
Speciality, *intrinsic*, 5
  particular, 79
Specie, *money*, 800
Species, *kind*, 75
  appearance, 448
Specific, *special*, 79
Specification, *description*, 594
Specify, *name*, 564
  tell, 527
Specimen, *example*, 82
Specious, *probable*, 472
  sophistical, 477
  plausible, 937
Speck, *dot*, 193
  small quantity, 32
  blemish, 848
Speckle, *variegated*, 400
  blemish, 848
Spectacle, *appearance*, 448
  show, 882
  prodigy, 872
Spectacles, *optical instrument*,
               445
Spectator, *spectator*, 444
Spectre, *vision*, 448
  ugly, 846
  ghost, 980
Spectroscope, *optical*, 445
  colour, 428
Spectrum, *colour*, 428
  appearance, 448
Speculate, *think*, 451
  suppose, 514
  chance, 621
  venture, 675
  traffic, 794
  view, 441
Speculum, *mirror*, 445
Speech, *speech*, 582
Speechless, *silence*, 581
Speed, *velocity*, 274
  activity, 682
  haste, 684
  to help, 707
  succeed, 731
Speedometer, *velocity*, 274
  measure, 466
Speedwalk, *way*, 627
Speer, *ask*, 461
Spell, *interpret*, 522
  read, 539
  period, 106

Stiff, *rigid*, 323
  resolute, 604
  difficult, 704
  restrained, 751
  severe, 739
  dear, 814
  affected, 855
  haughty, 878
  pompous, 882
  ugly, 846
  style, 572, 579
Stiff-necked, *obstinate*, 606
  resolute, 604
Stifle, *silence*, 403
  conceal, 528
  destroy, 162
  kill, 361
  sound, 405
Stigma, *disgrace*, 874
  blame, 932
Stigmatize, *accuse*, 938
Stile, *way*, 627
Stiletto, *piercer*, 262
  dagger, 727
Still, *ever*, 112
  silent, 403
  quiet, 174
  quiescence, 265
  photograph, 556
  calm, 826
  notwithstanding, 179
  compensation, 30
  vaporizer, 336
Still-born, *failure*, 732
  dead, 360
Stilted, *bombastic*, 577
  affected, 855
Stilts, *support*, 215
  height, 206
  journey, 266
  boasting, 884
Stimulate, *incite*, 615
  violence, 173
  energize, 171
  passion, 824
Stimulus, *zest*, 615
Sting, *pain*, 378
  sensation, 380
  pungent, 392
  suffering, 824, 830
  provoke, 900
Stingy, *mean*, 817
Stink, *stench*, 401
Stinkard, *stink*, 401
Stinking, *bad*, 649
Stinko, *drunk*, 959
Stint, *degree*, 26
  limit, 233
  scanty, 640
  parsimony, 819
Stipend, *salary*, 809
Stipendiary, *receiving*, 785
  subjected, 749
  magistrate, 967
Stipple, *engraving*, 558

Stipple, *variegation*, 440
Stipulate, *conditions*, 770
  bargain, 769
Stir, *move*, 264
  agitation, 315
  activity, 682
  energy, 171
  emotion, 824
  discuss, 476
  prison, 752
Stir up, *mix*, 41
  excite, 615
  violence, 173
Stirrup-cup, *departure*, 293
  intoxicant, 959
Stitch, *work*, 680
  to join, 43
  pain, 828
Stiver, *money*, 800
Stock, *cause*, 153
  store, 636
  materials, 635
  provision, 637
  property, 780
  money, 800
  merchandise, 798
  collar, 225
  offspring, 166
  relation, 11
  quantity, 25
  habitual, 613
Stock-still, *immovable*, 265
Stockade, *defence*, 717
Stocking, *dress*, 225
Stockpile, *store*, 636
  provide, 637
Stocks, *funds*, 802
  punishment, 975
  restraint, 752
Stocky, *short*, 201
  broad, 202
Stoic, *insensible*, 823
  inexcitable, 826
  disinterested, 942
Stole, *dress*, 225
Stolid, *dull*, 843
  stupid, 499
Stomach, *pouch*, 191
  taste, 390
  liking, 865
Stomacher, *dress*, 225
Stone, *dense*, 321
  hard, 323
  materials, 635
  missile, 284
  weapon, 727
  kill, 361
Stone-blind, *blind*, 442
Stone-coloured, *grey*, 432
Stone-wall, *hinder*, 706
Stonk, *bombardment*, 716
Stony broke, *poor*, 804
Stony-hearted, *cruel*, 900
Stooge, *substitute*, 147
  assistant, 711

Stooge, *deputy*, 759; *loaf*, 683
Stook, *assemblage*, 76
Stool, *support*, 215
Stool-pigeon, *deceiver*, 548
  informer, 527, 529
Stoop, *bow*, 308
  slope, 217
  humble, 879
  servile, 886; *porch*, 191
Stoor, *see* Stour
Stop, *close*, 67, 261
  halt, 265
  lodge, 186
  prevent, 706
  silence, 403
  continue, 141
  discontinue, 142
Stopcock, *stopper*, 263
Stopgap, *shift*, 626
  substitute, 634
  deputy, 759
  plug, 263
Stopper, *stopper*, 263
Store, *magazine*, 636
  provision, 637
  shop, 799
  the memory, 505
  greatness, 31
Storehouse, *store*, 636
Storey, *layer*, 204
  rooms, 191
Στοργή, *love*, 897
Storm, *wind*, 349
  violence, 173
  agitation, 315
  passion, 825
  convulsion, 146
  anger, 900
  to attack, 716
  assemblage, 72
Storm-stayed, *hindered*, 70
  restraint, 751
Story, *narrative*, 582, 594
  news, 532
  lie, 546
Stot, *rebound*, 277
Stound, *wonder*, 870
Stour, *dust*, 330
  dirt, 653
Stout, *strong*, 159
  lusty, 192
  brave, 861
Stove, *furnace*, 386
Stow, *locate*, 184
  desist, 142
Stow it, *silent*, 585
Stowage, *space*, 180
  location, 184
Strabismus, *dim sight*, 443
Straddle, *sit*, 215
  stride, 266
  trim, 607
Stradivarius, *violin*, 417
Strafe, *punish*, 972
  maltreat, 649

Submerge, *sink*, 162, 208
  plunge, 310
Submission, *surrender*, 725, 879
Submissive, *humble*, 725, 879
  enduring, 826
Submit, *surrender*, 725
  obey, 743
Subordinate, *inferior*, 34
  unimportant, 643
  servant, 746
  subjection, 749
Subordination, *order*, 58
Suborn, *hire*, 795
  bribe, 784
Subpoena, *mandate*, 741
Subscribe, *assent*, 488
  agree to, 762, 769
  give, 707, 784
Subscription, *donation*, 809
Subsequent, *in time*, 117
  in order, 63, 65
Subservient, *utility*, 644
  intermediate, 631
  aiding, 707
  servility, 886
Subside, *sink*, 306
  cave in, 252
  decrease, 36
  calm down, 826
Subsidiary, *tending*, 176
  means, 632
  auxiliary, 707
Subsidy, *pay*, 809
  gift, 784
  aid, 707
Subsist, *existence*, 1
  life, 359
  continuance, 141
Subsistence, *food*, 298
  livelihood, 803
Subsistence money, *loan*, 787
  advance, 809
Subsoil, *earth*, 342
  interior, 221
*Substance, *thing*, 3
  matter, 316
  interior, 221
  quantity, 25
  texture, 329
  compendium, 596
  meaning, 516
  important, 642
  wealth, 803
Substantial, *dense*, 321
  existence, 1
  true, 494
Substantially, *intrinsically*, 5
Substantiate, *demonstrate*, 478
  make good, 494, 924
Substantive, *substance*, 3
Substitute, *means*, 634
  deputy, 759
Substitution, *change*, 147
Substratum, *substance*, 3
  interior, 221

Substratum, *layer*, 204
  base, 211
  support, 215
  materiality, 316
Subsumption, *inclusion*, 76
Subterfuge, *lie*, 546
  sophistry, 477
  cunning, 702
Subterranean, *underground*, 208
Subtilize, *sophistry*, 477
Subtle, *cunning*, 702
  wise, 498
  rare, 322
  light, 320
  texture, 329
Subtract, *retrench*, 38
  diminish, 36
  arithmetical, 84
  to take, 789
Subtrahend, *deduction*, 38
  number, 84
Suburban, *environs*, 227
  distance, 197
Subvention, *aid*, 707
  gift, 784
Subvert, *invert*, 218
  depress, 308
  change, 140
  destroy, 162
Subway, *road*, 627
Succedaneum, *substitute*,
                147, 634
Succeed, *answer*, 731
  follow, 63
*Succès d'estime, *approbation*,
                931
Success, *success*, 731
Succession, *sequence*, 63
  transfer, 783
  continuity, 69
  of time, 109
  lateness, 117
Successor, *sequel*, 65
  posterior, 117
Succinct, *concise*, 572
Succour, *help*, 707
Succubus, *demon*, 980
Succulent, *juicy*, 333
  edible, 298
  semiliquid, 352
Succumb, *yield*, 725
  obey, 743
  fatigue, 688
Such, *similarity*, 17
Suck, *imbibe*, 296
  deprive, 789
Sucker, *dupe*, 547
Suckling, *youth*, 129
Suction, *imbibition*, 296
Sudatorium, *furnace*, 386
Sudden, *early*, 132
  abrupt, 508
  transient, 111
Suds, *froth*, 353
Sue, *demand*, 765

Sue, *at law*, 969
Suet, *fat*, 356
Suffer, *physical pain*, 378
  moral pain, 828
  to endure, 821
  to allow, 760
  disease, 655
  experience, 151
Sufferance, *permission*, 760
Sufficient, *enough*, 639
Suffix, *sequel*, 65
  adjunct, 39
Sufflation, *wind*, 349
Suffocate, *choke*, 361
Suffragan, *church*, 996
Suffrage, *vote*, 609
  prayer, 990
Suffragist, *dueness*, 924
Suffuse, *mix*, 41
  feel, 821
  blush, 874
Sufism, *religions*, 984
Sugar, *sweet*, 396
  to flatter, 933
Sugarloaf, *convexity*, 250
Suggest, *suppose*, 514
  advise, 695
  inform, 527
  recall, 505
  occur, 451
*Suggestio falsi, *equivocalness*,
                520
  falsehood, 544
Suggestion, *plan*, 626
Suggestive, *impure*, 961
*Sui generis, *special*, 79
  unconformity, 83
*Sui juris, *freedom*, 748
Suicide, *kill*, 361
Suit, *accord*, 23
  class, 75
  expedient, 646
  series, 69
  clothes, 225
  courtship, 902
  at law, 969
Suit-case, *receptacle*, 191
Suite, *series*, 69
  adjunct, 39
  sequel, 65
  retinue, 746
Suiting, *accord*, 23
Suitor, *love*, 897
Sulcated, *furrow*, 259
Sulky, *discourteous*, 895
  bad-tempered, 901
  gloomy, 837
Sullen, *discourteous*, 895
  bad-tempered, 901
  gloomy, 837
  misanthropical, 911
Sully, *deface*, 846
  dirty, 653
  dishonour, 874, 940
Sulphur, *colour*, 436

Sultan, *master*, 745
  noble, 875
Sultry, *heat*, 382
Sum, *total*, 50
  number, 84
  to reckon, 85
  money, 800
Sum up, *description*, 594
Sumless, *infinity*, 105
Summary, transient, 111
  early, 132
  concise, 572
  compendium, 201, 596
Summation, *numeration*, 85
Summer, *heat*, 382
  support, 215
Summer-house, *abode*, 189
Summit, *top*, 210
  climax, 33
Summon, *command*, 741
  accuse, 938
Summon up, *evoke*, 824
Sump, *marsh*, 345
  sink, 653
Sumptuary, *expenditure*,
                           800, 809
Sumptuous, *ostentation*, 882
Sun, *luminary*, 423
Sun-bonnet, *dress*, 225
Sun-up, *morning*, 125
Sunbeam, *light*, 420
Sundae, *food*, 298
Sunday, *rest*, 685
Sunder, *disjoin*, 44
Sundown, *evening*, 126
Sundowner, *tramp*, 268, 876
  loafer, 683
Sundries, *oddments*, 51
Sundry, *multitude*, 102
Sunk, *low*, 208
  vice, 945
Sunless, *dark*, 421
Sunlight, *light*, 420
  cheerful, 836
  pleasing, 827
  prosperous, 734
Sunny, *see* Sunlight
Sunshade, *shade*, 424
Sunshine, *see* Sunlight
Sup, *eat*, 296
  drink, 298
Super, *good*, 648
Superable, *facility*, 705
Superabundant, *sufficient*, 641
Superadd, *addition*, 37
  increase, 35
Superannuated, *age*, 128
Superannuation, *pension*, 803
Superb, *proud*, 845
Supercargo, *overload*, 694
*Supercherie, *deception*, 545
Supercilious, *haughty*, 878
  insolent, 885
  contemptuous, 929
Superdreadnought, *ship*, 273

Supereminence, *repute*, 873
Supererogation, *uselessness*, 645
  superfluity, 641
  activity, 682
Superexalted, *repute*, 873
Superexcellent, *goodness*, 648
Superfetation, *addition*, 37
Superficial, *shallow*, 209, 220
  ignorant, 491
Superficies, *face*, 220
Superfine, *best*, 648
Superfluity, *excess*, 641
  remainder, 40
Superfortress, *aircraft*, 273A
Superhuman, *divine*, 976
  perfect, 650
  great, 31
Superimpose, *cover*, 220
Superincumbent, *above*, 206
  weight, 319
  resting, 215
Superinduce, *production*, 161
  change, 140
  addition, 37
Superintend, *direction*, 693
Superintendent, *director*, 694
Superior, *greater*, 33
  important, 642
  good, 648
Superlative, *perfect*, 650
  great, 31
Superman, *hero*, 948
Supernal, *lofty*, 206
Supernatant, *overlying*, 206
Supernatural, *deity*, 976
  spiritual, 317
Supernumerary, *redundant*,
                           641
  remaining, 40
  actor, 599
Superpose, *addition*, 37
  cover, 222
Superscription, *mark*, 550
  writing, 590
  evidence, 567
Supersede, *disuse*, 678
  substitute, 147
Superstition, *credulity*, 486
  heresy, 984A
Superstratum, *exteriority*, 220
Superstructure, *completion*,
                           729
Supertax, *tax*, 812
Supervacaneous, *useless*, 645
  redundant, 641
Supervene, *happen*, 151
  succeed, 117
  addition, 37
Supervise, *direction*, 693
Supervisor, *director*, 694
Supine, *horizontal*, 213
  inverted, 218
  inert, 172
  sluggish, 683
  torpid, 823

Supine, *indifferent*, 866
Supper, *food*, 298
Supplant, *substitution*, 147
Supple, *soft*, 324
  servile, 886
Supplement, *adjunct*, 39
  completion, 52
  addition, 37
Suppletory, *addition*, 37
Suppliant, *petitioner*, 767
Supplicant, *petitioner*, 767
Supplicate, *beg*, 765
  pity, 914
  worship, 990
Supplies, *materials*, 635
  aid, 707
Supply, *give*, 784
  provide, 637
  store, 636
Support, *sustain*, 215
  operate, 170
  evidence, 467
  aid, 707
  preserve, 670
  endure, 821, 826
Supporter, *prop*, 215
Suppose, *supposition*, 514
Supposing, *provided*, 469
Supposition, *supposition*, 514
Supposititous, *false*, 544, 925
  non-existing, 2
Suppository, *remedy*, 662
Suppress, *conceal*, 528
  silence, 581
  destroy, 162
Suppurate, *fester*, 653
*Supra, *priority*, 116
Supranatural, *spiritual*, 317
Supremacy, *superior*, 33
  authority, 737
  summit, 210
Supremely, *great*, 31
Surcease, *cessation*, 142
Surcharge, *redundance*, 641
  dearness, 814
Surcingle, *fastening*, 45
Surd, *number*, 84
Sure, *certain*, 474
  assent, 488
  consent, 762
  safe, 664
Sure-footed, *careful*, 459
  skilful, 698
Surely, *wonder*, 870
Surety, *security*, 771
  evidence, 467
Surf, *foam*, 353
  tide, 458
Surf-riding, *navigation*, 267
Surface, *exterior*, 220
Surfeit, *satiety*, 869
  redundance, 641
Surge, *ocean*, 341
  rotation, 312
  swell, 305

Swim, *navigate,* 267
  vertigo, 503
Swim in, *abound,* 639
Swim-suit, *dress,* 225
Swimming, *successful,* 731
  buoyant, 320
Swimmingly, *easily,* 705
  prosperously, 734
Swindle, *peculate,* 791
  cheat, 545
Swindler, *defrauder,* 792
  sharper, 548
Swing, *space,* 180
  hang, 214
  play, 170
  oscillate, 314
  rhythm, 138, 413
  freedom, 748
Swinge, *punish,* 972
Swingeing, *great,* 31
Swinish, *intemperance,* 954
  gluttony, 957
Swink, *work,* 686
Swipe, *blow,* 276
Swish, *hiss,* 409
Switch, *scourge,* 975
  shift, 279
  whisk, 311, 315
Switchback, *obliquity,* 217
Swivel, *hinge,* 312
  cannon, 727
Swivel-eye, *squint,* 443
Swollen, *proud,* 878
  expanded, 194
Swoon, *fainting,* 160
  inactivity, 683
  fatigue, 688
Swoop, *seizure,* 789
  descent, 306
Swop, *see* Swap
Sword, *arms,* 722, 727
  sharpness, 253
Swordsman. *combatant,* 726
Swot, *to study,* 539
  scholar, 492
Sybarite, *intemperance,* 954
Sybo, *condiment,* 393
Sycophant, *servility,* 886
  assent, 488
  adulation, 933
  flatterer, 935
Syllable, *word,* 561
Syllabus, *list,* 86
  compendium, 596
Syllogism, *logic,* 476
Sylph, *sprite,* 979
Sylvan, *woody,* 367
Symbol, *sign,* 550
  metaphor, 521
  mathematical, 84
Symmetry, *form,* 252
  order, 58
  beauty, 845
  equality, 27
Sympathy, *kindness,* 906

Sympathy, *love,* 897
  friendship, 888, 891
  pity, 914
Symphonic, *harmony,* 413
Symphony, *music,* 415
Symposium, *feast,* 299
  festivity, 840
  discussion, 461
Symptom, *sign,* 550
Synagogue, *temple,* 1000
Synchronism, *time,* 120
Syncopate, *shorten,* 201
Syncopation, *rhythm,* 413
Syncope, *cut,* 160
  conciseness, 572
Syncretism, *heresy,* 984A
Syndic, *master,* 745
Syndicalism, *participation,* 778
Syndicate, *partnership,* 712, 797
  co-operation, 709
Synecdoche, *metaphor,* 521
  substitution, 147
Synod, *council,* 696
  church, 995
  assemblage, 72
Synonym, *nomenclature,* 564
  identity, 13
Synonymous, *equal,* 27
  interpretation, 522
Synopsis, *arrangement,* 60
  compendium, 596
Synovia, *lubricant,* 332
Syntax, *grammar,* 567
Synthesis, *combination,* 48
  reasoning, 476
Synthetic, *imitation,* 19
Syphon, *see* Siphon
Syren, *see* Siren
Syringe, *spray,* 348
Syrup, *sweet,* 396
Systaltic, *pulse,* 314
System, *order,* 58, 60
  plan, 626
Systole, *pulse,* 314
  contraction, 195
Syzygy, *contiguity,* 199

T

T.N.T., *arms,* 727
T-square, *angularity,* 244
T.V., *radio,* 599B
Ta, *thanks,* 917
Ta ta, *departure,* 293
Tab, *adjunct,* 39
Tabby, *variegated,* 440
Tabernacle, *temple,* 1000
Tabid, *morbid,* 655
  shrivelled, 195
  noxious, 649
Table, *stand,* 215
  layer, 204
  flatness, 251
  list, 86
  record, 551

Table, *repast,* 298
Table-cloth, *covering,* 222
Table-d'hôte, *food,* 298
Table-talk, *talk,* 588
Table-turning, *occult,* 992
Tableau, *painting,* 556
  scene, 824
Tableland, *plain,* 344
  flat, 213
Tablet, *record,* 551
  layer, 204
  flatness, 251
Taboo, *spell,* 992, 993
  prohibition, 761
Tabor, *music,* 417
Tabouret, *support,* 215
*Tabula rasa, *oblivion,* 506
Tabulate, *arrange,* 60, 69
  register, 86
*Tace, *silence,* 403
Tachometer, *velocity,* 274
Tachygraphy, *writing,* 590
Tacit, *hidden,* 526
Taciturn, *silent,* 585
Tack, *direction,* 278
  nail, 45
  to turn, 279
  change course, 140
Tack to, *add,* 37
  join, 43
Tackle, *gear,* 633
  fastening, 45
  to undertake, 676
  encounter, 720
  impact, 276
Tacky, *sticky,* 46
Tact, *skill,* 698
  wisdom, 498
  taste, 850
  discrimination, 465
Tactician, *proficient,* 700
Tactics, *conduct,* 692
  plan, 626
  skill, 698
  warfare, 722
Tactile, *touch,* 379
Taction, *touch,* 379
Tactless, *foolish,* 499
  discourteous, 895
Tactual, *touch,* 379
Tadpole, *young,* 129
Tag, *add,* 37, 39
  fastening, 45
  part, 51
  smallness, 32
  end, 67
  sequel, 65
  point, 253
  maxim, 496
Tail, *end,* 67
  back, 235
  adjunct, 37, 214
  sequel, 65
  follow, 281, 461
Tailor, *dress,* 225

Tatterdemalion, *commonalty*, 876

Tattle, *talk*, 588

Tattler, *newsmonger*, 532

Tattoo, *roll*, 407
  variegate, 440

Taunt, *reproach*, 938
  ridicule, 856
  hoot, 929

Tautology, *repetition*, 104
  identity, 13
  diffusiveness, 573

Tavern, *inn*, 189

Tawdry, *vulgar*, 851
  colour, 428

Tawny, *yellow*, 436
  brown, 433

Tax, *impost*, 812
  to accuse, 938
  require, 765
  impose, 741; *employ*, 677

Taxi, *vehicle*, 272

Tea, *food*, 298

Tea-gown, *dress*, 225

Tea-room, *food*, 298

Teach, *teaching*, 537

Teach-in, *lecture*, 595

Teachable, *learning*, 539

Teacher, *instructor*, 540

Team, *group*, 69
  party, 712

Teamster, *director*, 694

Tear, *separate*, 44
  destroy, 162
  violence, 173
  move rapidly, 274
  weeping, 839

Tear out, *extract*, 301

Tease, *annoy*, 830

Teaser, *poser*, 533, 704

Teat, *convexity*, 250

Technique, *skill*, 698
  musical, 415

Technology, *skill*, 698

Techy, *see* Tetchy

Teddy bear, *plaything*, 840

Teddy boy, *bad man*, 913, 949

Tedium, *fatigue*, 841

Teem, *abound*, 639
  numerous, 102
  productiveness, 168

Teeming, *assemblage*, 72

Teenager, *youngster*, 129

Teeny-weeny, *little*, 193

Teepee, *abode*, 189

Teeter, *oscillate*, 314

Teetotalism, *sobriety*, 958
  temperance, 953

Teetotum, *rotation*, 840

Tegument, *covering*, 222

Telecast, *radio*, 599B

Teledu, *stink*, 401

Telegenic, *radio*, 599B

Telegnosis, *occult*, 992

Telegraph, *signal*, 550

Telegraph, *news*, 532

Telegraphic, *concise*, 572
  velocity, 274

Telekinesis, *occult*, 992
  thought, 451

Teleology, *intention*, 620

Telepathy, *occult*, 992
  thought, 451

Telephone, *hearing*, 418
  news, 532

Teleprompter, *radio*, 599B

Telescope, *optics*, 445

Teleview, *radio*, 599B

Television, *publication*, 531
  radio, 599B

Tell, *inform*, 527
  count, 85
  influence, 175
  speak, 582
  describe, 594

Tell of, *mean*, 516

Tell off, *count*, 85
  reprimand, 932

Telltale, *evidence*, 467
  divulge, 529

Telly, *radio*, 599B

Temerity, *rashness*, 5
  state, 7
  elasticity, 323
  affections, 820
  to moderate, 174
  soften, 324, 826
  prepare, 673
  irascibility, 901

Temperament, *nature*, 5
  tendency, 176
  disposition, 820
  music, 413

Temperance, *moderation*, 953

Temperate, *moderate*, 174
  mild, 826

Temperature, *heat*, 382

Tempest, *violence*, 173
  wind, 349; *agitation*, 315
  excitement, 825

Tempestivity, *occasion*, 134

Temple, *church*, 1000
  side, 236

*Tempo, *melody*, 413

Temporal, *transient*, 111
  material, 316
  laical, 997

Temporary, *transient*, 111

Temporize, *cunning*, 702
  policy, 698
  diuturnity, 110
  delay, 133
  opportunity, 134

Tempt, *entice*, 615
  desire, 865; *try*, 676

Ten, *number*, 98

Tenable, *probable*, 472

Tenacious, *retentive*, 781
  avaricious, 819
  resolved, 604

Tenacious, *obstinate*, 606
  prejudiced, 481

Tenacity, *toughness*, 327

Tenancy, *possession*, 777

Tenant, *occupier*, 188
  possessor, 779
  present, 186

Tenantless, *empty*, 187
  solitary, 893

Tend, *aid*, 107
  train, 370
  contribute, 153
  conduce, 176
  direct to, 278

Tendentious, *misjudgment*, 481

Tender, *soft*, 324
  susceptible, 822
  loving, 897
  compassionate, 914
  to offer, 763; *ship*, 273
  vehicle, 272

Tenderfoot, *stranger*, 57
  learner, 541

Tendon, *fastening*, 45

Tendril, *infant*, 129
  filament, 205
  fastening, 45

Tenebrific, *darkness*, 421

Tenement, *house*, 189
  property, 780

Tenet, *belief*, 484
  creed, 983

Tenner, *money*, 800

Tennysonian, *poetry*, 597

Tenon, *dovetail*, 300

Tenor, *course*, 7
  degree, 26
  direction, 278
  meaning, 516
  musical, 413

Tense, *hard*, 323

Tensile, *elasticity*, 325

Tension, *strength*, 159
  length, 200
  hardness, 323
  strain, 686

Tent, *receptacle*, 189
  covering, 222

Tentacle, *instrument*, 633
  grip, 781

Tentative, *experimental*, 463
  essaying, 675

Tenterhooks, *expectation*, 507

Tenuity, *rarity*, 322
  thinness, 203
  smallness, 32

Tenure, *dueness*, 924
  possession, 777

Tepefaction, *heating*, 384

Tepid, *warm*, 382
  passionless, 823

Terce, *worship*, 990

Tercentenary, *period*, 138
  celebration, 883

Terebration, *opening*, 260

Thirst, *desire*, 865
Thisness, *speciality*, 79
Thistle, *sharpness*, 253
Thistledown, *light*, 320
Thither, *direction*, 278
Thole, *feeling*, 821
Thong, *join*, 45
Thor, *god*, 979
Thorn, *sharp*, 253
  painful, 830
  pain, 378
Thorny, *difficult*, 704
Thorough, *completeness*, 52
Thorough-bass, *music*, 413
Thorough-going, *greatness*, 31
Thorough-paced, *great*, 31
  complete, 52
Thoroughbred, *manners*, 852
Thoroughly, *great*, 31
Thorp, *abode*, 189
Though, *counteraction*, 179
  compensation, 30
  opposition, 708
  evidence, 468
Thought, *reflection*, 451
  maxim, 496
  small quantity, 32, 193
  idea, 453
Thoughtful, *reflecting*, 451
  wise, 498
Thoughtless, *incogitant*, 452
  careless, 460
  foolish, 499
  improvident, 674
  unskilful, 699
Thousand, *number*, 98
Thowless, *inactive*, 683
Thraldom, *slavery*, 749
Thrall, *slave*, 746
Thrapple, *air-pipe*, 351
Thrash, *beat*, 972
Thrash out, *inquire*, 461
Thrasonical, *boast*, 884
Thread, *tie*, 45
  filament, 205
  continuity, 69
  file, 60
  to pass through, 302
Thread one's way, *journey*, 266
  experiment, 463
Threadbare, *bare*, 226
  imperfect, 651
Threat, *threaten*, 909
Threaten, *future*, 121
  doom, 152
  alarm, 669
  danger, 665
Three, *number*, 92
Three-master, *ship*, 273
Threefold, *number*, 93
Threnody, *lament*, 830
Thresh, *see* Thrash
Threshold, *beginning*, 66
Thrice, *number*, 93
Thrift, *success*, 731

Thrift, *prosperity*, 734
  economy, 817
Thriftless, *prodigal*, 818
Thrill, *touch*, 379
  affect, 821, 824
Thriller, *story*, 594
Thrilling, *tingling*, 380
  charming, 829
Thrive, *succeed*, 731
  prosper, 734
  health, 654
Throat, *opening*, 260
  air-pipe, 351
Throb, *agitate*, 315
  emotion, 821
Throe, *violence*, 173
  agitation, 146, 315
  pain, 378, 828
Throne, *seat*, 215
  abode, 189
  authority, 747
Throng, *assembly*, 72
Throttle, *seize*, 789
  occlude, 261
  suffocate, 361
Through, *passage*, 302
  instrument, 631
  owing to, 154
  end, 66
Throughout, *totality*, 50
  time, 106
Throw, *propel*, 284
  eject, 297
  exertion, 686
Throw away, *lose*, 776
  relinquish, 782
Throw-back, *reversion*, 145
Throw down, *destroy*, 162
  overthrow, 308
Throw in, *add*, 300
Throw off, *eject*, 297
  do with ease, 705
Throw over, *desert*, 624
Throw up, *resign*, 757
  desert, 624
Thrum, *music*, 415
Thrush, *musician*, 416
Thrust, *push*, 276
  eject, 297
  attack, 716
Thrust in, *insert*, 300
  interpose, 228
Thud, *noise*, 406
Thug, *thief*, 792
  bad man, 949
Thuggism, *killing*, 361
Thumb, *finger*, 379
Thumb-nail, *little*, 193
Thumbscrew, *scourge*, 975
Thump, *beat*, 276
  punish, 972
  noise, 406
Thumping, *great*, 31
Thumping, *noise*, 404
  roar, 411

Thumping, *violence*, 173
  threaten, 909
Thunder-box, *toilet*, 191, 653
Thunder-storm, *violence*, 173
Thunder-struck, *awe*, 870
Thunderbolt, *prodigy*, 872
Thunderclap, *prodigy*, 872
Thundering, *size*, 192
Thurible, *rite*, 998
Thus, *reasoning*, 470
Thus far, *smallness*, 32
Thwack, *beat*, 276
  punish, 972
Thwart, *obstruct*, 706
  intersect, 219
Tiara, *diadem*, 747
  ornament, 847
  canonicals, 999
Tick, *sound*, 407
  oscillation, 314
  indicate, 550
  credit, 805
Tick off, *reprimand*, 932
Ticket, *indication*, 550
  permission, 760
  plan, 626
Tickle, *touch*, 380
  please, 377, 829
  laugh, 838
Tickled, *amused*, 827
Ticklish, *difficult*, 704
  uncertain, 475
  dangerous, 665
Tiddly, *drunk*, 959
Tide, *ocean*, 341
  flood, 348
  abundance, 639
Tidings, *news*, 532
Tidy, *clean*, 652
  trim, 673
Tie, *relation*, 9
  fasten, 43, 45
  security, 771
  equality, 27
  obligation, 926
  contention, 720
Tie-beam, *support*, 215
Tier, *continuity*, 69
  layer, 204
Tiff, *discord*, 713
  anger, 900
Tiffin, *food*, 298
Tiger, *violence*, 173
  courage, 861
  servant, 746
  wretch, 913
  miscreant, 949
Tight, *fast*, 43
  closed, 261
  smart, 845
  drunk, 959
Tight-lipped, *taciturn*, 585
Tike, *commonalty*, 876
Tile, *covering*, 222
  hat, 225

Till, *to cultivate*, 371
  coffer, 191, 802
  up to the time, 108
Tilt, *slope*, 217
  tumble, 306
  cover, 222
Tilt at, *attack*, 716
Tilt over, *obliquity*, 218
Timber, *materials*, 635
Timbre, *music*, 413
Timbrel, *musical instrument*, 417
Time, *period*, 106
Time-ball, *indication*, 550
Time-server, *servility*, 886
  apostate, 941
  cunning, 702
  expedient, 646
  irresolution, 605
  versatile, 607
  selfish, 943
Time-worn, *old*, 124
  exhausted, 659
Timelessness, *never*, 107
Timely, *early*, 132
  opportune, 134
Timepiece, *chronometer*, 114
Timid, *fearful*, 860
  cowardly, 862
  humble, 881
Timon of Athens, *recluse*, 893
Timorous, *see* Timid
Timpanist, *musician*, 416
Tin, *money*, 800
  to preserve, 670
Tin hat, *defence*, 717
Tin-opener, *open*, 260
Tinct, *colour*, 428
Tincture, *mixture*, 41
  to colour, 428
Tinder, *burn*, 388
Tine, *sharpness*, 253
Ting, *ring*, 408
Tinge, *colour*, 428
  mix, 41
Tingle, *pain*, 378, 828
  feeling, 821
Tingling, *titillation*, 380
Tink, *resonance*, 408
Tinker, *improve*, 658
Tinkety-tonk, *departure*, 293
Tinkle, *resonance*, 408
  faint sound, 405
Tinsel, *ornament*, 847
  glitter, 420
  display, 882
  tawdry, 851
  false, 544
Tint, *colour*, 428
Tintinnabulation, *resonance*, 408
Tiny, *little*, 32
  small, 193
Tip, *summit*, 210
  end, 67; *hint*, 527

Tip, *to give*, 784, 809
  reward, 973
  of iceberg, 193
Tippet, *dress*, 225
Tipple, *drink*, 296, 298
  drunkenness, 959
Tipstaff, *police*, 965
Tipsy, *drunk*, 959
Tiptoe, *high*, 206
  curiosity, 455
Tiptop, *summit*, 210
  first-rate, 648
Tirade, *disapproval*, 932
  declamation, 582
Tire, *weary*, 841
  worry, 830
  fatigue, 688
Tiresome, *wearisome*, 841
Tiro, *see* Tyro
Tirrivee, *agitation*, 315
Tissue, *texture*, 329
Tit, *small*, 193
  pony, 271
Tit for tat, *retaliation*, 718
  compensation, 30
Titanic, *greatness*, 31, 192
Titbit, *dainty*, 829
Tithe, *tenth*, 99
  dues, 812
Titillate, *touch*, 380
  please, 377, 838
Titivate, *dress*, 225
  beautify, 845
Title, *distinction*, 877
  name, 564
  mark, 550
  property, 780
  right, 924
Title-page, *beginning*, 66, 593
Titter, *laugh*, 838
Tittle, *small quantity*, 32
  little, 192
Tittle-tattle, *chat*, 588
  news, 532
Tittup, *frisk*, 266, 274
Titubation, *fall*, 306
  failure, 732
Titular, *title*, 564
Toad, *ugliness*, 846
Toad-eater, *servile*, 886
  flatterer, 935
Toady, *to flatter*, 933
Toast, *roast*, 384
  celebrate, 883
Tobacco, *tobacco*, 298A
Toccata, *music*, 415
Tocsin, *alarm*, 669
  indication, 550
Toddle, *walk*, 266
  limp, 275
Toddler, *child*, 129
Toe, *base*, 211
Toehold, *support*, 215
Toff, *notability*, 642
  fop, 854

Toffee, *sweet*, 396
Toffee-nose, *proud*, 878
Toga, *dress*, 225
Together, *added*, 37
  simultaneous, 120
  accompanying, 88
*Tohu-bohu, *tumult*, 315
Toil, *exertion*, 682, 686
  trap, 667
Toilet, *dress*, 225
  room, 191
Toilsome, *difficult*, 704
Token, *sign*, 550
Toledo, *arms*, 727
Tolerable, *endurable*, 651
Tolerant, *patient*, 826
Tolerate, *endure*, 821
  permit, 760
  licence, 750
  lenity, 740
  laxity, 738
Toll, *sound*, 407
  tax, 812
Tollbooth, *mart*, 799
  prison, 752
Tolling, *interment*, 363
Tomahawk, *arms*, 727
Tomb, *interment*, 363
Tomboy, *vulgar*, 851
Tome, *volume*, 593
Tomfoolery, *absurdity*, 497
  ridiculous, 856
  amusement, 840
Tommy, *soldier*, 726
Tommy-gun, *arms*, 727
Tompion, *stopper*, 263
Tom-tom, *drum*, 416, 722
*Ton, *taste*, 852
Tonality, *melody*, 413
Tone, *state*, 7
  affections, 820
  strength, 159
  sound, 402
  melody, 413
  minstrelsy, 415
  colour, 428
Tone down, *modify*, 174, 469
  discoloration, 429
Tone-poem, *music*, 415
Tong, *guild*, 712
Tongs, *grip*, 781
Tongue, *language*, 560
Tongue-tied, *dumb*, 581
Tongueless, *dumb*, 581
Tonic, *remedy*, 662, 656
  refresh, 689
  music, 413
Tonnage, *size*, 192
Tonsure, *canonicals*, 999
Tontine, *income*, 810
Too, *addition*, 37
Too much, *redundance*, 641
Tool, *instrument*, 631, 633
  adorn, 847
Toot, *sound*, 408

Unglue, *disjunction*, 44
  incoherence, 47
Ungodly, *irreligion*, 989
Ungovernable, *violent*, 173
  disobedient, 742
  passion, 825
Ungoverned, *freedom*, 748
Ungraceful, *ugly*, 846
  inelegant, 579
  vulgar, 851
Ungracious, *uncivil*, 895
  unfriendly, 907
Ungrammatical, *solecism*, 568
Ungrateful, *ingratitude*, 917
Ungratified, *pain*, 828
Ungrounded, *error*, 495
Ungrudging, *liberality*, 816
Unguarded, *neglected*, 460
  improvident, 674
  dangerous, 665
  spontaneous, 612
Unguent, *oil*, 356
Unguided, *ignorant*, 491
  unskilful, 699
Unhackneyed, *desuetude*, 614
Unhallowed, *irreligion*, 989
  profane, 988
Unhand, *liberation*, 750
Unhandsome, *ugly*, 940
Unhandy, *unskilfulness*, 699
Unhappy, *pain*, 828
Unhardened, *tender*, 914
  penitent, 950
  innocent, 946
Unharmed, *safety*, 664
Unharness, *disjoin*, 44
  liberate, 750
Unhatched, *non-preparation*,
                              674
Unhazarded, *safety*, 664
Unhealthy, *ill*, 655
  unwholesome, 657
Unheard-of, *ignorant*, 491
  exceptional, 83, 137
  impossible, 471
  improbable, 473
  wonderful, 870
Unheeded, *neglected*, 460
Unheralded, *inexpectation*, 507
Unheroic, *cowardly*, 862
Unhesitating. *resolution*, 604
Unhewn, *formless*, 241
  unprepared, 674
Unhindered, *free*, 748
Unhinge, *weaken*, 169
  derange, 61
Unhinged, *unsettled*, 605
  insane, 503
Unholy, *evil*, 989
Unhonoured, *disrespect*, 874
Unhook, *disjoin*, 44
Unhoped, *unexpected*, 508
Unhouse, *displace*, 185
Unhurt, *uninjured*, 670
Unicorn, *monster*, 83

Unicorn, *prodigy*, 872
Unidea'd, *unthinking*, 452
Unideal, *true*, 494
  existing, 1
Uniform, *homogeneous*, 16
  simple, 42
  orderly, 58
  regular, 82
  symmetrical, 242
  livery, 225
  insignia, 550
  uniformity, 23
Unify, *combine*, 48
  make one, 87
Unilluminated, *dark*, 421
  ignorant, 491
Unimaginable, *inconceivable*,
                              519
Unimaginative, *dull*, 843
Unimagined, *truth*, 494
Unimitated, *original*, 20
Unimpaired, *preserved*, 670
  sound, 648
Unimpassioned, *inexcitable*,
                              826
Unimpeachable, *innocent*, 946
  irrefutable, 474, 478
  inalienable, 924
  perfect, 650
Unimpeded, *facility*, 705
Unimpelled, *uninduced*, 616
Unimportant, *insignificant*, 643
Unimpressionable, *insensible*,
                              823
Unimproved, *deterioration*, 659
Uninfluenced, *unbiased*, 616
  obstinate, 606
Uninfluential, *inert*, 172
Uninformed, *ignorance*, 491
Uninhabited, *empty*, 187
  solitary, 893
Uninitiated, *unschooled*, 699
Uninjured, *good*, 648
  preserved, 670
  healthy, 644
Uninquisitive, *indifferent*, 456
Uninspired, *unexcited*, 823
  unactuated, 616
Uninstructed, *ignorant*, 491
Unintellectual, *ignorant*, 452
  imbecile, 499
Unintelligent, *foolish*, 499
Unintelligible, *difficult*, 519
  style, 571
Unintentional, *change*, 621
Uninterested, *incurious*, 456
  inattentive, 458
  indifferent, 823
  weary, 841
Uninteresting, *wearisome*, 841
  dull, 843
Unintermitting, *unbroken*, 69
  durable, 110
  continuing, 143
  active, 682

Uninterrupted, *continuous*, 69
  unremitting, 143
Uninvestigated, *unknown*, 491
Uninvited, *exclusion*, 893
Uninviting, *unattractive*, 866
  unpleasant, 830
Union, *junction*, 43
  combination, 48
  concord, 23, 714
  concurrence, 178
  marriage, 903
Union Jack, *flag*, 550
Unique, *special*, 79
  alone, 87
  exceptional, 83
  dissimilarity, 18
  non-imitation, 20
Unison, *agreement*, 23
  concord, 714
  uniformity, 16
  melody, 413
Unisonant, *harmony*, 413
Unit, *number*, 87
  troop, 726
Unitarian, *heterodoxy*, 984A
Unite, *join*, 43
  agree, 23
  concur, 178
  assemble, 72
  converge, 290
  league, 712
Unity, *singleness*, 87
  integrity, 50
  concord, 714
Universal, *general*, 78
Universe, *world*, 318
University, *school*, 542
Unjust, *wrong*, 923
Unjustified, *undue*, 925
Unkempt, *careless*, 653
  slovenly, 851
Unkennel, *turn out*, 185
  disclose, 529
Unkind, *malevolent*, 907
Unknit, *disjoin*, 44
Unknowable, *concealment*, 528
Unknown, *ignorant*, 491
  latent, 526
  to fame, 874
Unlaboured, *unprepared*, 674
  style, 578
Unlace, *disjoin*, 44
Unlade, *ejection*, 297
Unladylike, *vulgar*, 851
  rude, 895
Unlamented, *disliked*, 898
  unapproved, 932
Unlatch, *disjoin*, 44
Unlawful, *undue*, 925
  illegal, 964
Unlearn, *forget*, 506
Unlearned, *ignorant*, 491
Unleavened, *non-preparation*,
                              674
Unless, *circumstances*, 8

Unpretentious, *modest*, 881
Unprincipled, *vice*, 945
Unprivileged, *undueness*, 925
Unproclaimed, *latency*, 526
Unprocurable, *impossibility*, 471
Unproduced, *non-existent*, 2
Unproductive, *barren*, 169
  useless, 645
Unprofessional, *non-observance*, 614
Unprofitable, *useless*, 645
  inexpedient, 647
  bad, 649
  unproductive, 169
Unprogressive, *unchanged*, 141
Unprolific, *barren*, 169
Unpromising, *hopeless*, 859
Unprompted, *impulse*, 612
Unpromulgated, *latent*, 526
Unpronounced, *latent*, 526
Unpropitious, *hopeless*, 859
  inauspicious, 135
Unproportioned, *disagreement*, 24
Unprosperous, *adversity*, 735
Unprotected, *danger*, 665
Unproved, *sophistry*, 477
Unprovided, *scanty*, 640
  unprepared, 674
Unprovoked, *uninduced*, 616
Unpublished, *latency*, 526
Unpunctual, *tardy*, 133
  untimely, 135
  irregular, 139
Unpunished, *exempt*, 960
Unpurified, *uncleanness*, 653
Unpurposed, *chance*, 621
Unpursued, *relinquishment*, 624
Unqualified, *inexpert*, 699
  unentitled, 925
  unprepared, 674
  complete, 52
Unquelled, *violence*, 173
Unquenched, *violence*, 173
  burning, 382
Unquestionable, *certainty*, 474
Unquestioned, *certainty*, 474
  assent, 488
Unquiet, *excitement*, 825
Unravaged, *undamaged*, 648
Unravel, *untie*, 44
  straighten, 246
  unfold, 313
  decompose, 49
  solve, 462, 480A
  interpret, 522
  disembarrass, 705
  arrange, 60
Unravelled, *arranged*, 58
Unreachable, *distance*, 196
Unreached, *shortcoming*, 304
Unread, *ignorance*, 491
Unready, *non-preparation*, 674
  incompleteness, 53
Unreal, *non-existing*, 2

Unreal, *erroneous*, 495
  imaginary, 515
Unreasonable, *foolish*, 499
  exorbitant, 814
  unjust, 923
  impossible, 471
  erroneous, 495
Unreasoning, *material*, 450A
  instinctive, 477
Unreclaimed, *impenitence*, 951
Unreconciled, *discord*, 713
Unrecorded, *obliteration*, 552
Unrecounted, *exclusion*, 55
Unrecovered, *deterioration*, 659
Unrectified, *imperfection*, 651
Unredeemed, *greatness*, 31
Unreduced, *greatness*, 31
Unrefined, *vulgarity*, 851
Unreflecting, *impulse*, 612
Unreformed, *impenitence*, 951
Unrefreshed, *fatigue*, 688
Unrefuted, *demonstrated*, 478
  true, 494
Unregarded, *neglected*, 460
  unrespected, 929
Unregistered, *unrecorded*, 552
Unrehearsed, *impulse*, 612
Unrelated, *irrelation*, 10
Unrelaxed, *unweakened*, 159
Unrelenting, *malevolent*, 907
  revengeful, 919
Unreliable, *dubious*, 475, 485
  untrustworthy, 940
Unrelieved, *aggravation*, 835
Unremarked, *neglected*, 460
Unremembered, *forgotten*, 506
Unremitting, *continuing*, 69, 110
  industrious, 682
Unremoved, *location*, 184
Unremunerative, *inutility*, 645
Unrenewed, *unchanged*, 141
Unrepealed, *unchanged*, 141
Unrepeated, *fewness*, 103
  unity, 87
Unrepentant, *impenitent*, 951
Unrepining, *patient*, 831
Unreplenished, *insufficient*, 640
Unreported, *untold*, 526
Unrepressed, *violent*, 173
Unreproached, *innocence*, 946
Unreproachful, *forgiveness*, 918
Unreproved, *innocence*, 946
Unrequited, *owing*, 806
  ingratitude, 917
Unresented, *forgiven*, 918
Unresenting, *enduring*, 826
Unreserved, *frank*, 543
Unresisting, *obedience*, 743
Unresolved, *irresolute*, 605
Unrespected, *disrespect*, 929
Unresponsive, *insensibility*, 823
Unrest, *moving*, 264
  change, 140
  changeable, 149

Unrestored, *deterioration*, 659
Unrestrained, *free*, 748
  unencumbered, 705
Unrestraint, *intemperance*, 954
Unrestricted, *undiminished*, 31
  free, 748
Unretracted, *affirmation*, 535
Unrevealed, *concealed*, 528
Unrevenged, *jealousy*, 920
Unreversed, *permanence*, 141
  continuance, 143
Unrevoked, *continuance*, 143
Unrewarded, *debt*, 806
  ingratitude, 917
Unrhymed, *prose*, 598
Unriddle, *solve*, 462
  interpret, 522
  disclose, 529
Unrighteous, *evil*, 945
Unrip, *uncover*, 260
Unripe, *unprepared*, 674
Unrivalled, *goodness*, 648
Unrivet, *disjoin*, 44
Unrobe, *divest*, 226
Unroll, *straighten*, 246
  evolve, 313
  display, 525
  unravel, 47
Unromantic, *true*, 494
Unroof, *divest*, 226
Unroot, *pull up*, 162
Unruffled, *calm*, 174
  placid, 826
  unaffected, 823
  quiet, 265
  orderly, 58
Unruly, *disobedient*, 742
  obstinate, 606
  violent, 173
Unsafe, *dangerous*, 665
Unsaid, *unspoken*, 581
  untold, 526
Unsanctified, *unholy*, 988, 989
Unsanctioned, *undue*, 925
Unsanitary, *insalubrious*, 657
Unsated, *desire*, 865
Unsatisfactory, *discontent*, 832
  displeasing, 830
Unsatisfied, *discontent*, 832
Unsavoury, *unsavouriness*, 395
Unsay, *retract*, 607
Unscanned, *neglected*, 460
Unscathed, *health*, 654
Unschooled, *illiterate*, 491
  uneducated, 699
Unscientific, *ignorant*, 495
  unskilled, 699
Unscoured, *unclean*, 653
Unscreened, *danger*, 665
Unscrew, *disjoin*, 44
Unscriptural, *heterodoxy*, 984A
Unscrupulous, *evil*, 940
Unseal, *disclosure*, 529
Unseam, *disjoin*, 44
Unsearched, *neglect*, 460

INDEX

Variegation, *colour*, 440
Variety, *difference*, 15
  multiformity, 16A
  exception, 83
  class, 75
Variform, *difference*, 15
  variety, 81
Various, *different*, 15
  many, 102
  variation, 20
Varlet, *sinner*, 949
Varnish, *coat*, 222
  decorate, 845, 847
  semiliquid, 352
  sophistry, 477
  falsehood, 544
  excuse, 937
Vary, *differ*, 15
  diversify, 18
  modify, 20
  change, 140
  fluctuate, 149
Vasculum, *botany*, 369
Vase, *receptacle*, 191
Vassal, *servant*, 746
Vassalage, *subjection*, 749
Vast, *in quantity*, 31
  in size, 192
Vat, *receptacle*, 191
Vatican, *temple*, 1000
Vaticide, *killing*, 361
Vaticination, *prediction*, 511
Vaudeville, *the drama*, 599
Vault, *cellar*, 191
  sepulchre, 363
  to leap, 305, 309
Vaulting, *superiority*, 33
Vaunt, *boasting*, 884
*Vaurien, *sinner*, 949
Veda, *sacred books*, 986
Vedette, *safety*, 664
  warning, 668
Veer, *regression*, 283
  change, 140
  deviate, 279
  change intention, 607
Vegetable, *vegetable*, 365
  plant, 367
Vegetarian, *temperance*, 953
Vegetate, *grow*, 194
  exist, 1
  inactivity, 683
  insensibility, 823
  quiescence, 265
Vehemence, *violence*, 173
  emotion, 825
Vehicle, *vehicle*, 272
  instrumentality, 631
*Vehmgericht, *illegality*, 964
Veil, *mask*, 530
  to conceal, 528
  shade, 424
  covering, 225
Veiled, *invisible*, 447
  latent, 526

Vein, *humour*, 602
  tendency, 176
  cast of mind, 820
  mine, 636
Veined, *variegation*, 440
Velleity, *will*, 600
Vellum, *writing*, 590
Velocipede, *locomotion*, 266
Velocity, *swiftness*, 274
Velour, *smooth*, 255
  rough, 256
Velvet, *smooth*, 255
  rough, 256
  ease, 705
  physical pleasure, 277
  moral pleasure, 827
  profit, 618
Velveteen, *smooth*, 255
  rough, 256
Venal, *parsimony*, 819
  mercenary, 812, 943
Vend, *sell*, 796
Vendible, *sale*, 796
Vendetta, *feud*, 713
  revenge, 919
Vendor, *merchant*, 797
Veneer, *covering*, 222
  ostentation, 882
Venerable, *old*, 128
Veneration, *respect*, 928
  piety, 987
  worship, 990
Venery, *chase*, 622
Venesection, *ejection*, 297
Vengeance, *revenge*, 919
  (with a), *greatness*, 31
Vengeful, *revenge*, 919
Venial, *excusable*, 937
Venom, *bane*, 663
  malignity, 907
Venomous, *evil*, 649
  malignant, 907
Vent, *air-pipe*, 351
  opening, 260
  emit, 295
  disclose, 529
Vent-peg, *stopper*, 263
Ventilate, *perflate*, 349
  air, 338
  clean, 652
  discuss, 595
  examine, 461
  publicity, 531
Ventilator, *wind*, 349
Ventricle, *receptacle*, 191
Ventriloquism, *voice*, 580
Venture, *chance*, 156
  to try, 621, 675
  danger, 665
  courage, 861
Venturesome, *brave*, 861
  rash, 863
Venue, *place*, 182
Venus, *goddess*, 979
  beauty, 845

Venus, *love*, 897
Veracity, *truth*, 494, 543
Veranda, *portico*, 191
*Verb. sap., *advice*, 695
Verbal, *word*, 562
Verbatim, *imitation*, 19
  interpretation, 522
  word, 562
Verbiage, *diffuse*, 573
  nonsense, 497
Verbose, *diffuse*, 573
  loquacious, 584
Verdant, *green*, 435
  vegetation, 367
  credulous, 486
  ignorant, 491
Verd-antique, *green*, 435
Verdict, *opinion*, 480
  sentence, 969
Verdigris, *green*, 435
Verdure, *green*, 435
  plant, 367
Verecundity, *modesty*, 881
  humility, 879
Verge, *brink*, 230
  to tend, 278
  contribute, 176
Verger, *churchman*, 996
Veridical, *truthful*, 543
Verify, *test*, 463
  demonstrate, 478
  judge, 480
  warrant, 771
Verily, *positively*, 32
  truly, 494
Verisimilitude, *probable*, 472
Veritable, *truth*, 494
Verity, *truth*, 494
Verjuice, *sourness*, 397
Vermicular, *convolution*, 248
Vermiform, *convolution*, 248
Vermilion, *redness*, 434
Vermin, *base*, 876
  unclean, 653
Vernacular, *language*, 560
  familiar, 82
Vernal, *early*, 123
  spring, 125
*Vers de société, *poetry*, 597
*Vers libre, *poetry*, 597
Versatile, *changeable*, 605
  skilful, 698
Verse, *poetry*, 597
Versed, *skill*, 698
Versicolour, *variegation*, 440
Versifier, *poetry*, 597
Version, *interpretation*, 522
Verso, *left hand*, 239
Vert, *change belief*, 144, 484
  green, 435
Vertex, *summit*, 210
Vertical, *verticality*, 212
Vertigo, *insanity*, 503
Verve, *imagination*, 515
  feeling, 821

Visage, *front*, 234
    appearance, 448
Vis-à-vis, *front*, 234
    opposite, 237
Viscera, *interior*, 221
Viscid, *semiliquid*, 352
Viscount, *noble*, 875
    master, 745
Viscounty, *title*, 877
Viscous, *semiliquid*, 352
*Visé, *indication*, 550
Vishnu, *deity*, 979
Visible, *visibility*, 446
Vision, *sight*, 441
    imagination, 515
    apparition, 980
Visionary, *erroneous*, 495
    imaginary, 515
    impossible, 471
    heterodox, 984A
Visit, *sociality*, 892
    frequent, 136
    arrival, 292
Visitation, *pain*, 828
    disease, 655
    calamity, 830
Visiting-card, *indication*, 560
Visitor, *arrival*, 292
    director, 694
Visor, *concealment*, 528
Vista, *point of view*, 441
    prospect, 448, 507
Visual, *vision*, 441
Vital, *importance*, 642
Vitality, *life*, 359
    strength, 159
Vitals, *interior*, 221
Vitiate, *deteriorate*, 659
    debase, 945
Vitreous, *density*, 321
Vitrify, *density*, 321
    harden, 323
Vitriolic, *malevolent*, 907
Vituperate, *disapprove*, 932
    scold, 908
*Viva, *honour*, 873
Viva voce, *speech*, 582
Vivacious, *active*, 682
    sensitive, 822
    cheerful, 836
Vivarium, *taming*, 370
*Vive, *honour*, 873
Vivid, *light*, 420
    colour, 428
    lively, 375
    energetic, 171
    style, 574
Vivify, *life*, 359
Vivisect, *anatomize*, 44
Vixen, *scold*, 901
    fury, 173
Viz., *meaning*, 516
Vizier, *deputy*, 759
Vizor, *see* Visor
Vocable, *word*, 562

Vocabulary, *word*, 562
Vocal, *voice*, 580
    loudness, 404
    music, 415
Vocalist, *musician*, 416
Vocalize, *speech*, 580
Vocation, *business*, 625
Vociferate, *cry*, 411
    loudness, 404
    voice, 580
Vogue, *fashion*, 852
    custom, 613
    repute, 873
Vogue word, *neology*, 563
Voice, *speech*, 580
    grammar, 567
    sound, 402
    cry, 411
    choice, 609
    affirmation, 535
    opinion, 484
Void, *vacuum*, 2, 4
    absence, 187
    to emit, 297
    invalidate, 964
Voivode, *master*, 745
Volant, *flight*, 267
Volapük, *language*, 560
Volatile, *vaporizable*, 336
    changeable, 149
    irresolute, 605
Volatility, *caprice*, 608
Volcanic, *violence*, 173
    excitable, 825
Volitation, *flight*, 267
Volition, *will*, 600
Volley, *impulse*, 276
    attack, 716
    violence, 173
    collection, 72
Volplane, *descent*, 306
Volte-face, *recantation*, 607
Voluble, *loquacity*, 584
Volume, *bulk*, 192
    quantity, 25
    greatness, 31
    book, 593
Voluntary, *willing*, 600, 602
    music, 415
Volunteer, *endeavour*, 676
    offer, 600, 763
Voluptuary, *libertine*, 962
Voluptuous, *sensual*, 954
    pleasure, 377
    joy, 827
    delight, 829
Volute, *convolution*, 248
Vomit, *ejection*, 297
Vomitory, *opening*, 260
Voodooism, *occult arts*, 992
Voracity, *appetite*, 865
    gluttony, 957
Vortex, *rotation*, 312
    whirlpool, 348
Votary, *devotee*, 840, 865

Vote, *choice*, 609
    affirmation, 535
Vote for, *assent*, 488
Votive, *promise*, 768
Vouch, *testify*, 467
    assert, 535
Voucher, *evidence*, 467
    record, 551
    security, 771
Vouchsafe, *permit*, 760
    consent, 762
    ask, 765; *deign*, 879
Vow, *promise*, 768
    assert, 535
    worship, 990
Voyage, *journey*, 267
    motion, 264
Voyageur, *boatman*, 269
Voyeur, *curiosity*, 455
*Vraisemblance, *probability*,
    472
Vulcan, *god*, 979
Vulgar, *unrefined*, 851
    discourteous, 895
    commonalty, 876
Vulgarism, *solecism*, 568
    language, 560
Vulgate, *revelation*, 985
Vulnerable, *danger*, 665
Vulpine, *cunning*, 702
Vulture, *bane*, 663

W

W.C., *lavatory*, 653
Wabble, *oscillation*, 314
Wacky, *mad*, 503
Wadding, *lining*, 224
    softness, 324
    stopping, 263
Waddle, *slowness*, 275
    oscillation, 314
Wade, *swim*, 267
Wafer, *layer*, 204
Waft, *transfer*, 270
    blow, 267, 349
Wag, *oscillate*, 214
    agitate, 315
    wit, 844
Wage war, *contention*, 720
Wager, *chance*, 621
Wages, *expenditure*, 809
Waggery, *wit*, 842
Waggish, *merry*, 836
Waggle, *oscillation*, 314
    agitation, 315
Wagon, *vehicle*, 272
Wagonette, *vehicle*, 272
Waif, *outcast*, 893
Wail, *lamentation*, 839
Wain, *vehicle*, 272
Wainscot, *lining*, 224
    base, 211
Waist, *narrow*, 203
Waistcoat, *dress*, 225

Well-timed, *opportune*, 134, 646
Well-to-do, *prosperity*, 734
Well-wisher, *friend*, 890
Welladay, *lamentation*, 839
Wellington, *boot*, 225
Wellnigh, *almost*, 32
Welsh, *to cheat*, 545
Welsher, *deceiver*, 548
   swindler, 792
   defaulter, 808
Welt, *edge*, 230
Welter, *rotation*, 312
   agitation, 315
*Weltschmerz, *weariness*, 841
Wen, *convexity*, 250
Wench, *young girl*, 129
   woman, 374
Wend, *journey*, 266
Werewolf, *demon*, 980
Wersh, *tasteless*, 391, 866
   insipid, 575
West, *side*, 236
Wet, *water*, 337
   moisture, 339
Wet-nurse, *to pamper*, 954
Whack, *blow*, 276, 972
   share, 786
   try, 675
Whacked, *exhausted*, 160
Whacker, *size*, 31, 192
Whale, *monster*, 192
Whaler, *ship*, 273
Wham, *impact*, 276
Whang, *impact*, 276
Wharf, *anchorage*, 189
Whatnot, *receptacle*, 191
What's-his-name, *euphemism*, 565
Wheedle, *flatter*, 933
   coax, 615
   endearment, 902
Wheel, *circle*, 247
   circuition, 311
   deviation, 279
   rotation, 212
   instrument, 633
   means, 632
   money, 800
   torture, 378, 975
   pain, 830
   execution, 972
Wheel-chair, *vehicle*, 272
Wheelbarrow, *vehicle*, 272
Wheen, *plurality*, 100
   multitude, 102
Wheeze, *blow*, 349
   hiss, 409
   joke, 842
Whelm, *redundance*, 641
Whelp, *young*, 129
When, *time*, 119
Whence, *attribution*, 155
   inquiry, 461
   reasoning, 476

Whence, *departure*, 293
Whenever, *time*, 119
Whensoever, *time*, 119
Where, *presence*, 186
Whereabouts, *situation*, 183
   nearness, 197
Whereas, *reason*, 476
Wherefore, *reason*, 476
   attribution, 155
   inquiry, 461
   motive, 615
Whereupon, *futurity*, 121
Wherever, *space*, 180
Wherewith, *instrument*, 631
Wherewithal, *means*, 632
   money, 800
Wherry, *boat*, 273
Whet, *excite*, 824
   incite, 615
   sharpen, 253
   desire, 865
   meal, 298
Whey, *fluid*, 337
Whiff, *wind*, 349
Whiffy, *smelly*, 401
Whigmaleerie, *trifle*, 643
While, *duration*, 106, 120
Whilom, *preterition*, 122
Whim, *caprice*, 608
   prejudice, 481
   desire, 865
   imagination, 515
   wit, 842
Whim-wham, *trifle*, 643
Whimper, *lamentation*, 839
Whimsical, *fancy*, 515, 608
   ridiculous, 853
Whimsy, *desire*, 865
Whine, *cry*, 411
   complain, 839
Whinny, *animal cry*, 412
Whip, *to beat*, 276, 972
   scourge, 975
   rapidity, 274
   driver, 694
   trouble, 830
Whip-hand, *success*, 731
Whip off, *escape*, 671
Whip-round, *giving*, 784
Whip up, *snatch*, 789
Whipper-in, *director*, 694
   servant, 746
Whippersnapper, *youth*, 129
Whippet, *chase*, 622
Whipping-post, *scourge*, 975
Whirl, *rotation*, 312
Whirligig, *rotation*, 312
Whirlpool, *vortex*, 312
   eddy, 348
   danger, 667
   confusion, 59
Whirlwind, *wind*, 349
   vortex, 312
   agitation, 315
Whirlybird, *aircraft*, 273A

Whirr, *roll*, 407
Whisk, *rapidity*, 274
   circuition, 311
   agitation, 315
Whisker, *hair*, 256
Whisky, *vehicle*, 272
Whisper, *faint sound*, 405
   stammer, 583
   tell, 527
   prompt, 615
   remind, 505
Whist! *silence*, 403, 585
Whistle, *hiss*, 409
   music, 415
   instrument, 417
Whistle at, *depreciate*, 483
Whit, *point*, 32
   part, 51
   small, 193
White, *whiteness*, 430
   eye, 441
White feather, *coward*, 862
White horses, *wave*, 348
White lie, *equivocalness*, 520
   plea, 617
White-livered, *cowardice*, 862
Whitewash, *whiten*, 430
   adorn, 847
   vindicate, 937
   acquit, 970
   insolvency, 808
Whither, *tendency*, 176
   direction, 278
Whittle, *disjoin*, 44
   abbreviate, 201
Whiz, *sibilation*, 409
   expert, 700
Whizz-kid, *go-getter*, 682
Whodunit, *story*, 594
Whole, *entire*, 50
   complete, 52
   healthy, 654
Whole-hearted, *cordial*, 602
Wholesale, *greatness*, 31
   whole, 50
   indiscriminate, 465A
   plenty, 639
   barter, 794
Wholesome, *salubrity*, 656
Wholly, *great*, 31
   whole, 50
Whoop, *cry*, 411
   loud, 404; *weep*, 839
Whoopee, *merry*, 836
Whopper, *untruth*, 546
Whopping, *size*, 192
Whore, *libertine*, 962
   impurity, 961
Why, *reason*, 615
   inquiry, 461
   cause, 155
Wicked, *vice*, 945
   improbity, 940
Wicker, *crossing*, 219
Wicket, *entrance*, 66

Witticism, *wit*, 842
Wittingly, *purposely*, 620
Witty, *wit*, 842
Wive, *marriage*, 903
Wizard, *sorcerer*, 994
  oracle, 513
  good, 648
Wizardry, *occult*, 992
Wizened, *withered*, 193, 195
Wobble, *oscillate*, 314
Woden, *god*, 979
Woe, *pain*, 828
  evil, 619
Woebegone, *pain*, 828
  dejection, 837
Woeful, *painfulness*, 830
Wold, *plain*, 344
Wolf, *to devour*, 296
  alarm, 669
  philanderer, 902
Woman, *woman*, 131, 374
Womanish, *cowardly*, 862
Womanly, *weakness*, 160
Womb, *interior*, 221
  cause, 153
Wonder, *astonishment*, 879
  prodigy, 872
Wonderfully, *great*, 31
Wonderment, *prodigy*, 872
Wondrous, *wonder*, 870
Wonky, *imperfect*, 651
Wont, *habitual*, 613
  usual, 82
Woo, *desire*, 865
  courtship, 902
Wood, *plant*, 367
Wood-note, *animal cry*, 412
Woodcut, *engraving*, 558
Woodcutter, *forester*, 371
Wooer, *love*, 897
Woof, *texture*, 329
Wool, *hair*, 256
Wool-gathering, *folly*, 499
  inattention, 458
  madness, 503
Woolsack, *pillow*, 215
  authority, 747
  tribunal, 966
Wop, *alien*, 57
Word, *vocable*, 562
  intelligence, 532
  promise, 768
  revelation, 985
  Deity, 976
  maxim, 496
Wording, *expression*, 566
  style, 569
Wordless, *aphony*, 581
Words, *quarrel*, 713
Wordy, *diffuseness*, 573
Work, *product*, 154
  agency, 170
  to use, 677
  shape, 240
  adorn, 847

Work, *action*, 680
  book, 593
Work in, *introduce*, 37
Work off, *get rid of*, 545, 672
Work out, *conduct*, 692
  achieve, 729
Work up, *incite*, 615
  inflame, 824
Work upon, *influence*, 175
Workhouse, *poverty*, 804
Working, *activity*, 682
Workman, *agent*, 690
  originator, 164
Workmanlike, *skill*, 698
Workmanship, *produce*, 161
  handiwork, 680
Workshop, *workshop*, 691
World, *universe*, 318
  mankind, 373
  fashion, 852
  events, 151
  great, 31
Worldling, *selfish*, 943
Worldly, *selfish*, 943
  irreligious, 989
Worldwide, *world*, 318
Worm, *small*, 193
  animal, 366
  spiral, 248
Worm in, *insert*, 300
  interpose, 228
Worm out, *ascertain*, 480A
Wormeaten, *imperfect*, 651
  decayed, 659
Wormwood, *unsavoury*, 395
Worn, *imperfect*, 651
  decayed, 659
Worry, *vexation*, 828
  to tease, 830
  harass, 907
Worse, *badness*, 649
Worsen, *deteriorate*, 659
Worship, *religious*, 990
  title, 877
  servility, 886
Worshipful, *repute*, 873
Worst, *defeat*, 731
Worsted, *defeated*, 732
Worth, *goodness*, 648
  value, 644
  virtue, 994
  price, 812
Worth while, *utility*, 644
Worthless, *useless*, 645
  profligate, 945
Worthy, *virtuous*, 944
  good, 648
  saint, 948
Wot, *knowledge*, 490
Wound, *evil*, 619
  badness, 649
  injure, 659
  hurt, 900
Wrack, *evil*, 619
Wraith, *spirit*, 980

Wrangle, *dispute*, 713
  reason, 476
Wrangler, *scholar*, 492
Wrap, *cover*, 222
  circumscribe, 231
Wrapped in, *attention*, 457
Wrapper, *cover*, 222
  dress, 225
Wrapt, *see* Rapt
Wrath, *anger*, 900
Wreak, *inflict*, 918
Wreath, *trophy*, 733
  ornament, 847
  honour, 877
Wreck, *remainder*, 40
  destruction, 162
  failure, 732
Wrecker, *thief*, 792
Wrench, *extract*, 301
  seize, 789
  twist, 243
  draw, 285
Wrest, *seize*, 789
  twist, 243
  distort, 523, 555
Wrestle, *contention*, 720
Wrestler, *combatant*, 726
Wretch, *sinner*, 949
  apostate, 941
Wretched, *unhappy*, 828
  bad, 649
  contemptible, 643
  petty, 32
Wriggle, *agitation*, 315
  cunning, 702
Wright, *workman*, 690
Wring, *pain*, 378
  to torment, 830
  distort, 243
Wring from, *taking*, 789
Wrinkle, *fold*, 258
  hint, 527
Writ, *order*, 741
  in law, 969
Write, *writing*, 590
Write off, *cancel*, 552
Write up, *praise*, 931
  detail, 594
Writer, *lawyer*, 968
Writhe, *agitate*, 315
  pain, 378, 828
Writing, *book*, 593
Writing-case, *receptacle*, 191
Wrong, *evil*, 619
  badness, 649
  erroneous, 495
  vice, 945
  immoral, 923
  to injure, 907
Wrong-headed, *foolish*, 499
  obstinate, 606
Wrongdoer, *sinner*, 949
  evildoer, 913
Wrought up, *excitation*, 824
Wry, *oblique*, 217

Wry, *distorted*, 243
*Wunderbar, *wonder*, 870
Wynd, *abode*, 189
Wyvern, *monster*, 83

X

Xanthin, *yellow*, 436
Xanthippe, *shrew*, 901
Xebec, *ship*, 273
Xylography, *engraving*, 558
Xylophone, *musical instrument*, 417

Y

Y, *bifurcation*, 91
Yacht, *ship*, 273
　　navigation, 267
Yahoo, *commonalty*, 876
Yak, *carrier*, 271
Yammer, *cry*, 411
　　complain, 839
Yank, *jerk*, 285
Yap, *animal cry*, 412
Yard, *workshop*, 691
　　abode, 189
　　support, 215
Yardstick, *measure*, 466
Yarn, *filament*, 205
　　prate, 584
　　story, 594
　　exaggeration, 549
Yashmak, *dress*, 225
Yataghan, *arms*, 727
Yaw, *deviate*, 279
Yawl, *ship*, 273
Yawn, *open*, 260
　　gape, 198
　　fatigue, 688
　　insensible, 823
Yawp, *cry*, 411
Yea, *assent*, 488
Yeah, *assent*, 488
Year, *period*, 108
Yearly, *periodical*, 138
Yearn, *desire*, 865
　　pine, 828
　　pity, 914
　　love, 897
　　sad, 837
Yeast, *bubble*, 353
Yegg, *evildoer*, 913, 949
　　thief, 792
Yell, *cry*, 411
　　complain, 839
Yellow, *yellow*, 436
　　cowardly, 862
Yelp, *animal cry*, 412
Yen, *desire*, 865
Yeoman, *man*, 373
　　commonalty, 876
　　farmer, 371
Yeomanry, *army*, 726
Yep, *assent*, 488

Yes, *affirmation*, 488
　　consent, 762
Yes-man, *assent*, 488
Yesterday, *preterition*, 122
Yet, *exception*, 83
　　time, 106, 122
　　counteraction, 179
　　compensation, 30
Yield, *submit*, 725, 826
　　regress, 283
　　obey, 743
　　consent, 762
　　relinquish, 624
　　furnish, 784
　　produce, 161
　　gain, 810
　　price, 812
　　facility, 705
Yippy, *hippy*, 183
Yodel, *music*, 415
Yoga, *asceticism*, 955
Yogi, *priest*, 996
Yoke, *join*, 43
　　vinculum, 45
　　couple, 89
　　bond, 752
　　subjection, 749
Yokel, *clown*, 876
Yonder, *distance*, 196
Yore, *preterition*, 122
Yoshiwara, *brothel*, 961
Young, *age*, 127
Young man, *lover*, 897
Youngster, *youth*, 129
Younker, *youth*, 129
Youth, *age*, 127
　　newness, 123; *lad*, 129

Z

Zadkiel, *oracle*, 513
Zany, *fool*, 501
Zarathustra, *religious founder*, 986
Zareba, *defence*, 717
Zeal, *activity*, 682
　　feeling, 821
　　desire, 865
Zealot, *active*, 682
　　resolute, 604
　　obstinate, 606
Zealotry, *obstinacy*, 606
Zebra, *variegation*, 440
Zenana, *apartment*, 191
Zend-Avesta, *sacred books*, 986
Zenith, *summit*, 210
　　climax, 33
Zephyr, *wind*, 349
Zeppelin, *aircraft*, 273A
Zero, *nothing*, 4
　　naught, 101
Zest, *relish*, 390, 394
　　enjoyment, 827
Zetetic, *inquiring*, 461
Zeus, *god*, 979

Zigzag, *angle*, 244
　　obliquity, 217
　　deviation, 279
　　oscillation, 314
　　circuit, 629
Zion, *heaven*, 981
Zipper, *pendent*, 214
Zither, *musical instrument*, 417
Zodiac, *outline*, 229
　　universe, 318
Zoilus, *envy*, 921
*Zollverein, *compact*, 769
Zombie, *fool*, 501
Zone, *circle*, 247
　　belt, 229
　　region, 181
　　layer, 204
Zoography, *zoology*, 368
Zoological garden, *taming*, 370
Zoology, *zoology*, 368
Zoom, *deviation*, 279
　　ascent, 305
Zoophyte, *animal*, 366
Zootomy, *zoology*, 368
Zoroaster, *religious founder*, 986
Zouave, *combatant*, 726
Zymotic, *insalubrity*, 657

ORIGINAL INTRODUCTION

By Peter Roget

The present work is intended to supply, with respect to the English language, a desideratum hitherto unsupplied in any language; namely, a collection of the words it contains and of the idiomatic combinations peculiar to it, arranged, not in alphabetical order, as they are in a dictionary. but according to the *ideas* which they express.[1] The purpose of an ordinary dictionary is simply to explain the meaning of words; and the problem of which it professes to furnish the solution may be stated thus: The word being given, to find its signification, or the idea it is intended to convey. The object aimed at in the present undertaking is exactly the converse of this; namely, the idea being given, to find the word, or words, by which that idea may be most fitly and aptly expressed. For this purpose, the words and phrases of the language are here classed, not according to their sound or their orthography, but strictly according to their *signification*.

The communication of our thoughts by means of language, whether spoken or written, like every other object of mental exertion, constitutes a peculiar art, which, like other parts, cannot be acquired in any perfection but by long and continued practice. Some, indeed, there are, more highly gifted than others with a facility of expression, and naturally endowed with the power of eloquence; but to none is it at all times an easy process to embody in exact and appropriate language the various trains of ideas that are passing through the mind, or to depict in their true colours and proportions the diversified and nicer shades of feeling which accompany them. To those who are unpractised in the art of composition, or unused to extempore speaking, these difficulties present themselves in their most formidable aspect. However distinct may be our views, however vivid our conceptions, or however fervent our emotions, we cannot but be often

[1]See note on p.555

conscious that the phraseology we have at our command is inadequate to do them justice. We seek in vain the words we need, and strive ineffectually to devise forms of expression which shall faithfully portray our thoughts and sentiments. The appropriate terms, notwithstanding our utmost efforts, cannot be conjured up at will. Like 'spirits from the vasty deep,' they come not when we call; and we are driven to the employment of a set of words and phrases either too general or too limited, too strong or too feeble, which suit not the occasion, which hit not the mark we aim at; and the result of our prolonged exertion is a style at once laboured and obscure, vapid and redundant, or vitiated by the still graver faults of affectation or ambiguity.

It is to those who are thus painfully groping their way and struggling with the difficulties of composition, that this work professes to hold out a helping hand. The assistance it gives is that of furnishing on every topic a copious store of words and phrases, adapted to express all the recognizable shades and modifications of the general idea under which those words and phrases are arranged. The inquirer can readily select, out of the ample collection spread out before his eyes in the following pages, those expressions which are best suited to his purpose, and which might not have occurred to him without such assistance. In order to make this selection, he scarcely ever need engage in any elaborate or critical study of the subtle distinctions existing between synonymous terms; for if the materials set before him be sufficiently abundant, an instinctive tact will rarely fail to lead him to the proper choice. Even while glancing over the columns of this work, his eye may chance to light upon a particular term, which may save the cost of a clumsy paraphrase, or spare the labour of a tortuous circumlocution. Some felicitous turn of expression thus introduced will frequently open to the mind of the reader a whole vista of collateral ideas, which could not, without an extended and obtrusive episode, have been unfolded to his view; and often will the judicious insertion of a happy epithet, like a beam of sunshine in a landscape, illumine and adorn the subject which touches it, imparting new grace, and giving life and spirit to the picture.

Every workman in the exercise of his art should be provided with proper implements. For the fabrication of complicated and curious pieces of mechanism the artisan requires a corresponding assortment of various tools and instruments. For giving proper effect to the fictions of the drama, the actor should have at his disposal a well-furnished wardrobe, supplying the costumes best suited to the personage he is to represent. For the perfect delineation of the beauties of nature, the painter should have within reach of his pencil every variety and combination of hues and tints. Now the writer, as well as the orator, employs for the accomplishment of his purposes the instrumentality of words; it is in words that he clothes his thoughts; it is by means of words that he depicts his feelings. It is therefore essential to his success that he be provided with a copious vocabulary, and that he possess an entire command of all the resources and appliances of his language. To the acquisition of this power no procedure appears more directly conducive than the study of a methodized system such as that now offered to his use.

The utility of the present work will be appreciated more especially by those who are engaged in the arduous process of translating into English a work written in another language. Simple as the operation may appear, on a superficial view, of rendering into English each of its sentences, the task of transfusing, with perfect exactness, the sense of the original, preserving at the same time the style and character of its composition, and reflecting with fidelity the mind and the spirit of the author, is a task of extreme difficulty. The cultivation of this useful department of literature was in ancient times strongly recommended both by Cicero and by Quintilian as essential to the formation of a good writer and accomplished orator. Regarded simply as a mental exercise, the practice of translation is the best training for the attainment of that mastery of language and felicity of diction which are the sources of the highest oratory and are requisite for the possession of a graceful and persuasive eloquence. By rendering ourselves the faithful interpreters of the thoughts and feelings of others, we are rewarded with the acquisition of greater readiness and facility in correctly expressing our own; as he who has best learned to execute the orders of a commander becomes himself best qualified to command.

In the earliest periods of civilization, translations have been the agents for propagating knowledge from nation to nation, and the value of their labours has been inestimable; but, in the present age, when so many different languages have become the depositories of the vast treasures of literature and of science which have been accumulating for centuries, the utility of accurate translations has greatly increased, and it has become a more important object to attain perfection in the art.

The use of language is not confined to its being the medium through which we communicate our ideas to one another; it fulfils a no less important function as an *instrument of thought*, not being merely its vehicle, but giving it wings for flight. Metaphysicians are agreed that scarcely any of our intellectual operations could be carried on to any considerable extent without the agency of words. None but those who are conversant with the philosophy of mental phenomena can be aware of the immense influence that is exercised by language in promoting the development of our ideas, in fixing them in the mind, and detaining them for steady contemplation. In every process of reasoning, language enters as an essential element. Words are the instruments by which we form all our abstractions, by which we fashion and embody our ideas, and by which we are enabled to glide along a series of premises and conclusions with a rapidity so great as to leave in the memory no trace of the successive steps of the process; and we remain unconscious how much we owe to this potent auxiliary of the reasoning faculty. It is on this ground, also, that the present work founds a claim to utility. The review of a catalogue of words of analogous signification will often suggest by association other trains of thought, which, presenting the subject under new and varied aspects, will vastly expand the sphere of our mental vision. Amidst the many objects thus brought within the range of our contemplation, some striking similitude or appropriate image, some excursive flight or brilliant conception, may flash on the mind, giving point and force to our arguments, awakening a responsive chord in the imagination or sensibility of the reader, and procuring for our reasonings a more ready access both to his understanding and to his heart.

It is of the utmost consequence that strict accuracy should regulate our use of language, and that every one should acquire the power and the habit of expressing his thoughts with perspicuity and correctness. Few, indeed, can appreciate the real extent and importance of that influence which language has always exercised on human affairs, or can be aware how often these are determined by causes much slighter than are apparent to a superficial observer. False logic, disguised under specious phraseology, too often gains the assent of the unthinking multitude, disseminating far and wide the seeds of prejudice and error. Truisms pass current, and wear the semblance of profound wisdom, when dressed up in the tinsel garb of antithetical phrases, or set off by an imposing pomp of paradox. By a confused jargon of involved and mystical sentences, the imagination is easily inveigled into a transcendental region of clouds, and the understanding beguiled into the belief that it is acquiring knowledge and approaching truth. A misapplied or misapprehended term is sufficient to give rise to fierce and interminable disputes: a misnomer has turned the tide of popular opinion; a verbal sophism has decided a party question; an artful watchword, thrown among combustible materials, has kindled the flames of deadly warfare, and changed the destiny of an empire.

In constructing the following system of classification of the ideas which are expressible by language, my chief aim has been to obtain the greatest amount of practical utility. I have accordingly adopted such principles of arrangement as appeared to me to be the simplest and most natural, and which would not require, either for their comprehension or application, any disciplined acumen, or depth of metaphysical or antiquarian lore. Eschewing all needless refinements and subtleties, I have taken as my guide the more obvious characters of the ideas for which expressions were to be tabulated, arranging them under such classes and categories as reflection and experience had taught me would conduct the inquirer most readily and quickly to the object of his search. Commencing with the ideas expressing mere abstract relations, I proceed to those which relate to the phenomena of the material world, and lastly to those in which the mind is concerned, and which comprehend intellect, volition, and feeling; thus establishing six primary Classes of Categories.

1. The first of these classes comprehends ideas derived from the more general and ABSTRACT RELATIONS among things, such as *Existence, Resemblance, Quantity, Order, Number, Time, Power*.

2. The second class refers to SPACE and its various relations, including *Motion*, or change of place.

3. The third class includes all ideas that relate to the MATERIAL WORLD, namely, the *Properties of Matter*, such as *Solidity, Fluidity, Heat, Sound, Light*, and the *Phenomena* they present, as well as the simple *Perceptions* to which they give rise.

4. The fourth class embraces all ideas of phenomena relating to the INTELLECT and its operations, comprising the *Acquisition*, the *Retention*, and the *Communication of Ideas*.

5. The fifth class includes the ideas derived from the exercise of VOLITION, embracing the phenomena and results of our *Voluntary and Active Powers*, such as *Choice, Intention, Utility, Action, Antagonism, Authority, Compact, Property*, etc.

6. The sixth and last class comprehends all ideas derived from the operation of our SENTIENT AND MORAL POWERS, including our *Feelings, Emotions, Passions*, and *Moral and Religious Sentiments*.[1]

The object I have proposed to myself in this work would have been but imperfectly attained if I had confined myself to a mere

---

[1] It must necessarily happen in every system of classification framed with this view, that ideas and expressions arranged under one class must include also ideas relating to another class; for the operations of the *Intellect* generally involve also those of the *Will* and vice versa; and our *affections* and *emotions*, in like manner, generally imply the agency both of the *Intellect* and the *Will*. All that can be effected, therefore, is to arrange the words according to the principal or dominant idea they convey. *Teaching*, for example, although a Voluntary act, relates primarily to the Communication of Ideas, and is accordingly placed at No 537, under Class IV, Division II. On the other hand, *Choice, Conduct, Skill*, etc., although implying the co-operation of Voluntary with Intellectual acts, relate principally to the former, and are therefore arranged under Class V.

It often happens that the same word admits of various applications, or may be used in different senses. In consulting the Index the reader will be guided to the number of the heading under which that word, in each particular acceptation, will be found, by means of *supplementary words*, printed in italics; which words, however, are not to be understood as explaining the meaning of the word to which they are annexed, but only assisting in the required reference. I have also, for shortness' sake, generally omitted words immediately derived from the primary one inserted, which sufficiently represents the whole group of correlative words referable to the same heading. Thus the number affixed to *Beauty* applies to all its derivatives, such as *Beautiful, Beauteous, Beautify, Beautifulness, Beautifully*, etc., the insertion of which was therefore needless.

catalogue of words, and had omitted the numerous phrases and forms of expression, composed of several words, which are of such frequent use as to entitle them to rank among the constituent parts of the language.[1] Very few of these verbal combinations, so essential to the knowledge of our native tongue, and so profusely abounding in its daily use, are to be met with in ordinary dictionaries. These phrases and forms of expression I have endeavoured diligently to collect and to insert in their proper places, under the general ideas they are designed to convey. Some of these conventional forms, indeed, partake of the nature of proverbial expressions; but actual proverbs, as such, being wholly of a didactic character, do not come within the scope of the present work, and the reader must therefore not expect to find them here inserted.

For the purpose of exhibiting with greater distinctness the relations between words expressing opposite and correlative ideas, I have, whenever the subject admitted of such an arrangement, placed them in two parallel columns on the same page, so that each group of expressions may be readily contrasted with those which occupy the adjacent column, and constitute their antitheses. By carrying the eye from the one to the other, the inquirer may often discover forms of expression of which he may avail himself advantageously to diversify and infuse vigour into his phraseology. Rhetoricians, indeed, are well aware of the power derived from the skilful introduction of antitheses in giving point to an argument, and imparting force and brilliancy to the diction. A too frequent and indiscreet employment of this figure of rhetoric may, it is true, give rise to a vicious and affected style; but it is unreasonable to condemn indiscriminately the occasional and moderate use of a practice on account of its possible abuse.

The study of correlative terms existing in a particular language may often throw valuable light on the manners and customs of the nations using it. Thus Hume has drawn important inferences with regard to the state of society among the ancient Romans, from

[1] For example: To take time by the forelock; to turn over a new leaf; to show the white feather; to have a finger in the pie; to let the cat out of the bag; to take care of number one; to kill two birds with one stone, etc.

certain deficiencies which he remarked in the Latin language.[1]

In many cases, two ideas, which are completely opposed to each other, admit of an intermediate or neutral idea, equidistant from both: all these being expressible by corresponding definite terms. Thus, in the following examples, the words in the first and third columns, which express opposite ideas, admit of the intermediate terms contained in the middle column having a neutral sense with reference to the former.

Identity	*Difference*	*Contrariety*
Beginning	*Middle*	*End*
Past	*Present*	*Future*

In other cases, the intermediate word is simply the negative to each of the two opposite positions; as, for example:

Convexity	*Flatness*	*Concavity*
Desire	*Indifference*	*Aversion*

[1] 'It is an universal observation,' he remarks, 'which we may form upon language, that where two related parts of a whole bear any proportion to each other, in numbers, rank, or consideration, there are always correlative terms invented which answer to both the parts and express their mutual relation. If they bear no proportion to each other, the term is only invented for the less, and marks its distinction from the whole. Thus *man* and *woman, master* and *servant, father* and *son, prince* and *subject, stranger* and *citizen,* are correlative terms. But the words *seaman, carpenter, smith, tailor,* etc., have no correspondent terms which express those who are no seamen, no carpenters, etc. Languages differ very much with regard to the particular words where this distinction obtains; and may thence afford very strong inferences concerning the manners and customs of different nations. The military government of the Roman emperors had exalted the soldiery so high, that they balanced all the other orders of the state: hence *miles* and *paganus* became relative terms; a thing, till then, unknown to ancient, and still so to modern, languages.' 'The term for a slave, born and bred in the family, was *verna.* As *servus* was the name of the genus, and *verna* of the species without any correlative, this forms a strong presumption that the latter were by far the least numerous: and from the same principles I infer that if the number of slaves brought by the Romans from foreign countries had not extremely exceeded those which were bred at home, *verna* would have had a correlative, which would have expressed the former species of slaves. But these, it would seem, composed the main body of the ancient slaves, and the latter were but a few exceptions.'—HUME, *Essay on the Populousness of Ancient Nations.*

The warlike propensity of the same nation may in a like manner be inferred from the use of the word *hostis* to denote both a *foreigner* and an *enemy.*

Sometimes the intermediate word is properly the standard with which each of the extremes is compared; as in the case of:

Insufficiency   Sufficiency   Redundance

For here the middle term, *Sufficiency*, is equally opposed on the one hand to *Insufficiency* and on the other to *Redundance*.

The forms of correlative expressions would suggest the use of triple, instead of double, columns for tabulating this threefold order of words; but the practical inconvenience attending such an arrangement would probably overbalance its advantages.

It often happens that the same word has several correlative terms, according to the different relations in which it is considered. Thus to the word *Giving* are opposed both *Receiving* and *Taking*; the former correlation having reference to the *persons* concerned in the transfer, while the latter relates to the *mode* of transfer. *Old* has for opposite both *New* and *Young*, according as it is applied to *things* or to *living beings*. *Attack* and *Defence* are correlative terms, as are also *Attack* and *Resistance*. *Resistance*, again, has for its other correlative *Submission*. *Truth in the abstract* is opposed to *Error*, but the opposite of *Truth communicated* is *Falsehood*. *Acquisition* is contrasted both with *Deprivation* and with *Loss*. *Refusal* is the counterpart both of *Offer* and of *Consent*. *Disuse* and *Misuse* may either of them be considered as the correlative of *Use*. *Teaching*, with reference to what is taught, is opposed to *Misteaching*, but with reference to the act itself, its proper reciprocal is *Learning*.

Words contrasted in form do not always bear the same contrast in their meaning. The word *Malefactor*, for example, would, from its derivation, appear to be exactly the opposite of *Benefactor*, but the ideas attached to these two words are far from being directly opposed; for while the latter expresses one who confers a benefit, the former denotes one who has violated the laws.

Independently of the immediate practical uses derivable from the arrangement of words in double columns, many considerations, interesting in a philosophical point of view, are presented by the study of correlative expressions. It will be found, on strict examination, that there seldom exists an exact opposition between two words which may at first sight appear to be the counterparts of one another;

for, in general, the one will be found to possess in reality more force or extent of meaning than the other with which it is contrasted. The correlative term sometimes assumes the form of a mere negative, although it is really endowed with a considerable positive force. Thus *Disrespect* is not merely the absence of *Respect*; its signification trenches on the opposite idea, namely, *Contempt*. In like manner, *Untruth* is not merely the negative of *Truth*; it involves a degree of *Falsehood. Irreligion*, which is properly *the want of Religion*, is understood as being nearly synonymous with *Impiety*. For these reasons, the reader must not expect that all the words which stand side by side in the two columns shall be the precise correlatives of each other; for the nature of the subject, as well as the imperfections of language, renders it impossible always to preserve such an exactness of correlation.

There exist comparatively few words of a general character to which no correlative term, either of negation or of opposition, can be assigned, and which therefore require no corresponding second column. The correlative idea, especially that which constitutes a sense negative to the primary one, may, indeed, be formed or conceived; but, from its occurring rarely, no word has been framed to represent it; for in language, as in other matters, the supply fails when there is no probability of a demand. Occasionally we find this deficiency provided for by the contrivance of prefixing the syllable *non*; as, for instance, the negatives of *existence, performance, payment,* etc., are expressed by the compound words, *non-existence, non-performance, non-payment,* etc. Functions of a similar kind are performed by the prefixes *dis-*,[1] *anti-, contra-, mis-, in-,* and *un*[2]. With respect to all these, and especially the last, great latitude is allowed according to the necessities of the case, a latitude which is limited only by the taste and discretion of the author.

On the other hand, it is hardly possible to find two words having in all respects the same meaning, and being therefore interchangeable; that is admitted of being employed indiscriminately, the one or the

---

[1] The word *disannul*, however, had the same meaning as *annul*.

[2] In the case of adjectives, the addition to a substantive of the terminal syllable *less*, gives it a negative meaning : as *taste, tasteless; care, careless; hope, hopeless; friend, friendless; fault, faultless,* etc.

other, in all their applications. The investigation of the distinctions to be drawn between words apparently synonymous forms a separate branch of inquiry which I have not presumed here to enter upon; for the subject has already occupied the attention of much abler critics than myself, and its complete exhaustion would require the devotion of a whole life. The purpose of this work, it must be borne in mind, is not to explain the signification of words, but simply to classify and arrange them according to the sense in which they are now used, and which I presume to be already known to the reader. I enter into no inquiry into the changes of meaning they may have undergone in the course of time.[1] I am content to accept them at the value of their present currency, and have no concern with their etymologies, or with the history of their transformations; far less do I venture to thrid the mazes of the vast labyrinth into which I should be led by any attempt at a general discrimination of synonyms. The difficulties I have had to contend with have already been sufficiently great without this addition to my labours.

The most cursory glance over the pages of a dictionary will show that a great number of words are used in various senses, sometimes distinguished by slight shades of difference, but often diverging widely from their primary signification, and even, in some cases, bearing to it no perceptible relation. It may even happen that the very same word has two significations quite opposite to one another. This is the case with the verb *to cleave*, which means *to adhere tenaciously*, and also *to separate by a blow*. *To propugn* sometimes expresses *to attack*; at other times, *to defend*. *To ravel* means both *to entangle* and *to disentangle*. The alphabetical index at the end of this work sufficiently shows the multiplicity of uses to which, by the elasticity of language, the meaning of words has been stretched so as to adapt them to a great

---

[1] Such changes are innumerable; for instance, the words *tyrant, parasite, sophist, churl, knave, villain,* anciently conveyed no opprobrious meaning. *Impertinent* merely expressed *irrelative,* and implied neither *rudeness* nor *intrusion,* as it does at present. *Indifferent* originally meant *impartial*; *extravagant* was simply *digressive*; and *to prevent* was properly to *precede* and *assist*. The old translations of the Scriptures furnish many striking examples of the alterations which time has brought in the signification of words. Much curious information on this subject is contained in Trench's *Lectures on the Study of Words.*

variety of modified significations in subservience to the nicer shades of thought which, under peculiarity of circumstances, require corresponding expression. Words thus admitting of different meanings have therefore to be arranged under each of the respective heads corresponding to these various acceptations. There are many words, again, which express ideas compounded of two elementary ideas belonging to different classes. It is therefore necessary to place these words respectively under each of the generic heads to which they relate. The necessity of these repetitions is increased by the circumstance that ideas included under one class are often connected by relations of the same kind as the ideas which belong to another class. Thus we find the same relations of *order* and of *quantity* existing among the ideas of *Time* as well as those of *Space*. Sequence in the one is denoted by the same terms as sequence in the other, and the measures of time also express the measures of space. The cause and the effect are often designated by the same word. The word *Sound,* for instance, denotes both the impression made upon the ear by sonorous vibrations, and also the vibrations themselves, which are the cause or source of that impression. *Mixture* is used for the act of mixing, as well as for the product of that operation. *Taste* and *smell* express both the sensations and the qualities of material bodies giving rise to them. *Thought* is the act of thinking, but the same word denotes also the idea resulting from that act. *Judgment* is the act of deciding, and also the decision come to. *Purchase* is the acquisition of a thing by payment, as well as the thing itself so acquired. *Speech* is both the act of speaking and the words spoken; and so on with regard to an endless multiplicity of words. Mind is essentially distinct from Matter, and yet, in all languages, the attributes of the one are metaphorically transferred to those of the other. Matter, in all its forms, is endowed by the figurative genius of every language with the functions which pertain to intellect; and we perpetually talk of its phenomena and of its powers as if they resulted from the voluntary influence of one body on another, acting and reacting, impelling and being impelled, controlling and being controlled, as if animated by spontaneous energies and guided by specific intentions. On the other hand, expressions of which the primary signification refers exclusively to the properties and actions of matter are metaphorically applied to the phenomena of thought and volition, and even to the feelings and passions of the soul; and in speaking of a *ray of hope*, a *shade of doubt*, a *flight of fancy*, a *flash of wit*, the *warmth of emotion*, or the *ebullitions of anger,* we are scarcely conscious that we are employing metaphors which have this material origin.

As a general rule, I have deemed it incumbent on me to place words and phrases which appertain more especially to one head also under the other heads to which they have a relation, whenever it appeared to me that this repetition would suit the convenience of the inquirer, and spare him the trouble of turning to other parts of the work; for I have always preferred to subject myself to the imputation of redundance, rather than incur the reproach of insufficiency.[1] When, however, the divergence of the associated from the primary idea is sufficiently marked, I have contented myself with making a reference to the place where the modified signification will be found. But in order to prevent needless extension, I have, in general, omitted *conjugate words*[2] which are so obviously derivable from those that are given in the same place, that the reader may safely be left to form them for himself. This is the case with adverbs derived from adjectives by the simple addition of the terminal syllable *-ly*, such as *closely, carefully, safely*, etc., from *close, careful, safe*, etc., and also with adjectives or participles immediately derived from the verbs which are already given. In all such cases, an 'etc.' indicates that reference is understood to be made to these roots. I have observed the same rule in compiling the index, retaining only the primary or more simple word, and omitting the conjugate words

[1] Frequent repetitions of the same series of expressions, accordingly, will be met with under various headings. For example, the word *Relinquishment*, with its synonyms, occurs as a heading at No. 624, where it applies to *intention*, and also at No. 782, where it refers to *property*. The word *Chance* has two significations, distinct from one another: the one implying the *absence of an assignable* cause, in which case it comes under the category of the relation of Causation, and occupies the place No. 156; the other, the *absence of design*, in which latter sense it ranks under the operations of the Will, and has assigned to it the place No. 621. I have, in like manner, distinguished *Sensibility, Pleasure, Pain, Taste*, etc., according as they relate to *Physical* or to *Moral Affections*; the former being found at Nos. 375, 377, 378, 390, etc., and the latter at Nos. 822, 827, 828, 850, etc.

[2] By 'conjugate or paronymous words is meant, correctly speaking, different parts of speech from the same root, which exactly correspond in point of meaning' – *A Selection of English Synonyms*, edited by Archbishop Whately.

obviously derived from them. Thus I assume the word *short* as the representative of its immediate derivatives *shortness, shorten, shortening, shortened, shorter, shortly,* which would have had the same references, and which the reader can readily supply.

The same verb is frequently used indiscriminately either in the active or transitive, or in the neuter or intransitive sense. In these cases I have generally not thought it worth while to increase the bulk of the work by the needless repetition of that word, for the reader, whom I suppose to understand the use of the words, must also be presumed to be competent to apply them correctly.

There are a multitude of words of a specific character, which although they properly occupy places in the columns of a dictionary, yet, having no relation to general ideas, do not come within the scope of this compilation, and are consequently omitted. The names of objects in Natural History, and technical terms belonging exclusively to Science or to Art, or relating to particular operations, and of which the signification is restricted to those specific objects, come under this category. Exceptions must, however, be made in favour of such words as admit of metaphorical application to general subjects with which custom has associated them and of which they may be cited as being typical or illustrative. Thus the word *Lion* will find a place under the head of *Courage,* of which it is regarded as the type. *Anchor*, being emblematic of *Hope*, is introduced among the words expressing that emotion; and, in like manner, *butterfly* and *weathercock*, which are suggestive of fickleness, are included in the category of *Irresolution*.

With regard to the admission of many words and expressions which the classical reader might be disposed to condemn as vulgarisms, or which he, perhaps, might stigmatize as pertaining rather to the slang than to the legitimate language of the day, I would beg to observe that, having due regard to the uses to which this work was to be adapted, I did not feel myself justified in excluding them solely on that ground, if they possessed an acknowledged currency in general intercourse. It is obvious that, with respect to degrees of conventionality, I could not have attempted to draw any strict lines of demarcation, and far less could I have presumed to erect any absolute standard of purity. My object, be it remembered, is not to regulate the use of words, but simply to supply and to suggest such as may be wanted on occasion, leaving the proper selection entirely to the discretion and taste of the employer. If a novelist or a dramatist, for example, proposed to delineate some vulgar personage, he would wish to have the power of putting into the mouth of the speaker expressions that would accord with his character, just as the actor, to revert to a former comparison, who had to personate a peasant, would choose for his attire the most homely garb, and would have just reason to complain if the theatrical wardrobe furnished him with no suitable costume.

Words which have, in process of time, become obsolete, are, of course, rejected from this collection. On the other hand, I have admitted a considerable number of words and phrases borrowed from other languages, chiefly the French and Latin, some of which may be considered as already naturalized; while others, though avowedly foreign, are frequently introduced in English composition, particularly in familiar style, on account of their being peculiarly expressive, and because we have no corresponding words of equal force in our own language.[1] The rapid advances which are being made in scientific knowledge, and consequent improvement in all the arts of life, and the extension of those arts and sciences to so many new purposes and objects, create a continual demand for the formation of new terms to express new agencies, new wants, and new combinations. Such terms, from being at first merely technical, are rendered, by more general use, familiar to the multitude, and having a well-defined acceptation, are eventually incorporated into the language, which they contribute to enlarge and to enrich. *Neologies* of this kind are perfectly legitimate, and highly advantageous; and they necessarily introduce those gradual and progressive changes which every language is destined to undergo.[2] Some modern writers,

---

[1] All these words and phrases are printed in italics.

[2] Thus in framing the present classification I have frequently felt the want of substantive terms corresponding to abstract qualities or ideas denoted by certain adjectives, and have been tempted to invent words that might express these abstractions; but I have yielded to this temptation only in the four following instances: having framed from the adjectives *irrelative, amorphous, sinistral,* amd *gaseous* the abstract nouns *irrelation, amorphism, sinistrality*, and *gaseity*. I have ventured also to introduce the adjective *intersocial* to express the active voluntary relations between man and man.

however, have indulged in a habit of arbitrarily fabricating new words and a new-fangled phraseology without any necessity, and with manifest injury to the purity of the language. This vicious practice, the offspring of indolence or conceit, implies an ignorance or neglect of the riches in which the English language already abounds, and which would have supplied them with words of recognized legitimacy, conveying precisely the same meaning as those they so recklessly coin in the illegal mint of their own fancy.

A work constructed on the plan of classification I have proposed might, if ably executed, be of great value in tending to limit the fluctuations to which language has always been subject, by establishing an authoritative standard for its regulation. Future historians, philologists, and lexicographers, when investigating the period when new words were introduced, or discussing the import given at the present time to the old, might find their labours lightened by being enabled to appeal to such a standard, instead of having to search for data among the scattered writings of the age. Nor would its utility be confined to a single language, for the principles of its construction are universally applicable to all languages, whether living or dead. On the same plan of classification there might be formed a French, a German, a Latin, or a Greek Thesaurus, possessing, in their respective spheres, the same advantages as those of the English model. Still more useful would be a conjunction of these methodized compilations in two languages, the French and the English, for instance; the columns of each being placed in parallel juxtaposition. No means yet devised would so greatly facilitate the acquisition of the one language by those who are acquainted with the other: none would afford such ample assistance to the translator in either language; and none would supply such ready and effectual means of instituting an accurate comparison between them and of fairly appreciating their respective merits and defects. In a still higher degree would all those advantages be combined and multiplied in a *Polyglot Lexicon* constructed on this system.

Metaphysicians engaged in the more profound investigation of the Philosophy of Language will be materially assisted by having the ground thus prepared for them in a previous analysis and classification of our ideas, for such classification of ideas is the true basis on which words, which are their symbols, should be classified.[1] It is by such analysis alone that we can arrive at a clear perception of the relation which these symbols bear to their corresponding ideas, or can obtain a correct knowledge of the elements which enter into the formation of compound ideas, and of the exclusions by which we arrive at the abstractions so perpetually resorted to in the process of reasoning and in the communication of our thoughts.

Lastly, such analyses alone can determine the principles on which a

[1] The principle by which I have been guided in framing my verbal classification is the same as that which is employed in the various departments of natural history. Thus the sectional divisions I have formed correspond to natural families in botany and zoology, and the filiation of words presents a network analogous to the natural filiation of plants or animals.

The following are the only publications that have come to my knowledge in which any attempt has been made to construct a systematic arrangement of Ideas with a view to their expression. The earliest of these, supposed to be at at least nine hundred years old, is the AMERA CÓSHA, or *Vocabulary of the Sanscrit Language*, by Amera Sinha, of which an English translation, by the late Henry T. Colebrooke, was printed at Serampoor in the year 1808. The classification of words is there, as might be expected, exceedingly imperfect and confused, especially in all that relates to abstract Ideas or mental operations. This will be apparent from the very title of the first section, which comprehends '*Heaven, Gods, Demons, Fire, Air, Velocity, Eternity, Much*'; while *Sin, Virtue, Happiness, Destiny, Cause, Nature, Intellect, Reasoning, Knowledge, Senses, Tastes, Odours, Colours*, are all included and jumbled together in the fourth section. A more logical order, however, pervades the sections relating to natural objects, such as *Seas, Earth, Towns, Plants*, and *Animals*, which form separate classes, exhibiting a remarkable effort at analysis at so remote a period of Indian literature.

The well-known work of Bishop Wilkins, entitled *An Essay towards a Real Character and a Philosophical Language*, published in 1668, had for its object the formation of a system of symbols which might serve as a universal language. It professed to be founded on a 'scheme of analysis of the things or notions to which names were to be assigned'; but notwithstanding the immense labour and ingenuity expended in the construction of this system, it was soon found to be far too abstruse and recondite for practical application.

In the year 1797 there appeared in Paris an anonymous work, entitled *Pasigraphie, ou Premiers Éléments du nouvel Art-Science d'écrire et d'imprimer une langue de manière à être lu et entendu dans toute autre langue sans traduction*, of which an edition in German was also published. It contains a great number of tabular schemes of categories, all of which appear to be excessively arbitrary and artificial, and extremely difficult of application, as well as of apprehension.

strictly *Philosophical Language* might be constructed. The probable result of the construction of such a language would be its eventual adoption by every civilized nation, thus realizing that splendid aspiration of philanthropists – the establishment of a Universal Language. However Utopian such a project may appear to the present generation, and however abortive may have been the former endeavours of Bishop Wilkins and others to realize it,[1] its accomplishment is surely not beset with greater difficulties than have impeded the progress to many other beneficial objects which in former times appeared to be no less visionary, and which yet were successfully achieved, in later ages, by the continued and persevering exertions of the human intellect. Is there at the present day, then, any ground for despair that, at some future stage of that higher civilization to which we trust the world is gradually tending, some new and bolder effort of genius towards the solution of this great problem may be crowned with success, and compass an object of such vast and paramount utility? Nothing, indeed, would conduce more directly to bring about a golden age of union and harmony among the several nations and races of mankind than the removal of that barrier to the interchange of thought and mutual good understanding between man and man which is now interposed by the diversity of their respective languages.

[1] 'The languages,' observes Horne Tooke, 'which are commonly used throughout the world, are much more simple and easy, convenient and philosophical, than Wilkins's scheme for a *real character*; or than any other scheme that has been at any other time imagined or proposed for the purpose.' – "Επεα Πτερόεντα, p. 125.

—— A Dictionary of ——
OBSCENITY, TABOO AND EUPHEMISM
James McDonald

'Excuse me, I'm just going to the euphemism'

Why, for hundreds of years, have we been so embarrassed about going you-know-where? And why do we have so many words to describe people doing, well . . . *It*? And why, in God's name, do we swear so much?

The *Dictionary of Obscenity, Taboo and Euphemism* takes a scholarly, entertaining and enlightening look at the traditionally taboo subjects of bodily functions, sex and religion; and, in a fascinating foreword, arrives at some interesting conclusions about the amazing array of words relating to them. The dictionary itself lists definitions, origins, and changes in usage and meaning, with many entries supplemented by quotations from Chaucer, Shakespeare and other infamous ink-slingers. Where appropriate, other-language equivalents and rhyming slang evasions are given.

While many entries are as old as the hills — and Kiss Arse Hill in Cheshire is *old* — others are recent arrivals from Australia and the United States. And some, sadly, are obsolete: we may have stopped talking about firkytoodling (you'll have to look it up), but we still do it.

It would probably have caused Victorians to get their unmentionables in a twist, but to the modern etymologist and general reader alike, the Dictionary of Obscenity, Taboo and Euphemism will prove an illuminating, instructive and thoroughly entertaining read.

0 7474 0166 7   REFERENCE   £3.99

$\mathscr{D}$ICTIONARY $\mathscr{O}$F
THEATRE

ALAN ISAACS

Over 5000 entries provide a comprehensive guide to the
theatrical world, past and present. Concentrating heavily
on biographical information on playwrights, directors,
impresarios, actors and actresses, the dictionary also
covers technical terms and major plays. Clearly presented
and with cross-references linking playwrights, plays and
actors, it is a must for thespians, theatre-goers, and lovers
of all things theatrical.

0 7474 0019 9   SPHERE REFERENCE   £7.99

DICTIONARY OF

ALLUSIONS

ABRAHAM H LASS, DAVID KIREMIDJIAN
AND RUTH M GOLDSTEIN

allusions in this dictionary are words and phrases that compare aspects of people, places, things and ideas with their counterparts in history, mythology, scripture, literature and popular culture.

Many familiar allusions owe their existence to the Bible. The Land of Nod, for example, lay east of Eden, and had — surprisingly — nothing to do with sleep. And while 'a fly in the ointment' first appeared in Ecclesiastes, 'salt of the earth' was first mentioned in Matthew's Gospel.

People — real and fictitious — are also the source of allusions. The original Juggernaut was a Hindu god, a remover of sin, whose image was placed on a great car. And Svengali was a musician with almost magical powers of influence in *Trilby* (1894), a novel by George du Maurier.

With over 1,300 entries, and frequent cross-references, the *Dictionary of Allusions* will prove an enlightening read and an invaluable, original reference book.

0 7474 0412 7   REFERENCE   £3.50